WED 9:00

ROOM 211

CANADIAN MARKETING

SECOND EDITION

CASES & EXERCISES

SECOND EDITION

CANADIAN MARKETING

CASES & EXERCISES

CHARLES B. WEINBERG
University of British Columbia

GORDON H. G. McDOUGALL
Wilfrid Laurier University

McGraw-Hill Ryerson Limited
Toronto Montreal New York Auckland Bogotá Caracas Lisbon
London Madrid Mexico Milan New Delhi Paris
San Juan Singapore Sydney Tokyo

CANADIAN MARKETING: CASES & EXERCISES
Second Edition

Case material is made possible by the co-operation of business firms and other organizations which may wish to remain anonymous by having names, quantities, and other identifying details disguised while maintaining basic relationships. Cases are prepared as the basis for class discussion rather than to illustrate either effective or ineffective handling of an administrative situation.

ISBN: 0-07-551203-3

3 4 5 6 7 8 9 0 BG 0 9 8 7 6 5 4

Printed and bound in Canada

Care has been taken to trace ownership of copyright material contained in this text. The publishers will gladly take any information that will enable them to rectify any reference or credit in subsequent editions.

Sponsoring Editor: Kelly Smyth
Senior Supervising Editor: Lenore Gray
Proofreader: Jackie Barr
Cover & Text Design: Hania Fil
Technical Artist: New art by Pat Code
Typesetting: Q-Composition Inc.
Printing & Binding: Best Gagné Book Manufacturing
Text set in: Simoncini Garamond and Futura

CANADIAN CATALOGUING IN PUBLICATION DATA

Weinberg, Charles B.
Canadian marketing: cases and exercises

2nd ed.
ISBN 0-07-551203-3

1. Marketing – Canada – Case studies. I. McDougall, Gordon H. G., 1942– II. Title.

HF5415.12.C3W45 1991 658.8'00971 C90-095323-3

This book is dedicated to Joanne,
Beth, and Amy Weinberg, and to
Betty, Michael, and Sandy
McDougall.

CONTENTS

APPENDICES

PREFACE

The second edition of *Canadian Marketing: Cases and Exercises* builds on the successful first edition which has been adopted throughout Canada in a variety of educational settings. In preparing the second edition we sought to capture the breadth and depth of marketing management in a dynamic environment. "New and improved" may be an overworked phrase in marketing, often signifying little more than packaging and styling changes. However, we've made substantive changes in this new edition, using advice and suggestions from professors at many business schools in an effort to make a good product even better. In particular, we have added a separate section on international marketing and several of the new cases include challenges due to the increasing pressures in both home and foreign markets from international competitors. The new cases include marketing decisions faced by a number of high technology companies on one hand and well-known branded consumer products on the other. As well, a number of the new cases reflect societal and environmental concerns.

Of the 55 cases and exercises in this edition, 24 are new to *Canadian Marketing*, 8 that appeared earlier have been given improved classroom value through pruning or other revisions, and 23 have been retained without major changes. All textual materials have been rewritten to provide more depth of coverage. The optional computer software is now even more user friendly.

Reviewers for this second edition told us they wanted to continue to see a diversity of topics and settings covered. We have done this by continuing to feature a mix of services and goods marketing situations and including the marketing problems of nonprofit organizations.

The diversity of topics is amplified by the variation in length and complexity of the cases and exercises in this book. Our research for this book included discussions with many marketing instructors throughout Canada. The need for a mix of short and long cases, for single topic and multiple-issue teaching materials, for cases where the problem is well defined and for cases where finding the problem is the key challenge was repeatedly emphasized. The second edition of *Canadian Marketing: Cases and Exercises* provides a mix of cases that allows the instructor to adapt the book to the particular needs of his or her students.

A key strength of the book, we feel, has been our ability to enlist the aid of marketing faculty throughout Canada in the preparation of cases for this book. Not only have they told us what is needed, but they have responded enthusiastically to our call by sending us their best and most recent cases. And they have been gracious in allowing us to edit their cases so that the book can follow a common format, making the book more readable for students.

The first edition of this casebook broke new ground by presenting an optional package that enabled students to undertake computer-assisted analysis of many of the materials. The diskette developed by John D. Claxton and Charles B. Weinberg is again pathbreaking. The computer aids, formatted to be compatible with VP Planner and Lotus 1-2-3, are designed to reflect a marketing management viewpoint. Details of how to use the optional software are provided in Appendix 2. However, we want to emphasize that the data in all the cases and exercises in this book can be analyzed simply with the aid of a pocket calculator.

Many students using this book may be new to case analysis. While no universal formula for analyzing cases exists, we can help students learn to improve their case analysis skills. The introductory note, "Analyzing and Learning from Cases," provides suggestions to the student new to case analysis. The introductory material also includes a case, a student's written analysis of that case, and a critique of the student's report. These materials help a student become accustomed both to the demands of case analysis and the excitement generated from attempting to resolve difficult management problems.

We have prepared over half the materials in this book. The remaining cases have primarily been written by authors from a wide variety of Canadian academic institutions, including Alberta, Bishop's, Brock, Calgary, Concordia, Guelph, Hautes Études Commerciales, McMaster, Queen's, St. Francis Xavier, Toronto, and Western. We want to thank the following case authors for graciously allowing us to use their cases in our book: Talaat Abdel-Malek, Maryanne Bauer, Craig Baxter, Jacques M. Boisvert, John D. Claxton, E. Raymond Corey, Marc Dubuc, Carole Duhaime, Scott D. Edgett, Marc Filion, Thomas F. Funk, Katherine Gallagher, Daniel F. Gardiner, Peter Gilmour, E. Gimpel, O. Guindo, Eric J. Karson, Rick Jenkner, Mark S. Johnson, Roger A. Kerin, V. H. Kirpalani, Gordon J. Lucas, William F. Massey, David B. Montgomery, James E. Nelson, Robert E. M. Nourse, John R. Oldland, Grant N. Poeter, Craig R. Pollack, Richard W. Pollay, William A. Preshing, Marvin Ryder, Kenneth Shachmut, H. J. Simpkins, Douglas Snetsinger, Ian Spencer, Susan Spencer, Shirley Taylor, Mark Vandenbosch, Mary L. Volk, Harrie Vredenburg, Denise Walters, Shauna White, and John Yokom. We also want to thank Ken Wong for his assistance in identifying and developing case materials. Several of the cases are based on reports originally prepared by students in university courses; we wish to acknowledge here the following students for their primary research contributions: Lindsay Anderson, Janeen Cucheran, Bruno Curatole, Eduardo Gamba, Steven Hardy, Jason Kearns, Deanna Lee, Z. Kirby Leung, Jessica Ma, Tracey Renzullo, Ian Roe, Dan Singer, Clive Wallace, and Scott Williams. We also thank the copyright holders for giving us permission to reproduce their materials. We are particularly grateful to the managements of many organizations—sometimes disguised—that form the subjects of these cases, since it is only their willingness to share experience and data that make case development possible.

A great many people have assisted in the preparation and publication of the second edition of *Canadian Marketing: Cases and Exercises*. We wish to thank Christopher Lovelock for his wise counsel and important assistance in the planning and preparation of this book. The efforts of Katherine Gallagher who provided excellent guidance and first class editing and writing at many stages of manuscript development are appreciated. Special mention must be made to our friend and colleague John Claxton, for his innovative work in developing the optional computer disk that accompanies this book. We also want to acknowledge especially the talents of Douglas Snetsinger who authored or co-authored seven of the cases in this book. We thank James Forbes, Richard Pollay, and David Tse, who provided case ideas and reviews for this edition. We are particularly grateful for "beyond-the-call-of-duty" secretarial service and word processing assistance of Rosalea Dennie at the University of British Columbia and to Elsie Grogan, Janet Campbell, Lori

Kapshey, and Mavis Sheen at Wilfrid Laurier University. James Koehle's and Kevin Siluch's considerable help both in computer programming and case development is appreciated. The financial support of the Office of Research at Wilfrid Laurier University, The Max Bell Foundation Project on International Business, and the University of British Columbia is gratefully acknowledged. We're particularly appreciative of the important role played by our editor at McGraw-Hill Ryerson, Kelly Smyth, and we wish, also, to thank Lenore Gray for her excellent editing of the manuscript.

We thank the following reviewers for the many useful comments and suggestions they provided: Catherine Aitken, Arlene Bennett, Kevin Bittle, Ted Brown, Ian Fenwick, Thomas Funk, Barry Mills, Peter Pasold, Rosemary Polegato, Lynn Ricker, Marvin Ryder, Ian Spencer, and Dennis Sullivan.

Finally, we want to thank the many students we have had the privilege of teaching in Canada and around the world. Their enthusiastic response to case teaching has stimulated the development of this edition of our book. The fun and challenge of case teaching exists from the interaction between students and instructors.

ANALYZING AND LEARNING FROM CASES

Unlike methods of instruction that use lectures and textbooks, the case method of instruction doesn't present students with a body of tried and true knowledge about how to be a successful manager. Instead, it provides an opportunity for students to learn by doing.

As a student, you may find that dealing with cases is very much like working with the actual problems that people encounter in their jobs as managers. In most instances, you'll be identifying and clarifying problems facing the management of an organization, analyzing qualitative information and quantitative data, evaluating alternative courses of action, and then making decisions about what strategy to pursue for the future. You may enjoy the process more—and probably learn more—if you accept the role of an involved participant rather than that of a disinterested observer who has no stake or interest in resolving the problems in question.

The goal of case analysis is not to develop a set of "correct" facts, but to learn to reason well with available data. Cases mirror the uncertainty of the real-world managerial environment in that the information they present is often imprecise and ambiguous. You may perhaps be frustrated that there is no one right answer or correct solution to any given case. Instead, there may be a number of feasible strategies management might adopt, each with somewhat different implications for the future of the organization and each involving different trade-offs.

If you're using this book in a course or seminar, you'll be exposed to a wide range of different management situations within a relatively short span of time. As a result, the cases presented in this book collectively will provide a much broader exposure to marketing problems than most managers experience in many years on the job. Recognizing that the problems with which managers must deal are not unique to a particular institution (or even to a specific industry) forms the basis for developing a professional approach to management.

CASES AND THE REAL WORLD

It's important to recognize that even though case writers try to build realism into their cases, these cases differ from "real-world" management situations in several important respects. First, the information is prepackaged in written form. By contrast, managers accumulate their information through such means as memoranda, meetings, chance conversations, research studies, observations, news media reports, and other externally published materials—and, of course, by rumour.

Second, case writers tend to be selective in their reporting because most cases are designed with specific teaching objectives in mind. Each must fit a relatively short class period and focus attention on a defined category of management problem. To provide such a focus—and to keep the length and complexity of the case within reasonable bounds—the writers may need to omit information on problems, data, or personnel that are peripheral to the central issues of the case.

In the real world, management problems are usually dynamic in nature. They call for some immediate action, with further analysis and major decisions delayed until some later time. Managers are rarely able to wrap up their problems, put them away, and go on to the next "case." In contrast, discussing a case in class or writing an analysis of a case is more like examining a snapshot taken at a particular point in time—although sometimes a sequel case provides a sense of continuity and poses the need for future decisions within the same organization.

A third and final contrast between case analyses and real-world management is that participants in case discussions and authors of written case reports aren't responsible for implementing their decisions, nor do they have to live with the consequences. However, this doesn't mean that you can be frivolous when making recommendations. Instructors and classmates are likely to be critical of contributions that aren't based on careful analysis and interpretation of the facts.

You should make a particular effort to establish the significance of any quantitative data presented in the text of the case, or, more often, in the exhibits. See if new insights may be gained by combining and manipulating data presented in different parts of the case. But don't accept the data blindly. In the cases, as in real life, not all information is equally reliable or equally relevant. On the other hand, case writers won't deliberately misrepresent data or facts to try to trick you.

DEVELOPING RECOMMENDATIONS

At this point in the analysis, you should be in a position to summarize your evaluation of the situation and to develop some recommendations for management. First, identify the alternative courses of action that the organization might take. Next, consider the implications of each alternative, including possible undesirable outcomes, such as provoking responses from stronger competitors. Ask yourself how short-term tactics fit with longer-term strategies. Relate each alternative to the objectives of the organization (as defined or implied in the case, or as redefined by you). Then, develop a set of recommendations for future action, making sure that these recommendations are supported by your analysis of the case data.

Your recommendations won't be complete unless you give some thought to how the proposed strategy should be implemented.

- What resources—human, financial, and other—will be required?
- Who should be responsible for the implementation?
- What time frame should be established for the various actions proposed?
- How should subsequent performance be measured?

SMALL GROUP DISCUSSIONS

The best results in the early stages of case preparation are generally achieved by working alone. But a useful step, prior to class discussion, is to discuss the case with a small group of classmates. (In some instances, you may find yourself assigned to a small discussion group or you may be required to work with others to develop a written report for possible group presentation.)

These small groups facilitate initial testing of ideas and help to focus discussion on the main considerations. Within such a discussion group, present your arguments and listen to those of other participants. Except in the case of group projects, the aim of such a meeting is not to reach a consensus, but to broaden, clarify, and redefine your own thinking—and to help others do likewise.

Effective management of the marketing side of a business or other institution involves adjusting corporate resources to the changing character of the marketplace; this is different from just applying knowledge about what works and what doesn't work in marketing. Accordingly, the focus of small group discussions should be on analysis and decision making: What are the facts? What do they mean? What alternatives are available? What specifically should management do? How and when?

CLASS DISCUSSIONS

Courses taught by the case method emphasize inductive learning, with conceptual frameworks and strategic guidelines being developed from the analysis of a variety of real-world situations. This approach contrasts sharply with the deductive approach to learning used in lectures where the concepts are presented first and must then be applied to actual situations.

PREPARING A CASE

Just as there's no one right solution to a case, there is also no single correct way of preparing a case. However, the following broad guidelines may help familiarize you with the job of case preparation (Exhibit 1). With practice, you should be able to establish a working style with which you feel comfortable. The guidelines on initial analysis and on developing recommendations should also serve you well for preparing written case reports or case-based exams.

INITIAL ANALYSIS

First, it's important to gain a feel for the overall situation by skimming quickly through the case. Ask yourself,

- What sort of organization is the case about?
- What is the nature of the industry (broadly defined)?
- What is going on in the external environment?
- What problems does management appear to be facing?

An initial fast reading, without making notes or underlining, should provide a sense of what is going on and what information is being presented for analysis. Then you'll be ready for a very careful second reading. This time, seek to identify key facts so that you can develop a situation analysis and clarify the nature of the problems facing management. As you go along, try to make notes in response to such questions as:

- What decisions need to be made and who will be responsible for making them?
- What are the objectives of the organization itself and of each of the key players in the case? Are these objectives compatible? If not, can the problems be reconciled or will it be necessary to redefine the objectives?
- What resources and constraints are present that may help or hinder attempts by the organization to meet its objectives?

ROLE OF THE INSTRUCTOR

In class, you may find that the role played by an instructor using the case method usually differs significantly from that of a lecturer. The instructor's role in case discussions is often similar to that of a moderator—calling on students, guiding the discussion, asking questions, and periodically synthesizing previous comments. Teaching styles vary, of course, from one case instructor to another.

Many professors like to begin the class by asking a student to "lay out" the case, which may involve your being asked to identify key problems and opportunities, to present some preliminary data analysis, and perhaps to outline a possible plan of action.

Some instructors assign study questions in advance to help students with their case preparation, but others feel it is more realistic (albeit more demanding) to let students define for themselves how they should approach each new case.

RESPONSIBILITIES OF PARTICIPANTS

Instead of being a passive notetaker, as in lecture classes, you'll be expected to be an active participant in case discussions. Indeed, it's essential that you participate: if nobody participates, there can be no discussion! If you never join in the debate, you'll be denying

Exhibit 1
PREPARING A CASE: A BRIEF OUTLINE

I. Initial Fast Reading
- — no notes
- — get a feel for what's going on
- — think about major problems and forces present

II. A Second Careful Reading
- — make notes identifying: organizational objectives
nature of problem(s)
key facts
key decisions
- — evaluate and analyze case data

III. Development of Recommendations
- — identify alternative courses of action to meet objectives
- — consider implications of each action
- — provide recommendations, supported by analysis

other participants the insights that you may have to offer. Moreover, there's significant learning involved in presenting your own analysis and recommendations and debating them with your classmates, who may hold differing views or else seek to build on your presentation. But don't be so eager to participate that you ignore what others have to say. Learning to be a good listener is also important in developing managerial skills.

Occasionally, it may happen that you are personally familiar with the organization depicted in a case. Perhaps you are privy to additional information not contained in the case, or perhaps you know what has happened since the time of the case decision. If so, keep this information to yourself unless, or until, the instructor requests it. (This advice also holds true for written reports and case exams.)

Learning comes through discussion and controversy. In the case method of instruction, participants must assume responsibility not only for their own learning, but also for that of others in the class. Thus, it's important for students to be well prepared, willing to commit themselves to a well reasoned set of analyses and recommendations, and receptive to constructive criticism. Students unwilling to accept this challenge are likely to find the case method aimless and confusing. On the other hand, if you do accept it, we're confident that you'll experience in the classroom that sense of excitement, challenge, and even exasperation that comes with being a manager in real-world situations.

EXAMPLE OF A CASE ANALYSIS

There is no universal formula for analyzing cases, but there *are* ways to learn how to do better case analyses. The textual notes at the start of each section provide a review of the major issues in each section's cases and exercises. However, you should remember that management problems don't come in neatly classified packages. Cases almost always raise multiple issues, and students should recognize that identifying problems and establishing priorities are the keys to case analysis.

To help you become accustomed to the nature of case analysis, the following includes a case (Western Products Limited), a student's written analysis of that case, and a critique of the student's report.

WESTERN PRODUCTS LIMITED

Charles B. Weinberg

George Norrin, the majority owner of Western Products Limited of Victoria, faced an important decision: Should the company, for the first time in its 35-year history, begin a large advertising campaign?

The advertising campaign, if begun, would focus on the company's chain saw products. Western Products marketed a variety of power tools—pneumatic drills, generators, concrete vibrators—to the industrial and construction markets in the western provinces and three western states, Washington, Oregon, and California.

Western had entered the chain saw business 15 years ago when one of Mr. Norrin's closest friends, Jim Dagan, had decided to retire. Mr. Dagan had owned a small company which manufactured and marketed chain saws. Mr. Dagan asked his friend if he was interested in buying the company, Dagan Power Saws. The two men quickly worked out a reasonable price. Mr. Dagan remained a passive partner in the company and received 10% of the profits from the chain saw division of Western Products. Currently, chain saws accounted for 42% of Western's sales and 48% of the company's profits (Exhibit 1).

MARKET BACKGROUND

While no precise data were available, Western estimated that it held a 15% market share in its market area for gasoline-powered chain saws. It was the fourth largest manufacturer of these chain saws in its region.

Gasoline-powered chain saws were sold to loggers, farmers, large land owners (companies and institutions), and home-owners, who were primarily casual users, with many trees on their property. The home-owner market appeared to be something of a growth area. The logger market, on the other hand, was quite cyclical, rising and falling with the boom-and-bust cycle which seemed to characterize the forestry industry.

At the time that Dagan Power Saws was purchased, three-fifths of its sales were made through a distributor, Excelsior Sales, which owned a number of retail outlets and acted as a wholesaler to many other retail outlets throughout the West. It was Excelsior's wholesaling system that allowed Western to achieve distribution in both the United States and Canada. All sales to Excelsior carried the distributor's own brand names. The Excelsior name was used for sales through its own stores and the Harter brand name for sales through other companies. (The Harter brand name was solely owned and controlled by Excelsior.) Overall, Excelsior accounted for 59% of Western's chain saw sales; this percentage had been virtually constant over the past 15 years. Mr. Norrin thought that his relationship with Excelsior was excellent.

Exhibit 1
WESTERN PRODUCTS LIMITED INCOME STATEMENT

	$ in thousands	
Sales		$4,233
Cost of Goods Sold		
Materials	$1,901	
Shipping	278	
Labour	962	3,141
Contribution		$1,092
Manufacturing Overhead	$ 630	
Administrative Expenses	151	
Sales & Marketing	138	919
Net Profit (before tax)		$ 173

Mr. Norrin and his chief assistant, Kara Smith, regularly called on all major forestry companies, other companies and institutions that were likely to be buyers of gasoline-powered chain saws or involved in land-clearing operations, operators of lumber yards and building supply distributors, and occasionally large retailers. However, Mr. Norrin and Ms. Smith were not able to visit many of the dealers who sold chain saws. For example, of the 53 dealers in British Columbia who sold Dagan-brand chain saws, they had only called on 19 in the most recent year. Most dealers sold several brands of chain saws, but many limited themselves to two or three brands. All sales in these markets (41% of the chain saw business) were made under the Dagan brand name. The majority of these sales were made through wholesalers and retailers.

Western participated in a number of agricultural fairs, such as the Pacific National Exhibition in Vancouver, each year and sponsored log rolling and other contests. However, the company had never advertised either in trade journals to reach dealers or in magazines that might directly reach the people who were the buyers and users of chain saws.

Western manufactured a variety of chain saw models, but they differed primarily in the length of their chain saw blade and in horsepower. Trade association surveys showed that a number of other features were important to users. Weight of the chain saw, ease of controls, whether it had a gas protector, and the warranty were important to consumers, with safety being a critical—although unspoken—concern to many. The Dagan chain saws were at least as good as those of the major competitors on all these dimensions and had a slight advantage on weight. That is, for any given horsepower and blade length, the Western saw would weigh slightly less than that of its major competitors. However, this advantage was very difficult to notice unless someone worked with a chain saw for an extended period of time.

A typical gasoline-powered chain saw had a retail price of $500. Excelsior received a 30% discount on this price, as did most other distributors and wholesalers to whom

Dagan sold. On average, Excelsior or other wholesalers would take one-third of this discount (that is, $50), and the retailer would receive the remaining two-thirds (that is, $100).

Of Dagan's revenues, 48% represented materials (including preassembled components), 22% represented labour, and the remainder was contributed to overhead and before-tax profit. Because Excelsior picked up the chain saws from the Dagan factory, there were no shipping expenses.

THE ADVERTISING PROPOSAL

Two years ago, Mr. Norrin hired Kevin Style as marketing manager for Dagan chain saws. Mr. Style, a Bachelor of Commerce graduate from the University of British Columbia, had paid for his education by working as a logger in the summers. After graduation, he worked for five years as a sales representative with Canadian Faucets, a major marketer of plumbing fixtures and, then, spent two years as associate sales manager at the company's head office.

Mr. Style felt that Dagan could substantially increase sales of its own brand of gasoline-powered chain saws if it achieved a greater presence in the market place. He felt that brand name recognition would increase the company's sales, both because dealers would be more inclined to mention the brand to their customers

Exhibit 2

EXCERPTS FROM SURVEY OF RECENT BUYERS OF POWER TOOLS COSTING MORE THAN $100

How much time did you spend thinking about purchase?		
Less than 1 week	4%	
1 week to 1 month	15%	
1 month to 3 months	41%	
More than 3 months	40%	
How familiar were you with the product before you bought it?		
Very familiar	28%	
Somewhat familiar	43%	
Not too familiar	29%	
Did you have a brand in mind before your first visit to a dealer?		
Yes	57%	(40% said they bought this brand)
No	43%	
How great was the dealer's influence on your purchase?		
Considerable	44%	
Some	18%	
Hardly any	15%	
None	23%	

Source: Recent trade publication

and because customers would be more inclined to specify—or at least recognize—the Dagan brand name.

Recently, a trade journal had published the results of a market survey which dealt with how individuals bought power tools. Although Mr. Style could not determine what portion of the buyers were professionals, such as loggers or carpenters, and what portion were home-owners, he still felt the results were helpful. The magazine had sent out a questionnaire to 1,200 recent buyers of power tools and had received 800 replies. The main results of the survey are shown in Exhibit 2. In brief, Mr. Style noted from the findings that 57% of buyers had a brand of power tool in mind before buying it and that 44% said that the dealer had considerable influence on the brand that was purchased. He felt that these results supported his contention that advertising could pay off for Western.

Mr. Style had interviewed a number of ad agencies about the possibility of handling the Dagan account. After extensive discussion, he hired the Summit Advertising Agency to represent his company and prepare an advertising plan. He negotiated a one-year contract with a flat fee of $5,000 to the agency. He had done this rather than pay a commission on advertising dollars spent, because he didn't want the agency to have an incentive to recommend advertising expenditures just to increase their earnings.

Summit recommended that advertising would be an excellent investment for Dagan. However, they believed that if the Dagan brand name was to achieve recognition, a few small-space ads would not do much. Rather, the agency suggested that full-page ads should be used on a frequent basis. Summit had conducted some research and had identified a set of magazines and local papers that most loggers read, two trade journals that reached most retailers and wholesalers in Dagan's

Exhibit 3

SUMMARY OF SUMMIT ADVERTISING PROPOSAL

Market Target	Media Description	Intensity	Cost
Retailers & Wholesalers	2 monthly trade journals: *Lumber Wholesaler & Retailer* and *Store Management*	6 ads per year in each magazine	$16,400
Home Owners	3 magazines aimed at do-it-yourselfers: *Popular Crafts*, *Western Homeowner*, and *Canadian Homes*	ads in 2 issues of each magazine during heavy selling season	$18,500
Loggers	Local newspapers, and magazines, e.g., *Forestry Workers' News*	1 to 4 ads in selected newspapers and magazines	$10,100

market area, and three magazines that targeted the "do-it-yourself" home-owner who might make use of a chain saw. As shown in Exhibit 3, Summit proposed spending $45,000 on this campaign (of which 15%, the commission the media paid to Summit, would be rebated to Dagan). A key point in the advertising campaign would be the lighter weight of the Dagan chain saw.

Mr. Style thought this was an excellent proposal and heartily endorsed it. An expenditure of this magnitude would require the approval of Mr. Norrin, not only because of its size but also because of its novelty for this company.

STUDENT ANALYSIS OF WESTERN PRODUCTS LIMITED

ISSUE

Should Western begin a large advertising campaign for its chain saw products?

DISCUSSION

Mr. Style thinks that Western can substantially increase sales of Dagan brand name chain saws by undertaking a major advertising campaign in Western's market area. Although Mr. Style's past work experience provided him with knowledge of marketing procedures, he has not fully considered the implications of his proposal. At Canadian Faucets, his previous employer, Mr. Style was selling products in a market with many direct competitors (assumed). At Western, Mr. Style is selling products in a market with direct and indirect competitors (including Excelsior, with Excelsior and Harter brand names—see Exhibit 1). By increasing advertising for Dagan chain saws and thereby causing an increase in sales of Dagan chain saws (assumed), Excelsior's chain saw sales, under both their brand names, will likely suffer. This could serve to tarnish the excellent relationship that currently exists between the two companies and that has apparently existed for 15 years, as evidenced by the fact that Excelsior has continually accounted for approximately 60% of Dagan chain saw sales over this period.

If this relationship does deteriorate, Western has more to lose than gain by operating independently of Excelsior. Excelsior's distribution channels allow Western to sell its products in western provinces and states. Also, as indicated by the power tool buyer survey, many consumers tend to purchase well known brand name products. To capitalize on this fact, Western needs to have a well established name through which to sell its products, something that Excelsior provides in its large distribution channels. Excelsior also has a strong influence on Western's sales because of the influence retailers have on purchases (also indicated by the survey). Finally, because most of Western's sales are currently through retailers and wholesalers, who require the same margins as Excelsior, Western saves nothing in terms of lower margins to dealers by not selling through Excelsior. In fact, Western saves money by selling to Excelsior because the distributor absorbs the delivery costs of the chain saws, as shown in Exhibit 2.

Therefore, assuming that there are presently no threats to Western by Excelsior to stop selling Dagan chain saws under the Excelsior and Harter brand names, increasing advertising to improve Dagan chain saw sales could serve to cannibalize Excelsior's sales of Dagan chain saws. This would jeopardize the excellent relationship the two companies now have and, in the long run, cause Western to lose this powerful distribution channel that accounts for approximately three-fifths of its chain saw sales.

Exhibit 1
CURRENT SALES PATTERN

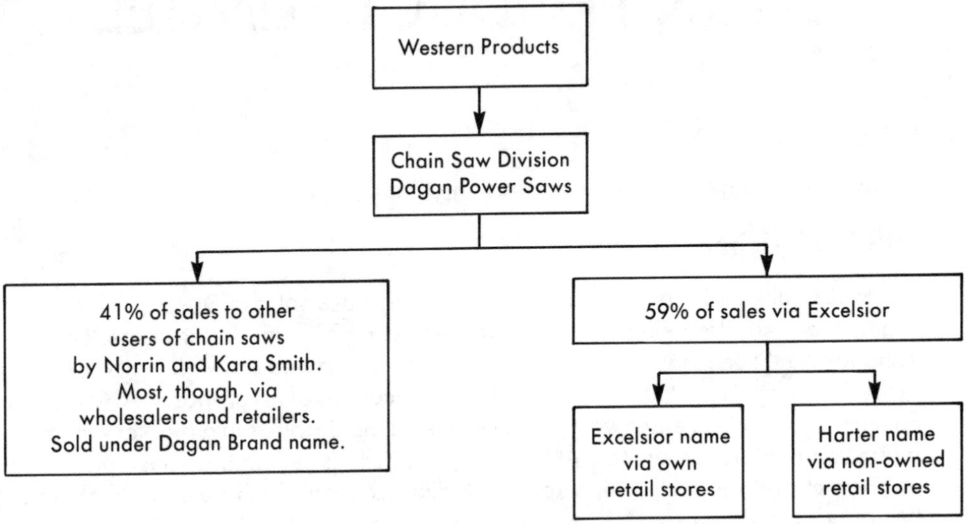

Exhibit 2
FINANCIAL ANALYSIS

Revenue to Western per Unit		
Retail Price		$500
Discount (30%)	$150	
Wholesaler margin (1/3 of 30%	50	
Retail margin (2/3 of 30%)	100	150
Revenue to Western/chain saw		$350

Western's Current Unit Sales	
Percentage of market	15%
Total dollar sales	$4,233,000
Percentage of revenue—chain saws	42%
Chain saw revenue	$1,777,860
Chain saw price	$500
Approx. chain saws sold (Western total)	3,555
Chain saws sold via Excelsior (59%)	2,100
Chain saws sold direct by Dagan	1,455
Total chain saw market (3555/0.15)	23,700 units

(continued)

Exhibit 2 continued

Calculation of Shipping Cost per Chain Saw Sold under Dagan Name		
Western's total shipping costs	$ 278,000	
Western's total revenue	$4,233,000	
Total chain saws sold	3,555	
Chain saws sold via Dagan name	1,455	
× price per chain saw	$500	
Revenue generated via Dagan chain saw sales (1,455 × $500)	$728,000	
Dagan name chain saws revenue as percentage of total revenue ($728,000/$4,233,000)	17%	
Approximate shipping costs/Dagan chain saw (17% × $728,000/1,455)	$33	per Dagan chain saw

Contribution per Chain Saw

	Dagan Name		Excelsior Name	
Revenue/chain saw		$350		$350
Materials (48%)	$168		$168	
Labour (22%)	77		77	
Shipping	33		0	245
		278		
Contribution/chain saw		$ 72		$105

Advertising Costs	
Flat fee	$ 5,000
Proposed spending	$45,000
15% returned to Western	⟨ 6,750⟩
Total advertising cost	$43,250

Extra Chain Saw Sales Required to Cover Advertising Cost

Contribution per chain saw under Dagan name	$ 72
Contribution per chain saw under Excelsior name	105
Chain saws required to sell under Excelsior name only:	Chain saws required to sell under Dagan name only:
$43,250/105	$43,250/72
411 ←	→ 600
Required % of market 411/23,700 units	Required % of market 600/23,700 units
1.73% ←	→ 2.53%

ALTERNATIVES

1. Proceed with advertising plans.
2. Propose co-op advertising with Excelsior for Excelsior's brand names in areas which Dagan brand name chain saws are not heavily promoted by Western.

ANALYSIS OF ALTERNATIVES

1. Proceeding with advertising plans could weaken the relationship between Western and Excelsior and cause Western to lose or have its powerful distribution channels obstructed in the future.
2. Proposed co-op advertising with Excelsior for Excelsior's brand names would allow Western to magnify its advertising dollar and perhaps increase sales for chain saws in areas in which Mr. Norrin and Kara Smith do not attempt strongly to sell Dagan chain saws.

RECOMMENDATION

Propose to Excelsior that co-op advertising for Excelsior brand name chain saws be undertaken in areas which Western does not heavily promote Dagan-named chain saws.

CLOSING NOTE

If Western does decide to advertise, either with or without Excelsior, the increase in sales of chain saws required to pay for the advertising will give Western an idea of the feasibility of the proposal. As indicated in Exhibit 2, to pay for an advertising cost of $43,250, Western would have to have an incremental increase in chain saw sales of 411 under the Excelsior name or 600 under the Dagan name. These numbers would represent a 1.73% and 2.53% increase in market share (out of a total market of 24,000 chain saws), respectively.

CRITIQUE OF STUDENT ANALYSIS OF WESTERN PRODUCTS LIMITED

OVERALL EVALUATION

Your analysis of the advertising campaign issue was thorough and clear. You should have widened the scope of your analysis, though, to capture some of the more subtle issues, such as, Is Western Products too dependent on Excelsior? What are the relative merits of advertising and personal selling? What market segments should be pursued?

ISSUE IDENTIFICATION

Your statement of the issue was clear and concise. However, you didn't develop a statement of the broader problems facing the company. Remember that what people think is the problem is often only a symptom of the real problem. In this case, Mr. Norrin was focusing on whether to advertise the Dagan brand of chain saws. You should have asked yourself why Mr. Norrin was even considering this change. After all, Western Products was not in any kind of obvious trouble. There must have been a good reason for contemplating an investment like this. Was the market changing, thereby making new forms of communication necessary? Did existing channels of distributions need to be supplemented? Was personal selling no longer feasible and/or effective?

Among the case facts to be considered helpful in identifying key issues are

- only 41% of sales are under the Dagan brand name
- Mr. Norrin and Ms. Smith lacked the time to call on a majority of other dealers and distributors
- brand preference is important to buyers
- dealers exert considerable influence on buyers

Always question whether what seems to be the issue actually is. Often, the problem goes deeper.

Your flow chart was very useful in clarifying the pattern of chain saw sales and Western's relation with Excelsior.

SITUATION ANALYSIS

You did not do a thorough situation analysis. It is usually a good idea to do one, because it helps you organize a lot of information and sheds light on the issues in the case. It also makes explicit the assumptions under which you are operating and lets you know what you *don't* know.

A situation analysis would have revealed, for example, that Western Products' relationship with Excelsior may be a mixed blessing. In your analysis, you did a very good job explaining the advantages of the relationship, but you overlook the associated threat. Western Products' dependence on a single major distributor puts it in a vulnerable position. That puts the advertising question in a different, more favourable light—not only might an advertising campaign generate some "pull" demand, it might also reduce Western Products' vulnerability. However, you did a good job in recognizing that the impact of Dagan's ad campaign on relations with Excelsior must be considered in making a decision.

ALTERNATIVES

Given your identification of issues, your list of alternative courses of action was fine. For completeness, it should have included the option, "Do nothing differently." Maybe even more critical, however, was your not considering the alternative of hiring an additional salesperson. The case mentions that the executives don't have the time to call on all the accounts, and the market research data show that the dealer's influence is important in the purchase process.

The second alternative (co-op advertising) you proposed was particularly good because it went beyond what had been suggested in the case; a creative solution like this is a big plus.

ANALYSIS OF ALTERNATIVES

Your analysis of the alternatives you suggested was concise. It is important to state the criteria against which you are evaluating the alternatives. To a certain extent you did this, but only in your "closing note." You seemed to evaluate the alternatives against different criteria. For example, what is the incremental financial cost of each alternative? What are the incremental financial benefits? What are the nonfinancial costs and benefits? These criteria should have been the logical result of your situation analysis. You need to examine each alternative systematically, so that you can see exactly how well each one does on each criterion. Then, if new circumstances change the firm's priorities (for example, should the relationship with Excelsior sour), it is easier to see how the alternatives stack up.

Your economic analysis of the advertising alternative was good. You generally made reasonable assumptions in evaluating the financial impact of the proposed advertising plan. It's a good idea, as you did, to translate the numbers into a market share target. For a company with a current market share of 15%, an incremental market share gain of 2.5% is a considerable challenge.

In your analysis, you might note that the $5,000 fee to Summit Advertising is already committed for this year, so it is not an incremental cost and would not be appropriate for the breakeven analysis. You were generally quite careful in your analysis, and it was correct to recognize the 15% rebate on media costs.

You should not be convinced too quickly that a particular alternative is superior. Avoid the temptation to try to find the one, "right" answer. Look at each possibility in as balanced a way as possible. For example, the alternative of co-op advertising still leaves Western Products quite dependent on Excelsior.

RECOMMENDATION

Your recommendation was clear and actionable. However, you could have been more specific by making recommendations which would have addressed the questions, What rate should be used to share the co-op ad costs? What's the budget? What is the likely outcome?

ORGANIZATION OF REPORT

You might have used a more formal approach or framework in your ''analysis'' or ''discussion'' section. As mentioned earlier, you did not do a ''Situation Analysis.'' Consider using subheadings, such as (a) consumer/buyer analysis, (b) market segmentation, (c) environmental analysis, and (d) company versus competition—strengths and weaknesses. While these categories may not always be appropriate, they help the reader to understand the presentation. Furthermore, the categories may help organize your thoughts and analysis. As an example, under ''Buyer Analysis,'' you might consider, How important is advertising in the buying decision for a chain saw? How important is personal selling? Are potential buyers aware of the Dagan brand name? The Excelsior brand name?

Lastly, the ''Closing Note'' catches the reader by surprise. This note should be presented earlier in the discussion so that the merits of your recommendations can be assessed.

TO RECAP

You have done a good job of examining one aspect of the case. If you had applied the same creativity to other issues and had approached the case more systematically, yours would have been a superior case analysis.

SECOND EDITION

CANADIAN MARKETING

CASES & EXERCISES

Section 1

THE NATURE OF MARKETING

Every reader of this book has been an active consumer for years, evaluating and purchasing a wide array of products from competing suppliers. The cases and exercises in this book place the reader in a different role, that of the marketing manager in a diverse group of organizations, responsible for helping to develop, price, and distribute their products and encouraging customers to purchase them.

In a purchase, the customer offers something of value (typically money, but also time and personal effort) in exchange for the value represented by the product. Managing and facilitating these transactions lie at the heart of marketing management. Success in this endeavour requires an understanding of how individuals and organizations make decisions relating to purchase behaviour and how this behaviour may be influenced.

Historically, the study of marketing emphasized the purchase and sale of physical goods in the private sector of the economy. The greatest sophistication was achieved in consumer packaged goods, with attention later being directed to marketing consumer-durable and industrial goods. Today, the situation is different in that marketing expertise is now also highly valued by managers of service firms (whose output accounts for approximately half of Canada's gross national product). In the public and nonprofit sectors, too, there is widespread interest in developing a stronger marketing orientation among organizations as diverse as disease-prevention agencies, transit authorities, museums, and performing arts programs. Most nonbusiness organizations market services, but some sell goods through retail stores or mail order catalogues, and many promote social issues and behaviour patterns—such as conserving scarce resources and voting in political campaigns. In this book, we will use the term *product* in its generic sense to include goods, services, and social behaviours.

MANAGEMENT AND CUSTOMER PERSPECTIVES

Success in developing a marketing program for any type of product requires the ability to understand both management and customer perspectives. The organization attempts to achieve profitability through the sale of its products (public and nonprofit organizations may seek to achieve social as opposed to *financial* profits and thus need to attract gifts or tax revenues to help cover their costs); customers are interested in what the product will do for them.

At one level, the marketing process is used by the organization to develop an overall product-market strategy. Decisions must be made on which customers to serve with what products in order to meet goals. Such decisions must be made in light of the company's resources and with regard to future as well as current market conditions. This perspective reflects the costs and benefits accruing to the marketer. At a second level, the marketing process is used to develop detailed marketing programs that reflect a good understanding of the needs of final customers and intermediary organizations. Managers should be asking: What specific combination of product features, delivery systems, pricing, and information dissemination will lead a specific customer (or group of customers) to purchase a specific product from us rather than from a competitor—or not at all?

The materials in this casebook are concerned with both levels of the marketing process. This dual focus requires, first, careful analysis and evaluation of each organization's product-market strategy. Is this strategy realistic and sound in the light of environmental trends, market characteristics, customer needs, and competitive activities? What modifications, if any, are required? Rarely is there one obvious strategy or plan. Widely varying solutions to a marketing problem may be appropriate, depending on the manager's knowledge and assessment of current and future conditions, creativity in generating plans of action, willingness to take risks, and judgement about the resources available and the goals to be met. Moreover, some strategies may be more difficult to implement than others. Although case analysis and discussion do not allow for actual implementation, the likelihood of successful implementation is an important criterion in assessing a strategy. Different strategies are, of course, likely to have different consequences down the road.

Developing a specific marketing plan emphasizes the second level of the marketing process, since here the focus is on resolving a particular marketing problem or taking advantage of a specific opportunity. A critical part of most marketing plans is using special skills (or "distinctive competences") that will make the firm particularly effective in its chosen product-market, relative to its competition. Developing a marketing plan usually proceeds in the following manner:

1. Identify and define the problem or opportunity.
2. Establish the marketing goals to be met.
3. Analyze relevant data on the market, customers, intermediaries, competitors, and other relevant environments.
4. Develop alternative approaches and plans of action.
5. Analyze the economic implications of alternative strategies as these relate to costs, revenues, and anticipated volumes. Consider other relevant criteria.
6. Use these analyses to select and justify a specific plan of action.

MARKETING TOOLS AND CONCEPTS

The cases in this first section of the book introduce various analytical tools and conceptual frameworks that are central to the development of marketing strategy. These include market analysis, market segmentation, buyer behaviour, competitive analysis, and the role of intermediaries. Many marketing decisions can be broken down into several elements that are collectively referred to as the marketing mix. These elements include product policy, pricing, distribution, and communication (for example, personal selling, advertising, direct mail, telemarketing, and promotion).

MARKET ANALYSIS

Central to the development of any marketing program is information on market size, structure, and dynamics. From this information, managers can gain insights into the performance of existing products relative to the competition and into the prospects for existing or proposed products in the future.

Among the most significant questions that the manager should seek to answer are

- How large is the market for the product in question?
- Is it growing, shrinking, or static?
- What are the major forces influencing the level of demand for this product?
- Can the market be broken down into segments? If so, what are the most useful bases for segmentation?
- At what stage in the product life cycle is this market? Are we dealing with a new-product category that is growing rapidly, a mature and well-established one, or an old-product category for which demand is falling?
- Is demand consistent over time or does it fluctuate sharply in response to random or cyclical factors?
- Who are the competitors serving this market? What is the basis of competition? Where is the competition vulnerable?

MARKET SEGMENTATION

The concept of market segmentation is implicit in decisions on what customer groups to serve and on how to combine marketing variables to appeal to a particular group of potential customers.

Market segmentation is based upon the following propositions:

1. Not all customers are alike—many customers (or institutional purchasers) differ from one another in marketing-relevant ways.
2. Segments of consumers can be identified and isolated within the overall market according to such factors as their personal characteristics, geographic location, lifestyles, the needs they seek to satisfy, their buying behaviour, and levels of usage of the product in question.

Most marketing organizations find themselves operating in "mass markets" of thousands or even millions of customers and prospective customers. Market segmentation represents a middle way between a strategy of market aggregation, in which all customers are treated similarly, and market disaggregation, in which each customer is treated uniquely. The goal is to combine the efficiencies of economies of scale with the attention to personal concerns that comes from focusing on the needs of individuals who share certain important characteristics. Effective marketing strategy requires an explicit choice of which segments to serve.

BUYER BEHAVIOUR

How does a customer decide to buy a product and then go about purchasing it? Managers need to understand buyer behaviour before they can move to strategy development. Some purchases are an impulsive act by a single individual, such as buying a magazine at a supermarket checkout counter. Other purchases entail more time and planning, whether they represent the decision of an individual or of a group. Large purchases in a family or institutional setting may involve several members who may act as a type of buying committee. Such a group is sometimes known as a decision-making unit, since its members arrive at the purchase decision collectively, even though a single individual may take responsibility for making the purchase or placing the order.

Individuals or decision-making units are often influenced in their purchase decisions by advice or information from other parties. Friends and relatives, for instance, may encourage or discourage a particular course of action, such as buying a new car. Large organizations may have a formal buying committee which is responsible for selecting a vendor or choosing which product to buy. Moreover, corporate executives outside the buying committee may influence the product "specs" in one way or another or impose requirements that specify which manufacturers and service suppliers represent approved vendors.

Although analysis of one's personal experiences in buying consumer goods and services may offer useful insights, it is unwise to generalize too broadly from these. Other people may approach similar purchases in different ways. The buying behaviour of industrial firms and other institutions is frequently somewhat different from that of household purchasers, the former involving substantially larger volumes, unfamiliar product categories, and formalized procedures for decision making.

A general set of questions for understanding buyer behaviour might include the following:

- Who initiates the buying process?
- What events or factors stimulate a need to purchase?
- What are the constraints associated with the decision?
- Is this a one-time or repetitive purchase situation?
- What criteria are used to evaluate alternative products?
- How are these criteria set? Which criteria are most important and how will they change over time?
- Whose opinions influence the evaluation of alternative purchases?
- Who makes the final buying decision, and does any one individual have effective veto power?
- Who implements the actual purchase transaction?
- Who uses the product once the purchase has been made?

COMPETITIVE ANALYSIS

Actions taken by competitors play a major role in determining whether a particular marketing program will be successful. At the outset, analysis of the market should identify and evaluate the relative strength of current competitors, using the following criteria:

- How long has each competitor been active in the market?
- What is its market share in both volume and financial terms? And has this share been rising or falling over time?
- Does each competitor appeal to a broad cross-section of customers, or does it pursue

a "niche" strategy, targeting its product(s) and marketing programs at one or more market segments?

- What are key strengths and distinctive competences of each competitor?

Determining the current competitive situation, however, is not sufficient. Any manager who presumes, without good evidence, that competing organizations will continue their present strategies into the future is most unwise. Marketers need to know enough about each competitor—its financial situation, marketing strengths and weaknesses, people resources, short- and long-term objectives, potential for innovation, cost structure, and management values—to predict, with reasonable accuracy, how it is likely to respond to new initiatives.

ROLE OF INTERMEDIARIES

Marketers of both consumer and industrial products may find it necessary, or simply advantageous, to delegate certain marketing functions to independent intermediaries. Thus, the design and execution of advertising campaigns are frequently contracted out to advertising agencies. Similarly, credit financing may be arranged through a financial institution such as a bank or credit card company. The most important use of intermediaries concerns the physical distribution of goods and the delivery of services (sometimes through franchising or the use of electronic channels for financial and information services). A major advantage of using intermediaries rather than doing the work oneself is that it substitutes variable costs for fixed overheads and semivariable costs.

Organizations that choose to market through intermediaries—such as wholesalers, retailers, distributors, brokers, or agencies—are looking for leverage. In return for a portion of the selling price, the original marketer gets the intermediary to offer customer benefits like greater convenience, expert advice, added service features, and one-stop shopping for related products. Additionally, the intermediaries may take full or partial responsibility for selling, advertising and promotional efforts, credit, and display. In some instances, selected intermediaries may receive exclusive rights to distribute a specific product, as in franchising or exclusive dealerships. In other instances, a qualified intermediary may be permitted to act as a distributor for the product in question.

Marketers should always remember that intermediaries are independent organizations which are free to enter into an agreement, or not, with primary suppliers of goods and services. The alternative for the marketer is to integrate vertically and operate its own distribution system—a strategy that is much more common in the service sector than in manufacturing, particularly for consumer goods. Some distributor relationships are highly structured, as in franchising, and give the original marketer a significant degree of control. In other relationships, as with a small manufacturer selling through a well-established retail chain, the power lies more strongly with the retail chain.

In certain respects, analyzing current and prospective intermediaries is analogous to customer analysis. Intermediaries can be segmented according to a variety of factors (size, target market, geographic location, hours of operation, and so forth). Their involvement with competitors' products can be studied. An analysis can—and should—be made of how an intermediary makes decisions on whether or not to distribute particular goods and services, what criteria its management employs in making such decisions, and which individuals comprise its decision-making unit. Finally, consideration should be given to what advantages might be gained over competitors by improving the margins provided to intermediaries, offering advertising and promotional assistance, providing market research data, and increasing contact with relevant managers.

THE MARKETING MIX

Putting together a marketing plan requires the manager to make strategic decisions in several important areas, which are collectively known as the marketing mix and include:

1. the product,
2. the distribution and delivery system through which products are made available to customers,
3. the price at which the product is sold, and
4. the communications by which prospective customers are informed about the product and encouraged to buy it.

Many people mistakenly equate marketing solely with communication activities—advertising, promotion, public relations, and personal selling. Viewed from the perspective of the marketing mix, we can see that the scope of the marketing function is considerably broader.

The marketing mix provides a very useful organizing framework for strategy development. First, product characteristics must be designed with reference to both customer needs and the requirement to differentiate the product from competing alternatives. Second, choices must be made on how to get the product delivered to the customer through physical or electronic channels. Third, a price must be set that will, at projected sales volumes, enable the marketer to cover costs and generate the level of profit desired. This price must also be set with reference to the prices of competing products and the ability and willingness of prospective customers to pay. Credit arrangements may be necessary to bring the product within reach of many would-be customers. Finally, the marketer must evaluate the most cost-effective ways of communicating with customers to tell them (or remind them) about the product and encourage them to buy it. This involves decisions about messages, advertising media, personal selling efforts, publicity and public relations, point-of-sale information, labelling, signing, and instructional materials. While this sequential approach may be a helpful first step, all marketing mix elements are ultimately interdependent and the marketing plan must recognize these interdependencies.

CONCLUSION

Marketing is the most externally directed of all the management functions, focusing on customers, intermediaries, competitors, and market dynamics. Successful marketers need to adopt multiple perspectives. They must understand the strengths and weaknesses of both their own organizations and those of their competitors, recognizing the goals that each seeks to achieve. They must also be able to see the world from the viewpoint of prospective customers and intermediaries, in terms of the needs that each seeks to satisfy and the criteria that they employ in evaluating alternative suppliers.

The first task of marketing is to establish an overall product-market strategy to meet organizational objectives. The second task is to develop a marketing plan including detailed substrategies for each element of the marketing mix. Decisions must be made on the features that the product should possess, how it is to be delivered to customers (should intermediaries be used?), how it is to be priced, and what information should be communicated through which media to potential customers. Each of these decisions must be oriented toward the needs and characteristics of the market segments at which the product is targeted. Managers should also take into account the strategies directed at each segment by competing organizations, to assess how much of a threat they represent. Sound plans should anticipate and counter or finesse competitive efforts. The third and final task—which is critical to the ultimate success of any plan—is to have the co-operation of all involved. The task is to persuade the organization to commit the necessary resources to the product and ensure that all managers, personnel, and intermediaries understand their role in helping to implement the plan.

1 B.C. PACKERS

Craig R. Pollack

Charles B. Weinberg

In February 1989, Mr. David McIvor, General Manager of the Export Canned Sales Division of British Columbia Packers Limited, was considering whether his division should launch a canned cat food product in the Canadian cat food market. Some categories in this market had experienced impressive growth in recent years, but Mr. McIvor recognized that competition was increasing; for his company to compete successfully he knew that B.C. Packers would have to enter the market fairly quickly or not at all.

COMPANY BACKGROUND

B.C. Packers was founded in 1923 as a private company. In 1984, it was purchased by George Weston Limited—a publicly traded multi-billion dollar conglomerate. B.C. Packers is best known for its canned tuna and salmon products; the company's Canadian product line includes the Cloverleaf, Rupert, Bumble Bee, and Paramount brands. Cloverleaf is the market leader in both canned salmon and tuna, holding more than a 35% market share on both brands. Sales for the Fisheries Division of Weston Resources (which includes B.C. Packers) for 1987 and 1988 were $564 million and $573 million respectively. Operating income for 1987 and 1988 was $42 million and $32 million respectively.

In the early 1980s, B.C. Packers entered into a joint venture agreement with the Philippines government and opened a canning facility in that country under the name of the Mar Fishing Company. The Philippines operation supplied canned fish products to various overseas markets as well as manufacturing a canned cat food product. The cat food, called "Lovely," had been produced for several years and was sold only in Japan.

CANADIAN CANNED CAT FOOD OPPORTUNITY

Management at B.C. Packers had been considering the possibility of entering the Canadian cat food market for a few years. The domestic cat food opportunity arose primarily because B.C. Packers was looking for more profitable alternatives for the fish by-product that was generated in the processing of their canned salmon and tuna. Currently, B.C. Packers either sells this by-product in bulk as fish meal (a commodity for which the firm just covers its costs) or as a cat food for the Japanese market. While selling a well-known brand of cat food in Japan had proved to be fairly profitable for B.C. Packers, competition was very heavy in this market. Also,

Note: Some of the data in this case are disguised.

the Philippines plant had a considerable amount of excess capacity in which to process the fish by-product; Mr. McIvor felt that it was unlikely that B.C. Packers could generate enough sales in Japan to utilize all the excess capacity.

In addition to B.C. Packers' successful experience with selling a branded, advertised cat food in Japan, there were other reasons that Mr. McIvor felt that marketing a cat food product in Canada might be viable for the firm. The reasons included: a considerable rise in the number of cats as household pets in North America over the last five years due to changing sociodemographic factors; B.C. Packers had an established network of brokers throughout Canada that distributed their canned salmon and tuna products; B.C. Packers was highly regarded by the Canadian retail trade; and Weston could provide product research support for a B.C. Packers cat food product.[1] Based on B.C. Packers' experience in Japan and the strength of Weston's research labs, Mr. McIvor was confident that his firm could formulate cat foods that were equal to that of any major cat food manufacturer and superior to many.

While Mr. McIvor recognized that these were quite compelling reasons, he realized that he needed more information about the Canadian cat food market before he could commit the firm to introducing a product. Consequently, Mr. McIvor formed a three-person management team to carry out a study of the Canadian cat food industry. The team took two months to research, write, and submit a report to Mr. McIvor. After looking at the report in detail, Mr. McIvor felt he had a good understanding of the market.

THE CAT FOOD INDUSTRY

According to the report, 1989 Canadian total pet food sales at retail prices were forecasted to be $625 million. Of this total, grocery store sales were placed at $500 million, while the remaining $125 million in sales would be generated by specialty pet food stores. These specialty stores accounted for $65 million in cat food sales in 1989. Cat food sales through specialty stores were estimated to be growing at a rate of 10% annually.

The team members noted that while they relied on the best available data, there was some uncertainty surrounding the figures. Limited statistics were compiled on pet/cat population (as well as of sales of pet-related products) in Canada by any one organization. Also, a significant portion of Canadian pet information was extrapolated from U.S. sources and was viewed by some industry experts as somewhat unreliable.

Of the estimated $500 million in grocery store sales for 1989, cat food sales were expected to account for 52% of the total. If achieved, this would be a 7% increase in dollar sales over 1988. Within the cat food category for 1989, total cat food sales by type were forecast as follows:

[1] Many of the major North American cat food manufacturers utilized large product research facilities in an attempt to gain a competitive advantage over their competition.

Canned	60.9%	$158.3 million
Dry	30.8	80.1 million
Semi-moist	8.1	21.1 million
Snacks	0.2	0.5 million
Totals:	100%	$260.0 million

The management team broke down the canned cat food category further in terms of the products' promoted images. The canned cat food found in grocery stores was classified into three distinct classes: gourmet, national, and price (including store) brands. See Exhibit 1 for a "store check" summary of some products from each brand category.

The gourmet class, less than two years old in Canada, consists of "extravagantly" flavoured canned cat food sold at a premium price. These brands are targeted to consumers who place a "higher value" on their cats and, therefore, are willing to spend more on a product that they believe to be superior. Although the flavour offerings provide improved palatability, gourmet products are not necessarily nutritionally superior. Nevertheless, consumers may buy these brands due to their perception that gourmet products are of higher quality. Examples of such brands are Fancy Feast and Whiskas Supreme. Flavours of Fancy Feast, which is sold in 85 g cans, include whitefish and tuna, salmon feast, tender beef, and cod, sole, and shrimp. The flavours of Whiskas Supreme include tuna and whitefish, salmon and crab, chicken and game, and turkey and giblets. The average retail price of the gourmet brands is $0.69 per can.

National brands come in a variety of beef, poultry, and seafood flavours that are competitively priced. They are targeted towards the average consumer encouraging

Exhibit 1

CANNED CAT FOOD STORE CHECK RESULTS

Brand	Category	Number of Flavours	Sizes	Regular Price	Feature Price
Fancy Feast	Gourmet	9	85g	0.69	0.59
Whiskas Supreme	Gourmet	10	105g	0.69	0.59
Whiskas	National	12	170g and 380g	0.79, 1.33	0.62, 1.09
9-Lives	National	13+	170g	0.49	0.39
Kal Kan	National	9	170g and 383g	0.68, 1.09	0.58, 0.99
Miss Mew	National	10	170g	0.62	0.49
Dr. Ballards	National	3	397g	1.09	0.99
Pamper	National	13+	170g and 380g	0.69, 1.09	0.59, 0.99
President's Choice	Store	6	170g and 397g	0.49, 0.89	n/a
No Name (Super-Valu)	Store	6	170g and 397g	0.43, 0.86	n/a

brand loyalty and offering a low-risk purchase through strong brand awareness. Miss Mew, 9-Lives, Puss 'n Boots, and Kal Kan are examples of national brands. Most of the dollar sales for national brands are accounted for by the 170 g can size, which has an average retail price of $0.59.

Price brands offer a limited selection of flavours and compete primarily on price. On average, they are sold at a retail price of $0.49 per 170 g can. Virtually no advertising money or promotional support is invested in these brands. A portion of this market consists of supermarket or generic brands in which the supermarket contracts with a packer to put the store's label on the product. Again, there is minimal advertising or promotion support behind these brands. An exception to this is President's Choice brand (sold in Loblaws and Real Canadian Superstores), which is positioned as a higher quality generic product.

According to industry sources, the 1989 expected grocery outlet market shares (and sales) of each class of canned cat food are as follows:

Gourmet brands	12.5%	$ 19.8 million
National brands	72.5	114.7 million
Price brands	15.0	23.8 million
Totals:	100.0	158.3 million

Although the bulk of sales in the cat food market is generated via the national brands, industry experts all support a polarization trend in the market. It appears that the fastest growth is occurring in the gourmet category with an estimated growth rate of 50% per annum during its initial two years on the market.[2] Similarly, the price brands experienced a strong growth of 17% during the same two-year time frame. These polarized segments have cannibalized the national segment which experienced an 8% decrease in dollar sales during 1987 to 1988.

Retail Distribution Channels

There are two primary retail distribution channels for pet foods. Grocery stores (supermarkets, superettes, convenience stores, and all other food stores) account for more than 75% of total pet food sales. Pet food is very important to the grocery trade as it is currently the second largest product category in terms of dollar sales in supermarkets.

The second type of retail distribution channel consists of specialty pet food stores, which were expected to account for an estimated $30 million (retail) of canned cat food sales in 1989. In addition to carrying a variety of gourmet, national, and price brands, these stores have the exclusive rights to sell premium brands that are

[2] Gourmet cat food products in the United States, which have been on the market for three to four years longer than their Canadian counterparts, experienced a growth rate of 50% during their first two to three years but then experienced considerable decline. In 1987, the U.S. gourmet cat food market grew at a 5% to 12% rate—the range was due to conflicting figures from different industry experts.

positioned as highly nutritious products. Examples of premium brands are Pro Plan and Science Diet. These brands are usually purchased by owners whose pets are either competitive "show pets" or have some kind of nutritional deficiency. Specialty store owners state that these premium brands account for a sizable portion of their sales, probably exceeding 30%. Gourmet brands are also said to do well in specialty stores, although somewhat below the level of the premium brands. National and price brands make up the remainder of their sales. Detailed data are not available on the share of market held by the various brands in these stores. However, most major brands are stocked by these stores.

PET FOOD MANUFACTURERS

Canadian cat food manufacturers can be divided according to the type of product they produce into national/gourmet, premium, or price brand producers.

National/Gourmet Manufacturers

Manufacturers in this category include firms that produce either or both a national or gourmet cat food. The leaders among the national brand manufacturers include: Nestle (Miss Mew), Effem (Whiskas and Kal Kan), Quaker Oats (Puss 'n Boots and Pamper), and Starkist (9-Lives). The major gourmet brand producers are Nestle (Fancy Feast) and Effem (Whiskas Supreme). Many of the gourmet and national firms are widely diversified into other grocery product lines. Virtually all the products in this category are available in numerous flavours. Many national brands are backed by annual million dollar (or more) advertising and promotion campaigns, while some gourmet products are also supported by large expenditures. Manufacturers in this category offer special deals and discounts to consumers and the trade at various times during the year. For example, in a one-month period two major brands were offering trade promotions—one at 8% off and the other at 20% off the wholesale price if specified volume and display requirements were met. Another brand was offering consumers one can free if two cans were purchased. Two brands had just finished offers of free gifts (e.g., a calendar with pictures of cats) if a sufficient number of labels were sent to the company.

Premium Manufacturers

Leaders in the premium cat food segment include Hill's Pet Products (Science Diet), Martin Feed Mills (Techni-Cal), and Ralston Purina (Pro Plan). IAMs, the dominant pet food manufacturer in the Canadian premium pet food segment, does not presently compete in the canned cat food market. Its pet food line includes products in the dry dog and cat food market. Premium products are also available from veterinary clinics in addition to being sold in specialty outlets. Cat food manufacturers in this category pursue a serious commitment to research and development; their products are positioned as highly nutritious. Marketing support typically includes limited advertising in trade journals and various training and nutritional programs for veterinarians and specialty retailers.

Exhibit 2

PROFILES OF CANADIAN CAT FOOD BUYERS

Premium Buyers:	upper income, professional, specialty store shopper, nutritionally oriented, very pet health conscious, pure-breed cat owner, regular veterinarian visits, strong attachment to cat
Gourmet Buyers:	generally female age 35 and over, affluent, upper income, supermarket shopper, personification of cat as a baby substitute, typically single cat owner, spoils cat after working all day, perceives high price to be quality, identifies with luxury image
National Buyers:	generally female 25 to 54, somewhat price sensitive, low-risk purchaser, conservative, some brand loyalty, perhaps multiple cat owner, family oriented
Price Buyers:	budget-constrained, price sensitive, possibly multiple cat owner, buys in volume, cat may have a smaller role in the household

Price Manufacturers

Price brands are manufactured by various regional manufacturers. Price products are lower priced, have minimal advertising support, and have a smaller number of flavour offerings. Manufacturing these brands is not a particularly difficult task, and there are a number of potential suppliers. In addition, supermarket chains that want to offer a private brand of pet food can easily arrange for a contract packer to produce whatever quantities are needed.

CONSUMER PROFILES

The time available to the management team had not permitted them to carry out a consumer survey. Nevertheless, they compiled their own profiles of Canadian cat food consumers using industry sources, trade periodicals, and some previously collected market data. The four major segments are described in Exhibit 2.

Shoppers who bought at grocery stores typically shopped once a week and bought seven to ten cans at a time. Specialty store shoppers usually bought twice as much and shopped two to three times a month. Specialty food store buyers were believed to make most of their purchases at one store, but do not necessarily always purchase the same brand. Among national and gourmet brand purchasers, there was believed to be a considerable amount of brand switching. Some buyers (or at least their cats) were thought to be loyal to flavours rather than to brands.

PET FOOD CERTIFICATION

The nonprofit Canadian Veterinary Medical Association (CVMA) offers the only third party nutritional quality assurance program for pet foods in Canada. Established in

1976, the CVMA is a very well-respected, credible association. However, not all pet food companies in Canada choose to have their products certified by this organization. This can be attributed to many factors, including the fact that certification is a voluntary process, and that gourmet and some national brands do not want to be "associated with" the price brands that obtain certification.[3]

OTHER FACTORS

As Mr. McIvor read the management team's report, some other factors that seemed important to him as they pertained to the Canadian pet and cat food industries were as follows:

- It is difficult to secure substantial distribution for many new pet food products as competition for store shelf space is intense.
- Some of the larger pet food companies utilize direct sales forces (versus brokers) in order to gain better exposure for their products with retailers.
- The pet food industry is characterized by competitive, aggressive pricing strategies; retailers frequently receive products at discounts ranging from 8% to 20% off the wholesale price. Over a year, these discounts typically averaged 4% of a manufacturer's sales.
- Most grocery stores carried two to three price brands of which one was usually a store brand.
- Nestle's national brand "Friskies" cat food, which was number three in canned cat food sales in the United States, is expected to be introduced in Canada in 1990.
- As a result of the Canada–U.S. Free Trade Agreement, competition in the Canadian pet food industry may increase because of imports of U.S. products by Canadian brokers and wholesalers.
- During the period of 1983 to 1987, the cat population in Canada increased 4.6% in total as compared to a 5.8% decrease in the dog population. The various factors contributing to this trend were: (1) an increase in real estate costs: people are moving into smaller dwelling units due to higher land costs and cats are viewed as more appropriate pets in smaller living quarters; (2) a rise in urbanization: houses are becoming more concentrated and smaller as more people are moving to city centres and cats appear to function better in less space than many dogs; and (3) changes in the family: more women are entering the work force and spending less time at home caring for the family and pets and cats tend to require less care than most dogs.

CONSIDERING THE CAT FOOD OPPORTUNITY

While Mr. McIvor felt that the management team's report was informative and helpful, he still had some hesitations about entering the Canadian canned cat food market. Mr. McIvor voiced his concerns to his superiors and together they decided

[3] CVMA's fee for certification was about $8000 for the initial listing (per flavour) and $5000 per year (per flavour) to monitor the product.

that Mr. McIvor and his export division staff should develop a business plan. The firm would use the plan as its basis in deciding whether B.C. Packers should enter the canned cat food market.

In developing the business proposal, Mr. McIvor was especially concerned with the questions of which product class market, if any, should B.C. Packers enter? While Mr. McIvor had many factors to consider, he recognized that a profitability analysis of each option would help him with his decision. In order to do this, Mr. McIvor estimated the contribution margins that B.C. Packers would likely achieve from each class. His estimates, before advertising and trade discounts, were a 57% contribution margin (on B.C. Packers' price) for gourmet brands, 48% for national brands, and 37% for generic brands. Mr. McIvor based these estimates on the average prices manufacturers were currently receiving for their products. Gourmet brands were sold by manufacturers for an average price of $11.50 per case of 24 cans (85 to 105 g size). National and price brands were typically sold in larger can sizes (170 g and 380 g). For national brands, manufacturers typically realized $9.24 for a case of 24 (170 g) cans. Manufacturers of generic brands typically sold their product to retailers at a price of $7.25 for a case of 24 (170 g) cans. Mr. McIvor felt that, initially, B.C. Packers would use those prices, depending on the product class.

After estimating the firm's prices and contribution margins, Mr. McIvor recognized that the promotion and advertising requirements needed for each product class should be included in the calculations. Mr. McIvor had asked B.C. Packers' advertising agency to estimate what would be required to succeed in the cat food market. Trinka James, the account manager, suggested that an expenditure of $650,000 would be required to achieve 10% of the gourmet market, but she said her estimate of share could be off by ±3%. She also said that the national brand market was much tougher. At least twice as much advertising and promotion would be needed to be heard above the clutter and even so only a fraction of the national market could be gained. She noted that one established national manufacturer had spent more than a million dollars and only achieved a 5% share (of the national market) in the first year. Less spending would be needed in subsequent years. Incremental marketing, general, and administrative costs would also be incurred. For this project, these items were estimated to be $150,000. (If B.C. Packers' cat food sales exceeded $2 million, these costs would likely rise by another $50,000.) Additionally, trade discounts had to be factored into any decision.

The fish processing plant in the Philippines had sufficient excess by-products to supply B.C. Packers with up to 800,000 cases (24 cans, 90 g each) per year. To make a complete product line, chicken and beef would be purchased from other divisions of the company.) Beyond that, an investment of $250,000 would be required to expand plant capacity.

Mr. McIvor knew that a number of other questions and issues also needed to be resolved. The following lists several of the more pressing ones.

- Could B.C. Packers secure shelf space in retail outlets? This was an extremely important consideration, as securing adequate shelf space is critical to the success of any packaged good product. Obtaining shelf space depended on many considerations including the number of competitors in the product category, a company's reputation within the packaged goods industry, the ability of a salesperson/broker to sell a product to a retail buyer, trade allowances provided by the brand, ad support behind the product, and the track record of the brand in other stores. Mr. McIvor wondered which product category would allow the firm to gain the most shelf space.

- How much money should B.C. Packers allocate for consumer promotions? Mr. McIvor not only wanted to know how much money the firm should spend on promoting and advertising a product during its introductory year, but also how much it should spend against a brand over the first three to five years. Also, Mr. McIvor wondered what media vehicles the firm should utilize in promoting a cat food. It appears that many national and gourmet brands spend considerable amounts on television and print advertising. Current advertising spending by competitors was not known.
- What would be an appropriate package size? Currently, the plant in the Philippines has the equipment to manufacture a 90 g can—the size of B.C. Packers' canned salmon and tuna products. If a gourmet line was to be introduced, this package size would be chosen. However, a product for the other categories would require a larger size can. (There would a one-time cost of $20,000 for each new can size). Another option was to package the cat food in a can with a pull-tab top that was shaped so that the can would then serve as the cat's feeding dish. This package would be viable only if B.C. Packers targeted the gourmet market where the small can size was comparable to a single meal for a cat. Adopting this option would involve a one-time cost of $50,000 for machine retooling, but would also add an estimated $0.60 to B.C. Packers' cost per case.
- Mr. McIvor had tentatively decided to use his current brokers to distribute the new cat food product if it were introduced. The brokers, who would be paid a 5% commission on sales (at the manufacturer's price), could cover both the supermarket and specialty store channels. However, he wanted to think again about the advantages and disadvantages of B.C. Packers hiring its own sales force. The biggest benefit of hiring and training its own sales force was that B.C. Packers would receive maximum exposure for the cat food product as brokers usually sell the products of numerous firms. The main disadvantage of using a sales force was that salespeople were not as cost efficient as brokers at lower volume levels. In addition, salespeople would require a partially guaranteed salary (at least initially) while brokers would be paid strictly on a commission basis.

While Mr. McIvor recognized that there were many difficulties to overcome, he did not want to let a profitable opportunity slip away. With these thoughts in mind, he began to prepare the business proposal.

2 WINDSOR MINIATURE GOLF

Gordon H. G. McDougall

In January 1987, John Smith and Sandra Brown, two high-school teachers, had just finished their analysis of a proposal for a miniature golf course in Windsor, Ontario. They had initially thought of the idea after watching a miniature golf tournament on television. After collecting data on the viability of the proposal, they were discussing whether they should actually invest more time and money and make the proposal a reality. John felt the proposal would make money no matter where they located or how they promoted the venture.

"Look, Sandra, there's no real competition and there's lots of people who would love to play miniature golf in Windsor. I think we've got a potential gold mine on our hands. I've calculated that our maximum capacity for the course is 864 rounds per day, based on the assumption that there would be four people per hole and they would take one hour to play one round. Given that there are 18 holes and the course will be open 12 hours per day, a total of (4 × 1 × 18 × 12) 864 rounds could be played every day."

Sandra Brown was more cautious: "I think there are two important factors: the location and how we market the idea to people. If we don't get the Devonshire Mall location, I wouldn't be too keen on the idea. Also, if we don't promote miniature golf properly, there's a chance that it won't succeed. I think we should have another look at our analysis and figure out if this idea could work and what's the best way to market it."

THE IDEA

John Smith and Sandra Brown had often discussed ways of getting into business during their lunch hours at school. The two teachers felt they could each invest $5,000 in a business venture if they could come up with a reasonable idea. After seeing the televised miniature golf tournament, they decided to do some research on miniature golf in Windsor. The research included an analysis of competition, potential locations, consumers' needs, the Windsor market, and the costs involved.

The Competition

A survey of the Windsor area revealed two existing miniature golf courses. The competitors were evaluated on a number of criteria (Exhibit 1), and the general conclusion reached by the partners was that both courses were of poor quality. It was felt that if a miniature golf course was constructed of high-quality materials and offered a fair degree of challenge, it would attract virtually all of the competitors' customers. The partners decided that if they went ahead with the venture they should

Exhibit 1
MINIATURE GOLF COURSES IN WINDSOR, 1987

		Competitor I (Gateway Plaza)	Competitor II (Suburban Go-Kart)
Location	Accessibility	excellent	poor
	Built-in clientele	very good	poor
Cost	Per eighteen-hole round	$2.00	$1.50
Course	Appearance	fair	poor
	Challenge offered	fair	poor
	Material quality	poor	very poor
Promotion	Advertising	little	none
	Tournaments	none	none
	Leagues	none	none
	Incentives	none	none
	Appeal to market segments	none	none
Return on investment		fair	in the red

consider constructing the best possible course in terms of challenge, materials, and craftsmanship.

Potential Locations

After looking at a number of areas, the partners concluded that any location should be readily accessible to the public. The basic idea was to "bring the game to the people" by having a convenient location. They felt that a location in or near a shopping mall would be good because of the high traffic flows. The manager of Cambridge Investments, a company that controlled Devonshire Mall, was contacted, and the idea of a miniature golf course located at the mall was discussed. Devonshire Mall was considered an ideal site as it was the largest shopping centre in Windsor, with over 150 stores and services in an enclosed mall located in the southern suburbs of the city. The number of people who shopped at Devonshire Mall each month was estimated at around 600,000. The mall had large areas of parking space (parking was available for 4,200 cars), and it was proposed that the golf course be located near one of the entrances to the mall. The manager, while interested in the proposal, did not commit himself to the venture. He suggested that the two partners return after they had finalized their plans. If they were allowed to locate at Devonshire Mall, their rental fee for the land would be 15% of gross sales.

Consumer Analysis

The next step in the project was to conduct a consumer analysis. The partners listed a number of consumer needs they felt miniature golf could satisfy and ranked them in terms of probable importance for three different consumer groups. The needs and rankings were

	Preteen and Teens	Male Adults	Female Adults
a) Recreational enjoyment	1	1	1
b) Family outing	4	4	2
c) Relaxation	5	5	4
d) Socializing	3	8	3
e) Challenge/competition	2	2	5
f) Time required to play	8	6	6
g) Status	6	7	7
h) Convenience	7	3	8

This analysis indicated the primary needs satisfied would be enjoyment, challenge, and socializing with friends or family. Further information was collected by conducting two consumer surveys. A questionnaire was drawn up and given to students at their school. The results, shown in Exhibit 2, indicated that most students would play miniature golf at Devonshire Mall if they were there. Approximately 50% would play miniature golf on a date, and 50% said they would come to the mall on Sunday and play. Approximately 77% said they felt that $2 was a reasonable price for golf. Only 17% felt $2 was too high a price.

The second survey, shown in Exhibit 3, asked 100 adults if they could see any use for a miniature golf course at Devonshire Mall. The results indicated that consumers might participate in miniature golf while shopping at the mall.

The Windsor Market

Windsor, Canada's fourteenth largest city, was primarily a heavy-industry community with large automobile assembly and feeder plants. The average weekly earnings in the city of 250,000 people were $498 compared to the Canadian average of $429. The proposed site at Devonshire Mall would be within a fifteen-minute drive for most of the population of the city.

An additional piece of information was collected: the average number of days with and without rain between May and September (Exhibit 4). On average, there were 104 days without rain during the period.

Cost Estimates

The partners calculated the costs of constructing the miniature golf course (Exhibit 5). The total estimated cost of $17,600 included the cost of building the eighteen holes plus a pro shop, fencing, and miscellaneous expenses. No cost was included for labour because the holes could be built by the industrial arts class at the high school where they taught. The only operating expenses they would incur would be advertising expenses and hiring someone to run the course. The cost of hiring someone was estimated at $4,368, based on paying them $3.50 per hour twelve hours per day for the season of 104 days. They had planned to have the course open from 10:00 a.m. to 10:00 p.m. each day.

Exhibit 2

STUDENT SURVEY RESULTS—AGE SIX TO EIGHTEEN (SAMPLE SIZE = 300)

1. Sex?

Male	144
Female	156
	300

2. Do you go to Devonshire Mall in the summer?

Yes	253
No	47
	300

a) If yes: Would you play miniature golf?

	Yes	No	Maybe
Male	99	12	7
Female	97	24	14

b) If no: Would you go to the mall for a recreational activity like miniature golf?

	Yes	No	Maybe
Male	4	11	11
Female	4	10	7

3. Do you think members of your family would play?

a) Older than yourself?

Yes	No	Maybe
85	61	154

b) Younger than yourself?

Yes	No	Maybe
126	33	141

4. Would you play miniature golf with your date?

	Yes	No	Maybe	No answer
Male	80	14	26	24
Female	82	10	32	32

5. Do you consider $2 a low price—reasonable price—high price?

	Low	Reasonable	High
Male	14	96	34
Female	4	134	18

6. Would you come to the mall on Sunday to play?

	Yes	No	Maybe
Male	70	42	32
Female	80	31	45

While they had collected some data on advertising rates, they had not decided on any advertising campaign. *The Windsor Star*, the local daily newspaper, had a city-wide circulation of 86,000. Cost of advertising for a full page, half page, a quarter page, and one-eighth page was $3,924, $1,962, $981, and $491, respectively. Radio advertising costs ranged from $60 for a thirty-second spot on prime time on CKLW (the local rock nostalgia station) to $32 for an equivalent spot on CKWW (the local teen-oriented rock station).

Exhibit 3
ADULT SURVEY RESULTS

1. (Sample size = 100; females = 50, males = 50)
2. Interviews were conducted at Devonshire Mall and with friends and colleagues.
3. The respondents were informed of the proposal (miniature golf) and asked if they could see any use for such a service.
4. Results—most frequent responses only (response was considered frequent if it occurred 10% of the time):
   a) I could see it as an advantage in that my children wouldn't mind coming shopping with us.
   b) Could serve as a family activity.
   c) Would play while waiting for my wife.
   d) I really don't have the time.

Exhibit 4
SELECTED STATISTICS—WINDSOR MARKET

A. Population (Metropolitan Windsor) Age Groups, 1986	Male	Female
0–4	8,495	8,325
5–9	8,755	8,335
10–14	9,430	9,305
15–19	10,585	10,105
20–24	11,735	11,610
25–34	20,715	20,935
35–44	17,275	17,430
45–54	12,660	12,865
55–64	12,290	13,515
65–69	4,175	5,405
70+	7,605	12,435
	123,720	130,265

Families, 1986: Number 67,595
Average no. per family 3.2

Households, 1986: Number 91,615
Average no. per household 2.7

(continued)

Exhibit 4 continued

B. Income (Average Weekly Earnings)

	Metro Windsor	Canada
1986	$498.47	$428.50
1985	446.78	417.08
1984	438.85	404.10

Taxation Statistics Income Class	1985
Under $2,500	17,460
2,500– 4,999	10,328
5,000– 7,499	10,749
7,500– 9,999	9,963
10,000–12,499	9,221
12,500–14,999	8,060
15,000–19,999	13,470
20,000–24,999	10,294
25,000–29,999	11,035
30,000–39,999	16,815
40,000–and over	12,455
Total	129,850
Average Income	$ 19,182

C. Weather

	Rainfall	
Month	Average number of days with rain*	Average number of days without rain
May	12	19
June	10	20
July	9	22
August	9	22
September	9	21
	49	104

Sources: *Financial Post, Canadian Markets*, and *Marketing Research Handbook*, Statistics Canada, Catalogue 63–224.

*Based on an accumulation of at least .01″. Averaged over last thirty years. Most likely time of rainfall: 3:00 p.m. to 7:00 p.m. during these months.

Exhibit 5

COST ESTIMATES FOR MINIATURE GOLF COURSE

Material Cost			
¾″ plywood	$32.50 per sheet		
2 by 4	0.30 per foot (linear)		
2 by 8	0.70 per foot (linear)		
paint	23.00 per gallon		
carpeting	22.00 square yard		
Average Cost per Hole			
Material cost			
2 by 4, 125′		$ 37.50	
2 by 8, 60′		42.00	
¾″ plywood (3 or 4 sheets)		115.00	
Carpeting (Kentucky blue grass), 11.25 square yards		247.50	
Miscellaneous (nails, sheet metal, batteries, motors, sand, shrubbery)		185.00	
Paint (1 gallon per hole)		23.00	
Total		$650.00	
Labour Cost per Hole			
All construction is to be done by the industrial arts class at the high school under the supervision of a qualified craftsman.			
Total cost per hole		$650.00	
Total cost for eighteen holes = 18 × $650			$11,700
Other Expenses			
Pro shop		$2,500	
Fencing		2,300	
Miscellaneous (putters, balls, cards, pencils)		1,100	
Total		$5,900	5,900
TOTAL COST			$17,600

DECISIONS

The partners faced a number of decisions. They had not decided on the price to charge, either $1.50 or $2 per round; what advertising should be done, if any; or what they should do if the manager of Devonshire Mall did not agree to their proposal. They estimated the total cost would probably be around $19,000, which would mean they would have to borrow $9,000 from the bank. Finally, the major decision had to be made. Should they invest in this venture?

3 VANCOUVER SYMPHONY ORCHESTRA

Daniel F. Gardiner

Charles B. Weinberg

Nothing in the arts has ever been accomplished with thinking whether it will sell.[1]

At a February 1, 1987 meeting in the Vancouver Symphony Orchestra (VSO) offices, three executives were discussing some of the marketing challenges they currently faced. Low attendance and weak revenues had already taken their toll. In January, the VSO's board had voted to cancel the four weeks of concerts from June 11 to July 8 so as to lower its anticipated deficit of $500,000 for the year. The shutdown, which affected about 80 musicians and the 21 members of the management staff, would not affect any concerts in the regularly scheduled season. A special Tchaikovsky Festival, for which tickets had not been sold as yet, would be cancelled. With about 40 performances left there was still time to turn around the fortunes of the VSO.

Dana Rome, Executive Director: "We've got to do something and do it fast to get out of this difficult situation. Time is running out for this season."

Andrea Reid, Director of Marketing: "From my point of view, I've got to find out who wants what: do subscribers want something different from nonsubscribers? If so, what? We've got all this information that needs analyzing, and I'm hoping it will be useful in marketing both this and next season."

D. Von Rogers, Director of Communications: "I've got to decide on an appropriate theme or themes to communicate to the segments we go after. What ads do we run? Are there any promotions we can develop? We've got to give the printers sufficient lead time to get out brochures for next year, so I need to know what to focus on."

Armed with the computer data from an audience survey conducted a month earlier, the three knew that they had to sift through the information very carefully. Within two weeks they had to come up with a set of specific and actionable recommendations that dealt with this year's problem.

All three agreed that their immediate task was to build ticket sales for the remaining four months (about 40 performances of 17 different programs) of the current season. Most of the VSO performances were grouped into four main series. The twelve-event Jubilee series ran from September to May, the five-event Musically

[1] Edo de Waart, conductor, Minnesota Orchestra, as quoted in Alan Rich "The Glorious Symphony," *Newsweek*, January 5, 1987, p. 54.

Exhibit 1
DESCRIPTION OF PERFORMANCES IN CELEBRATION SERIES*

CELEBRATION SERIES

Date	Soloist	Description
Feb. 7 (2 nights)	Igor Kipnis, Harpsichord	A stunning evening of the music of Bach including two concertos for harpsichord and orchestra; the Musical Offering and the Passacaglia and Fugue in C Minor.
Mar. 14 (2 nights)	Barry Tuckwell, French Horn	Britain's outstanding Barry Tuckwell teams with French conductor Georges Sebastian to perform horn concertos by Haydn and Mozart. And on the same program, Mozart's glowing Symphony No. 40, and Schubert's Symphony No. 9, known as "The Great."
Apr. 18 (2 nights)	Alicia de Larrocha, Pianist	The VSO debut of Japan's gifted conductor Tadaaki Otzka also brings the return of Spain's greatest pianist, Alicia de Larrocha. You will hear piano concertos by Haydn and Rachmaninoff, Dvořák's Carnival Overture, and Tchaikovsky's brilliant Symphony No. 4.
May 9 (2 nights)	Edith Mathis, Soprano	The sensational Swiss soprano Edith Mathis returns. Hear her again in soaring concert arias by Mozart and as the soloist in Mahler's sweeping Symphony No. 4.
May 30 (2 nights)	Christopher Parkening, Guitarist	A program inspired by the colour of Spain. The dazzling young guitarist Christopher Parkening in a performance of Rodrigo's Guitar Concerto and the VSO in Ravel's Symphonic Espagnole and De Fallas' Three-Cornered Hat.

* Celebration concerts are performed on Saturdays and Mondays at 8:00 p.m.

Speaking series from September to December, the five-event Celebration series from January to May, and the six-event Pops from February to May. Exhibits 1 and 2 present information from promotional brochures for the Pops and Celebration series. Since these were both spring series and somewhat "lighter" (particularly the Pops), the executives decided to concentrate their efforts on these two series. Exhibit 3 presents attendance data for these two series as of February 1. The executives hoped to raise ticket sales to 65% of capacity, an increase from 59% for the past fall's Musically Speaking series and from 55% for the seven already completed Jubilee concerts. The 65% level had been met by all four main series in 1984–85.

Exhibit 2
DESCRIPTION OF PERFORMANCES IN POPS SERIES*

Date	Description
Jan. 23 (4 nights)	CLEO LAINE AND JOHN DANKWORTH in concert.
Feb. 27 (4 nights)	JAZZ/SYMPHONY CROSSROADS with conductor John Dankworth.
Apr. 3 (4 nights)	THE CAMBRIDGE BUSKERS with conductor Richard Hayman.
Apr. 24 (4 nights)	MUSIC FOR LADIES AND LOVERS with conductor Mitch Miller.
May 22 (4 nights)	KISMET—a concert performance of the hit musical with conductor Jack Everly and world-renowned singers.
Jun. 5 (4 nights)	THE MUSIC OF GEORGE GERSHWIN with soprano Mavis Martin and pianist Boris Zarankin.

* Pop concerts are performed on Fridays, Mondays, and Tuesdays at 8:30 p.m. and Saturdays at 7:30 p.m.

Exhibit 3
TICKET SALES FOR CELEBRATION AND POPS SERIES (AS OF FEBRUARY 1, 1987)

Celebration	Nights	Subscription Sales	Single Tickets*
February 7	2	2953	452
March 14	2	2953	723
April 18	2	2953	203
May 9	2	2953	28
May 30	2	2953	72
Average Price per Ticket:		$12.51	$15.93
Pops			
January 23**	4	4747	2211
February 27	4	4747	415
April 23	4	4747	252
April 24	4	4747	86
May 22	4	4747	17
June 5	4	4747	49
Average Price per Ticket:		$12.68	$18.10

* Tickets were available in all price categories for all dates for which performances were scheduled.
** Already performed. Figures represent total sales.

Other performances scheduled for the next few months included five more events in the Jubilee series (very similar to the Celebration series), two dance performances by touring ballet companies with which the VSO performed, several matinees, and school concerts. A 65% goal was set for all remaining public performances.

BACKGROUND

The VSO, the third largest symphony orchestra in Canada, was one of the oldest cultural institutions in Vancouver, British Columbia, a growing city with a metropolitan area population of 1.4 million. Regular seasons were first offered in the 1930s, when the orchestra came under the patronage of a prominent local family. The orchestra's original repertoire included mostly big band music. Over the years, the repertoire expanded to reflect more classical and symphonic works, changing in response to the tastes of the various musical directors. The regular season was lengthened and the number of scheduled programs and series increased.

The orchestra, among the 20 largest in North America, had been plagued with financial, managerial, and artistic problems in recent years. Subscription revenue had declined steadily in the last five years, putting pressure on the symphony to emphasize sales of single tickets and to heavily promote each event. With 122 scheduled performances in the current season, a 15% decrease in regular subscribers (to the Jubilee and Musically Speaking series), a sluggish economic climate in Vancouver, and a deficit of more than $800,000 in each of the last two years, the VSO faced an enormous challenge just to maintain the status quo, let alone reduce its deficit (Exhibit 4).

Exhibit 4
SELECTED FINANCIAL RATIOS

	July 1, 1984 to June 30, 1985		July 1, 1985 to June 30, 1986	
	$000's	Percentage of Expenses	$000's	Percentage of Expenses
Expenses:				
Concert	7,354	87%	6,539*	86%
Administration	1,120	13%	1,082**	14%
Total Expenses	8,474	100%	7,621	100%
Earned Revenues	4,328	51%	3,665	48%
Private Sector Donations	1,345	16%	1,140	15%
Public Sector Grants	1,959	23%	1,996	26%
Loss for the Year	843	10%	811	11%

* These expenses could be further subdivided as follows: musicians, conductors, and soloists $4,456; theatre rent $680; stage and production $471; and publicity and promotion $932.

** Of the $1,082 administration expense, $350 could be attributed to fund raising.

Exhibit 5
PRICES FOR SINGLE SEATS AT VSO CONCERTS

Number of Seats Available	Matinee and Weekday Evenings	Weekend Evenings
610	$ 8	$10
942	$12	$14
958	$16	$18
251	$22	$25
2,761		

All concerts were held at the Orpheum, a beautifully restored hall with excellent acoustics, located six blocks from the centre of downtown Vancouver. There was ample parking within a few blocks of the Orpheum, but there was no parking garage in the Orpheum; the parking lots immediately across the street had a capacity of 600 cars. Many of the city bus lines stopped just outside the Orpheum, but late-night service was infrequent. The Orpheum had 2,761 seats. Exhibit 5 shows single seat ticket prices and the number of seats in each price block.

While small consolation, symphony orchestras throughout North America were going through difficult times. For example, a news magazine article reported that the Oakland Symphony in California had declared bankruptcy in September 1986 and closed its doors while others, such as the San Diego symphony, had suspended operations for a season or more. The Chicago Symphony, despite playing to a 98% seating capacity, met only 62% of its $20 million operating budget from single ticket and subscription sales. On the other hand, some symphonies, such as Montreal's orchestra, were enjoying greatly increased attendance levels and renewed financial support.

DECLINE IN ATTENDANCE

By the end of the 1970s, the VSO enjoyed record attendance and had one of the largest subscription bases of any orchestra in North America. However, since then the number of subscribers had steadily declined. In the previous year, subscriptions had dropped by 18%. In the current year, the decrease in subscriptions could approach 20%, for an overall decline of over 30% in two years. Subscribers presently received a discount of about 25% from the single ticket prices. While single ticket prices ranged from $8 to $25 depending on seat location and day of the week, most single ticket sales were in the $12 to $18 range. Plans were being made to revise the subscription packages for the upcoming season in order to reverse the downward sales trend.

Single ticket sales had also been decreasing, but at a slower rate than subscriptions and were becoming relatively more important in terms of total attendance. They accounted for 36,701 tickets sold in the previous year. Two years earlier, regular subscribers accounted for 79% of the total attendance. However, the proportion of subscribers for the current year was projected at only 70% of total attendance.

THE FREE CONCERT

The VSO executives knew that one way to offset declining revenues was to focus on non-subscribers. After a recording date for the VSO was postponed, it was decided that a free concert be given in order to obtain "trial" among nonsubscribers. This concert was held in the evening on Tuesday, January 6, 1987. People had to go to the VSO's administrative office located three miles away from the Orpheum where the VSO performed to pick up tickets. After being heavily promoted on a local FM radio station, the concert was an immediate "sellout" with all 2,761 tickets distributed. In order to obtain information about the concert-goers in a cost-effective manner, a questionnaire was developed and given to audience members. Because of time constraints, an initial draft of the questionnaire was pretested only on VSO office employees. A slightly condensed copy of the survey is shown in Appendix 1 along with relevant response frequencies for each question for the entire sample.[2] Respondents had the choice of dropping off the survey at various places in the Orpheum or mailing it in later. A total of 614 completed questionnaires from the 2,400 people actually in attendance were returned. Since almost everyone attended in groups of two or more, this was considered a good response rate by management. Of the 614 questionnaires, 19% were from current subscribers, 29% from former subscribers, and 52% from people who had never subscribed. The executives were quite pleased with this distribution, as their aim was to attract people who had previously not attended or had attended infrequently or not recently. The respondents were at least interested enough in classical music to attend a free concert—which could not be said of everyone.

Given all this information, the three executives sat down to analyze it and work on a report for the Board of Directors. They knew that any recommendations they made *must* be supported by the data.

[2] The data were stored on the VSO's computer system and could be further analyzed. Appendix 2, for instance, provides a breakdown of all answers that differ significantly by subscriber status. This variable was of particular interest to the executives.

Appendix 1
AUDIENCE QUESTIONNAIRE AND PERCENTAGE RESPONSES

VANCOUVER SYMPHONY ORCHESTRA
Audience Questionnaire

Dear Patron:

We at the Vancouver Symphony Orchestra want very much to provide the best possible musical experience for our audiences and the Vancouver community as a whole. In our continuing efforts to improve our performances and make your concert-going as satisfying and enjoyable as possible, we ask that you take a little time to answer the following questions. Your opinions and suggestions are extremely important and will be most useful in helping us to evaluate our programs, as well as our manner of presentation.

When you leave tonight's concert, please be so kind as to place the completed questionnaire in one of the special boxes located near the exits and the VSO Gift Shop. If you do not have time to complete it this evening, we would request that you mail it to us at your convenience. On behalf of the members of the orchestra and the staff, thank you very much for your assistance.

Dana Rome
Executive Director
Vancouver Symphony Orchestra

1. Are you a subscriber (i.e., purchase series tickets) to the VSO?
   19%* Yes, currently
   29% No, but formerly
   52% Never subscribed
2. Have you ever purchased tickets to an individual VSO event?
   22% Yes, since this past September
   51% Yes, but only before this past September
   26% No
3. Since this past September how many times have you attended a VSO performance?
   56% I haven't attended a VSO performance since September
   18% Attended once

* percent of all respondents

12% Attended 2 to 3 times
7% Attended 4 to 5 times
5% Attended more than 5 times

4. If you have ever attended previous VSO performances, we would like to know why. Please indicate the THREE most important reasons from the list below (1 = Most Important, 2 = Second-Most Important, 3 = Third-Most Important). Write 1, 2, or 3 on the appropriate lines.

i = most important
ii = 2nd or 3rd most important

i.	ii.	
42%	19%	I wanted to see and hear classical music performed live.
2%	16%	The VSO is an excellent orchestra.
7%	44%	I think the Orpheum is an excellent setting for great music.
13%	31%	The choice of music appealed to me.
13%	37%	I wanted to see famous guest artists and conductors.

Please list any additional reasons below.

____
____
____

5. Overall, what is your rating of the VSO on the following characteristics?

	Excellent	Good	Fair	Poor
Performance of Orchestra	65%	33%	1%	0%
Guest Artists	43%	53%	2%	2%
Music Selection	22%	59%	10%	8%
Acoustics in Orpheum	56%	39%	3%	1%
Prices of Tickets	13%	46%	35%	6%
Convenience of Parking	12%	41%	33%	13%
General Atmosphere of Orpheum	63%	34%	2%	1%
Service from Ticketron	26%	57%	13%	4%

6. Please give us your opinion about the amount of each type of music played by the VSO.

	Too Much	About Right	Too Little
Classical, (e.g., Bach, Mozart)	6%	72%	22%
Twentieth Century music, (e.g., Debussy, Stravinsky)	14%	71%	14%
Pops, (e.g., Mantovani, Williams)	20%	62%	18%
Contemporary, (e.g., Schaeffer)	24%	60%	16%

7. Below are presented eight pairs of events characterized by renown of performer, seating arrangements, and single ticket prices. Assuming everything else about each pair is identical, please check your preference in each case.

International Performers & $20 Price	**44% vs. 56%**	New, Promising Performers & $8 Price	Orchestra & $20 Price	**26% vs. 74%**	Balcony & $8 Price
Orchestra & $20 Price	**30% vs. 70%**	Balcony & $14 Price	International Performers & $20 Price	**63% vs. 37%**	New, Promising Performers & $14 Price
International Performers & $14 Price	**77% vs. 23%**	New, Promising Performers & $8 Price	Orchestra & $14 Price	**46% vs. 54%**	Balcony & $8 Price
International Performers & Balcony	**67% vs. 33%**	New, Promising Performers & Orchestra	International Performers & Orchestra	**59% vs. 41%**	International Performers & Balcony

8. What concert times do you prefer?

12% Matinees (2:30 p.m.)
34% 7:30 p.m.
55% 8:00 p.m.
7% 8:30 p.m.

9. What day of the week do you prefer to attend concerts?

18% Sunday
21% Monday
27% Tuesday
17% Wednesday
17% Thursday
25% Friday
32% Saturday

10. From where do you get most of your information about VSO events?

    47% From VSO mailings
    46% From ads in daily newspapers (e.g., *Sun, Province*)
    3% From ads in community newspapers
    32% From radio ads
    3% From television ads
    10% From reviews and feature stories
    12% Other—please specify (primarily word-of-mouth)

11. Which daily newspaper do you read most often?

    71% *Sun*
    24% *Province*
    13% Other—Please specify (primarily *Globe & Mail*)

12. Are you:

    39% Male
    61% Female

13. To which age group do you belong?

    2% Under 18
    6% 18–24
    16% 25–34
    17% 35–44
    21% 45–54
    22% 55–64
    19% 65 and over

14. Please specify your postal code __ __ __ __ __ __

15. If you prefer to purchase tickets to individual events (as opposed to subscription tickets) why is this so? Please indicate below.

    ____
    ____
    ____

16. All things considered, what would it take to get you to attend VSO performances on a regular basis?

    ____
    ____
    ____

THANK YOU FOR COMPLETING THIS QUESTIONNAIRE AND FOR YOUR PATRONAGE OF THE VSO.

Appendix 2
VSO RESPONDENT PROFILE BY SUBSCRIBER STATUS (SELECTED QUESTIONS)

The percentages represent the proportion of respondents within each subscriber group (e.g., Subscribers, Formers, Nevers) that responded to each of the questions. For example, with respect to individual ticket purchase, 38% of the current subscribers bought a ticket since September, compared to 24% of the formers, and 16% of the nevers.

	Current Subscriber	Former Subscriber	Never Subscribed
Number of Respondents	117	178	319
	Percentage Within Each Subscriber Group		
Q. 2			
Individual Ticket Purchase			
Yes, since this past September	38%	24%	16%
Yes, before this past September	53	59	47
No	9	18	37
Q. 3			
Attendance Since September			
Never	67	18	64
Once	19	10	22
2–3 times	11	18	10
4–5 times	2	30	2
6 or more	1	24	2
Q. 4			
Reasons for Past Attendance			
Live Music*			
Most important	54	46	35
2nd or 3rd most important	23	21	17
VSO Excellent*			
Most important	7	1	2
2nd or 3rd most important	27	21	10
Orpheum Good Place for Music			
Most important	6	8	6
2nd or 3rd most important	52	45	42
Choice of Music*			
Most important	7	20	12
2nd or 3rd most important	33	29	33
Famous Guest Artist or Conductors*			
Most important	18	12	13
2nd or 3rd most important	41	45	31

(continued)

Appendix 2 continued

	Current Subscriber	Former Subscriber	Never Subscribed
Number of Respondents	117	178	319
	Percentage Within Each Subscriber Group (Categories with less than 10% response not shown.)		
Q. 5 Rating of VSO's Characteristics			
Performance of Orchestra			
Good	38	33	32
Excellent	62	66	67
Guest Artists			
Good	55	54	51
Excellent	41	40	45
Music Selection*			
Poor to fair	20	21	16
Good	72	59	54
Excellent	8	20	30
Acoustics in Orpheum			
Good	41	38	39
Excellent	55	59	56
Price of Tickets*			
Fair	21	41	37
Good	62	44	40
Excellent	13	9	16
Convenience of Parking			
Poor	10	14	13
Fair	30	38	32
Good	51	37	40
Excellent	10	11	15
General Atmosphere of Orpheum*			
Good	41	40	27
Excellent	56	56	71
Service from Ticketron (automated box office)			
Fair	15	14	12
Good	55	56	58
Excellent	28	27	24
Q. 6 Opinion of Music Played by VSO			
Classical			
Too little	21	22	22
About right	72	70	73
Too much	6	8	5

(continued)

Appendix 2 continued

	Current Subscriber	Former Subscriber	Never Subscribed
Number of Respondents	117	178	319
	Percentage Within Each Subscriber Group		
Twentieth Century Music			
Too little	18	11	15
About right	73	69	73
Too much	9	20	12
Pops*			
Too little	10	16	25
About right	70	65	56
Too much	20	19	19
Contemporary*			
Too little	22	13	16
About right	48	58	68
Too much	30	29	16
Q. 10			
Information About VSO Events (all other sources less than 10% each)			
VSO mailings	46	42	17
Ads in daily newspaper	22	28	35
Radio ads	13	16	27
Q. 13			
Age of Respondents			
24 and under	4	4	12
25–34	11	10	21
35–44	9	10	20
45–54	21	23	17
55 and over	55	53	28

* Significant relationship to subscriber status ($p \leq .05$) for subcategories in Questions 4, 5, and 6.

4 DOMINION MOTORS & CONTROLS, LTD.

E. Raymond Corey

PRODUCT POLICY FOR OIL WELL PUMPING MOTORS

Dominion Motors & Controls, Ltd. (DMC), had acquired over 50% of the available market for oil well pumping motors in the northern Canadian oil fields since they were discovered in 1973. Although the company was a large supplier of motors and control equipment and had an excellent reputation for product quality, DMC executives believed it had been especially successful in this market because of one salesman, who had been hired in 1974. He was both aggressive and capable, and he could "talk the oil people's language." He had gained experience in Texas in electrical equipment sales and oil field electrical application engineering. At that time none of DMC's competitors had salespeople in the area with similar skills. The company had therefore been able to get a good early foothold and develop a strong market position.

Early in 1985, however, DMC was threatened with the loss of this market because of tests performed by the Hamilton Oil Company. Hamilton was the largest oil company active in Canada and owned and operated over 30% of the total producing wells. Mr. Bridges, head of Hamilton's electrical engineering department, who had been in charge of the motor testing program, had concluded that DMC's motor was third choice behind those offered by Spartan Motors, Ltd., and the Universal Motor Company of Canada, respectively. Thus, in March 1985 executives of DMC had to decide what action, if any, the company should take to maintain its share of the oil well pumping market.

COMPANY BACKGROUND

Dominion offered a line of motors ranging from small fractional horsepower (hp) units to large 2,000-horsepower motors. The company also produced motor control and panel-board units, which would automatically control and protect a motor. In 1984, DMC sales approximated $323 million and were distributed among product groups as indicated in Exhibit 1.

This case was prepared by Professor E. Raymond Corey as the basis for class discussion rather than to illustrate either effective or ineffective handling of an administrative situation.

Exhibit 1
SALES BY PRODUCT GROUPS, 1984

Product Group	Dollar Sales	Unit Sales
Controls and panel boards	$ 72,000,000	not applicable
Fractional horsepower motors	120,000,000	500,000
1–200 hp motors	85,000,000	22,000
250–2,000 hp motors	40,000,000	700

Source: Company records.

Exhibit 2
DISCOUNT SCHEDULE BY CLASS OF PURCHASER

Purchaser	Discount	List Price Multiplier
OEM	45%	0.55
Reseller	40	0.60
Large user	38	0.62
Small user	25	0.75

Source: Company records

About 80% of DMC sales were made directly by company salespeople to original equipment manufacturers (OEMs) and large industrial users, such as oil companies, paper mills, and mining concerns. Approximately 20% of sales were made to distributors for resale, primarily to small users (small drilling contractors and others) and small OEMs. The discount schedule for various classes of purchasers appears in Exhibit 2.

OIL WELL PUMPING MOTOR MARKET

Major oil fields were discovered in northern Canada late in 1973. By 1984, there were approximately 5,500 producing wells in these fields, of which 850 were started in operation that year. Hundreds of oil companies were active in the area, but only about 25 owned 50 or more wells.

According to industry estimates, an average of 1,000 new wells would enter production each year for the next five years. Estimators were careful to point out, however, the difficulty of making such forecasts with any degree of accuracy. Actually, many people intimately acquainted with the Canadian oil industry believed that this estimate might prove low. Because of rapid changes in world economic and political conditions and technology, forecasting was most difficult. Sales to this market were seasonal; over 80% were made between April and September.

Dominion's competition consisted of other well-known Canadian motor manufacturers and a number of foreign competitors (particularly British, German, and Japanese firms).[1] All the Canadian manufacturers maintained closely competitive pricing structures. Foreign competitors, however, usually sold 10% to 20% below the Canadians' established prices.

Dominion salespeople attempted to sell a motor and control unit as a package. Frequently, however, oil field customers bought the motor of one manufacturer and the controls of another. The majority of DMC's competitors did not offer motor controls. The main sources of motor control competition were control manufacturers.

From 1973 to 1984, DMC sold about 15% of the control and panel-board units used in oil well applications. The average pump system installed to deliver oil from a proven well cost about $34,000. Approximately $5,000 of this was invested in electrification of the pumping installation (motor, controls, wiring, installations, and so forth). The motor itself accounted for approximately one third of this $5,000 investment and the control and panel-board units another 30% of this amount.

THE BUYING AND SELLING OF OIL WELL MOTORS

Large Canadian oil producers were typically organized so that production (removing petroleum from the ground) was separated from refining (making the petroleum into usable products, such as gasoline and lubricants) and marketing. The production organization in the larger companies typically included field operations people, who managed the rigs themselves; engineers; purchasers, who actually ordered the equipment; geologists, who assessed the likelihood of finding oil in different locations; and standard administrative functionaries, such as personnel and legal staff. Field operations were generally organized geographically, with regional directors, district managers, rig supervisors, and foremen for each shift, and special functions such as maintenance. Rig supervisors were in charge of operating the rig itself and were viewed as important people. They typically were experienced hands who had worked up from entry level positions. They played a major role in rig operations, and their opinions about machinery were respected by other oil company personnel. Engineering designed and specified equipment, such as the rotating drilling platforms, and included primarily mechanical and a few chemical engineers.

Normally, salespeople called on their customers to keep them abreast of changes in the line and to nurture the relationships they had developed over the years. Specific people called on in the large companies varied; in some cases they were top executives; in others engineers; and in still others operations managers, rig superintendents, and a variety of related rig personnel. During these calls salespeople often obtained leads on companies believed to be contemplating expansion or overhauls.

The smaller companies had simpler organizations. The very small ones often consisted of only a few rigs, sometimes only one. These operators did no refining, but sold their petroleum to the large, integrated producers. Few small operators had separate engineering departments. They tended to be more oriented toward industry standards in their buying and often followed the larger companies in purchasing policy and equipment choice.

[1] Many U.S. motor manufacturers operated Canadian subsidiaries, which were considered Canadian competition.

DOMINION'S ADVERTISING AND PROMOTION PROGRAMS

Dominion had an advertising program which management considered of limited value in making sales, but useful in helping the salespeople. Trade journals were used to reach the different buying influences.

Although management did not expect its advertising actually to produce sales, it was strongly opposed to a mere business-card style of advertising in trade papers. It made every effort to present effective selling copy and layout. The advertisements often pictured actual installations with fairly long accompanying sales arguments.

Catalogues were important in DMC's promotional program. Each motor size was described in a general catalogue distributed to purchasing and engineering personnel. This single publication approach, in contrast to pamphlets describing each motor, was difficult to revise. But management believed that the catalogue was cheaper and more efficient than individual pamphlets because the product line was quite small and the motor designs and specifications were seldom changed.

FACTORS AFFECTING SPECIFICATIONS OF OIL WELL PUMPING MOTORS

Approximately 80% of the motors sold for oil well pumping applications since 1973 had been 10-hp NEMA[2] design C (high starting torque, low starting current), totally enclosed, fan-cooled units with moisture-resisting insulation. The remaining 20% of sales were motors of the same type but with higher or lower horsepower ratings.

Such factors as drilling depth, oil viscosity, water content of pumped fluid, underground pressure, and the government-controlled production allowables in the northern Canadian fields had determined the type of motor best suited for this area.[3] One particularly important determinant had been the low winter temperatures, which required a motor with a high starting torque.[4] To be assured of sufficient starting torque, many oil companies were using 10-hp motors, even though these were larger than were actually required to lift the oil to the surface. This practice was called "overmotoring."

During 1984 power companies serving the oil fields made two announcements which could affect the specifications of oil well pumping motors. First, their schedule of power rates was changed. The former flat rate, charged regardless of the horse-

[2] National Electrical Manufacturers Association, a nonprofit organization to which the great majority of electrical manufacturers in the United States and Canada belonged. It developed and promulgated standard specifications for electrical equipment. Adherence to the standards was entirely voluntary; neither members nor nonmembers were precluded from manufacturing or selling products that did not conform to them.

[3] The characteristics of oil fields yet to be discovered could easily differ from those of existing fields, and, therefore, other types of motors might come to be required.

[4] Starting torque, expressed in pounds-feet, was the twisting or turning power of the motor, which enabled it to overcome initial load resistance.

power of motors on a pumping installation, was replaced with a graduated schedule based on connected horsepower of an installation:

Horsepower of Installation	Monthly Base Charge per hp
5	$25.00
7½	21.50
10	20.00

Second, power companies demanded that their customers stop overmotoring and improve the "power factors" of their installations.[5] They did not at the time, however, indicate what, if any, penalty overmotoring would incur.

HAMILTON'S FIELD TEST PROGRAM

Following these announcements, John Bridges, Hamilton's chief electrical engineer, initiated field tests on oil pumping motors. His objective was to define the specifications of a motor which could be used most economically. The tests, therefore, were to determine (1) the horsepower required to lift the fluid, and (2) the maximum starting torque required to start the pumping units at low winter temperatures.

Although the tests were completed by early 1985, DMC executives only became aware of them in March through the reports of a salesperson calling on Hamilton. Although the salesperson was unable to obtain a memorandum describing the test procedures and findings, DMC executives pieced together what they believed to be a fairly accurate picture of the conclusions.

According to their information, Mr. Bridges had determined the following: (1) fluid-lifting requirements dictated a 3- to 5-hp motor; (2) starting torques in excess of 70 pounds-feet would energize the pumping units at temperatures as low as −50F; (3) this starting torque requirement would necessitate a 7½-hp motor; (4) because the Spartan 7½-hp motor had the highest starting torque of the motors tested (Exhibit 3) and the Universal 7½-hp motor had the second highest, these should be his company's first and second choices in the future. Dominion's 7½-hp motor was the third choice. Management at DMC also learned that Mr. Bridges planned to report his findings formally to Hamilton's executives in May.

[5] The "power factor" of an AC circuit was defined as the ratio of power-producing current to total current. In most AC circuits, both magnetizing current (which did no work) and power-producing current were conveyed. If no magnetizing current was present, the total current equaled the power-producing current and the power factor was unity or 100%. In motors working well below their rated capacity, much magnetizing current was present and the power factor was quite low. The lighter the load relative to the motor capacity, the lower the power factor.

The watt-hour meter used to determine a customer's power bill recorded only power-producing current, so when a utility system had to carry nonpower-producing current, its income and ability to carry payload, or power-producing current, were reduced. Consequently, more facilities were required to serve a low power-factor load than a high power-factor load of the same kilowatt (payload) demand.

Exhibit 3

MAXIMUM STARTING TORQUES OF MOTORS TESTED BY HAMILTON OIL COMPANY (IN POUNDS-FEET)

Horsepower	Starting Torque, by Motor Manufacturer			Minimum Starting Torque Required by NEMA Standards
	Spartan	Universal	Dominion	
5	68	65	60	57.7
7½	102	97	89	76.5
10	110	109	105	101.5

Dominion executives believed these tests had not produced data extensive or intensive enough to define oil pumping requirements accurately. They did believe, however, that the findings had provided rather specific indications of pumping needs under a given set of operating conditions.

DMC personnel were extremely concerned, nevertheless, about the probable effect on their company's market standing of Hamilton's endorsement of the Spartan and Universal motors. Mr. Bridges was known to be very influential in establishing Hamilton's purchasing policy.[6] In addition, because Hamilton was the only firm operating in the Canadian oil fields that maintained an electrical engineering staff, Mr. Bridges's recommendations would probably carry great weight in the entire industry. Most DMC executives believed, therefore, that they could not hope to stay in the oil well pumping market unless they responded somehow to Mr. Bridges's challenge.

POSSIBLE SOLUTIONS TO DOMINION'S PROBLEM

Four courses of action were developed by Dominion executives:

1. Reduce the price of DMC's 10-hp motor to that of the 7½-hp motor.
2. Re-engineer DMC's present 7½-hp motor to make its starting torque at least equal to that of the Spartan 7½-hp unit.
3. Undertake design of a definite-purpose motor for the oil well pumping market. This would ideally be a basic 5-hp motor with the starting torque of a 10-hp unit.
4. Attempt to persuade Mr. Bridges and Hamilton executives that the conclusions reached from their test results unduly emphasized obtaining the *maximum* starting torque available.

[6] All oil well pumping motors used by Hamilton Oil Company were procured through its Production Department, and most of the motors this department purchased were for oil well pumping. Other departments independently purchased large numbers of motors either directly from manufacturers or through contractors. Motors used in refineries, for example, were typically acquired as original equipment through the contractors who built the refineries. Motors for an average oil refinery in Canada cost between $250,000 and $1,000,000.

Alternative 1

Reducing the price of DMC's 10-hp motor to the level of its 7½-hp unit was advocated by several executives as a quick initial way to meet the problem. Such a move, they thought, could be taken either immediately or as late as May 1985. These executives pointed out that the oil well motor market was rapidly becoming active after its usual winter slump and that if the company wanted to share in the 1985 sales, DMC must gain a competitive position immediately. They recognized that this would not be a long-run solution. It did appear, however, because the savings from using a 7½-hp instead of a 10-hp motor were not large and because no oil company had yet been penalized for maintaining low power factors, that a 10-hp motor could continue to be acceptable for the short run. Exhibit 4 shows the costs and prices of the small motors in DMC's line.

Exhibit 4
COSTS AND PRICES OF SMALL INTEGRAL MOTORS

Horsepower	Manufacturing Cost*	Commercial Cost†	List Price	Prices to Large Users‡
5	$ 511.53	$ 571.20	$1,685.00	$1,045.00
7½	663.51	714.00	1,940.00	1,200.00
10	816.00	907.80	2,550.00	1,580.00
15	1,229.10	1,371.90	3,725.00	2,310.00

* Manufacturing cost includes direct labour, materials, and manufacturing overhead.

† Commercial cost includes manufacturing cost and charges for engineering, transportation, sales service, advertising, administrative overhead, and depreciation. It does not include salespeople's salaries and commissions, which amounted, on all sales, to approximately 8 percent of net sales billed.

‡ These prices are based on the discount schedule in Exhibit 2.

Some executives argued that there was no need to reduce the price of the company's 10-hp motor until Mr. Bridges delivered his formal report. They doubted that many oil companies would hear of the results until the formal report, so there might not be much effect on motor purchases for another two or three months. Dominion could sell its 10-hp motor at the usual price until it encountered objections and the market became aware of Hamilton's endorsement of the Spartan motor.

Executives who favoured this alternative believed it would immediately combat Hamilton's endorsement of the Spartan motor. It would be a useful temporary competitive measure until they could obtain and completely study Mr. Bridges's test results. Then DMC could reach a more satisfactory and reasoned strategy decision. They believed that adequate appraisal of Mr. Bridges's tests, results, and conclusions might require as much as one year, especially if company executives wanted to have DMC's own engineers make comparative tests.

Alternative 2

Several company executives believed that DMC's best opportunity to stay in the oil well market lay in re-engineering its present 7½-hp motor to give it a starting torque equal to or greater than that of the Spartan 7½-hp motor.[7] Initial investigations revealed two ways of increasing starting torque.

First, at least 105 pounds-feet of starting torque could be obtained by modifying the existing 7½-hp internal motor components. This motor would have the same frame size (i.e., mounting dimensions) as the existing 7½-hp motor, but its temperature rise would be greater than NEMA standards. This departure would not, according to DMC personnel, significantly alter the safety or operating characteristics of the motor, because they would use special high-temperature insulation. These executives were uncertain, however, how oil field users might react to an operating temperature above NEMA standards. A commercial cost of $790 would be incurred to manufacture this motor.

A second way to obtain the same starting torque was to use a larger motor frame. This motor would continue to meet or exceed all NEMA's minimum standard performance specifications, but not NEMA mounting dimensions for its rating. Executives at DMC believed, however, that standard motor mounting dimensions were not important in oil well pumping applications. They also believed that such a motor would meet less customer resistance than one that exceeded NEMA's maximum temperature rise. The commercial cost of this motor would be $867.

Neither of these methods would involve additional investment in plant or equipment. It would take approximately three months to begin shipment of the modified motor.

Advocates of altering the company's existing 7½-hp motor to increase starting torque believed this was the answer to the product problem. They pointed out that "souping-up" would give DMC a motor with the highest starting torque of any 7½-hp motor then available.

Not all DMC executives agreed that this alternative would be desirable, however. They pointed out that such a move would invite a "torque war," which could lead to unbalanced motor designs.[8] This would confuse motor buying practices and be detrimental to the motor industry as a whole. It had long been DMC's policy to support industry standards by not publicizing or claiming operating characteristics in excess of NEMA standards. The company had excellent testing facilities, which enabled engineers to design motors close to NEMA standards and thus reduce costs. One executive stated, "There is no point in building more margin into our motors than required by the NEMA standards. . . . Our better testing facilities allow us to design closer to NEMA standards than our competitors. . . . There is no point in building a large margin into our motors."

[7] Under this alternative DMC's present 7½-hp motor, with a starting torque of 89 pounds-feet, would continue to be manufactured and sold to customers who had no need for or interest in high starting torques.

[8] This was described by one executive as "technical inflation."

Alternative 3

A number of DMC's executives supported a move to design a definite-purpose motor for the oil well pumping market. They felt this was the only way to regain effective product leadership. They pointed out that the Hamilton tests indicated that the specific motor desired would have the running characteristics and rating of a 5-hp unit but the starting torque of a 10-hp motor. This motor would exceed minimum NEMA specifications. They reasoned that such a unit would have unquestioned competitive superiority in this market. Preliminary examination indicated that the motor could be produced for a commercial cost of approximately $665.

Executives believed that such a motor could be successfully sold at a net price of $1,045 to large users. They reasoned that the definite-purpose motor should be priced close to the 5-hp general-purpose motor because it was actually a 5-hp motor. Also, it would be priced below the 7½-hp general-purpose motor to give DMC a price advantage over the 7½-hp motors competing in the oil well market. Some managers, however, believed a definite-purpose motor could be sold for somewhat more than $1,045 and perhaps more than a current 7½-hp motor. An investment of $75,000 was believed adequate to provide the required engineering and testing. Executives believed only minor expenditures for plant and equipment would be necessary to produce the new motor. Engineers estimated that it would take four to five months for production to begin.

Those who favoured this alternative summarized its merits by noting that DMC would be offering the market *exactly* what it wanted. Furthermore, they believed that the first manufacturer to offer a definite-purpose motor, tailored to the needs of the market, would have an important tactical advantage over competitors which could be expected to last a long time. They felt that with such a motor DMC could increase its share of the oil well pumping market to approximately 60%.

With few exceptions the Canadian motor industry had adhered to general-purpose motors—motors designed to be acceptable for a number of applications. As a rule their performance characteristics exceeded the specific requirements of any individual application. Some industry executives believed that this philosophy (based on NEMA standards) had been the salvation of the Canadian motor industry. They pointed out that the Canadian motor market was only about one tenth the size of the U.S. market, making it economically difficult to justify small production runs of special-purpose motors. Manufacturers had concentrated on standard, general-purpose motors to achieve unit costs competitive with those of imported motors.

Alternative 4

Several members of DMC's management group believed that Mr. Bridges's conclusions were not completely accurate. They argued that before considering changes in product and market strategy, they should attempt to persuade Mr. Bridges and the executives of the Hamilton Oil Company that another set of conclusions could be drawn from the test results. Several DMC executives knew Hamilton's purchasing vice president socially and believed that perhaps they could approach him.

These executives pointed out that all 7½-hp motors tested had starting torques in excess of 80 pounds-feet (see Exhibit 3) and therefore should have been satisfactory, because 70 pounds-feet of torque was deemed capable of "breaking" a pump in the most extremely cold weather. Mr. Bridges had apparently reasoned that because starting torque was the most important feature in oil well pumping motor applications, he should get as much of it as possible. The Spartan motor was his first choice because it had the highest starting torque. Most DMC executives believed that the instances when 80 pounds-feet of torque would not start a motor would be extremely rare, but, as one expressed it, "Engineers love big margins whether they use them or not."

Many company executives believed that there was real reason for questioning Mr. Bridges's conclusions, but they did not know how to present different conclusions. Mr. Bridges was scheduled to present his conclusions early in May to Hamilton top management. Several DMC executives close to the situation reported that Mr. Bridges was convinced of the validity of his interpretations and evidenced an intense pride of authorship. They believed it would be very difficult to approach him directly. Some felt that nothing but ill will could be generated by any attempt to alter Mr. Bridges's recommendations.

Dominion executives were united in their concern that, although Mr. Bridges had begun his tests in October 1984, they had not known of them until March 1985. Most believed that the present problem would never have arisen had they known of Mr. Bridges's tests when they started. Although most executives were not in favour of encouraging a trend to definite-purpose motors, they did feel that when a customer was attempting to define its motor needs precisely, DMC personnel should work with the customer so the company could be in on the ground floor of subsequent developments.

Some executives believed that DMC personnel should go one step further and begin testing and defining the motor needs of the company's various market segments in preparation for when a customer (such as Hamilton) might conduct an investigation itself. Executives who supported this policy believed that such work could be looked on as a long-term investment in maintaining the company's future market position. Company engineers, however, were already overburdened; so this program would necessitate additional hiring.

Section 2

FINANCIAL AND ECONOMIC ANALYSIS IN MARKETING

A financial or economic analysis is necessary to evaluate all major courses of action in marketing. Introducing a new product, entering a new market, changing a price, or increasing the size of a sales force are all decisions that can have significant financial consequences.

In this section, we review some of the basic concepts of financial and economic analysis as applied to marketing decision making. We concentrate on simplified situations in order to focus on the key issues.

COSTS, PRICE, AND CONTRIBUTION

Variable costs (VC) change with the volume of the product produced or sold. For a manufacturer variable costs typically would include the costs of materials and labour; as more units are manufactured, total variable costs increase. Variable costs are usually expressed as VC per unit. This is often a good representation of the way such costs vary over the relevant range of sales for marketing decision making.

Fixed costs (FC) do not change with the volume and are those that would still be incurred, at least in the short run, even if no products were manufactured or sold. Fixed costs can include the rental of a building, the cost of display cases, the advertising budget, and other expenses which would not change, once committed, irrespective of the volume sold or produced. See Exhibit 1 for an example of variable and fixed costs.

Although in many analyses the two major cost categories are fixed and variable, in some situations a third type of cost, *semi-variable cost* (SVC), is important. Semi-variable costs tend to vary with the *capacity* to provide volume (often in stepwise fashion) as opposed to directly with volume itself. Such costs are particularly prevalent in service industries, for instance an airline might incur a semi-variable cost of $300 per flight (for fuel, salaries, and landing fees) when adding an extra flight a day on its Toronto to New York schedule; its variable cost might be only $6 per passenger boarded (for refreshments and ticketing costs). For theatre companies, the cost of running another performance of a show and for a retail store, the cost of opening an additional day are semi-variable costs. For a manufacturer, the decision to add an overtime shift to meet anticipated demand can involve semi-variable costs. Although we will not consider semi-variable costs explicitly in the remainder of this note, they are often quite important and need to be considered in an economic analysis of alternatives.

Exhibit 1
RELATIONSHIP OF VARIABLE AND FIXED COSTS

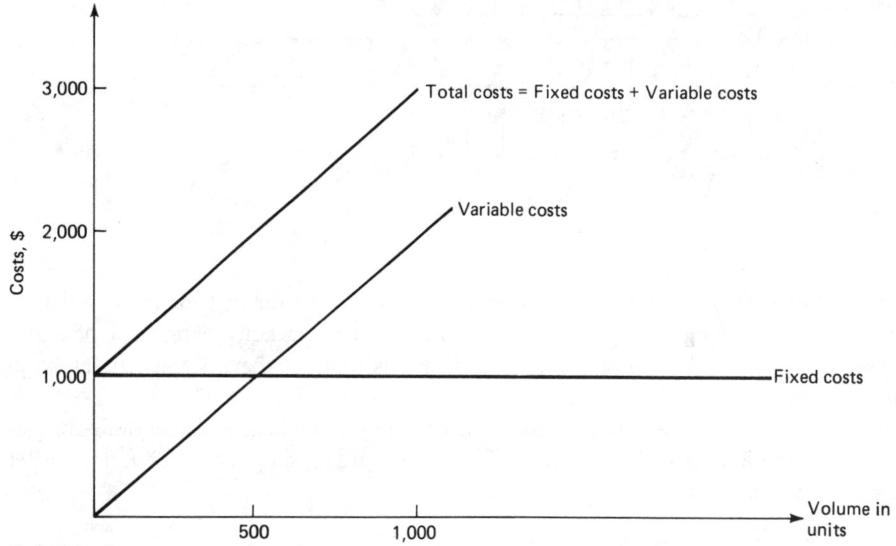

Exhibit 2
ILLUSTRATION OF BREAKEVEN ANALYSIS

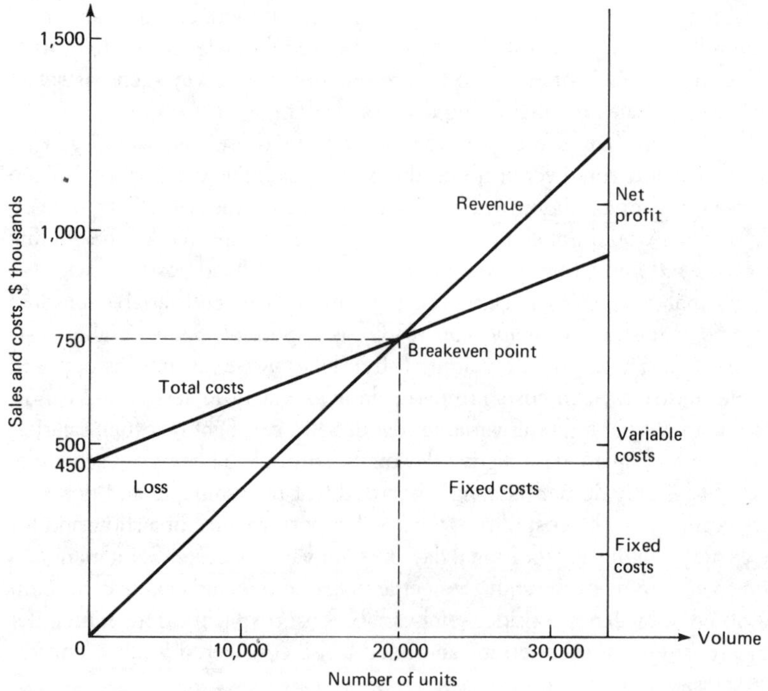

Price (P) per unit is the revenue obtained per unit, net of any discount offered to others in the distribution channel. Price per unit times *Volume* (V) sold gives the total (or gross) revenue realized by the seller.

Contribution or margin per unit is the difference between price per unit and variable cost per unit, that is,

$$\text{Unit Contribution} = \text{P per unit} - \text{VC per unit.}$$

Similarly, total (or gross) contribution is the product of unit contribution times volume. Net contribution is equal to unit contribution times volume less fixed cost, that is,

$$\text{Net Contribution} = [(\text{P} - \text{VC}) \times (\text{V})] - \text{FC.}$$

To illustrate these concepts, consider the example of a British Columbia fruit packer who is thinking of setting up a small factory to produce frozen raspberry juice. Rental costs for the factory and facilities, including such factors as utilities, insurance, and property taxes are $150,000 annually. Sales force, advertising, marketing, and other management operating costs are $200,000 per year. The costs of leasing specialized packing and freezing machinery, which has a useful life of five years, is $100,000 annually. The cost of raw materials and labour is $15 per case (12 large cans) of frozen raspberry juice. If the selling price of frozen raspberry juice is $37.50 per case, then we could calculate the following:

Fixed Costs	= $150,000 + $200,000 + $100,000
	= $450,000
Variable Costs per case	= $15
Selling Price per unit	= $37.50
Unit Contribution	= $37.50 − $15.00 = $22.50

If the company expects to sell 24,000 cases in a year, then estimated costs and revenues would be as follows:

Total VC	= 24,000 × $15 = $360,000
Total Revenue	= 24,000 × $37.50 = $900,000
Total Contribution	= $540,000
Net Contribution	= $540,000 − $450,000 = $90,000

Next we shall examine some concepts that can be used to help evaluate the economics of deciding whether to set up the frozen raspberry juice factory.

BREAKEVEN ANALYSIS AND PROFITABILITY

Breakeven analysis allows management to calculate the level of sales required to cover the fixed costs of making any significant marketing change (Exhibit 2). The breakeven volume is found by dividing the fixed costs by the unit contribution, that is,

$$\text{Breakeven Volume (in units)} = \frac{\text{Fixed Costs}}{\text{Unit Contribution}}$$

In the case of the raspberry juice packer, the breakeven volume is

$$\frac{\$450{,}000}{\$22.50} = 20{,}000 \text{ cases}$$

If the alternative being examined involves a change from a current one, then the fixed cost component of the breakeven calculation is replaced by the amount of the change in the fixed costs. The importance of breakeven calculation is that it puts the focus on the profitability of a product, not just its sales volume.

One test of a marketing initiative is the feasibility of attaining the breakeven volume. If the current market size is 50,000 cases, then selling 20,000 cases means getting a 40% market share unless the market is expected to grow rapidly. If high market share is necessary for success, then competitive reaction must be carefully considered.

For many marketing alternatives, such as the introduction of a new product, it would be unreasonable to expect the project to achieve breakeven in its first year. In such a case management may look at the feasibility of attaining breakeven within two, three, or more years.

While public and nonprofit organizations may seek to obtain only a breakeven volume, most businesses would not go ahead with a project unless a profit was likely. While the profit required can be set in many ways, one alternative is to specify it as a percentage of the investment required. Target profitability volume in units can be calculated as follows:

$$\text{Target Profitability Volume (in units)} = \frac{\text{Fixed Costs} + \text{Target Profit}}{\text{Unit Contribution}}$$

For example, if the raspberry juice producer had to invest $1 million to establish this business and set a target profit of 18% on the investment, then the number of units it would need to sell to achieve target profitability is calculated as follows:

$$\frac{\$450{,}000 + \$180{,}000}{\$22.50} = 28{,}000 \text{ cases}$$

CONDITIONAL SALES FORECASTS AND RESPONSE FUNCTIONS

In many ways, a breakeven analysis evaluates a marketing program from a different perspective than that used in formulating the plan itself. The breakeven analysis produces a target volume and asks how feasible its accomplishment is. In contrast, the development of a marketing plan forecasts that a certain level of sales is expected if the specified plan is implemented. In other words, sales are a function of a specific marketing plan. More succinctly, and in the context of the marketing mix, we can say that the plan represents a *conditional sales forecast* in that the sales are conditional on a particular marketing mix. A response function is the part of the conditional sales forecast that explicitly links a sales response to one or more elements of the marketing mix.

Take, for instance, the example of advertising expenditure level for the management of a regional movie chain. In the present marketing plan, a monthly advertising expenditure of $20,000 is expected to result in attendance of 60,000 people. However, increasing the ad budget by 50% to $30,000 is expected to increase the number of attendees to 66,000; increasing advertising by another $10,000 is expected, based on tests in other regions of the country, to raise attendance to 68,000 people. On the other hand, reducing advertising by $10,000 from the present budget of $20,000 is expected to reduce admissions to 50,000 people. Given these estimates then, a forecast of sales conditional on advertising would be as follows:

Advertising Budget	Estimated Attendance
$10,000	50,000
$20,000	60,000
$30,000	66,000
$40,000	68,000

As can be seen in Exhibit 3, attendance is much more sensitive to decreases than to increases in advertising. The profitability of changing the advertising level depends upon the contribution per ticket sold. If in this case the contribution were $3 per ticket sold, the following profitability analysis would help management to make a decision about the advertising budget:

(1) Advertising Budget	(2) Estimated Attendance	(3) = $3 × (2) Contribution Before Advertising	(4) = (3) − (1) Contribution After Advertising
$10,000	50,000	$150,000	$140,000
$20,000	60,000	$180,000	$160,000
$30,000	66,000	$198,000	$168,000
$40,000	68,000	$204,000	$164,000

As can be seen, the most profitable level of sales is obtained when advertising spending is $30,000 for a contribution, after allowing for the expense of advertising, of $168,000. It is evident from looking at the data that the highest level of sales is not the most profitable level in this case.

This section has illustrated one form of profitability analysis. At times more complex techniques may be needed to adjust for the time value of money, to allow for risk and uncertainty, and to account for possible competitive response.

Exhibit 3
ADVERTISING RESPONSE FUNCTION

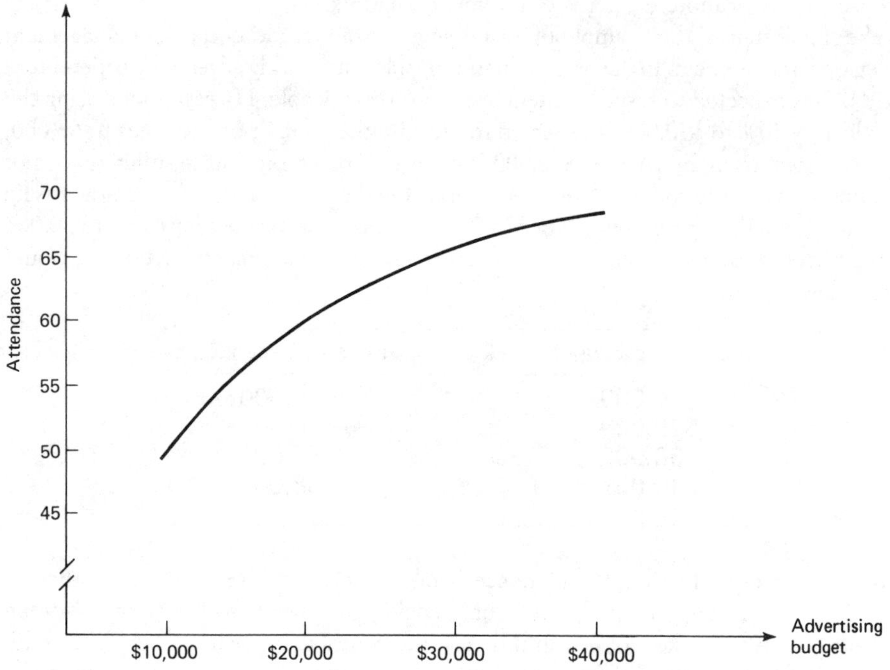

UNCERTAINTY

Marketing managers develop marketing plans with the expectation that certain sales outcomes will be achieved. But they cannot be certain of those outcomes. A furniture manufacturer may find that a particular advertising campaign was not as effective as anticipated or an amusement park operator may do better than planned due to unusually pleasant weather. Competitors may also take actions which keep firms from reaching their goals. Thus, a new brand of shampoo may achieve a promising 10% market share in its test markets, but only a 4% share when an established competitor engages in extensive promotional activity during the new brand's national launch.

There is no simple way to account for uncertainty. A good first step, however, is to identify the major sources of uncertainty in the marketing plan. In general, any uncertainties that have a significant impact on the final outcome need to be considered in depth. While no risk factor can be totally ignored, concentration should be placed on the critical ones. Market research may help to narrow the range of uncertainty.

One test of a marketing strategy is to examine its robustness in the face of difficulties. Consider, for example, an airline opening a new route using jumbo jets. The strategy would be robust if the airline could profitably substitute a smaller plane on the new route, using the jumbo jet on the charter market if traffic were not to develop as expected.

All risk cannot be eliminated from marketing decisions, but it can be reduced. While many approaches are available to deal with uncertainty, we will mention just two here. The first is to estimate a range of possible outcomes of a particular decision and determine if management is willing to live with the resulting risk. A typical approach is to construct three scenarios—optimistic, expected or most likely, and pessimistic. For example, suppose a shampoo marketer has developed a new line of shampoos to appeal to men whose hair is graying. To market the line, the company will need to invest in advertising and promotion. The company thinks it will sell 50,000 tubes annually, with a contribution margin of $2 per unit. However, if the product catches on, sales could go as high as 100,000 tubes. On the other hand, the product could make no headway at all in the market and sell only 10,000 units. Profitability under these three scenarios would be as follows:

	Optimistic	Most Likely	Pessimistic
Sales (Units)	100,000	50,000	10,000
Contribution	$200,000	$100,000	$ 20,000
Fixed Costs	$ 75,000	$ 75,000	$ 75,000
Net Profit (Loss)	$125,000	$ 25,000	$(55,000)

The company might look at these data and conclude that it could not afford a loss of $55,000 and would reject the project, at least in its present form, or it might feel that the chances of a profit are so much greater than the chances of a loss that the new shampoo should be launched. If it were to pursue this second course of action, the company would, of course, do whatever it could to prevent the pessimistic scenario.

A second approach to dealing with uncertainty is to try to estimate the probability of each outcome and then calculate an expected value. If the expected value is positive, then the company goes ahead with the project, assuming, naturally, that the firm has the funds required to invest in the project and that no better opportunities are available. While many pages could be devoted to a discussion of expected value, a common sense example is sufficient, for our purposes, to convey its meaning and illustrate its calculation. Suppose you make a bet with a somewhat naïve friend, saying that you will pay him $1 if a tossed coin comes out heads, but he will pay you $2 if the coin is tails. In the long run, half the coin tosses will result in heads and half in tails (assuming the coin is fair). So half the time you will pay a dollar and half the time you will win $2. Your expected value is therefore $0.50, calculated as follows:

$$\begin{aligned} \tfrac{1}{2}(-\$1) + \tfrac{1}{2}(\$2) &= -\$0.50 + \$1 \\ &= \$0.50 \end{aligned}$$

Probabilities are not so easy to determine for management decisions, but market research and test marketing do help. To return to the shampoo marketer, suppose the company estimated that there was a 10% chance of the optimistic scenario, a 10% chance of the pessimistic, and an 80% chance of the most likely sales outcome. Then the expected profit from the new shampoo would be

$$.10(\$125{,}000) + .80(25{,}000) + .10(-\$55{,}000) = \$27{,}000.$$

In this case, the new product launch has a positive expected value, so it looks like the firm should go ahead with its plans.

Uncertainty is a reality for a manager. To consider only the most optimistic outcomes would be foolhardy, but to consider only the worst results would paralyze a company into inaction. Approaches such as those discussed here, which try to balance risk against profit, help managers make decisions in the face of an uncertain environment.

LONGER TIME HORIZONS

For some marketers, the time between taking an action and its impact on sales is very short. For example, when a fast food chain advertises a special free drink with each hamburger ordered for one week only, then the company's return is almost immediate. Other actions, however, involve a longer time frame, and it may be years before an investment earns its full return. For example, if the fast food chain opened a new store, it might take several years before the store became profitable and even longer before the store's full potential was realized. To be more concrete, suppose opening the new store involved an investment of $90,000 on the company's part and produced a loss of $10,000 for the first year and an expected profit of $60,000 in each of the next two years. The company treasurer insists that all projects must pay for themselves within three years. Should the company open this new store?

The problem in answering this question is that money received a year or two from now is worth less than money available now. If you have money now, you can invest it and earn interest. If you do not have it now, you can try to borrow it from the bank and pay the banker interest. Suppose you go to a bank and the loan officer offers to lend you $90,000 now if you pay the bank $100,000 a year from now. Then, in financial terms, the "present value discount factor" is .90, and a dollar a year from now is equivalent to $0.90 now. Similarly, a dollar paid two years from now is worth $0.81; calculated as (.90)(.90) = $0.81. Using this notion of "present value," here is how we might calculate the return on the $90,000 investment in a new store:

Years From Now	Profit	Discount Factor	Value Now
1	−$10,000	.90	−$ 9,000
2	60,000	(.90)(.90) = (.81)	48,600
3	60,000	(.90)(.90)(.90) = (.729)	43,740
			$83,340

The return of $83,340 is less than the required investment of $90,000, so on economic grounds the company should not proceed with the investment.

How could the company change this outcome? If a longer time horizon for cost recovery were permitted, then perhaps the project would be viable. Another alternative would be to upgrade the value of future returns by attempting, for example, to borrow money more cheaply.

These actions require a careful consideration of the company's financial policies, particularly with regard to setting the terms for judging marketing plans that involve both expenditures and returns over several years. In this brief discussion we can only suggest the need for considering both the short- and long-term effects of marketing actions and point out that some way needs to be established for placing a value on future returns. Such policies generally involve deciding on a time horizon over which to measure returns and a means to discount the value of future returns.

CONCLUSION

Financial and economic analysis is an important part of the evaluation of all significant marketing alternatives. This section provides an introduction to some of the basic approaches that will be helpful in the cases included in this book. No one form of analysis, however, is sufficient to evaluate a course of action; the soundness of a plan must be judged against multiple criteria.

5 FINANCIAL EXERCISES FOR MARKETING DECISIONS*

1. Borden Manufacturing, located in the Regina, Saskatchewan area, enjoys a 4% share of a total market of 75,000 emergency power generators that are sold each year. Borden offers its retailers and wholesalers a combined margin of 35% on a retail price of $2,000 per generator.

Debra Stern, Borden's controller, estimates that variable production costs amount to $785 per generator and fixed manufacturing costs total $260,000 per year. In addition, shipping and packaging costs of $40 per unit must be paid by Borden. Management costs are $85,000 and the annual advertising budget is $80,000. The company employs one sales representative at a salary of $60,000 a year.

a) What are Borden's fixed costs?
b) What are Borden's variable costs per unit?
c) What is the unit contribution?
d) What is the breakeven volume for Borden (in units)?
e) What market share is needed to achieve this volume?
f) What are Borden's current profits?
g) If establishing the Borden company involved an investment of $1,100,000 and the company requires a return of 18% on its capital, is the generator line still profitable? Justify your answer.
h) What are the profits after allowing for the required return on capital?
i) Ted Rastelli, the firm's vice-president for marketing, estimates Borden can sell 4% more generators than it does presently by increasing its advertising budget from $80,000 to $100,000. Alternatively, if he reduces the advertising budget by $20,000, he expects to sell 75 fewer units. Should Borden raise or lower its advertising budget? Why?
j) What would be the breakeven level (in units) if the advertising budget were raised?
k) What would be the breakeven level (in units) if the advertising budget were lowered?
l) As an alternative to the change in advertising, Borden is considering offering one free safety light with every generator sold. These safety lights cost Borden $50 each. If this offer can increase generator sales by 150 units, what would be the change in total profits?

2. Jennifer Blumen, owner of Blumen's Florists, is preparing for a year-end review of the performance of her two stores. She opened the downtown store 20 years ago; the suburban store is only three years old. The following lists the financial data that have been collected:

* Written by the Marketing Faculty, School of Business and Economics, Wilfrid Laurier University.

	Suburban Store ($)	Downtown Store ($)
Sales	475,000	842,000
Flowers at cost	184,000	319,000
Depreciation	33,000	45,000
Advertising	6,000	70,000
Store help	28,000	63,000
Rent and utilities	9,000	30,000
Administrative salaries	25,000	35,000
Telephone	6,500	15,500
Delivery costs	40,000	105,000
Office expenses	7,000	10,000
Beginning inventory	86,000	235,000
Ending inventory	59,000	214,000
Investment	350,000	675,000
GST credits	13,000	22,000
GST due	23,100	47,000

a) Prepare operating statements for each Blumen Florist shop.
b) Using ratio analysis, compare the performance of the two outlets. What are the implications of this analysis?
c) Which shop would you close if forced to close one? Why?

3. The Li Tang Doll Corporation has completed development of a new line of collectable dolls. It expects to sell 15,000 of these dolls in the first year and 25,000 in the second year. The following financial and sales data have been assembled:

Retail selling price	$60
Retail margin	50%
Materials cost/unit	$4.50
Labour cost/unit	$6.25
Packaging cost/unit	$0.25
Sales force salaries/expenses	$145,000
Manufacturing overhead [allocated] (per unit)	$3.80
Administrative expenses	$68,000
Sales promotion (first year only)	$35,000

Prepare a two-year financial summary for the new doll including: variable cost per unit, contribution per unit, total contribution, total fixed costs, breakeven volume, gross margin, and net profit.

4. Montreal Gloves (MG) is considering the addition of a new line of water-proof gloves ("Water Smart") next year to its existing brand, "Stay Dry." First-year sales of the new line are projected at 300,000 pairs. The table below provides price and cost data. The sources of these sales are expected to be 20% from new customers, 40% from competitors' customers, and 40% (of the 300,000) from previous buyers of MG's other brand, Stay Dry. Sales of Stay Dry totalled 200,000 pair this year and are expected to remain at this level if the new line is not introduced. Ben Nadson, manager of the Gloves Division, is concerned about the cannibalization of Stay Dry sales by the new line. Should the new line be introduced?

	Current	Year 1 with New Line	
	Stay Dry	Stay Dry	Water Smart
Factory selling price	$22.00	$22.00	$27.50
Variable costs	$14.50	$14.50	$20.00
Fixed costs	$825,000	$645,000	$1,510,000

5. The Great Canadian Baking Company (GCBC) is a national manufacturer of baking products. Last year, GCBC's research department completed the development of an innovative ready-to-spread icing to replace the company's current product.

The new GCBC ready-to-spread icing offered the consumer a benefit not available from other products on the market—it contained real butter. "Blind" consumer tests indicated that the GCBC product had superior flavour and texture, when compared with the current GCBC icing and its competitors.

Hal Mira, New Product Manager for GCBC, needs to develop a pricing plan for the new icing. Market data have been collected (see the table "Competitive Market Data"). The product, promotion, and distribution components of the

Competitive Market Data: Ready-to-Spread Icing

Company	Retail Price (450 g pkg.)	Flavour	Consumer Perceptions Texture/Smoothness	Value	Market Share
GCBC (current product)	$2.19	High	High	High	35%
Duncan Hines	2.25	High	High	Medium	30%
Betty Crocker	2.19	Medium	High	Medium	25%
No-Name	2.05	Medium	Low	Low	10%

- Average retail price (weighted average)—$2.19.
- Total annual Canadian demand—3 million packages.
- Because of the "convenience" of this product, consumers are relatively price insensitive. Each $0.01 increase in the average price decreases total annual Canadian demand by only 50,000 packages.

marketing plan have been tentatively set and are shown in the table "Product Data." Price is the only remaining consideration.

a) Outline the factors that Mr. Mira should consider in setting the price for GCBC's new ready-to-spread icing.
b) What pricing methods should be considered for the new icing? What method do you recommend? Why?
c) What retail price do you recommend for the new icing? What market share do you estimate for the new product at this price? Justify your estimate.
d) What will the gross margin and net profit be for the new product in the first and second years, at your recommended price?

Product Data: New GCBC Ready-to-Spread Icing

Retail margin	20%
Wholesale margin	10%
GCBC costs	
—raw materials	\$0.46/pkg.
—packaging	\$0.35/pkg.
—direct labour	\$0.22/pkg.
—production overhead	\$60,000/year
—administrative expenses	\$80,000/year
—introductory advertising and promotion	\$400,000
—second year advertising and promotion	\$250,000

6. Locuster Industries (LI) is a major North American manufacturer of cleaning, baby, and personal care products. Jason Flynn, manager of the Personal Care Products (PCP) Division, has just had a disturbing conversation with Deborah Cermeil, brand manager for the Quintene line of shampoos and conditioners. The Quintene brand was successfully introduced two years ago as an exclusive (professional-formula), "natural" line of hair-care products. However, the market for upscale shampoos and conditioners has matured; competitors are flooding the market and consumers are becoming much more price sensitive.

After reviewing several strategies, Mr. Flynn and Ms. Cermeil narrowed their choice down to two options beyond what Locuster was currently doing. The table that follows presents data for each of these options.

Option A

Introduce the Essence line, lower-priced "natural" hair-care products, under the Locuster company name.

Option B

Manufacture a line of private-label (Style Brand) "natural" hair-care products for a major drug store chain. The Quintene line is still very profitable and will be maintained, so Locuster does not have the capacity to undertake both new projects. In fact, management is uncertain about making *any* changes.

	Current	Projected Year 1				
	Quintene Only	Quintene Only	Quintene and Essence		Quintene and Style	
Sales (millions bottles)	3.0	2.8	2.0	3.0	2.5	1.8
Retail price	$6.00	$6.50	$6.50	$4.79	$6.50	$3.59
Factory price	$2.90	$3.10	$3.10	$2.25	$3.10	$2.05
Variable cost/ bottle	$1.60	$1.70	$1.80	$1.10	$1.80	$1.00
Fixed Costs:						
Manufacturing	$ 700,000	$ 700,000	$700,000	$ 700,000	$700,000	$700,000
Administration	600,000	600,000	600,000	600,000	600,000	300,000
Marketing	1,000,000	1,000,000	600,000	1,800,000	800,000	200,000

a) The PCP Division currently makes a profit of $5.3 million on factory sales of $35 million. Any strategy chosen must maintain this ratio. Recommend a course of action based on the net profit percentage.
b) Outline the other factors that should influence PCP's choice of strategy.

7. Lisa Roberts, the owner of the Blanchard Beauty Parlor in downtown Winnipeg, has to decide whether or not to open a second shop in a suburban shopping mall. If she does so, she would incur a monthly cost of $3,000 for a rental of a fully equipped beauty parlor and would have to sign a minimum one-year lease. Since Ms. Roberts pays her employees on a commission basis, she estimates that each customer who comes to the store will provide a net return (contribution) to her of $3. She thinks it is most likely (about a 75% chance) that the suburban store will attract 1,000 customers a month, but there is a 10% chance that demand could be as low as 600 customers. On the upbeat side, she thinks there is a 15% chance of demand as high as 2,000 customers a month. Based on the experience of other beauty parlor owners, she believes that demand would not reach its full level until the third month of operation. The first two months would likely produce about half the sales of the other months, but would not be a good predictor of ultimate sales.

Should Ms. Roberts open the beauty parlor at the suburban mall?

8. Joshua Ross, the marketing manager of Electric Motor Company (EMC), was considering changing the company's distribution structure in Ontario. EMC was a medium-size manufacturer of standard electric motors. The motors, ranging in size from ¼ horsepower to 50 horsepower, were sold to a wide variety of industrial customers across Canada. EMC motors were sold primarily on the basis of price and reliability. Total company sales in the past year were $5,000,000 ($2,000,000 in Ontario).

Mr. Ross was considering replacing the six sales agents in Ontario with three company salespeople. The sales agents, who earned 7% commission on sales, sold EMC's product line as well as a number of complementary products. It was estimated that EMC's motors accounted for about 30% of the agents' total sales. Mr. Ross felt that sales in Ontario could be increased by hiring three salespeople who focused exclusively on EMC's products. He estimated that if the three salespeople were hired there was a 50% chance that sales would remain the same, a 30% chance that sales would increase by 10%, and a 20% chance that sales would increase by 20%. The cost for each person would be $70,000 ($50,000 salary and $20,000 expenses).

Mr. Ross discussed his plan with the president of EMC, Laura Jeffries. Ms. Jeffries replied, "I'm not sure about your estimates. Rather than a 50% chance of sales remaining the same, I think there's only a 25% chance that they will stay the same and a 25% chance that sales will decline by 20% if we go with our own sales force. This is because the sales agents will pick up another line of motors and compete with our own sales force. I agree with the rest of your estimates. However, I think if we offer the sales agents a bonus for increased sales, they might push our product a little harder. Why don't you work out some alternatives and we'll talk again."

a) As Mr. Ross, prepare and evaluate some alternatives.
b) What would you recommend?

9. Canadian Airways, one of the country's two major airlines, was considering operating an airplane shuttle service between Toronto and New York. The airline was to be named Executive Airlines, and all necessary operating arrangements had been made. Operating the airline would cost $900,000 per month for leasing of airplanes, management, and marketing.

In addition, the incremental costs were as follows:

Per Flight:	
Crew pay	$189.22
Fuel	179.38
Airport landing fees	23.76
Airport personnel	21.12*
Per Passenger:	
Food and drinks	1.23
Commissions	1.76
Passenger liability insurance	0.62

* Provided by Canadian Airways at the stated cost per flight.

Patrick O'Donnell, the manager in charge of Executive Air, believes that at a price of $60 per flight, he can run 12 flights per week day from 6 a.m. to 6 p.m. (6 each way), at an average of 68 passengers per flight. If Executive Air also runs the planes at night or on the weekends, the additional service would have to charge half-price and expect to attract 40 passengers per flight. Executive would run 4 flights each week night (2 each way) and 10 flights (5 each way), each weekend day. The entire operation would depend on 2 jet airplanes being totally dedicated to the service.

a) Assuming that no night and weekend flights are run, prepare a monthly income statement for Executive Airlines.
b) Assuming night and weekend flights are to be run also, prepare a monthly income statement for Executive Airlines.
c) What should Mr. O'Donnell do? Why?

6 CENTENNIAL COMMUNITY CENTRE

Charles B. Weinberg

Nora Harold, the executive director of the Centennial Community Centre (CCC) located in a large city in the Maritimes, needed to determine a pricing strategy and performance schedule for an upcoming event at its Duncan Auditorium. The Duncan Auditorium, an excellent facility, built and donated by a wealthy resident 15 years ago, was owned and operated by the CCC.

The CCC operated the Duncan Auditorium as a nonprofit performance hall. Its goal was to manage this facility so as to build as large an audience as possible without incurring a deficit. The Duncan, with a capacity of 300 seats, was booked for an average of 200 performances a year by both local and out-of-town groups. It typically scheduled events for up to three weeks of performances (eight performances per week), but some groups appeared for just two or three nights.

The highly regarded Western Drama Theatre of the Deaf (WDTD) had received a grant to fund a Canadian tour. The WDTD wished to include the CCC in its tour. WDTD's manager told Ms. Harold that, if a satisfactory schedule could be arranged, the WDTD would pay all production costs involved in its appearance and would charge $4 per ticket sold as a performance fee. It would perform as few as 2 times or as many as 25 times, but would like to have at least 50% of seats sold when it did perform. The CCC would be responsible for all marketing decisions (including advertising, pricing, and timing and number of performances) and expenditures. All revenues would go to the CCC, which in addition to the $4 charge by WDTD incurred costs of $6 per seat sold. While some costs were involved with putting on each performance, Western's definition of production costs included these expenses so it was not a factor for the CCC to consider.

Ten years ago, a computer programmer joined the CCC's board, and established a system for extensive recordkeeping. Using these data, CCC's management had developed estimates of the effect of different price and advertising strategies on demand (Exhibit 1). While the numbers were more precise than CCC's certainty of these results, management was quite confident that the estimates were "in the right direction."

1. Develop a number of performances, price, and advertising strategy for the CCC for the WDTD proposal.
2. Suppose the CCC is primarily concerned with locally based groups and only books others to earn money for its local groups. What strategy (number of

Note: Data and setting are disguised.

Exhibit 1

ESTIMATED DEMAND AND REVENUE AS A FUNCTION OF PRICE AND ADVERTISING

DEMAND (tickets)							
	ADVERTISING						
Price	$1,000	$3,000	$5,000	$7,000	$9,000	$11,000	$13,000
$5	4,800	7,200	7,200	7,200	7,200	7,200	7,200
$7	2,800	4,400	5,300	6,100	6,800	7,200	7,200
$9	1,900	2,900	3,600	4,100	4,500	4,900	5,200
$11	1,400	2,100	2,600	3,000	3,300	3,600	3,900
$13	1,000	1,600	2,200	2,400	2,500	2,700	3,000
$15	800	1,300	1,700	1,900	2,000	2,100	2,100
$17	700	1,100	1,300	1,500	1,600	1,600	1,600
$19	600	900	1,050	1,200	1,400	1,400	1,400
$21	500	800	900	1,000	1,200	1,200	1,200
$23	450	700	800	900	1,050	1,050	1,050
$25	400	600	700	800	900	900	900
$27	300	500	600	700	700	700	700
$29	250	400	500	600	600	600	600

NET REVENUE ($)							
$5	−25,000	−39,000	−41,000	−43,000	−45,000	−47,000	−49,000
$7	−9,400	−16,200	−20,900	−25,300	−29,400	−32,600	−34,600
$9	−2,900	−5,900	−8,600	−11,100	−13,500	−15,900	−18,200
$11	400	−900	−2,400	−4,000	−5,700	−7,400	−9,100
$13	2,000	1,800	1,600	200	−1,500	−2,900	−4,000
$15	3,000	3,500	3,500	2,500	1,000	−500	−2,500
$17	3,900	4,700	4,100	3,500	2,200	200	−1,800
$19	4,400	5,100	4,450	3,800	3,600	1,600	−400
$21	4,500	5,800	4,900	4,000	4,200	2,200	200
$23	4,850	6,100	5,400	4,700	4,650	2,650	650
$25	5,000	6,000	5,500	5,000	4,500	2,500	500
$27	4,100	5,500	5,200	4,900	2,900	900	−1,100
$29	3,750	4,600	4,500	4,400	2,400	400	−1,600

Note: At price of $5 and with advertising at $1,000, estimated demand is 4,800 tickets.
Costs are $4 × 4,800 + $6 × 4,800 + $1,000 = $49,000.
Net revenues are estimated at $24,000 − $49,000 = −$25,000.

performances, price, and advertising) should the CCC set if it seeks to earn the maximum returns possible from WDTD's tour?

3. The CCC can also use WDTD's tour to raise funds. If the CCC mounts a fund-raising campaign costing \$4,000, it can likely raise \$10,000 (before expenses). If the show proves popular, the CCC believes it can raise an additional \$5 per attendee, up to a maximum of \$20,000 (before expenses) in total. For example, if there were 1,000 attendees, CCC believes it could raise \$15,000 (\$10,000 + \$5 × [1,000]), or \$11,000 after expenses. What should the CCC do if it seeks to get the largest audience possible for WDTD, but not lose money (including donations)?

7 CANADIAN POPULATION AND HOUSEHOLD TRENDS: DRAWING IMPLICATIONS FOR MARKETING

Gordon H. G. McDougall

An important aspect of marketing is to determine the future implications of population and household trends. The three tables that follow provide past and future data on the Canadian population by age group, geographic area, and household. Analyze the tables and prepare a discussion of the marketing implications that are likely to occur in the decade from 1986 to 1996. Then contrast these changes with those that occurred in the decade from 1976 to 1986.

Exhibit 1

POPULATION, ACTUAL AND PROJECTED BY AGE GROUP 1951–2006 (THOUSANDS)

Year	Population	Under 9	10–19	20–34	35–49	50–64	65 & Over
Actual							
1951	14,010	3,120	2,190	3,260	2,610	1,740	1,090
1956	16,080	3,790	2,600	3,540	3,020	1,890	1,240
1961	18,240	4,340	3,290	3,670	3,400	2,150	1,390
1966	20,020	4,500	3,930	3,950	3,630	2,470	1,540
1971	21,570	4,070	4,420	4,790	3,760	2,780	1,750
1976	22,990	3,620	4,620	5,760	3,850	3,140	2,000
1981	24,340	3,560	4,240	6,560	4,220	3,400	2,360
1986	25,600	3,630	3,730	6,940	4,980	3,590	2,730
Projections							
1991	26,610	3,570	3,610	6,750	5,820	3,690	3,170
1996	27,350	3,260	3,680	6,240	6,560	4,030	3,580
2001	27,820	2,880	3,620	5,770	6,910	4,760	3,880
2006	28,090	2,670	3,310	5,680	6,740	5,550	4,410

Source: *Marketing Research Handbook*, Statistics Canada, Catalogue 63-224, various years. Projections based on moderate fertility rates, average net international migration, and a migration flow within Canada that partially reflects the late 1960s' pattern.

Exhibit 2

POPULATION, ACTUAL AND PROJECTED BY GEOGRAPHIC AREA 1951–2006 (THOUSANDS)

Year	Total Population	Maritime Provinces	Quebec	Ontario	Prairie Provinces	BC & Yukon/NWT
Actual						
1951	14,010	1,620	4,050	4,600	2,550	1,190
1956	16,080	1,760	4,630	5,410	2,850	1,430
1961	18,240	1,900	5,260	6,230	3,180	1,670
1966	20,020	1,980	5,780	6,960	3,380	1,920
1971	21,570	2,060	6,030	7,700	3,540	2,240
1976	22,990	2,180	6,240	8,260	3,780	2,530
1981	24,340	2,230	6,440	8,630	4,230	2,810
1986	25,600	2,320	6,630	9,110	4,510	3,030
Projections						
1991	26,610	2,440	6,790	9,620	4,590	3,170
1996	27,350	2,520	6,880	9,950	4,730	3,270
2001	27,820	2,590	6,900	10,170	4,830	3,330
2006	28,090	2,630	6,890	10,280	4,910	3,380

Source: *Marketing Research Handbook*, Statistics Canada, Catalogue 63-224, various years. Projections based on moderate fertility rates, average net international migration, and a migration flow within Canada that partially reflects the late 1960s' pattern.

Exhibit 3

HOUSEHOLDS, ACTUAL AND PROJECTED BY GEOGRAPHIC AREA 1966–2001 (THOUSANDS)

Year	Total Households	Maritime Provinces	Quebec	Ontario	Prairie Provinces	BC & Yukon/NWT
Actual						
1966	5,180	450	1,390	1,880	910	550
1971	6,030	500	1,600	2,230	1,020	680
1976	7,170	600	1,900	2,640	1,190	840
1981	8,280	670	2,170	2,970	1,450	1,020
1986	9,220	750	2,340	3,430	1,590	1,110
Projections						
1991	10,110	820	2,510	3,780	1,760	1,240
1996	10,680	860	2,590	4,020	1,870	1,340
2001	11,190	900	2,650	4,230	1,980	1,430

Note: Households include single-detached, single-attached, apartments and flats, and mobile homes.

Source: *Marketing Research Handbook*, Statistics Canada, Catalogue 63-224, various years. Projections based on moderate fertility rates, average net international migration, and a migration flow within Canada that partially reflects the late 1960s' pattern.

Section 3

MARKETING RESEARCH

Sound marketing decisions require accurate, timely information about markets, competitors, and consumer behaviour. Marketing research, which is one form of marketing information, is primarily concerned with special-purpose research projects, although the same techniques may be used repeatedly on the same or different classes of problems. Managers utilize marketing research to increase the likelihood of making more informed, and hence usually better, decisions. Every marketing research project should begin with a clear understanding of the organization's specific information needs. Given the uncertain, dynamic, and competitive nature of the marketing environment, no manager can hope to gain perfect understanding of the organization's market. Rather, the goal of marketing research is to reduce uncertainty to tolerable levels at a reasonable cost.

STEPS IN THE MARKETING RESEARCH PROCESS

Marketing research is properly viewed as a sequence of steps which can be termed the *research process*. A summary of the research process is presented in Exhibit 1. When beginning a study, managers are often tempted to go straight to the instrument design and data collection stages, without thinking through the prior steps. This is a serious mistake and often leads to market research reports that are not useful because the wrong questions are asked or the data collected turn out to be unreliable and inaccurate.

DEFINING THE PURPOSE OF THE RESEARCH

The primary questions to be asked before beginning any marketing research project are, "Why is this information needed?" and "What will the implications of this research be?" Only if the findings can influence management decisions, should the research be carried out.

The reasons for conducting marketing research can be categorized by examining the process of decision making. A useful three-stage model is

1. recognizing and defining problems,
2. generating and selecting alternative courses of action, and
3. monitoring performance.

The first stage of any decision is recognition that a problem exists. Often, the initial signals that managers receive are only vague indications or symptoms of a problem—but once detected, marketing research can be very useful in defining and understanding it.

Exhibit 1

THE MARKET RESEARCH PROCESS

1. Defining the Purpose of the Research—Why is information to be gathered?
2. Statement of Research Objectives—What information is needed?
3. Review of Existing Data—What is already known?
4. Value Analysis—Is the research worth the cost?
5. Research Design
   a. Exploratory
   b. Descriptive
   c. Causal
6. Methods of Primary Data Collection
   a. Communication
   b. Observation
7. Research Tactics—Sampling Procedures and Instrument Design
   a. Target population
   b. Sample selection
   c. Sample size
   d. Instrument design
   e. Pretesting
8. Field Operations—Data Collection
9. Data Analysis
10. Completion of the Project
    a. Interpretation of data
    b. Recommendations
    c. Final report

Following problem recognition, marketing research can help managers better understand the problem or opportunity as well as help search for and evaluate alternative courses of action. Much of the work done in this area is characterized by formal research procedures. Indeed, the careful gathering of descriptive data and the evaluation of specific alternatives through questionnaires and observational studies are probably the areas in which the most money is spent. Market surveys and test marketing are both examples of such studies.

Once a marketing plan is implemented, progress should be measured against the original purpose through performance monitoring. The information gathered should help ascertain not only whether the program is meeting its goals, but also *why* it is succeeding or failing. Performance monitoring may indicate a need for changes in a specific plan or its execution; moreover, it enables managers to learn from their mistakes and successes and to redirect the business accordingly.

STATEMENT OF RESEARCH OBJECTIVES

After establishing that the research will serve a useful purpose, the next step is to state explicitly the research objectives—what specific information is needed? In other words, this stage involves going from the general to the particular.

Information requirements should be stated in writing. These requirements can then be reviewed to see if they are specific enough to provide guidance to the researchers, set forth the issues to be investigated, and include all the relevant questions to be asked. Some managers determine their information requirements by stating their beliefs about the market as a set of hypotheses. For example, a brand manager might wish to test the hypothesis that increasing the advertising budget by 25% will expand sales by at least 20%. It's often helpful to prepare samples of possible outputs and see what issues the sample report raises. Are other data needed before the results can be used? For example, is it enough to know that an ad budget should be increased, or must the media be specified as well?

REVIEW OF EXISTING DATA

Before gathering new data, researchers should investigate the possibility of using data that already exist. Market researchers divide information into two classes, primary data and secondary data. *Primary* data are new information collected especially for the research project being undertaken; *secondary* data, in contrast, have previously been collected separately for other purposes. An organization's own internal recordkeeping system, the observations of staff, easily accessible published data, reports from the trade, and other kinds of information can often be readily assembled to give a good deal of valuable information. Federal and provincial governments gather and publish voluminous amounts of statistical data; government agencies also publish studies on a wide range of topics. A good general rule to follow is not to gather primary data until it becomes clear that no satisfactory secondary data are available. Even then, it's best to start with secondary data and restrict primary data collection to topics that remain unresolved.

In addition to internally generated accounting and transaction data, many companies use their sales force, distributors, and other employees or associates as important sources of market and competitive information. A formalized system of collecting and retrieving such data, along with adequate incentives for the sales force, is necessary to make the process useful.

Many trade associations and marketing service firms gather information about various markets and make it available to companies at a fee. Trade associations, for instance, typically report on market trends, industry sales, and government actions in documents that are restricted to their members. Market research firms offer many syndicated services. One such service compiles data collected from a panel of more than 5,000 households, who keep a weekly diary in which they record purchases (e.g., brand, price, quantity) of many items. A company selling toothpaste, for example, can then buy information on such factors as toothpaste buyers' brand loyalty, socioeconomic characteristics, and purchase frequency. Directories describing proprietary sources of marketing information may be found in many business libraries.

VALUE ANALYSIS

Management's next task is to ask whether the research is worth doing in terms of the value of the information obtained for decision making. Not all information is worth the monetary and time costs associated with its collection. No research project should be implemented unless management is committed to using the findings as an input to decision making. Before carrying out a research project, a manager should be satisfied that its findings will be useful in reducing the likelihood either that a bad (and costly) mistake will be made or that a marketing program will lack the fine tuning necessary to achieve its full financial potential. By relating the cost of the research to the estimated incremental value of improved decision making, a manager can then determine whether the proposed study represents a worthwhile investment.

A second consideration in value analysis is timeliness. Because of market dynamics and competitive pressures, marketing decisions often must be made quickly. Partial information that can be obtained next week may be worth more than detailed information that will be available next quarter. Similarly, a more expensive research project may be justifiable if it can deliver the required data more quickly.

RESEARCH DESIGN

A research design guides the collection and analysis of data. Although each study has its own specific purpose, it is useful to classify marketing research into three broad groupings:

1. exploratory,
2. descriptive, and
3. experiments and other causal studies.

EXPLORATORY STUDIES These are most often used in the problem discovery and definition phases of decision making. They are more informal and less rigidly controlled than standardized questionnaire interviews, and include such methods as

1. reviews of related literature,
2. interviews with experts,
3. in-depth interviews of small samples of typical consumers, and
4. detailed case histories.

Managers should not overgeneralize from the results of exploratory research. Caution is necessary since the results are not based on a representative sample of the population and cannot be projected to the entire market. The semi-structured nature of the research, the role of the interviewer in directing the responses, and the subjectiveness of the answers do not usually allow for unambiguous interpretation of the results. Qualitative research should be used to gain insights into the consumer perspective and suggest hypotheses for further testing and alternatives to pursue.

DESCRIPTIVE STUDIES These are used to

1. portray the attitudes, behaviour, and other characteristics of persons, groups, or organizations;
2. determine the extent of association among two or more variables and to draw inferences about these relationships; and
3. make predictions about the future and/or the results of different management actions.

In general, descriptive studies can be subdivided between cross-sectional and longitudinal studies. Cross-sectional studies examine the population of interest at one point in time. For example, one appliance company carried out a survey to determine whether such characteristics as income, number and age of children, and wife's employment status were associated with owning microwave ovens and other kitchen appliances. By contrast, a longitudinal or panel study investigates a fixed sample of people who are measured at a number of points in time. While cross-sectional or aggregate data describe total consumption, a panel allows researchers to monitor an individual's behaviour, such as a customer's brand loyalty, over time.

EXPERIMENTS These provide the best means for establishing a causal relationship. In an experiment, various levels of the causal factor—the treatment—are assigned on a statistically random basis to subjects. Then differences in response between those receiving the different treatments and those receiving no treatment—the controls—are measured and analyzed to see if there is evidence of a causal relationship.

TEST MARKETING The goal of test marketing, one form of experiment, is to determine how consumers react to a new product under market conditions. Test markets can be used to estimate the likely sales of a new product in order to help decide whether to launch the product nationally. Another use of test marketing is to evaluate several marketing plans. For instance, a company uncertain as to whether to use a standard or high promotion budget may test these alternatives in different cities. Test markets also help a company to study wholesaler and retailer response to its marketing program and to observe consumer purchasing patterns and foresee possible problems that could occur when the product is bought and used under normal buying conditions.

Competitive reactions to a test market, however, are somewhat problematic. A competitor who makes no reaction to a test market may later compete actively, perhaps with an imitative product. Other competitors may react aggressively to disrupt a test market in order to lower the value of information gained and to discourage a company from implementing its new product plans. Despite test marketing's costs and difficulties, test markets are usually helpful in increasing a good product's likelihood of success and avoiding major failures.

METHODS OF PRIMARY DATA COLLECTION

The two major methods of data collection are (oral and written) communication and observation. Observation involves the recording of behaviour or the identification of readily observable personal characteristics such as age or sex. In some cases subjects may not even be aware that they are being observed. Other characteristics such as a person's awareness and attitudes can be obtained only by asking. Also it is usually cheaper and faster to ask people about their behaviour through interviews or questionnaires than it is to observe it.

One advantage of observation is that it does not depend on the ability or willingness of the respondent to provide data. Some people may seek to hide from interviewers the fact that they buy cheaper, generic brands; others may try to overclaim their thriftiness. Observation describes actual behaviour.

RESEARCH TACTICS

TARGET POPULATION In choosing the subjects for a study, it is important to distinguish between the population or universe, the sampling frame, the sample, and the respondents. The target population is the group we wish to study. For example, if a bank is planning a financial services program for people over 65, then that is the target population.

SAMPLING FRAME The sampling frame specifies the members of the target population to be surveyed. It is not always easy to identify. For the bank's program, the sampling frame might be a list of all those who receive Canada Pension Plan payments. However, the frame may not be a perfect representation of the population, since not everyone who is over 65 receives CPP payments, yet some younger, disabled workers do receive them. A sampling frame is needed whenever a researcher wishes to conduct a survey of people who are preselected by name. If an interviewer is sent to a shopping centre to question every fifth person who enters, then a list of preselected names is not needed.

PROBABILITY SAMPLES In probability samples, every person in the frame has a known chance of being selected; the actual choices will be made probabilistically. (A random sample is one kind of probability sample in which each person has an equal chance of being selected.) The great advantage of probability sampling is that this known chance of selection allows the researcher to make a statistical estimate of the size of the sampling error and thereby determine how far the findings might differ from those that would be obtained by studying the entire population.

NONPROBABILITY SAMPLES In nonprobability samples, the interviewer has more discretion in selecting respondents. Convenience samples are composed of subjects who volunteer or who are readily available to the researcher, such as people walking through a shopping centre, church groups, or students in class. Quotas may be established to ensure that respondents reflect a mix of prespecified characteristics, such as being equally split between men and women.

One danger associated with giving interviewers control over the choice of respondents is that they will tend to choose those individuals who are easiest to interview—people who look friendly or live in convenient locations, e.g., apartment houses in "good" neighbourhoods. Such respondents may not be representative of the population as a whole, even though they may share some of that population's readily measurable characteristics.

In practice, researchers use nonprobability designs quite frequently. They are the logical choice for informal exploratory research and can save time and money in other studies. Also such samples may provide better control of error due to factors other than sampling.

SAMPLE SIZE "How large should the sample be?" is one of the most frequently asked and seemingly simple questions raised in planning research studies. The answer depends on the purpose of the research, the sampling design used, the characteristics being studied and their variation within the population, the precision desired from the estimate, the desired level of confidence in the accuracy of the estimate, the cost of the study, and the time available. Mathematical formulas can be used to help determine the optimal sample size.

In general, precision increases with the square root of the sample size, so doubling precision requires multiplying the sample size by four. Other factors, such as the nature of the analysis to be performed on the data, can be very important in setting sample size. Too small a sample in segmentation studies, for example, may make it impossible to conduct meaningful analyses of cross-tabulated data.

RESPONSE RATE People fail to respond to surveys for two reasons—either they are not reached by the researchers (not-at-homes in interviews, wrong address in mail surveys), or they refuse to participate. Mail questionnaires typically achieve response rates in the 10% to 50% range; personal and telephone interviews (with three or four callbacks) reach 50% to 80% of subjects. High response rates are needed to limit nonresponse bias because responders and nonresponders generally differ. Women who do not answer morning telephone calls, for instance, may be employed outside the home, in contrast to women who work at home who are easier to reach. The researcher needs to determine how significant these differences are and to make adjustments where appropriate.

Large sample sizes do not in themselves compensate for biases resulting from low response rates. Often, greater validity is achieved by increasing the response rate than by increasing the number of people sampled. Special incentives, prior mailings, a well-written, well-designed questionnaire, a combination of interview methods, and intensive follow-up efforts can lead to higher response rates.

METHODS OF ADMINISTRATION Telephone and personal interviews and mail questionnaires are the three major ways of collecting information, although various combinations of these methods can be used. While mail is usually the cheapest of the three, the cost of the data collection and analysis per completed mail questionnaire usually exceeds $5. Telephone can be two to four times as expensive, and personal interviews even more so. In addition to lower cost, mail questionnaires offer the advantage of uniformity of administration, since the interviewers themselves may add variation to personal and telephone surveys. In mail questionnaires respondents may also have greater confidence in their anonymity (when it is promised) than they feel when being interviewed. On the other hand, mail questionnaires usually cannot be used to probe the subject in great depth. Moreover, considerable time must be allotted for the mailing and return of questionnaires.

Although personal interviews are costly, they provide the researcher with considerable flexibility and control. Samples of the product can be shown. An interview is particularly appropriate for revealing information about complex, emotional subjects and for probing the sentiments that underlie expressed opinions.

Telephone interviews are less expensive than personal interviews and quicker to complete. Political candidates, for instance, often use telephone interviews to monitor voters' changing opinions before an election. Telephone interviews combine many of the advantages of the mail and personal methods. Of course, telephone interviews cannot use graphical materials and cannot be as rich in content or as long as personal interviews.

CONTENT AND WORDING OF THE QUESTIONS In designing a questionnaire, each individual question needs to be carefully constructed in order to obtain accurate data. For example, in wording questions, clear, simple words should be used, and leading or biased questions avoided. Answers to socially sensitive or personally embarrassing questions are potentially unreliable and particular care must be taken in asking for such information and the ordering of questions. Additionally, it's important to consider whether the respondent knows the answer or can get the requested information without too much time and effort. While unnecessary questions should be avoided, the researcher should make sure that all needed information is obtained.

PRETESTING The researcher should never expect that the first draft of a questionnaire will be usable. After completion, it must be re-examined as a whole and revised. Even then the design is far from complete; the key test of a questionnaire is how it performs in practice. Two types of pretesting are required. The first is conducted through personal interviews with a convenience sample to identify major errors. More critical is a pretest that simulates the actual administration of the questionnaire. Those who design a questionnaire are much closer to a topic than the respondents will be, and the pretest identifies problems that arise because of these vast differences in perception. Additionally, the researcher should attempt to tabulate the data from the pretest to see if, in fact, the analyses that were planned can be carried out. In brief, pretesting is a *must*.

FIELD OPERATIONS

Field operations include those parts of the research process during which the data are collected and coded. Since a number of professional market research firms specialize in these tasks, most organizations contract out all or part of the field work. As with all such tasks, management must ensure that it has an effective way to monitor the quality and performance of data collection and coding. Otherwise errors can occur. In one study of theatre attendance, 35% of the nonsubscribers were falsely classified as new subscribers because the analysts interpreted no reply to a question as equivalent to a check by the number 0, an answer which represented a new subscriber.

DATA ANALYSIS

Data analysis often involves complex, sophisticated techniques. The manager should not reject a specific technique just because it is complex, since it may contribute new insights to understanding a market. On the other hand, not all useful analysis techniques are necessarily complicated.

Although data analysis is one of the last steps in the market research process, its impact appears much earlier. For example, the type of analysis to be done often influences the content and form of the questions. It is often a good idea to create dummy versions of the tables that are expected to appear in the final report and to make sure that the questions included (and their format) lend themselves to the kind of analysis required to complete those tables.

INTERPRETATION OF DATA, RECOMMENDATIONS, AND REPORT WRITING

Depending on their skills, interests, and organizational policies, researchers and managers may share a good deal of the writing and interpretation, or none at all. Two cautions are in order. First, the interpretations of the data should be based on an analysis of what the survey actually discovered, not on what managers and researchers hoped would be found. Second, the report should be written clearly and concisely so that the newly discovered information and insights are communicated to the relevant decision makers. Graphic presentations of data are often more easily understood by decision makers than tables.

SUMMARY

Successful market research requires a disciplined approach to problem specification and data collection and analysis; it is not simply a matter of asking questions. Many market research projects fail to influence decision making because of weaknesses in planning, execution, analysis, and presentation. Both managers and researchers are more likely to obtain findings that will be useful for decision making if they follow a systematic approach to market research.

8 THE COORS DISTRIBUTORSHIP

James E. Nelson
Eric J. Karson

Larry Brownlow was just beginning to realize the problem was more complex than he had thought. The problem, of course, was giving direction to Manson and Associates regarding which research should be completed by February 20, 1989, to determine market potential of a Coors beer distributorship for a two-county area in southern Delaware. With data from this research, Larry would be able to estimate the feasibility of such an operation before the March 5 application deadline. Larry knew his decision on whether or not to apply for the distributorship was the most important career choice he had ever faced.

LARRY BROWNLOW

Larry was just completing his MBA and, from his standpoint, the Coors announcement of expansion into Delaware could hardly have been better timed. He had long ago decided the best opportunities and rewards were in smaller, self-owned businesses and not in the jungles of corporate giants. Because of a family tragedy some three years earlier, Larry found himself in a positiion to consider small business opportunities such as the Coors distributorship. Approximately $500,000 was held in trust for Larry, to be disbursed when he reached age 30. Until then, Larry and his family were living on an annual trust income of about $40,000. It was on the basis of this income that Larry had decided to leave his sales engineering job and return to graduate school for his MBA.

The decision to complete a graduate program and operate his own business had been easy to make. Although he could have retired and lived off investment income, Larry knew such a life would not be to his liking. Working with people and the challenge of making it on his own, Larry thought, were far preferable to enduring an early retirement.

Larry would be 30 in July, about the time money would actually be needed to start the business. In the meantime, he had access to about $15,000 for feasibility research. Although there certainly were other places to spend the money, Larry and his wife agreed the opportunity to acquire the distributorship could not be overlooked.

COORS, INC.

Coors' history dated back to 1873, when Adolph Coors built a small brewery in Golden, Colorado. Since then, the brewery had prospered and become the fourth-largest seller of beer in the country. Coors' operating philosophy could be summed up as "hard work, saving money, devotion to the quality of the product, caring about the environment, and giving people something to believe in.'' Company operation is consistent with this philosophy. Headquarters and most production facilities are still located in Golden, Colorado, with a new Shenandoah, Virginia, facility aiding in nationwide distribution. Coors is still family operated and controlled. The company had issued its first public stock, $127 million worth of nonvoting shares, in 1975. The issue was enthusiastically received by the financial community despite its being offered during a recession.

Coors' unwillingness to compromise on the high quality of its product is well known both to its suppliers and to its consuming public. Coors beer requires constant refrigeration to maintain this quality, and wholesalers' facilities are closely controlled to ensure that proper temperatures are maintained. Wholesalers are also required to install and use aluminum can recycling equipment. Coors was one of the first breweries in the industry to recycle its cans.

Larry was aware of Coors' popularity with many consumers in adjacent states. However, Coors' corporate management was seen by some consumers to hold anti-union beliefs (because of a labour disagreement at the brewery some ten years ago and the brewery's current use of a non-union labour force). Some other consumers perceived the brewery to be somewhat insensitive to minority issues, primarily in employment and distribution. These attitudes—plus many other aspects of consumer behaviour—meant that Coors' sales in Delaware would depend greatly on the efforts of the two wholesalers planned for the state.

MANSON RESEARCH PROPOSAL

Because of the press of his studies, Larry had contacted Manson and Associates in January for their assistance. The firm was a Wilmington-based general research supplier that had conducted other feasibility studies in the mid-Atlantic region. Manson was well known for the quality of its work, particularly with respect to computer modelling. The firm had developed special expertise in modelling such things as population and employment levels for cities, counties, and other units of area for periods of up to ten years into the future.

Larry had met John Rome, senior research analyst for Manson, in January and discussed the Coors opportunity and appropriate research extensively. Rome promised a formal research proposal (Exhibit 1) for the project, which Larry now held in his hand. It certainly was extensive, Larry thought, and reflected the professionalism he expected. Now came the hard part—choosing the more relevant research from the proposal—because he certainly couldn't afford to pay for it all. Rome had suggested a meeting for Friday, which gave Larry only three more days to decide.

Larry was at first overwhelmed. All the research would certainly be useful. He was sure he needed estimates of sales and costs in a form allowing managerial analysis, but what data in what form? Knowledge of competing operations' experience, retailer support, and consumer acceptance also seemed important for feasibility analysis. For example, what if consumers were excited about Coors and retailers indifferent, or the other way around? Finally, several of the studies would provide information that could be useful in later months of operation, in the areas of promotion and pricing, for example. The problem now appeared more difficult than before!

It would have been nice, Larry thought, to have had some time to perform part of the suggested research himself. However, there just was too much in the way of class assignments and other matters to allow him that luxury. Besides, using Manson and Associates would give him research results from an unbiased source. There would be plenty for him to do once he received the results anyway.

Exhibit 1

MANSON AND ASSOCIATES RESEARCH PROPOSAL

January 16, 1989

Mr. Larry Brownlow
1198 West Lamar
Chester, PA 19345

Dear Larry:

It was a pleasure meeting you last week and discussing your business and research interests in Coors wholesaling. After further thought and discussion with my colleagues, the Coors opportunity appears even more attractive than when we met.

Appearances can be deceiving, as you know, and I fully agree some formal research is needed before you make application. Research that we recommend would proceed in two distinct stages and is described below.

Stage One Research, Based on Secondary Data and Manson Computer Models:

Study A: National and Delaware Per Capita Beer Consumption for 1988–1992
Description: Per capita annual consumption of beer for the total population and for population age 21 and over in gallons is provided.
Source: Various publications, Manson computer model
Cost: $1,000

Study B: Population Estimates for 1986–1996 for Two Delaware Counties in Market Area
Description: Annual estimates of total population and population age 21 and over are provided for the period 1986–1996.
Source: U.S. Bureau of Census, Sales Management Annual Survey of Buying Power, Manson computer model
Cost: $1,500

Study C: Estimates of Coors' Market Share for 1990–1995
Description: Coors' market share for the two-county market area based on total gallons consumed is estimated for each year in the period 1990–1995. These data will be projected from Coors' nation-wide experience.
Source: Various publications, Manson computer model
Cost: $2,000

(continued)

Exhibit 1 continued

Study D: Estimates of Number of Liquor and Beer Licences for the Market Area, 1990–1995
Description: Projections of the number of on-premise sale operations and off-premise sale operations are provided.
Source: Delaware Department of Revenue, Manson computer model
Cost: $1,000

Study E: Beer Taxes Paid by Delaware Wholesalers for 1987 and 1988 in the Market Area
Description: Beer taxes paid by each of the six presently operating competing beer wholesalers are provided. These figures can be converted to gallons sold by applying the state gallonage tax rate ($0.06 per gallon).
Source: Delaware Department of Revenue
Cost: $200

Study F: Financial Statement Summary of Wine, Liquor, and Beer Wholesalers for Fiscal Year 1986
Description: Composite balance sheets, income statements, and relevant measures of performance for 510 similar wholesaling operations in the United States are provided.
Source: Robert Morris Associates Annual Statement Studies, 1987 ed.
Cost: $49.50

Stage Two Research, Based on Primary Data:

Study G: Consumer Study
Description: Study G involves focus-group interviews and a mail questionnaire to determine consumers' past experience, acceptance, and intention to buy Coors beer. Three focus-group interviews would be conducted in the two counties in the market area. From these data, a questionnaire would be developed and sent to 300 adult residents in the market area, utilizing direct questions and a semantic differential scale to measure attitudes toward Coors beer, competing beers, and an ideal beer.
Source: Manson and Associates
Cost: $6,000

Study H: Retailer Study
Description: Group interviews would be conducted with six potential retailers of Coors beer in one county in the market area to determine their past beer sales and experience and their intention to stock and sell Coors. From these data, a personal-interview questionnaire would be developed and executed at all appropriate retailers in the market area to determine similar data.
Source: Manson and Associates
Cost: $4,800

(continued)

Exhibit 1 continued

Study I: Survey of Retail and Wholesale Beer Prices
Description: In-store interviews would be conducted with a sample of 50 retailers in the market area to estimate retail and wholesale prices for Budweiser, Miller Lite, Miller, Busch, Bud Light, Old Milwaukee and Michelob.
Source: Manson and Associates
Cost: $2,000

Examples of the final report tables are attached [Exhibit 2]. This should give you a better idea of the data you will receive.

As you can see, the research is extensive and, I might add, not cheap. However, the research as outlined will supply you with sufficient information to make an estimate of the feasibility of a Coors distributorship, the investment for which is substantial.

I have scheduled 9:00 a.m. next Friday as a time to meet with you to discuss the proposal in more detail. Time is short, but we firmly feel the study can be completed by February 20, 1989. If you need more information in the meantime, please feel free to call.

Sincerely,

John Rome
Senior Research Analyst

Exhibit 2
EXAMPLES OF FINAL RESEARCH REPORT TABLES

Table A National and Delaware Residents' Annual Beer Consumption per Capita, 1988–1992 (gallons)

	U.S. Consumption		Delaware Consumption	
Year	Based on Entire Population	Based on Population Age 21 and Over	Based on Entire Population	Based on Population Age 21 and Over
1988				
1989				
1990				
1991				
1992				

Source: Study A

Exhibit 2 continued

Table B Population Estimates for 1986–1996 for Two Delaware Counties in Market Area

	Entire Population					
County	1986	1988	1990	1992	1994	1996
Kent						
Sussex						
	Population Age 21 and Over					
County	1986	1988	1990	1992	1994	1996
Kent						
Sussex						

Source: Study B.

Table C Estimates of Coors' Market Share for 1990–1995

Year	Market Share (%)
1990	
1991	
1992	
1993	
1994	
1995	

Source: Study C

Table D Estimates of Number of Liquor and Beer Licences for the Market Area, 1990–1995

Type of Licence	1990	1991	1992	1993	1994	1995
All beverages						
Retail beer and wine						
Off-premise beer only						
Veterans beer and liquor						
Fraternal						
Resort beer and liquor						

Source: Study D

Exhibit 2 continued

Table E Beer Taxes Paid by Beer Wholesalers in the Market Area, 1987 and 1988

Wholesaler	1987 Tax Paid ($)	1988 Tax Paid ($)
A		
B		
C		
D		
E		
F		

Source: Study E

Note: Delaware beer tax is $0.06 per gallon.

Table F Financial Statement Summary for 510 Wholesalers of Wine, Liquor, and Beer in Fiscal Year 1986

Assets	Percentage
Cash and equivalents	
Accounts and notes receivable, net	
Inventory	
All other current	
Total current	
Fixed assets, net	
Intangibles, net	
All other noncurrent	
Total	100.0
Liabilities	
Notes payable, short term	
Current maturity long-term debt	
Accounts and notes payable, trade	
Accrued expenses	
All other current	
Total current	
Long-term debt	
All other noncurrent	
Net worth	
Total liabilities and net worth	100.0

(continued)

Exhibit 2 continued

Income Data	
Net sales	100.0
Cost of sales	
Gross profit	
Operating expenses	
Operating profit	
All other expenses, net	
Profit before taxes	
Ratios	
Quick	
Current	
Debts/worth	
Sales/receivables	
Cost of sales/inventory	
Percentage profit before taxes, based on total assets	

Source: Study F (Robert Morris Associates, © 1987)

Interpretation of Statement Studies Figures

RMA recommends that Statement Studies data be regarded only as general guidelines and not as absolute industry norms. There are several reasons why the data may not be fully representative of a given industry:

1. The financial statements used in the Statement Studies are not selected by any random or statistically reliable method. RMA member banks voluntarily submit the raw data they have available each year, with these being the only constraints: (a) The fiscal year-ends of the companies reported may not be from April 1 through June 29, and (b) their total assets must be less than $100 million.
2. Many companies have varied product lines; however, the Statement Studies categorize them by their primary product Standard Industrial Classification (SIC) number only.
3. Some of our industry samples are rather small in relation to the total number of firms in a given industry. A relatively small sample can increase the chances that some of our composites do not fully represent an industry.
4. There is the chance that an extreme statement can be present in a sample, causing a disproportionate influence on the industry composite. This is particularly true in a relatively small sample.
5. Companies within the same industry may differ in the method of operations, which in turn can directly influence their financial statements. Since they are included in our sample, too, these statements can significantly affect our composite calculations.
6. Other considerations that can result in variations among different companies engaged in the same general line of business are different labour markets, geographical location, different accounting methods, quality of products handled, sources and methods of financing, and terms of sale.

For these reasons, RMS does not recommend that Statement Studies figures be considered as absolute norms for a given industry. Rather, the figures should be used only as general guidelines and in addition to the other methods of financial analysis. RMA makes no claim as to the representativeness of the figures printed in this book.

Exhibit 2 continued

Table G Consumer Questionnaire Results

	Percentage		Percentage
Consumed Coors in the past: Yes ____		No ____	
Attitudes toward Coors:	%	Usually buy beer at:	
Strongly like		Liquor stores	
Like		Taverns and bars	
Indifferent/no opinion		Supermarkets	
Dislike		Corner grocery	
Strongly dislike		Total	100.0
Total	100.0		
Weekly beer consumption:		Features considered important when buying beer:	
Less than 1 can		Taste	
1–2 cans		Brand name	
3–4 cans		Price	
5–6 cans		Store location	
7–8 cans		Advertising	
9 cans and over		Carbonation	
Total	100.0	Other	
Intention to buy Coors:		Total	100.0
Certainly will			
Maybe will			
Not sure			
Maybe will not			
Certainly will not			
Total	100.0		

Semantic Differential Scale, Consumers*

	Extremely	Very	Somewhat	Somewhat	Very	Extremely	
Masculine	____	____	____	____	____	____	Feminine
Healthful	____	____	____	____	____	____	Unhealthful
Cheap	____	____	____	____	____	____	Expensive
Strong	____	____	____	____	____	____	Weak
Old-fashioned	____	____	____	____	____	____	New
Upper-class	____	____	____	____	____	____	Lower-class
Good taste	____	____	____	____	____	____	Bad taste

Source: Study G

* Profiles would be provided for Coors, three competing beers, and an ideal beer.

Exhibit 2 continued

Table H Retailer Questionnaire Results

	Percentage		Percentage
Brands of beer carried:		Beer sales:	
Budweiser		Budweiser	
Miller Lite		Miller Lite	
Miller		Miller	
Busch		Busch	
Bud Light		Bud Light	
Old Milwaukee		Old Milwaukee	
Michelob		Michelob	
		Others	
Intention to sell Coors:		Total	100.0
Certainly will			
Maybe will			
Not sure			
Maybe will not			
Certainly will not			
Total	100.0		

Semantic Differential Scale, Retailers*

	Extremely	Very	Somewhat	Somewhat	Very	Extremely	
Masculine	____	____	____	____	____	____	Feminine
Healthful	____	____	____	____	____	____	Unhealthful
Cheap	____	____	____	____	____	____	Expensive
Strong	____	____	____	____	____	____	Weak
Old-fashioned	____	____	____	____	____	____	New
Upper-class	____	____	____	____	____	____	Lower-class
Good taste	____	____	____	____	____	____	Bad taste

Source: Study H

* Profiles would be provided for Coors, three competing beers, and an ideal beer.

Exhibit 2 continued

Table I Retail and Wholesale Prices for Selected Beers in the Market Area

Beer	Wholesale Six-Pack Price[a] (dollars)	Retail Six-Pack Price[b] (dollars)
Budweiser		
Miller Lite		
Miller		
Busch		
Bud Light		
Old Milwaukee		
Michelob		

Source: Study I

[a] Price at which the wholesaler sold to retailers.
[b] Price at which the retailer sold to consumers.

INVESTING AND OPERATING DATA

Larry was not completely in the dark regarding investment and operating data for the distributorship. In the past two weeks he had visited two beer wholesalers in his home town of Chester, Pennsylvania, who handled Anheuser-Busch and Miller beer, to get a feel for their operation and marketing experience. It would have been nice to interview a Coors wholesaler, but Coors management had instructed all of their distributors to provide no information to prospective applicants.

Although no specific financial data had been discussed, general information had been provided in a cordial fashion because of the noncompetitive nature of Larry's plans. Based on his conversations, Larry had made the following estimates:

Inventory		$240,000
Equipment:		
Delivery trucks	$150,000	
Forklift	20,000	
Recycling and miscellaneous equipment	20,000	
Office equipment	10,000	
Total equipment		200,000
Warehouse		320,000
Land		40,000
Total investment		$800,000

A local banker had reviewed Larry's financial capabilities and saw no problem in extending a line of credit on the order of $400,000. Other family sources also might loan as much as $400,000 to the business.

To get a rough estimate of fixed expenses, Larry decided to plan on having four route salespeople, a secretary, and a warehouse manager. Salaries for these people and himself would run about $160,000 annually, plus some form of incentive compensation he had yet to determine. Other fixed or semifixed expenses were estimated as follows:

Equipment depreciation	$35,000
Warehouse depreciation	15,000
Utilities and telephone	12,000
Insurance	10,000
Personal property taxes	10,000
Maintenance and janitorial service	5,600
Miscellaneous	2,400
Total	$90,000

According to the two wholesalers, beer in bottles and cans outsold keg beer by a three-to-one margin. Keg beer prices at the wholesale level were about 45 percent of prices for beer in bottles and cans.

MEETING

The entire matter deserved much thought. Maybe it was a golden opportunity, maybe not. The only thing certain was that research was needed, Manson and Associates was ready, and Larry needed time to think. Today is Tuesday, Larry thought—only three days until he and John Rome would get together for direction.

9 CANADIAN HOUSEHOLD PRODUCTS

Gordon H. G. McDougall

Ms. Wendy Jackson, marketing manager for Canadian Household Products, was planning to introduce a new brand of toothpaste named "Fresh" in Canada. Recently, the major competitors had introduced "pump" versions of their brands where the toothpaste was dispensed through a pump rather than squeezed out of a tube. Ms. Jackson decided to introduce the new brand, Fresh, in a pump dispenser. One decision to be made was the type of package to use for Fresh. After extensive design work, two packages (Package A and Package B) were developed. The problem was to determine which package would be the most effective in marketing Fresh.

Ms. Jackson decided to have some research conducted to assist her in making the package decision. She asked the company's marketing research department to design and implement research to collect information on the problem. The research department decided to run three different studies in order to increase the reliability and validity of the final results. The three studies are reported below.

RESEARCH STUDY NUMBER 1

A questionnaire was designed and pretested. Based on the pretest (twenty randomly selected respondents) a final questionnaire was developed. A sampling plan was designed on a completely random basis, and a sample size of two hundred was selected. Personal interviews were conducted, and after three callbacks, all two hundred respondents selected had been interviewed.

All respondents were asked a series of questions relating to attitudes towards and purchase of toothpaste. For the "Package Preference Question," respondents had been divided on a random basis into two subsamples. The first subsample was shown Fresh in Package A and the second subsample was shown Fresh in Package B. Respondents in each subsample were then asked the following two questions:

---

1. Do you think the package for Fresh toothpaste is:

   Attractive _____ _____ _____ _____ _____ Unattractive

   (1) (2) (3) (4) (5)

2. Would you ever buy Fresh toothpaste?

   Yes _____ No _____

The results for the two subsamples were:

(continued)

		Shown Package A	Shown Package B
Question 1.	Mean average	2.1	3.3
	Sample standard deviation	1.0	1.0
		Percent	
Question 2.	Yes	60	50
	No	40	50
		100	100

RESEARCH STUDY NUMBER 2

A laboratory experiment was conducted at the Canadian Household Products factory. Part of a room was set up to look like the shelves in a supermarket. A number of grocery products were put on the shelves, including a display of different brands of toothpaste. The entire staff of the plant (150 people) was randomly assigned to one of two groups of equal size (Group 1 and Group 2). The experiment, which was run on two consecutive working days, involved asking each respondent to imagine the shelves represented part of a supermarket. The respondents were asked to "buy" one of the brands of toothpaste. The respondents were told they didn't have to pay for the toothpaste, and that they could keep the brand they selected. After a respondent had selected a brand, the researcher replaced the brand so that each respondent viewed an identical shelf. On the first day, the different brands of toothpaste included Fresh in Package A and Group 1 participated in the experiment. The experiment was repeated on the following day with Group 2, and Fresh in Package B was used. The other brands of toothpaste remained the same for both days. The results of the two-day experiment were

	First Day	Second Day
Selected Package A	60	—
Selected Package B	—	50
Selected Other Brand	15	25
Total	75	75

RESEARCH STUDY NUMBER 3

A field experiment was conducted over a one-week period in four stores in a major city. The four stores (see description below) were typical of the type of store that sold toothpaste. The experiment involved selling Fresh in Package A in two of the stores (Large 1, Small 1) and Fresh in Package B in two of the stores (Large 2, Small 2) for a one-week period. The price was identical for both packages of Fresh.

- a large supermarket in a suburb of the city (Large 1)
- a large supermarket in the downtown shopping area of the city (Large 2)
- a small convenience store in a suburb of the city (Small 1)
- a small convenience store in the downtown shopping area of the city (Small 2)

The sales results for the one-week period were

Store	Package A	Store	Package B
Large 1	60 units	Large 2	100 units
Small 1	30 units	Small 2	40 units
	90 units		140 units

The results of the three studies were presented to Ms. Jackson. After examining the report, she wasn't sure what to conclude or what package to select. She called in her assistant, a recent business school graduate, and asked him to prepare a report which addressed the following issues:

1. A critical evaluation of the three studies in terms of:
   a) the strengths and weaknesses of each study;
   b) if there were weaknesses, how each of the studies could be modified to overcome the weaknesses; and
   c) what conclusions, if any, can be drawn from the studies.

2. Should additional research be conducted before a decision is made on the package to be used? If yes, what type of research? If no, what decision should be made?

3. What criteria should be used in deciding whether or not to conduct additional research?

Ms. Jackson eagerly awaited the report from her assistant.

10 DILLON CONTROLS, LTD.

James E. Nelson
Mark S. Johnson

"The choices themselves seem simple enough," thought Jack Dillon in January 1991, "either we enter the U.S. market in Pennsylvania and New York, we forget about the United States for the time being, or we do some more marketing research." Dillon was president of Dillon Controls, Ltd., located in Brantford, Ontario. The company was formed in 1980 and, after a slow start, had grown steadily to its present size of 25 employees and annual revenues of about $1.6 million. About 2% of these revenues came from sales to U.S. accounts.

THE AQUAWATCH SYSTEM

Dillon Controls' product line centred about its AquaWatch System, a design of computer hardware and software for the monitoring and control of pressurized water flows. Most often these water flows consisted of either potable water or sewage effluent as these liquids were stored, moved, or treated by municipal water departments.

The system employed an AquaWatch microcomputer installed at individual pumping stations where liquids were stored and moved. Pumping stations often were located many kilometres apart and linked geographically dispersed water users such as households and businesses to water and sewer systems. The microcomputer performed a number of important functions. It governed the starts, stops, and alarms of up to four pumps, monitored levels and available capacities of storage reservoirs, checked pump capacities and power consumptions, and recorded pump flows. It could even measure amounts of rainfall entering reservoirs and adjust pump operations or activate an alarm as needed. Each microcomputer could also be easily connected to a main computer to allow the remote control of pumping stations and the production of a variety of charts and graphs useful in evaluating pump performance and scheduling required maintenance.

The AquaWatch System provided a monitoring function that human operators could not match in terms of sophistication, immediacy, and cost. The system permitted each individual substation to control its own pumping operations; collect, analyze, and store data; forecast trends; transmit data and alarms to a central computer; and receive remote commands. Alarms could also be transmitted directly to a pocket-sized receiver carried by one or more operators on call. A supervisor could continually monitor pumping operations in a large system entirely via a computer terminal at a central location and send commands to individual pumps, thereby saving costly

Note: All dollar figures in the case are stated in Canadian currency. Some data are disguised.

service calls and time. The system reduced the possibility of overflows that could produce disastrous flooding of nearby communities or contamination of potable water.

Dillon Controls personnel would work with water and sewage engineers to design and install the desired AquaWatch System. Also they would train engineers and operators to work with the system and would be available 24 hours a day for consultation. If needed, a company engineer could be present to assist engineers and operators whenever major problems arose. Dillon Controls also offered its clients the option of purchasing a complete service contract whereby company personnel would provide periodic testing and maintenance of installed systems. The contract called for clients to pay Dillon for all direct costs of the service plus 15% for overhead.

An AquaWatch System could be configured a number of ways. In its most basic form, the system would be little more than a small "black box" that monitored two or three lift station activities and, when necessary, transmitted an alarm to one or more remote receivers. An intermediate system would monitor additional activities, send data to a central computer via telephone lines, and receive remote commands. An advanced system would provide the same monitoring capabilities but added forecasting features, maintenance management, auxiliary power back-up, and data transmission and reception via radio. Prices to customers for the three configurations in early 1991 were about $1,500, $2,800, and $4,800.

AQUAWATCH CUSTOMERS

AquaWatch customers could be divided into two groups: governmental units and industrial companies. The typical application in the first group would be a sewage treatment plant having about four to twelve pumping stations, with each station containing one or more pumps. Pumps would operate intermittently and—unless an AquaWatch or similar system were in place—would be monitored by one or more operators who would visit each station once or perhaps twice each day for about a half hour. Operators would take reservoir measurements, record running times of pumps, and sometimes perform limited maintenance and repairs. The sewage plant and stations typically were located in flat or rolling terrain, where gravity could not be used in lieu of pumping. If any monitoring equipment were present, it typically would consist of a crude, on-site alarm that would be activated whenever fluid levels rose or fell beyond a preset level. Sometimes the alarm would activate a telephone dialling function that alerted an operator some distance from the station.

Numerous industrial companies also stored, moved, and processed large quantities of water or sewage. These applications usually differed little from those in government plants except for their smaller size. On the other hand, there were a considerably larger number of industrial companies having pumping stations and so, Dillon thought the two markets offered nearly identical market potentials.

The two markets required essentially the same products, although industrial applications often used smaller, simpler equipment. Both markets wanted their monitoring equipment to be accurate and reliable, the two dominant concerns. Equipment should also be easy to use, economical to operate, and require little regular service or maintenance. Purchase price often was not a major consideration—as long as the price was in an appropriate range, customers seemed more interested in actual product performance than in initial outlays.

Future Demand

Dillon thought that world-wide demand for these types of systems would continue to be strong for at least the next ten years. While some demand represented construction of new pumping stations, many applications were replacements of crude monitoring and alarm systems at existing sites. These existing systems depended greatly on regular visits by operators, visits that often continued even after new equipment was installed. Most such trips probably were not necessary. However, many managers found it difficult to dismiss or reassign monitoring staff who were no longer needed; many were also quite cautious and conservative, desiring some human monitoring of the new equipment "just in case." Once replacements of existing systems were complete, market growth would be limited to new construction and, of course, replacements of more sophisticated systems.

Most customers (as well as noncustomers) considered the AquaWatch System to be one of the best on the market. Those knowledgeable in the industry felt that competing products seldom matched AquaWatch's reliability and accuracy. Experts also believed that many competing products lacked the sophistication and flexibility present in AquaWatch's design. Beyond these product features, customers also appreciated Dillon Controls' knowledge about water and sanitation engineering. Competing firms often lacked this expertise, offering their products somewhat as a sideline and considering the market too small for an intensive marketing effort.

The market was clearly not too small for Dillon Controls. While Dillon had no hard data on market potential for the United States, he thought that annual demand there could be as much as $30 million. In Canada, the total market was about $4 million in annual sales. Perhaps about 40% of this came from new construction, while the rest represented demand from replacing existing systems. Industry sales in the latter category could be increased by more aggressive marketing efforts on the part of competitors in the industry.

DILLON CONTROLS' STRATEGY

Dillon Controls currently marketed its AquaWatch System primarily to sewage treatment plants in Canada as opposed to industrial companies. Approximately 70% of its revenues came from Ontario and Quebec. The company's strategy could be described as providing technologically superior equipment to monitor pumping operations at these plants. The strategy stressed frequent contacts with customers and potential customers to design, supply, and service AquaWatch Systems. The strategy also stressed superior knowledge of water and sanitation engineering along with up-to-date electronics and computer technology. The result was a line of highly specialized sensors, computers, and methods for process controls in water treatment plants.

This was the essence of Dillon Control's strategy: having a special competence that no firm in the market could easily match. The company also prided itself on its being a young, creative company, without an entrenched bureaucracy. Company employees generally worked with enthusiasm and dedication; they talked with each other, regularly, openly, and with a great deal of give and take. Most importantly, customers—as well as technology—seemed to drive all areas in the company.

Dillon Controls' strategy in Canada seemed to be fairly well decided, that is, Dillon thought that a continuation of present strategies and tactics should continue to produce good results. However, one new aspect that would likely be introduced would be creating a branch office having both sales and distribution functions somewhere out west, most likely in Vancouver. The plan was to have such an office in operation well before the end of 1992. Having a branch office in Vancouver would greatly simplify sales and service in the western provinces, not to mention increase company sales.

U.S. Market

Beyond establishing the branch office, Dillon was considering a major strategic decision to enter the U.S. market. The recently signed Free Trade Agreement between Canada and the U.S. was prompting many Canadian companies to look southward. The agreement, which went into effect January 1, 1989, had, among other things, eliminated all tariffs on computer products traded between the two countries (such as the AquaWatch System). In addition, Dillon's two recent visits to the United States had led him to conclude that the market represented potential far beyond that of Canada and that the United States seemed perfect for expansion. Industry experts in the United States agreed with Dillon that the AquaWatch System outperformed anything used in the U.S. market. Experts thought that many water and sewage engineers would welcome Dillon Controls' products and knowledge. Moreover, Dillon thought that U.S. transportation systems and payment arrangements would present few problems.

Entry would most likely be in the form of a sales and service office located in Philadelphia. The Pennsylvania and New York state markets seemed representative of the United States and appeared to offer a good test of the AquaWatch System. The office would require an investment of some $200,000 for inventory and other balance sheet items. Annual fixed costs would total upwards of $250,000 for salaries and other operating expenses; Dillon thought that the office would employ only a general manager, technician, and secretary for at least the first year or two. Each AquaWatch System sold in the United States would be priced to provide a contribution of about 30%. Dillon wanted a 35% annual return on any Dillon Controls' investment, to begin no later than the second year. At issue was whether Dillon could realistically expect to achieve this goal in the United States.

MARKETING RESEARCH

To estimate the viability of a U.S. sales office, Dillon had commissioned the Browning Group in Philadelphia to conduct some limited marketing research with selected personnel in the water and sewage industries in the city and surrounding areas. The research had two purposes: to obtain a sense of market needs and market reactions to Dillon Controls' products and to calculate a rough estimate of market potential in Pennsylvania and New York. Results were intended to help Dillon interpret his earlier conversations with industry experts and perhaps allow a decision on market entry.

The research design itself employed two phases of data collection. The first consisted of five one-hour interviews with water and sewage engineers employed by local city and municipal governments. For each interview, an experienced Browning Group interviewer scheduled an appointment with the engineer and then visited his office armed with a set of questions and a tape recorder. Questions included

1. What procedures do you use to monitor your pumping stations?
2. Is your current monitoring system effective? Costly?
3. What are the costs of a monitoring malfunction?
4. What features would you like to see in a monitoring system?
5. Who decides on the selection of a monitoring system?
6. What is your reaction to the AquaWatch System?

Interviewers were careful to listen closely to the engineers' responses and to probe for additional detail and clarification.

Tapes of the personal interviews were transcribed and then analyzed by the project manager at Browning. The report noted that these results were interesting in that they described typical industry practices and viewpoints. A partial summary from the report appears below.

> The picture that emerges is one of fairly sophisticated personnel making decisions about monitoring equipment that is relatively simple in design. Still, some engineers would appear distrustful of this equipment because they persist in sending operators to pumping stations on a daily basis. The distrust may be justified because potential costs of a malfunction were identified as expensive repairs and cleanups, fines of $10,000 per day of violation, lawsuits, harassment by the Health Department, and public embarrassment. The five engineers identified themselves as key individuals in the decision to purchase new equipment. Without exception, they considered AquaWatch features innovative, highly desirable, and worth the price.

The summary noted also that the primary use of the interview results was to construct a questionnaire that could be administered over the telephone.

Telephone Questionnaire

The questionnaire was used in the second phase of data collection, as part of a telephone survey of 65 utility managers, water and sewage engineers, and pumping station operators in Philadelphia and surrounding areas. All respondents were employed by governmental units. Each interview took about ten minutes to complete, covering topics identified in questions one, two, and four above. The Browning Group's research report stated that most interviews found respondents to be quite co-operative, although 15 people refused to participate at all.

The telephone interviews had produced results that could be considered more representative of the market because of the larger sample size. The report had organized these results about the topics of monitoring procedures, system effectiveness and costs, and features desired in a monitoring system:

> All monitoring systems under the responsibility of the 50 respondents were considered to require manual checking. The frequency of operator visits to pumping stations ranged from monthly to twice daily, depending on flow rates, pumping station history, proximity of nearby communities, monitoring equipment in operation, and other factors. Even the most sophisticated automatic systems were checked because respondents "just don't trust the machine." Each operator was responsible for an average of 15 stations.
>
> Despite the perceived need for double-checking, all respondents considered their current monitoring system to be quite effective. Not one reported a serious pumping malfunction in the past three years that had escaped detection. However, this reliability came at considerable cost—the annual wages and other expenses associated with each monitoring operator averaged about $50,000.
>
> Respondents were about evenly divided between those wishing a simple alarm system and those desiring a sophisticated, versatile microprocessor. Managers and engineers in the former category often said that the only feature they really needed was an emergency signal such as a siren, horn, or light. Sometimes they would add a telephone dialer that would be automatically activated at the same time as the signal. Most agreed that a price of around $2,000 would be reasonable for such a system. The latter category of individuals contained engineers desiring many of the AquaWatch System's features, once they knew such equipment was available. A price of $5,000 per system seemed acceptable. Some of these respondents were quite knowledgeable about computers and computer programming while others were not. Only four respondents voiced any strong concerns about the cost to purchase and install more sophisticated monitoring equipment. Everyone demanded that the equipment be reliable and accurate.

Dillon found the report quite helpful. Much of the information, of course, simply confirmed his own view of the U.S. market. However, it was good to have this knowledge from an independent, objective organization. In addition, to learn that the market consisted of two apparently equally sized segments of simple and sophisticated applications was quite worthwhile. In particular, knowledge of system prices considered acceptable by each segment would make the entry decision easier. Meeting these prices would not be a major problem.

Market Potential

A very important section of the report contained an estimate of market potential for Pennsylvania and New York. The estimate was based on an analysis of discharge permits on file in government offices in the two states. These permits were required before any city, municipality, water or sewage district, or industrial company could release sewage or other contaminated water to another system or to a lake or river. Each permit showed the number of pumping stations in operation. Based on a 10% sample of permits, the report had estimated that government units in Pennsylvania and New York contained approximately 3,000 and 5,000 pumping stations for waste water, respectively. Industrial companies in the two states were estimated to add some 3,000 and 9,000 more pumping stations, respectively. The total number of pumping stations in the two states—20,000—seemed to be growing at about 2% per year.

Finally, a brief section of the report dealt with the study's limitations. Dillon agreed that the sample was quite small, that it contained no utility managers or engineers from New York, and that it probably concentrated too heavily on individuals in larger urban areas. In addition, the research told him nothing about competitors and their marketing strategies and tactics. Nor did he learn anything about any state regulations for monitoring equipment, if indeed any existed. However, these shortcomings came as no surprise, representing a consequence of the research design proposed to Dillon by the Browning Group some six weeks ago, before the study began.

THE DECISION

Dillon's decision seemed a difficult one. The most risky option was to enter the U.S. market as soon as possible. There was no question about the vast market potential of the U.S. However, the company's opportunity for a greatly increased bottom line had to be balanced against the threat of new competitors who were, for the most part, larger and more sophisticated than Dillon Controls. In fact, a friend had jokingly remarked that "a Canadian firm selling microprocessor controls in the U.S. would be like trying to sell Canadian semiconductors to the Japanese."

The most conservative option was to stay in Canada. Of course, Dillon Controls would continue to respond to the odd inquiry from the United States and would continue to fill orders that the company received from U.S. customers. However, it would not seek this sort of business in an aggressive fashion. Nor would it seek representation in the United States through an agent or distributor. The latter option put Dillon Controls out of the picture as far as controlling sales claims, prices, product installation, service, and other important aspects of customer relations.

In between the two extremes was the option of conducting some additional marketing research. Discussion with the Browning Group had identified the objectives of this research being to rectify limitations of the first study as well as to provide more accurate estimates of market potential. (The estimates of the numbers of pumping stations in Pennsylvania and New York were accurate to around plus or minus 20%.) This research was estimated to cost $40,000 and would take another three months to complete.

11 ETHICAL DILEMMAS IN MARKETING RESEARCH

Charles B. Weinberg

Marketing managers and marketing researchers are frequently confronted by ethical problems and dilemmas. Gathering, analyzing, and presenting information all are procedures that raise a number of important ethical questions in which the manager's need to know and understand the market in order to develop effective marketing programs must be balanced against an individual's right to privacy. The interpretation and use of data can also raise ethical questions.

The following scenarios present a set of ethical dilemmas that might arise in marketing research. Your assignment is to decide what action to take in each instance. You should be prepared to justify your decision. Bear in mind that there are no uniquely right answers; reasonable people may choose different courses of action.

1. As market research director of a pharmaceutical company, you are given the suggestion by the executive director that physicians be telephoned by company interviewers under the name of a fictitious market research agency. The purpose of the survey is to help assess the perceived quality of the company's products, and it is felt that the suggested procedure will result in more objective responses than if the company's name were revealed.

What action would you take?

2. Your company is supervising a study of restaurants conducted for the Department of Corporate and Consumer Affairs. The data, which have already been collected, include specific buying information and prices paid. Respondent organizations have been promised confidentiality. The ministry demands that all responses be identified by business name. Their rationale is that they plan to repeat the study and wish to limit sampling error by returning to the same respondents. Open bidding requires that the government maintain control of the sample.

What action would you take?

3. You are the market research director in a manufacturing company. The project director requests permission to use ultra-violet ink in precoding questionnaires in a mail survey. He points out that the accompanying letter refers to a confidential survey, but he needs to be able to identify respondents to permit adequate cross-tabulation of the data and to save on postage costs if a second mailing is required.

What action would you take?

4. You are employed by a marketing research firm and have conducted an attitude study for a client. Your data indicate that the product is not being marketed properly. This finding is ill-received by the client's product management team. They request that you omit that data from your formal report—which you know will be widely distributed—on the grounds that the verbal presentation was adequate for their needs.

What do you do?

5. You are a project director on a study funded by a somewhat unpopular federal policing agency. The study is on marijuana use among young people in a community and its relationship, if any, to crime. You will be using a structured questionnaire to gather data for the agency on marijuana use and criminal activities. You believe that if you reveal the name of the funding agency and/or the actual purposes of the study to respondents, you will seriously reduce response rates and thereby increase nonresponse bias.

What information would you disclose to respondents?

6. You are a student in a marketing research course. The professor assigns a project in which each student is required to conduct personal interviews with executives of high technology companies concerning their future plans. The professor has stated that all the information is confidential and will be used only in the research course. However, two days after the professor has assigned the project, you overhear him talking to a colleague where he mentions that this research project will be sold to a major technology firm in the industry.

What action would you take?

7. You are employed by a market research company. A clothing manufacturer has retained your firm to conduct a study. The manufacturer wants to know something about how women choose clothing, such as blouses and sweaters. The manufacturer wants to conduct group interviews, supplemented by a session which would be devoted to observing the women trying on clothing, in order to discover which types of garments are chosen first, how thoroughly they touch and examine the clothing, and whether they look for and read a label or price tag. The client suggests that the observations be performed unobtrusively by female observers at a local department store, via a one-way mirror. One of your associates argues that this would constitute an invasion of privacy.

What action would you take?

8. You are a study director for a research company undertaking a project for a regular client of your company. A study you are working on is about to go into the field when the questionnaire you sent to the client for final approval comes back drastically modified. The client has rewritten it, introducing leading questions and biased scales. An accompanying letter indicates that the questionnaire must be sent out as revised. You do not believe that valid information can be gathered using the revised instrument.

What action would you take?

9. A well-respected public figure is going to face trial on a charge of failing to report his part ownership of certain regulated companies while serving as a provincial minister. The defence lawyers have asked you, as a market research specialist, to do a research study to determine the characteristics of people most likely to sympathize with the defendant and hence to vote for acquittal. The defence lawyers have read newspaper accounts of how this approach has been used in a number of instances.

What action would you take?

10. You are the market research director for a large chemical company. Recent research indicates that many customers of your company are misusing one of its principal products. There is no danger resulting from this misuse, though the customers are wasting money by using too much of the product at one time. You are shown the new advertising campaign by the advertising agency. The ads not only ignore this problem of misuse, but actually seem to encourage it.

What action would you take?

Section 4
PRODUCT POLICY

An organization's choice of products to offer and markets to serve influences all the other elements in the marketing program. Product policy decisions centre on what goods and services the business should offer for sale and what characteristics these should have. These decisions involve matching the resources and goals of the company with market opportunities—hence the close link between market selection and product planning. Product decisions, therefore, require careful analysis of existing and potential products relative to the characteristics of both the market and the organization.

Appraising the need for changes in the product line is a continuing process, reflecting the dynamic nature of the marketplace as well as changes in the nature and resources of the company itself. One objective should be to eliminate or modify products which no longer satisfy consumer needs or fail to contribute significantly to the company's objectives. Another set of objectives relates to adding new products or product features which will meet consumer needs better, enhance the firm's existing product line, and improve utilization of present resources. Complacency in product management in the face of a dynamic, competitive environment is a sure road to ruin.

MARKET SELECTION

Product policy, along with market selection, is one of the central elements of marketing management. Product-market choice—what products to offer to which markets—is at the core of every organization's strategy. These decisions are closely linked, since different markets may have different needs, and not all products (or specific formulations of a particular product) will appeal to all markets. This section, therefore, will start with a discussion of the choice of which markets to serve. The following part emphasizes decisions on which products to offer.

Several companies in the same industry may make quite different market selection decisions. To illustrate, one cosmetics firm may concentrate on developing extensively advertised cosmetics sold in department stores at high prices to a style-conscious, upscale market, while another firm devotes its efforts to women who prefer the convenience and advice obtained from a sales representative who brings product samples to the customer's own home. A third company may concentrate on budget-minded individuals who shop in discount stores. Each firm, by choosing a different market target, is simultaneously making a decision about the marketing skills and resources required to succeed, the nature of competition likely to be encountered, the potential for growth and profitability to be obtained, and the threats and opportunities to be met in the external environment.

It is critical that marketing managers carefully choose the markets in which their firm will compete (Exhibit 1). Failure to do so may result in efforts scattered by attempting to be

Exhibit 1
FRAMEWORK FOR MARKET SEGMENTATION, TARGETING, AND POSITIONING

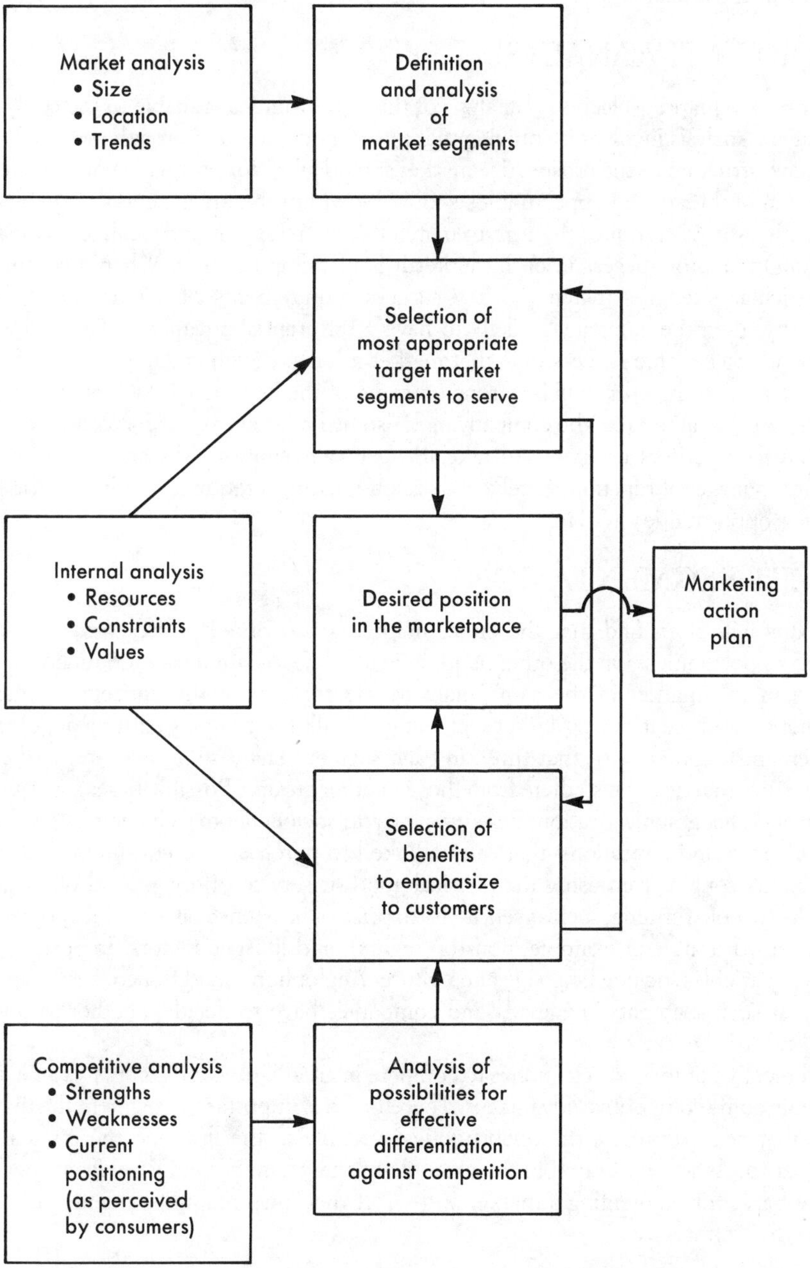

all things to all people—rarely a successful strategy. It may also result in lost opportunities to enter new markets or too much emphasis on old markets that are declining, unprofitable, or crowded with other competitors. A company's success is dependent on the opportunities available in the market or market segments it selects, as well as on how effectively it competes in those markets.

OPPORTUNITY ANALYSIS

An early step in market selection is analysis of the opportunities available to the company. Opportunity analysis involves identifying markets of good size and growth potential. The competitive structure of the prospective market should allow for profitable entry, while the environmental threats and opportunities should be within the organization's capabilities. Opportunity analysis requires the firm to match its own strengths and weaknesses against the requirements for success in each market it is planning to enter. When a company's own particular strengths match the key success requirements of a particular market opportunity, then the company is likely to have a differential advantage. This will allow the company to become successful in that market if it can design and implement a sound strategy. Quite often, a firm will be strong on some of the key success factors and weaker on others. At the same time, the company may also be uncertain as to what actions current and future competitors are going to take. Proper balancing of risks and rewards is an important managerial function: excellent decision making is required to identify the best marketing opportunities available.

MARKET SEGMENTATION

A company will often find that the entire market is too broad to serve as a basis for analyzing opportunities. On the other hand, individual needs often vary too much to treat everyone in the market in the same manner. Here is where the concept of market segmentation is of great value. Market segmentation calls for grouping existing or potential customers into segments, so that those in each segment share some relevant marketing characteristics that distinguish them from those in other groups. Possible bases for segmentation include geographic location; demographic and socioeconomic characteristics—such as age, income, and education—that can be linked to purchase and consumption behaviour; benefits sought from using the physical good or service offering; level of usage of the product; choice criteria, such as sensitivity to price or insistence on a product possessing a particular attribute (for example, nonstop flights); and lifestyle factors. Important segmentation variables include language and culture. Anglophones and francophones are the two largest such segments in Canada and companies have to decide whether to pursue one or both of these markets.

The objective of market selection is to compete in areas where the company can expect to maintain some competitive advantages. Therefore, it is important to segment the market in ways that will best reveal the opportunities available to the firm and the threats that may be faced. As was illustrated in the example of the cosmetics industry, firms may use different bases for segmenting a market and select their own unique segments on which to focus their efforts.

PRODUCT POSITIONING

To compete effectively in any given market a company must position its products appropriately relative to:

1. the needs of specific market segments,
2. the nature of competitive entries, and
3. its own strengths and weaknesses.

Exhibit 2 provides a listing of how product positioning can help management.

Exhibit 2
PRINCIPAL USES OF POSITIONING IN MARKETING MANAGEMENT

1. Provides a useful diagnostic tool for defining and understanding the relationships between products and markets by indicating:
   a. How the product compares with competitive offerings on specific attributes;
   b. How well the product performance meets consumer needs and expectations on specific performance criteria;
   c. The predicted consumption level for a product with a given set of performance characteristics offered at a given price.
2. Identifies market opportunities for:
   a. Introducing new products
      (i) What segments to target;
      (ii) What attributes to offer relative to the competition.
   b. Redesigning (repositioning) existing products
      (i) Appeal to the same segments or to new ones;
      (ii) What attributes to add, drop, or change;
      (iii) What attributes to emphasize in advertising.
   c. Eliminating products that
      (i) Do not satisfy consumer needs;
      (ii) Face excessive competition.
3. Aids making the other marketing mix decisions to pre-empt or respond to, competitive moves, for example:
   a. Distribution strategies
      (i) Where to offer the product (locations, types of outlet);
      (ii) What customer service to provide.
   b. Pricing strategies
      (i) How much to charge;
      (ii) What billing and payment procedures to employ.
   c. Communication strategies
      (i) What target audiences are most easily convinced that the product offers a competitive advantage on attributes important to them.
      (ii) What message(s). Which features should be emphasized.

An effective product positioning strategy requires careful analysis of market segments and an evaluation of how well competitors are meeting the needs of specific segments. Tylenol's successful positioning, for instance, is based on its ability to bring pain relief without the use of ASA. Sometimes positioning, or repositioning, represents a deliberate attempt to attack another firm's product and take away its market share; in other instances the objective is to avoid head-to-head competition by appealing to alternative market segments whose needs are not presently well served by existing products.

Product positions often reflect not only basic product characteristics but also such marketing mix elements as advertising and promotion, distribution strategy, pricing, or packaging. The Cadillac name carries different connotations for car buyers than does Chevrolet, although both are products of General Motors. Similarly, one reason the Bay purchased Zellers was to use Zellers as lower priced outlets. Different names differentiate the upscale stores from budget stores. Different positions, however, represent more than just names; each chain's position needs to be supported by a complete marketing plan; the chosen position establishes the basis for setting the marketing mix.

PRODUCT–ORGANIZATION FIT

Even if good opportunities exist for a new or repositioned product, this does not necessarily mean that the company should offer such a product. Unless there is a good "fit" between the proposed product and the firm's needs and resources, the net result of a "go" decision may be harmful or, at best, suboptimal.

The company must also consider how well the product matches the organizational mission and its impact on the firm's financial situation. Questions should be asked about the product's fit with other resource inputs, such as labour availability, management skills, and physical facilities. Other issues include the proposed product's impact upon the market position of other goods and services marketed by the company and its consistency with the firm's existing image. An evaluation should also be made of the feasibility of using the existing sales force, advertising media, and distribution channels or service delivery systems and of the consequences of introducing new alternatives.

PRODUCT DECISIONS

Virtually all manufacturing firms and service organizations produce a variety of different products. Policy decisions, therefore, may be approached from three possible levels:

- Individual product items.
- Product lines, namely a group of products which are related in the sense of satisfying a particular class of need, being used together, possessing common physical or technical characteristics, being sold to the same customer groups through the same channels, or falling within given price ranges.
- The product mix, which comprises all products offered for sale by an organization. Although a particular product item—or even an entire product line—may not be profitable in itself, it may contribute to the well-being of the firm by enhancing the overall product mix.

Product mix decisions should reflect not only market factors and corporate resources, but also the underlying philosophy of company management. Most organizations are faced with several options over time. Some choose to pursue a policy of diversity; others prefer to concentrate their efforts on a narrow mix offering a limited number of products in only a few sizes and varieties to a small set of targeted market segments. A diversified product mix reduces risk by spreading it across many different product lines, usually in different markets. Poor performance by one product or in one market should not have a drastic effect on overall performance. For the same reason that it reduces risk, however, a diverse product mix puts a ceiling on returns. A very successful product in a diversified mix will have much less of an impact than if it were part of a narrow, specialized mix.

Product strategy choices should be determined by management's long-run objectives concerning profit levels, sales stability, and growth, as modified by personal values and attitudes toward risk taking. Market opportunities determine the upper limits for potential profitability. The quality of the marketing program tends to determine the extent to which this potential is achieved.

THE PRODUCT LIFE CYCLE

It is important to recognize that new products and markets eventually mature and that different strategies are required over time. Many managers find it useful to divide a product's life cycle into four stages (Exhibit 3):

1. *Introduction* This is a period of typically slow growth in sales volume following the launch of the product. At this point, an innovative organization that is the first to market the product may have the field to itself. However, extensive communication efforts are often needed to build consumer awareness.
2. *Growth* Demand for the product begins to increase rapidly, reflecting repeated use by satisfied customers and broadening awareness among prospective customers who now try the product for the first time. Competition develops as other organizations introduce their own versions, transforming a single product into a product class of competing brands.
3. *Maturity* This is often an extended period during which sales volume for the product class stabilizes and astute marketers seek to position their own product offerings in ways that will differentiate them from those of competitors. Often this stage is characterized by market share battles. However, fad and fashion products may have very short life cycles in which demand grows extremely rapidly, peaks briefly, and then goes into sudden and precipitous decline.
4. *Decline* Sales volume for the product class declines as a result of environmental forces such as changing population profiles, changing consumer preferences, new legislation, or competition from new types of products that meet the same generic need. Some competitors, anticipating the death of the entire product class, kill off their own entries in the market.

The product life cycle concept suggests marketing strategies tailored to the life cycle stage the product is in. However, the product life cycle concept should not be employed without question. The life cycle of a product class often seems so long as to be meaningless. Further, in evaluating the relationship between marketing strategy and the product life

Exhibit 3
"TYPICAL" PRODUCT LIFE CYCLE

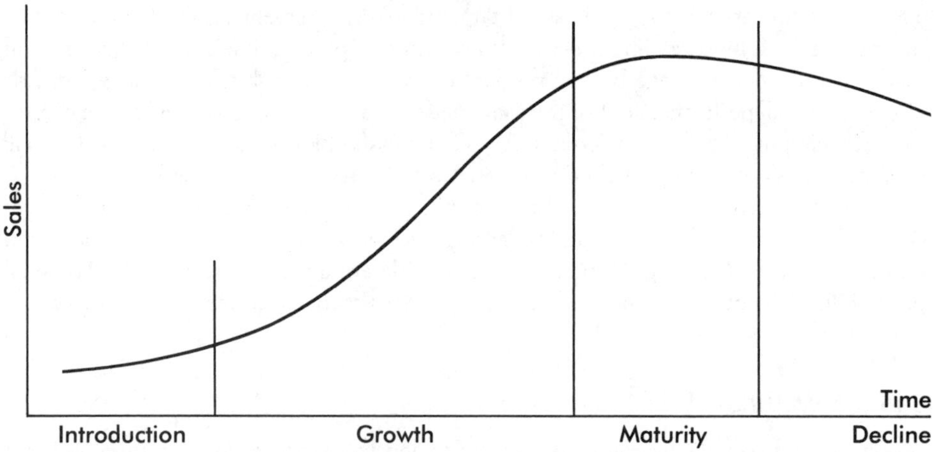

cycle, it is questionable whether the life cycle for a particular product or product class is an inevitable, independent force to which companies must adapt their marketing efforts, or whether marketing strategy can change the course of the life cycle.

Nevertheless, in order to manage its product mix effectively, every firm needs to have a sense of where its individual products stand in terms of their respective life cycles. It is particularly important to understand the life cycle of the product class in which individual offerings compete. Failure to do so can result in such mistakes as launching a new product when the product class is moving into decline or introducing an innovative product without sufficient communication support.

ADJUSTMENTS TO THE PRODUCT MIX

While the "ideal" product mix will vary from one business to another and may be hard to define, the following situations may indicate a suboptimal mix of products: chronic or seasonally recurring excess production capacity; a high proportion of profits coming from a small percentage of product items; competitors taking the initiative in markets; and steadily declining profits or sales.

Changes in product policy designed to correct any of the above situations or otherwise improve the firm's profitability can take one of the three basic forms:

- Product abandonment, involving discontinuing either individual items or an entire line;
- Product modification, involving changes in either tangible or intangible product attributes. It may be achieved by reformulation, redesign, repositioning, and addition or removal of certain features;

- New product introduction, involving the generation, development, evaluation, and introduction of new products or product lines.

NEW PRODUCT DEVELOPMENT

Designing and marketing new products is vital to a company's health. The new product development process should proceed systematically through a series of steps, beginning with a review of corporate objectives and constraints and continuing through to product introduction. Exhibit 4 summarizes these steps in diagrammatic form. The starting point is an assessment of:

- company and marketing objectives and constraints, and
- a situation analysis including information on the current and anticipated market, the competitive situation, and other environmental factors.

With this information, management can establish objectives for new products and develop suitable criteria for evaluating new product ideas.

Exhibit 4 lists other stages in the new product development process. First is the generation of new product ideas, since without this stage the rest of the process cannot exist. In idea generation, it is important to ensure that the source of new ideas comes from market needs (e.g., single serving food containers) as well as technological advances. Throughout the development process, there is a continuing interchange between evaluation and development. A company must set criteria that balance the risk of rejecting an idea that could become successful against accepting a project that later fails. As the financial commitment to the project increases, the evaluation becomes more extensive. In the early stages, ideas may just be checked to see if they meet new product development objectives and are within the company's capabilities. Profitability analysis becomes a critical part of the evaluation process. Later stages involve carrying out full scale evaluations of a product and its marketing strategy and may include test-marketing for consumer goods and services. At this critical stage, the concept is translated into reality—including how the product will be priced, distributed, and communicated.

The last stages of the new product development process involve market introduction and ongoing evaluation and improvement of the product and its marketing program. Management must recognize that its work is not done even if the product is successfully launched. Changing market needs, competitive thrusts, and technical developments all place continual pressure on the company to progress even further.

CONCLUSION

Product policy decisions are ongoing, reflecting the changing nature of the marketplace. Because an organization's choice of products has such important implications for every facet of the business, it tends to be of great concern to top management.

Product decisions are directly linked to market selection decisions. Without sound analysis of market needs and the development of a strong positioning strategy against competitors in targeted markets, products are unlikely to succeed.

Exhibit 4
NEW PRODUCT DEVELOPMENT PROCESS

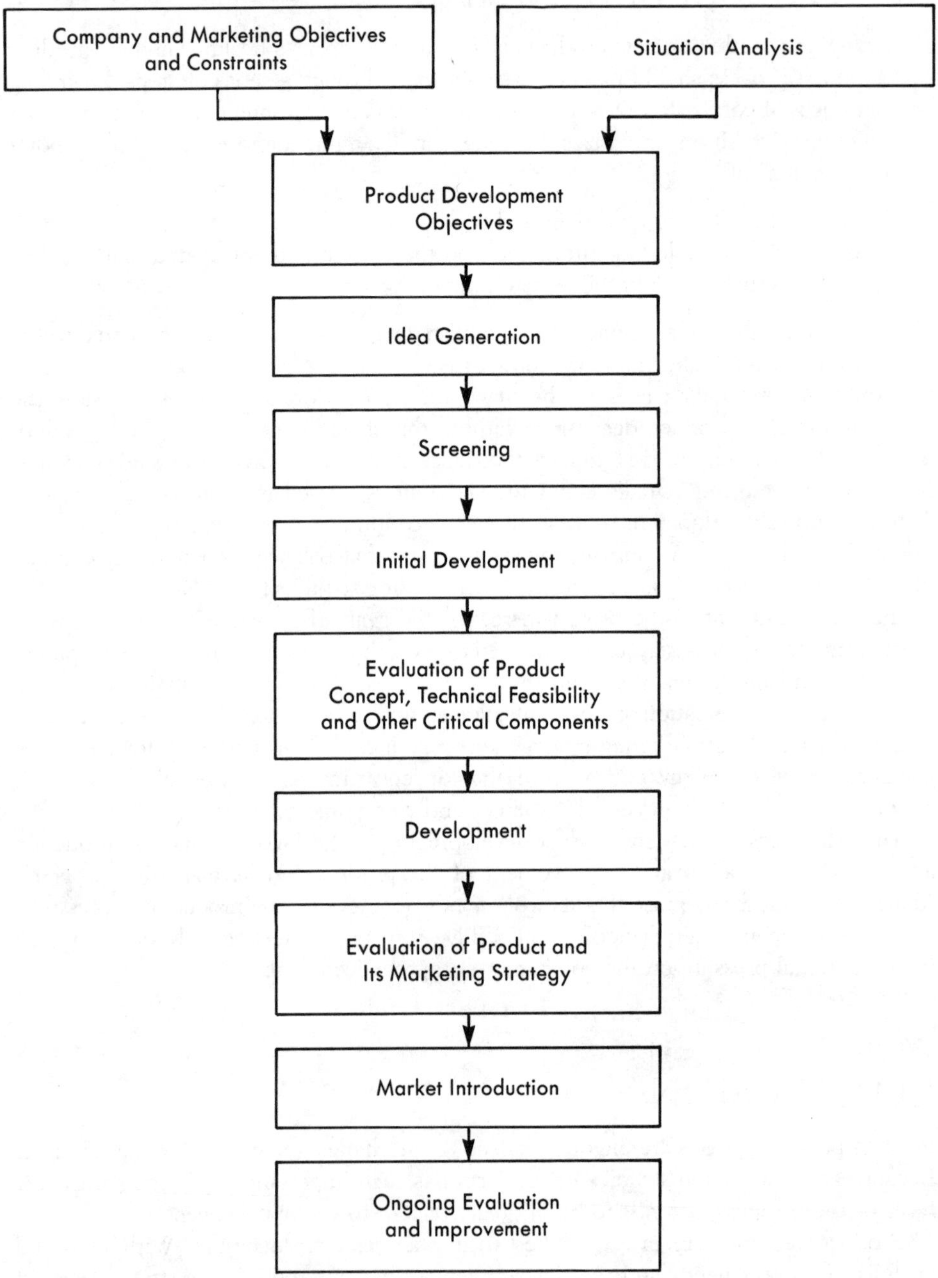

The resources of the firm, the corporate objectives established by management, the characteristics of existing and potential markets, the nature of the competition, and the existing product mix are all factors to be considered in making product policy decisions. It must be remembered, however, that virtually all products eventually lose their market appeal. Firms must abandon or modify products that are no longer competitive or serve a market need and develop an effective system for developing and introducing new products.

12 LOBLAWS

Gordon H. G. McDougall

Douglas Snetsinger

"It's been a year since we introduced green products at Loblaws and the decisions still are not getting any easier." In early July 1990, Scott Lindsay was reflecting upon his decision as to which, if any, of three possible products he would recommend for the G·R·E·E·N line: an energy-efficient light bulb, toilet tissue made from recycled paper, or a high-fibre cereal.

As Director of International Trade for Intersave Buying & Merchandising Services (a buying division for Loblaws), it was Scott's job to source and manage about 400 corporate brands (No Name, President's Choice, G·R·E·E·N)[1] for Loblaws in Canada. In four days Scott would have to make his recommendations to the buyers' meeting.

The "green line" for which Scott was sourcing products was a new concept for Loblaws and its customers. Launched in 1989 as part of the corporate President's Choice brands, green products had characteristics that were less hazardous to the environment and/or contributed to a more healthy lifestyle. At issue for Scott was deciding what was "green" and balancing the financial requirements of the company with the socially responsible initiative of the green line.

As well, his most pressing concern was his ability to convince the president, Dave Nichol, of the merits of his recommendations. Mr. Nichol was the driving force behind the corporate brands, and he maintained involvement and final authority on these important product decisions.

In preparation for the buyers' meeting, Scott had to have his written recommendations on Dave Nichol's desk that day. Dave Nichol required that recommendations include retail price and cost data, projected annual sales in units and dollars, as well as total gross margin expected. In addition to the expected results, best and worst case scenarios were also required. As well, primary reasons for and against the proposal needed to be given. Typically, the recommendations were made based on the Ontario market as it was the proving ground for new products.

The first product Scott was considering was a new energy-efficient light bulb, which had been successfully marketed in Germany. The bulb lasted at least ten times longer than a regular light bulb but was substantially more expensive. There was no

[1] No Name, President's Choice, and G·R·E·E·N are all trademarks, owned by Loblaw Companies Limited.

Note: Some data are disguised.

question in Scott's mind that the energy-efficient bulb had strong "green" characteristics and would enhance Loblaws green image. However, a potential consumer price of $20 and low retail margins were a troubling combination. He knew that store managers, who were measured on sales volume and profits, would not be enthusiastic about a product that would not deliver sales or profits. These store managers controlled the individual products and brands that were carried in their stores.

The second new product was, in fact, not a new product at all. Loblaws had been selling a toilet tissue manufactured with 100% recycled material under its No Name corporate label. The existing product could be repackaged under the G·R·E·E·N label and sold beside the No Name line of products. The green packaging might alert consumers sensitive to the recycled feature thereby generating greater volumes for the product. Further, Scott realized there was an opportunity to price the "green" toilet tissue at a higher price than the No Name, providing a higher profit margin.

The final product under consideration was a new corn flake product for the very "crowded" breakfast cereal category. The new cereal had an unusually high fibre content. The "body friendly" nature of the cereal was the basis for considering it for the green line. Its additional feature was that it could be sourced at a cost much lower than the national brands.

LOBLAW COMPANIES LIMITED

Loblaw Companies Limited is part of George Weston Ltd., a conglomerate of companies that operate in three basic areas: food processing, food distribution, and natural resources. George Weston is the sixth largest company in Canada with sales of $10.5 billion and net income of $988 million in 1989. The Loblaw Companies, an integrated group of food wholesaling and retailing companies, had total sales and net earnings in 1989 of $7,934 million and $70 million respectively (Exhibit 1).

At the wholesale level, divisions such as Kelly, Douglas & Company and Atlantic Wholesalers supplied over 1,280 corporate and franchise stores as well as over 12,300 independent retailers through its 54 company-owned warehouses. At the retail level, Loblaws operated both company-owned (corporate) stores, including Loblaws, Zehrs, Superstore, and Real Canadian Superstore and franchised operations including No Frills, Mr. Grocer, and Value Mart. Loblaws retail operations are spread across Canada, except in the province of Quebec, and in New Orleans and St. Louis in the United States. Eastern Canada generates approximately 50% of retail sales, western Canada approximately 33%, and the United States approximately 16% (Exhibit 1).

Two divisions within Loblaws co-ordinated the purchasing from outside suppliers for the corporate brands. Loblaw International Merchants under the direction of its president, Dave Nichol, was responsible for the development and merchandising of the corporate brands throughout the organization. These were approximately 3,000 corporate brands with about 200 new brands added each year. Intersave Buying and Merchandising Services was responsible for the procurement of goods from both foreign and domestic suppliers for the corporate brand program.

Exhibit 1

LOBLAWS—SELECTED FINANCIAL HIGHLIGHTS (1985–1989)

	1989	1988	1987	1986	1985
Operating Results ($ millions)					
Sales	7,934	8,308	8,631	7,839	6,931
Trading profit*	291	258	290	249	225
Operating income	191	160	190	163	152
Net earnings	70	26	74	74	67
Return on Sales (percent)					
Operating income	2.4	1.9	2.2	2.1	2.2
Earnings before income taxes	1.4	.8	1.5	1.5	1.7
Per Common Share ($)					
Net earnings	0.80	0.41	0.87	0.91	0.85
Earnings Ratios (percent)					
Return on common equity	11.7	5.9	12.5	14.6	15.6
Return on capital employed	13.8	11.2	13.6	14.3	17.0
Regional Sales ($ millions)					
Eastern Canada	3,988	3,705	3,602	3,070	2,781
Western Canada	2,650	2,340	2,087	2,028	1,887
United States	1,296	2,263	2,942	2,471	2,263
Total	7,934	8,308	8,631	7,839	6,931
Regional Operating Income ($ millions)					
Eastern Canada	90	76	106	74	72
Western Canada	67	56	47	56	45
United States	34	28	37	33	35
Total	191	160	190	163	152
Sales by Segment ($ millions)					
Retail	5,025	4,921	4,777	4,430	3,940
Wholesale	2,909	3,387	3,854	3,409	2,991
Total	7,934	8,308	8,631	7,839	6,931

Source: Company Records

* Trading profit is defined as operating income before depreciation.

THE RETAIL FOOD INDUSTRY

Loblaws operated in the extremely competitive retail food business, an industry that was both highly concentrated and fragmented. Over 13,000 retail stores competed for the Canadian consumer's food dollar, yet 50% of the $41 billion sales in 1989 went through only 4% of the outlets—the supermarket chains—including Loblaws,

Provigo, A&P, Oshawa, Safeway, and Steinberg. The approximately 4,800 convenience stores in Canada—Becker's, 7 Eleven, Mac's, and others—had sales of $2.3 billion. The over 8,000 independent retailers, ranging from small "mom and pop" corner stores to large independent supermarkets, generated sales of about $12.8 billion in 1989.The remaining industry sales, about $5.4 billion, were generated by specialty stores, such as bakeries and seafood stores ($3.2 billion) and a host of other types of stores, including drugstore retail outlets.

When adjusted for inflation, growth in the retail food industry was near zero for the past five years and forecasts for the early 1990s suggested a similar pattern. The low industry growth was due, in part, to little growth in the Canadian population and to increased expenditures by Canadians in fast-food and other restaurants. The intense competition within a mature industry meant that average net profit margins (pre-tax profits/sales) in the industry were low, averaging less than 2% in the past five years and only 1.5% in 1988. Consequently, the major chains were constantly examining new marketing and merchandising innovations as well as promotion incentives from manufacturers to build value for their customers and create store switching and preference.

The retail food business has seen a number of changes throughout the years including the following:

- While chain stores share of the market had been relatively stable, the sales per store had increased as some chains merged and closed stores during the past decade. For example, in early July 1990, Steinberg announced it was selling 69 Ontario stores (58 Miracle Food Marts and 11 Ultra Mart food and drug stores) to A&P. A&P already operated 194 stores in Ontario under the A&P and Dominion names.
- A variety of store formats had been introduced in response to changing consumer preferences, competitive pressures, and economic conditions. For example, "box" stores, warehouse stores, combination stores (selling both food and nonfood products), and superstores had been developed in the past fifteen years.
- Specialty stores, with their emphasis on quality and freshness, were increasing their market share.
- Generic (no-name) and store brands were increasing their share at the expense of national brands.
- Control in the industry had been shifting to the large chains, from the manufacturers. This trend was likely to continue as new sources of supply became available through free trade and as the chains reduced their emphasis on nationally branded products.

Six chains—Loblaws, Provigo, Oshawa, Steinberg, Safeway, and A&P—were the major competitors in the Canadian food business. In 1989, Loblaws was the largest of the six with total sales, wholesale and retail, of $7.9 billion, followed by Provigo ($7.4 billion), Oshawa ($4.9 billion), Steinberg ($4.5 billion), Safeway ($3.5 billion), and A&P ($2.2 billion).

While retail market share data was difficult to obtain because most of the chains operated both wholesale and retail divisions, industry sources estimated that Loblaws held the largest retail share in Canada at around 19%. Provigo held a 16% share, and it was estimated that the remaining chains held 10% or less of the market. Competition was regional in nature, with Provigo strong in Quebec, Safeway strong in western Canada, Loblaws and A&P with strengths in Ontario, and Sobey's (part of the Empire conglomerate) strong in the Maritimes.

The intense competition for market share was reflected by industry experts, who, over the past year, made the following observations:

- Food retailers are locked in a cutthroat industry, scrambling to hold on to a shrinking market. The population is aging, leaving smaller appetites to whet.
- The grocery business is a treacherous one, characterized by low margins and dominated by giant companies. Niche players crowd the corners.
- The economic slowdown has hit supermarkets as consumers cut down on grocery spending. Consumers are buying more food on special and switching to cheaper foods.

LOBLAWS CORPORATE STRATEGY

Against this background of intense competition, changing consumer preferences, and changing economic conditions, Loblaws has been guided by a corporate strategy that has led to dramatic alterations in the way it does business. Loblaws envisioned the road to sustainable competitive advantage through innovative marketing, low costs, and a large network of suppliers. Traditionally, retailers in the food industry relied on price discounting to generate increased volume sales thereby increasing market share. Loblaws views this way of thinking as valid but narrow. Loblaw's umbrella strategy was to be the best low cost, high quality food distributor in the industry. This strategy led to four substantial changes at Loblaws: (1) the introduction of generics, (2) the development of the President's Choice corporate product line, (3) a broad-scale investment program, and (4) a new marketing strategy.

The Introduction of Generics

First sold in the United States in 1977, generics are unbranded, plainly packaged, less expensive versions of common products such as spaghetti, paper towels, and canned peaches. Loblaws and a competing chain, Dominion, introduced generics in early 1978. Loblaws quickly became the leader in generic sales. In 15 months Loblaws expanded the line, called "No Name," from 16 to 120 products; by 1983, Loblaws carried over 500 generic products which accounted for about 10% of Loblaw's total sales. The generics appealed to price-sensitive consumers during an economic downturn in the Canadian economy.

Loblaws strategy with their generic line differed from competitors such as Dominion. Most food distributors positioned their generics as lower-priced products with lower quality than competing national brands. Loblaws produced a generic product that was of a higher quality. The quality of No Name products, coupled with lower prices, attractively packaged in an eye-catching yellow with heavy advertising against national brands led to the success of the line.

Development of The President's Choice Line

With the introduction of No Name, Loblaws recognized another unique marketing opportunity. Through internal market research in the early 1980s on the corporate brand philosophy, the company discovered that the target market for quality corporate products was the more affluent and educated consumer. It was found that this consumer did not require a national brand product to discern product quality and thus acceptability for purchase. It was at this time that Canada was also emerging from a recession. As consumer incomes rose, Loblaws saw an opportunity to meet the demands of this consumer. In 1984, President's Choice was introduced as a higher quality, high-value brand.

The President's Choice line was positioned directly against national brands. Loblaws plan was to develop consumer brand loyalty for this corporate line to such an extent that consumers would switch supermarkets to acquire President's Choice. An example of a very successful President's Choice product was the "Decadent" chocolate chip cookie. Based on product tests, Loblaws identified a lack of quality in the leading national brand chocolate chip cookie. The Decadent was made with a higher percentage (40%) of chocolate chips and real butter, and within a few months of its launch it was the best selling cookie in Ontario.

The increasing activity of Loblaws in developing corporate brands led to the establishment of the Weston Research Centre, a product testing laboratory. The centre was involved in the research and development of new products, quality control testing, and quality assurance programs. These activities were carried out on behalf of companies within the Weston and Loblaws group. By the late 1980s, the centre had 100 employees and spent over $20 million each year to ensure product quality for corporate brands. Typically, a buyer for Loblaws would identify a possible product for inclusion in the corporate line. The buyer would then find a manufacturer to produce the product and the manufacturer would work with experts from the Weston Research Centre to meet the required product quality standards. The product would then be launched as part of the President's Choice or No Name line.

The corporate line was well received by consumers. By 1989, approximately 2,200 No Name brands and 700 President's Choice brands made up 30% of Loblaw's total grocery sales. President's Choice and No Name brands earned an average 15% higher margin than the national brands. Approximately 200 new corporate brands were introduced annually with three-quarters of them being successful, as compared to a 10% success rate for national brands.

The Broad-scale Investment Program

In 1984, Loblaws began a broad-scale investment program that, over the next five years, involved expenditures of approximately $1.8 billion on systems and market expansion through store developments. This included the development of a highly sophisticated information system. Through this system the corporation used store level scanner data to obtain the sales of every product sold. This made it possible to monitor the effectiveness of their merchandising strategy as sales, promotion, and pricing information could be examined weekly to determine individual product profitability and to support inventory management.

Exhibit 2

LOBLAWS RETAIL OPERATIONS—SELECTED HIGHLIGHTS (1985–1989)

	1989		1988		1987		1986		1985	
	Stores	sq. ft. (millions)	Stores	sq. ft. (millions)	Stores	sq. ft. (millions)	Stores	sq. ft. (millions)	Stores	sq. ft. (millions)
Stores										
Beginning of year	311	10.6	361	11.3	380	10.8	363	9.2	381	9.2
Opened	55	1.2	21	1.2	20	1.2	60	2.4	18	0.6
Closed	(18)	(0.2)	(58)	(1.7)	(23)	(0.4)	46	(0.9)	26	(0.4)
Franchised:										
Transfer to:	(22)	(0.4)	(18)	(0.3)	(18)	(0.4)	13	(0.2)	19	(0.4)
Transfer from:	8	0.1	5	0.1	2	0.1	16	0.3	9	0.2
End of year	334	11.3	311	10.6	361	11.3	380	10.8	363	9.2
Average store size (in thousands)	33.9 sq.ft.		34.1 sq.ft.		31.4 sq.ft.		28.4 sq.ft.		25.3 sq.ft.	
Analysis by size										
> 60,000 sq. ft.	40		33		26		18		10	
40,000–60,000	48		44		47		46		33	
20,000–39,999	148		154		176		179		171	
10,000–19,999	64		68		93		112		129	
< 10,000 sq. ft.	34		12		19		25		20	
Total	334		311		361		380		363	
Sales										
Annual sales (in millions)	$5,025		$4,921		$4,777		$4,430		$3,940	
Annual average sales per gross sq. ft.	$458		$440		$440		$457		$432	

Market expansion was accomplished through substantial expenditures to upgrade existing stores, as well as to build new stores in strategic locations. To put this massive investment program in perspective, between 1985 and 1989, Loblaws opened 174 new stores, closed 130 stores, transferred 90 company-owned stores to franchise operations, and transferred 40 franchised stores to company-owned operations (Exhibit 2). Thirty-two of the new stores opened during this period were "superstores." Loblaws had identified superstores, also called combination stores or supercentres, as the "wave of the future" and the key to future success in the retailing industry. Superstores (typically over 130,000 square feet) were up to four times the size of conventional supermarkets. Approximately one-third of the space was devoted to nonfood items. For example, Real Canadian Superstore, which opened in Calgary in late 1988, was over 135,000 square feet, larger than two football fields, and stocked over 45,000 items.

Throughout the aggressive expansion program, Loblaws' management stressed they would maintain the company's financial objectives including: (1) to increase earnings per common share at an average of 15% per year over any five-year period, (2) to provide an average return on common shareholders' equity of 15% per year over any five-year period, and (3) to have less total debt than total equity in the business.

Through all this activity, the company was able to maintain a debt/equity ratio of 1:1 and shareholder returns averaging 12%. Although Loblaws did not meet its goals of a 15% average shareholder return and a 15% average annual increase in earnings per share over the 1984 to 1989 period that coincided with the repositioning and investment program, the results were still impressive compared to many firms in the industry.

The New Marketing Strategy

Dave Nichol, the president of Loblaws International Merchants, was the driving force behind the No Name and President's Choice concepts. He travelled the world to identify new product opportunities for Loblaws. While market research was used to assist in the selection and launch of new products, it was Dave Nichol's innate sense of customer likes which underlay the selection—and success—of many of the corporate brands.

The communication campaign for the corporate brands was unique. From the beginning of the No Name launch, Dave Nichol was involved in advertising these products, often appearing in television campaigns to promote the No Name line. As a result, he became well known to many Canadian consumers. Nichol also introduced the *Insider's Report*, a multicoloured, comic-book size booklet that featured corporate brands and offered consumers shopping tips. Ten million copies of each issue were circulated four times a year as an insert with newspapers across Canada in areas where Loblaws or its affiliates had stores.

The main goals of the *Insider's Report* were to provide news of product availability and to highlight promotions. By consolidating advertising expenditures through the use of the *Insider's Report*, Loblaws spent considerably less on their advertising campaigns than did the national brands. The advertising-to-sales ratios for Loblaws brands was about 3%, less than half of that spent by many national brand manufacturers.

THE GREEN IDEA

The G·R·E·E·N line launch had its origins in one of Dave Nichol's buying trips to Germany in 1988, where he was struck by the number of grocery products that were being promoted as "environmentally friendly." He discovered that *The Green Consumer Guide*, a "how-to" book for consumers to become environmentally responsible, had become a best-seller in England. In late 1988, Loblaws began collecting information on Canadian attitudes about the environment. The results suggested that an increasing number of Canadians were concerned about environmental issues, and some expressed a willingness to pay extra to purchase environmentally safe products. Further, many said they were willing to change supermarkets to acquire these products (Exhibit 3).

As well, increased attention was being drawn to Canada's environmental problems. The news media and environmental groups such as Greenpeace and Pollution Probe were providing Canadians with many disturbing facts. For example, Canadians use more energy per capita than any other nation in the world. Canadians also produce approximately 15 tonnes of carbon dioxide per person per year, the primary cause of the "greenhouse effect" (the warming of the world's atmosphere). On a per capita basis, Canadians are found to be one of the worlds greatest contributors to acid rain, air and water pollution, and the degeneration of the ozone layer.

THE G·R·E·E·N LAUNCH

Armed with this supportive data, in late January 1989, Loblaws management decided to launch by July 1989 a line of 100 products that were either environmentally friendly or healthy for the body. These products would be added to the family of the corporate line and called G·R·E·E·N. Although the task was considered ambitious, the corporation believed it had the requisite size, strength, influence, network, imagination, and courage to be successful. Loblaws contacted a number of prominent environmental groups to assist in the choice of products. These groups were requested to make a "wish list" of environmentally safe products. Using this as a guide, Loblaws began to source the products for the G·R·E·E·N launch.

A few products, such as baking soda, simply required repackaging to advertise the already existing environmentally friendly qualities of the product. Intersave Buying and Merchandising Services were able to source some products through foreign suppliers, such as the Ecover line of household cleaning products, to be marketed under the G·R·E·E·N umbrella. All G·R·E·E·N products were rigorously tested as well as screened by environmental groups such as Pollution Probe and Friends of the Earth. This collaboration was developed to such an extent that a few of the products were endorsed by Pollution Probe.

The G·R·E·E·N product line, consisting of about 60 products, was launched on June 3, 1989. Initial G·R·E·E·N products included phosphate-free laundry detergent, low-acid coffee, pet foods, and biodegradable garbage bags (Exhibit 4). A holistic approach was taken in selecting these initial products; for example, the pet food

Exhibit 3
CONSUMER ATTITUDES ON ENVIRONMENT

1. National survey on issues.

What is the most important issue facing Canada today?

Issues	1985	1986	1987	1988	1989
Environment	*	*	2	10	18
Goods and services tax	*	*	*	*	15
Inflation/Economy	16	12	12	5	10
Deficit/Government	6	10	10	6	10
National unity	*	*	*	*	7
Free trade	2	5	26	42	7
Abortion	*	*	*	*	6
Employment	45	39	20	10	6

Source: Maclean's/Decima Research

* Not cited by a significant number of poll respondents.
Note: Survey conducted in early January of each year.

2. National survey on willingness to pay for cleaner environment.

Would you be willing to pay:

50% more to clear garbage (67%)[1]
10% more for groceries (66%)
$1,000 more for a car (63%)
5¢ a litre more for gas (63%)
$250 more to clean sewage (58%)
10% tax on energy (57%)

Source: Angus Reid Group

[1] The numbers in brackets represent the percent of those surveyed who agreed with each statement.
Note: Survey conducted in early 1989.

3. Loblaws customers surveys.

How concerned are you about the environment? (%)

Extremely(32), Quite(37), Somewhat(24), Not Very(5), Don't Care(2)

How likely is it that you would purchase environmentally friendly products?

Very(49), Somewhat(43), Not too(2), Not at all(4)

How likely is it that you would switch supermarkets to purchase environmentally friendly products?

Very(2), Somewhat(45), Not too(24), Not at all(10)

Note: Survey conducted in early 1989.

Exhibit 4
THE INITIAL G·R·E·E·N PRODUCTS

Food
Just Peanuts Peanut Butter
Smart Snack Popcorn
"The Virtuous" Soda Cracker
Cox's Orange Pippin Apple Juice
White Hull-less Popcorn
Reduced Acid Coffee
Boneless and Skinless Sardines
"Green" Natural Oat Bran
Naturally Flavoured Raisins: Lemon, Cherry, Strawberry
"Green" Turkey Frankfurters
100% Natural Rose Food
Norwegian Crackers
Turkey Whole Frozen
Gourmet Frozen Foods (low-fat)
"If the World Were PERFECT" Water

Cleaning/Detergent Products
All-Purpose Liquid Cleaner with Bitrex
"Green" Automatic Dishwasher Detergent
Ecover 100% Biodegradable Laundry Powder*
Ecover Dishwasher Detergent
Laundry Soil and Stain Remover with Bitrex
Drain Opener with Bitrex
Ecover Fabric Softener
Ecover 100% Biodegradable Toilet Cleaner
Ecover 100% Biodegradable Wool Wash
Ecover Floor Soap
"Green" 100% Phosphate Free Laundry Detergent

Pet Food
Low Ash Cat Food
Slim & Trim Cat Food
All Natural Dog Biscuits

Cooking Products
"The Virtuous" Canola Oil
"The Virtuous" Cooking Spray
Baking Soda

Paper-Based Products
Bathroom Tissue
"Green" Ultra Diapers
"Green" Foam Plates
Swedish 100% Chlorine-Free Coffee Filters
"Green" Baby Wipes
"Green" Maxi Pads

Oil-Based Products
Biodegradable Garbage Bags
Hi-Performance Motor Oil
Natural Fertilizer
Lawn and Garden Soil

Other Products
Green T-Shirt/Sweatshirt
Green Panda Stuffed Toy
Green Polar Bear Stuffed Toy
Cedar Balls

* The Ecover brands are a line of cleaning products made by Ecover of Belgium. These products are vegetable oil based and are rapidly biodegradable. Loblaws marketed these products under the G·R·E·E·N umbrella.

products were included because they provided a more healthful blend of ingredients for cats and dogs. The G·R·E·E·N products were offered in a distinctively designed package with vivid green colouring. When the package design decisions were being made, it was learned that 20% of the Canadian population is functionally illiterate. Management felt that the distinct design would give these consumers a chance to readily identify these brands.

The G·R·E·E·N launch was supported with a $3 million television and print campaign. Consumers were informed of the new product line using the June 1989 issue of the *Insider's Report*. In an open letter to consumers, Mr. Nichol addressed Loblaws motivation for the G·R·E·E·N launch (Exhibit 5). Part of this motivation was also to offer consumers a choice which could, in the longer term, provide educational benefits for consumers on specific green issues. As well, by offering the choice, consumers could ''vote at the cash register'' and, in a sense, tell Loblaws what they were willing to buy and what green products they would accept.

The *Report* provided descriptive statements for many of the G·R·E·E·N products (Exhibit 6) and noted that Loblaws would continue to carry a broad range of products including national brands and President's Choice. The G·R·E·E·N line was to be typically priced below national brand products. The G·R·E·E·N introduction was not without its problems. Shortly after the launch, members of Pollution Probe rejected their previous endorsement of the G·R·E·E·N disposable diaper. These members felt that the group should not support a less than perfect product. The G·R·E·E·N diaper was more environmentally friendly than any other disposable brand. However, it was not, in Pollution Probe's opinion, environmentally pure. Further, it was felt that endorsing such products compromised the integrity and independence of the organization. This prompted the resignation of Colin Issac, the director of Pollution Probe. The group subsequently discontinued its endorsement of the diaper, but continued its support of six other G·R·E·E·N products.

Controversy also arose around the introduction of the G·R·E·E·N fertilizer. Greenpeace, a prominent environment group, rejected Loblaw's claims that the fertilizer had no toxic elements and therefore was environmentally pure. The group did not know that Loblaws had spent substantial funds to determine that the product was free of toxic chemicals.

Both incidents, although unfortunate, focused the attention of Canadians on the G·R·E·E·N product line. The media highlighted Loblaws as the only North American retailer to offer a line of environmentally friendly products. This publicity also prompted letters of encouragement from the public who supported Loblaws' initiative. Surveys conducted four weeks after the line introduction revealed an 82% awareness of the G·R·E·E·N line with 27% of the consumers actually purchasing at least one of the G·R·E·E·N products. In Ontario alone, the G·R·E·E·N line doubled its projected sales and sold $5 million in June 1989.

THE FIRST YEAR OF GREEN

The launch of G·R·E·E·N was soon followed by a virtual avalanche of ''environmentally friendly'' products. Major consumer goods companies like Proctor & Gamble, Lever Brothers, and Colgate-Palmolive introduced Enviro-Paks, phosphate-free

Exhibit 5
THE INSIDER'S REPORT—OPEN LETTER

SOMETHING <u>CAN</u> BE DONE!

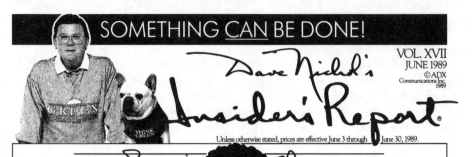

Dave Nichol's Insider's Report®

VOL. XVII
JUNE 1989
©ADX Communications Inc. 1989

Unless otherwise stated, prices are effective June 3 through June 30, 1989.

President's Choice

G·R·E·E·N™

An Open Letter To Canadian Consumers about President's Choice G•R•E•E•N Products

Over the last year, while travelling the world looking for new products, I was astounded at the level of consumer interest in environmentally friendly products. For example, the best-selling book in England last year was an environmental handbook ranking retailers and their products.

Back in Canada, I noticed that every public opinion poll indicated that the environment was the number one concern of Canadian consumers — confirming what my mail had been telling me for at least a year.

Convinced that this concern was genuine, the Insider's Report team met with executives of many of Canada's leading environmental groups and asked them what products they would like to see us create that would in some way help to reduce pollution. Their guidance was the genesis of the G•R•E•E•N "Environment Friendly™" product program and in many cases we actually worked with these groups to develop specific products which they then felt confident in endorsing.

At the same time we also began development of "Body Friendly™" (low calorie, high fibre, low fat, low cholesterol, etc.) products under the G•R•E•E•N label. This Insider's Report highlights the first wave of our new President's Choice **G•R•E•E•N product program.**

Here are a few points of clarification about the program.

1. With few exceptions, President's Choice **G•R•E•E•N** products are priced at, or below the price of the national brand to which they are an alternative.
2. We do not intend to censor products that some may feel are "environmentally-unfriendly." We see our role as providing a choice **so you may decide for yourself.**
3. Protecting the environment is a young and therefore, imprecise science. As a result, not all groups agree on what the best products are to help control pollution. For example, some advise us to use paper pulp trays for all eggs while others say recyclable, ozone-friendly foam trays made with pentane instead of chlorofluorocarbons (C.F.C's) are a better solution. We accept the fact that it is inevitable that not **all** environmental groups will agree with **all** of our President's Choice **G•R•E•E•N** products.
4. Some may accuse us of being "environmental opportunists." **WE SEE OUR ROLE AS PROVIDING PRODUCTS THAT PEOPLE WANT.** That's why we created **No Name products** when Canada's food inflation was running at 16%. That's why we created **President's Choice products** when a demand for superior-quality products arose. And that's why we've created **G•R•E•E•N products** when the overwhelming concern of Canadians is the environment.

   We invite you to read about our new President's Choice **G•R•E•E•N** products in this Insider's Report and decide for yourself whether or not they fill a real need in our society.
5. A number of our **G•R•E•E•N** products are products that we've carried for years (such as baking soda). Putting them under the **G•R•E•E•N** label was in response to environmental groups who chided us by saying, "You have a number of products in your stores right now that could help fight pollution **but you have to bring them to your customers' attention and then explain how to use them.**"

We acknowledge that we are not environmental experts and we readily admit that **we do not have all the answers.** However, we feel strongly that these products are a step in the long journey toward the solution of our enormous environmental problems. If **G•R•E•E•N** products do nothing more than help raise awareness of the need to address environmental issues **NOW,** and give Canadians hope **that SOMETHING CAN BE DONE,** then in the end, they will have made a positive contribution.

Dave Nichol

David Nichol, President
Loblaw International Merchants

Loblaws superCentre zehrs no frills

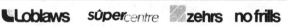

Selected products also available at Mr. Grocer, valu-mart®, freshmart™ and Your Independent Grocer®.

PRINTED ON RECYCLED NEWSPRINT

Exhibit 6

EXAMPLES OF PROMOTION FOR THE G·R·E·E·N LINE IN *THE INSIDER'S REPORT*

SOMETHING CAN BE DONE!

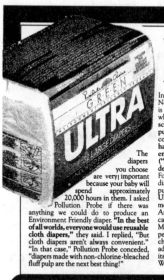

Look For Pollution Probe's Endorsement On Every Package

THESE DIAPERS COULD SAVE 500,000,000 TREES A YEAR!!

The diapers you choose are very important because your baby will spend approximately 20,000 hours in them. I asked Pollution Probe if there was anything we could do to produce an Environment Friendly diaper. **"In the best of all worlds, everyone would use reusable cloth diapers,"** they said. I replied, "But cloth diapers aren't always convenient." "In that case," Pollution Probe conceded, "diapers made with non-chlorine-bleached fluff pulp are the next best thing!"

In order to produce "whiter-than-white" diapers, most North American fluff pulp (that's the diaper padding) is bleached with chlorine-based chemicals. But at what cost to our environment?! **Two years ago, scientists discovered that chlorine in the pulp-bleaching process combines with natural compounds in wood to form a startling variety of hazardous waste products, including environment-threatening furans and dioxins. ("TCDD," one of 75 dioxins known to exist, is the deadliest toxin ever synthesized by man!!)**

Fortunately, it is no longer necessary to produce diapers using chlorine-bleached fluff pulp. The fluff pulp in our **NEW President's Choice G.R.E.E.N Ultra Diapers** is produced in Canada by one of the most technologically advanced mills in North America. The mill produces a very special type of pulp, called B.C.T.M.P. (Bleached Chemi-Thermal Mechanical Pulp), which is bleached with hydrogen peroxide instead of environment-threatening chlorine. Pollution Probe explained that the advantage of bleaching with hydrogen peroxide is that its primary waste products are OXYGEN AND WATER. THE ELIMINATION OF CHLORINE MEANS THAT ENVIRONMENT-THREATENING FURANS AND DIOXINS ARE LESS LIKELY TO BE CREATED IN THE PRODUCTION OF OUR FLUFF PULP. As a result, water pollution is kept to a minimum! Unlike the artificial whiter-than-white color of chlorine-bleached diapers, **the natural creamy color of the fluff pulp in our diapers is proof of their Environment Friendly manufacturing process!**

BUT THAT'S NOT ALL! **The special B.C.T.M.P. process gets double the number of diapers from a tree compared to conventional chlorine-bleached pulp production.** THIS MEANS THAT IF EVERYONE IN THE WORLD USING DISPOSABLE DIAPERS SWITCHED TO DIAPERS MADE FROM B.C.T.M.P., NON-CHLORINE-BLEACHED FLUFF PULP, AS MANY AS 500,000,000 TREES WOULD BE SAVED ANNUALLY! (According to the Financial Times of London, worldwide diaper manufacturing currently consumes 1 billion trees per year!)

Superior-quality President's Choice G.R.E.E.N Ultra Diapers FIT COMFORTABLY, HELP KEEP BABY DRY and PROTECT AGAINST DIAPER RASH. Until June 30, they're introductory-priced at just $9.99 for **44 MEDIUM** (12 to 24 lb), **32 LARGE** (over 22 lb) or **28 LARGE PLUS** (over 27 lb) diapers. Look for Pollution Probe's endorsement on every package.

P.S. WE'RE ALSO IN THE PROCESS OF PUTTING NON-CHLORINE-BLEACHED FLUFF PULP INTO OUR NO NAME ULTRA DIAPERS. Just $8.99 for a bag of 44 Medium, 32 Large or 28 Large Plus diapers. Ø Look for our new **"Non-Chlorine-Bleached Fluff Pulp"** sticker to identify those No Name diapers that have already been converted.

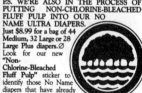

AT LAST!! ENVIRONMENT FRIENDLY BABY WIPES!!

Like conventional disposable diapers, the main component in most baby wipes is chlorine-bleached pulp. We searched the world to find a non-chlorine-bleached pulp product from which we could make quality baby wipes. At the last minute, we found a significantly more Environment Friendly, **OXYGEN-BLEACHED** pulp in Sweden and flew it to Canada just in time for the break of our G.R.E.E.N Insider's Report! **NEW President's Choice G.R.E.E.N Baby Wipes with lanolin (unscented, alcohol-free) are formulated for baby's delicate skin. AND, FOR EXTRA SOFTNESS, THEY CONTAIN 33% NATURAL COTTON FIBRE!** Introductory-priced at just $3.99 for 84 sheets in a convenient "one-hand" dispenser (so that you can hold baby with the other!). Ø

---

detergents, and biodegradable cleaning products. Competing supermarket chains had varied responses from launching their own "green" line (Miracle Mart introduced three "Green Circle" products, Oshawa Foods introduced about 10 "Greencare" products) to highlighting environmentally sensitive products in their stores (Safeway) to improving its internal practices through recycling and other activities (Provigo).

As well, companies from McDonald's to Labatt's positioned themselves in one way or another as environmentally responsible. These marketing activities created some consumer skepticism about whether some of these products were truly environmentally friendly. In addition, various companies had different ideas about what was environmentally friendly, which also created some consumer confusion. Part of the problem was that it was very difficult to determine what is and isn't environmentally safe. Serious environmentalists argued that to accurately assess the environmental impact of a product, it was necessary to conduct a "cradle-to-grave" analysis—a detailed review of the product, how it was manufactured, how it is used, and how it is disposed. Others argued that if a product were environmentally "better" than other brands (for example, a biodegradable disposable diaper versus a regular disposable diaper) then the consumer should be offered that choice.

It appeared that Loblaw's actions had an impact on corporations and consumers. For example, in a national survey of 1,500 Canadians conducted in November 1989, 56% of respondents answered "yes" to the question: "Over the past year, have environmental concerns influenced your purchase decisions?" Of those who answered yes, and were than asked "In what way?", it was found that 23% purchased environmentally friendly products, 21% avoided the purchase of hazardous products, 11% didn't purchase pesticides, and 7% boycotted certain products.

During the year, Loblaws continued to develop and promote the G·R·E·E·N product line. In the first year of G·R·E·E·N, Loblaws sold approximately $60 million worth of G·R·E·E·N products and "broke even" on the line.

THE DECISIONS

As Scott began to make his decisions on the three products, he reflected on the past year. He thought that $60 million in sales for the G·R·E·E·N line was reasonable, but he had hoped the line would do better. He remembered some of the products that just didn't fit in the line such as "green" sardines. "I don't think we sold 20 cans of that stuff." Scott and the other buyers at Intersave were very concerned when a product didn't sell. Individual store managers, who were held accountable for the sales and profits of their store, did not have to list (that is, stock in the store that he or she managed) any product, including any in the G·R·E·E·N line. If a store manager thought the product was unsuitable for the store, it wasn't listed. As well, if a buyer got a product listed and it didn't sell, his or her reputation with the store managers would suffer.

One thing that had changed was the product opportunities. When the G·R·E·E·N line was launched, Scott and the other buyers had to actively search to find products that could qualify as "green." Now it seemed that all kinds of suppliers were jumping on the "environmental bandwagon." However, the environmental advantages of many of these product proposals were difficult to verify. Some, despite good sales potential, could only be considered "pale green," a term used to describe products that had debatable or small positive impacts on the environment.

Light Bulb

The proposal by Osram, a well-known German manufacturer, was a true green product. The Osram light bulb was a compact fluorescent bulb that could replace the traditional incandescent light bulb in specific applications. The unique aspect of this product was that while fluorescent light technology was commonplace (these long-tube lights were common in office buildings), only recently had the product been modified to use it as a replacement for traditional light bulbs. The major benefits of fluorescent light bulbs were that they used considerable less energy than incandescent light bulbs (for example, a 9 watt fluorescent bulb could replace a 40 watt incandescent bulb and still provide the same lighting level, while using only

Exhibit 7
THE OSRAM LIGHT BULB

22.5% of the energy) and it lasted at least 10 times longer (an estimated 2,000 hours versus 200 hours for the incandescent bulb). To date, the major application for compact fluorescents had been in apartment buildings in stairwells where lights remained on 24 hours a day. Apartment building owners purchased them because the bulbs lowered both energy costs and maintenance costs (less frequent replacement).

The compact fluorescent had limited applications in the home. Because of its unique shape it could not be used with a typical lampshade (Exhibit 7). The main application was likely to be in hallways where it was difficult to replace a burned-out bulb. Even in these situations, a new fixture (that is, an enclosure) might be required so that the compact fluorescent would fit.

The bulb's energy efficiency and long-lasting features were well tested and had been sold for specialized industrial use for several years. The bulb was making satisfactory in-roads in Germany even though it was priced at the equivalent of $40 Canadian.

Loblaws sold a variety of 60 and 100 watt No Name and Phillips light bulbs in packages of four. In total the light bulb category generated over $1 million in gross margin for Loblaws in 1989 (Exhibit 8).

The initial Osram proposal was to sell the product to Loblaws at $19.00 per bulb. Even if the mark-up was set at 5%, Loblaw's retail price would be $19.99. Scott talked this over with a number of people at Loblaws and concluded that the price was too high to be accepted by Canadian consumers. At this time, Ontario Hydro entered the picture. Ontario Hydro was extremely concerned about its ability to meet the power demands of its customers in the next decade and was engaged in aggressive energy conservation programs. Ontario Hydro was prepared to offer a $5 rebate for every light bulb that was sold in Ontario in the three months following the launch. Although it meant customers would have to request the rebate by mail it reduced the effective price of the bulb to the consumer to $14.99.

Scott felt that the combination of the rebate, a retail price at only half that paid by German consumer's and a strong environmental message had strong merchandising appeal that could be exploited in the launch of the bulb. Nevertheless, the sales potential was still unclear. Loblaws' annual sales in Ontario were nearly four million bulbs or $2.7 million. Because this product was unique and new, Scott had difficulty estimating its sales potential. His best guess was that Loblaws might sell anywhere from 10,000 to 50,000 Osram bulbs in one year. Scott thought that half the sales would come from regular customers and the other half from customers coming to Loblaws specifically to buy the bulb. Scott also felt that after three months, the price should be raised to $24.99 retail to generate a reasonable margin for Loblaws.

Scott thought that if half the volume were generated at the higher price, it would certainly be easier to maintain the support of the store managers. At the $24.99 price, the margin would be $5.99 per bulb. Even considering the cannibalization issue, the margin on the higher priced Osram would be about four times higher than the margin for a four pack of regular bulbs. However, it would be necessary to

Exhibit 8
LIGHT BULBS (1989)

	Average Retail Price[1] ($)	Average Cost ($)	Annual Sales ($000)	Total Gross Margin ($000)	Market Share (%)
Loblaws					
60 Watt	2.25	1.25	470	209	18
60 Watt Soft	2.75	1.50	426	193	16
100 Watt	2.25	1.25	294	130	11
100 Watt Soft	2.75	1.50	279	127	11
Total Loblaws			1,468	659	56
Phillips					
60 Watt	2.40	1.50	367	138	14
60 Watt Soft	3.20	1.65	341	165	13
100 Watt	2.40	1.50	236	88	9
100 Watt Soft	3.20	1.65	210	102	8
Total Phillips			1,153	493	44
Total			2,621	1,152	100

[1] Based on four packs (that is, four light bulbs in a package).Total unit sales were 1,019,000 (four packs).

calculate the contribution for the year to see what the net effect would be for the line. The shelf space required for these bulbs was minimal and could be handled by some minor changes to the layout of the existing bulbs.

BATHROOM TISSUE

The bathroom tissue category was a highly competitive, price-sensitive market. The category was one of the largest in the Loblaws lineup, generating over $31 milliion in retail sales in Ontario and $7 million in contribution (Exhibit 9). Bathroom tissue was more important to Loblaws than just a volume generator. It was one of the few

Exhibit 9
BATHROOM TISSUE (1989)

	Average Retail Price[1] ($)	Average Cost ($)	Annual Sales ($000)	Total Gross Margin ($000)	Market Share (%)
Loblaws[2]					
President's Choice	2.50	1.95	1,542	339	5
No Name White	1.75	1.15	3,084	1,052	10
No Name Coloured	1.80	1.35	386	96	1
Loblaws Total			5,012	1,487	16
Royale					
White	1.85	1.55	10,795	1,751	34
Coloured	2.00	1.60	3,855	771	12
Royale Total			14,650	2,522	46
Cottonelle					
White	1.85	1.45	4,627	1,000	15
Coloured	1.95	1.50	4,627	1,068	15
Cottonelle Total			9,254	2,068	30
Other Brands					
Capri	1.50	0.90	945	378	3
April Soft	1.40	0.95	721	232	2
Jubilee	1.35	0.70	386	186	1
Dunet	2.45	1.60	405	140	1
White Swan	1.55	1.00	463	164	1
Other Brands Total			2,920	1,100	8
Total			31,836	7,177	100

[1] Statistics for the prices, costs and sales have been collapsed over the various sizes and reported in equivalent four-roll packs. Total unit sales were 17,125,000 (four-roll packs).

[2] With respect to colours and sizes, Loblaws offered six varieties, Royale (eight varieties), Cottonelle (eight varieties), Capri (four varieties), April Soft (three varieties), Jubilee (two varieties), Dunet (one variety), and White Swan (eight varieties).

product categories that would draw price-conscious buyers into the store. Loblaws listed 40 different sizes and colours from various manufacturers. There were six Loblaws brands in the category. Loblaws was aggressive at delisting any competitive or corporate brand that did not meet turnover or profitability goals. Manufacturers were just as aggressive at providing allowance and merchandising incentives to ensure satisfactory margins for Loblaws and to facilitate retail price reductions which in turn would enhance turnover and maintain volume goals. Two national brands—Royale and Cottonelle—held shares of 46% and 30% respectively.

For 1989, Loblaws' brands held 16% of the market with No Name White providing a total gross margin of over $1 million. Loblaw's No Name White was sourced for an average cost of $1.15 for a 4-roll package. These lower costs were largely based on the fact that the tissue was manufactured with totally recycled material. This product feature made it a candidate for G·R·E·E·N line consideration. The existing product could simply be repackaged with the distinctive G·R·E·E·N labelling and an emphasis placed on the recycled character of the product. No development or testing costs would be required, and art work and new labelling costs would be minimal.

Several decisions needed to be considered with respect to the repackaging of the No Name product. Should the new product replace the old or simply be added to an already crowded category? Should the price of the new product be set higher than that set for the old? Should the product be launched at all? If it is launched should it get prominence in the quarterly *Insider's Report*? Should it be positioned against some national brands? How much inventory should be ordered, and what was the expected profitability?

READY-TO-EAT CEREAL

Loblaws sold more than $14 million worth of family cereals (that is, cereals targeted at the "family" market) in Ontario in 1989 (Exhibit 10). Loblaws corporate brand share of the family cereal segment, at 14%, was lower than corporate objectives for this category. One of Scott Lindsay's goals was to increase Loblaws share for this category. The major obstacle was the dominance of the well-known national brands marketed by Kellogg's, Nabisco, General Mills, and Quaker Oats (Exhibit 10). The brand leaders, such as Kellogg's Corn Flakes, Nabisco Shreddies, and General Mills' Cheerios, were as familiar to shoppers as any other product or brand in a store. With decades of advertising and promotional suppport, these brands had become thoroughly entrenched in the minds and pantries of generations of Canadians.

The brand names of these market leaders provided the manufacturers with strong protection against competitors. However, the manufacturing process did not. The manufacturing processes were well known in the industry, and many firms could produce identical products at favourable costs. Loblaws had found several products from domestic sources that appeared to be as good if not better than the national brands. One such product was a corn flake product which had a very high fibre content. The new product would appeal to those customers who had been primed by the health claims of high fibre diets. In sensory tests it had proven to have an

Exhibit 10
FAMILY CEREALS (1989)

	Average Retail Price[1] ($)	Average Cost ($)	Annual Sales ($000)	Total Gross Margin ($000)	Market Share (%)
President's Choice					
Bran with Raisins	2.35	1.50	1,051	380	7.4
Honey Nut Cereal	3.00	1.40	324	173	2.3
Toasted Oats	3.00	1.45	221	114	1.5
Corn Flakes	1.75	1.20	193	60	1.4
Crispy Rice	3.20	1.50	263	139	1.8
Loblaws Total			2,052	866	14.3
Kellogg's					
Corn Flakes	2.30	1.80	1,436	312	10.1
Raisin Bran	2.75	2.00	1,236	324	8.7
Honey Nut Corn Flakes	3.95	2.70	460	141	3.2
Rice Krispies	3.95	2.52	899	315	6.3
Common Sense	4.40	2.70	433	167	3.0
Mini-Wheat	3.30	2.00	326	129	2.3
Variety Pack	5.90	3.90	309	105	2.2
Other Kellogg's	3.41	2.26	258	87	1.8
Kellogg's Total			5,357	1,580	37.5
Nabisco					
Shreddies	2.35	1.70	2,725	754	19.1
Apple/Cinnamon	2.25	1.50	169	57	1.2
Raisin Wheat	3.30	2.10	139	50	1.0
Nabisco Total			3,033	861	21.2
General Mills					
Cheerios	3.80	2.60	1,171	370	8.2
Cheerios/Honey Nut	3.90	2.60	1,017	339	7.1
General Mills Total			2,188	709	15.3
Quaker					
Corn Bran	3.50	2.25	389	139	2.7
Life	3.15	2.10	358	119	2.5
Oat Bran	4.10	2.80	281	89	2.0
Muffets	2.65	1.60	92	36	0.6
Quaker Total			1,120	383	7.8
Others	2.40	1.45	573	227	4.0
Total			14,323	4,626	100.0

[1] Based on 500 gram size. Total unit sales were 4,950,000 (500 gram size).
Cereals are packaged in several different sizes. Some brands like Kellogg's Corn Flakes could have four different sizes (e.g. 350g, 425g, 675g, 800g) on the shelf at one time. To facilitate comparisons, all figures have been converted to a standard 500 g size and where brands had multiple sizes, the figures are reported as averages, weighted by the sales volume of the size.

excellent taste and texture profile and was equal to or preferred in blind taste tests to some of the market leaders. Moreover, the product could be obtained for $1.40 per 500 g package.

The President's Choice brands were beginning to make in-roads in this market, and this new product could increase the share. However, it was not clear how to position the high-fibre corn flake product. Should it go in the regular President's Choice line as a line extension of the current corn flake product or should it be packaged as a G·R·E·E·N product? As a regular President's Choice product it would be positioned directly against Kellogg's as an all-round cereal with extra value. As a G·R·E·E·N product it would be positioned less against Kellogg's and much more towards a health/"good-for-you claim." G·R·E·E·N positioning might also minimize any cannibalization of the President's Choice corn flakes. The lower sourcing costs provided some flexibility on pricing. It could be priced as low as $1.75, like the current President's Choice corn flakes, and still maintain good margins or it could be priced as high as Kellogg's Corn Flakes at $2.30 and generate superior margins.

Having reviewed the three proposals, Scott began the process of preparing his recommendations. "I'll start with the financial projections," thought Scott, "then consider the pros and cons of each proposal. Then it's decision time."

13 NABOB SUMMIT

John R. Oldland

"I'm running the most successful new brand that Nabob has introduced in the last twenty-five years, and now you're telling me my sales are too high," Bruce McKay, Summit's product manager complained. "I feel like the proverbial Canadian grain farmer, the more I sell the less I make."

"That's right. Summit's not making enough money, and you've until year end to solve the problem," John Bell, Nabob's General Manager, told the upset product manager, and, as Mr. Bell left the room, he delivered a parting comment, "And don't destroy the brand while you're solving that problem!"

Despondently Mr. McKay looked at the packages and documents that cluttered his office. His eye was caught by the bright blue Summit Decaffeinated package, the line extension that had just been successfully introduced. Beside it was the March/April, 1987, A.C. Nielsen report which had arrived that morning. It was open at the section revealing performance in the critical Metro Toronto market. The Summit share had shot upwards and was now close to 8%. The other document that caught his attention was the latest cost analysis and profitability statement. It confirmed his worst fears. The profitability per case of Nabob Tradition was 30% greater than that of Summit. Every Tradition user who switched to Summit cost the company money.

THE NABOB STORY

Although Nabob had been making food products for 70 years, nothing in its history was as momentous as the purchase of the company in 1976 by Jacobs Suchard of Zurich, Switzerland. Nabob, which made over 150 products, had been owned by Weston, the large grocery retailer and bread manufacturer. After Jacobs purchased it, Nabob either stopped manufacturing many small brands that had been private labels for Super Valu, a Weston company, or sold those with a solid franchise to other companies. By 1984 the product line had been reduced to only two businesses, ground coffee and tea. Tea was sold only in Alberta and British Columbia. Nabob ground coffee was sold nationally but with very little penetration in Quebec. The size of the Canadian ground coffee market was 78 million pounds and, at an average retail price per pound of $3.50, the dollar value of the market was $275 million.

Jacobs brought to Nabob a singlemindedness of purpose, enthusiasm for the products it sold, and a marketing entrepreneurial zeal with which to take on far larger competitors. This was Jacobs's first entrance into North America, and the company had no intention of remaining content with its dominant position in the Western Canada ground coffee market. Klaus Jacobs, the parent company's chairman, explained one of his management philosophies, "To set high expectations and performance standards for everyone in everything we do," by saying, "We want to be not just as good as our competitors but better. We have to be, in order to equalize their greater size and scale. If they are the Goliaths, we have to be the David." Nabob was Jacobs's window on the North American market.

In 1978, Nabob entered the Ontario market with its Tradition brand of roast coffee. The coffee was packaged in a unique vacuum package, quite different from the soft paper bag packaging that then dominated the Eastern Canadian market.

Nabob test marketed Tradition in Peterborough and Kingston and then rolled out the brand to the rest of Ontario with heavy promotional support and extensive advertising. Memorable advertising copy had the Nabob spokesperson compare the difference between Nabob's hard packaging and the competitor's soft paper bags while delivering the message, "Nabob comes in a hard vacuum pack, not in a soft paper bag that lets in stale air. Nabob's fresh flavour and aroma can't get out until you release it. Want a fresher better tasting cup of coffee? Start with a fresher better tasting coffee. Nabob." The introductory "Microphone" commercial is provided in Exhibit 1.

The major competitor was Maxwell House, from General Foods, with a 15.5% share of the market in 1978 (Exhibit 2). Ground coffee was considered by many to be a commodity business with pricing as the dominant marketing factor. Maxwell House was also able to rely on the halo effect from heavy advertising behind its instant coffee brand.

By 1982, Nabob had reached an Ontario market share of 22.5%, just below the 24.4% share of Maxwell House, while keeping its 30% market share in Western Canada. During 1982, Nabob introduced a better tasting Tradition as a result of new high-yield roasting technology, and in 1983 Tradition Decaffeinated was added to the line, giving further impetus to brand growth.

By 1983, Maxwell House had moved to vacuum packaging and was supporting the brand with heavy advertising, featuring the company's long-term spokesperson, Ricardo Montalban. In Ontario, Maxwell House remained the best known brand and had been able to build its market share in the face of Nabob's dramatic growth in this market. Maxwell House Decaffeinated was added in 1982, just months before Nabob Decaffeinated was launched. General Foods also marketed three other ground coffee brands—Sanka, Brim, and Chase and Sanborn.

Nabob, drawing from its European experience, believed that the Canadian roast coffee market, although seemingly a commodity business, could be segmented. "Our objective," said John Bell, "is to segment the roast coffee market as much as we can." Nabob set about testing two premium roast coffees. The first was Signature, a fine blend of arabica coffees featuring high quality beans from Kenya, test marketed in Alberta. The name, package graphics, and advertising signalled a luxury positioning, reflecting the quality of the coffee. The brand failed to meet its targets. Consumers were accustomed to the taste of their regular brands, often found the premium taste too bitter, and were unwilling to pay the premium price.

The second brand was Select Discoveries, a family of four flavours: Mocha Java, French Bistro, Columbian Classic, and Swiss Chocolate Café. They were sold in 200 gram tins (rather than 369 gram vacuum packaging) and were introduced in Ontario in 1983. A small market developed for this specialty product, but there did not appear to be the same desire for premium quality coffees as in Europe.

Exhibit 1
THE MICROPHONE COMMERCIAL

NABOB

Nabob Foods Limited
Tradition Roast Coffee
60 Second Television
Commercial "Microphone"

MAN: Inside these ordinary, old-fashioned, soft paper bags . . .

. . . is ground coffee. You can smell the coffee inside, on the outside.

Stale air keeps getting in, flavour and aroma keep getting out. That's bad. Now for the good news.

Inside this <u>extraordinary</u> . . .

. . . hard (knock, knock) foil vacuum pack is a truly superior blend of ground coffee, Nabob. Western Canada's leading fresh ground coffee.

You can't smell a thing. Stale air can't get in, so Nabob's famous flavour and aroma <u>can't</u> get out.

But listen . . .

WHOOSH.

Smell that . . . <u>that's</u> fresh aroma.

Now I ask you, which one do you think makes a better, fresher cup of coffee?

You're absolutely right.

Exhibit 2

ROAST COFFEE SHARES IN EQUIVALENT POUNDS (NATIONAL)

	Percentages							
	1978	1979	1980	1981	1982	1983	1984	1985
Nabob								
Tradition	13.4	17.3	21.8	21.3	22.9	24.9	23.5	21.4
Tradition Decaffeinated						2.0	2.4	2.7
Other Nabob	1.0	0.6	0.2	0.1	0.9	0.4	0.5	0.4
Total Nabob	14.4	17.9	22.0	21.4	23.8	27.3	26.4	24.5
Maxwell House								
Regular	15.5	16.5	16.9	17.2	17.0	18.7	19.0	19.0
Decaffeinated				0.1	0.9	1.3	1.3	1.3
Gold						0.9	1.2	0.9
Total Maxwell House*	15.5	16.5	16.9	17.3	17.9	20.9	21.5	21.2
Sanka*			1.1	1.2	1.7	1.8	1.9	1.6
MJB	3.8	4.4	4.5	5.5	5.2	5.5	5.0	5.2
Chase & Sanborn*	8.3	8.5	8.3	9.6	8.7	5.9	4.6	4.6
Melitta	4.4	4.5	4.4	4.7	4.4	4.4	5.2	4.6
Brooke Bond	5.3	4.5	4.0	3.9	2.6	1.9	2.0	2.4
Hills Bros.			2.0	4.2	3.5	3.1	3.1	2.9
Private Label	39.4	33.9	30.9	26.3	26.6	24.1	26.2	28.5
All other	8.9	9.8	5.9	5.9	5.5	5.2	4.1	4.5
TOTAL	100.0	100.0	100.0	100.0	100.0	100.0	100.0	100.0

Source: A.C. Nielsen National Food Index

* Brands marketed by General Foods

Note: 1 pound = 453.6 grams

Maxwell House, in anticipation of an expansion of Nabob Signature from the Alberta test market into Ontario, had launched a premium brand of its own, Maxwell House Gold, sold in a one-pound tin. This brand achieved around a 1% share of the market, making it more difficult for Nabob to introduce another premium brand.

THE DEVELOPMENT OF SUMMIT

It was at this stage that John Bell, then Vice-President of Marketing and Sales, Roger Barnes, the Market Research Manager, and Bruce McKay, the Product Manager, met to evaluate new product opportunities. The concept that seemed to offer the greatest promise was coffee that used 100% Colombian beans.

This was not an original idea. General Foods had introduced a premium Colombian coffee, Yuban, in the early seventies that had a lacklustre career in the market, peaking at only a 2% share and discontinued in 1978. It still survived as a strong premium regional brand in parts of the United States. To match the Yuban launch in Canada, Nabob rushed its own premium Colombian brand to market, Boban (Nabob spelt backwards). Needless to say this brand name creativity was not appreciated by consumers and the brand was quickly withdrawn from the market. Even Safeway entered this market with its own premium Colombian coffee, but it, too, was discontinued in a short time.

Nabob decided to launch a separate brand but one still clearly within its stable of brands. In a study that probed the strength of the Colombian beans proposition, it was found that 65% of a national sample believed that Colombian coffee was the best tasting in the world, and that 93% recognized Colombia as a coffee-producing country. This high level of awareness had been developed by the National Federation of Colombian Coffee Growers, which had been spending more than $1.5 million annually on television and print advertising in Canada.

Summit, prepared with 100% Colombian beans, was launched in October 1985. Each aspect of the marketing mix had been carefully developed.

Name and Packaging

Summit, as a name, had many advantages. It was short, not used by other manufacturers, and carried the connotation of high quality. Also, the best beans were grown on the high mountainsides in subtropical countries, and there was an appreciation of this through previous advertising. Consideration was given to calling the brand Nabob Colombian. However, this use of a generic name would have inhibited the development of a distinct brand image and could have been easily matched by the competition. The packaging had to be clearly positioned within the Nabob family. The pack retained the key Nabob logo elements and was red (distinct from the green for Tradition and brown for Tradition Decaffeinated) in order to reinforce Summit's subtropical mountain imagery and stand out strongly on the shelf.

Advertising

Creative copy themes were developed to communicate to coffee drinkers that Colombian coffees were known for their rich and distinctive taste and that new Nabob Summit was the best tasting Colombian coffee. The advertising was to have the same tone consumers had come to associate with Nabob advertising—confident, demanding, and assertive.

Summit's copy strategy was clearly stated on the package: "Like all great tasting Nabob coffees, Nabob Summit must meet our strict standards for flavour and aroma. That means we don't just pick 100% pure Colombian coffee beans. We go further by choosing only the few that pass Nabob's test. Only then will you find the rich, distinctive flavour that makes Colombian coffees both legendary and good enough for Nabob."

To provide continuity, Nabob once again turned to Mike Reynolds, spokesperson for the Nabob brand since its 1978 introduction in Ontario. The "Sword" commercial (Exhibit 3) was tested, using the "Day-after recall" technique to measure memorability of the advertising and its ability to communicate the copy strategy. Two hundred women between the ages of 18 and 64 were contacted by telephone the day after the commercial was aired in major centres across Canada. The commercial was remembered as well as the average thirty-second commercial (see following).

	Norm for 30 Second Commercials
Unprompted Recall of Ad	20
Prompted Recall	60

There was concern that the visual device of the sword dominated the commercial and obscured the message that this was a new brand named Summit and that it was made exclusively from Colombian beans. The idea that Nabob uses only the best beans in their coffee, a communication objective in all Nabob advertising, was the strongest message recalled in the commercial.

Pricing and Promotion

Summit trade pricing was at parity with Tradition in spite of the fact that Colombian beans were a more expensive blend than regular tradition. Retail pricing would be slightly above Tradition because retailers would take a higher margin. It was also hoped that Summit could benefit from the leverage of the popular Tradition brand to generate strong retail advertising, merchandising, and price feature support for the new brand.

A $0.55 direct mail coupon was sent to three million households in Canada in February/March 1986 to initiate trial buying. Total costs including printing, handling, and redemption expenses were expected to amount to $250,000.

Ground coffee was sold extensively on promotion. Summit was to be promoted simultaneously with Tradition so that the new brand could benefit from the merchandising leverage that the larger brand offered. Approximately $0.30 per unit would be offered to the trade, and this was expected to generate trade support and feature pricing at least one week every month.

If, for example, the regular list price to the retailer was $3.19 for a 369 gram package, an off-invoice reduction of $0.20 a unit would be offered on an almost continuous basis to produce a net regular price of $2.99. A fluctuating merchandising allowance would also be offered on a regular basis and could be paid to those retailers who would feature price the brand. The usual merchandising allowance was $0.10 a unit bringing the cost to the retailer down to $2.89. The feature retail price target would be $2.99. The merchandising allowance might change as the regular list price changed to achieve this feature price. Since ground coffee was often a loss leader for retailers, this slim retail margin was acceptable. In addition, other allowance promotions might be run in specific regions and would be used to pay for the retail advertising that supported coffee promotions. Lastly there was a co-operative allowance of 3% off the regular list price. This allowance, based on volume, was accumulated and available to retailers who supported the brand with promotional activity.

Exhibit 3
THE SWORD COMMERCIAL

NABOB

CLIENT: NABOB
PRODUCT: Summit
TITLE: "Sword"
LENGTH: 30 sec. T.V.

MIKE: This . . . is 100% Colombian coffee, famous for its legendary flavour.

And this is also 100% Colombian, New Nabob Summit.

They're both 100% Colombian, so they both taste the same, right?

Wrong.

Some of these Colombian coffee beans simply don't measure up . . .

to Nabob's standards for flavour and aroma.

Ah, but the ones that do make all the difference in Nabob Summit.

A taste we'd call,

a cut above.

Media

The media plan called for 1800 Gross Rating Points (GRPs) of television advertising in the major television markets in Ontario and Western Canada. The advertising ran in two flights. The introductory flight lasted 12 weeks starting in mid-December. The second, sustaining flight, at a lower weight level of 60 GRPs a week, ran for a further ten weeks in the fall of 1986.

Nabob, in allocating its media dollars, took into consideration the sales per capita of the regular coffee market by region, its own share of market provincially and the cost of purchasing air time in each city area (Exhibit 4). Summit advertising, scheduled to begin in January, was brought forward to December as distribution had grown faster than was anticipated. To maximize Summit awareness, GRP levels were raised to 150 GRPs in mid-January. In March Summit advertising was replaced by Tradition Decaffeinated advertising.

As well, the National Federation of Colombian Coffee Growers was prepared to subsidize Nabob Summit advertising, up to $0.12 U.S. per pound.To earn the maximum subsidy, Nabob had to spend $0.17 U.S. per pound and, if it did would receive a rebate from the National Federation of $0.12 U.S. per pound.[1]

SUMMIT'S FIRST YEAR

The Summit launch must be viewed in the context of worldwide coffee commodity prices. The 1985 Brazilian coffee harvest had been a disaster and had a dramatic effect on coffee futures. Between August 1985 and February 1986, the commodity price of roast coffee rose by 70%. Commodity prices peaked at $3.20 per pound. Consumer prices were to some extent cushioned from this volatile market. The large companies stopped buying at the higher prices. Also, manufacturers squeezed margins as prices rose, hoping to increase them once the prices started to fall. As a result, the retail price of coffee increased from $3 to just over $4 per pound during the first six months of Summit's launch. This spiralling cost of coffee was of grave concern to Nabob, as it could have adversely affected early trial of Summit. Retailers had stocked up with coffee just prior to the Summit launch in anticipation of higher prices. In an escalating price market consumers could also be expected to either reduce their purchases or stock up on their regular brand before prices rose. Exhibit 5 provides information about Summit pricing through 1986.

These pricing concerns proved to be illusory. The signals of success were almost immediate. The retail trade was quick to appreciate the value offered by the product and decided to give shelf space to the brand immediately. The trade saw that Nabob was going to market the brand aggressively. As well, ground coffee was a very visible product in that it was heavily promoted, the pricing was extremely competitive, and many retailers used it as a loss leader.

The parity pricing strategy and accompanying trade support plan proved important in determining the product's rapid success and overcoming "price increase" fears. In its first full Nielsen audit, Summit exceeded 50% distribution in all areas

[1] At that time, $1.00 U.S. = $1.35 Canadian

where it was marketed, reaching a high of 89% distribution in Alberta. The trade, in turn, supported the product, and a 2% national share was achieved in the first audit. This share was the minimum level at which the trade would begin to give the brand ongoing support. By comparison, the best share ever reached by Signature was 1.9%. In Alberta and British Columbia, market shares of 3.4% and 4%, respectively, were reached. This was achieved before advertising and coupon support had a chance to make an impact. Despite price increases, the trade aggressively priced Summit, averaging only a $0.10 per pack premium for the year. In addition, the brand was co-op advertised (featured in weekly supermarket advertisements) and displayed. Summit's share of weighted co-op averaged 10%, an excellent result for a new product.[2]

By the end of the year, Summit had exceeded all the marketing objectives set out for it, as the following shows (Exhibits 6 to 8 provide further details of Year 1 performance).

	Objective	Actual
Year 1 Share	2.7	3.3
Distribution Where Marketed	80%	82%
Trial of Coffee Buying Households	12%	12%
Repeat Purchase	35%	42%

In early May 1986, an awareness, attitude, and usage survey was conducted in Vancouver, Calgary, and Toronto. Nabob contacted by telephone 130 principal grocery shoppers (the individual in the household primarily responsible for grocery shopping), in each of the three cities, who were 18 years and over and who had purchased ground coffee in the last month. At that stage, awareness and trial were still relatively low. Results were more favourable in Calgary than either Vancouver or Toronto (see below).

	Unaided Awareness		Summit Total Unaided & Aided Awareness	Summit Purchase
	Total Nabob	Summit		
Vancouver	65%	4%	35%	9%
Calgary	72	13	48	15
Toronto	62	4	25	6

Overall perceptions of Summit were favourable among those who were aware of the brand and prepared to comment. Summit was seen as a "top-of-the-line," "richer," "better" coffee. Summit advertising was reinforcing the consistent message of Nabob advertising—that Nabob used only the best beans in its coffee.

[2] Co-op advertising is retail advertising in which the cost is shared by the retailer and the national advertiser. Weighted co-op is the percentage of times that a brand, like Summit, was featured in a given time period compared to all coffee brands that were featured.

Exhibit 4
NABOB—1986 MEDIA PLANNING INDEX

Market	CPM(1)	MDI(2)	CPM Index(3)	MDI/CPM Index	1985 Weekly GRP Levels(4)
Ottawa E	11.30	100	134	75	50
Barrie	8.50	100	101	99	50
Sudbury	9.60	100	115	87	50
Kingston	11.40	100	136	74	50
Peterborough	9.05	100	107	93	50
Sault Ste. Marie	9.30	100	110	91	50
Kitchener	7.75	100	92	109	60
London	6.50	100	78	128	50
Toronto	7.00	100	84	119	60
Thunder Bay	13.30	180	159	63	50
Winnipeg	6.50	180	78	230	100
Regina	8.00	180	95	189	60
Brandon	12.35	180	147	122	—
Swift Current	18.50	180	221	81	—
Prince Albert	12.50	180	149	121	—
Yorkton	7.60	180	91	198	90
Saskatoon	7.50	180	89	202	70
Lloydminster	6.40	180	76	236	90
Medicine Hat	6.60	179	198	90	—
Red Deer	8.85	179	106	169	80
Edmonton	10.30	179	123	145	70
Calgary	10.50	179	125	143	60
Vancouver	6.45	175	77	227	100
Okanagan	12.50	175	149	117	50
Prince George	17.20	175	205	85	—
Dawson Creek	25.70	175	307	57	—
Weighted Average	8.38				

(1) CPM is the cost per thousand messages delivered against a target group in a television market over a 52 week period. The target group is women 18+.

(2) MDI is the market development index for ground coffee, with the Ontario index 100. It reflects the much higher development (sales per capita) of ground coffee in Western Canada. The main reason for this is the lower consumption of instant coffee in the West.

(3) CPM index is the cost per thousand divided by the CPM weighted average.

(4) A rating point is a percent of the viewing households tuned in to a television market. If 10% of the potential audience sees the commercial, it has a rating of 10. GRPs are the totals of the ratings for commercials shown during a given period.

(continued)

Exhibit 4 continued

SUMMIT MEDIA SCHEDULE (GRPS PER WEEK)

Market	1985 December		1986 January				February					March
	16	23	30	6	13	20	27	3	10	17	24	3
All markets Numbers of GRPs per week	←—60—→			←—150—→				←—100—→				

GRP (Gross Rating Point). A rating point is the percentage of the viewing households tuned in to a television market. If 10% of the potential audience sees the commercial, it has a rating of 10. GRPs are the totals of the ratings for commercials shown during a given period.

In the competitive Toronto market where Maxwell House and Nabob Tradition were close rivals, Nabob had after nine years achieved a very strong image. Nabob conducted periodic attitude and image studies which measured consumer perceptions of Nabob and Maxwell House on a number of attributes. In the past, Maxwell House had a strong reputation in the market, based, in part, on the fact that Maxwell House marketed both ground and instant coffee and heavily advertised both product categories. While Maxwell House was still considered the best selling brand, over the years Nabob had steadily improved its reputation on all taste and quality attributes to the extent that the Maxwell House image advantage had now been eliminated.

Competitor reaction was swift. General Foods reformulated and repackaged its Maxwell House Gold brand. The brand moved from packaging in tins to vacuum packaging and was offered in two varieties, Colombia and Arabica. The pricing strategy was changed from premium to parity with Summit. Maxwell House Gold share increased from 1% in December/January 1986, to 2.2% in December/January 1987. MJB, an important brand in Western Canada, introduced MJB Colombian, and several generics also introduced Colombian varieties.

THE IMPACT OF THE PRICING DECISION

Success can be your worst enemy. Nabob had planted the seeds for continued growth for 1987. Research conducted on a decaffeinated Colombian product had yielded favourable results. Accordingly, Summit Decaffeinated had been introduced in late 1986 to capitalize on the momentum of the brand.

An aggressive marketing plan had been approved to enhance the Summit brand. For example, spending on advertising at $0.17 U.S. per pound on Summit in 1987 would generate advertising support for the brand almost equivalent to that of the main brand, Tradition.

If Nabob continued to fuel the marketing fires behind Summit, the brand would continue to grow. Unfortunately, much of that growth would probably be at the expense of the more profitable Tradition brand. The cost premium for an all-Colom-

Exhibit 5

SUMMIT AVERAGE RETAIL PRICE (369 GRAM UNITS)

	1986												Total
	Jan.	Feb.	Mar.	Apr.	May	June	July	Aug.	Sept.	Oct.	Nov.	Dec.	1986
Tradition	$3.08	3.37	3.65	3.91	3.86	3.97	3.87	3.64	3.50	3.67	3.75	3.59	3.59
Summit	$3.05	3.52	3.54	4.05	4.12	4.15	4.07	3.74	3.48	3.60	3.89	3.48	3.69
Difference vs. Tradition	−0.03	+0.15	−0.11	+0.14	+0.26	+0.18	+0.20	+0.10	−0.02	−0.07	+0.13	−0.11	+0.10

Exhibit 6

GROUND COFFEE SHARES

	Total 1985	Dec./Jan. 1986	Feb./Mar.	Apr./May	June/July	Aug./Sept.	Oct./Nov.	Total 1986	Dec./Jan. 1987
Nabob									
Tradition (369 gram)	21.4	19.5	17.0	19.0	18.8	20.7	17.7	18.8	15.9
Tradition (200 gram)	—	—	—	—	0.1	1.4	1.7	0.6	1.7
Tradition Decaffeinated	2.7	2.3	2.5	2.6	2.6	2.6	2.7	2.6	2.6
Summit	—	2.0	3.0	3.7	3.1	4.2	4.0	3.3	3.9
Summit Decaffeinated	—	—	—	—	—	—	—	—	0.2
Other Nabob	0.4	—	—	—	—	—	—	—	—
Total Nabob	24.5	23.8	22.5	25.3	24.5	28.9	26.1	25.3	24.3
Maxwell House									
Regular	19.0	18.3	16.1	17.4	19.3	17.7	17.5	17.7	18.5
Decaffeinated	1.3	1.1	1.4	1.4	1.4	1.3	1.4	1.3	1.3
Gold	0.9	1.0	1.0	1.7	2.0	1.6	1.7	1.5	2.2
Total Maxwell House	21.2	20.4	18.5	20.5	22.7	20.6	20.6	20.5	22.0

Source: A.C. Nielsen Food Index

Exhibit 7
SUMMIT FACT SHEET

	DJ 86	FM 86	AM 86	JJ 86	AS 86	ON 86	DJ 87	TOTAL 1986
Market Shares*								
National	2.0	3.0	3.7	3.1	4.2	4.0	3.9	3.3
Ontario	1.6	3.8	4.7	3.5	5.5	5.3	4.8	4.0
Man./Sask.	1.6	1.8	2.5	3.2	3.1	2.7	3.4	2.4
Alberta	3.4	4.6	5.7	4.7	5.2	6.3	5.3	5.0
B.C.	4.0	4.1	3.7	3.4	4.7	3.9	4.9	4.0
Distribution**								
National	44	51	54	54	55	55	55	
Ontario	54	70	75	77	77	78	78	
Man./Sask.	58	68	77	69	69	74	70	
Alberta	89	91	99	88	89	81	82	
B.C.	78	83	85	82	83	86	89	
Share of Weighted Co-op***								
Tradition								
National	24	17	16	21	21	18	16	20
Ontario	31	28	20	22	26	21	15	25
Man./Sask.	47	15	37	33	40	22	34	27
Alberta	38	25	23	31	31	29	22	29
B.C.	18	16	26	23	21	17	19	20
Summit								
National	6	10	11	10	11	9	10	10
Ontario	7	17	14	11	16	18	14	15
Man./Sask.	14	14	13	19	10	5	13	12
Alberta	11	10	18	12	15	12	13	20
B.C.	7	9	13	15	11	6	14	11

Source: A.C. Nielsen National Food Index

* in equivalent pounds

** in stores accounting for X% of the business

*** percent of stores providing retail advertising support

bian blend of beans was 10%. However the cost gap could widen depending on fluctuating commodity markets, and quite possibly a premium of up to 20% might have to be paid. The Tradition user who switched to Summit might be a satisfied customer but, at the same time, a less profitable one for Nabob. The company, in developing its own projections, had forecasted that a third of Summit volume would be cannibalized from Tradition. The latest figures, particularly from the Toronto market, showed a cannibalization rate in excess of 50%. In 1986, the Summit share was 3.3%, but corporate share had edged ahead only 2%.

Exhibit 8

SUMMIT COFFEE—CUMULATIVE TRIAL AND REPEAT PURCHASE FREQUENCY, 1986

	Jan.	Feb.	Mar.	Apr.	May	June	July	Aug.	Sept.	Oct.	Nov.	Dec.
Monthly Household Buying	1.8%	1.8	1.9	1.6	2.1	1.7	1.0	2.1	2.2	1.5	1.7	2.0
New	100.0	85.5	68.4	54.1	55.3	48.4	63.4	44.6	52.6	33.5	32.7	37.3
Repeat	0	14.5	31.6	45.9	44.7	51.6	36.6	55.4	47.4	66.5	67.3	62.7
Cumulative Households Buying	1.8	3.4	4.7	5.6	6.7	7.6	8.2	9.2	10.3	10.8	11.4	12.1
Households Buying Once	94.9	83.1	76.4	69.3	67.2	64.9	65.7	60.5	60.6	58.9	58.0	58.1
Repeating once	5.1	14.0	17.2	21.5	18.5	20.4	19.4	22.8	22.1	22.2	22.4	21.0
Repeating twice	—	2.9	4.9	5.4	9.0	7.9	8.2	9.5	8.7	9.4	8.7	7.3
Repeating 3 times	—	—	1.5	2.6	4.3	2.8	2.2	2.8	4.3	4.4	3.2	5.9
Repeating 4 times	—	—	—	1.2	0.0	2.2	2.1	0.6	0.6	1.2	3.9	1.8
More than 4 times	—	—	—	—	1.0	1.8	2.4	3.8	3.7	3.9	3.8	5.9

Source: Consumer Panel of Canada

Nabob case prices (each case contained twelve 369 gram packages) varied depending on order quantity, as the following shows:

Case Order Quantity	Price
25–99	39.81
100–199	39.05
200–399	36.66
400 case plus	38.28

The relative cost and profit ratios on Summit and Tradition were as follows:

	Tradition	Summit
	%	%
Gross sales	100	100
Gross profit	50	42
Marketing cost	30	25
Administrative and other	10	10
Profits before tax	10	7

In May 1987, General Foods reintroduced all its decaffeinated ground coffees in smaller 300 gram packages at parity with their regular coffees. Apart from the obvious absolute reduction in price, the big advantage to General Foods was that regular and decaffeinated coffees could now be jointly promoted.

A further complication was the fact that the Federation of Colombian Coffee Growers was starting to put pressure on Nabob to raise the price of Summit. While they found Canadian results satisfactory, they believed that parity pricing was inconsistent with the premium image they were trying to create worldwide. In every previous instance when the Federation had supported and endorsed a Colombian coffee, they had been able to achieve premium pricing.

Mr. McKay felt extremely uncomfortable about the current predicament. He had gained enormous satisfaction from the brand's success and knew it had more potential. Summit Decaffeinated was a superb new coffee. The small retail price differential with Tradition was narrowing as the trade support of the brand was increasing. New copy had been developed that he felt was stronger than the introductory "Sword" commercial. Was it right to put the brakes on the brand before its full potential was realized? Was Nabob over the long haul right to muzzle a brand that was in fact a superior coffee to its leading brand? What would be the repercussions to his own career if he placed the brand's profitability in front of the brand's volume? With these thoughts in mind, he began to decide the future strategy for Summit.

14 CNCP TELECOMMUNICATIONS

Scott J. Edgett

Gordon J. Lucas

Mary L. Volk

In early 1988, the executive team of CNCP Telecommunications faced an uncertain financial future: the mainstay of the company's revenues, Telex, was experiencing rapid declines, and none of the newly developed product initiatives were about to show large revenue gains in the upcoming year. Dick Cuthbert, vice-president of marketing for CNCP, had investigated several potential opportunities for the company and felt that a venture into Third Party Maintenance (TPM)[1] services would be a positive move for the company. However, he wanted to consider the implications of this move and what strategy CNCP should pursue if it entered the TPM market.

BACKGROUND

Moving into the late 1980s, the management of CNCP Telecommunications faced changes on the technical, regulatory, and ownership fronts.

Historically, Telex had been the principal source of revenue and profits for the firm. Based on technology developed in Germany in the 1930s, Telex is a telegraphic service where subscribers lease the use of a teleprinter. With this printer device, a message can be received or sent 24 hours per day. Telex, a reliable message service, was widely used by both large organizations, such as banks and manufacturing firms, and by smaller enterprises such as florists and travel agencies. CNCP dominated the Telex business with a market share of over 80% of the Canadian market of nearly $200 million in 1985. Telex was so well established as a brand name in the consumers' minds that competing services found advertising to be counter-productive. If Bell Canada advertised the benefits of TWX (a competing telegraphic service), CNCP's sales of Telex went up!

The Telex business was based on old switches, old terminals, and old transmission lines. As a result of using old, fully depreciated equipment to deliver a regulated service, CNCP was very profitable. However, this stability and large market share also contained the seeds of some serious problems. Telex was becoming obsolete.

[1] TPM is defined as the servicing of equipment which has not been sold by the servicing organizations.

DECLINE OF TELEX

New technical developments were eroding the use of Telex. One threat came from the introduction of computer networks that connected offices such as banks and travel agents around the world. These networks had been developed to automate money transfer and airline reservations. Once in place, the networks could also be used for the transmission of messages.

At the same time, in-house computers were being used for sending messages within the organizations that owned the computers. Telex was squeezed between these networks connecting related organizations on the one hand and in-house electronic mail systems on the other hand. These innovations had contributed to a dramatic decline in Telex revenue to $138 million in 1986 and a further decline to $120 million in 1987 (Exhibit 1).

Another change threatened to further accelerate the demise of Telex: facsimile transmission of documents had become practical. The development of a modern-looking, easily used fax machine sold by aggressive sales forces became known as the "fax revolution." Based on these developments, Telex revenues were forecast to be approximately $70 million in 1988.

ATTEMPT TO ENTER THE LONG DISTANCE BUSINESS

By the mid-1980s, CNCP's management had recognized the vulnerability of Telex revenues as the main financial support of the organization. The top management of CNCP had little industrial selling experience. Searching for a response to the threatened decline in Telex revenues, they did not see a likely victory in a confrontation with the telephone companies for the data transmission business of large organizations. They saw the prospect of relief in another direction—permission from Canada's federal regulators, the Canadian Radio-television and Telecommunications Commission (CRTC)[2], to provide competitive long distance telephone services.

The regulatory agencies in the United States had recently allowed competition in long distance voice services, and Canada had just elected a Conservative government. The road to regulatory change was long and difficult, but CNCP management was confident they could enter the telephone business. Competitive long distance was a booming industry in the United States, Canadians were frequent telephone users, and the prices of telephone services in Canada were over twice the comparable prices in the United States. Management spared no effort, but CNCP's application for permission to sell long distance services was rejected by the CRTC in 1986.

CNCP ENVIRONMENT

The evolution of CNCP Telecommunications is intertwined with the history of Canada. In 1881, the Canadian Pacific Railway was given the right by Parliament to build a telegraph line along its railway line. In 1886, the first trans-Canada telegram was

[2] The CRTC is responsible for administering all telecommunication and broadcast laws and regulations in Canada.

Exhibit 1
CNCP SELECTED FINANCIAL STATISTICS (1983 TO 1987)

	1987	1986	1985	1984	1983
Selected income and expense items ($000):					
Revenue[1]	316,522	343,757	349,124	338,093	315,014
Expenses excluding income taxes and unusual items	300,205	312,223	313,006	306,334	289,646
Unusual items before taxes[2]	21,460	—	—	—	—
Depreciation	47,058	52,226	49,124	46,809	44,753
Debt costs	15,796	16,562	16,469	15,683	16,349
Net income (loss)	(2,420)	13,975	16,584	15,524	12,506
Selected financial position items ($000):					
Net fixed assets	401,661	380,190	372,273	351,567	350,093
Capital expenditures	80,263	61,100	71,797	52,663	44,743
Total assets	450,830	431,821	433,713	414,085	401,925
Debt due to partners	153,493	139,387	145,044	134,619	154,508
Equity	203,085	206,581	199,564	194,290	175,014
Financial statistics:					
Debt ratio	43.0%	40.3%	42.1%	40.9%	46.9%
Return on average total capital					
Income before unusual items	6.4%	8.8%	9.8%	9.5%	8.6%
Net income	3.5%	8.8%	9.8%	9.5%	8.6%
Miscellaneous statistics:					
Employees	3,371	3,633	3,906	3,937	3,969
Salaries and wages ($000)	106,787	111,598	111,675	102,535	104,614
Revenue per employee ($)	93,896	94,621	89,381	85,876	79,369

Source: Company records

[1] Telex revenue was approximately $160 million in 1985, $138 million in 1986, and $120 million in 1987.

[2] The unusual items related to an early retirement program offered in 1987 and the write-down of assets related to obsolescent terminal and switching equipment.

transmitted from New Westminster, British Columbia to Canso, Nova Scotia, on Canadian Pacific's telegraph network. Similarly, the Canadian National Railway also developed a telegraph network, and for many decades the two companies competed for the telegraph business in Canada. As well, both provided national teleprinter services, and in the 1930s and1940s both added private line voice and teletype services.

In 1947, Canadian Pacific Telegraph (CPT) and Canadian National Telegraph (CNT) agreed to pool their operations in private wire services. Over the next two decades, the companies merged other parts of their operations and adopted the name of CNCP. By 1976, the two companies had rationalized their telecommunication networks and facilities. In 1980, CNCP Telecommunications was formed as a result of the formal merger of CPT and CNT. It was jointly owned by Canadian Pacific Limited (50%) and Canadian National Railways (50%).

CNCP Telecommunication's objective was to determine the communications needs of Canadians and to design solutions to these needs that are cost effective and employ affordable technical advances. The company fulfilled these objectives by providing a full range of voice and data services to the business community and a telegraph service to the general public. The principal revenue generating product had historically been the Telex.

Telex, a teleprinter network, had a tremendous impact on business-to-business communications in Canada when CPT and CNT introduced the service in 1956. The service grew rapidly, and, at its peak in 1985, reached more than 2,200 communities across Canada.

While Telex was the mainstay of CNCP's business for many years, CNCP had also introduced and offered a range of telecommunication services including:

- a Canada-wide microwave network (1964) that allowed for high speed transmission of data;
- computer message switching services (1964);
- Telenet (1966) which permitted communication between a Telex terminal and a user's private network;
- Broadband Exchange (1967), the first Canadian network capable of handling voice and high-speed data transmissions;
- Infodat (1978), a data network equipped with digital transmission technology;
- Infoswitch (1980), a hybrid public switched digital service.

More information on these and other more recent CNCP services are provided in Appendix 1.

The only other major provider of telecommunication operations was Telecom Canada. This company was an umbrella organization for provincial telephone companies (for example, B.C. Telephone), with Bell Canada as its largest member. Bell Canada had become Bell Canada Enterprises (BCE), owner of Northern Telecom, TransCanada Pipelines, and others. BCE was one of Canada's largest corporations, and in 1987 BCE had sales of $14.6 billion and net income of $1.1 billion. In the same year, Canadian Pacific had sales of $12.2 billion and net income of $640 million. BCE and other Telecom Canada members were the forces confronted by CNCP.

COMPANY ORGANIZATION

Since 1980, CNCP had been functionally organized. The emphasis was on operational control over quality of service and expenses. The sales and operations management in regions such as western Canada reported to separate superiors in Toronto and seldom worked together on customer situations or business plans.

In 1987, marketing was reorganized to concentrate on the needs, directions, and satisfaction of three groups of customers: large business users, general business users, and consumers. Marketing was designated as the central co-ordinating function: forecasting revenues, arranging co-ordination of the organization's resources to meet customer needs, and advising how to increase the market orientation of CNCP. In all other respects, CNCP remained functionally organized.

A NEW MANAGEMENT ERA

Within a three-year period (1986 to 1988), all of CNCP's senior executives retired. A new president, George E. Harvey, a senior executive from the computer and communications industry, was appointed in early 1987. On arrival at CNCP, Mr. Harvey took inventory of the situation. While all the energy of the management had been focused on a breakthrough in long distance telephone services, the Telex had continued to decline. By the summer of 1987, while Mr. Harvey was assembling a sales and marketing oriented executive team, CNCP had slipped to a breakeven financial position.

A key member of the new executive team was Dick Cuthbert. Raised and educated near Washington D.C., with early management experience with large U.S. firms including Texas Instruments and Xerox, he had lived in Canada for approximately ten years. He had been involved in technical management with Bell Northern Research and then in product management at CNCP. New service offerings introduced under his direction, were the bright spots in a tough situation in late 1987. Still, Mr. Cuthbert was very concerned that while Telex was declining, no clear successors were approaching the growth or maturity stage.

With energy and imagination, Mr. Harvey and his new sales executives were rejuvenating the sales force and leading it into major accounts and the next tier of prospective buyers. They were selling the services Mr. Cuthbert had been developing in his years as a product manager. However, these services were early in their development, and they were not expected to become established before the early 1990s. For example, in 1987, the company had experienced some growth in revenue from electronic mail and voice and data services (Dialcom), but this growth was not sufficient to replace the loss in Telex revenue.

CNCP's regulatory staff had regrouped after their long distance telephone setback and had submitted an application to the CRTC for permission to offer a facsimile transmission service. However, the application had been before the CRTC for nearly six months with no firm date for a ruling and no assurance of a favourable decision when it did come. Besides, facsimile transmission was another infant service, albeit one with substantial potential.

PLANNING FOR 1988

In a 1987 meeting with his team of marketing managers, Mr. Cuthbert conducted a brainstorming session. Emerging from this session was a list of ideas which responded to customer needs, had significant short-term margin potential, and used major CNCP strengths to achieve results. This list of ideas included emphasis on Third Party Maintenance (TPM) and the hiring of a consulting firm with marketing and computer services expertise to evaluate the prospects for TPM. The consultants provided the following information on TPM.

Exhibit 2
PROJECTED TRENDS IN MAINTENANCE PROVIDERS

	Market Share (%)	
	1986	1991
TPM Companies	9	22
Manufacturers	54	45
Distributors	37	33
Totals	100	100

Source: *Communication News*, based on data provided by Frost and Sullivan, a New York market research firm.

THIRD PARTY MAINTENANCE

Until the early 1980s, most purchasers of computer equipment had contracted with their computer vendors for the maintenance of that equipment. As the price of computer hardware declined, computer vendors increasingly relied on computer maintenance and software fees to maintain their revenues. At the same time, computer architecture had become more standardized so that a maintainer of one brand of computers could expand its capabilities to other brands without much difficulty.

Additionally, the organizations that serviced high-technology products enjoyed healthy growth rates which out-paced the other service sectors in the early 1980s. As a result of high and growing margins, the once captive service business of equipment vendors became vulnerable to other service organizations. This vulnerability gave rise to the TPM industry.

The TPM market supported a diversity of companies from small regional service organizations to the large mainframe manufacturers who regarded TPM service as a principal source of profit growth.

In the next several years, it was projected that the TPM service companies would gain market share from both manufacturers and their distributors (Exhibit 2).

In the immediate future, it was expected that the cost of TPM services would decrease, primarily due to the increased reliability of hardware coupled with the improvement of field service systems. Projections indicated that the healthy profits experienced in the TPM services would continue into the 1990s.

THE TPM MARKET IN CANADA

The TPM market in Canada was large and growing. Revenue forecasts for 1988 were projected at $248 million, $290 million for 1989, and $340 million for 1990.

Mergers and acquisitions had become a factor in TPM, as in other high technology areas. The following major ownership and other changes affected the Canadian TPM market:

- Bell Canada purchased TRW Data Systems (renamed Bell Technical Services Inc.);
- General Electric purchased AABEX Electronic Services;

- Apple purchased Miscoe Data Inc.;
- Sorbus (itself owned by Bell Atlantic, a U.S. company) used its sister company, MAI Canada Ltd., to market TPM in Canada.

The market had a large number of suppliers and no clear leader. While Bell Technical Services Inc., was significant in size, its revenues in 1987 represented only 13% of total Canadian services revenue and was essentially the same as that of the second largest service company, Computerland. In fact, the ten largest service companies' combined revenues represented less than 60% of the industry's 1987 total revenue (Exhibit 3).

When Mr. Cuthbert examined this information on the top service companies in Canada, he noticed that CNCP's market share would have been 3% of the total. He saw that this was a market without a leader and contrasted the TPM market situation with that of Bell Canada in long haul data traffic and with IBM Canada in mainframe computers. In those markets more than 60% went to the leader.

Mr. Cuthbert's consultants also pointed out that, according to Frost and Sullivan, Inc., the communications equipment TPM market was growing quickly in the United States. Exhibit 4 shows the sectors of TPM communications growth in the United States.

Since the competition for the TPM market in Canada had no clear leader, Mr. Cuthbert projected that competition was best understood by considering customers' expressed needs and how current and expected competitors would stack up against those needs. The consultant's report indicated that response time was the most

Exhibit 3
TOP SERVICE COMPANIES (1987 revenue in millions of dollars)

	Rank and Organization	TPM Service Revenue	Market Share
1	Bell Technical Services	$ 22.8	12.6%
2	Computerland Corp.	22.5	12.4
3	Richard Bessner & Assoc.	9.0	5.0
4	GE Computer Services	8.3	4.6
5	NCR Canada	7.8	4.3
6	Datatech Systems	7.6	4.2
7	Xerox Canada	7.2	4.0
8	Miscoe Data (Apple)	6.2	3.4
9	Honeywell Bull	6.1	3.3
10	CNCP	5.4	3.0
11	Testpoint	4.5	2.5
12	Computer Maintenance Co.	4.3	2.4
	All Other	69.7	38.3
	Total	$181.4	100.0

Sources: Evans Research, a Toronto market research firm, and CNCP's TPM revenue.

important factor followed by reputation (Exhibit 5). In Canada, fast response time posed a problem for many of the smaller regional service companies since many large TPM buyers required a wide range of geographic coverage. Also of concern to the Canadian buyer was the size of the TPM provider, which many buyers equated to reputation. Some buyers felt that smaller firms might not have the expertise to provide a quality service which would increase the risk of service disruption. A competitive price was important, but buyers seemed willing to pay a premium for a service that met their other demands. Finally, one-stop service (the ability of the service provider to fix all types and brands of equipment, regardless of the vendor)

Exhibit 4

UNITED STATES COMMUNICATIONS EQUIPMENT TPM REVENUES (in millions of U.S. dollars)

	1986	1991
Private branch telephone exchange (PABX)	$ 35	$ 188
Key/hybrid system	16	53
Local area network (LAN)	140	1199
Modem	55	186
Other	31	142
Totals	$277	$1768

Source: Frost and Sullivan, Inc.

Definitions*:

Private branch telephone exchange (PABX): a private automatic telephone exchange that provides for the transmission of calls to and from the public telephone network. For example, a business might install its own PABX which would be connected with Bell Canada for outside calls.

Key/Hybrid system (small telephone exchange): an arrangement of key telephone stations and associated circuitry, located in an organization/business, providing combinations of certain voice communication arrangements, such as multi-line pickup and call line status lamp signals. Typically, these key systems are located in small businesses.

Local area network (LAN): a system linking together computers, word processors, and other electronic office machines to create an inter-office, or inter-site network. These networks usually provide access to external networks, for example, public telephone and data transmission networks, information retrieval systems, and so on.

*Modem (**mo**dulator/**dem**odulator)*: a device that modulates and demodulates signals which allows computers to communicate using ordinary telephone lines.

* Source: Jerry M. Rosenberg, *Dictionary of Computers*, John Wiley and Sons, New York, 1987.

Exhibit 5
CANADIAN TPM BUYING CRITERIA

Need	Rank in 1987	Rank in 1985
Response time	1	1
Reputation	2	2
Price	3	4
One-stop service	4	3

Source: Evans Research

Exhibit 6
CNCP'S RELATIVE STRENGTHS BY USER CRITERION

	Response Time	Reputation	Price	One-stop Service
Modem maintenance	Equal except strong in remote locations	Good	Should be a strength	Can be a strength
Workstation maintenance	Same as above	Weak	Can be a strength	Can be a strength

had become a growing maintenance requirement in response to the proliferation of multiple vendors' equipment at most sites.

The Evans Research findings were used to establish a reasonable set of criteria in the evaluation of CNCP's competitive needs in two segments which were important in 1988—service to personal computers and other workstations[3] and service of modems. Mr. Cuthbert then decided to rank CNCP against its competitors and found that CNCP's principal competitive strengths for modem and workstation business were price in major centres and coverage in remote areas (Exhibit 6).

Another promising market for TPM services was local area network (LAN) systems (Exhibit 4). The market situation in LAN maintenance appeared to be rather different from that in modem and workstation maintenance. LAN technology was in its infancy and many firms (both suppliers and users) were "learning as they went along." Servicing LANs required a broad range of diagnostic, maintenance, and repair skills since both the machines and their inter-connections had to be serviced. However, in the LAN area, there were competitors in Canada who had experience installing and servicing LANs (Lanpar, Bell Technical Services, and a large number of small firms),

[3] A workstation consists of the hardware that permits interaction with a computer system, be it a mainframe or a multi-user micro. A simple keyboard/monitor combination and a microcomputer are both workstations.

Exhibit 7
LOCAL AREA NETWORK (LAN) MAINTENANCE NEEDS

Profile	Service	% Stated as Need	% Very Satisfied[1]
Large corporation	Additions to network	82	43*
	Hardware support	73	75
	Software support	64	71
	Consulting	64	66
	User training	64	38*
Medium corporation	Hardware support	83	70
	Software support	67	33*
	Additions to network	67	63
	User training	52	28*
Government	Hardware support	63	83

Source: York Enterprise Development Corporation, LAN Maintenance Survey

[1] Items shown with asterisks indicate areas where a significant service need was poorly met.

but the consultants' interviews suggested that users still felt a need for service that was not being provided. Exhibit 7 presents the major service requirements and user satisfaction levels with the levels of service being provided in the LAN maintenance market.

THE CNCP SITUATION

Armed with the consultants' information on the Canadian market size, growth, and areas of opportunity, Mr. Cuthbert turned his analysis to his company's current position. He knew that TPM was not an entirely new market opportunity for CNCP. In 1987, CNCP obtained $5.4 million in TPM revenues (Exhibit 8). Of that amount, $3.4 million was from the servicing of Telex equipment.

Mr. Cuthbert observed the following from his analysis of CNCP's maintenance revenues in 1987:

- CNCP's telecommunications equipment maintenance was dominated by the servicing of modems for CNCP and "Others" which represented 86% of CNCP's $2,509,000 telecommunications maintenance revenue.
- CNCP's "Other" TPM telecommunications revenue was dominated by three major customers whose modems CNCP maintained.
- CNCP did not perform LAN maintenance, the largest telecommunications maintenance sector with a strong projected growth rate.

Mr. Cuthbert concluded that CNCP was positioned relatively well to enter the TPM market in comparison to many potential competitors. CNCP's main relevant strengths, which the definition of the TPM strategy took into account, were summarized as:

- a known professional service company with broad geographic dispersion;
- an existing customer base which contained large, growing customers with a predominance in certain vertical markets (financial, transportation, and government);
- proven equipment maintenance expertise, dominated by modem maintenance and encompassing other vendors' equipment; and
- a potential for the addition of supplementary services based on current field services, resources, and skills.

In considering how he would bring about CNCPs entrance into the TPM market, Mr. Cuthbert summarized his thoughts as follows:

- CNCP was already a significant participant in a growing market that had no clear leader, but many aggressive participants.
- Modem maintenance, where CNCP was a large participant already, was very price competitive but offered CNCP the opportunity to sell remote service at enhanced prices.
- CNCP did not enjoy a proven reputation in PC-based and other workstation maintenance, which was a fiercely price-competitive market. Again, CNCP could sell remote maintenance at enhanced (but still low) prices.
- Maintenance of private network equipment (for example, PABX and key/hybrid systems as shown in Exhibit 4) presented an opportunity for CNCP to establish leadership in an emerging segment and to reap better profits than the above segments in both populated centres and remote locations.
- LAN TPM represented an opportunity for CNCP to take a position of competitive leadership although it might require a strategic partnership arrangement.

THE DECISION

While Mr. Cuthbert felt that an aggressive entry into the TPM market was possible, he was not certain how this market would evolve over the next few years. A further question was whether CNCP should attempt to service all of the segments of the TPM market or focus their efforts on one or two segments. As well, if any or all of these TPM segments were entered, he wondered what share CNCP could realistically achieve.

The more Mr. Cuthbert thought about the situation, the more questions came to mind. Should CNCP focus only on doing the maintenance it already knew how to do (for example, modems) and leave the more complex LAN and private network maintenance to more entrepreneurial companies? Would a strategy related to special maintenance services in a small number of major centres work better? How would CNCP train its technicians across the country in all these technologies? What kind of extra costs would be involved in implementing this strategy? Could the service be made attractive enough that the CNCP sales team would aggressively go after the TPM business? Would the service grow if he allowed it to be managed from within the existing CNCP organization? How could he help the new business unit succeed quickly, both within CNCP and in the market? Did it make overall sense to recommend another service initiative as part of the response to CNCP's business situation? Did other recommendations make more sense? "Questions, questions, questions" Mr. Cuthbert thought, "now it's time for answers and decisions."

Exhibit 8
CNCP'S 1987 MAINTENANCE REVENUES (in thousands of dollars)

Equipment	CNCP[1]	Other[2]	Total
Telex	$ —	$3,411	$3,411
Data communication/transmission	358	650	1,008
Office automation	—	10	10
Telecommunications	1,252	1,257	2,509
Service	119	83	202
Other	161	38	199
Total	$1,890	$5,449	$7,339

Source: Data provided by CNCP Strategic Market Information

[1] Maintenance of equipment owned and operated by CNCP (for example, earth stations owned and operated by CNCP).

[2] Maintenance of equipment operated by other business firms (for example, maintenance of Telex machines that were operated by banks, florists, or other businesses).

These revenue categories include

- *telex*: self-evident
- *data communication/transmission*: terminals, printers (for example, primarily involved with maintaining peripheral equipment such as keyboards, printers, monitors)
- *office automation*: teletex (word processing capabilities)
- *telecommunications*: modems, multiplexors, earth stations (for example, primarily involved with maintaining equipment used to transmit data over long distances)
- *services*: education, CNCP's software maintenance, administration fee
- *other*: unknown, not categorized

Appendix 1
CNCP PRODUCTS AND SERVICES

Message Services

WP Mail is a high-speed messaging service designed to meet the telecommunications requirements of the integrated electronic office. It provides for communication between word processing terminals of different manufacturers.

*Telepost** is offered jointly by CNCP and Canada Post. CNCP transmits messages electronically to the post office nearest the destination for next-day delivery. Input from Telex, telephone, and message centre services is available.

*Teletex** is a high-speed, letter-quality text communication that transmits information from desk-to-desk and continent-to-continent in seconds.

Telex is a teleprinter service offered throughout Canada and the world.

*Dialcom** is both a messaging service and a gateway to a number of the largest data bases in the world.

Data Services

*Infoswitch** is a public digital network that integrates networks and protocols into one high-performance, pay-for-use network.

Infodat is a private, digital data transmission service offering dedicated circuitry for terminal-to-computer and computer-to-computer communications for large organizations. Its applications include reservation systems, inventory control, and credit verification.

*Mach III** consists of integrated digital telecommunications products that handle a wide variety of customer communications needs, including private line voice networking, wideband data transmission, and the integration of voice, data, and video traffic over the same channels.

Voice Services

Broadband Exchange Service is a long distance voice and data network. The service offers quality transmission across Canada as well as access to the United States public telephone network.

*VoiceLine** a voice concentration technology that allows two long distance voice communications to occur simultaneously over a single channel, while at the same time maintaining voice quality and integrity over each path.

Source: Company Records

* Introduced since 1980.

15 CINEMA V REPERTORY THEATRE

Harrie Vredenburg

Mr. Thiery Martin sat in his office in January 1985, looking at the customer survey data he had recently received. He hoped it contained information on which he could build a new marketing program that he could present to Mr. Custom, the General Manager.

Cinema V, a repertory film theatre, was feeling the effects of its shrinking primary market, the English-speaking population of Montreal. Mr. Martin, Cinema V's Program Director and Assistant General Manager, was also worried about the possible impact of some of the new developments in the cinema industry. Cinema V would have to do some serious marketing, he felt, to increase its average utilized capacity from its present low of 35% to 50% within two years.

THE THEATRE

Cinema V Repertory Theatre was located on Sherbrooke Street, an important commercial and shopping street, near Décarie Boulevard in the west end of Montreal. It was approximately four kilometres west of the downtown core. The theatre was well served by public transit as it was located on the subway (metro) line and on a major bus route. Residential areas surrounding the theatre were predominantly English-speaking, although in recent years the proportion of French-speaking residents had been increasing. Within a three-kilometre radius of the theatre, there were approximately 14,000 occupied dwellings containing 12,000 English-speaking, 3,000 French-speaking, and 25,000 bilingual residents.

The theatre was owned by Mr. Michael Custom, a local entrepreneur who held interests in a number of Montreal enterprises, including two popular restaurants on the city's main downtown shopping street. Mr. Custom had been involved in the cinema business for a number of years, having at one time owned 18 theatres in the Montreal area.

Cinema V was a repertory theatre as opposed to a "first-run" theatre. Repertory film theatres specialized in showing films which had already had a first showing as a new release in a first-run theatre. Repertory cinemas obtained "second-run" films at a lower cost than first-run theatres and charged admission prices substantially lower than first-run theatres. Rather than showing one film for a week or longer as most first-run theatres did, repertory theatres generally showed different films each night of the week. As well, in one evening several films would generally be shown in different screening rooms at different times.

Cinema V had two screening rooms with seating capacities of 538 and 332. On most evenings two showings were held in each screening room. Besides the two screening rooms, the theatre had a large main lobby in which a concession stand was located. There was an additional area in the main lobby which was not being used. Mr. Martin was unsure as to how he might make this high traffic area productive, although he and Mr. Custom had discussed the possibility of using the space for a small in-house restaurant or a video cassette rental outlet.

Four employees were normally required to operate the theatre: a projectionist/night manager, a concession operator, a cashier, and a doorman. Daily cleaning of the theatre was contracted out and maintenance was contracted for as required. Total fixed costs for 1985, including all salaries, cleaning, heating/air conditioning, maintenance, and miscellaneous expenses were estimated at $150,000. In 1984, the technical facilities had been upgraded including the installation of a new $25,000 Dolby stereo system and an $8,000 state-of-the-art projection system. The new projection system eliminated the need for a second projectionist and had resulted in a saving of $25,000 per year in 1984.

HISTORY

The Cinema V premises were first opened in the 1920s as a nightclub. Known as the Empress, the theatre featured silent movies as well as vaudeville acts on the stage. Over the years the theatre earned a reputation for raciness bordering on bawdiness. Through the 1950s and 1960s, the theatre was operated as a first-run movie theatre showing newly released films.

In 1974, Mr. Custom was approached by a Mr. Friedman and a Mr. Miller who proposed to convert the theatre into a repertory cinema and manage it for a 50% share of the profits. Messrs. Friedman and Miller had observed the success of the Outremont Repertory Theatre, the first such theatre in Montreal, which had been in operation for a short time. As this theatre was located in the east central area of the city and catered to a predominantly French-speaking clientele, they felt that a repertory cinema in the west end, catering to the English-speaking population, would be equally successful.

For the following eight years Messrs. Friedman and Miller co-managed Cinema V, while Mr. Custom was not involved in its management. In 1982, Messrs. Friedman and Miller left Cinema V in order to start a competing repertory theatre several blocks away, which they named "The Monkland." Mr. Custom, who had taken over active management of Cinema V, was determined not to lose customers to his new rival and cut his prices. The Monkland theatre closed within a year and no new competitors had since appeared in the city's west end.

For a brief period, Mr. Custom employed a general manager for the day-to-day management of the theatre but then decided the business required his own attention. Mr. Martin was hired in 1983 as Program Director and Assistant General Manager, reporting to Mr. Custom.

INDUSTRY BACKGROUND

The film theatre industry has traditionally suffered from a high level of sales and earnings volatility. This volatility was attributed to the individual nature and popularity of each film and to rapidly changing public tastes. Industry sources maintained that the single most important factor influencing theatre attendance was the public's judgement of a particular film's entertainment and artistic merits.

Theatre revenues have historically not shown any correlation with economic conditions. Some industry sources argued that there might be an inverse relationship with economic conditions. Since going to the movies was a relatively inexpensive form of entertainment, people would go to the movies more during difficult economic times and reduce their expenditures on more expensive forms of entertainment.

Summer and Christmas were generally acknowledged as the most important seasons in the cinema industry. These were the leisure seasons, especially for the principal movie audience, persons under the age of 24. Between 1979 and 1983, 32.5% of annual Canadian box office receipts were generated during the summer months.

Canadian film theatre revenues continued to grow modestly during the late 1970s and early 1980s (Exhibit 1). Per capita expenditures increased by 39% from 1975 to 1983. A consolidation of the number of theatres was occurring; in Quebec the number of theatres declined by 27% between 1980 and 1983. Concurrent with this was a general trend towards an increased number of screening rooms per theatre. This allowed operators to increase the variety of films shown and to decrease the financial risk resulting from very unpopular films.

A number of individuals in the cinema theatre industry were becoming concerned about the possible impact of developments in the broader film industry. Home viewing of films was becoming a threat to the cinema theatre industry. In 1979, worldwide theatre showings accounted for 80% of a film's gross revenues. By 1984, it was estimated that the theatre portion had dropped to 60%. Significant increases in the film revenue generation had taken place in pay television, which in 1984 accounted for 17% of all movie revenues. Home video and disk systems grew from zero to an 8% share of film revenues between 1979 and 1984, and by the end of 1984 it was estimated that 28% of all Canadian households had a video cassette recorder.

Estimates of the future growth and importance of these alternative film distribution channels varied widely among industry sources. There was some evidence that the new channels were becoming more influential in film production and distribution decisions; films appeared to be being released for home viewing earlier than in the past. Some industry sources suggested that with an aging population the convenience of home viewing would become increasingly important.

THE MONTREAL CINEMA THEATRE INDUSTRY

The theatre industry in Montreal differed from other Canadian cities in that it reflected the bilingual nature of the city. First-run cinema theatres were targeted to either the French or English-speaking market. Films for the French-speaking market could be French language original films, or English or other language films dubbed or subtitled in French. Films for the English-speaking market were usually English language original films with the occasional non-English language film dubbed or subtitled in English. There were 33 French language cinemas with 58 screening rooms in the area known as the Montreal Urban Community. In addition, there were 19 English

Exhibit 1
CANADIAN BOX OFFICE STATISTICS

	1975	1976	1977	1978	1979	1980	1981	1982	1983
Number of Theatres									
Canada	1173	1129	1094	1079	1070	1037	1036	983	899
Quebec	345	333	322	310	299	280	264	235	205
Net Receipts from Admissions									
Canada ($ millions)	182.14	192.46	197.81	218.36	239.35	271.13	279.22	316.74	298.41
Quebec ($ millions)	44.04	46.95	46.58	49.70	51.43	54.11	54.03	58.59	62.92
Average Capacity Utilized									
Canada (%)	16	15	16	18	18	20	19	19	17
Quebec (%)	13	13	13	16	16	17	16	17	17
Average Admission Price									
Canada ($)	2.16	2.34	2.59	2.68	2.78	3.05	3.29	3.59	3.82
Quebec ($)	2.27	2.45	2.69	2.42	2.75	2.93	3.38	3.64	3.95
Per Capita Expenditures									
Canada ($)	10.04	10.49	10.48	11.20	12.16	13.01	13.81	14.98	13.94
Quebec ($)	8.63	9.09	9.01	9.73	10.32	9.77	10.49	10.94	11.65

Source: Canadian Film Digest, 1985

language theatres with 46 screening rooms in Montreal. The total population in the Montreal area exceeded 2.9 million people; approximately 500,000 were English-speaking (many of whom were bilingual), and approximately 1.9 million were French-speaking (many of whom were bilingual).

Unlike the first-run cinemas, which showed films either exclusively in French or in English, the repertory cinemas occasionally showed films in the second language. There were five French language repertory cinemas in Montreal and three English language repertory cinemas.

DEVELOPMENTS IN REPERTORY CINEMA

A number of changes in the film industry had a direct impact on repertory cinemas. Newly released films were becoming available for second-run showings much more quickly than in the past. Generally, new releases now become available for second-run showing about eight weeks after initial release in a market.

Repertory cinemas also began to obtain certain first-run films. These films tended to be "small budget," as opposed to Hollywood extravaganzas and covered unusual topics. They usually did not have mass market appeal. These films were available to repertory theatres because the major first-run cinema chains were not interested in them.

The earlier availability of newly released films and the availability of some first-run films were not exclusive to repertory cinemas. The video cassette industry had similar access to these films. Often films appeared in repertory cinemas and on the shelves of video cassette outlets at the same time. In some instances exclusive rights had been granted to video cassette producers, preventing repertory theatres from showing the films at all.

CINEMA V FILM PROGRAMMING

Cinema V showed a wide variety of films and did not focus on any particular genre. Foreign films, classics, cult films, documentaries and lesser known films all had their place on the schedule. As well, recent "first run" box office hits were regularly shown.

Periodically, film festivals were held. During a film festival, films in a certain category were exhibited frequently for a period of 6 to 8 weeks. These film festivals were given priority with respect to promotion.

Films were shown daily throughout the week. There were four showings each evening at 7:00, 7:15, 9:00 and 9:30. On Sundays there were also four matinee showings featuring children's films.

Cinema V obtained films from film distributors. There were 35 film distributors in Quebec, although only about ten were of a significant size. Distributors generally demanded a fee of 37.5% of the box office receipts. Box office receipts were verified by the distributors sending "checkers" to a cinema on unannounced visits. Once a film was booked with a distributor, the booking theatre had exclusive rights to the film in the Montreal area. This policy often resulted in theatres competing for the rights to certain films. This was especially prevalent when the film in question was a recent first-run box office hit. Cinema V typically booked films two weeks prior to releasing its bimonthly film schedule.

CINEMA V PRICING

Mr. Custom believed that his repertory cinema prices should be about 50% of the price of admission to first-run theatres, which ranged from $5 to $5.50. In addition, he felt that because of his west end location he should keep his prices below those of his downtown competitors.

The price of admission to most films was $2.50. For some festival films, usually those which were first-run, the price of admission was raised to $5. A senior citizen and children's price of $0.99 existed. In addition, regular filmgoers could purchase a package of 10 admission tickets for $20. The $2.50 ticket price included a $0.23 amusement tax. Attendance averaged about 4,000 persons per week, with the weekend accounting for the largest numbers (Exhibit 2). Precise sales data for the concession stand were not available. Based on industry estimates, the average movie-goer spent $1.50 on concessions, which generated a contribution margin of $0.50.

Exhibit 2

MONTHLY ATTENDANCE AT CINEMA V FROM JUNE 1982 TO MAY 1984

	1982–83	1983–84
June	16,500	13,800
July	14,300	17,800
August	18,900	19,200
September	18,200	20,100
October	13,100	19,000
November	11,200	18,000
December	10,500	13,800
January	15,200	20,200
February	11,500	13,500
March	11,600	16,700
April	15,300	16,500
May	14,100	18,000

AVERAGE DAILY ATTENDANCE AT CINEMA V FROM JUNE 1983 TO MAY 1984

Sunday	787
Monday	456
Tuesday	416
Wednesday	430
Thursday	406
Friday	606
Saturday	867
Average per day	567
Average per week	3,968

CINEMA V PROMOTION

The primary promotional vehicle used was the printed film schedule. The schedule consisted of a two-month calendar printed on an 11½ × 18 inch double-sided poster. Under each day and date the titles of the films to be shown were listed along with a short description of the film. A sample program is provided in Exhibit 3.

Approximately a million schedules were printed every eight weeks and were distributed to some 250 locations throughout the downtown and west end areas. Schedules could be picked up in magazine and record stores, restaurants, public areas in the four local universities, public libraries, and other places. Costs associated with the schedules were as follows: layout $300, typesetting $250, printing $3,500, and distribution $600, for a total cost of $4,650.

Cinema V also provided a phone-in service. Customers dialing the theatre's telephone number heard a recorded message describing the movies to be shown that evening and the times at which they were to be shown. The cost of this service was approximately $40, consisting of the monthly telephone charge and the one-time cost of the tape recorder/answering machine.

All the local repertory cinemas received a free listing of their daily programs in the two main daily newspapers, *La Presse* and *The Gazette*. Paid newspaper advertisements were occasionally used by Cinema V to promote a film festival or a premiere showing of a popular film. The cost of a 4 × 5 inch daily advertisement was about $350. The cost of an advertisement was often split between the theatre and the film distributor, who would also stand to gain from higher attendance.

Although advertisements were normally placed in the English-language daily, *The Gazette*, Mr. Martin had recently tried an advertisement in the French-language *La Presse*. To his surprise, he found that attendance at the promoted films appeared to have increased.

THE COMPETITIVE ENVIRONMENT

There were seven other repertory cinemas in Montreal: five of these were primarily French language, and two were primarily English language theatres.

None of the French language repertory cinemas were located in the downtown area, although all were easily accessible by public transit. The number of screens and seating capacities of the repertory cinemas is shown in Exhibit 4. The Outremont theatre was the most successful of the French language repertories. It was the oldest of the Montreal's repertories, had the greatest seating capacity, and was very well maintained. Recently it had opened a video cassette rental operation on the theatre premises.

Both of Cinema V's English language competitors, the Conservatoire d'Art Cinématographique and the Seville, were located in the downtown area. The Seville was located on Ste. Catherine Street, Montreal's busy downtown shopping street, where it could benefit from a high volume of pedestrian traffic.

The Conservatoire d'Art Cinématographique was operated by Concordia University. It operated on a year-round basis as a repertory cinema, unlike most university-based student cinemas. Movies shown differed from those of other repertory cinemas

Exhibit 3
EXAMPLE OF CINEMA V SCHEDULE

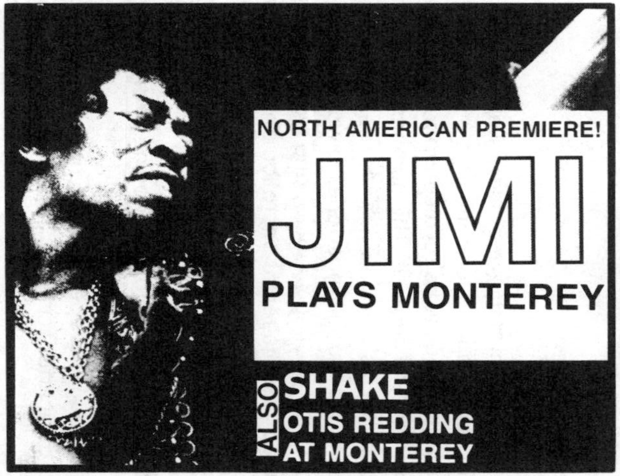

CINEMA V

"SHOULD BE SEEN BY ANYONE WISHING TO
UNDERSTAND THE NATURE OF THE ATOMIC AGE"
—ROLLING STONE
HALF LIFE
1954.
Marshall Islands.
South Pacific.
Code Name: BRAVO

SEPTEMBER

23 SUNDAY AUGUST

1:00 **THE LORD OF THE RINGS**
(1978 USA) 130 min. (G) D: Ralph Bakshi. Animated version of the classic J.R.R. Tolkien tale of Hobbits, Middle-earth and the ring that gives unlimited power.

2:00 **BODY HEAT**
3:30 **RADIO DAYS**
4:00 **THE GODS MUST BE CRAZY**
5:30 **CASABLANCA**
7:00 **THE GODS MUST BE CRAZY**
(1983 Botswana) 109 min. (G) D: Jamie Uys. W: Xao (as the Bushman), Marius Weyers. A coca-cola bottle thrown out of an airplane lands in the desert. Considering it as an unwanted gift from the Gods, a Bushman goes looking for the edge of the world to return it.

7:15 **RADIO DAYS**

9:15 **CASABLANCA**
(1942 USA) 102 min. (G) D: Michael Curtiz. W: Humphrey Bogart, Ingrid Bergman, Peter Lorre, Claude Rains. A classic blend of romance, intrigue, suspense, humour and Hollywood.

9:30 **BODY HEAT**
(1981 USA) 113 min. (18) D: Lawrence Kasdan. W: William Hurt, Kathleen Turner. Murder, lust, avarice and betrayal, plenty of sex, sweat and smart talk.

24 MONDAY AUGUST

7:00 **A TOUCH OF EVIL**
(1958 USA) 108 min. (14) D: Orson Welles. W: Charlton Heston, Orson Welles, Janet Leigh, Marlene Deitrich. "Narc Heston and corrupt cop Welles tangle over murder investigation in sleazy Mexican border town, with Heston's bride Leigh the pawn of their struggle. Fantastic, justifiably famous opening shot merely commences stylistic masterpiece, dazzlingly photographed by Russell Metty."—Leonard Maltin

7:15 **LOVE AND DEATH**
(1975 USA) 85 min. (G) D: Woody Allen. W: Woody Allen, Diane Keaton, Zvee Scooler. Woody Allen plays a Russian trying to avoid the draft in the Napoleonic War. A brilliant parody of every film made from a Russian novel.

9:00 **EDWARD MUNCH**
(1976 Norway/Sweden) 167 min. (G) D: Peter Watkins. W: Geir Westby, Gro Fraas. An obsessively detailed and meticulously researched study of the tortured Expressionist painter. Through montage it creates a life and madness of its own.

9:15 **RADIO DAYS**

25 TUESDAY AUGUST

7:00 **THE QUIET EARTH**
(1985 New Zealand) 100 min. (G) D: Geoff Murphy. W: Bruno Lawrence, Alison Routledge, Pete Smith. A scientist wakes up one day to find his top-secret energy project has evidently eliminated the rest of humanity. He finds two other survivors, and the scene is set for a struggle in this unusual, strikingly photographed film.

7:15 **TWIST AND SHOUT**
(See August 9)

9:15 **THE ASSAULT**

9:45 **THE TENANT**
(1976 USA) 124 min. (14) D: Roman Polanski. W: Roman Polanski, Isabelle Adjani, Shelley Winters. A man rents an apartment in which the previous tenant committed suicide and is driven mad by his new environment.

26 WEDNESDAY AUGUST

7:00 **BOB DYLAN DONT LOOK BACK**
(1967 USA) 96 min. (G) D: D.A.Pennebaker. W: Bob Dylan, Joan Baez, Donovan, Alan Price, Albert Grossman, Allen Ginsberg. Bob Dylan on tour through Engand in 1965, performing and reacting to his newfound popularity. "A running, jumping, and standing still portrait of the American rock star as a young oracle...DON'T LOOK BACK is blessed with the spontaneous and untapped comic talent of Dylan himself." — New York Times

7:15 **PROVIDENCE**
(1977 G.B.) 104 min. (14) D: Alain Resnais. W: Dirk Bogarde, John Gielgud, Ellen Burstyn, David Warner. A writer tries to complete his final novel, and mixes his imagined thoughts with real-life encounters.

9:15 **GARDENS OF STONE**
(See August 25)

9:30 **ANDY WARHOL'S BAD**
(1976 USA) 105 min. (18) D: Jed Johnson. W: Carroll Baker, Perry King, Susan Tyrrell. A gross comedy of chic disgust; a housewife heads a gang of assassins for hire. A picture with something to offend absolutely everybody.

27 THURSDAY AUGUST

7:00 **HALF LIFE**
(See September 7)

7:15 **WOODY ALLEN'S Sleeper**
(1973 USA) 88 min. (14) D: Woody Allen. W: Woody Allen, Diane Keaton. Woody Allen is frozen and awakens in 2173, where people are tortured by being forced to watch reruns of Howard Cossell on TV.

9:15 **PARIS, TEXAS**
(1984 Germany/France) 145 min. (G) D: Wim Wenders. W: Harry Dean Stanton, Nastassja Kinski, Dean Stockwell, Hunter Curson. inner of the Palme d'Or at the 1984 Cannes Film Festival. After a four-year absence, a man turns up to claim his young son and start a search for his wife. Music by Ry Cooder.

9:30 **STRANGER THAN PARADISE**
(1984 USA) 89 min. (G) D: Jim Jarmusch. W: John Lurie, Eszter Balint, Richard Edson. An oddly touching offbeat comedy about two losers

28 FRIDAY AUGUST

7:00 **FELLINI'S 8 1/2**
(1963 Italy) 137 min. (G) D: Federico Fellini. W: Marcello Mastroianni, Anouk Aimée. A stupendous, brilliant and baffling filmic psychoanalysis by Fellini of the fantasies and real life happenings of a director having artistic difficulties. One of the truly great films of modern times.

7:15 **FELLINI'S AMARCORD**
(1973 Italy France) 123 min. (18) D: Federico Fellini W: Tonino Guerra, Federico Fellini. A memory, as only Fellini can remember, of a year in the seaside town of Rimini in the 30's.Dazzling, remarkable imagery.

9:15 **ON COMPANY BUSINESS**
(1981 USA) 180 min.(G) D: Allen Francovich. A powerful and detailed exposé of the "dirty tricks" used by the CIA over the last thirty years to influence international politics by intervening in the internal events of foreign governments. **Admission: $5.00 (Members $4.00)**

9:30 **MY DINNER WITH ANDRÉ**
(1982 USA) 111 min. (G) D: Louis Malle. W: André Gregory, Wallace Shawn, Jean Lenauer. A fascinating film of a conversation which becomes increasingly surrealistic.

29 SATURDAY AUGUST

4:00 **RAISING ARIZONA**

4:15 **84 CHARING CROSS ROAD**

7:00 **MONTEREY POP**

7:15 **84 CHARING CROSS ROAD**
(See July 30)

9:15 **RAISING ARIZONA**
(See July 26)

9:30 **STEAMING**
(See July 26)

11:45 **SUPER VIXENS**
(1975 USA) 105 min. (18) D: Russ Meyer. W: Shari Eubank, Charles Napier. Monstrous women roam the desert, brutalizing hapless males.

12:00 **THE ROCKY HORROR PICTURE SHOW**
(1975 G.B.) 100 min. (18) D: Jim Sharman. W: Tim Curry, Susan Sarandon, Barry Bostwock, Richard O'Brien. An outrageously kinky horror movie spoof, spiced with sex, transvestism, and rock music, about a straight couple stranded in an old dark house full of weirdos from Transylvania.

Exhibit 4
MONTREAL AREA REPERTORY CINEMAS

Cinema	Language	Admission Price	Number of Screens	Seating Capacity	Number of Showings Per Week
Cinema V	English	2.50	2	538/332	28
Seville	English	2.99	1	922	16
Conservatoire d'Art Cinématographique	English	2.00	1	700	11
Outremont	French	3.25	1	1291	18
Ouimetoscope	French	3.00	2	641/275	31
Cinémathèque Québécoise	French	3.00	2	411/330	13
Cinéma Parallèle	French	3.00	1	75	14
L'Autre Cinéma	French	3.25	2	222/144	28

in that older and foreign films made up the largest portion of the program. Popular films were not shown. Each eight-week schedule had a theme, such as Japanese cinema or Russian cinema. Subtitles were generally in English.

Cinema V's most significant competitor was the Seville. The Seville catered to an English-speaking audience and showed a range of films similar to Cinema V. The two theatres constantly competed for the rights to popular first-run films as they became available to repertory cinemas.

The Seville had only one screening room, with a seating capacity of 922. As a result, only two films could be shown per evening. Unlike Cinema V, the Seville had not switched to the more up-to-date Dolby sound system, but still used the older technology Kintek system. The Seville advertised a "giant screen," although the screen's actual size was only marginally larger than those at Cinema V.

The Seville charged an admission price of $2.99 for most films. Senior citizen and children's prices were the same as those at Cinema V. The Seville offered regular customers a one-year membership for $5. Membership entitled one to buy regular admission tickets for $2 and to obtain discounts on special events like film festivals.

The Seville had traditionally printed and distributed a schedule similar to Cinema V's (Exhibit 5). In addition to distributing to the same locations as Cinema V's schedules, the Seville distributed theirs to downtown highrise apartment buildings. Recently the schedule was changed to a four-page magazine format and included paid advertisements. The Seville also operated a recorded telephone message service.

In addition to monitoring his repertory cinema competitors, Mr. Martin also kept a watchful eye on the activities of one of the first-run cinema chains. The Cineplex chain operated one outlet in Montreal but was rumoured to be planning further expansion in the city. The current Cineplex outlet was located downtown and consisted of nine screening rooms. Cineplex was using practices which blurred the traditional lines between first-run cinemas and repertory cinemas. Cineplex was showing films for much longer runs than traditional first-run cinemas. It was also

Exhibit 5
FROM MAIN COMPETITOR'S SCHEDULE

FESTIVAL
SEVILLE
GIANT SCREEN
2155 O. rue Ste. Catherine St. W.
1 Block East of Atwater Metro
Bus Terminus and the Forum
Bus lines: 90, 115, 15, 37, 144, 138, 24
After midnight: 105, 106
TEL.: 932-1139 (24 hrs)
PLEASE: call ahead to confirm showings.
S.V.P. Veuillez nous téléphoner à l'avance pour confirmer les représentations des films.
REGULAR ADMISSION $2.99
MEMBERS $2.00
Golden Agers and Children 12 and under:
L'Âge d'Or et les enfants de 12 ans ou moins: 99¢*

* typical schedule would follow

showing some lesser known films in several screening rooms. The chain also appeared to be prepared to cut prices below those of traditional first-run cinemas; it had recently started charging an admission price of $2 on Tuesdays.

THE CUSTOMER SURVEY

Mr. Martin felt that the Montreal cinema theatre industry was undergoing some profound changes. He sensed that unless Cinema V became much more proactive, it could become a victim of these changes. The first step to proposing a strategic plan for survival, he thought, was to develop a better understanding of Cinema V patrons. With the help of a well-known business school located in the city, a survey was carried out in November 1984.

Data was gathered on customer demographics (Exhibit 6) and customer awareness of and attitudes to various aspects of Cinema V operations (Exhibits 7 to 12). Due to cost constraints it was not possible to collect data on customers who, for whatever reasons, no longer attended the theatre. A stratified sample was taken of current patrons over a period of seven days. The proportion of the sample drawn on each evening was equivalent to the proportion of weekly customers attending that particular evening (for example, on average, 25% of weekly attendance was on Saturday evening, thus 25% of the sample was drawn on that night). The total sample size was 200.

A systematic random sampling plan was used in which every third customer in line to view a film was approached by one of two researchers to fill in a self-administered questionnaire. On average, it took about five minutes to fill in the questionnaire. Non-response was virtually zero as customers were interested in the survey topic and were not occupied with any other activity.

Mr. Martin glanced at his desk calendar. He would be meeting with Mr. Custom at the end of the month. Given the lead times required to negotiate with film distributors, design a program, and have schedules printed and delivered, he would have to have his recommendations ready for this month's meeting, if changes were to be implemented for the important summer season.

Exhibit 6
DEMOGRAPHIC PROFILE OF CINEMA V FILMGOERS

	Number	Percentage
Age		
15–24	100	50.3
25–34	54	27.1
35–50	30	15.1
51–65	10	5.0
65 +	5	2.5
	199	100.0
Occupation		
Employed	93	47.2
Unemployed	20	10.2
Student	75	38.1
Other	9	4.5
	197	100.0
Language Spoken Most Often		
English	129	67.2
French	48	25.0
Other	15	7.8
	192	100.0
Mode of Transportation		
Walk	55	28.4
Bus/Metro	71	36.6
Car	65	33.5
Other	3	1.5
	194	100.0

Exhibit 7
MOVIE GOING HABITS OF CINEMA V FILMGOERS

	Number	Percentage
Attend Movies Frequently (More Than Twice a Month)		
Yes	147	73.5
No	53	26.5
	200	100.0
Language of Films Most Often Seen		
English	157	84.0
French	26	13.9
Other	4	2.1
	187	100.0
First Time Seeing Film in Attendance for		
Yes	165	84.2
No	31	15.8
	196	100.0
Main Reason for Attending Particular Showing at Cinema V		
For the Film	117	66.1
Lower Price	23	13.0
Night Out	26	14.7
Closest Cinema	8	4.5
Other	3	1.7
	177	100.0

Exhibit 8
ADVERTISING EFFECTIVENESS AS SEEN BY CINEMA V FILMGOERS

	Number	Percentage
How Learned Which Film Was Playing		
Cinema V Schedule	112	53.3
Telephone	19	9.1
Newspaper Listing	59	28.1
Friend	16	7.6
Other	4	1.9
	210*	100.0
Schedule Seen in Last Two Months		
Yes	141	71.2
No	57	28.8
	198	100.0
Aware of Cinema V Pass		
Yes	117	58.8
No	82	41.2
	199	100.0

* Exceeds 200 because of multiple answer possibilities

Exhibit 9
EXPANSION PREFERENCES OF CINEMA V FILMGOERS

	Number	Percentage
Type of Expansion Desired by Cinema V Filmgoers		
Video Rental Shop	35	22.6
Small Restaurant	90	58.1
Other	30	19.3
	155	100.0

Exhibit 10

CINEMA V FILMGOERS' SATISFACTION WITH PRESENT SITUATION

	Number	Percentage
Satisfied with Service		
Yes	178	94.2
No	11	5.8
	189	100.0
Satisfied with Cleanliness		
Yes	123	65.8
No	64	34.2
	187	100.0
Satisfied with Price		
Yes	186	97.4
No	5	2.6
	191	100.0
Satisfied with Projection (Focus, Sound, Etc.)		
Yes	127	68.3
No	59	31.7
	186	100.0
Satisfied with Overall Selection of Films		
Yes	141	73.4
No	51	26.2
	192	100.0

Exhibit 11
COMPARISON OF CINEMA V TO COMPETITORS BY CINEMA V FILMGOERS

	Number	Percentage
Repertory Cinemas Visited in Last 12 Months		
Cinema V	180	90.0*
Seville	119	59.5
Outremont	46	23.0
Ouimetoscope	26	13.0
C.A.C.**	38	19.0
Repertory Cinema Most Often Visited		
Cinema V	131	68.9
Seville	31	16.3
Outremont	16	8.4
Ouimetoscope	4	2.1
C.A.C.	8	4.2
	190	99.9
Number of Times Attended Cinema V in Last 12 Months		
1 to 3	66	33.8
4 to 6	51	26.2
7 or more	78	40.0
	195	100.0

* Using base of 200
** (C.A.C.: Conservatoire d'Art Cinématographique)

Exhibit 12
FILM TASTES OF CINEMA V FILMGOERS

	AGE GROUPS											
	Total		15–24		25–34		35–50		51–65		65+	
Type of Films	Mean	Std. Error	Mean	Std. Error	Mean	Std. Error	Mean	Std. Error	Mean	Std. Error	Mean	Std. Error
Comedies	4.0	0.07	4.1	0.10	4.1	0.13	3.9	0.18	3.5	0.43	3.8	0.37
Dramas	3.9	0.08	3.7	0.12	4.3	0.11	3.8	0.23	4.5	0.22	4.4	0.40
Science Fiction	2.9	0.10	3.1	0.14	3.1	0.19	2.5	0.25	2.0	0.42	2.4	0.51
Cult Films	2.4	0.09	2.6	0.14	2.4	0.16	2.0	0.24	1.9	0.48	1.4	0.25
Foreign Films	3.4	0.10	3.3	0.14	3.4	0.17	3.8	0.24	3.8	0.39	3.4	0.75
Musicals	2.8	0.10	2.6	0.14	2.7	0.18	3.0	0.25	3.3	0.42	4.4	0.60
Sample Size	n = 193		n = 98		n = 50		n = 30		n = 10		n = 5	

NOTE: Based on 5-point attitudinal scale,

Don't Like		Fair		Like a Lot
1	2	3	4	5

16 VARITY CORPORATION

Thomas Funk

Maryann Bauer

Craig Baxter

It was August 10, 1988, and Bud Cruise, president of Varity Corporation, was seated comfortably in his first-class seat on Air Canada flight 634 from Kansas City to Toronto. As he reflected on some of the facts and information he had just gathered from farmers and equipment dealers throughout the midwestern United States, he realized the decisions he faced were even more difficult than expected.

The Central Electronics Group, a division of Varity Corporation, was in the process of developing what they called a Field Optimization System (F.O.S.) that would monitor the moisture content and yield of grain within a farmer's field. This would provide information that would help the farmer better manage crop production activities. One component of the F.O.S., a grain mass-flow monitor had been developed and was ready for market. The engineering department had developed the monitor technology and was confident of its future success. Barney Watt, vice-president of marketing, was not so certain. He felt the potential for the monitor was limited, and that this product represented "another monument to engineering." On the other hand, the director of engineering, Dan Detwheeler argued that "marketing was a brake on the wheel of progress." He felt for years that farmers had been waiting for a workable monitor. Mr. Cruise had heard these opinions many times before.

The decision concerning whether to market the monitor was critical to Varity. It required that Mr. Cruise consider many questions. What is the market potential for the monitor? At what price should the product be introduced? Who is the target market? Should the monitor be marketed in the Original Equipment Market (O.E.M.) or aftermarket or both? How should the monitor be promoted? All of these questions had to be answered before the next meeting of the Board of Directors in two weeks time.

THE COMBINE INDUSTRY

Combines, sophisticated machines costing as much as $200,000, are used by farmers to harvest a wide variety of crops. While the basic combine is relatively standard, farmers typically buy them with a variety of features to customize the machine. This can either be for functional purposes (based on the crop) or for other

This case is based on research conducted by Peter Evans for his M.Sc. Thesis at the University of Guelph.

reasons (air conditioning for the cab). Combines are a major visible item purchased by farmers and are a source of pride to them, much as automobiles are to many of their owners.

In recent years, declining combine sales characterized the North American farm equipment market. Major manufacturers experienced a 47% reduction in total combine sales over the past five years. In Canada, the number of units decreased from a high of 4,915 units five years ago to a low of 2,601 in the current year; similar figures for the United States were 26,831 and 8,407 respectively. Many industry observers argued that declining incomes among farmers, due to falling commodity prices and rising interest rates, caused these trends.

Manufacturers were hoping that combine sales would rise as more and more farmers would have to replace their old combines. Five years ago, the average age of combines throughout North America was between 10 and 12 years. Given the expected 15-year product lifespan for combines, manufacturers predicted that it was about time for the downward sales trend to be reversed. There were, however, no signs of this occurring yet. It appeared that farmers were prepared to continue repairing their combines instead of buying new ones. As well, some farmers purchased used combines that became available due to farm bankruptcies or other farmers' trade-ins on new combines. Thus, combine sales continued to decline with manufacturers experiencing grossly under-utilized production capacities. At the present time, only 20% of the industry's total production capacity was being used. The massive slowdown resulted in widespread layoffs, corporate bankruptcies, and a drastic consolidation of manufacturing capacities.

Over the past several years, the market shares held by the leading combine manufacturers had remained relatively stable. For years, John Deere held the largest share of the market. Other full-line equipment manufacturers included Massey-Ferguson, Case-IH (formed when Case and International Harvester merged), Allis Chalmers, and New Holland. Currently, John Deere was thought to hold a 40% market share, Case-IH 28%, Massey-Ferguson 14%, Allis Chalmers 14%, and New Holland 5%. Each manufacturer had a local dealer in most farming areas and customer loyalty was tied to the dealer as well as the manufacturer.

THE COMPANY

Massey-Ferguson had for many years been considered an institution among farmers. It was believed that the company made an excellent product and was usually the first to introduce new advances in harvesting technology. Declining company sales, however, particularly for combines, were a major concern at Massey-Ferguson. Last year the combine division lost $12 million dollars. It soon became apparent to management that the company's survival was no longer ensured through the sale of farm equipment alone.

Massey-Ferguson began to diversify in an attempt to take advantage of other opportunities, to minimize risk, and to achieve overall success for the company. Massey-Ferguson's new direction was ultimately symbolized by a change in the company's name from Massey-Ferguson to Varity Corporation. The entire company was restructured. This included setting up the combine operation as a new company called Massey Combines in which Varity held a 45% interest. In addition, another new division called Central Electronics Group (C.E.G.) was established with the mandate of developing new electronic systems for all Varity divisions and affiliated companies. Its first assignment was the Field Optimization System.

THE TECHNOLOGY

The Central Electronics Group at Varity had been investing a great deal of time and money in the development of the Field Optimization System. The system provided a significant competitive advantage that other companies could not easily imitate. The F.O.S. is an advanced technology that enables a farmer to conveniently and accurately monitor (1) the moisture content, and (2) the yield of a crop during harvest. These factors were currently measured by farmers in far less sophisticated ways. Farmers often complained, however, that current methods (see below) generated inaccurate information and were a nuisance to use. Obtaining such information in a convenient way was a need frequently voiced by farmers.

Moisture Content

Information about the moisture level of a crop is important to the farmer. The level of moisture is critical to the length of time grain can be stored while still maintaining acceptable quality. As a result, grain elevators that purchase grain from farmers pay according to how close the moisture level is to an optimal level. Because of its importance, farmers currently use a variety of methods to estimate moisture levels. These range from the simple to the complex, and reflect different levels of accuracy. Among the simplest methods is for the farmer to walk through a field, obtain samples of grain, and simply "feel" the samples. A more accurate estimate can be obtained by measuring the moisture of the samples with a moisture meter which can be located on the farm. Meters, which are similar to those used at grain elevators, are accurate, but expensive; therefore, only the large-scale farmers typically purchase a meter for on-farm use. Another drawback of this method is that proper sampling can be a time-consuming procedure. As a result, many farmers tend to avoid taking enough samples for an accurate measurement.

Yield

Information on crop yield is of obvious value to the farmer. There are a number of inputs such as seed, pesticides, and fertilizer involved in maximizing the potential for a bumper crop. What the farmer needs is some method of objectively assessing the output, or yield, of the crop. With this information, the farmer can determine how crops respond to different levels and types of inputs. This, of course, allows the farmer to make improved decisions on input use in the future.

There are four methods that farmers currently use to estimate yields. Three, however, provide only rough estimates. In the first, visual observation, the farmer simply compares the height or density of the crop in one area of the field with another area. Understandably, this approach is extremely inaccurate; quite often the height or density of plants is not related to yield. A second method is more accurate, but also more time consuming. It involves hand harvesting small areas of a field, weighing the grain from these areas, and then using conversion charts to calculate yields on a per acre or per hectare basis. The third method occurs during harvest. The farmer simply notes the amount of grain in the holding bin on his combine after each section of his land has been harvested. Sometimes this information is documented by the farmer and the low-yield areas may be managed differently next year.

The fourth method is more accurate, but somewhat inconvenient. It involves marking the field off in grids and actually weighing loads of grain from each grid to get an accurate estimate of yield variability throughout a field. In using this method, the moisture level of each load must also be obtained. If moisture corrections are not made, the weight of water in the grain can be mistaken for dry matter, and this will distort the actual yield estimate. With the first three methods no corrections are made for moisture. While the final method for estimating yield provides superior information, farmers seldom have the time during harvest season to carry out such a tedious procedure.

PRODUCT DEVELOPMENT

The C.E.G. had invested nearly $1.5 million in the development of the F.O.S. over the past three years. Research efforts to date had concentrated on one component of the F.O.S., the grain mass-flow monitor, which was ready for market. The critical component of the monitor was an electronic probe that continually analyzed the grain as it was harvested. The probe sends a signal to the monitor located in the cab of the combine. The monitor can display the following information:

1. *Total Grain Harvested*—The pounds or kilograms of grain taken off the field up to that point in the harvest.
2. *Harvest Rate*—The number of pounds or kilograms being harvested per unit length at the current time.
3. *Instant Grain Moisture*—The moisture content of the grain at the current time.
4. *Total Area Harvested*—The area in square feet, acres, or hectares that has been harvested since the unit was last initialized.
5. *Instantaneous Yield per Unit Area*—The yield, corrected for moisture, at that instant during the harvest.
6. *Average Yield*—The total weight of grain taken off the field divided by the area over which that grain was harvested.

The monitor was quite similar to the dashboard computerized systems available on some cars. At the push of a button the dashboard would show a digital display of fuel consumption, level of fuel in the tank, how far one could travel at the current rate of consumption, and many other convenient and important bits of information. Comparable information would be provided to the farmer using the monitor.

Yield calculations are possible because the mass of grain passing by the probe is linked to a ground-speed sensor and the width of the combine. The farmer has the option of purchasing a printer which can provide a printed copy of the information being monitored. Varity anticipated selling the printer at a price of $200, which would give Varity a mark-up of 30% on the printer.

Tests conducted by the C.E.G. determined that the monitor was quite accurate in measuring both mass and moisture. The accuracy of the moisture readings was comparable to most on-farm moisture meters. Moreover, field tests had shown that once installed the unit was completely stable and required minimal maintenance. The mass-flow monitor was designed to fit on all makes and models of combines.

The Central Electronics Group felt there were a number of practical uses for the F.O.S. that could become strong selling points. These uses included

1. year-to-year comparisons of crop yields throughout the field;
2. identification of trouble spots (poor yield areas) which might be due to: salinity, poor drainage, insect damage, high weed populations, poor soil fertility, poor seed germination, erosion or poor soil structure; and
3. identifying the "best" time to harvest the crop based on moisture level measurement.

MARKET ANALYSIS

Mr. Cruise wondered how interested farmers would be in the sophisticated technology of the monitor. Having grown up on a farm, he was all too aware of traditional farming practices. He couldn't help but chuckle as he pictured himself explaining the benefits of the technology to his father who had been farming for nearly 40 years. He was almost certain that his father, like many other farmers, relied on intuition and experience when making farming decisions. Although these thoughts were firm in Mr. Cruise's mind, he had come to the realization that some farmers may have the desire to implement the monitor into their current management program. He could see how certain farmers would be interested in the technology, not only because of increased efficiency and accuracy, but more importantly because it was a new and interesting piece of equipment. Mr. Cruise's experience in farming made him aware that there were often a few farmers in any community who prided themselves on being the first to buy anything. Prior marketing research done at Varity consistently found that there were approximately two to three percent of all farmers who could be classified as innovators. Exhibit 1 summarizes the characteristics and behaviour of various adopter categories taken from an Iowa State University bulletin recently obtained by the marketing department at Varity.

In thinking about a target for the new product, the marketing group at Varity came to the tentative conclusion that the greatest potential for the monitor was on large farms. They felt that large-scale farmers were in a position to benefit most from the increased accuracy and efficiency of the monitor. In addition, they felt that large-scale farmers often had more working capital, which would make the purchase of this type of technology more feasible.

The marketing department obtained data on the number of corn and wheat farmers by size category in Canada and the United States (Exhibits 2 to 4). The department felt that corn farmers with more than 500 acres of corn, and wheat farmers with more than 1000 acres of wheat might be interested in the product. As

Exhibit 1

CHARACTERISTICS AND BEHAVIOUR OF ADOPTER CATEGORIES

Characteristics	Innovators	Early Adopters	Early Majority	Late Majority	Late Adopters
Time of Adoption	First 2% to 3% to adopt ideas	Next 13% to adopt new ideas	Next 34% to adopt new ideas	Next 34% to adopt new ideas	Last 16% to adopt new ideas
Attitudes and Values	Scientific and venturesome	Progressive	More conservative and traditional	Skeptical of new ideas	Agricultural magic and folk beliefs
Abilities	High level of education; ability to deal with abstractions	Above average education	Slightly above average education	Slightly below average education	Low level of education; difficulty dealing with abstractions
Group Membership	Leaders in organizations outside the community	Leaders in organizations within the community	Many informal contacts within the community	Little travel outside the community; little activity in organizations	Few memberships in formal organizations other than the church
Social Status	Highest social status, but their farming practices may not be accepted	High social status; looked to by neighbours as good farmers	Above average social status	Above average social status	Lowest social status
Farm Business	Largest, most specialized and efficient	Large farms, slightly less specialized and efficient	Slightly larger than average	Slightly smaller than average	Small farms; low incomes; often do not own farm
Sources of Information	Scientists; other innovators; research bulletins	Highest contact with sources of information; farm magazines	Farm magazines; friends and neighbours	Friends and neighbours	Mainly friends and neighbours; farm radio shows

Source: Iowa State University

Exhibit 2
UNITED STATES CORN AND WHEAT FARMS BY SIZE

Acre Categories	Number of Corn Farms	Number of Wheat Farms
1 to 9	3,762	1,011
10 to 49	44,727	20,030
50 to 69	22,075	12,015
70 to 99	41,133	25,387
100 to 139	43,906	27,855
140 to 179	47,668	33,111
180 to 219	33,557	21,826
220 to 259	33,380	21,612
260 to 499	121,200	93,049
500 to 999	79,083	90,729
1,000 to 1,999	26,693	56,540
2,000 and more	8,264	32,764

Exhibit 3
CANADIAN CORN FARMS BY SIZE

Acre Categories	Number of Farms
1 to 47	17,187
48 to 127	10,402
128 to 362	4,911
363 to 572	634
573 to 947	300
948 and more	109

Exhibit 4
CANADIAN WHEAT FARMS BY SIZE

Acre Categories	Number of Farms
1 to 32	8,929
33 to 72	13,911
73 to 127	18,347
128 to 192	17,485
193 to 362	28,174
363 to 697	16,147
698 to 1,197	3,945
1,198 to 2,997	974
2,998 and more	44

well, some members of the marketing group felt that many of these "large" farmers with older combines would not be interested in the product because the useful life of the combine was relatively short. It was estimated that approximately half of the larger farmers had older combines.

Because the product concept was so new and innovative, no one at Varity felt really comfortable in predicting the probable rate of adoption for this technology. They were aware of previous studies that determined that new agricultural chemicals often were adopted by most farmers in a couple of years, while more complex technologies could take five to ten years for most farmers to adopt.

The marketing group thought that because the target group was large-scale farmers, it was more likely that these farmers would be more progressive than the general farm population. One member of the marketing group spent some time analyzing the Iowa State University bulletin and other innovation studies and then prepared a rough estimate of the percent of target (large) farmers by adopter category. His estimates were; innovators (20%), early adopters (30%), early majority (30%), late majority (20%), and late adopters (0%).

Although Varity had extensive experience working with farmers of all types, it was common practice to learn as much as possible about markets prior to launching new products. For this reason, it was decided to conduct some basic marketing research. This research involved focus-group interviews with 120 "large" farmers in various regions of Canada and the United States. A brief summary of the methodology and results of this research is included in Appendix 1.

PRICE

It was crucial that Varity introduce the monitor at a price that would be perceived by farmers as providing good value for their money. Mr. Cruise knew that farmers, in general, were "price takers." They normally look at the price of equipment and, based on the benefits they perceive, estimate a payback period. Through marketing research conducted by Varity, it was discovered that skeptical farmers prefer a one- to two-year payback period, whereas more confident farmers feel that a payback period of four to five years is acceptable. Payback periods were difficult to estimate because they depend on the size of the farm, the crops grown, and, most importantly, the management skills of the farmer.

The pricing decision became even more involved because, being an entirely new product idea, there was no price reference. Varity desires a 15% return on its investment in new products, but this is irrelevant if farmers are not willing to pay a price that will generate such a return. Some Varity executives felt that the monitor should be priced as low as possible to maximize the change of a successful launch. They felt it was important to establish Varity's name in the market to lay the ground work for a new line of innovative products.

Because of the importance of the price issue, this was explored to some extent with farmers in the marketing research done for the product. At the conclusion of each group interview, the farmers were asked to fill in a sheet indicating whether or not they might be interested in purchasing the unit at a certain price. One-third of the farmers were given a price of $1,200; one-third a price of $1,400; and the final one-third a price of $1,600. The percentage of farmers indicating interest at the three price levels is shown in Appendix 2.

DISTRIBUTION

Varity reasoned that it had four distribution options, some of which could be used in combination. The four options were

1. Sell to other combine manufacturers so the product could be built into their combines, most likely as an extra-cost option.
2. Sell to Massey Combines to be used as an extra-cost option on their combines.
3. Sell through the Massey-Ferguson dealer network.
4. Sell direct to farmers.

Original Equipment Market (O.E.M.)

The first two distribution options involve selling the mass-flow monitor to original equipment manufacturers to be built into new machines. Under the first option, all competing manufacturers would be approached to include the product as an option or accessory on their combines. The current depressed state of the combine market meant that the total potential of this approach would be approximately 11,000 units a year if every combine were fitted with the mass-flow monitor. Of course, not all farmers would be interested in purchasing a combine with this option. Mr. Cruise wondered whether making the product available to competitors was really a good idea. Perhaps the monitor should be used to increase the attractiveness of Massey combines alone, and further position Massey as a leader in combine technology. Balancing this point of view, however, was the additional units which might be sold if a competing company decided to purchase the item.

Aftermarket

The third and fourth distribution options involve selling to the aftermarket. Regardless of whether or not the product was sold in the O.E.M. market, Mr. Cruise felt that the large number of existing combines on farms make the aftermarket very attractive. In the aftermarket, owners of all makes and models of combines could be approached to purchase a monitor. Essentially there were two ways of reaching this market. The first method involved selling the product through the large network of Massey-Ferguson dealers throughout North America. At the present time, Massey-Ferguson maintained a network of almost 1,200 franchised dealers that sold a complete line of Massey-Ferguson equipment. Typically, companies like Varity had a ratio of one salesperson to service 50 dealers. These dealers were located in all farming areas of Canada and the United States with major concentrations in the key corn and wheat areas. All Massey dealers sold new and used equipment, maintained a supply of parts, and had a service department staffed with trained mechanics. Many dealers sold some additional lines of equipment not manufactured by Massey-Ferguson such as feed mills, grain augers, and fertilizer tanks. Only a few dealers specifically sold electronic equipment, although most modern farm equipment contained some electronic parts. Because of the current downturn in combine sales, most dealers were quite anxious to find new products to sell. The standard dealer mark-up for equipment of this type was 30% of the retail price which would provide the dealer \$360 to \$480 at a retail price of \$1,200 to \$1,600.

The second option for reaching the aftermarket was through a direct selling approach. Here Mr. Cruise envisioned using trained salespeople who would call directly on farmers in the target market and attempt to sell them the monitor. Because the product was easy to install, the same person could mount it on the farmer's machine either at the time of sale or on a subsequent visit. Any follow-up service could be handled by the local Massey dealer at a nominal fee.

Mr. Cruise felt that a key advantage of direct selling was the flexibility and face-to-face contact that would enable objections and skepticism about the technology to be dealt with most effectively. In addition, Mr. Cruise was confident that with direct selling, efforts could be focused directly on the target group. On the other hand, Mr. Cruise questioned if it was wise to limit effort to a small group, particularly since it was not entirely clear who the target should be. Lastly, Mr. Cruise was aware of the high costs of personal selling. The average cost of a salesperson was close to \$70,000, including expenses, salary, and training.

PROMOTION

One of the overriding factors determining the success of the monitor would be the effectiveness of the promotional plan developed for the product. Mr. Cruise had witnessed many products progress from mere ideas into marketable products and then turn out to be unpopular among customers. Mr. Cruise felt, more often than not, that this was the result of a poorly designed and administered promotional plan. There were a number of ways the monitor could be promoted.

One promotional approach was the use of mass media such as farm magazines and possibly television. Mr. Cruise recognized that the effectiveness of mass advertising relied on a combination of timing and message. An example of this could be found in the use of television. It may be an excellent advertising media for the product and target market, but if the ads are not run when the desired audience is watching, or if the message is not of interest to the target, the effectiveness of the media is dramatically reduced. By using local television stations, a considerable degree of targeting to farm communities could be achieved. With this in mind Mr. Cruise began to review the available information on media types including their costs and audiences. The company's advertising agency, Bauer, Baxter and Associates, presented Mr. Cruise with some minimum costs for the two media being considered. In order to achieve minimum first year awareness, the agency thought it would cost \$500,000 on either television or farm magazines for a North American campaign. Of course, more than one type of media could be used to increase the overall effectiveness and create higher levels of awareness.

Although television and magazines had many advantages as media for promoting the monitor, Mr. Cruise wondered whether these media were capable of adequately communicating the full range of benefits offered by the product. Mr. Cruise knew that promotions, such as local demonstrations, could be very effective in communicating benefits and encouraging farmers to purchase the monitor.

Following the harvest season, each year there were more than 80 major exhibitions and farm shows throughout North America. Mr. Cruise wondered if some of the $500,000 would be more effectively spent on promotions (for example, display booths and demonstrations) during these shows.

Sales promotions were also considered attractive because they could be used effectively throughout the entire distribution channel. Mr. Cruise strongly believed that he could encourage dealers to push the product to a much greater extent if, for example, they were given a promotion allowance.

MANUFACTURING

It had already been decided that the manufacturing of the product would be contracted to an outside company. Because the monitor was so different from any of the other products Varity manufactured, all the necessary equipment would have to be purchased. The contracting arrangement would avoid the risk of purchasing equipment for an unproven product. An arrangement was reached with Thorne Electronics whereby the cost per unit of the mass-flow monitor would vary with the number of units ordered during each year. The following chart shows the unit cost for different volumes.

Annual Volume	Unit Cost
Less than 5,000	$600
5,000 to 9,999	$550
10,000 to 19,999	$500
20,000 and more	$450

The company controller was asked to estimate the level of other costs associated with the project. Administrative costs were estimated at $200,000 until sales started to increase above 2,000 units. At this point, experience showed that additional costs would be incurred. These additional costs were estimated at three percent of sales revenue. Other costs involved financing inventory and accounts receivable. The controller estimated that the company would have to carry inventory an average of six months, and receivables an average of three months.

THE DECISION

Mr. Cruise knew there were many critical decisions to be made in a short period of time. He had to decide how much of the information from engineering and marketing was based on fact, and how much was based on pride. Both groups at Varity were very excited about the impact this technology could have on the company. In addition, he wondered about the accuracy of the marketing research information generated in the focus groups. Should he put a lot of confidence in this information, or should he rely more heavily on his intuition and experience, and that of his key managers? Deciding on a target market, an introductory price level, a distribution plan, and a promotional package were all integral to the success of this product. Even the product itself could be changed. Mr. Cruise wondered if there were product changes that should be made to better meet farmer needs. No attention had yet been paid to the issues of a warranty and repair procedures. These issues could be important considerations to both prospective dealers and end users.

All these considerations had to be made in light of the substantial financial losses being incurred in recent years. The company could not afford any mistakes at this point. Was the market really ready for this type of technology? What effect might it have on Massey Combines? Could the product be a big winner and provide much needed cash for the company? Mr. Cruise was deep in thought as the plane made its final approach to the Toronto airport.

Appendix 1
MARKET RESEARCH RESULTS

Market research to support the introduction on the mass-flow monitor consisted of 14 focus-group interviews conducted in four main regions of North America. The region and the number of groups per region are shown below.

Region	Number of Groups
Wheat area of the U.S. (Kansas, Nebraska, South Dakota)	5
Corn area of the U.S. (Illinois, Indiana, Ohio)	6
Wheat area of Canada (Saskatchewan)	2
Corn area of Canada (Ontario)	1

Altogether 120 farmers attended the 14 meetings. Farmers were selected by Massey-Ferguson dealers in their respective areas. The guidelines established for farmer selection were

- ''progressive farmers'';
- approximately one-third young, one-third middle-aged, and one-third older;
- represent a cross-section of farming in the area;
- represent a broad spectrum of combine type and brand ownership; and
- have more than 2,000 acres of wheat or 500 acres of corn.

The format used at each meeting consisted of an introduction in which the mass-flow monitor was thoroughly explained to those in attendance, followed by a structured discussion of the monitor. At the conclusion of each session, each participant was asked to complete a short questionnaire to determine purchase interest at different price levels. All the focus groups were taped to facilitate subsequent analysis of the information. A number of extremely useful ideas were obtained from the groups. These are summarized below.

(continued)

Appendix 1 continued

- There was substantial interest in the mass-flow monitor in all areas.
- By far, the greatest interest was in knowing instant moisture levels when combining. This was of special interest to farmers in corn areas where it is necessary, in most years, to dry the crop. Some comments from the groups illustrate this point:

  "The moisture testing would be very useful to me."

  "If you're putting your grain in a bin or selling it to the elevator, knowing the moisture would be really useful."

  "Knowing the moisture first thing in the day would be really useful. You would know when it was dry enough without running a sample into the elevator for a test."

  "I think the yield information is a luxury we really cannot afford."

  "If I know what the moisture is running as I'm combining, I can move over a few rows in the field to a drier area."

  "I already have an acreage meter on the combine. When I fill the hopper, I know how many bushels I have and the yield I'm getting right now."
- Farmers also showed a lot of interest in knowing the average moisture level of a field. They indicated that this information could be used to determine whether or not the grain they are putting in a bin needs aeration or drying.
- Farmers were not overly interested in knowing total grain harvest. Most indicated they already had methods to determine this. Farmers who normally store grain on their farms were much more interested in this feature than farmers who sell their grain to elevators immediately after harvest.
- In general, farmers in the wheat areas were more interested in information relating to yields than farmers in the corn areas.
- Farmers in areas where yields are fairly uniform were less enthusiastic about knowing instantaneous and average yields. Most farmers felt this information was interesting, but certainly not essential.
- Many farmers raised the issue of accuracy, particularly in the area of moisture testing. The general consensus was that the moisture tester needed to provide estimates within 0.5% if it were to be useful.
- Several farmers expressed concern over the perceived complexity of the monitor. They pointed out that they wanted products that are "idiot proof' and extremely simple to understand and use.
- The focus groups also explored the general performance criteria farmers would use to evaluate the mass-flow monitor. The following general factors emerged:

(continued)

Appendix 1 continued

—high level of accuracy,
—trouble-free operation,
—simple to set up and operate,
—knowledgeable dealers and service personnel, and
—adaptable to any make or model of combine.

Appendix 2
PURCHASE INTEREST IN THE MONITOR AT VARIOUS PRICES

Retail Prices	Percentage of Corn Growers Interested in Purchasing	Percentage of Wheat Growers Interested in Purchasing
$1,200	45%	60%
$1,400	35%	55%
$1,600	25%	50%

17 PALPAC

Gordon H. G. McDougall

Leo Fitch, owner of Precision Tool and Gauge (P. T. and G.) of Adelaide, South Australia, was concerned as he reviewed the latest sales figures for PALPAC, the company's new pressed steel pallet.[1] PALPAC had been designed to replace wooden pallets but sales were considerably below expectations. Although the pallet was regularly priced at $40 (less for volume purchases), roughly double the cost of wooden pallets (see Exhibit 1), it had a number of advantages in that it was lighter, stronger, had a longer life, and was non-combustible. Further, when PALPAC was shown to potential buyers, they initially expressed interest but did not purchase the product.

Mr. Fitch wondered how a product that had won the 1983 Australian Design Award and had generated a great deal of enthusiasm at a materials handling trade show was selling so poorly. He decided to meet with the local sales representative of the distributor, Gerrard Strapping Systems, to review their marketing program and decide if the plan should be revised.

PRECISION TOOL AND GAUGE

Leo Fitch had purchased P. T. and G. in July, 1982, for approximately $1.3 million after it had been in receivership for 18 months. The firm had been in business for over 50 years and specialized in the design and manufacture of tools, jigs, fixtures, and dies for pressed metal components. As well, the firm had an extensive metal stamping facility which could test dies made in the plant and make pressed metal products on site. In 1978, the company lost $150,000 on sales of $3 million. By 1981, the losses exceeded $300,000, and the company was placed in receivership. When Leo Fitch was approached to purchase the company the receiver offered his opinion that the main reasons for the company's problems were poor management and inefficiencies in production. After assessing the operation, Mr. Fitch felt the company could be turned around with new management and some restructuring. As well, he noted that the plant had four large metal stamping presses with a replacement value of $500,000 and contracts with automotive firms to supply various stamped components (e.g., brackets, fuel tanks, cross members).

From relatively humble beginnings Leo Fitch had successfully bought and sold a number of companies over the past 15 years. He regarded himself as an entrepreneur who could take a poorly run firm and turn it into a profitable venture. Although he had no experience in the tool and die and metal stamping field, he felt that it

[1] A pallet is a tray or platform for goods being lifted or stored. Typically, goods are placed on a wooden pallet and then a fork lift truck moves the goods on the pallet from one location to another.

wouldn't be very difficult to learn about the business and make a profit within a short time.

After he purchased the company, Mr. Fitch's objectives were to improve production efficiency and to reduce the firm's dependence on the highly volatile automobile industry. When he took over he brought in Ken and Cathy Bowditch who had worked with him in previous ventures. Ken, his nephew, had extensive financial and accounting experience and handled the financial aspects of the business. Cathy, Ken's wife, had a mathematics background and was placed in charge of scheduling in the press shop. Over the next six months, they reduced the workforce from 90 to 41 and eliminated a number of unprofitable production and design activities. By the end of 1983 profits exceeded $150,000 on sales of $2.5 million and similar results were achieved in 1984. For the first six months of 1985, profits were considerably higher. They also considered ways for the firm to reduce its dependency on the automobile industry where sales fluctuations were common due to the "boom or bust" nature of car sales in Australia.

One possibility was a metal pallet. Mr. Bob Dunk, the company's general manager since 1978, had been considering the idea for some time. He had remained with the company and had discussed the product with Mr. Fitch and the Bowditches on several occasions. Mr. Dunk pointed out the many problems of wooden pallets (e.g., easily broken, splintering, loose nails that could tear the goods, etc.) and noted that many firms were dissatisfied with wooden pallets. He felt that a new metal pallet, if properly designed, could have a real impact in the marketplace. Mr. Fitch liked the idea as metal pallets did have some definite advantages over wooden pallets and it would allow the company to diversify. In August 1982, he approved the project, now called PALPAC.

PALPAC

The design and production of PALPAC took place over the next two years. Exhibit 2 details the main events that occurred. The research and development process was not without problems. The objective was to design a metal pallet that satisfied market as well as production requirements. During the research and development process, repeated trials with a variety of shapes and metal compositions were tested. John Lysaght Ltd., a leading Australian steel manufacturer, was of considerable assistance in supplying metal sheets for the prototype tryouts. Lysaght Ltd., developed a new galvanized deep drawing steel which was ideally suited for the manufacture of PALPAC. As well, C.S.I.R.O., a government research and development agency, using their Sirostrain-Grid Square Analysis System, were able to measure and display metal flows during a press forming operation and to determine the appropriate metal pressing sequence.

During the research and development phase two important events occurred. First, a prototype PALPAC was shown at a national materials handling conference in Melbourne in June 1983. The following month, the major Australian materials handling magazine, *Plantline*, ran an article on PALPAC and other business magazines also mentioned the new type of pallet. Over 300 enquiries resulted from firms interested in learning more about the product, buying it, or distributing it.

Exhibit 1
PALPAC BROCHURE

TRANSPORT

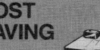

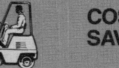

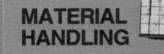

LIGHTWEIGHT:
Weighing only 22 kg — Palpac is less than half the weight of a timber pallet, saving over 30 kg on every pallet shipment you make.

SAVE ON PALLET RETURNS:
A 10 tonne truck can carry 450 empty Palpacs and a semi-trailer — 1000. Over 3 times the number of timber pallets.

4 WAY ENTRY:
Makes loading and unloading quicker and easier.

MATERIAL HANDLING

LIGHTWEIGHT:
At 22 kg Palpac is easily handled by one person.

PRESSED STEEL:
No nails or broken timber to cause injury or product damage and Palpac will not absorb moisture.

4 WAY ENTRY:
Make handling quicker and easier.

STACKABILITY:
Minimal space required for empty pallet storage. 100 Palpac can be stored in less space than 10 traditional pallets which means fewer trips required to provide packing areas with empty pallets.

PRECISE DIMENSIONS:
Palpac dimensions are always precise — ideal for automated handling situation.

HYGIENIC:
Palpac can be easily cleaned and can be exposed to extremes of heat and cold.

LESS RISK OF INJURY:
Less weight reduces the risk of back injury while injuries from protruding nails and slithers of timber are eliminated with Palpac.

COST SAVING

LONGER LIFE:
Palpac is pressed from a single sheet of steel — no nails to work loose — no timber to split — and not effected by the environment.

LOW MAINTENANCE:
Palpac cannot fall apart and will require little or no maintenance.

TRANSPORT:
By using Palpac the weight of each pallet load is reduced by around thirty kilograms, reducing transport costs.

WORKERS COMPENSATION:
Back injuries are a major cause of workers compensation claims. Reduced weight — less back injuries.

INSURANCE:
Palpac is non combustible and eliminates a major fire risk — timber pallets.

SPECIFICATION:
WEIGHT: Approx. 22 kg.
MATERIAL: Pressed from Galvabond Australian Steel.
SIZE: 1165 mm x 1165 mm x 100 mm.
ENTRY: 4 Way.

IAN TECHNOLOGY • • AUSTRALIAN STEEL • • AUSTRALIAN MANUFACTURE • • AUSTRALIAN DESIGN AWARD • • AUSTRALIAN TECHNOLOGY • •

SPACE SAVING
. . . Stackability 10:1

SAVING SPACE:

Palpacs nest together when empty.

- 100 Palpacs can be stored in less space than 10 traditional pallets, saving valuable storage area.
- As Palpac is non-combustible, inside storage represents no fire risk.
- Return transport costs can be drastically reduced.

Australian design award.

AWARDED 1983 Australian Design Award by the Design Council of Australia.

RACKING SYSTEMS:

Racking systems can be easily and quickly modified for Palpac.
The fitment is designed so that Palpac or traditional pallets can be used in the rack.

To establish the benefits to your company from the adoption of Palpac contact the GERRARD branch in your State:

QUEENSLAND
1130 Kingsford Smith Drive,
EAGLE FARM, QLD 4007
P.O. BOX 262,
HAMILTON CENTRAL, QLD 4007
Telephone: (07) 268 5611 Telex: AA42384

NEW SOUTH WALES
203 Woodpark Road,
SMITHFIELD, N.S.W. 2164
P.O. BOX 319,
SMITHFIELD, N.S.W. 2164
Telephone: (02) 609 1555 Sales: (02) 609 5955
Telex: AA26930

VICTORIA
Cnr. Geelong and Little Boundary Roads,
BROOKLYN, VICTORIA 3025
Telephone: (03) 314 0888 Telex: AA31427

TASMANIA
241 Hobart Road,
LAUNCESTON, TASMANIA 7250
P.O. BOX 66,
SOUTH LAUNCESTON, TAS. 7250
Telephone: (003) 44 2436 Telex: AA58700

SOUTH AUSTRALIA
168 Grote Street,
ADELAIDE, S.A. 5000
Telephone: (08) 51 2380 Telex: AA82322

WESTERN AUSTRALIA
9 Keegan Street,
O'CONNOR, W.A. 6163
P.O. BOX 41, MELVILLE, W.A. 6165
Telephone: (09) 331 2744 Telex: AA93579

The information in this literature is correct at time of printing. However, specifications and recommendations are subject to change without notice.

GERRARD STRAPPING SYSTEMS PTY. LTD.
P.O. Box 4568, MELBOURNE, VIC. 3001 AUSTRALIA
Telephone: (03) 314 0888 Telex: AA31427

Australian technology makes a breakthrough in materials handling

PALPAC™

All-Australian steel pallet

- Lighter and stronger.
- Empty Palpacs nest together saving space and transport costs.
- 4 way fork truck entry.
- Minimal maintenance required.
- Hygienic — easily cleaned.
- Non-combustible — no fire risk.
- Safer — less risk of injury.

Exhibit 2

RESEARCH AND DEVELOPMENT OF PALPAC PALLET

Date	Major Activities
August 1982 to December 1982	—Concept of metal pallet discussed (design and cost structures studied) —Decision made to use a four-way entry nine pod design —Materials testing and various design modifications to product shape and size
January 1983 to May 1983	—Further design modifications to improve strength and edge curls —Produce further prototypes for evaluation (painted, zinc plated, hot dip galvanized, uncoated) —Test prototypes for point loads and fork lift utilization —Co-ordinate testing with outside agency —Begin building production dies —World-wide patent production on the design obtained
June 1983 to January 1984	—Meetings with steel supplier to field test prototype —Field test prototypes —Release PALPAC prototype pallet for materials handling exhibition in Melbourne —Review exhibition results and begin to design modified systems —Submit PALPAC to Design Council of Australia competition —PALPAC receives the 1983 Design Council of Australia Award —Build additional dies —Test dies in production press —Further design modifications —Further field tests, poor galvanizing results in problems —Review and rework design and materials —Second production trial —Post galvanizing quality improved but requires further work
February 1984 to September 1984	—Revised galvanizing —Further field tests —Distribution contract signed with Gerrard Strapping Systems

Unfortunately, P. T. and G. was not ready for these activities as PALPAC was still in the prototype stage and the companies were sent a letter informing them of this fact. Second, Ken Bowditch sent an application in to the Design Council of Australia for their awards competition. PALPAC won an Australian Design Award in 1983 and received the Prince Philip Prize for Australian Design for 1984. This award was presented to P. T. and G. by the Prime Minister of Australia, Mr. Bob Hawke in early 1984. Considerable publicity surrounded the event leading to more enquiries including many from overseas companies wishing to market the product in other countries. Again, the companies were told that the Australian marketing decision had not been finalized and overseas arrangements would be left until that was completed.

After these events, Mr. Fitch recognized that P. T. and G. had little marketing expertise and decided to have PALPAC marketed by an outside firm. During the research and development phase information about the pallet market in Australia and elsewhere had been collected. Prior to deciding on which distributor to use, Mr. Fitch and other P.T. and G. personnel reviewed this information.

THE PALLET MARKET IN AUSTRALIA

Australia, a country equivalent in geographic size to the United States, has a population of approximately 15 million people. Of these, 70% reside in eleven major cities, the largest being Sydney, Melbourne, Brisbane, Adelaide, and Perth. Because the country has one of the world's highest urban concentrations of population, considerable transportation activity is required to move goods to the various cities. As well, Australia has a relatively high level of export/import trade.

Few statistics existed on the pallet market in Australia. This was due, in part, to the fact that one firm dominated the existing wooden pallet market (the firm, Chep, was estimated to hold between 60% and 80% of the market) and was reluctant to release any information. Rough estimates of the total market were in the range of 13.5 million units in 1984, but it was not clear how many pallets were produced during any given year. Over 80% of all pallets were rented, as opposed to purchased. The cost of renting a pallet was approximately 3.9 cents/day, but large users could negotiate considerably cheaper rates; the cost of purchasing a standard wooden pallet was $14 for softwood and $20 for hardwood. Firms that rented pallets often did not keep close control of their stock, and losses were common. The interesting aspect of this situation was that these firms continued to pay the rent on the pallets they lost because the pallet supplier (usually Chep) would charge them $24 for every lost pallet. Firms would actually rent more pallets to make up for the missing ones. The main reason for this phenomenon was that the individual responsible for pallets did not want to appear to be inefficient.

As shown in Exhibit 3, pallets varied in form and use. Standard wooden pallets dominated the Australian market, and most companies who employed them even for closed circuit use within a particular plant, factory, or retail/wholesale establishment tended to rent rather than purchase. When firms did purchase wooden pallets and they fell into disrepair, a worker within the factory was assigned to fix them. Virtually all pallets in open circuit use tended to be rented because the company could not easily retrieve them. Typically, a firm would send its goods to another company on pallets and get an equivalent number of pallets back in exchange. By renting the pallets, the firm reduced its capital costs and could regulate its pallet stocks to its seasonal needs. One of the problems faced by firms like Chep who manufactured and returned pallets was that companies frequently kept "good" pallets for their own use and sent damaged pallets back to the pallet rental firm.

A small but growing market existed for specialty pallets. Firms that manufactured high density weight products required pallets that could support heavy loads. Other

Exhibit 3

USE AND TYPE OF PALLETS

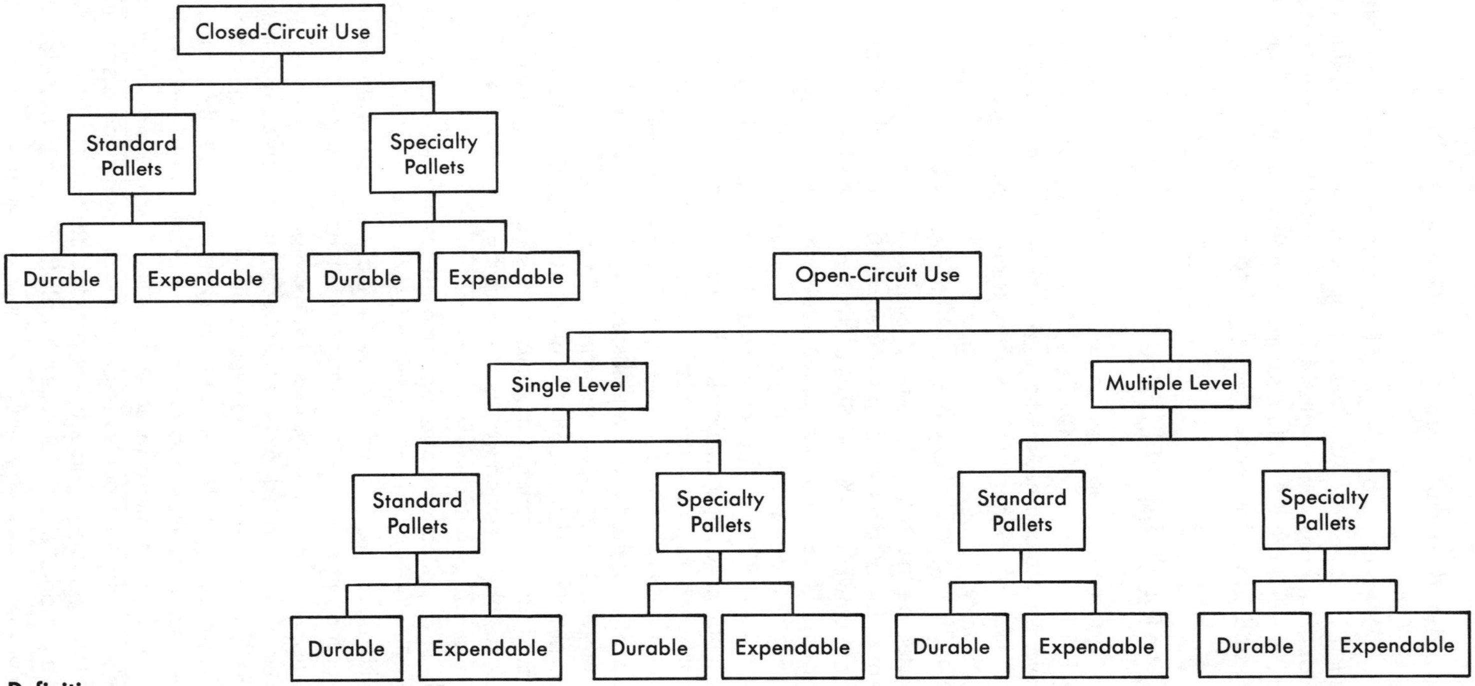

Definitions

- Closed-circuit use—pallets stay on the premises of the company.
- Open-circuit use—pallets move from one company to another (loaded pallets are sent out of company's immediate control).
- Standard pallet—typically wooden, durable pallets (depth and width = 1165 mm; height = 50.8 mm).
- Specialty pallets—may be made from a variety of materials including wood, plastic, steel or aluminium. Come in variety of shapes and sizes. Examples—where hygiene or sterilization standards apply.
- Single-level—loaded pallet shipped from one company to another (e.g., glass bottle manufacturer ships to food manufacturer).
- Multiple-level—loaded pallet shipped from one company to another (e.g., manufacturer ships to wholesaler, ships to retailer).
- Durable—pallet designed for continuous use.
- Expendable—pallets of light, low cost construction intended to be discarded after one trip.

firms that had uniquely shaped products (e.g., beer kegs from brewing companies) developed pallet designs to "fit the shape." As well, many firms in the food business (e.g., meat and dairy) had hygiene and sterilization standards which, at times, could only be met by pallets that could be washed and cleaned.

Finally, part of the pallet market consisted of expendable pallets which were low cost, relatively flimsy and designed to haul products on one trip. Major appliance manufacturers frequently used expendable pallets to transport refrigerators, stoves, etc., from their plants to retailers.

P. T. and G., in conjunction with the steel manufacturer Lysaght Ltd., did some preliminary market research and thought that a price of $30 would not be a deterrent to entering market areas where pallets were used in closed circuits. The food processing industry represented a good potential market as the possibility existed that future legislation might be passed banning the use of wooden pallets. These potential markets were estimated at one million pallets.

A further conclusion of the research was that because PALPAC would be about twice the price of a wooden pallet, it would be difficult to penetrate rental markets. An inherent problem of pallet rental is control of pallet ownership and numbers on hand, as theft of pallets or reward for pallets returned by drivers was common. One alternative was to convert selected high usage areas in open circuits to semicaptive or closed circuit type operations by promoting more strict or sophisticated control and materials handling systems.

TRENDS IN THE WORLD PALLET MARKET

Ken Bowditch was able to collect some general information on the world pallet market. In its simplest form, a pallet is essentially little more than a cargo-carrying platform, which, when loaded, may be easily lifted and so enable the load to be moved with maximum safety and minimum trouble. The two critical characteristics of a pallet are strength/stiffness and friction. When a loaded pallet is lifted and/or stacked, considerable stress may be placed on the pallet. Consequently, it must be constructed to carry the load without deflecting or "flexing" to an unacceptable degree. In terms of friction, it must have a high enough coefficient of friction between pallet deck and goods and between pallet and fork to reduce slippage to an acceptable level.

Pallet associations had been formed in various countries and occasionally met to discuss problems and opportunities. The results of a conference held in 1977 provided some information as to the number of pallets in production and use in various countries (Exhibit 4). A recent study of the pallet industry in the United Kingdom compared the wooden pallet against a number of alternative pallets (Exhibit 5). A wide range of pallets made from various materials have been manufactured in attempts to overcome the problems of the wooden pallet. The study concluded that "there is as yet no design of pallet in an alternative material equivalent in price and performance to the ordinary middle-price timber pallet. The competing designs are, in the main, either of slightly lower cost and substantially lower strength, or of higher cost with some advantage over the timber pallet such as longer life, or better resistance to contamination."

Exhibit 4
SELECTED DATA ON PALLET MARKET—BY COUNTRY

Country	Estimated Annual Pallet Production (Millions)	Estimated Pallets in Use (Millions)	Most Popular Size Pallet (mm)	Comments
France	20	N/A	N/A	N/A
Italy	7	N/A	1,200 × 1,000	Plastic pallets recently introduced, vast majority wood.
Japan	30	120	800 × 1,100 1,100 × 1,100	N/A
United Kingdom	14	N/A	1,200 × 100	Sixty-nine different types of plastic and other substitute pallets for sale, none having a major impact.
U.S.A.	205	N/A	1,200 × 1,000	A few plastic sold, 98% wood.
West Germany	25	40–45	1,200 × 1,000	A few plastic and paperboard pallets, vast majority wood.
Canada	N/A	N/A	N/A	Some plastic pallets in use, vast majority wood.
Australia	N/A	N/A	N/A	N/A

Source: The Status of the Pallet Throughout the World, Third World Congress, Blackburg, Virginia, 1977.

Based on this review, Leo Fitch decided that the marketing of PALPAC should be handled by a large national distributor who had expertise in materials handling. After examining proposals from a number of companies the decision was made to award the distribution rights for Australia to Gerrard Strapping Systems.

GERRARD STRAPPING SYSTEMS

Gerrard Strapping Systems, a large manufacturing and distribution firm (sales exceeded $50 million annually) with head offices in Melbourne, Victoria, specialized in designing and installing efficient distribution systems for its customers. Gerrard sales representatives would study a company's current distribution system and offer products and services designed to better utilize storage space, lower freight rates through higher density packs, reduce damage during the shipments, and increase handling efficiency. As an example, they developed a unique system which compressed and strapped bales of wool for shipment. Gerrard's major business was in strapping machines which were used to bind parcels, packages and/or boxes together prior to transportation. The most profitable aspect of the business was the

Exhibit 5
COMPARISON OF WOODEN VERSUS SUBSTITUTE PALLETS

Wooden Pallets Readily produced in a wide range of sizes; strength, stiffness, and friction, usually satisfactory; deterioration a problem—bottom boards fractured, nails protruding; weight sometimes a problem; cost relatively low.

Metals (steel and aluminum alloys) Steel pallets can be lightweight; friction a problem; unless galvanized, rusting a problem; expensive; used to a limited extent for handling fertilizer and other corrosive material. Aluminum used in certain areas (e.g., meat distribution) because of resistance to contamination and ease of cleaning; very expensive; longer life.

Plastics Usually moulded; shape changes over time; complex designs; high investment costs; usually expensive; small number in use.

Wood Products (cellular boards, chipboard pressings, plywood) With cellular boards humidity can cause loss of strength; with chipboard pressings moisture can cause warping and loss of strength; plywood is resistant to distortion which makes it attractive for automated handling systems demanding close dimensional tolerances; high initial cost.

Composites (steel and timber, paper and plastic, glass fibre and plastics, etc.) A wide range of composite pallets have been tried, few have made inroads into the standard wooden pallet market.

Source: *Materials Handling: Pallet Usage and Wastage*, Department of Industry, London, 1977.

sale of the binding material (e.g., plastic or steel tape) to firms who used Gerrard strapping machines. For example, a strapping machine would be sold for $20,000, but each year the firm might use $40,000 or more worth of binding material.

Gerrard offered complete market coverage of potential customers for PALPAC in Australia. Their sales force of 50 representatives called on all the major industries and sold carton closures or bundles, pallet securement systems, product protection, and unitization and/or bailing systems. Gerrard viewed PALPAC as a major opportunity to obtain a significant share of the pallet market. After a series of discussions a contract was signed between P. T. and G. and Gerrard Strapping Systems. The main terms of the contract were as follows:

- Gerrard would have the exclusive marketing rights to PALPAC for Australia for a period of five years;
- Gerrard would handle all marketing activities, including promotion, advertising, and personal selling;
- P. T. and G. would sell PALPAC pallets to Gerrard for approximately $24.50 per unit, F.O.B. factory. Gerrard would then resell the units to final customers at a price to be determined by Gerrard (the initial price was set at $40 per unit) which, according to a value analysis conducted by Gerrard, would still offer economic benefits if PALPAC were purchased (Exhibit 6);
- Gerrard would place orders for PALPAC in multiples of 1,000 (to allow P. T. and G. to achieve economical production runs).

Exhibit 6

VALUE ANALYSIS—PALPAC VERSUS STANDARD WOODEN PALLET

	PALPAC	Wooden
1. Total pallets in system	1,000	1,000
2. Total pallets replaced by year	15	333
3. Turnover percentage (2 − 1)	1.5%	33%
4. Average life of one pallet	20 years	3 years
5. Total repair cost annually	$225.00	$1,250.00
6. Cost per pallet per year of repair (5 − 1)	$0.23	$1.25
7. Cost of repair per pallet (6 × 4)	$4.60	$3.75
8. Purchase price of pallet	$40.00	$20.00
9. Cost of pallet including repairs over total of life (7 + 8)	$44.60	$23.75
10. Rebates after useful life (scrap value)	$2.00	$0.00
11. Cost after rebate (9 − 10)	$42.60	$23.75
12. Cost per year (11 − 4)	$2.13	$7.92

Source: Prepared by Gerrard Strapping Systems

In summary, P. T. and G. would manufacture PALPAC and Gerrard Strapping Systems would market the product. Members of both companies were very optimistic about the future of PALPAC when the contract was signed in August 1984, and Gerrard had estimated sales as high as 90,000 units in the first year.

Ken Bowditch had prepared some financial estimates of the profitability of PALPAC. Although the dies required to make PALPAC had cost $400,000, these costs were written off in the year they were incurred, so were ignored in the calculations. For each PALPAC unit, the cost of the steel was $17, labour and press time was estimated at $3.50, and cleaning each pallet (it had an oil residue after leaving the presses) cost $1.40 for a total manufactured cost of $21.90. Mr. Bowditch felt that if the sales were anywhere near the forecast, PALPAC could prove to be a profitable product.

INITIAL MARKETING EFFORTS

In August, Gerrard hired a product manager who had previous experience in the packaged goods industry. He was assigned the responsibility of marketing PALPAC throughout Australia. Six sales representatives were hired at an average salary of $18,000 and expenses of $5,000 to cover each of the six states in Australia. Sales representatives for Gerrard were offered these positions but only one, Michael Craft, accepted the position in South Australia. The remaining five representatives were all new employees. They spent approximately 95% of their time on PALPAC and reported to the new product manager. Their general sales approach was to call on existing Gerrard customers and talk to them about PALPAC. If the customer showed some interest, a PALPAC demonstration was arranged, and the salesperson then attempted to sell them PALPAC units. Brochures (Exhibit 1) were left with all businesses contacted by the salespeople.

An advertising campaign was launched and approximately $30,000 was spent in the first six months, primarily on ads in magazines and weekly business newspapers. For example, an ad was run in the *Financial Review*, a publication that reached a large number of middle and upper level managers. Similar ads were run in the major packaging and industry magazines (e.g., *Plantline, Factory Equipment News*). In some cases, the ad contained a clip-out coupon which could be returned to receive more information on PALPAC. The results of this advertising campaign were disappointing. Fewer than 100 enquiries were received in total, and an ad placed in *Australian Packaging*, considered the prime magazine to reach materials handling personnel, resulted in only 26 enquiries.

As well, sales were disappointing. Fewer than 1,000 pallets had been sold by the end of January 1985, six months after launch. General changes were made in the marketing of PALPAC which included the firing of the product manager (he was considered to have too little experience in the materials handling business) and the appointment of Michael Craft as product development manager. Mr. Craft continued his responsibility for selling PALPAC in South Australia. The other sales representatives now reported to the district sales managers for Gerrard in the various states.

By June 1985, the sales picture for PALPAC had not improved. In total, only about 5,000 PALPAC units had been sold. Leo Fitch had become increasingly concerned about this situation and decided to have a meeting with Michael Craft to review the matter.

The Meeting

In the course of the discussion with Michael Craft, Leo Fitch made the following notes:

- The most successful sale made by Michael Craft was to an automotive component manufacturer who used the pallets to move insulation material, a light flat product. A manager in another department saw a PALPAC unit and contacted Mr. Craft. Unfortunately, the fork lift trucks currently used in that department had "fixed forks" which were too wide to carry PALPAC. Mr. Craft, on his own initiative, found a fork lift truck that could do the job and convinced the manager to purchase two new fork lift trucks and 200 PALPAC units.
- Mr. Craft was also pleased to announce that a brick manufacturer in Darwin had just placed an order for 5,500 units at $30 each. This was the largest sale of PALPAC units and Mr. Craft felt it could be the breakthrough they had been looking for. The brick manufacturer had purchased the units because of their strength and low maintenance costs. As well, Darwin was in a tropical zone and wooden pallets tended to rot during the wet season. The manufacturer would also have the company name stamped on the units to prevent theft.
- A sale that Mr. Craft was optimistic about closing was with an irrigation supplier who manufactured water pipes and various irrigation sprayers. Company managers were enthusiastic but would need to alter their racking system in order to use PALPAC. To date, they had not done this but Mr. Craft remained optimistic. The potential existed to sell 1,300 units to this company.

- A customer who was impressed with PALPAC was the manager of a major motor car company who could use the pallets to move inventory and finished parts within the firm. However, after considerable discussion, the company decided the price ($40 per pallet) was too high and continued to rent pallets.
- In Mr. Craft's opinion the major reasons PALPAC was not selling were
  a) a minor flexing problem—when the pallet was stacked with a very heavy load the edges tended to bend and occasionally some of the load would drop off;
  b) racking system problems—current racking and materials handling systems were designed for standard wooden pallets. In many cases, PALPAC was not compatible with the current system and modifications would be required if PALPAC was to be used;
  c) in some cases when a PALPAC pallet was tried in a plant it was found that the pallet was too wide for the doors;
  d) PALPAC needed to be seen before any customer interest was generated. For example, brochures on PALPAC were sent to 43 fish processing companies who had to meet strict hygiene standards. No enquiry resulted from the mailings;
  e) one of the major advantages of the pallet was its light weight (PALPAC weighted 22 kilograms versus a wooden pallet at approximately 60 kilograms). This could offer substantial savings to companies who had light products that were transported a considerable distance (i.e., over 500 kilometres). However, because of the inability of firms to control pallets at the destination, the lightweight advantage was negated by the control problem;
  f) the price of PALPAC, at $40 per unit, was a major stumbling block for many companies. Not only did the absolute price of the pallet create an obstacle, but for many firms expenditures exceeding $5,000 (the equivalent of 125 pallets) required board of director or senior management approach. Thus, the decision to purchase or rent pallets which had traditionally been done by a purchasing agent now required higher approval if PALPAC pallets were to be purchased;
  g) the final problem involved block stacking of loaded pallets. In many instances, PALPAC pallets could not be loaded and stacked on top of one another because the pods of the upper pallets sank into the product below, sometimes resulting in instability.
- It was Michael Craft's opinion that PALPAC could best be sold to customers who were concerned about cleanliness (e.g., food processors), lightweight (e.g., customers who had light products), or those who used pallets on a closed circuit basis. He mentioned that the Gerrard name was an asset because the potential customers knew the company and were quite willing to listen to him talk about PALPAC. In fact, because PALPAC was made of steel and looked quite different from the traditional wooden pallet, he usually attracted quite a crowd when he was showing PALPAC in a factory.

Leo Fitch reviewed his notes and began considering his options regarding PALPAC. While he was pleased with the large sale that had just been made, he wondered if they had been taking the wrong approach to marketing the product; was Gerrard the right company to sell the product; and did the product need further design changes? Whatever the problem, he had to make a decision soon because the present situation was unsatisfactory for all concerned.

18 PORT-A-PAD

William A. Preshing
Denise Walters

In late 1986, Mr. Mark Tanner, a successful Canadian entrepreneur, purchased the Canadian rights to manufacture and distribute a reusable chemical heating pad named Port-A-Pad. The product—a vinyl bag containing chemicals which produced a constant level of heat—had a variety of therapeutic uses, including treatment of muscle injuries and relief from arthritic pain. The task facing management was to develop a strategy for Port-A-Pad in a market that had not changed in a number of years.

THE COMPANY

Mr. Tanner owned The Tanner Company, which operated three businesses in Western Canada—a peat-moss company, a mini-warehouse operation, and a landfill site. While attending a new business seminar, he met the inventor of Port-A-Pad and, after considerable investigation, paid $250,000 for the Canadian manufacturing and distribution rights. Mr. Tanner also obtained a patent on the product in Canada which would last 17 years.

THE PRODUCT

Port-A-Pad consisted of a vinyl bag containing a sodium acetate solution and a small stainless steel trigger. Activating the trigger caused the solution to crystallize, producing a predictable and constant level of heat. Since the concentration of the sodium acetate solution could be varied, the pad was available in two temperature settings: 117 and 130 degrees Fahrenheit (47 and 54 degrees Celsius). The preset temperature could not be exceeded. The pad gave off heat at its preset temperature for about 20 minutes, then started to cool but still produced enough heat to have therapeutic value for up to three hours. Use of the felt cover, which came with the pad, prevented rapid heat loss. The pad could be prepared for reuse by immersing it in boiling water for 15 minutes or autoclaving it in a chemical (but not a steam) autoclaving unit. An autoclaving unit acted in a similar manner to a pressure cooker. The pad could be reused hundreds of times until the vinyl wore out.

The Port-A-Pad could be marketed in rectangles of various sizes (8″ × 18″, 8″ × 8″, 4″ × 4″) and in the shape of a mitt. The vinyl bags, which would be produced by an outside contractor, were stamped from a die and could be made in virtually any size and shape at an average cost per bag of $0.50. Each die cost about $1,000 (which would be paid for by the Tanner company). It could be made in less than three weeks, enabling the company to respond quickly to changing market demand.

The sodium acetate solution would be purchased from an Ontario supplier at an average cost per bag of $1. Port-A-Pad obtained an inventory of 150,000 triggers, on consignment from the inventor, which did not have to be paid for until the pads were sold. The triggers were required to "start" the Port-A-Pad the first time it was used. The inventor had guaranteed to provide a future supply of triggers at a cost of $1.50 per unit. The felt covers and packaging were available from local suppliers at a cost per bag of $0.75.

The filling and sealing process was simple and neither labour nor capital intensive. This work would be done in the mini-warehouse to maintain quality control. One welder and three unskilled workers could produce 150 pads per hour or 22,000 per month. The combined wages of the welder and three workers would be $37.50 per hour. The company had purchased two welding machines, one as back-up in case of mechanical failure. As production needs increased, new welding machines could be purchased for approximately $7,500 each.

THE MARKET

Shortly after obtaining the rights to Port-A-Pad, Mark Tanner hired Richard McKay at a salary of $40,000 per year as the marketing manager. He had extensive sales experience including the introduction of a number of new products to the Canadian market. Mr. McKay's first assignment was to conduct an analysis of the market potential for Port-A-Pad.

Because of Port-A-Pad's versatility, it could be sold in three broad segments: (1) the medical treatment market, (2) personal warmth (for example, seat cushions, survival clothing, hand warmers), and (3) heating of inanimate objects (for example, food service, industrial equipment). After evaluating these market segments, Mr. McKay felt the medical treatment segment had the greatest potential for the immediate future, and he collected further information on this segment.

THE MEDICAL TREATMENT MARKET

The application of heat was a well-known treatment for relief from pain and increased mobility in cases of arthritis and traumatic joint or muscle injury. This market can be divided into two segments: the institutional and the home market.

Within the institutional market there were a number of market subsegments including active treatment hospitals, auxiliary hospitals, nursing homes,and physiotherapy and chiropractic clinics. Mr. McKay estimated that the total annual usage for these facilities would be 29,232 units. He arrived at this estimate by phoning 20 hospitals in the Calgary and Edmonton area and asking how many of these pads of all types (Exhibit 1) would be ordered each year. On average, 24 pads were currently used by each hospital. Using Statistics Canada data he found there were 1,218 hospitals in Canada and then projected the annual usage rate at 29,232.

Mr. McKay felt that the home use market would be reached primarily through retail pharmacies and secondarily through medical and surgical supply stores. There are about 2,700 such outlets in Canada, and he estimated demand through them at 189,000. This estimate was based on a telephone survey of 25 retail pharmacies and 10 medical supply stores. He explained the product to each respondent and asked how many they might sell in one year. On average, the respondents said they would sell 70 units each year. Based on this information, Mr. McKay estimated that the total home use market was 189,000 pads of all types annually.

As well, Mr. McKay felt that three market trends indicated a positive future for Port-A-Pad. Heat had been under-utilized as a means of treatment because of problems with burns, electrical shocks from heating pads, inconvenience and high cost. The Port-A-Pad, with its unique design and features, could surmount these problems. Secondly, the mean age of the Canadian population was rising and the "baby boom" generation was now approaching middle age. As people got older, the incidence of arthritis and other associated disorders would increase, leading to a more extensive personal use of the Port-A-Pad. Finally, as more people became fitness-conscious and participated in physical activities, athletic injuries that could be treated with heat would also increase.

Competition

No new products had been introduced in the industry in recent years and market shares were stable among competing firms. Port-A-Pad would compete with four existing products: electric heating pads, hot water bottles, instant hot packs, and reusable hot packs. Mr. McKay prepared a competitive analysis for these products (Exhibit 1). The companies producing these competing products were divisions of large multi-product firms, such as 3M and Johnson and Johnson, fabricated rubber manufacturers, and electrical goods manufacturers.

Electric heating pads applied controlled heat over large areas of the body. The pads could cause burns, especially in older patients with decreased skin sensitivity. There was a slight electric shock hazard with the pads and, as they required electricity to operate, were not truly portable.

Hot water bottles were portable and inexpensive but less convenient to use. The temperature was hard to regulate and heat was lost quickly, requiring frequent refilling. As with electric heating pads, there was some danger of burns or scalding from hot water.

Instant hot packs worked on an exothermic chemical reaction principle. A larger bag contained water as well as a smaller bag full of chemicals. When the entire bag was crushed the chemicals were released and combined with water to produce heat. These packs were easy to use and were inexpensive. However, they gave off uneven heat that could cause burns and the chemicals were often toxic. They were not reusable.

Reusable hot packs were of two types: institutional and home use. The institutional market leader was the Hydropack, a canvas pack filled with gel that was heated in a steam or hot water autoclave. The pack was wrapped in towels and applied to the patient. The main advantages of the pack were control (it was available in different sizes and the temperature could be regulated by proper heating) and long equipment life—in excess of 20 years. The disadvantages were the high initial cost, specialized heating equipment that was required, higher laundry bills (due to use of towels), and inability to produce "dry" rather than "moist" heat.

Exhibit 1
COMPETITIVE ANALYSIS

Product Type	Safety	Temperature Control	Selling Price	Heat Retention	Portability, Convenience	Weight, Pliability
Electric Heat Pad	Burn and shock possible	Controlled even	$10+	Indefinite	Fair, needs electricity	Fair
Hot Water Bottle	Burn possible	Uneven	$4+	15–25 min.	Fair, needs refilling	Poor
Instant Hot Pack	Burns, toxic	Uneven	$2+	10–20 min.	Good	Poor
Reusable Hot Pack	Good	Good	$30	35–40 min.	Fair, needs reheating	Fair
Home Pack	Good	Low heat	$1.50	15–25 min.	Good	Fair
Port-A-Pad	Good	Good	$20	2 hours	Good	Very Good

The home use packs contained chemicals that were activated by hot water or steam. They were portable and provided a controlled temperature, but the heat output was lower and lasted a shorter time than Port-A-Pad.

The Port-A-Pad had features that made it superior to all these products. It was truly portable, easy to use, and did not require specialized equipment. The temperature was absolutely controlled to reduce the possibility of burns, there were no toxic chemicals involved, and the pad produced therapeutic heat levels for two or more hours.

Based on his assessment of the competitive products, Mr. McKay felt that with a good marketing program Port-A-Pad could achieve a market share of up to 50%. However, he knew that this was a "guesstimate" at best, and the actual market share obtained might be quite different. In particular, he was concerned about the need to change traditional patterns of use.

Focus Groups

To initiate some ideas as to how to market the product, Mr. McKay conducted five focus-group sessions. The five groups consisted of three groups of consumers who were likely users (for example, people suffering from arthritis, people in extended care facilities, and physiotherapists). In each session people were shown a sample of the product and asked about its uses, important features, suggested selling price, and where it should be sold. Selected results from the focus groups are provided in Exhibit 2.

INITIAL MARKETING IDEAS

Based on his analysis of the market, competition, and focus group results, Mr. McKay developed a preliminary marketing plan for Port-A-Pad. He felt that the product could have a retail price of $20, which was in line with the price consumers appeared willing to pay for a reusable pad with Port-A-Pad's features. Retailers would probably expect a margin of 25% on retail selling price.

Successful marketing of Port-A-Pad in both the institutional and home markets probably required acceptance by the medical profession. In the institutional market the physician must order the heat treatments before there would be a demand for the pads. The home user often bought products on the basis of a doctor's recommendation.

Existing competitive products were marketed through three distributors. Canadian Hospital Products was the only Canadian company that distributed to the institutional market. The company prided itself on carrying Canadian-made products. Northern Medical was a national distributor that would distribute the pad to pharmacies and surgical supply stores. In Quebec there was resistance to a product distributed from outside the province, and because of this, a Quebec distributor would be chosen. All three distributors would require margins of 15% on their selling price. Mr. McKay considered adding three salespeople to push the distribution of the product; each salesperson would be responsible for servicing either the home, institutional, or

Quebec market. Salary and travel expenses for each salesperson were estimated at $30,000 per year.

Mr. McKay was uncertain about advertising but knew that the institutional market could be accessed on two levels: through the doctors and other medical personnel and through advertising aimed at purchasing agents for hospitals, nursing homes, and clinics. Considering the home market, promotional considerations would include the type of packaging and the product literature enclosed, as well as the type of advertising that would best reach the home market, which is primarily composed of older people.

Based on the information he had collected, Mr. McKay began preparing a marketing plan for Port-A-Pad. He was optimistic about the success of the venture and looked forward to presenting the plan for approval to Mr. Tanner.

Exhibit 2

SUMMARY OF FOCUS GROUP DISCUSSIONS

The summary is grouped into three categories: (1) consumers as users (particularly the arthritic and home market); (2) the institutional market (extended care facilities and hospitals); and (3) the physiotherapy group (personal and sports-related use).

1. THE CONSUMER MARKET

Key Uses

a. Substitution for other sources of heat.
b. Apply heat to ease the pain.
c. Arthritic users indicate that the pain is so substantial they will try anything on the market to seek relief.
d. Arthritic users tend to be sensitive to the word arthritic, thus anything that indicates relief will catch their attention. This is true with respect to advertisements, packages, discussions on talk shows, meetings with other arthritics, word-of-mouth, etc.
e. Major use occurs at any time but there was substantial interest in the fact that the product could be used in the night without significant preparation.

Key Product Features

a. Portability and controlled heat.
b. Variable temperature at purchase time (product line question).
c. Flat product—very useful when user is lying down.
d. Product durability.
e. Reusable, therefore only pennies per use.
f. Length of time heat lasts, particularly when covered in a towel, was viewed to be very positive.

(continued)

Exhibit 2 continued

g. Product could be packed in a suitcase or purse and used when travelling (in a car, plane, etc.).
h. Product is safe to use (unlike the hot wax treatment for arthritis).
i. Product is flexible and can be shaped to meet the user's needs.
j. The product does not leak (unlike a water bottle).

Price

a. Arthritics were prepared to spend in the order of $20 retail for the product, and many indicated they would consider more than one product.
b. The group indicated a warranty would be critical to initial purchase decision.
c. Some felt a towel cover could be provided for an additional sum.

Outlet

a. The majority of the group felt the product would be best suited to availability in a drug store or a department store. The great advantage of the department store was the implicit guarantee provided by the store as part of their retail policy.

2. INSTITUTIONAL MARKET

The discussion with people in the extended care facilities indicated that they received treatment from the central physiotherapy units. In addition, many were arthritic and indicated they would like to have such a product in their room for use during the night. A major factor in the new product is safety and reliability with respect to temperature control. This is particularly significant for older people because of a reduction in sensitivity to temperature on their skin (they tend to like heat that is too strong and thus harmful to the skin).

The major entry would be through the purchasing activity of the institutions. Individual pads may be acquired but payment would be personal. Price is thus a major factor for older people on restricted incomes.

Product acquisition varied greatly depending on whether the individual worked in a private clinic or in a hospital. The distinctions were also made by nurses who attended a focus group earlier. That is, the staff who use the product are important to the decision, but the central purchasing group also assumes a key role. It was indicated that the *major* factor in the minds of central purchasing people in the institution was the ability to show cost effectiveness and advice was given to use this part of the presentation to individual buyers for institutions. The private clinics indicated they also consider cost effectiveness and would look at the new product as the supply of existing heating pads was used up.

(continued)

Exhibit 2 continued

3. PHYSIOTHERAPISTS

The focus group with physiotherapists indicated that they spend substantial amounts of money on heating pads and are looking for cost-effective products.

Use

a. Useful where heat is the treatment medium.
b. Use in emergency cases of hypothermia.
c. Do not use in cases of inflammation or where internal bleeding may be present. Use in cases of inflammation after an initial treatment period where ice was used as the treatment medium.
d. Good potential for treatment of seniors because of temperature control which is essential due to poor circulation.
e. Good potential for in-home use after physiotherapy treatment program.

Benefits

a. Convenient.
b. Cost effective.
c. Safety due to constant temperature (point made was that heat is damaging, ice will not damage the skin because the person will stop using the ice due to the cold).
d. Warranty is essential to remove product liability from the user, particularly the user in private clinics. In essence they indicated a need to guarantee treatment time and product life.

Section 5

PRICING

Through pricing, management attempts to recover the costs of the separate elements in the marketing mix—the product itself, associated advertising and personal selling expenses, and the various services provided to consumers by the channels of distribution—as well as to generate profits and the funds necessary to operate the company.

Price is a very visible part of the marketing mix—easily observed by both customers and competitors. Establishing an appropriate pricing strategy is thus a critical part of any marketing plan. The foundations of pricing strategy are like a tripod, with the three legs representing:

1. the costs incurred by the marketer,
2. the prices charged by competitors, and
3. the value of the product to prospective purchasers.

From a consumer viewpoint, the price of a product is the amount paid or to be paid for the benefits offered by the "bundle" of attributes represented by the product and its supporting services. Changes in the nature of this bundle may increase or reduce not only the marketer's costs, but also the product's perceived value and thereby the price that consumers are willing to pay.

It is important to recognize that consumers may view a product according to its perceived and not actual value. A product may be of very high quality but customers may consider it as being "cheap," possibly because of a low price or a poorly designed package. Conversely, consumers may regard an expensive well-packaged product as being of high quality when in fact it is of poor quality. Repeat sales of such a product, however, may be limited.

Pricing policy should consequently be seen as only one of several interdependent elements in the marketing mix. Economic theorists have historically tended to overemphasize the role of price as a determinant of demand at the expense of such nonprice variables as product attributes, communication activities, and distribution. In addition, the economic concept of pricing generally emphasizes the level of price charged, overlooking such important marketing considerations as how products are paid for by consumers. "Can I charge it?" or "What terms can you give me?" may be equally, or more, important in some purchase decisions than the basic "How much is it?"

An organization's pricing objectives are normally derived from its overall marketing strategy and may change over time in response to changing conditions, both in the marketplace and in the firm's own resources. A tradeoff often has to be made between short-run profits and market-share targets which may reduce profits in the short run, but enhance them in the long run.

Pricing strategies must take into account not only the response of the ultimate consumer or industrial buyer but also the needs and characteristics of intermediaries in the channels of distribution. Sufficient margins must be offered at each level of distribution to make it financially attractive for the distributor to carry the goods or to represent the service organization in question.

Finally, pricing policies may reflect a communication objective. Many firms cultivate a "value-for-money" image. For example, ABC laundry detergent (with its advertising line, "I can't see a difference. Can you see a difference?") positions itself as being equivalent in quality to higher priced brands. Taking this policy a step further, some firms may offer one or more "loss leaders"—perhaps on just a temporary basis—to attract attention to the entire product line. At the other end of the spectrum are situations in which the marketer seeks to enhance the quality image of the product by deliberately charging a relatively high price.

SETTING PRICES

Assuming that the company has identified its target markets, the first step in setting prices is to establish the company's objectives for each target market. What segments does the company want to compete in and what goals has it set for each segment? In some segments, for example, the company may be determined to become the market share leader and to keep out new market entrants. In other segments, the company may be content with its current position and seek to maximize the cash flow generated from that market. Each of these goals requires a different marketing plan and marketing mix.

The next step is to determine the role of price within the marketing mix. If, for example, the firm has decided on a plan placing great emphasis on service by the retailer, then the pricing policy needs to allow for sufficient retailer margins. If, on the other hand, the plan is to become the dominant supplier for high volume customers, then prices must be set low enough to meet that goal. Within this framework, the company must then determine its pricing strategies and policies. Factors influencing these decisions are discussed in the next section.

Pricing involves a number of tactical decisions. Particularly for consumer products, these include such elements as when to run promotions, whether to price at or below critical pricing points (for example \$0.99 versus \$1), and whether to develop price lines. For example, including a high-price model in a line might make the medium-price model seem more reasonably priced. Other factors include how to communicate prices, what types of discounts to provide, and, for retailers, whether to use credit cards and allow payment over time. These tactical issues are quite important; neglecting them can make an otherwise sound pricing policy ineffective.

FACTORS INFLUENCING PRICING STRATEGIES AND POLICIES

Apart from marketing goals, a number of other factors also influence the determination of pricing strategies and policies. Key elements are the cost structure of the firm, the price elasticity of both primary (overall market) and selective (secondary or brand level) demand, and the competitive structure of the industry in which the company is competing. Other important considerations include product characteristics, the interrelationship among the

Exhibit 1
A SUMMARY OF INPUTS TO PRICING DECISIONS

1. Target market objectives and plan
2. Costs—both variable and fixed—associated with the product
3. Availability of funds to finance new products, competitive battles, and long-term plans
4. Total capacity available
5. Alternative products offered by the company
6. Extent and nature of competition
7. Pricing policies of competitors
8. Potential market size for a specific product offering, reflecting:
   - Type of offering
   - Location
   - Scheduling
9. Price elasticity of potential customers, reflecting:
   - Different market segments
   - Variations in product characteristics
   - Value of product (and product variations) to customers
10. Additional costs (beyond purchase price) incurred by patrons or consumers
11. Purchasing behaviour of potential customers
    How far in advance is purchase/use decision made?
    Preferred payment/reservation procedures
    - Payment made directly to originating organization versus payment through retail intermediary
    - Cash versus cheque or credit card
12. Reactions of distribution channels to pricing policies
13. Legal and regulatory considerations
14. Changes in the external environment that may affect:
    - Customer's ability or willingness to pay
    - Nature of competition
    - Size of market (and segments within that market)
    - Company's costs and financial situation
    - Ability of organization to determine preferred pricing policies without third-party "interference"

products in the company's product line, the availability of supply relative to demand, and government regulation. Exhibit 1 summarizes factors to consider when reading a pricing decision.

COST STRUCTURE

Several aspects of an organization's cost structure need to be considered:

1. the level of variable costs per unit and the extent to which these are likely to form a high proportion of the selling price,
2. the level of fixed costs,

3. the potential for economies of scale,
4. the possibility of changing cost structures over time, and
5. the firm's costs relative to those of its competitors.

When a company has high fixed costs and relatively low costs per unit of sale, such as with a computer service bureau or airline, the incremental cost of accommodating new customers or sales is comparatively low in relation to the prices charged. Under such circumstances, earnings may rise sharply if sales increase. Alternatively, for some businesses the reverse may be true; fixed costs may be comparatively low and variable costs per unit very high. Clothing products and certain foodstuffs are examples of products which may require substantial material or labour cost, or both. In these cases, since competition tends to force prices down, unit contribution is often low and even a substantial increase in sales volume by itself may not improve earnings dramatically. However, even here, the potential for economies of scale presents opportunities for some organizations, since manufacturing, marketing, or administrative efforts toward efficiency may result in reduced costs per unit as the scale of operations increases. This situation provides an opportunity to enhance both profits and unit market share. In some industries, such as electronics, increasing cost savings over time, due to technological and other advances, has an important influence on both short- and long-term pricing strategies.

PRICE ELASTICITY OF DEMAND

A key factor influencing pricing decisions for any product is the sensitivity of demand to changes in selling prices. If demand rises sharply when prices are lowered (or falls when they are increased), then demand is said to be highly elastic. Conversely, if demand is little affected by price changes, it is said to be inelastic.

The price sensitivity of demand for a particular product category reflects the importance of the product for consumers, the income level of present consumers, the existence of substitute products, the extent to which potential exists for increasing consumption (that is, whether demand is close to saturation), and whether or not demand for the product is dependent on sales of another product (such as in the link between jet engine and airplane sales). Price elasticity may vary sharply between market segments. For instance, business travellers are likely to be less sensitive to a change in hotel prices than are tourists, since the former may have little choice but to travel and, in any case, their employers will be paying the bills.

The price sensitivity for a given product category is not necessarily the same as that for an individual brand within that category. For example, if the price of Brand A's soap is raised, people may switch to another brand, decreasing Brand A's sales. However, if the prices of all brands of soap are raised, the sales of all brands may decline, but Brand A's sales will decline less than it would were it the only company to raise prices. The less individual brands are differentiated in consumers' eyes, the more difficult it is for a marketer to charge premium prices without losing substantial market share. Conversely, a small price cut by one organization may lead to substantial increases in selective demand. Such situations tend to lead to destructive price competition unless one of the firms in the industry is able to act as a price leader and stabilize prices.

COMPETITIVE STRUCTURE OF THE INDUSTRY

The number of firms in an industry often has a direct effect on pricing policy. When many competitors are selling an undifferentiated product—such as agricultural produce—individual marketers have little discretionary power to influence the prices at which they sell. In the absence of government regulation or a cartel, price is set by free-market conditions, and the marketer has little option but to accept it. Marketing boards for commodities such as eggs, chickens, and milk are one approach used in a number of Canadian agricultural industries to limit price competition.

At the other extreme are marketers who face no direct competition for a much needed product like electricity. In theory, these monopolists have complete discretionary power to establish their own selling prices. However, in practice, government regulatory bodies often monitor rate structures.

In oligopolistic situations, where there are relatively few competitors, like Canadian airlines, one or two of the principal firms may act as price leaders. Other firms are often content to follow their lead, settling for a stable market share in return for an acceptable margin of profits. Although the industry leaders have some discretionary influence over selling prices in such situations, they risk losing this role if their own prices stray too far from those dictated by underlying supply and demand forces in the industry.

In addition to evaluating the nature and extent of existing competition, the marketing manager must also evaluate the possibility of new companies entering the market. If barriers to entry are high—because of the need for substantial capital investments and/or access to scarce resources or expertise—then the prospect of new entrants may be remote. However, high prices and earnings within an industry may attract new competitors who are prepared to make the necessary investment for entry now in order to earn profits in the long run. Recognizing this, many firms in oligopolistic industries adopt low, "keep-out" prices, preferring lower short-run earnings to more competitors.

Typically, a firm attempts to escape from the constraints that the industry structure imposes on general pricing policy by differentiating other elements of the marketing mix. An analysis of competitive offerings, distribution channels, advertising and promotion options, and consumer needs (by segment) can provide insights into the realistic and operational feasibilities of such differentiation.

A further consideration is the level of the company's costs relative to those of the competition. A low-cost situation makes it possible to choose among such alternatives as:

1. enjoying extra profits;
2. allocating more resources to marketing activities, including research and development, in an effort to build sales and satisfy consumers better; or
3. initiating an aggressive, low-price strategy.

A firm with relatively high costs lacks this flexibility and will probably seek to avoid a low-price strategy which will put it at a financial disadvantage relative to competitors.

The most extreme example of competitive pricing concerns markets in which firms compete on the basis of bids, such as in the case of government procurement and the supply of certain industrial goods and services. While nonprice factors such as service, reliability, and product features can sometimes influence the outcome, the contract usually goes to the firm offering the lowest price for a product that meets the customer's specifications. For the marketer, cost and competition are the key factors in preparing a bid. If the company bids too low, it may not cover its costs; as the price increases, the chances of a competitor underbidding the company increase. Of course, the company does not know what its competitors will bid, so the company must trade off its chances of winning at a given price against the profit it would earn if it did win, in order to calculate its expected profit at different prices and to set its bid. Analysis of competitors is thus quite important in setting the appropriate bid price.

PRICING POLICIES FOR NEW PRODUCTS

In establishing the price for a new product, managers should recognize that the characteristics of the product itself play a central role. If it is merely a "me-too" item, not strongly differentiated from competitive offerings, then the level of existing prices may prove the crucial determinant. However, greater price discretion may be available to the marketer of a distinctively different product which has no close substitutes and is not likely to be imitated in the short term.

Other inputs to the pricing decision include an analysis of the market, prospective consumer segments, existing or potential competitors, and the needs of intermediaries in the distribution channel. Management must estimate potential demand in each major segment and the speed with which it will develop. Demand may be sensitive to changes in both price and the level of marketing effort. Sometimes a new product may be test-marketed at different prices in matched cities in order to obtain a better feel for the product's price sensitivity. An evaluation of competitive activity, if any, should provide details of the competitors' price range and the terms they offer to intermediaries. It may also help the marketer evaluate the possibility of price retaliation by firms that are marketing products likely to be displaced by the newcomer.

Communication and distribution decisions likewise have implications for pricing. The larger the communication budget, the higher fixed costs will be; further, the margin requirements of different distribution channels may influence the factory selling price and/or the recommended retail selling price.

By reviewing all these factors and undertaking a sensitivity analysis of the economic implications of alternative strategies, the marketing manager may be able to resolve the question of whether to adopt a "skim" or "penetration" policy.

Skimming is usually limited to distinctively different products. It involves setting a high initial price which skims the cream of demand at the outset, yielding high profits during the period before competition enters the market and prices start to fall. (High initial prices are sometimes also employed as a means of restricting demand at a time when product supply is limited.)

Market penetration is the opposite approach. It involves use of a low price to stimulate market growth and enable the firm to gain a dominant position; the goal is to pre-empt competition and ensure long-run profitability.

As the product matures and competitive activity increases, periodic evaluations are necessary to ensure that the pricing policy is realistic in the light of market conditions and the objectives of the firm.

CONCLUSION

When establishing pricing policies, marketing managers must be aware of the costs to be recovered, the prices charged by competitors for broadly similar products, and the value of the product to prospective purchasers. In a strict economic sense, the price set must yield a sufficient contribution so that, at the anticipated volume of sales, it will cover fixed costs and yield a satisfactory profit. Setting a price, however, is more complex than simply choosing a dollar amount to charge for a particular good or service. All pricing decisions must be made within the context of a marketing plan, which includes a clear specification of the objectives for each of the company's selected target markets and the linkage of pricing to other elements of the marketing mix.

19 CASCADE FOODS LTD.

Charles B. Weinberg

Sylvia Boaz, product manager for the newly formed fruit drinks division of Cascade Foods, was addressing her product management team in early March 1984.

> We've now completed the last of the test market experiments for the new line of fruit drinks in aseptic packages or "paper bottles," as many people call them. Although this packaging system is new to our market, it's been well accepted in Europe for a number of years and has gained market share rapidly in several U.S. cities. We've all agreed that the test market results are favourable for launching the product, but we can't make a final recommendation to top management until we settle on a pricing strategy. We might like to charge a premium for these fruit drinks but not if it'll damage sales too severely or open up the market for competition. It's ironic: here's a drink that tastes better than fruit drinks in cans, but is actually cheaper to package and ship in aseptic cartons. Do we price on cost or on value?

With these comments, Boaz began a meeting with Harold Mann, market research manager for Cascade Foods; Pierre Latouche, her product assistant; and Scott Green, an experienced marketing consultant who had worked for Cascade Foods a number of times in the past. Cascade had been considering entering the fruit drink market for a number of years, but had not been able to find a profitable niche in the market. The advent of aseptic packaging methods in which a container was made of laminated paperboard appeared to offer the opportunity that Cascade had been waiting for.

COMPANY BACKGROUND

Cascade Foods was founded in 1959 by Jacques Tremblay, the son of the controlling owner of Tremblay Stores, a leading regional supermarket chain. Jacques Tremblay had worked in various executive positions, becoming president of Tremblay Stores in 1952. In 1958, the Tremblay supermarkets were sold to an expanding national company. Although asked to remain as a senior executive in the company Jacques Tremblay resigned shortly after the takeover. He neither wanted to move from his home city nor work as an employee in a large company.

Jacques Tremblay began Cascade Foods as a regional marketer of branded packaged goods to supermarkets and other food stores. While many product categories—such as cereals, cake mixes, detergents, and toothpastes—were dominated by a few large companies that competed nationally, other product categories—such as many dairy products, baked goods, and several varieties of fruit juices—did not have nationally dominant brands. This is commonly observed by people who move from one region of Canada to another and cannot find their favourite brands. In the early 1980s, for example, Sealtest milk, a leading brand in Ontario, and Dairyland, a leader in the West, were generally not available in each other's main markets.

Based on his years in the supermarket business, Jacques Tremblay believed that there was considerable opportunity for a good regional marketer in many product categories. Some of the companies that sold to Tremblay Stores were professionally managed, but others maintained their position mainly due to a lack of effective competition.

Cascade Foods soon prospered. Its first products were baked goods (breads, rolls, cakes, etc.) and paper products (paper towels, napkins, toilet tissue, paper plates, etc.), but it soon developed a wider range of products. Different brand names were used in different product categories. Tremblay's strategy was to concentrate on the marketing of branded supermarket products and to use contract packers to manufacture the products sold by Cascade. Cascade presently used more than two dozen contract packers and monitored them under very tight quality control standards.

Cascade used brand advertising, primarily on local television and in newspapers, to establish strong brand images for its products. Coupled with an efficient distribution system, the company had earned a favourable reputation with the supermarket chains and food stores in the area. Although Cascade had experienced some costly failures, such as its brand of packaged cookies and line of tomato sauces, more than 60% of its product introductions were still on the market. Two product lines had been bought by a national food manufacturer who wanted to use the brand name and positioning strategy to launch nationwide brands.

At present, Cascade Foods marketed only one beverage product, apple juice. The product had been marginally successful with an approximately 7% market share in Cascade's region over the past five years. Although total volume of apple juice sold had grown in recent years, Cascade's market share had remained flat. About a year ago, a sales representative from the Montreal office of Tetra Pak Inc., the major supplier of aseptic packages ("paper bottles") in North America, had demonstrated the advantages of its packaging system to Cascade for its apply juice. Cascade management had quickly recognized that being first to use this system in the region's fruit drink market was a great opportunity.

ASEPTIC PACKAGING

Aseptic packaging was a dramatically different process for packaging milk, wine, fruit juices, drinks, and other liquid and semi-liquid products. Tetra-Pak, a family-owned Swedish company with almost $1.5 billion in sales in 1983, was the inventor of this packaging system and the dominant supplier of aseptic packages world-wide. In Western Europe, almost 50% of all milk was sold in Tetra-Pak containers, which allowed milk to be kept unrefrigerated for up to five months without loss of nutritional value or flavour. Not only did this provide a benefit for customers, but there were important savings in not having to use refrigerated shipment and storage. Up to 60% of a typical supermarket's energy bill was for refrigeration.

Although the refrigeration savings and longer shelf life were of limited application in the fruit juice and fruit drink industries, aseptic paper cartons cost less than bottles and cans. One-litre aseptic boxes were estimated to cost only about 30% as much as bottles and 50% of the cost of cans. Although the filling process for aseptic containers was more complicated (both the container and contents needed to be sterilized), one research firm estimated that the cost of filling juice concentrate in 250 mL Brik Pak boxes was 18% less than that for bottles or metal cans. Similar savings prevailed for larger sizes.

Cost savings were just one of the advantages of putting fruit drinks in the compact Brik Pak, Tetra-Pak's most popular shape, which came in two main sizes—a 250 mL box with a drinking straw attached for the convenience market—and a one-litre container. (Other sizes were available, and in 1984 Tetra-Pak was working on advancements such as a resealable 2 L package for milk.) Aseptic packaging required only flash sterilization during packing, rather than the longer heating process for canned and bottled goods (juice was usually pasteurized after bottling). Consequently, for fruit juices and drinks, the flavours were reported to be truer than in cans and bottles. On the other hand, some people felt that the sterilization process for milk gave it a slightly "cooked" flavour. The rectangular shape of the Brik Pak (whose shape fit its name quite well) allowed it to be easily stacked. Twelve Brik Paks in the one-litre size took only about two-thirds as much supermarket display space as 12 one-litre bottles. However, Brik Paks lacked the rigidity necessary for packaging carbonated beverages.

Convenience was a particularly critical factor for the 250 mL Brik Pak carton that measured approximately 6.3 cm wide × 10 cm tall × 3.8 cm deep. It appeared to be just the right size for lunch boxes and snacks and was being sold in specially designed vending machines in some markets. According to a senior executive of Ocean Spray Cranberries Inc. in the United States, a pioneer in the marketing of aseptic packaged drinks (such as Cranapple), "The kinds of products we offer suddenly become portable." One company reported a 20% increase in fruit drink sales due to aseptic packaging and classified these volume gains as almost completely incremental. Some soft drink bottlers had begun selling aseptic packages of fruit drinks and stocking them next to soda in supermarkets.

Tetra-Pak Inc., the Canadian subsidiary of Tetra-Pak, had recently built a large manufacturing plant in Ontario to produce aseptic packages for the Canadian market. In addition there were several other North American companies either producing or planning to produce aseptic packages in the near future. After Scott Green had reviewed the aseptic packaging industry, Cascade had decided to use Brik Pak cartons for its proposed entry into the fruit drink market. Cascade, in fact, would not do the manufacturing itself but would buy the finished product from a contract packer who would prepare the product according to Cascade's specifications. Cascade had successfully used this contract packer for several other product lines and had been extremely pleased with the quality and service provided by this firm.

FRUIT DRINK MARKET

Background

Fruit drink sales in Cascade's market area had grown 80% in the past five years (Exhibit 1). Fruit drinks were only one type of beverage refreshment. The most immediate competitors were fruit juices (which had a higher fruit content than fruit drinks) and powdered fruit drink mixes, to which a consumer added water and sometimes sugar. Other competitors included carbonated beverages, plain and flavoured milks, and bottled or tap water. Few brands competed in more than one of these markets, although some companies had brands in more than one of these markets.

The fruit drink market was very competitive with a number of national and regional brands available; market share data are reported in Exhibit 2. Despite its competitive

Exhibit 1

FRUIT DRINK SALES IN CASCADE MARKET AREA

Year	Quarter (000s of Cases)*			
	1	2	3	4
1979	428	415	452	413
1980	456	463	532	479
1981	502	543	627	568
1982	715	699	732	701
1983	768	750	791	731

* 1 case = 12 litres of fruit drinks

Exhibit 2

MARKET SHARE DATA FOR FRUIT DRINKS (ALL SIZES AND FLAVOURS), BASED ON VOLUME IN CASCADE'S MARKET AREA

	1980	1981	1982
Brand A	26%	26%	25%
Brand B	12%	13%	13%
Brand C	12%	9%	7%
Brand D	1%	5%	10%
Store brands and private labels	21%	24%	26%
Other brands	28%	23%	19%

intensity, the market seemed to promise high profitability. At current prices, a national brand was estimated to have a gross contribution margin of $3 per case (before advertising, promotion, and other marketing costs).

Although the brands differed in the number of flavours offered and competed, at times, by introducing new flavours, three accounted for the bulk of sales. These were apple, grape, and mixed fruit. The fruits combined in the mixed fruit drink differed from brand to brand, and some consumers showed a strong preference for the taste of a particular brand's mixed fruit drink. Often, the mixed fruit drink was the company's main focus in advertising and the basis on which the brand had been launched. The apple, grape, and other drink flavours often had been introduced to provide variety and satisfy the taste preferences of consumers.

The national brands were heavily advertised. Although Pierre Latouche, the product manager's assistant, could not obtain estimates of advertising and promotion levels on a regional basis, he was able to obtain estimates of expenditures for one national brand for three recent years:

	Cases Sold (000s)	Advertising (000s)	Promotion (000s)
1980	970	$ 950	$680
1981	1300	1340	870
1982	1560	1500	950

About 25% of the market was accounted for by store brands. These brands competed primarily on price; one litre of a store brand fruit drink would typically sell for about $0.20 less than a nationally advertised brand retailing at $1.29. Store brands were more successful in the grape and apple flavours than in mixed fruit flavours.

Entry into the Market

Sylvia Boaz led a new product team to investigate the possibility of using aseptic packaging systems as a vehicle for entry into the fruit drink market. Although some products, such as the Ocean Spray Cranberry drinks, were already sold in Cascade's market, as yet there was only limited availability of fruit drinks in aseptic packages. Boaz had estimated that Cascade, by moving quickly, could be the first major brand in its area to use the Brik Pak system. The major consumer benefits to be featured would be the flavour of the product and the convenience of the package. Senior management approval had been given to carry the project through the test market stage and Boaz was appointed product manager in charge of the product.

Cascade had tentatively decided on an initial three flavour line (mixed fruit, grape, and apple) in 250 mL and 1 L Brik Pak cartons. In consultation with its contract packer, Cascade had developed the fruit drinks. Harold Mann, the market research manager, had conducted a number of taste tests for the new product and found that the Cascade drinks were favoured, on average, by about 65% of respondents in paired comparison taste tests in which subjects did not know the brand name of the product they were drinking. This was considered a very strong score.

The marketing plan for the first year called for an aggressive advertising and promotion budget of $500,000 for advertising and $350,000 for consumer and trade promotion. (Generally, Cascade budgeted about 50% more funds for a new brand introduction than would be required to maintain an established brand at the same volume of sales.) Sales force costs were estimated at $225,000; distribution costs were included in the production costs and not charged against the contribution. The only other charge against the contribution margin was the $250,000 budget for the product management team, which included the salaries of Boaz and Latouche, costs for market research and consultants, and similar expenses incurred by Boaz and her group. At Cascade, entries into new product categories were not expected to break even until the second or third year of marketing.

PRICING DECISIONS

Sylvia Boaz and her team had recognized that pricing was one of the most critical decisions to be made. If Cascade were priced on a par with other branded versions of fruit drinks (equivalent to $1.29 per litre and $0.40 per 250 mL carton), the cost savings from aseptic packaging would allow a gross contribution margin of $4 per case—$1 per case greater than that presently estimated to be earned by the leading advertised brands. Assuming the introductory advertising and promotion policy described above, market research tests conducted under the supervision of Harold Mann and Scott Green had estimated a market share of 10% of the fruit drink market at the end of the first year. Cascade had developed a relatively sophisticated market research, simulation, and test market system to forecast the sales of new products. In the past, that system had estimated the share of market obtained by the new entrant at the end of one year within 1.5% of the actual share 80% of the time. In other words, Cascade believed there was an 80% probability that Cascade fruit drinks would have a market share between 8.5% and 11.5% at the end of one year with the planned introductory campaign.

Parity pricing was not the only alternative. Latouche had argued strongly that Cascade should charge a premium price for the product. Cascade's real strength, he suggested, was its ability to market branded products in its regional area. Here was a product with superior flavour and convenience, so the customer should be willing to pay more for it. Latouche had claimed that "if it cost more to manufacture than canned drinks, we would charge a higher price without question. Why shouldn't Cascade take the extra profit for itself? Furthermore, a premium price will help convey to consumers the superiority of the product. With a strong advertising campaign, we can position ourselves at the top of the market. If we set the price as the first entrants, others will price at our level. There's very little price variation among major brands at present."

Scott Green had questioned that approach. "High prices only provide an umbrella for competition to enter the market. Besides, why would consumers pay more? A high price could really depress sales. The package itself is novel enough, without imposing a price barrier as well for consumers. Pricing below current prices for canned drinks might even provide an incentive for initial trial, but Cascade shouldn't have to do that in the long run."

The product management group recognized that the pricing decision was too important to be left to guesses. Market research data might help narrow down some of the issues. Harold Mann, the market research manager, had over time built Cascade management's appreciation of both the value and limits of market research. While market research could not eliminate all uncertainty, it could often reduce some of it.

Two years ago, Cascade had run an experiment for its apple juice brand on the effect of short-term price promotions on sales. This study is summarized in the Appendix. It clearly showed that price reductions had a significant impact on sales, especially when combined with special supermarket displays.

However, the apple juice test, while helpful, was not directly relevant to the fruit drink market. Here Cascade was concerned with a permanent price for a new product. As a result, Boaz asked Mann to use the test market not only to assess the likely success of the product and its expected first-year market share, as reported earlier, but also to test the effect of different prices on sales of fruit drinks. As a group, the product management team helped design an experiment. Three price levels were tested:

Low:	\$1.19/L; \$0.35/250 mL
Regular:	\$1.29/L; \$0.40/250 mL
High:	\$1.39/L; \$0.45/250 mL

A change in the retail price of \$0.10/litre and \$0.05/250 mL was equivalent to a change of \$0.90 in Cascade's contribution per case, given the mix of sizes likely to be sold.

In addition, there was considerable discussion about the effect of advertising on price sensitivity. Some believed that higher levels of advertising decreased price sensitivity by establishing a strong brand image. Others felt that higher advertising expenditures expanded the potential market for the brand, but that the additional potential consumers were more price sensitive. Hence, they argued for a strategy of high advertising and low prices. Recognizing the importance of this factor, the test market was designed to test two levels of introductory advertising:

Normal:	annual rate of \$500,000
High:	annual rate of \$1,000,000

These six different price and advertising levels (3 prices × 2 ad budgets) were tested in 24 supermarkets in four cities. Two cities received high advertising levels, and two received low levels. Because price could be set individually by store, high, regular, and low prices were tested in two stores in each of the four cities used. Sales in units (normalized for store volume) were recorded bimonthly for each size and flavour for the four months that the test ran. There were no major differences in sales among flavours and sizes, so the data were summarized more compactly as shown in Exhibit 3. These data showed a clear effect of price and advertising on sales, but did not fully resolve the issue of the price and advertising levels to use.

Exhibit 3
PRICE AND ADVERTISING EXPERIMENT

Sales in Units for Months 1 & 2	Sales in Units for Months 3 & 4	Price	Advertising
331	280	L	N
394	256	L	N
329	279	L	N
403	217	L	N
662	430	L	H
478	357	L	H
552	337	L	H
665	474	L	H
253	247	R	N
289	190	R	N
276	270	R	N
335	203	R	N
351	224	R	H
535	394	R	H
409	203	R	H
424	305	R	H
252	220	H	N
293	151	H	N
255	181	H	N
210	156	H	N
221	148	H	H
321	254	H	H
310	172	H	H
312	249	H	H

Note: Sales in each store were adjusted for the overall volume of fruit drinks sold in each supermarket. The prices tested were Low ($1.19, $0.35), Regular ($1.29, $0.40) and High ($1.39, $0.45); the advertising budgets tested were Normal ($500,000) and High ($1 million).

A week after receiving these data, Boaz convened a meeting of the product management group. She had asked both Latouche and Green independently to prepare recommendations on a pricing strategy for Cascade fruit drinks in aseptic packages. The purpose of the meeting was to hear both presentations and resolve the issue of the right pricing strategy. Boaz would then need to prepare a report for senior management with a recommendation on whether to enter the fruit drink market and, if so, with what marketing plan and goals.

Appendix
APPLE JUICE EXPERIMENT

In conjunction with one supermarket chain, Cascade had conducted an extensive test of the impact of price promotions and display space on sales of its Cascade brand of apple juice. In brief, Cascade tested three price levels—its regular price level of $1.59 per litre of apple juice and prices of 10 and 20 cents off—and two display types, regular shelf space and a special end-of-aisle display. Thus there were six different conditions (3 price levels × 2 display levels). The experiment was conducted in six stores over a 12-week period. In alternate weeks 2, 4, 6, 8, 10, and 12 each store was randomly assigned one of the six treatments, and over the six experimental weeks, each store received each combination of price and display once. In the alternate weeks, price and display space were set at their normal levels. The impact on units sold were as follows (where 100 represents the level of sales at the regular price and with the normal display):

	Normal Display	End-of-Aisle Display
Regular price	100	131
10 cents off	124	143
20 cents off	136	157

In the week immediately following an experimental treatment, sales of apple juice declined about 10% in all cases except for the combination 20 cents off and end-of-aisle display where sales in the week following the experiment declined almost 20%. After the experiment ended, Cascade apple juice sales returned to their normal levels.

20 FRASER COMPANY

Charles B. Weinberg

Alice Howell, president of the Columbia Plastics Division of the Fraser Co., leaned forward at her desk in her bright, sunlit office and said, "In brief, our two options are either to price at a level that just covers our costs or to risk losing market leadership to those upstart Canadians at Vancouver Light. Are there no other options?" Tamara Chu, Columbia's marketing manager, and Sam Carney, the production manager, had no immediate reply.

Columbia Plastics, based in Seattle, Washington, had been the area's leading manufacturer of plastic moulded skylights for use in houses and offices for almost 15 years. However, two years earlier Vancouver Light, whose main plant was located in Vancouver, British Columbia, 240 km to the north of Seattle, had opened a sales office in the city and sought to gain business by pricing aggressively. Vancouver Light began by offering skylights at 20% below Columbia's price for large orders. Now Vancouver Light had just announced a further price cut of 10%.

COMPANY BACKGROUND

The primary business of the Fraser Co., which had recently celebrated its fiftieth anniversary, was the supply of metal and plastic fabricated parts for its well-known Seattle neighbour, Boeing Aircraft. Until the 1960s Boeing had accounted for more than 80% of the company's volume, but Fraser then decided to diversify in order to protect itself against the boom and bust cycle which seemed to characterize the aircraft industry. Even now, Boeing still accounted for nearly half of Fraser's \$50 million[1] in annual sales.

Columbia Plastics had been established to apply Fraser's plastic moulding skills in the construction industry. Its first products, which still accounted for nearly 30% of sales, included plastic garage doors, plastic gutters, and plastic covers for outdoor lights, all of which had proved to be popular among Seattle home-builders. In 1968, Columbia began production of what was to be its most successful product, skylights for homes and offices. Skylights now accounted for 70% of Columbia's sales.

THE SKYLIGHT MARKET

Although skylights varied greatly in size, a typical one measured 1 m × 1 m and was installed in the ceiling of a kitchen, bathroom, or living-room. It was made primarily of moulded plastic with an aluminum frame. Skylights were usually installed by homebuilders upon initial construction of a home or by professional contractors as part of a remodelling job. Because of the need to cut through the roof to install a skylight and then seal the joint between the roof and skylight so that water would

[1] All prices and costs are in U.S. dollars.

not leak through, only the most talented "do-it-yourselfers" would tackle this job on their own. At present 70% of the market was in home and office buildings, 25% in professional remodelling, and 5% in the do-it-yourself market.

Skylights had become very popular. Home-owners found the natural light it brought to a room attractive and perceived skylights to be energy conserving. Although opinion was divided on whether the heat loss from a skylight was more than light gained, the general perception was quite favourable. Home-builders found that featuring a skylight in a kitchen or other rooms would be an important plus in attracting buyers and often included at least one skylight as a standard feature. Condominium builders found that their customers liked the openness a skylight provided. Skylights were also a popular feature of the second homes that many people owned on Washington's lakes or in ski areas throughout the area.

In Columbia Plastics' primary market area of Washington, Oregon, Idaho, and Montana, sales of skylights had levelled off in recent years to about 45,000 units per year. Although Columbia would occasionally sell a large order to California home-builders, such sales were made only to fill slack in the plant and, after including the cost of transportation, were break-even propositions at best. No sales were made to Canada.

Four home-builders accounted for half the sales of skylights in the Pacific Northwest region of the United States. Another five bought an average of 1,000 units each, and the remaining sales were split among more than 100 independent builders and remodellers. Some repackaged the product under their own brand name, and many purchased only a few dozen or less.

Columbia would ship directly only to builders who ordered at least 500 units per year, although it would subdivide the order into sections of one gross (144) for shipping. Most builders and remodellers bought their skylights from building supply dealers, hardware stores, and lumberyards. Columbia sold and shipped directly to these dealers, who typically marked up the product by 50%. Columbia's average factory price was $200 when Vancouver Light first entered the market two years ago.

Columbia maintained a sales force of three people who contacted builders, remodellers, and retail outlets. The sales force was responsible for Columbia's complete line of products which generally went through the same channels of distribution. The cost of maintaining the sales force, including necessary selling support and travel expenses, was $90,000 annually.

Until the advent of Vancouver Light, there had been no significant local competition for Columbia. Several California manufacturers had small shares of the market, but Columbia had held a 70% market share until two years ago.

VANCOUVER LIGHT'S ENTRY

Vancouver Light was founded in the early 1970s by Jennifer McLaren, an engineer, Carl Garner, an architect, and several business associates in order to manufacture skylights. They believed there was a growing demand for skylights. Their assessment proved correct, and because there was no ready source of supply available in western Canada, their business was successful.

Two years ago the Canadian company announced the opening of a sales office in Seattle. Jennifer McLaren came to this office two days a week and devoted her attention to selling skylights only to the large volume builders. Vancouver Light announced a price 20% below Columbia's with a minimum order size of 1,000 units to be shipped all at one time. It quickly gained all the business of one large builder, True Homes, a Canadian-owned company. In the previous year that builder had ordered 6,000 skylights from Columbia.

A year later one of Columbia's sales representatives was told by the purchasing manager of Chieftain Homes, a Seattle-based builder who had installed 7,000 skylights the previous year, that Chieftain would switch to Vancouver Light for most of its skylights unless Columbia was prepared to match Vancouver's price. Columbia then matched that price for orders above 2,500 units, guessing that smaller customers would value highly the local service that Columbia could provide. Chieftain then ordered 40% of its needs from Vancouver Light. Two smaller builders had since switched to Vancouver Light as well. Before Vancouver's latest price cut had been reported, Tamara Chu, Columbia's marketing manager, projected that Vancouver Light would sell about 11,000 units this year, compared to the 24,000 that Columbia was now selling. Columbia's volume represented a decline of 1,000 units per year in each of the last two years, following the initial loss of the True Homes account.

Columbia had asked its lawyers to investigate whether Vancouver Light's sales could be halted on charges of export dumping, that is, selling below cost in a foreign market, but a quick investigation revealed that Vancouver Light's specialized production facility provided a 25% savings on variable costs, although a third of that was lost due to the additional costs involved in importing and transporting the skylights across the border from Canada to the United States.

THE IMMEDIATE CRISIS

Alice Howell and her two colleagues had reviewed the situation carefully. Sam Carney, the production manager, had presented the cost accounting data which showed a total unit cost of $135 for Columbia's most popular skylight. Vancouver Light, he said, was selling a similar model at $144. The cost of $135 included $15 in manufacturing overheads, directly attributable to skylights, but not the cost of the sales force nor the salaries, benefits, and overheads associated with the three executives in the room. General overheads, including the sales force and executives, amounted to $390,000 per year at present for Columbia as a whole.

Tamara Chu was becoming quite heated about Vancouver Light by this time. "Let's cut the price a further 10% to $130 and drive those Canadians right out of the market! That Jennifer McLaren started with those big builders and now she's after the whole market. We'll show her what competition really is!"

But Carney was shocked: "You mean we'll drive her *and us* out of business at the same time! We'll both lose money on every unit we sell. What has our sales force been doing all these years if not building customer loyalty for our product?"

"We may lose most of our sales to the big builders," cut in Alice Howell, "but surely most customers wouldn't be willing to rely on shipments from Canada? Maybe we should let Vancouver Light have the customers who want to buy on the basis of price. We can then make a tidy profit from customers who value service, need immediate supply, and have dealt with our company for years."

21 CLASSY FORMAL WEAR

V. H. Kirpalani

H. J. Simpkins

Stephen Hecht, grandson of Marcus Hecht, the founder of Classy Formal Wear, and now executive vice-president and chief operating officer of the firm, was considering how his new line of tuxedos, made in Korea but carrying the Yves Saint Laurent Label, should be priced. It was June 1989. A large quantity of the new, black, pure-wool tuxedos would be arriving in early 1990 at a cost which would permit a retail price well below any comparable tuxedo in the market. However, a low price might have an unfavourable impact on the firm's marketing image among its most important customers. Stephen Hecht was pondering both the tactical and strategic consequences of alternative prices, in preparation for choosing a price for the new line.

HISTORY AND GROWTH

Marcus Hecht had founded the firm in 1919 as one of the first formal wear rental stores in Canada. At that time, formal wear—tuxedos; full dress, black, tail coat outfits; and morning suits—was worn almost exclusively by well-to-do men. They wore formal attire to such events as weddings, balls, concerts, and school graduations. Hecht felt that the appeal of this type of clothing could be broadened if quality formal garments were made available at prices that the growing middle class could afford and, hence, he founded Classy as a formal wear rental company. By renting tuxedos, tail coats, and morning suits at a fraction of their retail selling prices, Hecht believed that he could attract substantial numbers of new customers who would otherwise not dress in formal wear.

From a one-store operation located near Montreal's downtown core, he gradually expanded the business so that by the late 1940s there were five stores in the city as well as one in Ottawa. By the 1950s his sons had assumed management positions in the company and stores were opened in Toronto and Hamilton. During the 1960s, Marcus Hecht handed the presidency of the company over to his eldest son Jack who continued Classy's expansion with the successful opening of stores in Vancouver and Quebec City.

Parallel to the growth in formal wear rentals in the six cities where Classy had stores, the company began to offer formal wear for sale on a limited basis. A narrow range of shirts were made available and tuxedos were offered for sale on a made-to-order basis with an average delivery time of six weeks.

THE MARKET AND THE COMPETITION

By the 1970s, retail sales accounted for just 5% of total company volume and were basically regarded as an add-on as opposed to a mainstream contribution to corporate revenues from rentals. Towards the latter part of that decade, there was a levelling off in the number of weddings taking place. This phenomenon occurred because the baby boom generation, born in the late 1940s and early 1950s, had now passed the usual marriage age. Close to 80% of formal wear rentals were for weddings and the stabilization in the number of weddings was not encouraging. (The other 20% of the market was split about evenly between school graduations and other formal occasions.)

In 1978, Jack Hecht passed away and left no heirs. His brother Joseph became Classy's president and the trends in the marketplace concerned him as well as his son Stephen, who had been appointed executive vice-president and chief operating officer in the early 1980s. A recent MBA graduate from the University of Western Ontario, Stephen brought a pronounced marketing emphasis to Classy's way of doing business. His research and analysis of the formal wear market showed that the levelling off in the number of weddings was being more than offset by an increasing number of weddings "going formal." In other words, although there was no growth in weddings actually taking place, there were more formal weddings. However, he could not be sure how long this phenomenon would continue.

CLASSY'S STRATEGY

Stephen decided to establish two fundamental marketing objectives for Classy. The first was to significantly increase the company's share of the formal wear rental market across the country. The second was to increase substantially the level of Classy's retail sales.

One of the key strategic tools the company used to help it achieve these objectives was the location and design of Classy stores. First, the company opened stores in new cities, namely Edmonton, Calgary, Winnipeg, and Kitchener. Also, it added stores in Vancouver, Toronto, Ottawa, and Montreal. Third, all the new stores were located in prime retail areas, either in downtown cores or in major regional shopping malls. Finally, all of the company's stores, including the older ones, were fitted with retail merchandising fixtures such as suit racks, shirt display units, and point-of-purchase shelving for formal wear accessories.

Another key strategic action Classy deployed was to increase the availability and inventory levels of its retail merchandise. All stores now carried and displayed a basic line of tuxedos priced from $399 to $599, formal shirts from $39 to $49, and bow tie and cummerbund accessory sets priced at $37. By comparison, very few of Classy's competitors carried any retail stock whatsoever, although they all offered used as well as custom-ordered tuxedos for sale.

Classy currently had 38 retail stores and was the dominant formal wear company in the country. Retail sales now accounted for about 10% of company revenues. But, in Stephen Hecht's assessment, Classy had barely scratched the surface of the potential retail sales market. Moreover, he felt the company was now well positioned to dramatically increase its sales revenues.

PLANNING ITS SALES REVENUES

It was with this in mind that Stephen Hecht developed an aggressive plan to make Classy the leading Canadian formal wear retailer. In early 1989, he visited a number of manufacturers of men's suits in Korea. During his three-week stay in that country, he discovered that the quality of suits being produced there was equal to and, in many cases, better than that being made in Canada. He also determined that any of the major Korean manufacturers could make quality tuxedos at about 60% of the cost of Classy's Canadian suppliers. The same cost structure proved to be the case with the Korean shirt manufacturers. Toward the end of his trip, Stephen Hecht placed an order for 2,000 black, pure-wool tuxedos with one of the suit manufacturers, for delivery in early 1990. He also placed a substantial order for formal shirts.

On his return to Canada, he actively pursued and secured the exclusive licence for the Yves Saint Laurent name and pattern. As a result of this, all of the tuxedos he had ordered from Korea would carry the Yves Saint Laurent label, and Classy would be the only formal wear specialist in Canada permitted to sell Yves Saint Laurent tuxedos.

The total landed cost to Classy for these Korean-produced Yves Saint Laurent tuxedos came to $137.50 including licencing fees. To begin the process of developing a pricing strategy for the new tuxedos, Stephen Hecht called a meeting of his three key executives on June 26, 1989.

MARKETING DECISION TIME

Attending the meeting were Stephen Hecht and Classy's three vice-presidents of finance, operations, and marketing. Stephen opened the meeting by reviewing the highlights of the plan he had put together. He stated that the company's goal should be to sell 2,000 tuxedos during the next year. He then asked the group for suggestions in regard to a retail selling price for the tuxedos.

The vice-president of finance remarked that this purchase of tuxedos by Classy was the largest investment in retail stock that the company had ever made. He went on to say that the company's overall objectives would be best served by recouping this investment as quickly as possible, so that funds for expansion would not be tied up for any appreciable amount of time.

The vice-president of operations expressed his agreement with this point of view, but was quick to add that the company had never sold more than 500 tuxedos in any one year.

The vice-president of marketing added that while the quality and designer name associated with the new tuxedos were inherently attractive, there were three key factors to consider when pricing them. First, consumer research in the United States indicated that the typical tuxedo purchaser was over 35 years of age and was most likely to go to a men's wear or department store, rather than to a formal wear store, for his purchase. Second, most of Classy's current customers were under 35 years of age. Third, within the past two years there had been strong competition in the retailing of tuxedos. According to the vice-president of marketing, competition could be categorized as in the following table (he also included Classy's proposed line).

Type of Store	Types of Tuxedos Offered	Designer Labels	Retail Prices
Better men's wear stores	Very high quality 100% wool Italian, German, and American imports	Giorgio Armani Mario Valentino Gianni Versace Hugo Boss Polo by Ralph Lauren	$749–$1,500
Better department stores	High quality 100% wool Italian and British imports and Canadian garments	Mani by Giorgio Armani Emmanuel Ungaro Hardy Aimies	$499–$749
Regular men's wear stores	Good quality polyester/wool blends from Korea and Canada	Private label	$295–$349
Discount men's wear stores and boutiques	Adequate quality polyester/wool blends from Korea and Eastern Europe	Private label	$179–$229
Classy	Good quality 100% wool from Korea	Yves Saint Laurent	?

Finally, he pointed out that Classy is not perceived as a formal wear retailer by the 35 and over age group and that in establishing a retail selling price, the average rental price of $85 should be kept in mind. The vice-president of operations reminded the group that the $85 rental price included a shirt, bow tie, and cummerbund or vest, as well as cuff links and shirt studs, and that this should be kept in mind as well.

The next issue that came up at the meeting was the market size. How many men are there who are considering a tuxedo purchase? Should the retail price be set at a low enough level to attract those men who have not as yet considered buying a tuxedo, or should it be set to appeal mainly to those who are already thinking about buying one? Given the company's objective of turning over the 2,000 tuxedos now on order in one year, it was agreed to set a price that would be attractive to both groups.

At this point the vice-president of operations suggested a $299 retail selling price. The vice-president of marketing supported this suggestion since it seemed to offer broad appeal to potential consumers and, from an advertising standpoint, could create a strong impact. The vice-president of finance remarked that the 54% mark-up level now being generated by Classy's other retail items. Therefore, he also supported the $299 price.

As the meeting began to wind down, Stephen Hecht said that the $299 price was deserving of consideration. But he was going to take a few days to think about it before making a firm recommendation to Joseph Hecht, Classy's president. In Stephen's mind, there were a number of questions that remained to be answered. First and foremost was his concern that Classy might be missing a major short-term profit opportunity by not pricing the tuxedos higher, say at $349 or $379 or $399. Given the high quality, pure-wool fabrication of the garments, he felt that the market may be willing to pay up to $100 more. He was also concerned about supply lines. If the tuxedos sold out very quickly, Classy would be caught in an out-of-stock situation. The lead time for delivery from Korea was six months. The last thing Stephen Hecht wanted was to have to turn away customers because there were no $299 Yves Saint Laurent tuxedos left for sale. On the other hand, he did not want the company to be holding large quantities of unsold stock at the end of the year.

Finally, Stephen Hecht realized that the price would have strategic implications for the kinds of customers that Classy might appeal to, and the image that Classy might create relative to the competition. But he was less sure of the best marketing strategy for Classy to pursue, and how alternative prices might help or hinder the chosen strategy.

22 ALIAS RESEARCH INC.

Douglas Snetsinger
Susan Spencer

"I can't believe they did it again!" exclaimed Isaac Babbs, district sales manager for the southwestern United States for Alias Research Inc. For the fourth time in 1990 he had lost a sale to Wavefront, his major competitor in the animation software market. He had worked on this sale for a month and he felt confident that the prospective customer was ready to buy Alias's $100,000 software. But Wavefront had stepped in at the last moment, cut their price from $55,000 to $25,000, and obtained the sale. Wavefront, a California-based company, seemed determined to dominate the region, while Alias, based in Toronto, was at least equally determined to make further inroads into the California market. "How does Toronto expect me to compete if they won't give me some flexibility on pricing," Babbs lamented as he thought about Alias's rigidly enforced policy of not permitting any price discounting on its products. With a sigh of resignation, he reached for the phone to call Toronto and let them know that another sale was lost to a price-cutting competitor.

THE HIGH-END GRAPHICS MARKET

Alias Research Inc., a software company located in Toronto, was a recognized market leader in high-end, three-dimensional (3D) computer graphics. Its product, ALIAS, was used in film animation, industrial design, architecture, education, medical and scientific visualization, packaging and product design, flight or space simulation, and a number of other applications. Seventy percent of the world's automobile manufacturers used ALIAS in their design processes. Some of its customers in other industries included Goodyear, Timex, Kraft, Motorola, Northern Telecom, Johnson & Johnson, and Industrial Light and Magic. Alias had sales offices in Boston, Princeton, Los Angeles, Chicago, and Detroit, as well as in France and Germany. The corporate officers for Alias are listed in Exhibit 1.

The total size of the market served by Alias was estimated at $81 million (U.S.) in 1990, of which Alias held a 15% share. Industry experts had forecast that the market would increase to $300 million by 1992. Virtually all of the growth was in the field of industrial design which currently accounted for 40% of the market. The remaining 60% was in the animation field, which was growing at a rate of only 1% each year. The animation market was saturated with a variety of competing products.

Alias's three main competitors were Wavefront Technologies, Thompson Digital Image (TDI), and Evans and Sutherland Computer Corporation (E&S). Originally a private custom software builder, Wavefront entered the video animation market in 1985 at approximately the same time as Alias. It had recently modified its package to provide some industrial design capability. However, Wavefront's product did not easily translate into manufacturable designs, and it required extensive training before any of its advanced tools could be properly used. Wavefront's major advantage was that their product could be run on many different types of computers, as opposed to Alias's which could only be run on Silicon Graphics hardware or IBM workstations.

Based in Paris, France, Thompson Digital Image (TDI) was Alias's principal competitor in the European market. TDI was a subsidiary of the Thompson Group, though 56% of TDI was owned by the French government. TDI's primary market, accounting for 80% of sales, was the video animation market. It was estimated that TDI had approximately 20 clients in the video post-production industry. TDI was also pursuing industrial design customers and had been successful with some leading French firms including Renault, the automobile manufacturer. TDI was currently overhauling its design software based on a similar technology to the Alias product.

Evans and Sutherland (E&S) was a large, multi-divisional computer hardware and software company with total sales of $129 million (U.S.). Based in Salt Lake City, they were engaged in the development of interactive super-computers for large-scale scientific and technical computations, modelling, and simulations. The Graphics Products Group designed and built high performance three-dimensional graphics hardware and specialized software. E&S's closest product to ALIAS was the Conceptual Design and Rendering System, a turn-key, computer-aided design system that was introduced in 1988. The system was developed in partnership with Ford and Chrysler. It was based on Alias-type technology and was priced at $200,000 (U.S.) to $250,000 (U.S.) and ran only on proprietary hardware manufactured by E&S.

Exhibit 1
ALIAS RESEARCH INC.—EXECUTIVE OFFICERS AND DIRECTORS

Name	Age*	Position
Stephen R.B. Bingham	40	President, Chief Executive Officer and Chairman of the Board of Directors
Susan I. McKenna	31	Executive Vice-President and Director
William J. McClintock	38	Vice-President Finance, Secretary, Treasurer, and Chief Financial Officer
Arthur W. Bell	34	Vice-President Marketing
Martin I. Tuori	38	Vice-President Research and Development
Gregory S. Hill	35	Vice-President Business Development
David N. Macrae	34	Vice-President Sales
Brian J. Conway	31	Director
William S. Kaiser	34	Director
Barry L. Stephens	50	Director

* Ages are as of July 1990.

ALIAS HISTORY

The Beginning

Alias Research Inc. was founded in 1983 by Stephen Bingham, Nigel McGrath, Susan McKenna, and David Springer. With few resources, they borrowed $500,000 of computer graphic equipment from McGrath's company and rented an office in an old elevator shaft for $150 per month. Though starting small in scope, the owners of this fledgling company had a big dream: to create an easy-to-use software package that would produce realistic 3D video animation for the advertising industry post-production houses.

Many companies in this industry had difficulty raising start-up funds and Alias was no exception. The problem was that it required substantial time and effort to develop software to the point where it was "debugged" and ready to be sold to customers. As much as 150 person-years of research and development effort might go into making the first working piece of software. Thus, investors were reluctant to provide funds on promises, as opposed to finished products.

However, Alias was able to obtain a $61,000 grant from the National Research Council, which, when combined with the limited funds of the founders, allowed work to begin. Other financial support was gained from the federal government through Scientific Research Tax Credits (SRTCs). A SRTC was actually a contract that allowed an investor to hire Alias to do a specified amount of research, in return for which the investor would get a tax credit for their own company. This sort of arrangement yielded two benefits for Alias. It provided much needed start-up funding and it allowed the four founders to maintain control of the company. It also allowed Alias to earn money by doing the research that was required for its own project.

Development of the software continued until mid-1985. One of the early decisions made was building the software based on a relatively new form of modelling technique which used cardinal splines rather than traditional polygonal lines.[1] Silicon Graphics, a small hardware firm based in California, produced a workstation that was specifically designed to work with spline technology. Silicon Graphics soon became a staunch supporter of Alias as they saw the opportunity for enhanced applications for their workstation.

The product, ALIAS, was unveiled at the Special Interest Group on Graphics (SIGGRAPH) show in July of 1985. The annual SIGGRAPH show was attended by many people who were involved in design (for example, designing products, labels, packages) and by many people who could help the designers (for example, software companies like Alias). For a company like Alias, the SIGGRAPH show provided an important opportunity to introduce and market new products. Many of the Alias group would attend the show and work long hours to generate leads for the ALIAS system. In fact, sales of ALIAS could often be traced to an initial meeting at the SIGGRAPH show.

[1] A cardinal spline is based on the first derivative of the modelling equation, while polygonal lines are based on the actual equation. The results that were achieved from cardinal splines, in terms of computer graphics, were a much smoother, more realistic line or surface than had been possible from a polygonal line.

The first sale, to a post-production house, came on July 15th. Then the unexpected occurred; General Motors Inc. (GM) expressed an interest in buying a system. GM was looking for a system that was compatible with their spline-based computer-aided-design (CAD) systems, and ALIAS was the only spline-based system available. Initially, the Alias group were reluctant to enter this new market; industrial design applications had not been part of the corporate objective and seemed too distant from their animation market. Further, GM wanted the package to run on basis-splines (b-splines)[2] which would require yet another significant investment by Alias in research and development (R&D). However, when GM kept dropping broad hints about 20 systems, potentially representing millions of dollars of revenue, Alias decided to go ahead and, in November 1985, the deal with GM was signed.

Once again, money was required to finance the research. However, Alias now had a major customer, more or less in hand, which reduced the risk of the venture in the eyes of potential investors. Early in 1986, Crownx, a venture capital company associated with Crown Life, invested $1.2 million for a 20% stake in Alias.

By early 1986, the company had sold ALIAS to a number of firms. Most of the sales were to small production houses in the video animation market, but sales were also made to Kraft, Motorola, and NASA. By the middle of 1986, there were 70 people working for the company, of whom 40 were programmers, Morale was high and the employees were beginning to see the fruits of their labours in print and on video. The work environment was flexible and relaxed—purposely designed to facilitate and stimulate creativity. Improvements and upgrades to the original package were constantly being developed, and a new release of the software (with a b-spline base) was planned for mid-1986. Staff increased to 80 in April of 1987, with the opening of three sales offices in the United States. In the same year, almost $3 million in new venture capital was received from two American companies. Everything was moving quickly and the members of Alias were looking forward to a promising future.

The Downturn

The development of ALIAS/2 (using b-splines) took much longer than had been expected and the product was not released until late in 1986. Initial sales were strong, but a problem was discovered with the new system. The final rendered picture was not matched to the original design on a consistent or reliable basis. While Alias could fix the bug on the installed systems on a patchwork basis, the sales force would find it next to impossible to sell new installations of ALIAS/2 until the problem was solved. The company immediately pulled members of the marketing and R&D staff together with a product management group to fix the software.

The first half of 1987 saw the beginnings of what was to become a major downturn in the animation industry as a whole. Premium, high-end systems, like those of Alias, were particularly affected by the slump. At the same time, personnel changes and budget cuts at GM had reduced the number of systems purchased from the expected

[2] B-splines are based on the second derivative of the modelling equation and were generally regarded as producing the smoothest lines and surfaces available in computer graphics.

number of 20 to only 4. Some of the new investors in Alias were dissatisfied with the company's performance and were demanding cuts in investment, particularly on R&D spending and personnel. Mr. Bingham and the other original owners still retained control and resisted the pressure. However, by late summer of 1987, Alias was forced to lay off 12 employees from marketing and administration.

The Recovery

Following the layoffs, quarterly company meetings were instituted in which the status of the company as a whole, plans for the future, and the past quarter's performance were reviewed with all employees. Day-long meetings of the management team (vice-president level and above) were held monthly. Efforts at clearing the lines of communication between departments were made to build a more cohesive team atmosphere than had existed previously. Although the culture of the company remained informal, the methods of control and the way of doing business became more formalized, with more attention being paid to earnings and profit. Although Alias experienced an operating loss in fiscal 1989, it was considerably less than in fiscal 1988 (the corporate year end is January 31).

In the summer of 1989, for the first time in two years the company began to hire people for new positions. A new vice-president of finance, Bill McClintock, took over the financial aspects of the company and tightened the purse strings on all expenditures. Staff were added to R&D, customer support, and marketing. For over two years, marketing of ALIAS had been handled primarily by the vice-president of marketing and communications, Arthur Bell. People were now hired to fill the positions of product manager, CAD marketing manager, distributor marketing manager, and communications manager. These people came from a variety of different backgrounds, not necessarily in computer-related industries. Mr. Bell, who was very enthusiastic about his new recruits, commented:

> So often, people who market software come directly out of R&D, or they are engineers. They are way too "techi" for most of our customers, who are designers. I wanted people who understood marketing, but who did not necessarily know computers. Peter Goldie (formerly senior brand manager for Crisco at Procter & Gamble) understands shelf space and everything that leads up to getting that shelf space. No one knows it better. He knows how to market, no matter what, and he can do that for us.

Perhaps most important of all were the changes made to the software itself. Because of all of the "bugs" in ALIAS/2, R&D immediately went to work on a "bug-fix" version, known as ALIAS/2.1. Other versions followed, which in some cases included only bug-fix material, and in other cases, included new applications or improved processes. By the summer of 1989, Version 2.4.2 was being used by most Alias customers. At that time, Alias had $3 million in the bank. The income statements for 1988 to 1990 are provided in Exhibit 2.

Exhibit 2

ALIAS RESEARCH INC.—CONSOLIDATED STATEMENT OF OPERATIONS ($000 U.S.)

	1988	1989	1990	First three months of fiscal 1991
Revenue:				
Products	5,709	6,466	10,962	3,106
Maintenance and services	451	774	1,044	271
Total revenue	6,160	7,240	12,006	3,377
Costs and expenses:				
Direct cost of products*	2,861	2,131	1,810	336
Direct cost of maintenance and services	448	509	615	198
General and administration	842	910	1,956	533
Sales and marketing	1,716	2,172	3,527	1,100
Research and development	1,150	954	973	525
Depreciation and amortization	480	500	560	145
Total costs and expenses	7,497	7,176	9,441	2,837
Operating income (loss)	(1,337)	64	2,565	540
Interest income (expense)	(39)	(20)	134	73
Other income (expense)	13	(9)	163	13
Income (loss) before income taxes	(1,363)	35	2,862	626
Provision for (recovery) income taxes	(43)	0	1,229	258
Net income (loss)	(1,320)	35	1,633	368

* Hardware purchased for resale

Alias Culture

The culture at Alias was by design relaxed and informal. Everyone, from the programmer in the R&D department to the president, appeared in jeans most of the time. Suits were worn only when people were expected from outside the company. In the words of Bill McClintock: "There are very few 'ties' around here, never mind 'suits,' and that is the way it should be." Friday was known as "shorts day," and throughout the summer, anyone not wearing shorts on a Friday had better have been expecting company.

Employees referred to themselves as "Alians," and the term was expressed with affection and pride. A friendly rivalry existed between the R&D and the administrative sides of the company, each housed in separate sections of the office. Employee birthdays were celebrated by all, with cake, drinks, and the occasional Elvis impersonator supplied by the company. Team spirit abounded and everyone regarded it as a great place to work. This was reflected in an article that appeared in the August 1990 *Report on Business Magazine* which described the company, its culture, and the software industry (Appendix 1).

ALIAS MARKETING

In many ways, marketing software is unlike marketing any other product. For example, security is a serious problem. Once the product has been sold, it is always possible that the product will be copied or even copied and resold. Once the product has been purchased, customers have to be kept up to date on new developments. When new versions and developments occur, the decision needs to be made whether current customers should be given free upgrades or not. Selling expenses are very high in the industry. Customers are geographically dispersed and sales are often achieved over an extended period and with the support of a number of individuals. As was the case with the Isaac Babbs sale that fell through, or the GM installations that were slow in coming, significant resources were invested in a potential sale which might evaporate at the most inopportune time.

Having a professional marketing and sales team was critical. As well, knowing how much to spend on marketing and in what areas was a perplexing task. Another difficult task was deciding how much R&D should be spent and on what projects. The company needed to determine how much customer service and support to provide and at what price, if any, to charge for that support and service. The potentially crippling problem of bugs needed to be considered and what actions were to be taken if, and when, they occurred. How should the product be priced in the first place? Should all the R&D, marketing, and overhead be factored into the price? How flexible should the company be with its pricing strategy?

The ALIAS Product

When a data tape containing the ALIAS product left Toronto, it contained a "hole" or a missing line of code which must be filled in before the software would operate. This line of code, called an encryption string, was twelve digits long and could contain numbers, punctuation marks, and upper or lower case letters. The string was unique to one tape of software and to the one piece of hardware upon which it would run. In other words, the same data tape could not be used to start up several different machines.

When customers purchased the software, they purchased customer support for that software. Phone support was provided 12 hours a day, as well as free upgrades and bug-fixes for a period of one year. The support contract had to be renewed each year by the customer if continuing support was to be received. No services were provided until the contract was renewed and payment was received.

A major advantage with the ALIAS system over other software was that ALIAS was easy to learn and easy to use. See Exhibit 3 for a comparison of Alias and Wavefront products. Those who were not computer literate, and even those who regarded computers with suspicion, were able to make use of most of the system's tools after

Exhibit 3
A COMPARISON OF WAVEFRONT AND ALIAS

Dimension	Wavefront	Alias
Ease of Use	Not easy Requires substantial training to use advanced functions	Pioneer in the development and improvement of making the product easy to use
Price	Negotiable Approximately U.S. $55,000 Discounts as much as 50% to make a sale	Fixed Base price is approximately U.S. $65,000 Discounts to educators and co-developers only
Primary Market	Animation Some industrial features recently added	Industrial Design but also has found wide application in animation
Basic Technology	Polygonal lines	Basis splines
Hardware	Runs on many different kinds of hardware	Dedicated to Silicon Graphics and IBM workstations (industry standards)

Source: Company Records

only a few days of training. Like Apple products, ALIAS was menu-driven, and most "drawing" was done with the aid of a mouse. Once the design, or "modelling" process was finished, the information could be sent to a variety of media. The information could be fed to a plotter, which gives a flat wireframe picture of the object, or it could be directly linked to a CAD machine, which was then used to construct the object from the computerized data. Other options included creating a surface and background for the object and outputting the picture or pictures to slides or videotapes, or even to a stereolithography vat[3] where a plastic prototype is created. In any case, ALIAS shortened the time between the conception of an idea and its appearance on the market, be that idea a car, a building, a piece of jewellery, or a special effect for a movie.

Customers, in general, had responded favourably to the flexibility and ease of use of ALIAS and its convenient access to a wide range of powerful options. Designers had liked the way ALIAS reduced the time between the conception of their ideas and having prototypes built, as well as having the capability of examining more iterations, improvements, and changes at the early stage of product development. Engineers had found that ALIAS provided a precise reading and measurement of designers' concepts and took advantage of its ability to directly link into CAD/CAM systems.

[3] A stereolithography vat is a vat filled with molten plastic and equipped with a pinpoint laser. The path that the laser takes is determined by the instructions in ALIAS. The result is a perfectly proportioned, solid, three-dimensional plastic model of the original computerized design.

Exhibit 4

ALIAS RESEARCH INC.—SALES HISTORY BY LINE OF BUSINESS ($000 U.S.)

	1987	1988	1989	1990
Industrial Design Market:				
Sales	790	3,374	5,320	10,186
Percent of Revenue	17%	55%	73%	85%
Animation Market:				
Sales	3,970	2,786	1,920	1,820
Percent of Revenue	83%	45%	27%	15%
Total Sales	4,760	6,160	7,240	12,006

The fundamental source of ALIAS's strength had been as a communication tool. It had given designers and engineers a common language to speak, and in the process, sped up the design-to-market cycle. The enthusiastic response of designers and engineers had led to the steady shift of Alias's revenue from animation into industrial design markets (Exhibit 4). While this trend was expected to continue, there are no plans to abandon the animation market.

Marketing and Sales

Alias promoted its products through participation in trade shows like SIGGRAPH, an annual world demonstration tour, articles and advertisements in industry publications, live demonstrations, television advertising, and sponsorship of cultural events. These activities were augmented by print and videotape sales support materials. A direct sales force was employed in North America and Europe. This group, which also managed Alias's distributor and dealer network, consisted of 19 people. There were sales offices in five cities in the United States, as well as in France and Germany. Alias' network of 16 dealers and distributors represented the product in 11 countries. This network generally specialized in design and engineering hardware and software complementary to the ALIAS product.

Pricing the Product

As is shown in the consolidated income statement for 1990 (Exhibit 3), the direct costs of sale amounted to only 20% of revenue. Almost all of the direct costs were for hardware purchased for resale, for maintenance, and for other services. The direct cost of the software was negligible. Using a cost-based approach to pricing would give Alias substantial room to manoeuvre on price. However, that was not their approach.

The approach used was to price the software at parity to the hardware upon which it was mounted. For example, a Silicon Graphics Personal IRIS Workstation cost the customer approximately $100,000 (U.S.). The ALIAS tape installed on that workstation would cost another $100,000 (U.S.). This method of pricing put ALIAS at or near the top of what the market would bear. A stripped-down version of ALIAS could sell for as little as $65,000 (U.S.), while the version with every option could run as high as $150,000 (U.S.). Once a system was installed, further options could be added at a cost of $10,000 (U.S.) to $30,000 (U.S.) per option. Customer support was provided on a two-tier pricing schedule. The first tier, which included software release updates and installation only, was provided for an annual fee equal to 10% of the then current software price. A second tier, in addition to incorporating the services of the first tier, provided hotline support and could be purchased for an annual fee of 15% of the then current software price. Training and consultant services were provided on a per day or per task rate (usually about U.S. $500 per person per day).

BACK TO THE FIELD

As Isaac Babbs drove down Highway #1 on the California coast to meet a new prospect at Boeing his thoughts wandered back to his telephone call with Arthur Bell. Arthur had expressed his disappointment over the lost sale, but had refused to make any changes in the pricing policy.

Isaac Babbs had a lot of confidence in the company. Alias management had made some tough calls over the history of the company and been proven right. However, Toronto was a long way from California and he felt he knew his customers better than anyone did. He disliked losing any sale, and he was still smarting from this last one. He understood why Alias had not engaged in price cutting in the past, but he was unsure if he could continue to compete against aggressive price-cutters, like Wavefront. Maybe it was time for a change. How many times had he heard about what a flexible company Alias was, he thought. Perhaps the pricing policy was the correct one, but he could not help worrying over the long-term implications of this rigid policy.

Arthur Bell had been disappointed to have received the news from Babbs. Babbs was one of his best field representatives and had been very successful in cultivating the lucrative southwestern market. Arthur Bell respected Babbs's opinions and was not pleased to hear about his concern over the lost sales and the inflexible pricing policy. The morale and commitment of any member of the sales force could not be treated lightly. Mr. Bell wondered if he came across as too intransigent on the issue of pricing. Perhaps it was time to review the pricing policy and bring it forward at the next management meeting. As he began preparing the memo, Stephen Bingham, the president walked by. Arthur told him about California incident and his interest in putting the pricing policy on the agenda. "Sure let's take a look at the issue," said Stephen. "I think our current pricing policy is just fine, but I am prepared to listen. However, I don't think we can look at price in isolation from the other marketing policies. It would be more useful if it was in the context of a review of the entire marketing program."

Appendix 1
EXCERPTS
Daniel Stoffman, "Big Dreams, No Backers," *Report on Business Magazine*, August 1990, pp. 47–51.

- Unlike cars or clothes or bread, no raw material is required to manufacture software. It is purely a creation of the mind, which is why it (Alias) attracts people that include a former comedian, a French horn player, and a former cabinet-maker.
- When the Honda Accord became the first car made by a foreign manufacturer to head the U.S. best-seller list last year, it was more than just another triumph for Japanese industry. Only a few insiders knew that it was also a triumph for Alias. All of Honda's cars, like those of BMW and Volvo, are designed on three-dimensional graphics software created at Alias.
- Canada produces almost no original industrial design—there is no such thing as a Canadian-designed car—but the eccentrics at Alias have created a wonderful tool for industrial designers. Until their software was developed in 1985, these designers did their work the old-fashioned way—with pencil and paper and clay models. Now the designers for such Alias customers as Timex, Motorola, Mitsubishi, British Telecom, and Goodyear can create moving, three-dimensional designs on their computer screens. The models are so realistic that a designer can see how light will reflect off a watch face or a car body long before the actual objects exist. Using Alias software can shave precious months, even years, off the time it takes to create a product.
- Good software is a living thing, constantly growing and adapting to meet its users' needs. That means long nights in front of computer screens. The Alias office contains two eating areas because software developers don't have time to go out for lunch or dinner. On a typical evening, the company will order in large quantities of chicken or pizza. Then the denizens of the factory might amuse themselves for a while playing the latest computer games or reading. A favorite writer at Alias is Vancouverite William Gibson, who writes science fiction novels about "cyber-punks" with computer chips embedded in their brains.
- In the software industry, tiny companies can grow into billion-dollar giants like Lotus and Microsoft almost overnight. That's exactly the sort of future the president, Stephen Bingham, has in mind for Alias, and he is off to an impressive start. Sales were just $12 million last year, but more than a third of those sales were to the Japanese—not known to deal with bantam-weights unless they have very good reasons to do so. The company even managed to forge a strategic alliance with mighty IBM. But for all its successes, there is no guarantee that Alias will make it. In fact, the odds are stacked against it. Software companies in Canada are starved for capital. Without money they can't grow, and in this business if you don't grow fast, you're dead.
- The sale is only part of the story. After you sell someone a $150,000 hardware and software package, you don't just wander off in search of the next customer. Software must be continually enhanced, and most of the enhancements are suggested by the users. Alias personnel meets regularly with their biggest customers.

Investing in software is a commitment, and customers are anxious to know where the company is going long term.Several have visited Alias's offices. ''The Japanese were impressed that we can turn out so much new technology so quickly,'' Mr. Bingham says. ''A visitor from Honda said we had 20 people doing the work of 200.''

- Alias got early support from Montreal ''angel'' Jim Muir, a friend of one of the partners, and Crownx Inc. of Toronto. Two Boston-based venture capitalists who specialize in high-tech also chipped in. But the company's growth has been largely financed through its own sales. Banks have so far refused to offer more than a small line of credit, saying they do not wish to finance foreign receivables which are the only kind Alias has. Banks also like to have collateral in case a loan goes sour—and by collateral they mean some real estate or a yard full of steel ingots. They don't mean a numeric code on a computer disc—software—which is where the wealth of a company like Alias resides.
- It's not hard to understand why lenders shy away from technology companies. Just look at the record of those high-tech darlings of the '70s—companies like Mitel and Lumonics. More recently, Canada's biggest software firm, Cognos, lost $17 million in fiscal 1990 after several years of good earnings. From an investor's viewpoint, the problem is the rapid rate of change. One banker notes: ''In a traditional borrowing relationship, you might analyze the company's record over the last five years. With high-tech companies, I look at the last five quarters. They go through the same cycles as a traditional firm but they do it at an accelerated pace. The products they were selling two years ago are now all obsolete and they've got new products.''

Section 6

ADVERTISING, PROMOTION, AND PERSONAL SELLING

Communication, which includes advertising, promotion, and personal selling, is the most visible or audible of marketing activities. Through communications, the marketer is able to inform existing or prospective customers about the product and its features, its price, and where to buy it and other distribution details; to create (where appropriate) persuasive arguments for using the service or buying the goods; and to remind people of the product.

THE COMMUNICATION PROCESS

Communication means sending a message through one or more media to a receiver in order to generate a response. The messages sent, however, may not reach the target audience; either they miss some people altogether or get lost in the general clutter or "noise" of everyday life. Even if a message reaches a specific individual, it may not be understood as intended or may not be remembered long enough to result in the response desired by the sender. Of course, consumers, their interest whetted by need or curiosity, may be actively seeking information. While this curiosity increases the chance of their receiving communication on a topic of interest, it does not guarantee it.

CRITERIA FOR EFFECTIVE COMMUNICATION

What factors determine whether a marketing communication will be effective in stimulating an individual to behave in ways desired by the marketer?

First, a communication strategist must understand the day-to-day behaviour of the target audience, so that messages can be delivered in places and at times likely to result in exposure. For mass-media advertising, this requires an understanding of the media habits of the target audience—the specific newspapers and magazines they read; the times at which they are likely to watch television or listen to the radio, together with the types of broadcasts they are most likely to turn to; and the routes and transportation modes they use for travelling to work and on shopping or recreational trips. A sales representative needs to schedule calls for times at which prospects are likely to be willing to listen to a presentation.

Second, the placement, scheduling, format, and content of the communication must be designed in such a way that it stands out from competing stimuli, thereby gaining the target audience's attention. Success in this area involves skill in copywriting, design, and production. A visual ad that looks different (or an audio ad that sounds different) from other advertisements in the selected medium is one way of achieving this goal.

Next, the message must be stated in terms the target audience will understand. The symbols used in communication are many; they include verbal language, body language, colour, shape, music, and other sounds. But for communication to be effective, both communicator and audience must place similar interpretations on these symbols. Effective salespeople tailor their presentations to the characteristics of the prospect.

It is also very important that the communication be remembered by the receiver long enough to have the desired result. Essentially, the message must be designed to strike some responsive chord in the target audience. Good copywriting, like effective personal selling, requires an understanding of the needs, wants, concerns, and even fears of the audience.

THE COMMUNICATION MIX

The term "communication mix" is sometimes used to describe the array of communication tools available to marketers. Just as marketers need to combine the elements of the marketing mix (including communication) to produce a marketing program, they also need to select the most appropriate ingredients for the constituent communication program.

The elements of the communication mix fall into four broad categories:

1. personal selling,
2. advertising,
3. public relations/publicity, and
4. promotional activities.

Personal selling involves representatives of the marketer engaging directly in two-way communication with customers, either in person or via electronic media. The latter three elements are all one-way communication—from the marketer to the customers.

PERSONAL COMMUNICATION

Communication between individuals has a powerful advantage over mass-media communication in that the message usually goes directly from sender to recipient. A second major advantage is that personal communication is usually reciprocal, with the recipient being able to ask the sender (salesperson, retail clerk, or telephone operator) for clarification or additional information. A sender can adapt the content and presentation of the message to the characteristics of the recipient, and to that individual's needs and concerns as revealed during the interaction.

Different communication channels may be relatively more effective in moving consumers from one stage of the purchase decision process to another. At the beginning of the process, the use of mass media is likely to be the most cost-effective channel for stimulating awareness and providing background knowledge. As consumers move towards evaluation and purchase, however, they may actively seek out two-way personal communication to enable them to ask specific questions that will help them make their final decisions.

IMPERSONAL COMMUNICATION

Although personal communication provides a powerful channel for messages, it is also costly and time-consuming. Much information can be delivered far more cheaply through impersonal sources, particularly when the objective is to generate initial awareness. Broadcast and print are the principal impersonal communication channels available to marketers.

Television is a powerful communication medium because it combines both audio and visual images. On the other hand, the high cost of producing quality commercials and buying air time put television outside the price range of many smaller or regional firms. Radio messages are less expensive than television messages, but radio messages leave more to the listener's imagination, because no visual images can be shown. Radio, however, can often reach people at times and in locations where television sets are unlikely to be found—for instance, while they are driving cars or at the beach.

A key characteristic of both television and radio is that broadcast messages are fleeting; they cannot be retained for later reference. Radio advertising is often used for short reminder advertising to encourage people to take action after previous messages, perhaps in other media, have built up awareness and knowledge of the product.

The print medium may be more effective than broadcasting for transmitting messages containing a great deal of information. Newspaper and magazine ads may be clipped for future reference; direct mail not only provides a message in tangible form but also offers the advantage that the content of the message can be personalized to meet the particular situation of the recipient. Like personal communication, a printed message is sometimes used to close the sale—typically, through the use of an order coupon in the body of the ad or an order form and postage paid envelope in a direct-mail communication.

Promotional ingenuity knows few bounds. A wide variety of promotional activities are available to the marketer. Coupons, premiums, contests, and price-packs (cents-off deals, two-for-one offers, etc.) are some of the short-term incentives offered to consumers to stimulate purchase of a product. These promotions all focus on the buying act itself, and not on such prior steps as building awareness of a brand. Even more targeted are point-of-purchase displays and in-store demonstrations which call the shopper's attention to the brand being promoted. While "buying" promotions are many and diverse, the majority of these promotional activities can be classified into one of three categories:

1. Trial—encouraging consumers to "try" a product for the first time.
2. Stocking—encouraging consumers to buy more of a product.
3. Continuity—encouraging consumers to buy a product on a regular basis.

In addition to consumer promotions, marketers also use trade promotion to gain wholesaler and retailer co-operation for their marketing programs. Trade promotions include buying allowances (discounts on each unit of the product bought during a specified time period), free goods (for example, one case free for every twelve cases ordered), and display allowances (payments for devoting store space to and setting up retail displays). While all elements of a marketing communication plan need to be integrated, this is particularly true for promotional activities. If used indiscriminately, promotions can detract from a product's positioning strategy. Used wisely, promotional activities help support a longer term marketing strategy and deal with immediate problems that arise when sales goals are not being met.

Exhibit 1
MARKETING COMMUNICATION DECISIONS

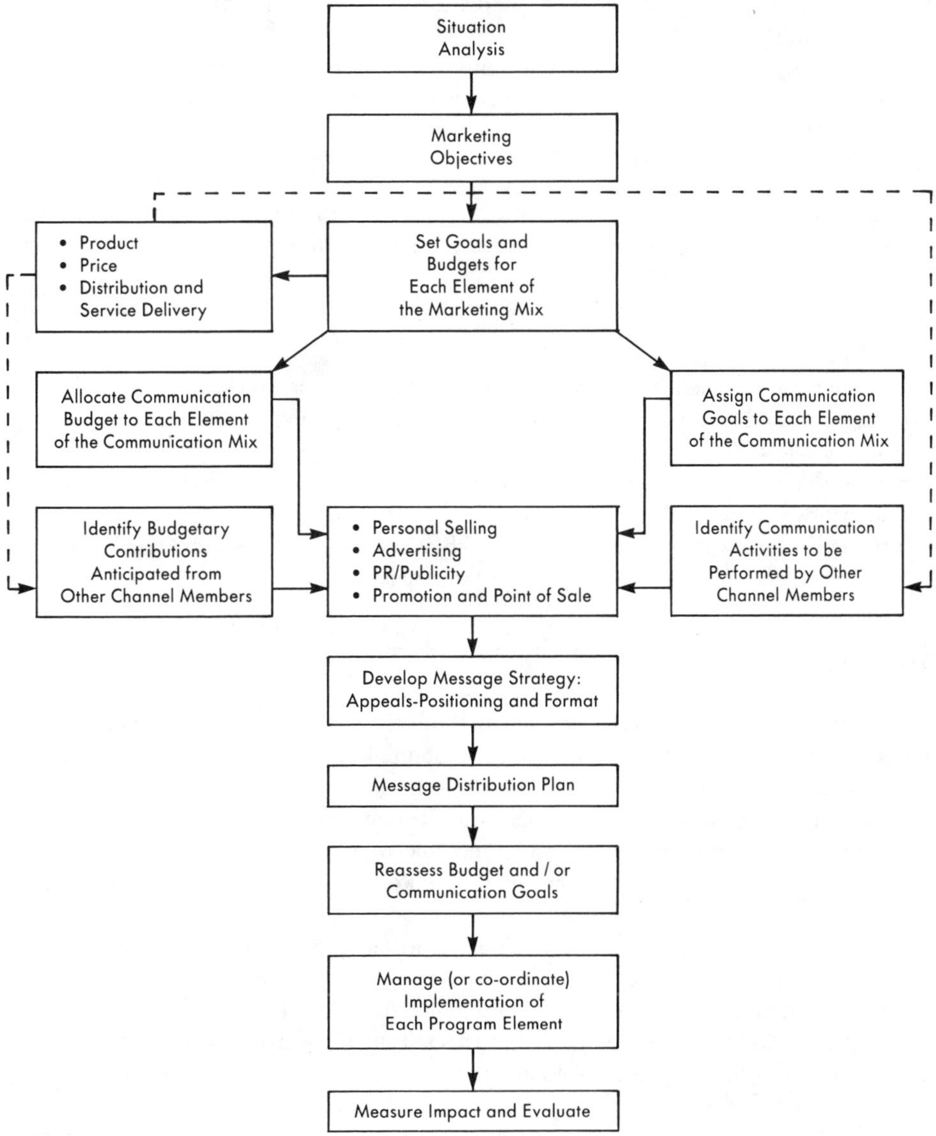

MAKING COMMUNICATION DECISIONS

SITUATION ANALYSIS

The starting point for making communication decisions as shown in Exhibit 1 is a situation analysis. This analysis should include an appraisal of:

- the organization's strengths, weaknesses, and objectives;
- product characteristics, pricing, and distribution systems;
- market segment characteristics and behaviour;
- strategy and marketing activities of competitors, and their anticipated responses to new initiatives;
- nature of suppliers and intermediaries, and their own marketing strategy;
- possible constraints on future use of specific communication elements.

MARKETING OBJECTIVES

Based on the situation analysis, marketing opportunities and problems can be identified. Marketing objectives can then be set for the organization as a whole and for specific products (or product lines).

The objectives for individual products should relate to a specific time frame and may include:

- a positioning statement identifying the market segments at which the product is to be targeted and its distinctive features relative to competing alternatives;
- sales goals in terms of volume and revenues during the period;
- market share goals at specific points in time, with careful delineation of the market boundaries within which these shares will be computed;
- intermediate measures of performance, such as increased awareness, knowledge, preference, and intention to buy among target customers.

GOALS AND BUDGETS FOR COMMUNICATION MIX ELEMENTS

From establishment of overall marketing goals, managers must move to establish specific goals and strategies for each element of the communication mix, with tentative budgets being allocated for the substrategy associated with each communication mix element.

In any given campaign, each communication element should be assigned a specific role to play in achieving overall objectives. Communication goals may refer to the states of mind that a prospective customer may go through or the actions that a person may take in response to advertising, a sales presentation, or another communication activity. Often different elements in the communication mix are assigned different goals, such as moving a customer from unawareness to awareness of a product, from awareness to interest, from interest to brand preference, and from preference to purchase.

Setting the communication budget—both overall and for each element of the communication mix—is a difficult decision. Many companies appear to budget for the next year based on what they spent in the previous year. Some do this just by extrapolating the dollar level from the previous year, and others relate expenditures to sales, usage, or some other activity. This assumes both that previous decisions were correct and that there have been no significant changes in the marketplace.

A related budgeting philosophy is to spend according to what a firm can afford. This assumes, at the extreme, that advertising and sales are unrelated and the value of advertising cannot be shown.

Another approach is to base expenditures on what competitors are doing. Paying attention to competition is important, and such information can play an important role in budget setting. But this approach of "competitive parity" ignores the differing goals, media efficiencies, and market segments of competitors. Moreover, this method implicitly assumes that competitors are spending optimally.

A frequently used approach is the "objective-and-task" method in which sub-objectives are established for the communication program (and its constituent elements), and a budget is set and allocated in terms of the tasks deemed necessary to achieve the assigned objectives. This is a sound approach when based on a detailed situation analysis, good understanding of the response of communication targets (for example, awareness, knowledge, attitude) to different advertising levels, and careful evaluation of the worth of achieving different goals.

How can a marketing manager co-ordinate such varied communication activities as advertising copywriting, management of sales territories, and liaison with media outlets for publicity purposes? The answer lies in taking decisions across the entire communication mix in four key areas:

1. Communication goals,
2. Message appeals-positioning,
3. Message format,
4. Message distribution plan.

The balancing of goals, positioning, format, and distribution must reflect the current situation and available budget and may need to be changed over time in light of the product's performance in the marketplace as well as competitive responses and initiatives.

MESSAGE APPEALS-POSITIONING

Message strategy consists of two parts: what to say (appeals-positioning) and how to say it (format). A campaign's appeals-positioning, sometimes called the "copy platform" or "message idea," should be based on the notion that each audience segment will be motivated by specific appeals or product features. The statement of appeals-positioning or copy platform provides the framework or "blueprint" on which specific copy messages are built.

MESSAGE FORMAT

Given a goal and a copy platform, what form should the message take? Should the advertising be humorous, use testimonials, include a demonstration, create fantasy, or evoke concern? What types of salespeople are needed and what should be included in their presentations to customers? Should the publicity release include pictures or not? Is there a role for a short-term sales promotion to dramatize some feature of the product?

Development of a message format is a creative process; many managers look for professional advice to help in copy execution. Suppliers of creative marketing services—such as advertising agencies, public-relations firms, and promotional specialists—can be retained to design and implement the necessary steps.

MESSAGE DISTRIBUTION PLAN

Once messages have been developed, the task is to decide how they should be sent. Advertising agencies are often well placed to allocate the budget in the most effective way, and they typically work with management to develop a media plan.

The objective of the media plan is to reach the desired target audience most efficiently within a limited budget. Generally, a mix of media vehicles is required because achievement of communication goals usually requires that a message (or set of messages) be seen more than once and because only rarely can one medium reach all members of a segment.

PERSONAL SELLING AND SALES FORCE MANAGEMENT

Sales force management is, in many ways, similar to advertising management. Both are forms of communication and must address the fundamental question of "who says what to whom." Both advertising and sales force managers need to be concerned with designing messages, choosing communications targets, and working within the budget constraints and communication goals of a marketing plan. The fundamental difference is that personal selling involves people—who must be recruited and trained—to deliver the message and to interact directly with customers or prospects.

The big advantage of personal selling as a communication or promotional tool is that it involves person-to-person contact with a potential user. This allows the sales representative to tailor the message to fit a particular customer's concerns and interests. During a sales call—which may take place in person or by phone—communication flows in both directions, allowing the salesperson to respond to immediate feedback from the customer. Questions and objections can be met and answered, and alternative approaches can be tried when the initial ones do not seem to be working. Sales representatives can also communicate a large amount of complex information in one or a series of sales calls. Visual aids and working models can also be used. By calling on the same client repeatedly, the salesperson can educate the client over time about the particular advantages of the product or company. Regular contact over an extended period is particularly important when offering a product that can be tailored to the needs of an individual user. When the customer is a regular user of the company's products, personal contact can be used to deepen and strengthen that loyalty, as well as to deal with any operational problems and concerns that may arise from time to time.

The major advantages of personal over impersonal communication are often offset by the major disadvantage of cost. Heavy monetary costs are incurred in paying, managing, and providing support for a sales force. In many selling situations of a technical nature, average costs exceeding $100 per call are quite common.

ORGANIZATION

A major organizational decision is whether the sales force should be organized on a geographic, product, or market basis or some combination of these. Among companies whose salespeople travel over wide areas to visit accounts, geography almost always becomes a basis for organization at some level. One problem that arises is how to coordinate local geographic efforts with the nation-wide concerns of major customers.

A related organizational concern is determining the number of levels of sales management to use and the number of individuals who will report to each type of manager—what is called the *span of control*. Lowering the number of sales representatives reporting to a manager allows for closer supervision but also increases the proportion of the personal selling budget spent on non-selling tasks. Also, too narrow a span of control can lead to overcontrol and can reduce salesperson initiative and motivation. On the other hand, personal selling activities need to be monitored carefully to keep them on target.

DEPLOYMENT OF PERSONAL SELLING RESOURCES

Once the basic sales organization has been determined, decisions must be made about how the sales force should be deployed. The issues include the assignment of accounts to sales representatives—the territory design problem—and allocation of sales force time to accounts, product lines, and activities such as opening new accounts versus servicing existing ones. Proper territorial design is a persistent problem for sales management. The needs of sales representatives—particularly senior ones who often have strong preferences and long-term ties to certain accounts—must be balanced against the requirements of the marketing plan and current market forces.

RECRUITING AND SELECTION

Clearly defining the role that personal selling is to play in the marketing program and the specific tasks that salespeople will be assigned can suggest the types of individuals needed, likely sources for recruitment, and appropriate selection criteria. Corporate resources, sales force size, and job requirements often determine whether the company should hire experienced or inexperienced people.

TRAINING

Almost all firms must do some training. For newly hired, inexperienced salespeople, training should cover selling skills, a detailed understanding of customers and their needs, and extensive knowledge of the company's products and its policies and procedures in general. Besides an initial program of familiarization, experienced sales personnel may benefit from more intensive training to improve their selling skills, inform them about new products and policies, or prepare them for more responsible positions within the sales organization.

REWARDS AND INCENTIVES

Rewards and incentives include both financial and nonfinancial elements. Rewards can be subdivided into two main categories, intrinsic and extrinsic. The former include such intangibles as feelings of competence, completion, and self-worth. Managers are paying increasing attention to the importance of intrinsic rewards. This can be done by defining jobs and responsibilities carefully, providing feedback, and, more generally, by trying to understand a salesperson's view of his or her job and role in the company.

Extrinsic rewards—tangible external elements controlled by the company—include financial and other benefits. Compensation systems should be designed to encourage the types of behaviour desired by the firm. Guaranteed salaries, commissions, and bonuses should be combined in appropriate proportions. There is growing concern by sales managers about too much reliance on commissions, since these may cause sales representatives to focus on the short term and not pay sufficient attention to building long-term account relationships. Company recognition, such as distinguished-service awards for successful salespeople, can often be an important motivator. The design of the compensation system plays an important role in attracting and retaining qualified people for the sales force.

EVALUATION AND CONTROL

Procedures are needed for sales executives to monitor the performance of individuals and sales groups against certain standards. Information on performance compared to targets can then be fed back to the involved parties so that any necessary corrective action can be taken. The standards may take the form of measures of input (such as the number of sales calls to be made, the number of new accounts to be contacted, and the level of a salesperson's knowledge) or measures of output (such as dollar sales achieved as compared to sales quotas for different products, market segments, etc.). Performance against some of these standards can be measured quite objectively, while performance against others must often rely on the subjective judgement of the field sales manager. A good evaluation and control system provides both the field sales manager and the salesperson with an opportunity to identify areas of strength and weakness and develop programs to correct any deficiencies that are identified.

SUMMARY

Communication decisions should be made across the full array of communication mix elements instead of being compartmentalized, element by element. This poses the need for an integrated approach to advertising, personal selling, public relations, and promotional activities, instead of treating these as unrelated tools that are independent of one another. Interdependence and synergy should be the watchwords of communication planning. In particular, marketers should note the use of different elements to move the target audience through a sequence of stages—becoming aware of a problem, learning about a solution to that problem, and actually doing something to help resolve it.

A systematic approach to communication planning should begin with a situation analysis and proceed to a definition of marketing objectives, establishment of size of a total communication budget, and selection of a tentative budget mix for each element. Subsequent steps involve clear definitions of goals for each communication element, determination of message appeals-positioning, selection of message format, and choice of message-distribution plan. Mass-media advertising has the advantage of low cost per impression, but to be successful it must make its way through a great clutter of competing messages. Personal selling is expensive, but it has the advantage of allowing direct two-way contact between the salesperson and the prospective customer.

23 VANCOUVER PUBLIC AQUARIUM

Grant N. Poeter

Charles B. Weinberg

Richard Knight, public relations director for the Vancouver Public Aquarium, reread the memo he had just received from Elizabeth Dewey, the aquarium's educational programs co-ordinator. Ms. Dewey had proposed that, starting the following fall, the Vancouver Aquarium restrict weekday admissions to only school tours during the hours from 10:00 a.m. to 3:00 p.m., and exclude the general public during those hours.

During the 1986–87 school year, the Vancouver Public Aquarium (VPA) offered five formal educational programs for students from kindergarten to grade 12. Further, the aquarium's trained guides (docents) gave children guided tours which included various performances offered to the general public. Though these tours were successful, there was evidence that both individual visitors and the schools felt that the aquarium could be better utilizing their facilities. For instance, some members of the general paying public found it irritating to browse through the galleries with "all the screaming kids around." Also, the teachers felt that the feeding performances, one of the highlights of the aquarium, could be geared more to the predominantly younger weekday market. Because the school market was important to the aquarium and weekday attendance by the general paying public was low, Mr. Knight felt that he must examine the proposal fully before giving Ms. Dewey a response.

BACKGROUND

The VPA opened its doors on June 3, 1956, in Vancouver's Stanley Park, a popular recreational area adjacent to downtown Vancouver (Exhibit 1). Accessible by bus or car, the park was centrally located within the Greater Vancouver Regional District (GVRD), an association of Vancouver and its surrounding communities (Burnaby, North Vancouver, Richmond, West Vancouver, and others). Most of the GVRD's population of 1.3 million people lived within ten miles of Stanley Park.

The aquarium's facilities had undergone numerous renovations in the 30 years following its opening. In 1967, the B.C. Telephone Pool was constructed to hold dolphins, but the aquarium acquired a killer whale (orca) instead. It quickly became evident that the pool was unsuitable for such a large mammal, and so in 1972, the killer whale pool was opened. In conjunction with these outdoor "gallery" changes, the aquarium continued to improve its indoor exhibits. Perhaps the most significant indoor change was the addition of the Amazon Gallery, which recreated the environ-

Exhibit 1
AQUARIUM LOCATION MAP

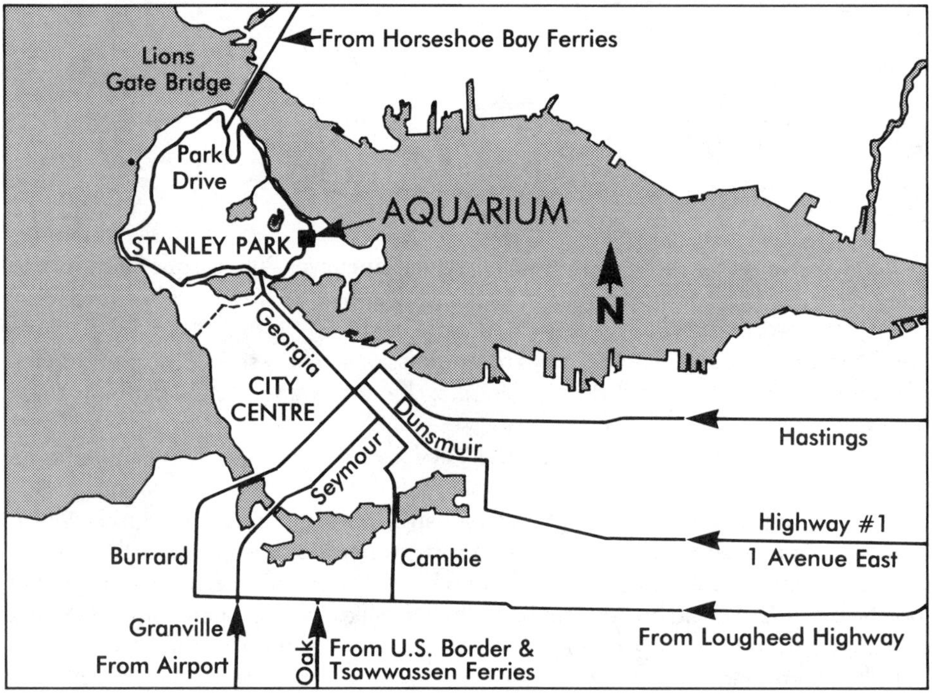

ment of an Amazon River valley. Opened in 1983 by Queen Elizabeth II, the Amazon Gallery, with its 2,200 specimens, was the only indoor exhibit of its kind in the world. Designed and constructed to house only killer whales, this exhibit set what many experts viewed as the world standard in both exhibit philosophy and animal husbandry.

With Expo '86, Vancouver's 100th birthday, and the aquarium's 30th birthday, 1986 was a record year for attendance with 876,825 visitors (Exhibit 2). Increasing attendance beyond that level was a challenge that faced Mr. Knight.

CURRENT OFFERINGS

In 1987, the aquarium housed some 7,100 specimens (669 species) of marine and aquatic life. Its sea otter breeding program was most successful and had helped to preserve this once endangered species; since 1983, five pups had been born at the aquarium. The aquarium saw itself as being on the leading edge of both marine research and display of mammals and Northern Pacific marine species.

The main product offered to visitors by the aquarium was the opportunity to see its collection of aquatic life. Related species were housed in "galleries," usually by

Exhibit 2
ANNUAL ATTENDANCE, 1982–1986

Attendance	1982	1983	1984	1985	1986
Paid					
Adults	216,161	257,400	237,312	248,742	329,334
Youths & Senior Citizens	76,123	84,276	70,713	79,285	—
Groups	43,465	45,665	46,605	34,983	55,280
Education Programs	10,580	6,226	8,983	14,638	—
Family Rate	166,696	181,107	166,736	120,409	196,481
Children & Seniors	—	—	—	—	86,186
Youths	—	—	—	—	22,784
	513,025	574,674	530,349	498,057	690,065
Other Attendance					
Members	54,783	91,891	73,604	66,963	73,148
Other	70,399	89,003	99,614	87,162	113,612
TOTAL	638,207	755,568	703,567	652,182	876,825
Single Admission					
Adults	$ 4.25 ea	$ 4.50 ea	$ 4.50 ea	$ 5.00 ea	$ 5.25 ea
Senior Citizens	$ 2.00 ea	$ 2.25 ea	$ 2.25 ea	$ 2.50 ea	$ 2.75 ea
Youths (5–18 yrs.)	$ 2.00 ea	$ 2.25 ea	$ 2.25 ea	—	—
Youths (12–18 years)	—	—	—	$ 3.75 ea	—
Youths	—	—	—	—	$ 4.00 ea
Children	—	—	—	$ 2.50 ea	$ 2.75 ea
Group Admission					
Family	$10.00	$11.00	$11.00	$13.00	$13.25
Adults, 10–34 persons	$ 3.00	$ 3.25	$ 3.25	—	—
35 or more	$ 2.50	$ 2.75	$ 2.75	—	—
Adults, 10 or more	—	—	—	$ 3.75	$ 4.00
Youths, 10 or more	$ 1.25	$ 1.50	$ 1.50	$ 2.00	$ 2.25

geographic region. In addition, the aquarium offered whale shows, films, tours, and special showings (such as "Fishes of China"), all included in the admission price. There were no restaurants or food services on the aquarium's grounds, although a number of food stands were located nearby in Stanley Park.

The aquarium also offered several secondary products. It had rented its facilities for social functions; companies could have staff parties, meetings, and dinner/dances in the various galleries; for children, birthday parties, complete with cake, were available. The aquarium also offered special lectures and school programs on aquatic life. Members could take advantage of whale watching tours, beach walks, and special previews. These programs had been very successful.

The aquarium also ran a retail operation, the Clam Shell Gift Shop, which sold aquarium-related books, animal prints, nature calendars, and numerous aquarium souvenirs.

MISSION

The VPA stated its mission as follows:

> The Vancouver Aquarium is dedicated to the preservation and enhancement of aquatic life through education, recreation, and research. It is a private, non-profit society, and is completely self-supporting.

This mission statement was the driving force behind the aquarium. Every program had to fit into one of the three categories in the statement; all staff were required to follow its guidelines. As expressed by VPA staff and literature, the aquarium's main business was to educate the public about aquatic life. The aquarium accomplished this through such activities as demonstrations and interpretive programs. In particular, the VPA offered numerous programs—such as lectures, tours, and beach walks—to educate school children, teens, and adults.

MARKETS

During the past two years, the aquarium's average weekday attendance in winter had been 550 patrons per day (Exhibit 3). Weekends were busier, with Saturdays averaging 1,300 patrons and Sundays averaging 2,100. Mr. Knight felt that Saturday's attendance could be higher, possibly reaching Sunday's levels.

During the summer, there was still a difference between weekdays and weekends but general attendance levels were higher. In fact, the weekday levels were more than double those of the winter months.

The aquarium had at least six significant markets: schools, members, general admissions, donors, volunteers, and scientists. Mr. Knight felt that the first five markets would be affected by any decision relating to school tour admissions.

Members

By the end of 1986, the Vancouver Public Aquarium Association had 39,360 members, based on the sale of 15,077 memberships (up from 11,850 in 1985) to individuals, couples, and families. Members accounted for 73,148 of the aquarium's total attendance of 876,825.

Diverse programs were offered to this group, which ranged from special educational programs to free admission to the aquarium; educational programs included whale watching in Johnstone Strait, previews of special displays, Galiano Island beach walks, and behind-the-scenes tours. Members received a 10% discount on giftshop purchases and an informative newsletter, called the *Sea Pen*, about once a month.

Mr. Knight realized that the membership was vital to the aquarium's finances and philosophy. He wondered how the members would react to not being allowed to use "their" aquarium on demand.

General Admissions

According to the 1986 Annual Report, the general admissions category accounted for 61% of revenues (Exhibit 4). A recent study of summer visitors found that 97% of those surveyed felt they had received good value for their entertainment dollar. The aquarium offered various programs to educate and entertain this public. For example, there were feeding shows, interpretive talks, films, and volunteers to answer exhibit enquiries. In addition, the aquarium was open for extended hours during the summer.

The VPA's primary market was the Greater Vancouver Regional District. This area accounted for 28% of summer admissions and for 65% of off-season visitors (see Appendix). A second market was the province of British Columbia, outside Greater Vancouver.

Other areas served included the Pacific Northwest of the United States to the south and the province of Alberta to the east. Though no programs were designed for these markets, visitors from these areas did patronize the aquarium during the summer months.

During the summer months, visitor parking, although free, could be a problem. Unfortunately, the VPA could do little to alleviate this problem because adjacent land in Stanley Park could not be appropriated for extra parking.

Donors

The donor market was seen as very important for the aquarium. Without donor support, many of the aquarium's capital projects could not have been completed. For instance, some 17,000 individuals, 130 corporations, 4 foundations, and the federal government contributed more than $4.3 million to build the Max Bell Marine Mammal Centre. The aquarium recognized donors in various ways, including plaques, exhibit names (like the H.R. MacMillan Tropical Gallery), and publication of donors' names in VPA publications.

Volunteers

The 180 VPA volunteers, made up of Aquarium Association members and their families, volunteered 13,000 hours to the aquarium in 1986. They supervised educational tours, served as docents for school tours, and worked in the Clam Shell gift shop. Management believed that the main attractions for volunteers were their sense of pride in the aquarium and genuine concern for its success.

Schools

Over 7,500 students took part in the following VPA educational programs in the most recent year:

Water Wonders	Kindergarten, Grades 1 and 2
Secrets of Survival	Grades 3 and 4
Mysterious Marine Mammals	Grades 5, 6, 7

Exhibit 3

VANCOUVER PUBLIC AQUARIUM AVERAGE DAILY ATTENDANCE FOR 1985 AND 1986

1985 Month	Monday	Tuesday	Wednesday	Thursday	Friday	Saturday	Sunday	Holidays	Total Month
January	436	493	400	391	434	1,399	2,157	1,036	26,147
February	725	545	395	376	949	1,301	2,622	0	26,644
March	832	712	707	818	1,042	2,139	2,866	1,293	44,267
April	928	812	746	858	888	1,944	2,508	2,420	54,335
May	1,458	1,041	1,085	1,214	1,283	2,144	3,081	3,105	50,452
June	1,883	2,157	1,646	1,882	2,155	2,365	3,189	0	66,664
July	4,361	3,314	3,822	3,694	3,357	3,858	4,181	4,052	119,047
August	3,731	3,801	4,221	3,477	3,268	4,161	4,992	5,436	123,214
September	957	1,121	1,081	968	1,489	2,287	3,265	3,883	49,136
October	957	678	578	419	957	1,764	1,694	1,687	28,271
November	405	274	498	378	347	925	1,961	2,831	21,916
December	340	341	359	249	254	532	1,475	1,482	29,263
Winter Av.*	616	507	491	439	664	1,343	2,129	1,388	29,418
Total Av.	1,418	1,274	1,296	1,227	1,369	2,068	2,833	2,269	53,280

* January, February, March, October, November, December

(continued)

Exhibit 3 continued

1986 Month	Monday	Tuesday	Wednesday	Thursday	Friday	Saturday	Sunday	Holidays	Total Month
January	447	401	350	311	535	1,426	2,289	1,452	28,341
February	475	401	585	494	750	1,027	1,675	0	21,622
March	687	523	553	709	758	1,798	2,596	2,633	41,076
April	672	641	684	635	586	1,261	1,741	2,162	34,483
May	1,614	1,997	2,613	2,080	1,928	3,244	3,366	4,746	79,204
June	3,396	3,825	3,711	3,662	3,496	4,409	4,763	0	117,200
July	6,342	5,615	5,819	5,173	5,715	6,472	6,950	4,609	182,367
August	6,238	5,810	6,142	5,290	4,944	5,450	6,622	7,550	180,315
September	2,152	1,966	2,361	2,711	2,231	3,417	4,304	5,209	82,848
October	688	978	1,041	869	1,202	2,005	2,813	2,740	43,540
November	406	442	535	327	555	1,029	1,277	1,840	22,021
December	434	443	341	382	307	523	1,216	1,832	29,402
Winter Av.*	523	531	568	515	685	1,301	1,978	1,750	31,000
Total Av.	1,963	1,920	2,061	1,887	1,917	2,672	3,301	2,898	71,868

* January, February, March, October, November, December

Exhibit 4
ANNUAL FINANCIAL REPORTS FOR VANCOUVER PUBLIC AQUARIUM, 1982–1986 (IN 000s)

	1982		1983		1984		1985		1986*	
Revenue	$	%	$	%	$	%	$	%	$	%
Admissions	$1,612	70%	$1,989	70%	$1,855	71%	$1,937	69%	$2,786	61%
Gross margin/store	268	12	303	11	308	12	313	11	894	20
Membership fees	198	9	300	10	278	11	288	10	409	9
Deferred income transfer	101	4	100	4	—	—	—	—	—	—
Donations & grants	84	4	84	3	83	3	148	5	226	5
General operating revenue	44	2	69	2	74	3	134	5	232	5
	$2,308	100%	$2,844	100%	$2,599	100%	$2,820	100%	$4,548	100%
Expenditure										
Specimen care & display	$ 670	29%	$ 868	31%	$ 790	30%	$ 563	20%	$ 941	25%
Engineering & operations	597	26	714	26	668	25	751	27	—	—
Administration	359	15	414	15	392	15	673	24	—	—
Attendance & membership	353	15	398	14	414	15	385	14	—	—
Education & research	344	15	404	14	425	16	407	15	—	—
Life support/bldg. operations	—	—	—	—	—	—	—	—	875	23
Administration & svcs.	—	—	—	—	—	—	—	—	652	17
Store & admissions	—	—	—	—	—	—	—	—	513	14
Education & visitor services	—	—	—	—	—	—	—	—	339	9
Promotion	—	—	—	—	—	—	—	—	229	6
Member services	—	—	—	—	—	—	—	—	130	3
Scientific studies	—	—	—	—	—	—	—	—	109	3
	$2,323	100%	$2,798	100%	$2,698	100%	$2,779	100%	$3,789	100%

* In 1986, the VPA implemented a new accounting system with redefined accounts.

Spineless Wonders (a laboratory program)	Grades 5, 6, 7
B.C.'s Marine Invertebrates (a laboratory program)	Grades 11 and 12
Royaume Aquatique	French-speaking groups
Travelling Teacher	Outreach program—an aquarium teacher visiting schools

In addition to these formal programs, tours of the aquarium, films, and interpretive workshops were offered to school groups. To accommodate French immersion classes, the aquarium offered French-language tours. There was also a "travelling teacher," employed by the aquarium, who toured the province teaching students in out-of-town schools about aquatic life and the work being done by the aquarium.

To make teachers aware of the aquarium's programs, each school in the Vancouver area received a descriptive brochure at the beginning of the school year. During the third week of September, the VPA offered an "Open House for Educators" that gave teachers the opportunity to participate in workshops, preview the programs offered, and pick up various resource materials. Afterwards, teachers could book their classes into the programs and tours.

These programs were very popular. Usually most available spaces for the formal programs were filled by the second week in October. During the school year, the aquarium averaged five school tours per day. At present, the aquarium could handle no more than six tours in a day. Though school groups were given special group rates and a volunteer was provided to guide the tours, no other special accommodations were offered by the aquarium.

Ms. Dewey's memo offered one possible response to the popularity of these programs. Her memo read, in part, as follows:

> During the recent professional development programs, held by my department, many teachers expressed some disappointment in their inability to book their students into the aquarium's programs . . . With such a demand for these programs, an increase in service to the children of Vancouver will be beneficial to both parties. First, if the aquarium were to offer more programs, the aquarium would increase exposure and also help revenues. Second, the children would be more aware of the work done by the aquarium and may become active aquarium members in the future.
>
> To accomplish this increase in school programs, we would need to set aside certain hours for the use by students. Since most school tours are conducted in the mornings and early afternoons, we propose that these tours be run between the hours of 10 a.m. and 3 p.m. During these hours only children and their supervisors would be able to view the galleries . . . This would at least double our current capacity for handling school tours. If such a program were adopted, the feedings and interpretive segments could be targeted to a younger population. Though it would be more work at the beginning, I feel that such a program could be very successful.

Ms. Dewey's proposal would require the VPA to alter its presentations (such as the killer whale feedings) to better suit a school-age audience and to restrict the VPA's galleries to school children until 3 p.m. on weekdays. Closing the galleries to the general public on school days would have two effects on the VPA's operation. First, the "conflict" between the general public and school tours would be eliminated; the public would not be fighting the crowds of school children. However, the frustrations of aquarium members and the general admission market might shift from annoyance with the school children to anger at not being allowed admission at all. Secondly, the Clam Shell Gift Shop's hours of operation could be reduced; the shop would not need to be open during the hours of school tours. Currently, the aquarium used two full-time salaried employees and one part-time staff member, in addition to volunteers, to handle admissions and run the gift shop during weekdays. If the proposal were adopted, the aquarium's staffing needs could be reduced by at least one paid position during the school tour periods.

Mr. Knight sat down to do a preliminary study to see if the proposal was economically feasible. During the winter months, an average of 550 people per day visited the aquarium on weekdays. Of these 550, roughly 70% were "General Admissions" (385 persons). A "typical" weekday group consisted of two adults ($5.50 each) and one child ($3). Mr. Knight felt that for the school proposal to be implemented, revenues from the school programs would have to be increased to cover at least part of the $1,700 loss of general admissions revenues. Of course, some proportion of the weekday visitors would come another time. There was also the possibility of opening the aquarium to general admission after 3 p.m., but currently few winter visitors came at that time.

School admissions were priced at $2.50 per student and the average school group's size was 34 students. Mr. Knight wondered if the aquarium, particularly the volunteer guides, could handle a significant increase in school tours. If not, could the aquarium attract new volunteer docents? He was relatively confident that the aquarium would not have to hire more paid staff.

PRICING AND PROMOTIONS

VPA's prices were to be increased by an average of 10% on April 1, 1987 (Exhibit 5). Adult admission would then cost $5.50, a price that included both the killer whale and beluga whale shows, tours, seal feedings, films, and entrance to all galleries.

Pricing policy was ultimately determined by the Vancouver Public Aquarium Association membership through its Board of Governors. Though the board had the final say, most pricing changes were initiated by VPA staff. The pricing policy was cost-oriented. The aquarium budgeted its expenditures for the coming year and then set ticket prices, membership fees, etc., to balance these expenses. Discounting practices were usually reserved for the aquarium's membership and groups of ten people or more.

The aquarium had two short-term promotional pricing programs. Both were offered in December and were marketed as the aquarium's gift to the city. During the first week in December, general admission was free. In 1986, 6,906 people took advantage of this opportunity. There were occasional other free days. For example, on March 9, 1987, the aquarium had a free day to thank Vancouver for its generous

Exhibit 5

THE VANCOUVER PUBLIC AQUARIUM'S PRICE LIST (AS OF APRIL 1, 1987)

General Admission	Price	Membership Fee	Price
Adult	$ 5.50	Adult	$20.00
Youth or Senior	$ 4.25	Special[1]	$15.00
Child	$ 3.00	Couple[2]	$30.00
Family	$14.00	Family	$35.00
Groups (10+):			
Adult	$ 4.25		
Child	$ 2.50		
School	$ 2.50		

Source: Vancouver Public Aquarium's Annual Report

[1] This group included students, out-of-province residents, and seniors.

[2] A senior couple could purchase a membership for $15.00.

support of the Tropical Fish Gallery restocking. An astounding 12,000 people visited the aquarium.

The second promotion was the Christmas train program, which the aquarium participated in for the first time in 1986. In conjunction with Vancouver's Stanley Park Zoo, the aquarium had special nightly openings during one week of the Christmas holiday period. Patrons purchased a train ticket, entitling them to ride on a specially decorated miniature train. The train ride ran through a portion of Stanley Park as a tourist and family attraction. For most of the year, the train was run only during daylight hours. After the ride, the VPA offered admission to the aquarium and special performances of killer whale shows at a reduced price. The program helped increase awareness of the aquarium, but rain during four of the five nights kept attendance down to only 860 people.

Communication

The aquarium's communication objective was to increase awareness of VPA programs. The membership was kept informed through special direct mail communication and regular quarterly editions of *Sea Pen* magazine. The local, non-member segments were exposed to PSA advertisements on both radio and television. In addition, newspaper advertising was used to promote special events/exhibits. Aquarium brochures were available at Tourist Information Centres, Grayline Tour Booths, and at the Vancouver Travel Infocentre. During the summer months, billboard advertising was used.

Advertising budgets were set in December for the following year, with few changes in the mix from year to year (Exhibit 6).

Relations with the media were very good—so good that sometimes things got a little hectic. Along with regular coverage of aquarium events by local news media, major promotions generated wider coverage. The opening of the new Killer Whale

Exhibit 6

FISCAL BUDGET 1986: PUBLIC RELATIONS/ADVERTISING

	Jan.	Feb.	March	April	May	June	July	August	Sept.	Oct.	Nov.	Dec.	Total
Radio			600		700	700	500	500	300	300	500	500	4,600
Television				1,500									1,500
Newspapers			500		500	200	500		500	300		500	3,000
"Thank-you"*					5,000								5,000
Magazines	18,860	1,670	170	580	7,580	1,980	1,910	860	580	720	670	1,220	36,800
Brochures		3,000	20,000										23,000
Brochure dist.	325	325	325	325	729	729	729	729	379	379	325	325	5,624
Photography		1,000	1,000	1,000	1,000	1,000							5,000
Passes		250			250			250			250		1,000
Billboards						6,300	6,300	6,300					18,900
Store displays		200			400		400		400		400		1,800
Schedules				5,000									5,000
Contingency	1,000	1,000	1,000	1,000	1,000	1,000	1,000	1,000	1,000	1,000	1,000		11,000
Total Month	20,185	7,445	23,595	9,405	17,159	11,909	11,339	9,639	3,159	2,699	3,145	2,545	122,224

* "Thank-you" was budgeted as a full-page advertisement to thank contributors for their support in building the Max Bell Marine Mammal Centre.

Habitat, the appearance of the killer whales in the Vancouver Bach Choir/Vancouver Symphony Orchestra's "In Celebration of Whales" concert, the birth of two sea otters, and the major "Fishes of China" display all received national coverage in 1986. When an act of vandalism wiped out almost the entire tropical marine collection in late 1986, media around the world picked up the story. In addition to news coverage, TV programs like "Midday," "Sesame Street," and "The Nature of Things" featured segments on the Vancouver Public Aquarium. "Danger Bay," the CBC/Disney series, was filmed at the aquarium for a third season in 1986, continuing the adventures of Grant Roberts and his family.

The aquarium had recently started to track its visitors and ask how they found out about the aquarium. For instance, in a summer 1986 survey, 24% of people surveyed stated that they had seen an aquarium brochure. However, 54% stated that they hadn't seen any advertising. With a 1987 budget of $120,000, Mr. Knight wondered how he could be more effective in increasing awareness.

OPERATING HOURS

The aquarium had three distinct sets of operating hours. During the summer, the aquarium was open from 9:00 a.m. to 9:00 p.m., seven days per week. VPA managers felt that the extended summer hours increased attendance and also took advantage of the longer daylight hours. However, a 1982 study found that only 28% of visitors were aware of the extended summer hours. During the spring and fall, the aquarium was open from 10:00 a.m. to 6:00 p.m. Management felt that the public would not patronize the aquarium during winter evenings, so for winter months, the hours were further reduced to 10:00 a.m. to 5:00 p.m. To increase revenues, the aquarium offered evening and restricted daytime rentals of the facilities from September to May. The typical fee ranged from $100 for a luncheon meeting using a small room in the aquarium to $1,700 for use of the entire facility during an evening. (Food was provided by outside caterers.) In 1986, the VPA received more than $200,000 in rental revenue.

Though the aquarium had used these opening hours in the past, Mr. Knight had heard of other nonprofit groups who had altered their hours to "fit" the working public. In essence, these institutions would not be open in the mornings or early afternoons but would keep their facilities open during the evening to accommodate the working public.

Weekend hours could be kept as is or extended into the evening. This might allow the aquarium to keep its present weekend customers, and if the public knew that the aquarium was open until the same hour every night, awareness of the later hours would increase. If management were to set the same operating hours for the whole year, much of the confusion caused by the changing hours might be alleviated.

THE DECISION

At February's board meeting, various alternatives for more effective use of aquarium facilities had been raised. Board approval would be required prior to implementation of any recommendation to change opening hours significantly. Also, all programs had to be compatible with the aquarium's mission statement. Though the VPA had been successful in the past, Mr. Knight felt that a new approach to marketing could improve usage of the aquarium.

He recognized that Ms. Dewey's proposal had merit and that the survey results might help the aquarium better target its winter markets.

As Mr. Knight drove home, he wondered, "Can I solve these problems?" Specifically, he needed to answer these questions:

1. How could the $120,000 promotional budget be better spent?
2. How could the aquarium boost its attendance on weekdays and on Saturday?
3. Should Elizabeth Dewey's school program proposal be implemented? If so, what communications would have to be done to minimize the risks associated with it and maximize the benefits? If not, how should the issues Ms. Dewey raised be addressed?

Appendix
SELECTED RESULTS FROM JANUARY, 1987, QUESTIONNAIRE*

		Weekday	Weekend
1. Are you a resident of the Greater Vancouver Regional District?	Yes	71	60
	No	51	20
2. Are you currently a member of the Vancouver Public Aquarium?	Yes	26	34
	No	96	46
3. Is this your first visit to the aquarium?	Yes	47	23
	No	75	57
4. Was your last visit to the aquarium within the last two years?	Yes	23	46
	No	52	11
5. On average, how much time did you spend on this visit?	Less than ½ hour	0	0
	½–1 hour	44	30
	1–3 hours	72	50
	Over 3 hours	6	0
6. Are you alone or are you visiting with others?	Alone	9	4
	Others	113	76
7. How did you first learn about the aquarium?	Friend/Relative	29	15
	TV	9	0
	Radio	2	0
	Tourist magazine	2	0
	Brochure	8	4
	Newspaper	0	1
	Magazine article	2	0
	Billboard	0	0
	"Discovered"	14	10
	"Just knew"	40	40
	Other	16	10
8. Do you feel that you have received your entertainment dollar value at the aquarium?	Yes	122	78
	No	0	2
9. Sex:	Male	85	47
	Female	37	33
10. What is your age group?	18–25	22	4
	26–30	34	18
	31–35	14	18
	36–40	22	14
	41–50	10	10
	51–60	12	8
	Over 61	8	8

Source: Based on a survey conducted during 2 weeks in January 1987. Interviewers were stationed near the exit and asked visitors, as they were leaving, to answer a brief questionnaire.

* Total Respondents: Weekdays: 122 Weekends: 80

24 STRATFORD INDUSTRIES (I)

Roger A. Kerin

Late in the evening of August 8, 1990, Charlton Bates, president of Stratford Industries, called Dr. Thomas Berry, a marketing professor at an Ontario university and a consultant to the company. The conversation went as follows:

Bates: Hello, Tom. This is Chuck Bates. I'm sorry to call you this late, but I wanted to get your thoughts on the tentative 1991 advertising program proposed by Mike Hervey of Hervey and Bernham, our ad agency.

Berry: No problem, Chuck. What did they propose?

Bates: The crux of their proposal is that we should increase our advertising expenditures by $400,000. They suggested that we put the entire amount into our consumer advertising program for ads in several shelter magazines.[1]

Berry: That increase will nearly double your spending on consumer advertising. Also, it will push you slightly above your policy of budgeting no more than 5% of expected sales for total promotion expenditures. Hasn't Karen Bott [vice-president of sales] emphasized the need for more sales representatives?

Bates: Yes, Karen has requested additional funds. You are right about the 5% figure too, and I'm not sure if our sales forecast isn't too optimistic. Your research has shown that our sales historically follow industry sales almost perfectly, and trade economists are predicting about a 13% increase for 1991. Yet, I'm not too sure.

Berry: Well, Chuck, you can't expect forecasts to be always on the button. The money is one thing, but what else can you tell me about Hervey's rationale for putting more dollars into consumer advertising?

Bates: He contends that we can increase our exposure and tell our story to the buying public—increase brand awareness, enhance our image, that sort of thing. He also cited data from *Home Furnishing* magazine which showed that the newly affluent baby boomers [consumers between the ages of 30 and 45] are almost three times as likely to buy dining-room furniture and twice as likely to buy living-room furniture as their elders in the next year. All I know is that my contribution margin will fall to 25% next year because of increased labour and material cost.

[1] Shelter magazines feature home improvement ideas, new ideas in home decorating, and so on. *Better Homes and Gardens* is an example of a shelter magazine.

Note: Names and data are disguised.

Berry: I appreciate your concern. Give me a few days to think about the proposal. I'll get back to you soon.

After the parting remarks, Dr. Berry began to think through Charlton Bates's summary of the proposal, Stratford's present position, and the furniture industry in general. He knew that Bates expected a well thought-out recommendation on such issues and a step-by-step description of the logic used to arrive at that recommendation.

THE COMPANY

Stratford Industries manufactures medium- to high-priced wood living-room and dining-room furniture. The company was formed at the turn of the century by Bates' grandfather, George Martin. Charlton Bates assumed the presidency of the company upon his father's retirement in 1982. Forecasted year-end gross sales in 1990 were $50 million; before-tax profit was $2.7 million.

Stratford sells its furniture through 1,000 high-quality department stores and furniture specialty stores across Canada and in several midwestern states (primarily Michigan and Illinois), but all stores do not carry the company's entire line. The company is very selective in choosing retail outlets. According to Bates, "Our distribution policy, hence our retailers, should mirror the high quality of our products."

The company employs ten full-time salespeople and two regional sales managers. Sales personnel receive a base salary and a small commission on sales. A company sales force is atypical in the furniture industry; most furniture manufacturers use sales agents or representatives who carry a wide assortment of noncompeting furniture lines and receive a commission on sales. "Having our own sales group is a policy my father established 25 years ago," noted Bates, "and we've been quite successful having people who are committed to our company. Our people don't just take furniture orders. They are expected to motivate retail salespeople to sell our line, assist in setting up displays in stores, and give advice on a variety of matters to our retailers and their salespeople." He added, "It seems that my father was ahead of his time. I was just reading in the *Financial Post Outlook* for household furniture that the competition for retail floor space will require even more support, including sales training, merchandising, inventory management, and advertising."

In 1989, Stratford allocated $2.5 million for total promotional expenditures for the 1990 operating year, excluding the salary of the vice-president of sales. Promotion expenditures were categorized into four groups:

1. sales expense and administration,
2. co-operative advertising programs with retailers,
3. trade promotion, and
4. consumer advertising.

The co-operative advertising budget is usually spent on newspaper advertising in a retailer's city. Co-operative advertising allowances are matched by funds provided by retailers on a dollar-for-dollar basis. Trade promotion is directed toward retailers and takes the form of catalogues, trade magazine advertisements, booklets for consumers, and point-of-purchase materials such as displays, for use in retail stores. Also included in this category is the expense of participating in manufacturers' expositions (that is, trade shows). Stratford is represented at two major expositions per year, one in Toronto and one in High Point, North Carolina. Consumer advertising is directed at potential consumers through shelter magazines. The typical format used in consumer advertising is to highlight new furniture and different living-room and dining-room arrangements. The dollar allocation for each of these programs in 1990 is shown in Exhibit 1.

Exhibit 1

ALLOCATION OF PROMOTION DOLLARS, 1989

Sales expense and administration	$ 737,500
Co-operative advertising allowance	1,052,500
Trade advertising	290,000
Consumer advertising	422,000
Total	$2,502,000

Source: Company records

THE INDUSTRY

The household furniture industry is composed of over 1,400 firms. Industry furniture sales at manufacturers' prices were forecasted to reach $8.6 billion in 1990 in the markets covered by Stratford (Canada and the midwestern United States). Ontario and Quebec are the major furniture-producing provinces in Canada, although Stratford also competes with United States furniture manufacturers to a limited extent. With the advent of the Free Trade Agreement between Canada and the United States in 1989, the 15% tariff on furniture—the tariff existed between both countries—was being phased out over a five-year period. Because Stratford had operated in several states in the United States for a number of years, company executives saw the agreement as a greater opportunity than a threat. In general, Charlton Bates did not see the agreement as having a major impact on the company. In fact, company executives considered shipping costs more important than tariffs in setting market boundaries. Major well-known furniture manufacturers include Sklar-Peppler, Kaufman, Sealy, and Kroehler. No one firm holds more than 5% of the total household furniture market.

The buying and selling of furniture to retail outlets centres around manufacturers' expositions held at selected times and places. At these marts, as they are called in the furniture industry, retail buyers view manufacturers' lines and often make buying commitments for their stores. However, Stratford's experience has shown that sales efforts in the retail store by company representatives traditionally account for 50% of the company's sales in any given year. The salespeople were paid an annual salary of $50,000 plus 0.5% commission on the sales they made in retail stores. The major manufacturer expositions for Stratford occur in Toronto in October and High

Point in April. Regional expositions are also scheduled during the June–August period in locations such as Vancouver and Detroit.

FURNITURE BUYING BEHAVIOUR

Results of a consumer panel sponsored by *Better Homes and Gardens* and composed of *Better Homes and Gardens* subscribers provide the most comprehensive information available on furniture buying behaviour. Selected findings from this consumer panel are reproduced in the Appendix. Other findings arising from this research are as follows.

- 94% (of the subscribers) enjoy buying furniture somewhat or very much
- 84% believe "the higher the price, the higher the quality" when buying home furnishings
- 72% browse or window-shop at furniture stores even if they don't need furniture
- 85% read furniture ads before they actually need furniture
- Retail outlets used by subscribers break down as follows:
  32% use furniture specialty stores
  28% use furniture gallery stores
  14% use department stores
  8% use Sears and K mart
  7% use discount furniture outlets
- 99% agree with the statement, "When shopping for furniture and home furnishings, I like the salesperson to show me what alternatives are available, answer any questions, and let me alone so I can think about it and maybe browse around."
- 95% say they get redecorating ideas or guidance from magazines
- 41% have written for a manufacturer's booklet
- 63% say they need decorating advice to "put it all together"

THE BUDGET MEETING

At the August 8 meeting attended by Hervey and Bernham executives and Stratford executives, Michael Hervey proposed that the expenditure for consumer advertising be increased by $400,000 for 1991. Co-operative advertising and trade advertising allowances would remain at 1990 levels. Hervey further recommended that shelter magazines account for the bulk of the incremental expenditure for consumer advertising.

Karen Bott, Stratford's sales vice-president, disagreed with the budget allocation and noted that sales expenses and administration costs were expected to rise by $50,000 in 1991. Moreover, Bott believed an additional sales representative was needed to service Stratford's accounts, since 50 new accounts were being added. She estimated that the cost of the additional representative, including salary and expenses, would be at least $50,000 in 1991. "That's about $100,000 for sales expenses that have to be added into our promotional budget for 1991," Bott noted. She continued:

> We expect sales of about $50 million in 1990 if our sales experience continues throughout the remainder of the year. If we assume a 13% increase in sales in 1991, that means our total budget will be about $2,825,000 if my figures are right, a $325,000 increase over our previous budget. And I need $100,000 of that. In other words, $225,000 is available for other kinds of promotion.

Hervey's reply to Bott noted that the company planned to introduce several new styles of living-room and dining-room furniture in 1991, and that these new items would require advertising to be launched successfully. He agreed with Bott that increased funding of the sales effort might be necessary and thought that Stratford might draw funds from co-operative advertising allowance and trade promotion.

Bates interrupted the dialogue between Bott and Hervey to mention that the $400,000 increase in promotion exceeded the 5% percentage-of-sales policy by $75,000. He pointed out that higher materials costs plus a recent wage increase were forecasted to squeeze Stratford's gross profit margin and threaten the company objective of achieving a 5% net profit margin before taxes. "Perhaps some juggling of the figures is necessary," he concluded. "Both of you have good points. Let me think about what's been said and then let's schedule a meeting for a week from today."

As Bates reviewed his notes from the meeting, he realized that the funds allocated to promotion were only part of the question. How the funds would be allocated within the budget was also crucial. Perhaps a call to Tom Berry would be helpful in this regard, too.

Appendix

SELECTED FINDINGS FROM THE *BETTER HOMES AND GARDENS* CONSUMER PANEL REPORT—HOME FURNISHINGS*

Question: If you were going to buy furniture in the near future, how important would the following factors be in selecting the store to buy furniture?

Factor	Very Important	Somewhat Important	Not too Important	Not at all Important	No Answer
Sells high-quality furnishings	62.6%	31.0%	3.8%	1.1%	1.5%
Has a wide range of different furniture styles	58.5	29.2	8.2	2.9	0.9
Gives you personal service	60.1	29.9	7.8	0.9	1.3
Is a highly dependable store	85.1	12.7	1.1	—	1.1
Offers decorating help from experienced home planners	26.5	35.9	25.4	10.9	1.3
Lets you "browse" all you want	77.1	17.8	3.3	0.7	1.1
Sells merchandise that's a good value for the money	82.0	15.6	0.9	0.2	1.3
Displays furniture in individual room settings	36.3	41.2	18.7	2.4	1.3
Has a relaxed, no-pressure atmosphere	80.0	17.1	1.6	—	1.3
Has well-informed salespeople	77.5	19.8	1.6	—	1.1
Has a very friendly atmosphere	68.2	28.1	2.4	—	1.3
Carries the style of furniture you like	88.0	10.0	0.9	—	1.1

* Reprinted courtesy of the *Better Homes and Gardens* Consumer Panel. Results are based on responses from 449 panel members.

Question: **Please rank the following factors as to their importance to you when you purchase or shop for case-goods furniture, such as a dining-room or living-room suite, 1 being the most important factor, 2 being second most important, and so on, until all factors have been ranked.**

	1	2	3	4	5	6	7	8	9	10	No Answer
Construction of item	24.1%	16.0%	18.5%	13.1%	10.5%	6.9%	4.9%	1.6%	0.2%	1.1%	3.1%
Comfort	13.6	14.7	12.9	12.3	12.7	10.9	8.2	4.5	4.0	2.4	3.8
Styling and design	33.6	19.8	11.1	9.6	4.7	7.3	4.5	1.6	2.9	1.6	3.3
Durability of fabric	2.2	7.6	9.8	14.5	15.1	14.7	12.9	5.6	5.8	7.8	4.0
Type and quality of wood	10.9	17.8	16.3	15.8	14.7	5.8	5.3	3.1	4.9	2.0	3.4
Guarantee or warranty	1.6	3.8	1.6	5.3	8.7	10.0	13.8	25.2	14.5	11.1	4.4
Price	9.4	6.2	8.7	8.5	10.0	12.5	14.2	11.8	6.9	8.0	3.8
Reputation of the manufacturer or brand name	6.2	3.6	4.7	5.6	6.2	6.2	12.7	17.1	22.7	11.6	3.4
Reputation of retailer	1.6	1.8	1.6	2.4	4.0	7.3	7.4	13.6	22.0	34.5	3.8
Finish, colour of wood	4.7	7.6	10.2	8.0	8.9	13.4	10.7	10.0	10.2	12.7	3.6

Question: Below is a list of 15 criteria that may influence what furniture you buy. Please rank each from 1 as most important to 5 as least important.

	1	2	3	4	5	No Answer
Guarantee or warranty	11.4%	11.1%	26.3%	16.9%	5.3%	29.0%
Brand name	9.1	6.5	14.3	25.6	11.6	32.9
Comfort	34.7	27.8	14.5	8.5	4.7	9.8
Decorator suggestion	4.0	2.4	2.7	8.2	44.8	37.9
Material used	14.9	24.1	14.9	13.4	6.2	26.5
Delivery time	0.7	0.5	1.3	2.9	55.2	39.4
Size	7.6	10.7	13.6	30.9	4.0	33.2
Styling and design	33.4	17.8	21.8	13.6	2.2	11.2
Construction	34.3	23.6	13.1	11.4	2.9	14.7
Fabric	4.0	25.6	24.9	14.0	4.5	27.0
Durability	37.0	19.4	13.6	6.9	4.9	18.2
Finish on wooden parts	5.8	14.7	16.7	10.7	16.7	35.4
Price	19.4	21.8	16.0	10.9	15.4	16.5
Manufacturer's reputation	4.2	9.1	15.4	22.9	14.3	34.1
Retailer's reputation	2.2	4.7	10.5	21.2	26.5	34.9

Question: Listed below are some statements others have made about their homes and the furniture pieces they particularly like. Please indicate, for each statement, how much you agree or disagree with each one.

Statement	Agree Completely	Agree Somewhat	Neither Agree nor Disagree	Disagree Somewhat	Disagree Completely	No Answer
I wish there were some way to be really sure of getting good quality in furniture.	61.9%	24.7%	4.7%	4.2%	3.6%	0.9%
I really enjoy shopping for furniture.	49.2	28.3	7.6	9.8	4.2	0.9
I would never buy any furniture without my husband's/wife's approval.	47.0	23.0	10.9	9.8	7.1	2.2
I like all the pieces in the master bedroom to be exactly the same style.	35.9	30.7	12.7	11.1	7.6	2.0
Once I find something I like in furniture, I wish it would last forever so I'd never have to buy again.	36.8	24.3	10.0	18.9	9.1	0.9
I wish I had more confidence in my ability to decorate my home attractively.	23.1	32.3	12.5	11.6	18.7	1.8
I wish I knew more about furniture styles and what looks good.	20.0	31.0	17.1	13.4	16.7	1.8
My husband/wife doesn't take much interest in the furniture we buy.	6.5	18.0	12.3	17.89	41.4	4.0
I like to collect a number of different styles in the dining room.	3.3	10.5	15.2	29.8	38.3	2.9
Shopping for furniture is very distressing to me.	2.4	11.6	14.3	18.0	51.9	1.8

Question: **Listed below are some factors that may influence your choice of furnishings, 1 being most important, 2 being second most important, and so on, until all factors have been ranked.**

	1	2	3	4	5	No Answer
Friends and/or neighbours	1.3%	16.9%	15.8%	22.1%	41.7%	2.2%
Family or spouse	62.8	9.4	14.3	9.8	2.0	1.7
Magazine advertising	16.3	30.3	29.6	17.6	4.2	2.0
Television advertising	1.1	6.7	14.7	32.5	42.3	2.7
Store displays	18.9	37.2	22.1	14.0	5.6	2.2

Question: **When you go shopping for a major piece of furniture or smaller pieces of furniture, who, if anyone, do you usually go with? (Multiple responses allowed.) Who, if anyone, helps you decide? (Multiple responses allowed.)**

	Usually Go With		Helps Decide	
	Major Pieces	Other Pieces	Major Pieces	Other Pieces
Husband	82.4%	59.5%	86.0%	63.5%
Mother or mother-in-law	6.2	9.1	2.4	4.5
Friend	12.0	18.9	3.6	8.0
Decorator	4.2	1.6	3.1	2.7
Other relative	15.6	15.4	10.0	12.9
Other person	2.9	3.3	1.6	1.8
No one else	5.1	22.3	7.1	24.3
No answer	0.9	3.1	0.9	2.2

25 STRATFORD INDUSTRIES (II)

Roger A. Kerin

In November 1990, Stratford Industries merged with Meadows Furniture, a manufacturer of upholstered furniture for living-rooms and family-rooms. The merger was not planned in a conventional sense. Meadows' owner died suddenly in August 1990, leaving his daughter, a lawyer, with controlling interest in the firm. The merger proceeded smoothly, since the two firms were located on adjacent properties, and the general consensus was that the two firms would maintain as much autonomy as was economically justified. Moreover, the upholstery line filled a gap in the Stratford product mix, even though it would retain its own identity and brand names.

The only real issue that continued to plague Bates was merging the selling effort. Stratford had its own sales force, but Meadows Furniture relied on sales agents to represent it. The question was straightforward, in his opinion: "Do we give the upholstery line of chairs and sofas to our sales force, or do we continue using the sales agents?" Ms. Karen Bott, Stratford's sales vice-president, said the line should be given to her sales group; Mr. Martin Moorman, national sales manager of Meadows, said the upholstery line should remain with sales agents.

MEADOWS FURNITURE

Meadows Furniture is a small manufacturer of upholstered furniture for use in living-rooms and family-rooms. The firm is over seventy-five years old. The company has some of the finest fabrics and frame construction in the industry, according to trade sources. Net sales in 1990 were \$3 million. Total industry sales of over 1,400 furniture manufacturers in 1990 were approximately \$8.6 billion. Company sales for Meadows had increased 15% annually over the last five years, and company executives believed this growth rate would continue for the foreseeable future.

Meadows Furniture employed 15 sales agents to represent its products. These sales agents also represented several manufacturers of non-competing furniture and home furnishings. Often a sales agent found it necessary to deal with several buyers in a store in order to represent all lines carried. On a typical sales call, a sales agent would first visit buyers. New lines, in addition to any promotions being offered by manufacturers, would be discussed. New orders were sought where and when it was appropriate. A sales agent would then visit a retailer's selling floor to check displays, inspect furniture, and inform salespeople about furniture. Meadows Furniture paid an agent commission of 5% of net company sales for these services. Moorman thought sales agents spent 10 to 15% of their in-store sales time on Meadows products.

The company did not attempt to influence the type of retailers that agents con-

Note: Names and data are disguised.

tacted. Yet it was implicit in the agency agreement that agents would not sell to discount houses. All agents had established relationships with their retail accounts and worked closely with them. Sales records indicated that agents were calling on furniture and department stores. An estimated 1,000 retail accounts were called on in 1990.

STRATFORD INDUSTRIES[1]

Stratford Industries is a manufacturer of medium- to high-priced living-room and dining-room wood furniture. The firm was formed in 1902. Net sales for 1990 were $50 million. The company employed ten full-time sales representatives who called on 1,000 retail accounts in 1990. These individuals performed the same function as sales agents, but were paid a salary plus a small commission. In 1990, the average Stratford sales representative received an annual salary of $50,000 (plus expenses) and a commission of 0.5% on net company sales. Total sales administration costs were $112,500.

The Stratford sales force was highly regarded in the industry. The salespeople were known particularly for their knowledge of wood furniture and willingness to work with buyers and retail sales personnel. Despite these points, Bates knew that all retail accounts did not carry the complete Stratford furniture line. He had therefore instructed Karen Bott to "push the group a little harder." At present, sales representatives were making ten sales calls per week, with the average sales call running three hours. Remaining time was accounted for by administrative activities and travel. Bates recommended that the call frequency be increased to seven calls per account per year, which was consistent with what he thought was the industry norm.

MERGING THE SALES EFFORT

In separate meetings with Bott and Moorman, Bates was able to piece together a variety of data and perspectives on the question. These meetings also made it clear that Bott and Moorman differed dramatically in their views.

Karen Bott had no doubts about assigning the line to the Stratford sales force. Among the reasons she gave for this approach were the following. First, Stratford had developed one of the most well-respected, professional sales groups in the industry. Sales representatives could easily learn the fabric jargon, and they already knew personally many of the buyers who were responsible for upholstered furniture. Second, selling the Meadows line would require only about 15% of present sales call time. Thus, she thought the new line would not be a major burden. Third, more control over sales efforts was possible. She noted that Stratford had developed the sales group 25 years earlier because of the commitment it engendered and the service "only our own people are able and willing to give." Moreover, our people have the Stratford "look" and presentation style that is instilled in every person. Fourth, she said it wouldn't look right if we had our representatives and agents calling on the same stores and buyers. She noted that Stratford and Meadows

[1] Additional background information on the company and industry can be found in the case entitled "Stratford Industries (I)."

overlapped on most of their accounts. She said, "We'd be paying a commission on sales to these accounts when we would have gotten them anyway. The difference in commission percentages would not be good for morale."

Martin Moorman advocated keeping sales agents for the Meadows line. His arguments were as follows. First, all sales agents had established contacts and were highly regarded by store buyers, and most had represented the line in a professional manner for many years. He, too, had a good working relationship with all 15 agents. Second, sales agents represented little, if any, cost beyond commissions. Moorman noted, "Agents get paid when we get paid." Third, sales agents were committed to the Meadows line: "The agents earn a part of their living representing us. They have to service retail accounts to get the repeat business." Fourth, sales agents were calling on buyers not contacted by Stratford sales representatives. He noted, "If we let Stratford people handle the line, we might lose these accounts, have to hire more sales personnel, to take away 25% of the present selling time given to Stratford product lines."

As Bates reflected on the meetings, he felt that a broader perspective was necessary beyond the views expressed by Bott and Moorman. One factor was profitability. Existing Stratford furniture lines typically had gross margins that were 5% higher than those for Meadows upholstered lines. Another factor was the "us and them" references apparent in the meetings with Bott and Moorman. Would merging the sales efforts overcome this, or would it cause more problems? Finally, the idea of increasing the sales force to incorporate the Meadows line did not sit well with him. Adding a new salesperson would involve restructuring of sales territories, potential loss of commission to existing people, and "a big headache."

26 CASTLE COFFEE LIMITED (I)

William F. Massy
David B. Montgomery
Charles B. Weinberg

In May of 1982, Adrian Van Tassle, advertising manager for Castle Coffee Ltd., contemplated the latest market share report. This was not one of his happier moments. "I've got to do something to turn this darned market around," he exclaimed, "before it's too late for Castle—and me. But I can't afford another mistake like last year . . . "

Indeed, William Castle (the president and a major stockholder of the Castle Company) had exhibited a similar reaction when told that Castle Coffee's market share was dropping back toward 5.4%—where it had been one year previously. He had remarked rather pointedly to Van Tassle that if market share and profitability were not improved during the next fiscal year, "some rather drastic actions" might need to be taken.

Adrian Van Tassle had been hired nearly two years ago by James Anthoney, vice-president of marketing for Castle. Prior to that time he had worked for companies in Montreal and Toronto and had gained a reputation as a highly effective advertising executive. Now, he was engaged in trying to reverse a long-term downward trend in the market position of Castle Coffee.

CASTLE'S MARKET POSITION

Castle Coffee was an old, established company in the coffee business. The company had at one time enjoyed as much as a 15% share of the market. These were often referred to as the "good old days," when the brand was strong and growing and the company was able to sponsor popular radio programs.

The company's troubles began when television replaced radio as the primary broadcast medium. Although Castle Coffee was an early television advertiser, the company experienced competitive difficulty as TV production and time costs increased. Further problems arose as several other old-line companies were absorbed by major marketers. For example, Nabob was bought by the internationally prominent Swiss coffee firm, Jacobs Suchard, joining General Foods Corporation (Maxwell House, Sanka, and Yuban brands of coffee) in the ranks of Castle's most formidable competitors. Finally, the advent of freeze-dry and the increasing popularity of instant coffee put additional pressure on the company, which had no entry in these product classes.

The downward trend in share continued during the 1970s; the company had held 12% of the market at the beginning of the decade but only about 5½% at the end. Share had held fairly stable for the last few years. This was attributed to a "hard-core" group of local buyers plus an active (and expensive) program of consumer promotions and price-off deals to the trade. Anthoney, the vice-president of marketing, believed that the erosion of share had been halted just in time. A little more slippage, he said, and Castle would begin to lose its distribution. This would have been the beginning of the end for this venerable company.

OPERATION BREAKOUT

When William Castle succeeded his father as president four years previously, his main objective was to halt the decline in market position and, if possible, to effect a turnaround. While he seemed to have achieved success in reaching the first objective, both he and Anthoney agreed that the same strategy, that is, intensive consumer and trade promotion, would not succeed in winning back any appreciable proportion of the lost market share.

Both executives believed that it would be necessary to increase consumer awareness of the Castle brand and develop more favourable attitudes towards it if market position were to be improved. This could only be done through advertising. Since the company produced a quality product (it was noticeably richer and more aromatic than many competing coffees), it appeared that a strategy of increasing advertising might stand some chance of success. A search for an advertising manager was initiated, which culminated in the hiring of Adrian Van Tassle.

After a period of familiarizing himself with the Castle Company and the coffee market, Van Tassle began developing a plan to revitalize Castle's advertising program. First, he "released" the company's current advertising agency and requested proposals from a number of others interested in obtaining the account. While it was generally understood that the amount of advertising would increase somewhat, the heaviest emphasis was on the kind of appeal and copy execution to be used. Both the company and the various agencies agreed that nearly all the advertising weight should go into television. No other medium could match TV's impact for a product like coffee. (There is a great deal of newspaper advertising for coffee, but this is usually placed by retailers under an advertising allowance arrangement with the manufacturer. Castle Coffee included such expenditures in its promotional budget rather than as an advertising expense.)

The team from Ardvar Associates, Ltd., won the competition with an advertising program built around the theme, "Only a Castle is fit for a king or a queen." The new agency recommended that a 30% increase in the quarterly advertising budget be approved, in order to give the new program a fair trial. After considerable negotiation with Castle and Anthoney and further discussion with the agency, Van Tassle decided to compromise on a 20% increase. The new campaign was to start in the autumn of 1981, which was the second quarter of the company's 1982 fiscal year (the fiscal year started July 1). It was dubbed "Operation Breakout."

PERFORMANCE DURING CURRENT YEAR

Castle had been advertising at an average rate of $200,000 per quarter for the last several years. Given current levels of promotional expenditures, this was regarded as sufficient to maintain market share about its current level of 5.4%. Castle's annual expenditure of $800,000 represented somewhat more than 5.4% of industry advertising, though exact figures about competitors' expenditures on ground coffee were difficult to obtain. This relation was regarded as normal, since private brands accounted for a significant fraction of the market, and these received little or no advertising. Neither Van Tassle nor Anthoney anticipated that competitive expenditures would change much during the next few years regardless of any increase in Castle's advertising.

Advertising of ground coffee followed a regular seasonal pattern, which approximated the seasonal variation of industry sales. The relevant figures are presented in Exhibit 1. Total ground coffee sales for all brands averaged 22 million pounds per quarter (in all container sizes) and were expected to remain at that level for several years. Consumption in winter was about 15% above the yearly average, while in summer the volume was down by 15%.

Advertising expenditures by both Castle Coffee and the industry in general followed the same basic pattern, except that the seasonal variation was between 80% and 120%—somewhat greater than the variation in sales. The "maintenance" expenditures on advertising, shown in Exhibit 1, was what the company believed it had to spend to maintain its "normal" 5.4% share of the market in each quarter. Van Tassle had wondered whether this was the right seasonal advertising pattern for Castle, given its small percentage of the market, but decided to stay with it. Therefore, the 20% planned increase in quarterly advertising rates was simply added to the "sustaining" amount for each quarter, beginning in the second quarter of the year, as shown in Exhibit 1.

Exhibit 1
INDUSTRY SALES AND CASTLE'S ADVERTISING BUDGET

	Industry	Sales	Maintenance Advertising		Planned Advertising	
Quarter	Pounds*	Index	Dollars*	Index	Dollars*	% Increase
1 Summer	18.7	0.85	0.160	0.80	0.160	0%
2 Autumn	22.0	1.00	0.200	1.00	0.240	20
3 Winter	25.3	1.15	0.240	1.20	0.288	20
4 Spring	22.0	1.00	0.200	1.00	0.240	20
Average	22.0	1.00	0.200	1.00	0.232	16

* in millions

Exhibit 2
AUGUST MEMO

August 1

Memo to: W. Castle, President

From: I. Gure, Controller

Subject: Proposed 20% Increase in Advertising

I think that Adrian's proposal to increase advertising by 20% (from a quarterly rate of \$200,000 to one of \$240,000) is a good idea. He predicts that a market share of 6.0 percent will be achieved compared to our current 5.4 percent. I can't comment about the feasibility of this assumption: that's Adrian's business and I presume he knows what he's doing. I can tell you, however, that such a result would be highly profitable.

As you know, the wholesale price of coffee has been running about \$2.72 per pound. Deducting our average retail advertising and promotional allowance of \$0.16 per pound, and our variable costs of production and distribution of \$2.11 per pound, leaves an average gross contribution to fixed costs and profit of \$0.45 per pound. Figuring a total market of about 22 million pounds per quarter and a share change of from 0.054 to 0.060 (a 0.006 increase), we would have the following increase in gross contribution:

$$\text{Change in gross contribution} = \$0.45 \times 22 \text{ million} \times 0.006 = \$0.06 \text{ million.}$$

Subtracting the change in advertising expense due to the new program and then dividing by this same quantity gives what can be called the advertising payout rate:

$$\begin{aligned}\text{Advertising payout rate} &= \frac{\text{change in gross contribution} - \text{change in advertising expense}}{\text{change in advertising expense}}\\ &= \frac{\$0.02 \text{ million}}{\$0.04 \text{ million}} = 0.50\end{aligned}$$

That is, we can expect to make \$0.50 in net contribution for each extra dollar spent on advertising. You can see that as long as this quantity is greater than zero (at which point the extra gross contribution just pays for the extra advertising), increasing our advertising is a good deal.

In speaking with Castle and Anthoney about the proposed changes in the advertising program, Van Tassle had indicated that he expected to increase market share to 6% or perhaps a little more. This sounded reasonable to Castle, especially after he had consulted with the company's controller. Exhibit 2 presents the controller's memorandum on the advertising budget increase. While a fraction of a share point might seem like a small gain, each additional share point was worth nearly $400,000 in annual gross contribution (before advertising) to the company.

Van Tassle had, of course, indicated that the hoped for 6% share was not a "sure thing" and, in any case, that it might take more than one quarter before the full effects of the new advertising program would be felt.

The new advertising campaign began as scheduled on October 1, the first day of the second quarter of the fiscal year. Adrian Van Tassle was somewhat disappointed in the commercials prepared by the Ardvar agency and a little apprehensive about the early reports from the field. The bi-monthly store audit report of market share for September–October showed only a fractional increase in share over the 5.4% of the previous period. Nevertheless, Van Tassle thought that, given a little time, things would work out and the campaign would eventually reach its objective.

The November–December market share report was received in mid-January. It showed Castle's share of the market to be 5.6%. On January 21, Van Tassle received a copy of the controller's memorandum to the president (Exhibit 3).

Exhibit 3
JANUARY MEMO

January 20

Memo to: W. Castle, President

From: I. Gure, Controller

Subject: Failure of Advertising Program

I am most alarmed at our failure to achieve the market share target projected by Adrian. The 0.2 point increase in market share achieved in November–December is not sufficient to return the cost of the increased advertising. Ignoring the month of October, which obviously represents a start-up period, a 0.2 point increase in share generated only $20,000 in extra gross contribution on a quarterly basis. This must be compared to the $40,000 we have expended in extra advertising. The advertising payout rate is thus only −0.50: much less than the breakeven point.

I know Adrian expects shares to increase again next quarter, but he has not been able to say by how much. The new program projects an advertising expenditure increase of nearly $50,000 over last year's winter quarter level. I don't see how we can continue to make these expenditures without a better prospect of return on our investment.

On Monday, January 24, Anthoney telephoned Van Tassle to say that the president wanted an immediate review of the new advertising program. Later that week, after several rounds of discussion in which Van Tassle was unable to convince Castle and Anthoney that the program would be successful, it was decided to return to fiscal 1981 advertising levels. The TV ad contracts were renegotiated and by the middle of February advertising had been cut back substantially toward the $240,000 per quarter rate that had previously been normal for the winter season. The advertising agency complained that the efficiency of their media "buy" suffered significantly during February and March, due to the abrupt reduction in advertising expenditure. However, they were unable to say by how much. The spring 1982 advertising rate was set as the normal level of $200,000. Market share for January–February turned out to be slightly under 5.7%, while that for March–April was about 5.5%.

PLANNING FOR FISCAL 1983

So, in mid-May of 1982, Adrian Van Tassle was faced with the problem of what to recommend as the advertising budget for the four quarters of fiscal 1983. He was already very late in dealing with this assignment, since additional media buys would have to be made soon if any substantial increase in advertising weight were to be implemented during the coming summer quarter. Alternatively, fast action would be needed to reduce advertising expenditures below their tentatively budgeted "normal" level of $160,000.

During the past month, Van Tassle had spent considerable time reviewing the difficulties of fiscal 1982. He had remained convinced that a 20% increase in advertising should produce somewhere around a 6% market share level. He based this partly on "hunch" and partly on a number of studies that had been performed by academic and business market researchers with whom he was acquainted.

One such study which he believed was particularly applicable to Castle Coffee's situation indicated that the "advertising elasticity of demand" was equal to about ½. He recalled that the definition of this measure when applied to market share was:

$$\text{Advertising elasticity of demand} = \frac{\text{percent change in market share}}{\text{percent change in advertising}}$$

One researcher, whose judgment Van Tassle trusted, assured him that it was valid to think of "percent changes" as being deviations from "normal levels" (also called maintenance levels) of advertising and market share. However, any given value of advertising elasticity would be valid only for moderate deviations from the norm. That is, the value of ½ he had noted earlier would not necessarily apply to (say) plus or minus 50% changes in advertising.

Van Tassle noted that his estimate of share change (6.0 − 5.4 = 0.6 percentage points) represented about an 11% increase over the normal share level of 5.4 points. Since this was to be achieved with a 20% increase in advertising, it represented an advertising elasticity of 11%/20% = 0.55%. While this was higher than the 0.5 found in the study, he had believed that his advertising appeals and copy would be a bit better than average. He recognized that his ads may not actually have been as great as expected, but noted that, "even an elasticity of 0.5 would produce 5.94% of the market within striking distance of 6%." Of course, the study itself might be applicable to Castle Coffee's market situation to a greater or lesser degree.

One lesson which he had learned from his unfortunate experience the year before was the danger inherent in presenting too optimistic a picture to top management. On the other hand, a "conservative" estimate might not have been sufficient to obtain approval for the program in the first place. Besides, he really did believe that the effect of advertising on share was greater than implied by performance this past autumn. Alternatively, if Castle and Anthoney had good reason for doubting this judgement, he wanted to know about it—after all, they had been in the coffee business a lot longer than he and were pretty savvy guys.

Perhaps the problem lay in his assessment of the speed with which the new program would take hold. He had felt it "would take a little time," but had not tried to pin it down further ("That's pretty hard, after all," he thought). Nothing very precise about this had been communicated to management. Could he blame the controller for adopting the time horizon he did?

As a final complicating factor, Van Tassle had just received a report from Ardvar Associates about the quality of the advertising copy and appeals used the previous autumn and winter. Contrary to expectations these ads rated only about 0.90 on a scale which rated an "average ad" at 1.0. These tests were based on the so-called "theatre technique," in which the various spots were inserted into a filmed "entertainment" program and shown to a sample of consumers brought together in a theatre. The effect of an ad was tested by a questionnaire designed to measure brand purchasing behaviour. Fortunately, the ads currently being shown rated about 1.0 on the same scale. A new series of ads scheduled for showing during the autumn, winter, and spring of 1983 appeared to be much better. Theatre testing could not be undertaken until production was completed during the summer, but "experts" in the agency were convinced that they would rate at least as high as 1.15. Van Tassle was impressed with these ads himself, but recalled that such predictions tended to be far from perfect. In the meantime, a budget request for all four quarters of fiscal 1983 had to be submitted to management within the next week.

27 ZEST

Gordon H. G. McDougall

Douglas Snetsinger

The first major assignment for Mr. George Mann, the new brand assistant for Zest, was to plan the 1986 Canadian sales promotion campaign. Mr. Mann, a recent business school graduate, joined Procter and Gamble (P&G) in the summer of 1985 and worked closely with Peter McTeer, the brand manager for Zest. He spent his first three months on various tasks involving Zest, one of five bar soaps sold by P&G (Ivory, Coast, Safeguard, and Camay were the others). Mr. Mann knew that Mr. McTeer was concerned about the sales performance of Zest which had lost share in recent years. One reason for the decline was that competing brands, particularly Irish Spring, were outspending Zest in the sales promotion area.

Mr. Mann conducted an extensive review of the sales promotion activities of Zest and competing brands. The review involved a detailed analysis of the results of the 1984 campaign and the year-to-date results for 1985 by region and by time period. All of the Zest promotion activities were assessed in terms of volume shipped and market share to determine their cost effectiveness. Based on this analysis and after a number of meetings, it was decided to increase the sales promotion budget for Zest to $1.2 million for 1986. Mr. McTeer then asked Mr. Mann to plan the sales promotion campaign for 1986 and focus on three decisions:

1. the amount allocated for trade allowances versus consumer sales promotions,
2. the specific sales promotions to be used, and
3. any new promotions to be tried.

Mr. Mann wanted to design the best plan possible to increase Zest's sales. As well, he also had a personal objective of introducing new, speculative promotions which would show his creative ability. However, speculative promotions would have to be justified on the basis of cost effectiveness. With these thoughts in mind, he began reviewing the material he had analyzed.

COMPANY BACKGROUND

Procter and Gamble is one of the most successful consumer goods companies in the world. It operates in 26 countries and had sales of $13.6 billion and net earnings of $635 million in 1985. The Canadian subsidiary contributed $1 billion in sales and $49 million in net earnings in 1985. This was an increase in sales of $60 million, but a decline in net earnings of $11 million over 1984. The profit decline was attributed to increased spending by the firm on a number of new product introductions and line extensions. The subsidiary was recognized as a leader in the Canadian packaged goods industry, and its consumer brands led in 13 of the 16 categories in which the company competed. P&G products can be found in nine out of ten Canadian homes.

While world-wide company sales had been more than doubling every ten years, the Canadian subsidiary's growth was even more rapid. In the past five years sales had doubled on both dollar and unit bases. P&G executives attributed the company's success to a variety of factors, including:

1. dedicated and talented human resources,
2. a reputation for honesty that won them the trust and respect of their suppliers and customers,
3. prudent and conservative management that encouraged thorough analysis prior to decision making,
4. innovative products offering superior benefits at competitive prices, and
5. substantial marketing expertise.

P&G has three operating divisions, organized by product type: Bar Soap and Laundry Products (brands include Ivory, Camay, Zest, Tide, and Bounce); Personal Care Products (brands include Crest, Head and Shoulders, Secret, Pampers, and Luvs); and Food and Household Cleaning Products (brands include Crisco, Duncan Hines, Joy 2, Cascade, Spic and Span, Comet, and Mr.Clean). Each division has its own Brand (or Advertising) Management, Sales, Finance, and Product Development line management groups. These groups report directly to the general manager of the operating division. The three general managers report to the president of P&G. The divisions use centralized staff departments for other services.

The Advertising Department was formed in 1930 when P&G initiated its brand management system. This system allowed P&G to aggressively market several brands in the same product category by assigning the marketing responsibility for each brand to a single Brand Manager. He or she leads a brand group that includes Assistant Brand Managers, and/or Brand Assistants, depending on the dollar volume and marketing complexity of the product. This group plans, develops, and directs the total marketing effort for its brand.

THE BAR SOAP MARKET

On a unit basis, the bar soap market had grown 2% per year for the past ten years and was expected to continue at this rate. For 1985, the total unit market was estimated at approximately 1.6 million statistical cases[1] and P&G's share was 46%, up from 41% in 1975.

The bar soap market can be divided into four segments: complexion (beauty), refreshment/deodorant, all purpose/price, and liquid. P&G is well represented in each of these segments (Exhibit 1). While these segments are quite distinct in terms of product characteristics, there is no strong correlation between segments and

[1] One statistical case or unit equals 540 ounces of soap. This figure is used by A.C. Nielson, the research company, to determine shares of the various brands of bar soaps. Because bar soaps are sold in different sizes it is necessary to use a common measure to determine share. One ounce equals 28.3 grams. One statistical case would be equivalent to approximately 153 bars of soap weighing 100 grams each.

family income or size. As well, while one family member may prefer a brand from one segment, another may prefer a brand from another segment. Consequently, families typically have brands from different segments in the home at any one time.

Exhibit 1
BAR SOAP MARKET

	1985[a]	1980	1975
Total Market (Statistical Cases)[b]	1,600,000	1,410,000	1,265,000
P&G Share	46%	43%	41%
By Segment (Share) (%)			
All Purpose Bars			
Ivory*	23.0	20.5	19.6
Other	23.8	23.6	19.5
	46.8	44.1	39.1
Beauty Bars			
Camay*	5.4	6.5	7.2
Dove	6.9	6.3	6.3
Caress	—	—	0.4
Lux	Restaged	5.2	7.3
Palmolive	3.2	4.9	6.0
	15.5	22.9	27.2
Deodorant Bars			
Zest*	11.2	13.2	13.5
Safeguard*	0.9	1.0	1.1
Lifebuoy	2.0	3.5	5.3
Dial	5.3	6.8	7.0
	19.4	24.5	26.9
Refreshment Bars			
Coast*	5.2	1.3	—
Irish Spring	5.0	6.4	6.8
Fresh	0.9	0.8	—
Shield	0.9	—	—
	12.0	8.5	6.8
P&G Share—Deodorant/Refreshment	17.3	15.5	14.6
Deodorant/Refreshment (total)	31.4	33.0	33.7
Liquid Soaps	6.3	—	—

Source: Company Records

[a] Preliminary estimates for 1985.

[b] One statistical case or unit equals 540 ounces of soap.

* P&G Brands

The traditional complexion bars, Camay and Dove, drew largely from a female target, particularly for face washing. The major refreshment/deodorant bars (Zest, Coast, Dial, and Irish Spring) tended to be used for showering and bathing. While use of these bars was skewed to the male market, women also liked their strong fragrances, associating them with cleanliness and refreshment. The all-purpose segment, which was dominated by Ivory and also included private label and store brands, tended to be used by the whole family. Ivory, in particular, had a family appeal, as parents felt it could be used with very young children.

The Refreshment/Deodorant Segment

Zest compared with all brands in the bar soap market but particularly with Dial and Irish Spring in the deodorant/refreshment segment. The total share of this segment had declined from 33% in 1980 to 31.4% in 1985 in spite of the introduction of three new brands. Share loss had also occurred in the beauty segment, while gains had been achieved in the all-purpose segment and the liquid soap segment.

Irish Spring, a Colgate-Palmolive brand, held a 5% share of the bar soap market in 1985. The brand had experienced share losses each year since 1980, including the first half of 1984. However, in the second half of 1984, a new, more aggressive strategy was adopted by the brand manager for Irish Spring. The brand was restaged, accompanied by a new "Richer Lather, Fresher Clean" advertising campaign and significant increases in sales promotion expenditures. In the second half of 1984, Irish Spring experienced sales increases of 7% compared to the same period in 1983.

In the first half of 1985, Irish Spring continued with heavy advertising and sales promotion efforts. Advertising expenditures for the July 1984 to July 1985 period were estimated at $1 million. Substantial trade allowances were offered; a bonus pack was introduced (three for the price of two), and a $0.50 coupon was offered through newspaper ads. This "triple" promotion plus the advertising support resulted in Irish Spring's share indexing at 111% for the first half of 1985 (11% more sales than the first half of 1984). Exhibit 2 details the competitive activities for Zest, Irish Spring, and Dial for the first half of 1985.

Zest's other major competitor in the deodorant market, Dial, held 5.3% of the total market in 1985. Dial had also experienced share declines in recent years and was pursuing a more aggressive strategy to alter the situation. Dial had been restaged and was currently running an "Improved Deodorant Protection" advertising campaign as well as extensive sales promotions in the form of trade allowances (Exhibit 2). It was estimated that Dial's advertising expenditures for 1985 would be approximately $800,000. On the basis of the data contained in Exhibit 2 and other competitive information, it was estimated that total trade promotion expenditures for Irish Spring for 1985 would be approximately $1 million and for Dial, approximately $900,000. Consumer promotions for 1985 for Irish Spring were estimated at $300,000 and for Dial at $280,000. Thus, advertising, trade and consumer promotions for Irish Spring were likely to total $2.3 million for 1985, and for Dial the total would be $1.98 million.

Exhibit 2

COMPETITIVE PERFORMANCE OF ZEST, DIAL, AND IRISH SPRING FIRST HALF, 1985

	Zest	Dial	Irish Spring
Share	11.2(98)[a]	5.3(102)	5.0(111)
% off Carload Allowance[b]	6.6(127)	11.2(121)	15.1(113)
Share of Weighted Co-op[c]	12.8(90)	7.5(59)	14.1(120)
Share of Display[d]	13.8(103)	14.2(66)	13.3(105)

Source: Company records

[a] Index versus a year ago. For example, Zest's share of 11.2% for the first half of 1985 was at 98% compared to the first half of 1984.

[b] A straight trade allowance. When Zest offered a trade allowance, on average the price to the retailer was discounted by 6.6%. If the regular price to the retailer was $70 per case, the average discount would be $4.62 per case. It was estimated that Zest was sold "on deal" about 60% of the time and both Dial and Irish Spring were sold "on deal" about 80% of the time.

[c] A trade allowance for co-op advertising. The national advertiser and the retailer share the cost of the retail ad. For bar soap manufacturers the expenditure results in a brand like Zest being featured in the weekly newspaper ad for a supermarket. Co-op share is the percentage of times that Zest was featured in a given time period. For the first half of 1985, Zest was featured 12.8%, Dial 7.5%, and Irish Spring 14.1%. A.C. Neilsen, the research firm, samples newspapers and counts the number of times each brand is mentioned, then determines the respective percentage mentions.

[d] A trade allowance for display space. The bar soap manufacturers provide the retail store with an allowance to obtain extra shelf space or superior shelf position. A.C. Neilsen conducts a periodic store audit and measures the amount of shelf space devoted to each bar soap brand.

The net effect of these competitive activities for the first half of 1985 was that Zest's share was marginally down (index at 98), Dial's share was slightly up (index at 102), and Irish Spring's share was higher (index at 111). Brand managers at Procter and Gamble, while concerned, wondered if the cost of these competitive activities wasn't seriously affecting the profitability of Irish Spring and Dial. All three companies probably faced similar cost structures (Exhibit 3), but it was estimated that the increased marketing expenditures of Dial and Irish Spring were likely to reduce their profit margins. Regular prices to the trade were similar for all three brands. In 1985, the regular price for a case of the complexion size of Zest (36 packs of four bars at 95 g each) was $72.70, or approximately $0.51 per bar. This would be equivalent to a statistical case selling for $81.31. Because of the competitive activities, it was predicted that none of the major brands would increase prices in 1986.

ZEST

Zest, launched in Canada in 1958, was the second leading brand in the bar soap market, Zest's market share peaked in 1978 at 14% and since then had declined slowly but steadily to the current 11%. Share losses could be traced to increased competition both in the number of brands and the intensity of promotion competition in the deodorant/refreshment segment, price competition in the all-purpose seg-

Exhibit 3

COST STRUCTURE FOR AN AVERAGE BAR SOAP (%)

Manufactured cost	57
Distribution	7
Selling and general administration	5
Marketing expenditures*	17
Profit	14
	100

Source: Company records.

* Includes advertising, trade and consumer promotion, and brand management expenses.

Note: It was estimated that the manufactured cost, distribution, and selling and general administration expense (69%) consisted of variable costs of 41% and fixed costs of 28%.

ment, and the development of the liquid soap segment. While Zest had lost share, unit sales had shown less decline due to the moderate market growth. For example, in 1980 the brand shipments totalled 186,000 statistical cases (13.2% share). The current estimate for 1985 was 179,000 cases (11.2% share), which was below the budget of 184,000 cases.

The brand's share performance differed dramatically in different water hardness areas. Zest's share strength was in the hard water regions (that is, Southwestern Ontario and Manitoba/Saskatchewan) where the product had significant rinsing superiority versus ordinary soaps. Zest, unlike competing brands, was a synthetic detergent bar, not a soap and, consequently, left no soap film. In addition, Zest provided a lighter, "airier" lather, and its volume of lather was superior to other brands. In soft water regions, competitive brands did not leave a film, and the primary benefit of Zest was not as relevant. The product formula had not been changed in 18 years. Estimates for 1985 were that Zest's shares across Canada would be: Maritimes, 7.4%; Quebec, 5%; Ontario, 12.7%; Manitoba/Saskatchewan, 30.6%; Alberta, 16.4%; and British Columbia, 6.6%. The brand was sold in three sizes, Super (200 g), Bath (130 g), and Complexion (95 g), which represented 12%, 42%, and 46% of Zest's unit sales, respectively.

ZEST'S 1985 MARKETING PLAN

Zest's long-term strategy was to maintain its leading share position in the deodorant/refreshment segment and its number two position in the bar soap category. The 1985 objectives were to attain market share of 11.5% and unit sales of 184,000 statistical cases. This was to be accomplished through:

1. maintenance of effective media/copy support,
2. superior display prominence and greater advertising emphasis in hard water regions,
3. continued development of the soft water regions with a new copy strategy, and
4. maintenance of existing sales and consumer promotion support.

Zest was positioned nationally as the bar soap that provided superior rinsing and lathering benefits for the whole family's bathing needs. The purchase target continued to be women 18 years of age and over.

Advertising Strategy

Zest's 1985 advertising strategy was to convince consumers that Zest was a unique bar which provided a superior feeling of freshness and cleanliness versus ordinary soap. Zest continued the theme of ''Clean Plus'' which had been run since August 1983.

Zest's media strategy was to efficiently maximize reach[2] among women 18 years of age and older. Spending was aligned to brand development which meant that a proportionally greater amount was spent in the hard water regions and was skewed seasonally in accordance with brand consumption. To maintain historical reach levels of 60% over a 52-week schedule the advertising budget was set at $775,000, a 12% increase over the last year's spending. The advertising budget translated to an expected spending level of $4.16 per statistical case.

Promotion Program

Zest's promotion objective in high brand development (BD) regions was to increase usage and trial among current users. In low brand development regions, Zest's promotion objective was to increase usage among infrequent and light users.

The promotion strategy was based on considerable analysis of the successes and limitations of past years' promotions programs, competitive activity, and current objectives. A significant portion of the promotion budget was allocated to trade events which included allowances, support for co-operative advertising, and support for display prominence. The 1985 promotion plan budgeted for seven allowance events in high BD markets, three of which provided additional funds to induce superior display. These events ran for four-week periods (Exhibit 4). In general, expected sales were affected by promotion offers, as well as other marketing activities, competitive activities, seasonal buying habits, and general economic conditions. In low BD markets, the plan called for five allowance events, four of which included display monies.

In line with 1985 objectives, a trial-oriented sampling program was initiated in July in Alberta. This program distributed 100 g samples through a household drop in cities with the hardest waters. This program was supplemented by a September sampling program distributed on bottles of Scope, another P&G product. The distribution of samples was expected to reach 30% of Alberta households.

A bonus pack program was instituted in 1985 which gave consumers four bars for the price of three. This April event was run across all high BD regions. A mailed coupon program was run in October in all high BD markets and in the Maritimes and British Columbia. This event represented an expansion over the previous year in

[2] Reach is the percentage of different households or members of a target market exposed to one or more advertising messages during a specified period of time, usually four weeks.

Exhibit 4
1985 ZEST PROMOTION PROGRAM AND SCHEDULE

Month	Area	Promotion	(1) Dollar Offer Per Statistical Case ($)	(2) Expected Cases Sold on Deal	(1) × (2) Total Cost ($)
January	HBD-ONT	allowance	7.00	8,600	60,200
	HBD-PRA	allowance	5.00	5,600	28,000
March	LBD	allowance	7.00	6,100	42,700
	HBD	allowance	6.50	13,400	87,100
	HBD	Bonus Pack (4/3)			267,000
April	LBD	allowance & display	9.00	6,900	62,100
	HBD	allowance & display	6.00	8,000	48,000
June	LBD	allowance & display	7.50	5,800	43,500
	HBD	allowance & display	5.50	7,300	40,150
July	Alberta	sampling—test			19,600
August	LBD	allowance & display	8.50	6,500	55,250
	HBD	allowance & display	5.50	8,200	45,100
September	Alberta	sampling—test			10,500
October	LBD	coupon—on pack			45,000
	HBD	coupon—on pack			75,000
November	HBD	allowance	6.00	10,800	64,800
	LBD	coupon—on pack			12,300
December	LBD	allowance	5.00	1,000	5,000
	HBD-ONT	allowance	7.00	7,300	51,100
	HBD-PRA	allowance	5.00	6,600	33,000
Total				102,100	1,095,400

Notes: Low brand development regions (LBD) encompass British Columbia, Quebec, and the Maritimes. High brand development regions (HBD) encompass the Prairies and Ontario.

The allowance events include money for reduction in the case price and for co-operative advertising. Some allowance events provide additional monies to induce display prominence. The value of the offers are reported in dollars per statistical case to facilitate comparison across events.

which the Prairies were excluded from couponing events. One additional November coupon event was run in low BD regions and distributed on Zest packages.

Total promotion spending was set at $1.1 million in 1985—up 5% from the previous year. It was expected that 102,000 statistical cases would be sold through allowance programs which represented about 56% of forecasted sales at an estimated cost of about $6.50 per case.

EARLY 1985 RESULTS

Mr. McTeer and Mr. Mann were not encouraged by the first-half results of the 1985 program. Zest sales were lagging forecast by 3%, and it appeared that annual sales would be closer to 179,000 statistical cases, not 184,000 as budgeted. They discussed these matters on a number of occasions and, based on their review and analysis, decided that the sales promotion budget should be increased by 10% for 1986 to $1.2 million. This decision was approved in principle at a budget meeting when the Zest brand review was held. The task of allocating the budget remained. They discussed several options, including increasing trade allowances to become more competitive with Irish Spring, using more consumer promotions in soft water areas where share was low, and offering fewer larger trade allowances or more, smaller trade allowances.

Finally, Mr. Mann wanted to bring some fresh, if not creative, approaches to his assignments. However, he had to be cautious in the use of new programs. First, his proposals might not get past the budget committees, and he would have to redo his plans; second, promotion plans were expected to achieve reasonable revenue goals. Using tried and true programs had the advantage in that they would achieve a relatively certain return for Zest.

SALES PROMOTIONS

Generally, Mr. Mann knew that sales promotions could accomplish a number of objectives. For consumers, objectives include encouraging more use and purchase of larger-size items or multiple purchases, getting nonusers to try the product, and attracting users of competitors' brands. For retailers, they include encouraging the retailer to carry new items and higher levels of inventory and related items, offsetting competitive promotions, building the retailer's brand loyalty, and gaining entry into new retail outlets. General objectives for the sales force are encouraging support of a new product, encouraging more sales calls, and stimulating sales in off-season.

The key was to match the objectives with the right blend of the myriad of sales promotion tools at his disposal. He could choose from coupons (certificates that entitle the bearer to a stated saving on the purchase of a particular product), price packs (includes offers to consumers of multiple units in a pack with a special price, such as four for the price of three), premiums (merchandise offered at a relatively low cost or free as an incentive to purchase a particular product), samples (offers of a free amount or trial of a product to consumers), refunds or rebates (certificates attached to the product which can be redeemed by the consumer for a stated amount), and contests or sweepstakes (offers of a chance to win a prize by submitting an entry). As well, sales promotions could be directed at the trade and included point-of-purchase displays, co-op advertising allowances, and trade allowances (offer of money off on each case purchased during a stated time period).

THE DECISION

While knowledge of the general sales promotion tools and objectives was useful, Mr. Mann had to make some specific decisions. With this in mind he jotted down a few notes:

- One of a brand assistant's key responsibilities must be to establish the appropriate mix between trade allowances, (straight trade, advertising, co-op advertising, and display allowances) and consumer promotions (direct-to-consumer spending) for an effective, balanced promotion plan.
- Both Irish Spring and Dial had substantially increased their trade allowances in 1985. Mr. Mann was not certain how the trade would react if the allowances for Zest were not increased.
- A major benefit of consumer promotions such as bonus packs (for example, four for the price of three) or coupons (for example, $0.30 on pack) was that the consumer received the entire savings. This means there was a direct, visible reduced price for the consumer. On the other hand, trade allowances might be passed on to the consumer, but this was not guaranteed. Zest had been fortunate in the past in that every $1 provided in trade allowances resulted in a $2 saving to the consumer because supermarkets had also reduced their margin (in the hope of generating more sales). This was not always true for the competition. In fact, in the first half of 1985. Zest offered a number of trade allowances with an average discount of 6.6%. Supermarkets who took advantage of this trade allowance also reduced the price to the consumer resulting in an average saving to the consumer of 12.9% off the regular price. Irish Spring offered trade allowances with an average discount of 15.1% which translated into consumer savings of 18%. Dial offered trade allowances of 11.2% which resulted in consumer savings of 13.1%.

Next Mr. Mann worked out some details on the three major sales promotion vehicles. Trade allowances would probably be the major vehicle. While the breakdown to the different types of trade allowances had to be considered (for example, what proportion of the funds to be given as straight trade versus co-op advertising allowances and/or display support allowances), Mr. Mann was more concerned about the percentage of the budget which should be allocated to trade allowances in total. He recognized that the consumer promotions were, in a sense, a supplement to the trade allowance structure.

Three possible coupon programs could be run, and specific costs and anticipated results were calculated (Exhibit 5). Finally, two different in-store merchandising events were considered—bonus packs and preassembled displays (PAD) (Exhibit 6). The PAD idea was new and was the result of considerable thought and effort by P&G executives. A major problem with the bar soaps was the difficulty in obtaining interesting, inexpensive displays. It takes a store clerk very little time to construct an end-of-aisle or special display of laundry soap, or soft drinks, or potato chips. However, because of the shape and size of bar soaps, stores were very reluctant to devote time to putting up end-of-aisle displays. The PAD concept addressed this problem. The display (Exhibit 7 provides an illustration of a PAD) was self-contained

Exhibit 5
ALTERNATIVE COUPON PROGRAMS

	FSCI[a]		In-Ad[b]		Direct Mail[c]	
Face value ($)	0.40	0.50	0.40	0.50	0.40	0.50
Redemption (%)	5	6	1	1	11	13
Cost ($000)	95	125	55	64	209	313
Cost/Redemption ($)	0.56	0.62	0.59	0.68	0.53	0.64
Expected statistical cases sold on deal (000)	19	24	20	20	34	44
Cost/Stat case ($)	5.00	5.21	2.75	3.20	6.15	7.11

[a] A free-standing coupon insert (FSCI) is a coupon and ad pre-printed on heavy paper and inserted loose into a newspaper or magazine. (These estimates are based on national coverage delivered in newspapers.)

[b] An in-ad coupon is a coupon in a weekly supermarket newspaper advertisement. The consumer clips the ad from the newspaper and presents it to the cashier at the supermarket that ran the ad. (These estimates are based on national coverage delivered in newspapers.)

[c] A direct-mail coupon is a coupon delivered by mail to households. The usual method is for a series of coupons from a number of advertisers to be delivered in one envelope. (These estimates are based on coverage of approximately 40% of households.)

Exhibit 6
IN-STORE MERCHANDISING EVENTS

	Bonus Packs[a]		PAD[b]	
	Regional HBD Mkts.	National	Regional HBD Mkts.	National
Cost (foregone profit in $000)	240	310	0	0
Artwork ($000)	9	9	5	5
Added factory ($000)	0	0	108	143
Total cost	249	319	113	148
Expected cases sold ($000)	20	27	18	25
Cost/Stat case ($)	12.45	11.81	6.28	5.92

[a] Bonus packs are two or more units sold on a "buy two or more, get one free" basis. These estimates are based on the complexion size (95 grams) where the consumer buys four bars and gets one free.

[b] Pre-assembled displays are specially prepared displays which involve minimum effort on the part of store personnel to set up the display.

and all store personnel had to do was to cut or slip open the box and place it at the end of the aisle. While this was a unique selling feature of the brand, Mr. Mann wondered whether the cost (approximately) of $6 per statistical case would translate into sufficient sales to be profitable. While the forecast sales were based on the results of a small test market, Mr. Mann was concerned that the consumer would not be receiving a direct incentive (for example, price pack, coupon) to purchase the product. With these thoughts in mind, Mr. Mann began developing the plan.

Exhibit 7
PAD DISPLAY

28 TRANS CANADA BANK

John Yokom

Mr. James Koehle, the newly hired marketing manager of Trans Canada Bank, one of Canada's big five, must set a promotion strategy. The latest "deposit share" results indicate that Trans Canada's share of the total funds on deposit in the total Canadian market has continued to decline. Trust companies are becoming more aggressive with advertising, promotion, and longer hours of service. Putting a premium on obtaining quick results, Trans Canada's management has decided to use a promotional contest to try to stop the erosion and is willing to spend the funds needed if an exciting promotion can be implemented.

Mr. Koehle, has been looking into the "deposits" problem since his first day on the job and has just received the results of a major bank industry study suggesting that *seniors* (defined as those 50 years and older) are the key to deposits. In fact, across Canada this age group accounts for roughly 20% of bank customers but over 60% of funds on deposit. The question facing Mr. Koehle is how can he motivate seniors to transfer deposit dollars to Trans Canada.

Mr. Koehle realizes the difficulty of this challenge. There is a lot of noise and promotional clutter to be overcome if Trans Canada's promotion is to work. To succeed, he will need a powerful promotion. More importantly, Mr. Koehle knows that he is going to have to reach out to the target market and motivate them on a personal level. He wants them to transfer at least $5,000 to an account at Trans Canada.

Mr. Koehle was asked by Brent Johnson, vice-president of marketing, to evaluate three promotion ideas submitted by three different agencies that specialized in running promotions. Mr. Johnson had said that he wasn't quite happy with any of them, so he thought Mr. Koehle might want to revise the proposals. Mr. Johnson asked Mr. Koehle to have a recommendation in one week. Budgets for each promotion are virtually identical so the cost of the campaign is not the issue. Exhibit 1 shows the suggested visuals for the three promotions.

PROMOTION IDEAS

Promotion Agency #1

Procter & Gamble (U.S.) and General Motors ran a tie-in promotion, "Win One of 750 Chevrolets" with a "key" packed in specially marked Procter & Gamble products. This agency has built on this concept to develop a promotion. It's "Here's Your Key to Win a Mercedes Benz." The plan is to mail special Mercedes Benz keys to seniors who live near each of the Trans Canada branches. Seniors will be invited to come into the branch and transfer a $5,000 deposit from another bank. If they do,

Exhibit 1
DRAFT VISUALS TO ILLUSTRATE PROMOTIONS

Promotion
#1

Promotion
#2

Promotion
#3

they will get to try their key in the special Mercedes Benz lock. If it opens, they win the car.

Promotion Agency #2

Based on their experience, this agency believes that seniors like bank passbooks. In fact, in this electronic age of the automatic teller machine, agency personnel think that seniors have become quite concerned that many banks seems to be moving away from this ''old-fashioned'' concept. To capitalize on this trend, the agency has developed the ''Passbook to Paradise'' promotion.

Seniors in each branch trading area will receive a real passbook with a special account number. To win, all a senior needs to do is transfer $5,000 to the branch, then match his or her passbook number against the prize numbers at the branch. Prizes include a two-week trip for two to a South Pacific paradise plus $5,000 in cash. Other prizes are five one-week Caribbean cruises for two, and 20,000 other cash prizes, ranging from $1 to $1000. The agency notes that it has run many successful sweepstakes promotions using this formula of one ''big'' grand prize plus lots of ''smaller'' prizes.

Promotion Agency #3

Scratch-and-win promotions have proven to be consistent winners. This agency's past experience with campaigns aimed at seniors suggest that this segment likes the fun and excitement of the instant-win concept. This agency proposes such a program. Seniors in each branch trading area will be mailed a ''Double Your Deposit or Double Your Savings'' scratch-and-win game card. To win, a senior must transfer $5,000 to the branch, and then scratch the card in front of a bank employee. Five depositors will instantly win double their deposits. The remaining contestants can enter a second-chance ''Double Your Savings'' sweepstakes. Five more double-your-account-balance prizes will be awarded.

The agency summarized its presentation by saying, ''This promotion has fun and excitement combined with the most powerful motivator known—cash!''

THE DECISION

Now that Mr. Koehle has had a chance to review the three proposals, his task is to select the one that will deliver the largest business gain (that is, increase in share of seniors' deposits). James knows that he may want to combine elements from each of the proposals, though he will have to be careful in deciding which agency actually gets the account. He has prepared a summary of research findings on seniors (Appendix 1) to help him make these choices.

By the end of the week, Mr.Johnson wants Mr. Koehle to have the promotions ranked, with suggested revisions and the reasons for his decision.

Appendix 1
A NOTE ON SENIOR CITIZENS

Articles describing the expanding consumer segment of senior citizens have been increasing in number over the past few years. Marketers are now realizing that seniors are a very lucrative market. Canadians over 50 years of age represent 55% of the discretionary spending power of Canadians and control 80% of all assets—physical and financial. However, only a small portion of all media spending is aimed directly at this segment. Marketers now recognize that they must develop campaigns aimed at seniors, who represent 35% of the Canadian adult population.

Canadians over 50 are among the heaviest consumers of expensive lifestyle products. They travel widely and are the leading purchasers of luxury condominiums, large cars, and such convenience products as microwave ovens. They are also living longer, healthier lives. They are among the largest consumers of newspapers and magazines, and indeed their buying power helps to support several Canadian publications specifically for those over 50, including Toronto-based *Today's Seniors* and Vancouver-based *Maturity*.

Seniors should not be stereotyped into a homogeneous group. Lifestyle research has been undertaken to identify the subgroups in this important sector of the population. It is the attitudes, actions, and activities within the demographic groups that are the real marketing trends. Based on a study by Grey Advertising, New York, three target groups among seniors are as follows:

Master Consumers (the largest and most important) are fit, active, secure, and fulfilled. Rather than seeking a fountain of youth, they are looking forward to their future and see retirement as a time to do all the things they put off in the past.

Maintainers are financially comfortable, not as active as they could be, and lack the sense of purpose needed to push them beyond the status quo.

Simplifiers are older, less affluent, less active, and relatively light consumers.

The agency offers the following guidelines when advertising to the 50-plus market:

- Don't use euphemistic name tags, such as the ''golden-harvest gang,'' etc., which they dislike.
- Treat them like grown-ups. They've been around long enough to know what they want. Hype, fluff, and a patronizing attitude will turn them off.
- Show how your product meets 50-plus needs, not how needy you find 50-plus consumers.
- Be fresh, but not frenetic. Think linear, be more literal, and less abstract.
- Capture their spirit. They believe life goes on and keeps getting better.
- Sex—yes. The libido lives on after 50, and so does romance.
- Put a twinkle in their eye—a chuckle, a wink, a light touch can make your message much more palatable.
- Tune them in. Music can be the bridge that spans generations—if it's the right music.
- As consumers, they are the voice of authority, so make them your spokespeople and role models.

When designing campaigns targeted to older demographic groups, creative people should keep in mind that what works for younger target groups won't always have the right appeal for the 50-plus market. One advertising industry expert recommends the following when targeting the older demographic groups:

- Show older consumers being active, not sitting down.
- Use actors ten years younger than the target group for the ad, since mature consumers think of themselves as younger than they actually are.
- Don't use cartoons or negative selling messages.
- Steer clear of muted browns and grays and of loud oranges, reds, and yellows. Mature consumers associate loud tones with garishness. They like cool blues and greens.

29 ASHMAN & BIRI ADVERTISING LIMITED

Gordon H. G. McDougall

Douglas Snetsinger

In late spring of 1988, Mr. Bill Jorch, newly appointed media director of Ashman & Biri Advertising Limited (A & B), faced a challenging media scheduling assignment. He needed to prepare the 1988–89 media plan for the Corda, a new subcompact which was to be introduced to the Canadian market in September 1988. The car was designed by a leading Canadian automobile manufacturer to compete in the "sporty" subcompact segment of the market.

A & B had obtained the advertising account for the Corda in an intense competition with three other advertising agencies. A & B's creative team had developed a "hot," visually-oriented campaign that everyone at the agency and the client's management group was excited about. However, the cost of developing the campaign had exceeded the budgeted level, so Mr. Jorch was under more pressure than usual to allocate the media budget efficiently. Mr. Jorch's task was to develop a media plan to accomplish the advertising objectives set out by the manufacturer. A total media budget of $1 million had been established, and a further $150,000 had been spent preparing television commercials and other advertisements for the campaign.

THE INDUSTRY

In the past few years, approximately 1 million cars were sold annually in Canada, and sales for 1988–89 were expected to be in that range. While overall car sales had remained flat, in recent years sales of compacts and subcompacts had increased at the expense of large models. The Corda was designed to compete in the subcompact segment, which accounted for 45% of total car sales. In the past two years, total sales of compacts on a regional basis were as follows: Maritimes (8%), Quebec (25%), Ontario (40%), and western Canada (27%). The largest single market for subcompacts was Toronto, which accounted for 26% of total national sales.

The comparable regional distribution of the the Canadian population was as follows: Maritimes (9%), Quebec (26%), Ontario (36%), and western Canada (29%). Toronto had 13% of Canada's population. On a regional basis, total car sales closely approximated population figures.

The leading car models sold in the subcompact market against which the Corda would compete included the Ford Escort EXP, Volkswagen Golf FTI, Honda CRX, Mazda RX-7, Pontiac Fiero, and the Toyota MR2. These models could be described as "sporty" subcompacts. In 1987, the competing manufacturers spent as much as $1.8 million and as little as $200,000 on advertising these "sporty" compacts. The largest advertisers tended to spend up to 80% of their budget on television, while the smaller advertisers used magazines almost exclusively.

THE CORDA

The Corda was positioned as a sporty car with the benefits of exciting styling, superior road handling, and excellent value. The car was designed and priced to provide consumers with an exhilarating, yet affordable, driving experience.

During the design and development of the Corda, the automobile manufacturer conducted a number of marketing research studies. The research included market tests of the car with a wide variety of potential customers. Based on this marketing research, the primary market for the Corda was identified as females, aged 18 to 34, in clerical or professional occupations with good income potential. In fact the research had indicated that over 60% of Corda sales were likely to be to women. With respect to psychographics, these females were outgoing, active, energetic, success-oriented, and in control of their lives. The secondary target was males, aged 18 to 34, in blue collar occupations with average income potential. They regarded themselves as modern, cheerful, and were moderately outgoing.

In a subsequent study of consumers planning to buy a new "sporty" subcompact (see table below), those who preferred the Corda tended to be single and younger.

	Preference for Corda	Preference for Other "Sporty" Subcompacts
Single	60%	35%
Under 18	2%	2%
18 to 24	51%	29%
25 to 34	41%	28%
35 to 44	6%	37%
Over 44	0%	4%
University degree	35%	37%

Those who preferred the Corda were interested in sports and social activities. For both target markets, female and male, the major appeal of the Corda was its great styling and that it looked like it was fun to drive. As well, females viewed the car as an extension of their personalities, while males were impressed by its value for money.

COMMUNICATION OBJECTIVES

Communication objectives were established to promote two consumer benefits. One was to communicate the excitement of driving a fun car and the social satisfaction derived from being seen in it. The Corda should be seen as an extension of the buyer's lifestyle. Second, a factual appeal was required to provide consumers with a reason to purchase on dimensions where the Corda had a competitive advantage.

More specifically, the four benefits were value for money, low maintenance, ease of handling, and safety. A research study had been conducted with individuals who rated new cars for various automotive publications. Based on their experience driving prototypes of the Corda, these "experts" had rated the car very favourably on the four benefits.

THE MEDIA BUDGET

After extensive analysis and discussion between A & B personnel and Corda management, the advertising media budget for the 1989 model year—September 1988 to August 1989—had been set at $1 million. This figure was based on an analysis of previous results for other brands in the car maker's product line, competitive analysis, and recognition that building first-year sales for the Corda was a major priority of the client. As well, the budget determination included an assessment of how much spending was needed to build awareness of the Corda and to motivate potential consumers to take the first step—going into a Corda dealership.

Mr. Jorch had been actively involved in the budget setting process. "Not all media buyers get to play an active role in budget setting, but at A & B my inputs are significant," he said. "No question about it, this is a budget I can live with."

THE MEDIA OBJECTIVES

Media objectives were established to guide the media selection process. The main objectives were:

1. Efficiently deliver impressions on a national basis in the hope of targeting all people interested in buying a car.
2. Direct media weight to the most likely targets, (a) women, single, 18 to 34, $20,000 + income, and (b) men, single, 18 to 34, $20,000 + income.
3. Match the emotional and factual appeals to the appropriate media.
4. To the extent that the budget allows, extra weight should be applied in markets where subcompact sales are high (in order of priority, Toronto, Montreal, Vancouver).

MEDIA PLANNING

Mr. Jorch's task was to select a media mix that accomplished the communication objectives within the guidelines established for the media plan. As Mr. Jorch viewed it, media selection consisted of two important decisions. First, how should the budget be allocated over the various media (that is, television, radio, newspapers, magazines, billboards) and second, what specific vehicles (for example, *Time, Maclean's, Chatelaine*) within media types should be used? A major problem faced by all media buyers was the difficulty in making comparisons across media. As shown in Exhibit 1, media measures vary across television, magazines, newspapers, and billboards. With these thoughts in mind, Mr. Jorch began reviewing the available information on the major media and their costs and audiences.

He first concentrated on making broad choices among the various media types.

Exhibit 1
DESCRIPTION OF MEDIA MEASURES

Television—measured in terms of gross rating points (GRPs) which are an aggregate of the total ratings of a given advertising schedule, usually in a weekly period, within a predetermined target group. GRPs equal reach times frequency. Reach is a measurement of the total unduplicated target audience potentially exposed one or more times to the advertiser's schedule of commercial messages in a given time frame, (for example, one week). *Reach* is usually expressed as a percentage of the target population in a geographically defined area, (for example, a metro area). *Frequency* is the average number of exposures among those reached. One weekly GRP would be achieved if 1% of the target population saw the ad once in a week. One hundred and twenty GRPs would be achieved if 30% of the market saw the ad four times in a week, or if 60% of the market saw the ad twice.

Magazines and Newspapers—measured in terms of circulation and primary readers. *Circulation* is the average number of copies per issue of a publication that is (1) sold through subscription, (2) distributed free to predetermined recipients, (3) carried within other publications, or (4) made available through retail stores. A *primary reader* is a person who qualified as a reader, living (working) in the household (or office) in which the publication is initially received.

Billboards—measured in terms of GRPs. GRPs express the net circulation generated by only those persons living within the specified market, as a percentage of the market's population.

While Mr. Jorch knew the main features of the different media types,he needed to use that information to narrow his focus. Because of the visual nature of the ad campaign he had decided that radio was unsuitable for the Corda. Similarly, he felt that given the size of the budget available, TV advertising required strong consideration. Based on his previous experience, he knew that television time should be purchased on a station-by-station basis, as opposed to purchasing time through a network (for example, CBC). These station-by-station purchases, referred to as spot buys because they guaranteed a "spot" within a particular time period (for example, prime time), cost considerably less than network purchases. Mr. Jorch thought that at least one-half the budget should be spent on television advertising and probably much more.

Mr. Jorch was of two minds about newspapers. On the one hand, newspaper ads could be used to target local markets quite precisely and could help support local Corda dealers. On the other hand, he would use only black and white quarter-page ads because the colour reproduction in newspapers was not appropriate to illustrate the Corda. Black and white ads would not have a strong visual appeal. In any case, if he decided to use newspaper advertising, no more than $100,000 would be spent in this medium.

Billboards were a major imponderable. Seen mostly by people in cars, they would seem to be a prime advertising vehicle. Their large size and big splash of colour were ideal for conveying the look of a Corda. But little beyond that exciting look could be shown.

Magazines had the advantage of brilliant colour, and the ad copy could be well presented in a magazine ad. Magazines also had a degree of permanency, as they remained in the household for a period of time. As well, magazines appeared to be effective at reaching the target market.

Mr. Jorch's assistant had compiled an extensive set of data on the audiences and rates of major Canadian media, as shown in Exhibits 2 through 8. As well, his assistant had prepared some information on the media habits of Canadians.

THE MEDIA DECISION

Mr. Jorch realized it was now time for him to do what he was best at doing—combining an intuitive feel for the media requirements that a campaign's creative theme demanded with a detailed analysis of masses of data to develop a highly efficient media plan. While not underestimating the importance of other aspects of the agency's work, Mr. Jorch knew that the only successful campaigns were those that reached their audience.

Exhibit 2

SPOT TELEVISION BUY IN SELECTED CITIES WITH POPULATIONS EXCEEDING 100,000 (1987 ESTIMATES)*

Metropolitan Area	Total Population	Percentage of Total Population Who are Female 20–34	Percentage of Total Population Who are Male 20–34	Cost/GRP**
Halifax	309,000	30.6	30.1	$ 25
Quebec City	615,000	29.0	29.7	40
Sherbrooke	124,000	28.7	29.2	19
Montreal (French)	1,899,000	27.2	28.1	105
Montreal (English)	1,016,000	27.8	27.9	95
Ottawa/Hull	809,000	29.0	28.9	65
Sudbury	148,000	23.6	24.2	17
Toronto	3,377,000	28.0	27.5	165
London	286,000	28.4	28.0	30
Kitchener	308,000	27.7	27.7	35
Winnipeg	614,000	27.2	27.8	35
Regina	177,000	29.0	30.0	25
Saskatoon	170,000	31.1	31.5	22
Calgary	664,000	34.3	36.9	55
Edmonton	703,000	32.6	34.3	58
Vancouver	1,392,000	27.6	28.2	83
Total	12,611,000	28.6	28.9	$874

Source: *The Canadian Media Directors' Council Media Digest, 1987/88, Market Research Handbook*, Statistics Canada, Catalog 63-224, and *Canadian Advertising Rates and Data*

* Spot television buys are the purchase of broadcast time on a station-by-station basis. The costs are based on prime time purchases (6:30 p.m. to 11:00 p.m.).

** Cost/GRP is the cost of one gross rating point. Gross rating point is a measurement of advertising derived by multiplying the number of people exposed to an advertisement by the average number of exposures per person. It costs $25 to expose 1% of Halifax's total population to one 30-second television ad. It costs $874 to expose 1% of the total population (12,610,000) to one 30-second television ad, of which 28.6% are females, aged 20 to 34 and 28.9% are males aged 20 to 34.

Exhibit 3

MAGAZINE COVERAGE AND RATES (1987 ESTIMATES)

	Circulation	Rate for Full Page 4 Colour	(CPM) Cost per Thousand	Estimated Readership Men 18+	Estimated Readership Women 18+
National					
Maclean's	649,281	$19,965	$30.75	585,000	500,000
*Time**	372,239	$10,870	$29.20	323,000	249,000
Chatelaine (E)	1,109,695	$24,580	$22.15	456,000	1,262,000
Canadian Living	515,756	$14,950	$28.99	214,000	590,000
*Marquee***	501,200	$ 8,915	$17.79	299,000	236,000

(continued)

Exhibit 3 continued

	Circulation	Rate for Full Page 4 Colour	(CPM) Cost per Thousand	Estimated Readership Men 18+	Women 18+
French language					
L'Actualité	265,732	$ 8,650	$32.55	224,000	332,000
Chatelaine (F)	304,313	$ 8,420	$27.67	130,000	337,000
Toronto Life	97,353	$ 5,778	$59.35	82,000	83,000
Starweek (T.V. magazine)	806,193	$12,825	$15.91	661,000	804,000
Sunday Sun TV	461,260	$ 6,128	$13.29	410,000	431,000

Source: *The Canadian Media Directors' Council Media Digest, 1987/88*

* *Time* is a U.S. publication that is not eligible for tax-deductible expenses for Canadian advertisers as per Bill C-58. The equivalent cost for a Canadian advertiser requires a 50% surcharge be added to the above cost figures.

** *Marquee* is a free bulk distribution publication and reported numbers have not been verified.

Exhibit 4
QUALITATIVE ASSESSMENT OF SELECTED MAGAZINES

Maclean's	Weekly news publication, estimated 93% duplication of audience with *Time*, 29% with *Marquee*, 90% with *Chatelaine* (English), 19% with *Toronto Life*
Time	Weekly news publication, estimated 28% duplication with *Marquee*, 47% with *Chatelaine* (English), 17% with *Toronto Life*
Chatelaine (E)	Women's monthly publication
Canadian Living	Readers may be somewhat older than target market
Marquee	Entertainment monthly publication, provided free to consumers at movie theatres across Canada
L'Actualité	Weekly French magazine
Chatelaine (F)	Women's monthly magazine
Toronto Life	Monthly general interest magazine, upscale
Starweek	Television weekly publication in Toronto, small size may not produce ads well
Sunday Sun TV	Television weekly publication in Toronto, small size may not produce ads well

Exhibit 5
HOURS VIEWING TELEVISION PER WEEK, PERCENTAGE

Number of Hours	Total Canada	Income Over $20,000
Less than 8	18	24
8–14.9	19	25
15–21.9	19	23
22–32.5	23	16
Over 32.5	21	12
	100	100

Magazines Read Per Month, Percentage

Number Read	Total Canada	Income Over $20,000
One or none	17	5
2 or 3	19	12
4 or 5	20	20
6 or 7	19	26
More than 7	25	37
	100	100

Source: *BBM Fall 1986 "BG" Report*

Exhibit 6
BILLBOARD COVERAGE AND RATES, TOP 10 MARKETS, OUTDOOR

	Estimated Population (000)	25 GRPs Daily Number of Panels	25 GRPs Daily Four Week Rate $	50 GRPs Daily Number of Panels	50 GRPs Daily Four Week Rate $
Top Three					
Toronto/Hamilton/ Oshawa	4,043.9	59	34,338	118	65,372
Montreal	3,128.5	47	28,435	94	54,050
Vancouver	1,467.9	23	12,581	45	24,435
Total–Top Three	8,640.3	129	75,354	257	143,857
Next Seven					
Edmonton	827.8	14	8,330	27	15,120
Calgary	819.9	14	8,400	28	15,960
Ottawa/Hull	798.7	17	10,965	33	20,592
Winnipeg	657.1	8	4,432	17	8,976
Quebec City	622.5	16	7,200	32	14,080
Kitchener	533.3	15	8,025	30	15,750
St. Catharines	457.9	17	9,095	33	17,325
Total–Top Ten	13,357.8	230	131,801	457	251,660

Exhibit 7
NEWSPAPER COVERAGE AND RATES

Metropolitan City	Major Newspaper	Circulation*	Rate for Black & White Quarter Page	(CPM) Cost Per Thousand
Halifax	*Chronicle-Herald*	80,274	$1,278	$15.92
Quebec City	*Le Soleil*	117,235	1,710	14.58
Sherbrooke	*La Tribune*	39,786	846	21.26
Montreal (F)	*La Presse*	201,875	2,610	12.93
Montreal (E)	*The Gazette*	48,943	2,250	45.97
Ottawa/Hull	*Ottawa Citizen*	188,483	1,994	10.58
Sudbury	*Sudbury Star*	26,803	540	20.14
Toronto	*Toronto Star*	523,458	5,661	10.81
Hamilton	*Hamilton Spectator*	118,522	1,494	12.61
London	*London Free Press*	128,085	1,755	13.70
Kitchener	*Kitchener-Waterloo Record*	77,844	797	10.24
Winnipeg	*Winnipeg Free Press*	172,246	1,841	10.69
Regina	*Leader Post*	73,253	734	10.02
Saskatoon	*Star Phoenix*	59,785	702	11.74
Calgary	*Calgary Herald*	134,553	1,598	11.88
Edmonton	*Edmonton Journal*	170,707	1,827	10.70
Vancouver	*Vancouver Sun*	230,297	4,113	17.86

Source: *Canadian Advertising Rates and Data*

* Average based on Monday to Friday

Exhibit 8
NEWSPAPER AUDIENCE REACH BY DEMOGRAPHICS (30 LARGEST MARKETS)

Group	Percentage Average Reach (Weekday)
Adults (18+)	63
18–24	55
18–34	57
18–49	60
Under $10,000	49
$10–15,000	55
$15–20,000	58
$20–25,000	60
$25–35,000	65
$35,000+	71
Males	68
Females	58

Source: *The Canadian Media Directors' Council Media Digest, 1987/88*

30 LONDON LIFE INSURANCE COMPANY

Marvin Ryder

Ralph Simmons, the regional manager of the Toronto branch of the London Life Insurance Company, was reviewing the monthly activity reports for four of his salespeople. It was May 1988, and he was trying to determine what, if any, action was needed to improve the selling performance for the four salespeople. A friend had told him about the three Rs as applied to sales staff problems—retrain, relocate, and replace. He remembered these as he thought about what could be done to help the salespeople achieve their full capabilities.

COMPANY BACKGROUND

London Life, Canada's largest life insurance company, operated nation-wide through a network of regional offices in major cities. Policies were sold by a sales and management team of over 2,700 professional sales representatives. In 1987, total income was a record $2 billion, double the company's 1981 revenue, while earnings, assets, and shareholder income showed healthy increases.

London Life sold a comprehensive range of personalized financial security products and services including: life, health, and disability insurance; retirement savings plans; annuities; and pension policies and contracts. More than two million London Life policies and contracts were owned by Canadians. London Life also sold and managed group benefit plans for more than 16,000 businesses coast to coast.

The corporate mission statement, revised in 1987, said: "Our Corporate Mission is to be the leader in meeting the needs of Canadians for personalized financial security. We recognize that corporate integrity and superior service are essential in serving our individual and business customers. Everything we do supports our mission."

THE INSURANCE INDUSTRY

At the end of 1987, Canadians owned $819 billion of life insurance, an increase of $79 billion in the past year and nearly seven times the amount owned in 1970. The industry administered 14.2 million individual life insurance policies in Canada and almost 94,000 group life insurance policies, covering 29.4 million certificates at the end of 1987.

The author gratefully acknowledges the support of the Life Underwriters Association of Canada Research Grant which funded this work.

Individual life insurance could be broken down into two basic types of protection—whole life (permanent) and term insurance. Whole life insurance offered more than death protection. Unlike term policies, it built cash value that could help families meet financial emergencies, pay for special goals, or provide retirement income. Cash value of whole life insurance policies was a by-product of the level premium system. As the mortality rate increased with age, the cost of life insurance increased. Under the level premium approach, the annual premium remained the same, despite the increased risk of death.

Although the premium charged in a whole life policy's earlier years was higher than the actual cost of the insurance, in later years, it was substantially lower than the actual cost of protection. In the early years, the excess amount of each premium was held in reserve, which, along with interest earned and future level premiums, assured that funds would be available to cover the increased risk of death as the policyholder grew older. The policyholder who decided to give up the protection by surrendering the policy was entitled to a share of the company's reserves. The measure of this share was the cash value plus policy dividends.

Term insurance policies offered protection only and most did not build up cash value. The premiums were initially lower than whole life policies of the same amounts, but increased with each renewal of the term policy, reflecting higher mortality rates at older ages.

During 1987, Canadians purchased $135 billion worth of life insurance. Of that total, 61% was bought on an individual basis, that is, by personal or family decisions usually through a life insurance agent. Although the market share of individual insurance was down from 65% in 1986, purchases of individual life insurance totalled $82 billion, an increase of 5% for the year.

A study of the individual life insurance policies bought by Canadians during 1987 showed that 54% were bought by people with incomes under $25,000. Three in four policies were bought by persons aged 15 to 44, one in three by those 25 to 34. Compared to earlier years, more women were buying life insurance. In 1987, 40% of policies covered females, versus 29% in 1970. The face amount of these policies on females was 29% of the 1987 total, compared to 13% in 1970.

THE TORONTO BRANCH

There were two sources of salespeople for the Toronto branch. Each year universities were visited by representatives from the London Life head office. Local managers would join these representatives to conduct initial interviews and to screen potential candidates. While students in commerce or business programs were usually recruited for sales positions, it was not unusual to interview students from humanities or social sciences as well. A second source of salespeople was referral from agents and other managers both from within London Life and from other insurance companies. Some salespeople work better in some environments than in others. Moving people from one branch to another or from one company to another might help them reach their full selling potential. At no time were salespeople solicited through advertising.

When recruiting a potential salesperson, Mr. Simmons looked for seven key factors. These were as follows:

1. An interest in people—concern, caring, being able to relate to someone's feeling, and ability to establish trust.
2. Good, sound judgement—when to act, when to listen.
3. Ability to handle rejection—not consider rejection to be personal when someone isn't interested in a product.
4. Imagination—someone needs imagination to turn the intangible benefits of insurance into something tangible, plus good verbal communication skills to express these benefits.
5. Motivation—in some ways this is the spirit of entrepreneurialism yet it should not be "greed" driven. He looked for people who wanted to achieve goals.
6. Intelligence—not measured in grades achieved while taking courses, but seen as common sense—"street smart."
7. Ethics/Morals—insurance is a product that people cannot really understand so one needs an agent who will not take advantage of someone's ignorance. As well, when people need the product, they are usually facing a crisis and could be easily preyed upon.

Insurance involved a personal interaction between the salesperson and the client. It was important that the salesperson understand a client's feelings and interests, and then translate these into financial opportunities. It required more than simply "niceness." Salespeople could be nice, yet not have someone's basic interests at heart. As Mr. Simmons often said, "An ounce of interest was worth a pound of niceness."

According to Mr. Simmons, salespeople had to keep one overriding objective in mind. London Life existed to help people achieve the financial security or freedom to allow them to do what they want. Salespeople worked to help clients achieve this freedom on their own terms.

The Toronto branch had approximately 30 salespeople. London Life tried to keep a ratio of one manager for every eight salespeople. This did not imply that a manager "managed" a specific eight salespeople. "Telling people what to do is not managing them." Rather each of the four managers were specialists in recruiting, training, advancement, and motivation.

All salespeople and managers attended a monthly meeting. Each person's activity report for the month was displayed for the group to see, and someone was chosen to make constructive, but critical (if necessary), comments. While quotas were set by the head office for each agency, these were not directly translated into quotas for each salesperson. Activity targets were set on a personal basis taking into account each person's strengths and goals.

THE MONTHLY ACTIVITY REPORTS

Mr. Simmons was examining the monthly activity reports for the four salespeople (Exhibit 1). The first section of the report looked at telephone activity. The first column within the section listed the number of telephone numbers dialed for the month. The next column listed the number of completed calls. From statistical evidence, one of every three calls should be completed. The third and fourth columns listed the number of appointments that were made. "New" appointments were people with

Exhibit 1

MONTHLY ACTIVITY REPORTS FOR THE FOUR EMPLOYEES

	TELEPHONING				FROM LUNCHES					ALL ACTIVITIES				
Roy Girard	Dialed	Reached	New	Old	No.	Suspects	Fact Sheets	Cases Open	Closed	Suspects	Fact Sheets	Cases Open	Closed	Effic. Points
January	455	143	30	39	16	11	7	9	10	32	20	30	24	106
February	401	126	27	31	14	10	8	6	9	28	18	26	26	98
March	375	130	28	37	13	8	5	6	7	22	17	29	20	90
April	362	134	25	29	10	7	5	3	6	24	18	24	19	83
	TELEPHONING				FROM LUNCHES					ALL ACTIVITIES				
Linda McCallum	Dialed	Reached	New	Old	No.	Suspects	Fact Sheets	Cases Open	Closed	Suspects	Fact Sheets	Cases Open	Closed	Effic. Points
January	500	117	19	26	10	7	4	8	11	28	15	29	30	98
February	464	92	15	25	8	5	4	9	10	34	19	27	30	101
March	525	97	15	27	11	8	6	10	8	36	16	35	28	108
April	517	102	13	24	8	6	4	12	8	30	19	34	22	98
	TELEPHONING				FROM LUNCHES					ALL ACTIVITIES				
Donald Widner	Dialed	Reached	New	Old	No.	Suspects	Fact Sheets	Cases Open	Closed	Suspects	Fact Sheets	Cases Open	Closed	Effic. Points
January	830	280	91	48	15	12	9	12	13	58	41	51	49	185
February	793	270	85	55	18	14	11	9	9	66	45	57	51	200
March	801	265	88	46	16	13	9	13	12	62	39	48	49	180
April	824	290	86	62	18	15	12	11	11	70	51	62	57	223
	TELEPHONING				FROM LUNCHES					ALL ACTIVITIES				
David Southcott	Dialed	Reached	New	Old	No.	Suspects	Fact Sheets	Cases Open	Closed	Suspects	Fact Sheets	Cases Open	Closed	Effic. Points
January	351	108	22	37	15	8	5	11	12	28	13	32	31	105
February	275	83	14	30	8	3	3	5	4	36	13	28	28	95
March	409	130	24	39	16	9	3	11	12	48	14	29	23	106
April	346	115	21	34	8	6	5	6	1	44	16	30	24	98

whom the agent had no previous contact; the agent had had some previous contact with "old" appointments. Based on historical data, about one of every two completed calls should result in an appointment.

The second section of the report looked at lunch-time activity. After-hours selling was frequently associated with this industry but Mr. Simmons did not believe in it. He felt the hours after work belonged to the agent and that he or she should spend that time with family and friends. Instead, he suggested that many of the sales contacts should be made at lunch-time. In fact, London Life served lunch in their offices in downtown Toronto. Over some sandwiches and soft drinks, the agents could talk with their contacts. In this section of the report the first column showed the number of lunch-time appointments—contacts—that were made. Not all contacts turned out to be prospective purchasers. Those contacts who were prospective purchasers were called "suspects." The second column showed the number of suspects that were determined from the lunch-time meeting. The third column showed the number of fact sheets that were completed. A fact sheet took roughly an hour to complete and listed a lot of personal information about a suspect. The fourth column showed the number of open cases, while the fifth column showed the number of closed cases. An open case was a suspect with whom the agent had ongoing relations. An open case might mean a suspect was considering the purchase of life insurance, an agent was still putting together a presentation for that person, or that they had simply agreed to meet and talk again. A closed case indicated that the agent and suspect had finished their transaction. This might mean that some insurance had been sold or that the person had decided not to purchase any insurance.

The next section of the report detailed the same information, but summed over all time periods including lunch. In other words, the number of suspects shown under "All Activities" included those suspects "From Lunches." The final section listed an agents "Efficiency Points." To determine this number, an agent received one point for a lunch appointment, one point for a completed fact sheet, one point for open cases, one point for closed cases, and a half-point for suspects. As a rule of thumb, an agent should generate five efficiency points per working day or roughly 100 efficiency points each month. It should be noted that this was a measure of efficiency and not effectiveness. Effective agents did more than simply "process" suspects.

THE FOUR SALESPEOPLE

Roy Girard joined the company eight months ago after graduating with a Bachelor of Commerce degree from the University of Toronto. In the summer of 1987, he went to Europe and travelled for four months before starting work in September. Mr. Girard was very athletic. He played slow pitch and coached a junior girl's softball team in the summer. In the winter,he played racquetball three times a week and was a forward with a hockey team in a corporate "No-Body-Contact" league. In February, Mr. Girard became engaged to a public health nurse in London, Ontario. They planned to be married in about a year.

Linda McCallum joined the company twenty-two months ago after graduating with a Bachelor of Arts degree in Economics from Queen's University. As far as Mr. Simmons knew, she led a rather quiet life. She was quite fond of the symphony and was also interested in antiques. When she took a vacation in 1987, she travelled through New England. She returned with six new goblets for her early Victorian glass collection. Ms. McCallum was engaged to be married, but Mr. Simmons knew very little about her fiance or when she planned to be married.

Donald Widner joined the company three years ago after working for two years with an investment company. He had a community college diploma in Marketing and Sales Management. For the past eighteen months, Mr. Widner had been the top salesperson in the branch. Intensely competitive, he seemed to thrive on the demands of personal selling. He often stated that "he would do whatever it took" to remain number one. He was a member of two service clubs (Rotary and Lions), an elder with his church, and President of the Parent-Teacher Association. His wife was a neurosurgeon at the Hospital for Sick Children in Toronto. They lived in a beautiful penthouse condominium in downtown Toronto, and they also had a cabin in northern Ontario, though they did not seem to visit it often. They had no children.

David Southcott was one of the senior salespeople within the company. He joined the company after getting his Bachelor of Commerce degree in 1978 from the University of Toronto. He had been offered promotions to Assistant Sales Manager, but he had turned them down as they would have meant leaving the Toronto branch. Many people felt that he was waiting for a vacancy within the branch before accepting a promotion. He was active in the community serving on the Boards of Directors for the United Way and for Big Brothers. He also helped organize the annual corporate fitness challenge which London Life had won last year. His wife had been a public school teacher, but she currently chose to stay at home and help raise their three children. Southcott's oldest son had just finished his first season of hockey. He never missed one of his son's games.

THE DECISION

The activity reports showed salesperson efficiency. Effectiveness could largely be measured by the volume of life insurance sold and premiums generated. All four salespeople were candidates for the Million Dollar Round Table. One way to qualify for membership in the Million Dollar Round Table was for a life insurance salesperson to sell $4,000,000 worth of whole life insurance during the year. As an example, a salesperson would qualify for the Round Table if he or she sold 40 people whole life insurance policies with a face value of $100,000 each. The Round Table was an independent organization that promoted the life insurance industry. If an individual qualified for membership, for a fee of $50 he or she could join. Upon joining he or she received a plaque, a magazine, and the opportunity to attend conferences and seminars on such topics as motivation and selling skills. In a given year, approximately 25% of the salespeople in the life insurance industry qualified for membership in the Round Table.

Like most companies in the industry, London Life paid their salespeople on the basis of sales performance. The salespeople received a combination of commissions and bonuses and no base salary. The commission rate was one percent of the value of a whole life policy. For example, the sale of a $100,000 whole life policy translated to a commission of $1,000. Bonuses were based on the commissions received for the year and increased on a sliding scale from 5% to 15%. As shown in Exhibit 2, a salesperson earning $25,000 in commissions received a 5% bonus, while a salesperson earning commissions of $150,000 (or more) received a bonus of 15%. While salespeople earned one percent commission on a new policy, if that policy was renewed by the customer in the next year, the salesperson received a reduced commission on the renewal. The commission structure on renewals was as follows: 0.5% for first-year renewal, 0.25% second year, 0.15% third year, 0.12% fourth year, 0.08% fifth year, and 0.005% thereafter.

Mr. Simmons estimated that if the four salespeople continued their current level of sales performance for the year that Roy Girard would receive approximately $39,000 in commissions and bonuses, while Linda McCallum would receive approximately $45,000. Virtually all of their commissions and bonuses would be the result of new business. Donald Widner would earn between $75,000 and $80,000 with a small portion of the commission and bonus coming from renewal business. David Southcott would earn about $60,000 for the year with a significant portion of that in renewal commissions.

As Ralph Simmons examined the activity reports he wondered what recommendations, if any, he should make to these salespeople.

Exhibit 2
BONUS STRUCTURE

Salesperson Commission ($)	Bonus (%)	Bonus ($)	Total Commission and Bonus
25,000	5	1,250	$ 26,250
50,000	7	3,500	53,500
75,000	9	6,750	81,750
100,000	11	11,000	111,000
125,000	13	16,250	141,250
150,000	15	22,500	172,500

31 ADAMS BRANDS

Gordon H. G. McDougall

Douglas Snetsinger

Mr. Ken Bannister, Ontario regional manager for Adams Brands, was faced with the decision of which of three candidates he should hire as the key account supervisor for the Ontario region. This salesperson would be responsible for working with eight major accounts in the Toronto area. Mr. Bannister had narrowed the list to the three applicants and began reviewing their files.

THE COMPANY

Warner-Lambert Inc., a large diversified U.S. multinational, manufactured and marketed a wide range of health care and consumer products. Warner-Lambert Canada Ltd., the largest subsidiary, had annual sales exceeding $200 million. Over one-half of the Canadian sales were generated by Adams Brands, which focused on the confectionery business. The major product lines carried by Adams were

1. chewing gum with brands such as Chiclets, Dentyne, and Trident,
2. portable breath fresheners, including Certs and Clorets,
3. cough tablets and antacids such as Halls and Rolaids, and
4. several other products including Blue Diamond Almonds and Sparkies Mini-Fruits.

In these product categories, Adams Brands was usually the market leader or had a substantial market share.

The division was a stable unit for Warner-Lambert Canada with profits being used for investments throughout the company. Success of the Adams Brands was built on:

1. quality products,
2. strong marketing management,
3. sales force efforts on distribution, display, and merchandising, and
4. excellent customer service.

Adams was organized on a regional basis. The Ontario region, which also included the Atlantic provinces, had 46 sales representatives whose responsibilities were to service individual stores. Five district managers co-ordinated the activities of the sales representatives. As well, three key account supervisors worked with the large retail chains (for example, supermarkets) in Ontario and the Atlantic area. The key account supervisor in the Toronto area had recently resigned his position and joined one of Adams' major competitors.

THE MARKET

The confectionery industry included six major competitors who manufactured chocolate bars, chewing gum, mints, cough drops, chewy candy, and other products. The 1986 market shares of these six companies are provided in Exhibit 1.

In the past few years, total industry sales in the confectionery category had been flat to marginally declining in unit volume. This sales decline was attributed to the changing age distribution of the population (that is, fewer young people). As consumers got older, their consumption of confectionery products tended to decline. While unit sales were flat or declining, dollar sales were increasing at a rate of 10% per annum as a result of price increases.

In the confectionery business it was critical to obtain extensive distribution in as many stores as possible and, within each store, to obtain as much prominent shelf space as possible. Most confectionery products were purchased on impulse. In one study it was found that up to 85% of chewing gum and 70% of chocolate bar purchases were unplanned. While chocolate bars could be viewed as an indirect competitor to gum and mints, they were direct competitors for retail space, and were usually merchandised on the same display. Retailers earned similar margins from all confectionery products (25% to 36% of retail selling price) and often sought the

Exhibit 1
MAJOR COMPETITORS IN CONFECTIONERY INDUSTRY

Company	Market Share (%)	Major Product Lines	Major Brands
Adams	23	gum, portable breath fresheners, cough drops	Trident, Chiclets, Dentyne, Certs, Halls
Cadbury/Nielson	22	chocolate bars	Caramilk, Crunchie, Dairy Milk, Crispy Crunch
Rowntree	15	chocolate bars	Black Magic, Kit-Kat, Smarties, Turtles
Nabisco/Hershey	14	gum, chocolate bars, chewy candy	Lowney, Reese's Pieces, Lifesavers
Wrigley's	9	gum	Hubba Bubba, Extra, Doublemint
Effem Foods Ltd.	9	chocolate bars, chewy candy	Mars, Snickers, M&M's, Skittles
Richardson-Vicks	2	cough drops	Vicks
Others	6		

Source: Company records and industry data

best-selling brands to generate those revenues. Some industry executives felt that catering to the retailers' needs was even more important than understanding the ultimate consumers' needs.

Adams Brands had always provided store display racks for merchandising all confectionery items including competitive products and chocolate bars. The advantage of supplying the displays was that the manufacturer could influence the number of prelabelled slots which contained brand logos and the proportion of the display devoted to various product groups, such as chewing gum versus chocolate bars. The displays were usually customized to the unique requirements of a retailer, such as the height and width of the display.

Recently, a competitor, Effem, had become more competitive in the design and display of merchandising systems. Effem was regarded as an innovator in the industry, in part because of their limited product line and new approach to the retail trade. The company had only eight fast-turnover products in their line. Effem had developed their own sales force, consisting of over 100 part-time merchandising sales people and eight full-time sales personnel, and focused on the head offices of "A" accounts. "A" accounts were large retail chains such as Mac's, Beckers, Loblaws, A & P, Food City, Miracle Food Mart, K mart, Towers, and Zellers. Other than Adams, Effem was one of a few companies that conducted considerable research on racking systems and merchandising.

THE RETAIL TRADE

Within the Adams Brands over two-thirds of confectionery volume flowed through wholesalers. The remaining balance was split between direct sales and drop shipments to retailers. Wholesalers were necessary because, with over 66,000 outlets in food, drug, and variety stores alone, the sales force could not adequately cover a large proportion of the retailers. The percentage of Adams sales through the various channels is provided in Exhibit 2.

The volume of all consumer packaged goods sold in Canada had increasingly been dominated by fewer and larger retail chains. This increased retail concentration resulted in retailers becoming more influential in trade promotion decisions, including dictating the size, timing, and numbers of allowance, distribution and co-op advertising events. The new power of the retailers had not as yet been fully wielded against the confectionery business. Confectionery lines were some of the most profitable lines for the retailer. Further, the manufacturers were not as reliant on listings from any given retailer as were other food and household product manufacturers.

The increased size of some retail chains also changed the degree of management sophistication at all levels including the retail buyers—those responsible for deciding what products were carried by the retail stores. At one time, the relationship between manufacturers' sales representatives and retail buyers was largely based on long-term and personal associations. Usually the sales representative had strong social skills, and an important task was to "get along well" with the buyers. Often when the representatives and buyers met to discuss various promotions or listings, part of

Exhibit 2
ADAMS BRAND SALES BY DISTRIBUTION CHANNEL

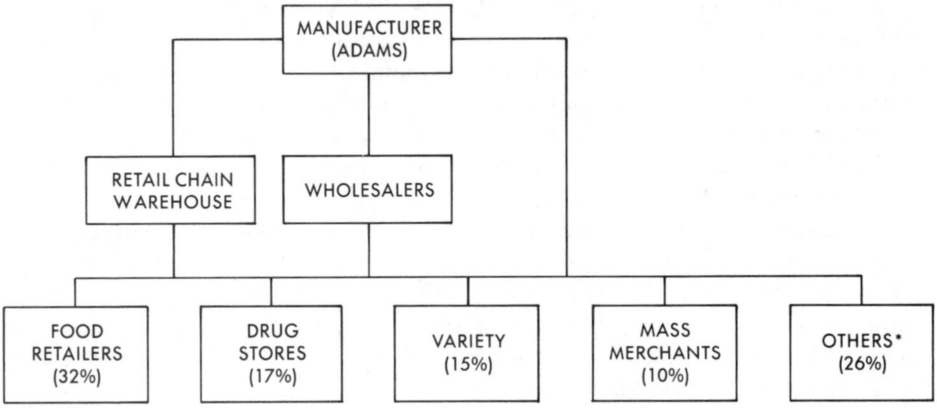

* Consists of a wide variety of locations, including vending machines, restaurants, cafeterias, bowling alleys, resorts.

the conversation dealt with making plans for dinner or going to a hockey game. The sales representative would be the host for these social events.

More recently, a new breed of buyer was emerging in the retail chains. Typically the new retail managers and buyers had been trained in business schools. They often had product management experience, relied on analytical skills, and used state-of-the-art, computer-supported planning systems. In some instances, the buyer was now more sophisticated than the sales representative with respect to analytical approaches to display and inventory management. The buyers were frequently requesting detailed plan-o-grams with strong analytical support for expected sales, profits, and inventory turns. The buyer would also at times become the salesperson. After listening to a sales presentation and giving an initial indication of interest, the buyer would attempt to sell space—space on the store floor and space in the weekly advertising supplements. For example, the buyer for Shopper's Drug Mart could offer a dump bin location in every store in the chain for a week. In some instances, both the buyer and the representative had the authority to conclude such a deal at that meeting. At other times, both would have to wait for approval from their respective companies.

The interesting aspect of the key account supervisor's position was that the individual would have to feel comfortable dealing with the "old" and "new" school of retail management. The task for Mr. Bannister was to select the right candidate for this position. The salary for the position ranged from $25,000 to $48,200, depending on qualifications and experience. Mr. Bannister expected that the candidate selected would probably be paid somewhere between $32,000 and $40,000. An expense allowance would also be included in the compensation package.

THE KEY ACCOUNTS SUPERVISOR

The main responsibility of the key accounts supervisor was to establish and maintain a close working relationship with the buyers of eight "A" accounts whose head offices were located in the Toronto area. An important task was to make presentations (15 to 30 minutes in length) to the retail buyers of these key accounts every three to six weeks. At these meetings, promotions or deals for up to five brands would be presented. The supervisor was responsible for all Adams brands. The buyer might have to take the promotions to his buying committee where the final decision would be made. In addition, the supervisor used these meetings to hear from the buyer about any merchandising problems occuring at the store level.

Mid-year reviews were undertaken with each account. These reviews, lasting for one hour, were focused on reviewing sales trends and tying them into merchandising programs, listings, service, and new payment terms. Another important and time-consuming responsibility of the key accounts supervisor was to devise and present plan-o-grams and be involved with the installation of the displays. The supervisor also conducted store checks and spent time on competitive intelligence. Working with the field staff was a further requirement of the position.

Mr. Bannister reflected on what he felt were the attributes the ideal candidate would possess. First, the individual should have selling and merchandising experience in the retail business in order to understand the language and dynamics of the situation. On the merchandising side, the individual would be required to initiate and co-ordinate the design of customized display systems for individual stores, a task that involved a certain amount of creativity. Second, strong interpersonal skills were needed. The individual had to establish rapport and make effective sales presentations to the buyers. Because of the wide range of buyer sophistication, these skills were particularly important. Mr. Bannister made a mental note to recommend that whoever was hired would be sent on the Professional Selling Skills course, a one-week program designed to enhance listening, selling, and presentation skills. Finally, the candidate should possess analytic skills because many of the sales and performance reports (from both manufacturer and retailer) were or would be computerized. Thus, the individual should feel comfortable working with computers. Mr. Bannister hoped that he could find a candidate who would be willing to spend a minimum of three years in the job in order to establish a personal relationship with the buyers.

Ideally, the candidate selected would have a blend of all three skills because of the mix of buyers he or she would contact. Mr. Bannister felt it was most likely these characteristics would be found in a business school graduate. He had advertised the job internally (through the company's newsletter) and externally (in the *Toronto Star*). A total of 20 applications were received. After an initial screening, three possible candidates for the position were identified. None were from Warner-Lambert.

In early August 1987, Mr. Bannister and a member of the personnel department then interviewed each of the candidates. After completing the interviews, brief fact sheets were prepared (Exhibit 3). Mr. Bannister began reviewing the sheets prior to making the decision.

Exhibit 3
LYDIA COHEN

Personal:	Born 1956; 168 cm; 64 kg; single
Education:	B.B.A. (1978), Wilfrid Laurier University; active in Marketing Club and intra-mural sports
Work:	1985–87, Rowntree Mackintosh Canada Inc.—District Manager Responsible for sales staff of three in Ottawa and eastern Ontario region. Establish annual sales plan and ensure that district meets its quota. 1978–1984, Rowntree Mackintosh Canada Inc.—Confectionery Sales Representative Responsible for selling a full line of confectionery and grocery products to key accounts in Toronto (1983–84) and Ottawa (1978–82). 1984 Sales Representative of the Year for highest volume growth.
Interests:	Racquet sports
Candidate's Comment:	I am interested in working in the Toronto area and I would look forward to concentrating on the sales task. My best years at Rowntree were in sales in the Toronto region.
Interviewer's Comment:	Lydia presents herself very well and has a strong background in confectionery sales. Her record at Rowntree is very good. Rowntree paid for her to take an introductory course in Lotus 1-2-3 in 1984, but she has not had much opportunity to develop her computer skills. She does not seem to be overly ambitious or aggressive. She stated that personal reasons were pre-eminent in seeking a job in Toronto.

JOHN FISHER

Personal:	Born 1960; 190 cm; 88 kg; single
Education:	B.A. (Phys. Ed.) (1985), University of British Columbia While at U.B.C. played four years of varsity basketball (team captain in 1983–84). Assistant Coach, Senior Basketball at University Hill High School, 1981–1985. Developed and ran a two-week summer basketball camp at U.B.C. for three years. Profits from the camp were donated to the Varsity Basketball Fund.
Work:	1980–86, Jacobs Suchard Canada Inc. (Nabob Foods)

Six years' experience (full-time, 1985–86, and five years part-time, 1980–85 during school terms and full-time during summers) in coffee and chocolate distribution and sales; two years on the loading docks, one year driving truck, and three years as a sales representative. Sales tasks included calling on regular customers, order taking, rack jobbing, and customer relations development.

1986–87, Scavolini (Professional Basketball)

One year after completing studies at U.B.C., travelled western Europe and northern Africa. Travel was financed by playing professional basketball in the Italian First Division.

Candidate's Comments: I feel the combination of educational preparation, work experience, and my demonstrated ability as a team player and leader make me well suited for this job. I am particularly interested in a job, such as sales, which rewards personal initiative.

Interviewer's Comments: A very ambitious and engaging individual with a good record of achievements. Strong management potential is evident, but interest in sales as a career is questionable. Minored in Computer Science at U.B.C. Has a standing offer to return to a sales management position at Nabob.

BARRY MOORE

Personal: Born 1947; 180 cm; 84 kg; married with two children

Education: Business Administration Diploma (1972), Humber College

While at school was active participant in a number of clubs and political organizations. President of the Young Liberals (1971–72).

Work: 1984–87, Barrigans Food Markets—Merchandising Analyst

Developed merchandising plans for a wide variety of product categories. Negotiated merchandising programs and trade deals with manufacturers and brokers. Managed a staff of four.

1981–84, Dominion Stores Ltd.—Assistant Merchandise Manager

Liaison responsibilities between stores and head office merchandise planning. Responsible for execution of merchandising plans for several food categories.

1980, Robin Hood Multifoods Inc.—Assistant Product Manager

Responsible for the analysis and development of promotion planning for Robin Hood Flour.

1975–80, Nestlé Enterprises Ltd.—Carnation Division Sales Representative

	Major responsibilities were developing and maintaining sales and distribution to wholesale and retail accounts.
	1972–75, McCain Foods Ltd.—Inventory Analyst
	Worked with sales staff and head office planning to ensure the quality and timing of shipments to brokers and stores.
Activities:	Board of Directors, Richview Community Club Board of Directors, Volunteer Centre of Etobicoke Past President of Etobicoke Big Brothers Active in United Way Yachting—C&C 34 Canadian Champion
Candidate's Comments:	It would be a great challenge and joy to work with a progressive industry leader such as Adams Brands.
Interviewer's Comments:	Very articulate and professionally groomed. Dominated the interview with a variety of anecdotes and humorous stories; some of which were relevant to the job. Likes to read popular books on management, particularly books which champion the bold gut-feel entrepreneur. He would probably earn more money at Adams if hired.

32 GENERAL ELECTRIC APPLIANCES

Richard W. Pollay

John D. Claxton

Rick Jenkner

Larry Barr had recently been promoted to the position of District Sales Manager (B.C.) for G.E. Appliances, a division of Canadian Appliance Manufacturing Co. Ltd. (CAMCO). One of his more important duties in that position was the allocation of his district's sales quota amongst his five salespeople. Barr received his quota for 1978 in October 1977. His immediate task was to determine an equitable allocation of that quota. This was important because the company's incentive pay plan was based on the salesperson's attainment of quota. A portion of Barr's remuneration was also based on the degree to which his sales force met their quotas.

Barr graduated from the University of British Columbia in 1969, with the degree of Bachelor of Commerce. He was immediately hired as a product manager for a mining equipment manufacturing firm because of his summer job experience with that firm. In 1972, he joined Canadian General Electric (C.G.E.) in Montreal as a product manager for refrigerators. There he was responsible for creating and merchandising a product line, as well as developing product and marketing plans. In January 1975, he was transferred to Coburg, Ontario, as a sales manager for industrial plastics. In September 1976, he became Administrative Manager (Western Region), and when the position of District Sales Manager became available Barr was promoted to it. There his duties included development of sales strategies, supervision of salespeople, and budgeting.

BACKGROUND

CAMCO was created in 1976 under the joint ownership of Canadian General Electric Ltd. and General Steel Wares Ltd. (G.S.W.). CAMCO then purchased the production facilities of Westinghouse Canada Ltd. Under the purchase agreement the Westinghouse brand name was transferred to White Consolidated Industries Ltd., where it became White-Westinghouse. Appliances manufactured by CAMCO in the former Westinghouse plant were branded Hotpoint.

The G.E., G.S.W., and Hotpoint major appliance plants became divisions of CAMCO. These divisions operated independently and had their own separate management staff, although they were all ultimately accountable to CAMCO management (Exhibit 1). The divisions competed for sales, although not directly, because they each produced product lines for different price segments.

Exhibit 1
ORGANIZATION CHART

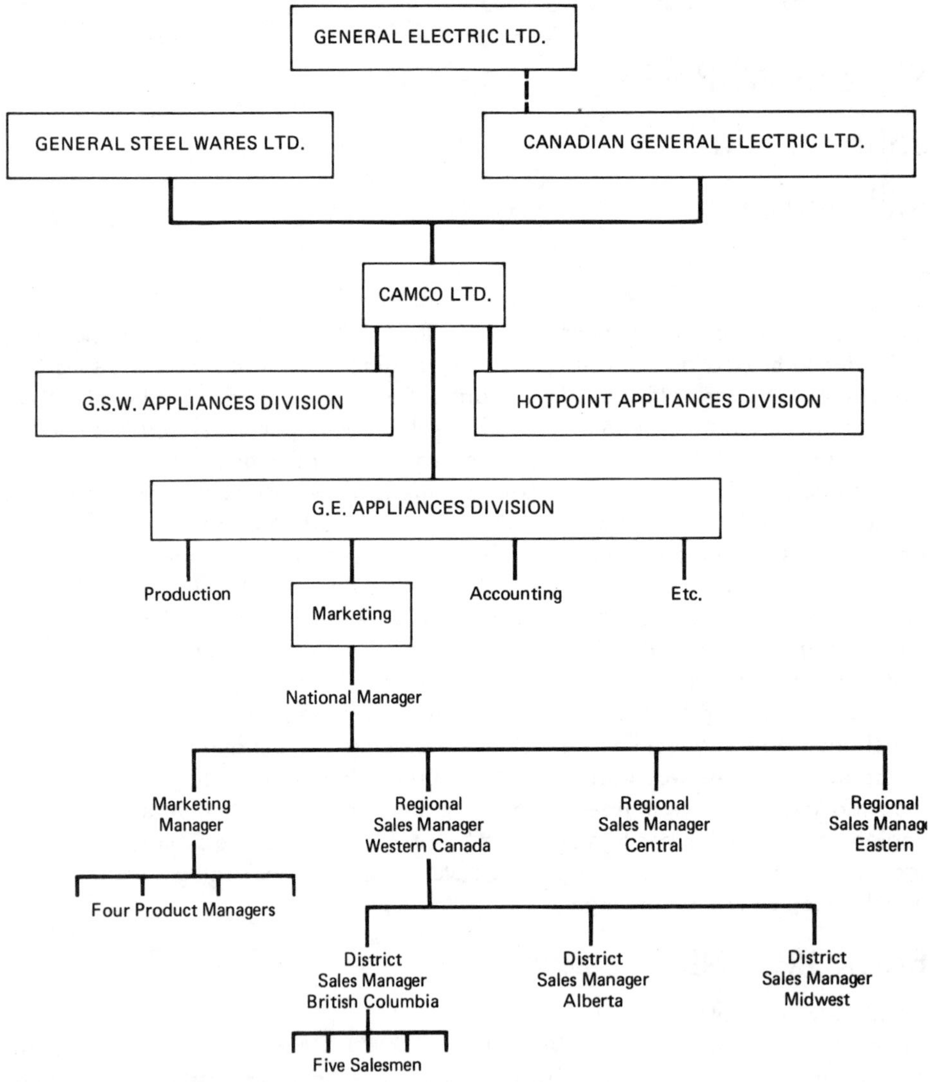

COMPETITION

Competition in the appliance industry was vigorous. CAMCO was the largest firm in the industry, with approximately 45% market share, split between G.E., G.S.W. (Moffat & McClary brands), and Hotpoint. The following three firms each had 10 to 15% market share: Inglis (washers and dryers only), W.C.I. (makers of White-

Westinghouse, Kelvinator, and Gibson), and Admiral. These three firms also produced appliances under department store brand names such as Viking (for Eaton's), Baycrest (for The Bay), and Kenmore (for Sears), which accounted for an additional 15% of the market. The remainder of the market was divided among brands such as Maytag, Roper Dishwasher, Gurney, Tappan, and Danby.

G.E. marketed a full major appliance product line, including refrigerators, ranges, washers, dryers, dishwashers, and television sets. G.E. appliances generally had many features and were priced at the upper end of the price range. Their major competition came from Maytag and Westinghouse.

THE BUDGETING PROCESS

Canadian General Electric was one of the most advanced firms in the consumer goods industry in terms of sales budgeting. Budgeting received careful analysis at all levels of management.

The budgetary process began in June of each year. The management of G.E. Appliances division assessed the economic outlook, growth trends in the industry, competitive activity, population growth, and so forth in order to determine a reasonable sales target for the next year. The president of CAMCO received this estimate, checked and revised it as necessary, and submitted it to the president of Canadian General Electric, where final authorization rested. G.E. Appliances was considered an "invest and grow" division, which meant that it was expected to produce a healthy sales growth each year, regardless of the state of the economy. As Barr observed, "This is difficult, but meeting challenges is the job of management."

The approved budget was expressed as a desired percentage increase in sales. Once the figure had been decided it was not subject to change. The quota was communicated back through CAMCO and G.E. Appliances, where it was available to the District Sales Managers in October. Each district was then required to meet an overall growth figure (quota), but each sales territory was not automatically expected to achieve that same growth. Barr was required to assess the situation in each territory, determine where growth potential was highest, and allocate his quota accordingly.

THE SALES INCENTIVE PLAN

The sales incentive plan was a critical part of General Electric's sales force plan. Each salesperson agreed to a basic salary figure called "planned earnings." The planned salary varied according to experience, education, past performance, and competitive salaries. A salesperson was paid 75% of his planned earnings on a guaranteed regular basis. The remaining 25% of salary was at risk, dependent upon the person's sales record. There was also the possibility of earning substantially more money by selling more than quota. (See Exhibit 2.)

The bonus was awarded such that total salary (base plus bonus) equalled planned earnings when the quota was just met. The greatest increase in bonus came between 101% and 110% of quota. The bonus was paid quarterly on the cumulative total quota. A holdback system ensured that a salesperson was never required to pay

Exhibit 2

APPLICABLE INCENTIVE EARNINGS SCHEDULE SALES INCENTIVE EARNINGS SCHEDULE: MAJOR APPLIANCES & HOME ENTERTAINMENT PRODUCTS

Sales Quota Realization %	% of Base Salary Total	Sales Quota Realization %	Incentive % of Base Salary Total
70	0	105	35.00
71	0.75	106	37.00
72	1.50	107	39.00
73	2.25	108	41.00
74	3.00	109	43.00
75	3.75	110	45.00
76	4.50	111	46.00
77	5.25	112	47.00
78	6.00	113	48.00
79	6.75	114	49.00
80	7.50	115	50.00
81	8.25	116	51.00
82	9.00	117	52.00
83	9.75	118	53.00
84	10.50	119	54.00
85	11.25	120	55.00
86	12.00	121	56.00
87	12.75	122	57.00
88	13.50	123	58.00
89	14.25	124	59.00
90	15.00	125	60.00
91	16.00	126	61.00
92	17.00	127	62.00
93	18.00	128	63.00
94	19.00	129	64.00
95	20.00	130	65.00
96	21.00	131	66.00
97	22.00	132	67.00
98	23.00	133	68.00
99	24.00	134	69.00
100	25.00	135	70.00
101	27.00	136	71.00
102	29.00	137	72.00
103	31.00	138	73.00
104	33.00	139	74.00
		140	75.00

back previously earned bonus by reason of a poor quarter. Because of this system, it was critical that each salesperson's quota be fair in relation to the other salespeople. Nothing was worse for morale than one person earning large bonuses while the others struggled.

Quota attainment was not the sole basis for evaluating the salespeople. They were required to fulfill a wide range of duties including service, franchising of new dealers, maintaining good relations with dealers, and maintaining a balance of sales among the different product lines. Because the bonus system was based on sales only, Barr had to ensure that the salespeople did not neglect their other duties.

A formal salary review was held each year for each salesperson. However, Barr preferred to give his salespeople continuous feedback on their performances. In this way, he hoped to avoid problems which could lead to dismissal of a salesperson and loss of sales for the company.

Barr's incentive bonus plan was more complex than the salespeople's. He was awarded a maximum of 75 annual bonus points broken down as follows: market share, 15; total sales performance, 30; sales representative balance, 30. Each point had a specific money value. The system ensured that Barr allocate his quota carefully. For instance, if one quota was so difficult that the salesperson sold only 80% of it, while the other salespeople exceeded quota, Barr's bonus would be reduced, even if the overall area sales exceeded the quota. (See Appendix, "Development of a Sales Commission Plan.")

QUOTA ALLOCATION

The total 1978 sales budget for G.E. Appliances division was about $100 million, a 14% sales increase over 1977. Barr's share of the $33 million Western region quota was $13.3 million, also a 14% increase over 1977. Barr had two weeks to allocate the quota amongst his five territories. He needed to consider factors such as historical allocation, economic outlook, dealer changes, personnel changes, untapped potential, new franchise or store openings, and buying group activity (volume purchases by associations of independent dealers).

SALES FORCE

There were five sales territories within British Columbia (Exhibit 3). Territories were determined on the basis of number of customers, sales volume of customers, geographic size, and experience of the salesperson. Territories were altered periodically in order to deal with changed circumstances.

One territory was comprised entirely of contract customers. Contract sales were sales in bulk lots to builders and developers who used the appliances in housing units. Because the appliances were not resold at retail, G.E. took a lower profit margin on such sales.

G.E. Appliances recruited M.B.A. graduates for their sales force. They sought bright, educated people who were willing to relocate anywhere in Canada. The company intended that these people would ultimately be promoted to managerial positions. The company also hired experienced career salespeople in order to get a

Exhibit 3

G. E. APPLIANCES—SALES TERRITORY

Territory Designation		Description
1	Contract (Jim Wiste)	Contract sales in Vancouver, Victoria. All contract sales outside of Interior region (50–60 customers)
2	Greater Vancouver (Garth Rizzuto)	Hudson's Bay, Firestone, K mart, McDonald Supply, plus seven major independent dealers
3	Interior (Dan Seguin)	All customers from Quesnel to Nelson, including contract sales in area (50 customers)
4	Coastal (Ken Block)	Eaton's, Woodward's, plus Vancouver Island north of Duncan and upper Fraser Valley (east of Clearbrook) (20 customers)
5	Independent and Northern (Fred Speck)	All independents in greater Vancouver area (except those specifically assigned elsewhere) and South Vancouver Island (including Victoria) plus northern B.C. and Yukon (30 customers)

blend of experience in the sales force. However, the typical salesperson was under thirty, aggressive, and upwardly mobile. G.E.'s sales training program covered only product knowledge. It was not felt necessary to train recruits in sales techniques.

ALLOCATION PROCEDURE

At the time Barr assumed the job of D.S.M., he had a meeting with the former sales manager, Ken Philips. Philips described to Barr the method he had used in the past to allocate the quota. As Barr understood it, the procedure was as follows:

The quota was received in October in the form of a desired percentage sales increase. The first step was to project current sales to the end of the year. This gave a base to which the increase was added for an estimate of the next year's quota.

From this quota, the value of contract sales was allocated. Contract sales were allocated first because the market was considered the easiest to forecast. The amount of contract sales in the sales mix was constrained by the lower profit margin on such sales.

The next step was to make a preliminary allocation by simply adding the budgeted percentage increase to the year-end estimates for each territory. Although this allocation seemed fair on the surface, it did not take into account the differing situations in the territories, or the difficulty of attaining such an increase.

The next step was examination of the sales data compiled by G.E. Weekly sales reports from all regions were fed into a central computer, which compiled them and printed out sales totals by product line for each customer, as well as other information. This information enabled the sales manager to check the reasonableness of his initial allocation through a careful analysis of the growth potential for each customer.

The analysis began with the largest accounts, such as Firestone, Hudson's Bay, and Eaton's, which each bought over $1 million in appliances annually. Accounts that size were expected to achieve at least the budgeted growth. The main reason for this was that a shortfall of a few percentage points on such a large account would be difficult to make up elsewhere.

Next, the growth potential for medium-sized accounts was estimated. These accounts included McDonald Supply, K mart, Federated Co-operative, and buying groups such as Volume Independent Purchasers (V.I.P.). Management expected the majority of sales growth to come from such accounts, which had annual sales of between $150 thousand and $1 million.

At that point, about 70% of the accounts had been analyzed. The small accounts were estimated last. These had generally lower growth potential but were an important part of the company's distribution system.

Once all the accounts had been analyzed, the growth estimates were summed and the total compared to the budget. Usually, the growth estimates were well below the budget.

The next step was to gather more information. The salespeople were usually consulted to ensure that no potential trouble areas or good opportunities had been overlooked. The manager continued to revise and adjust the figures until the total estimated matched the budget. These projections were then summed by territory and compared with the preliminary territorial allocation.

Frequently, there were substantial differences between the two allocations. Historical allocations were then examined and the manager used his judgement in adjusting the figures until he was satisfied that the allocation was both equitable and attainable. Some factors which were considered at this stage included experience of the salespeople, competitive activities, potential store closures or openings, potential labour disputes in areas, and so forth.

The completed allocation was passed on to the Regional Sales Manager for his approval. The process had usually taken one week or longer by this stage. Once the allocations had been approved, the District Sales Manager then divided them into sales quotas by the product line. Often, the resulting average price did not match the expected mix between higher and lower priced units. Therefore, some additional adjusting of figures was necessary. The house account (used for sales to employees of the company) was used as the adjustment factor.

Once this breakdown had been completed, the numbers were printed on a budget sheet, and given to the Regional Sales Manager (R.S.M.). He forwarded all the sheets for his region to the central computer, which printed out sales numbers for each product line by salesperson by month. These figures were used as the salesperson's quotas for the next year.

CURRENT SITUATION

Barr recognized that he faced a difficult task. He felt that he was too new to the job and the area to confidently undertake an account by account growth analysis. However, due to his previous experience with sales budgets, he did have some sound general ideas. He also had the records of past allocation and quota attainment (Exhibit 4), as well as the assistance of the R.S.M., Anthony Foyt.

Exhibit 4
SALES RESULTS

1975

Territory	1975 Quota (000s)	% of Total Quota	1975 Actual (000s)	Variance from Quota (V%)
1	$2,440	26.5	$2,267	(7)
2	1,790	19.4	1,824	2
3	1,624	17.7	1,433	(11)
4	2,111	23.0	2,364	12
5	1,131	12.3	1,176	4
House	84	1.1	235	—
TOTAL	$9,180	100.0	$9,299	1

1976

Territory	1976 Quota (000s)	% of Total Quota	1976 Actual (000s)	Variance from Quota (V%)
1	$2,587	26.2	$ 2,845	10
2	2,005	20.3	2,165	8
3	1,465	14.8	1,450	(1)
4	2,405	24.4	2,358	(2)
5	1,334	13.5	1,494	12
House	52	.8	86	—
TOTAL	$9,848	100.0	$10,398	5

Barr's first step was to project the current sales figures to end of year totals. This task was facilitated because the former manager, Philips, had been making successive projections monthly since June. Barr then made a preliminary quota allocation by adding the budgeted sales increase of 14% to each territory's total (Exhibit 5).

Barr then began to assess circumstances which could cause him to alter that allocation. One major problem was the resignation, effective at the end of the year, of one of the company's top salespeople, Ken Block. His territory had traditionally been one of the most difficult, and Barr felt that it would be unwise to replace Block with a novice sales representative.

Barr considered shifting one of the more experienced salespeople into that area. However, that would have involved a disruption of service in an additional territory, which was undesirable because it took several months for a salesperson to build up a good rapport with customers. Barr's decision would affect his quota allocation because a person new to a territory could not be expected to immediately sell as well as the incumbent, and a novice would require an even longer period of adaptation.

Barr was also concerned about Rizzuto's territory. The territory comprised two large national accounts and seven major independent dealers. The buying decisions

Exhibit 5
SALES PROJECTIONS AND QUOTAS, 1977–1978

Projected sales results, 1977

Territory	Oct. 1977 Year to Date	1977 Projected Total (000s)	1977 Quota (000s)	% of Total Quota	Projected Variance from Quota (V%)
1	$2,447	$ 3,002	$ 2,859	25.0	5
2	2,057	2,545	2,401	21.0	6
3	1,318	1,623	1,727	15.1	(6)
4	2,214	2,625	2,734	23.9	(4)
5	1,394	1,720	1,578	13.8	9
	132	162	139	1.2	—
TOTAL	$9,474	$11,677	$11,438	100.0	2

Preliminary allocation, 1978

Territory	1977 Projection (000s)	1978 Quota* (000s)	% of Total Quota
1	$ 3,002	$ 3,422	25.7
2	2,545	2,901	21.8
3	1,623	1,854	13.9
4	2,625	2,992	22.5
5	1,720	1,961	14.7
House	162	185	1.3
TOTAL	$11,677	$13,315	100.0

* 1978 Budget = territory projections + 14% = $13,315.

for the national accounts were made at their head offices, where G.E.'s regional sales representatives had no control over the decisions. Recently, Barr had heard rumours that one of the national accounts was reviewing its purchase of G.E. Appliances. If they were to delist even some product lines, it would be a major blow to the salesperson, Rizzuto, whose potential sales would be greatly reduced. Barr was unsure of how to deal with that situation.

Another concern for Barr was the wide variance in buying of some accounts. Woodward's, Eaton's, and McDonald Supply had large fluctuations from year to year. Also, Eaton's, Hudson's Bay, and Woodward's had plans to open new stores in the Vancouver area sometime during the year. The sales increase to be generated by these events was hard to estimate.

The general economic outlook was poor. The Canadian dollar had fallen in value compared to the U.S. dollar and unemployment was at about 8%. The government's anti-inflation program, which was scheduled to end in November 1978, had managed to keep inflation to the 8% level, but economists expected higher inflation and increased labour unrest during the post-control period.

The economic outlook was not the same in all areas. For instance, the interior of B.C., particularly the Okanagan region, was a very depressed area. Tourism was down and fruit farmers were doing poorly. Vancouver Island was still recovering from a 200% increase in ferry fares, while the greater Vancouver area appeared to be in a relatively better position.

In the contract segment, construction had shown an increase over 1976. However, labour unrest was common. There had been a crippling eight-week strike in 1976, and there was a strong possibility of another strike in 1978.

With all of this in mind, Barr was very concerned that he allocate the quota properly because of the bonus system implications. How should he proceed? To help him in his decision, he reviewed a note on development of a sales commission plan which he had obtained while attending a seminar on sales management the previous year (see Appendix).

Appendix
DEVELOPMENT OF A SALES COMMISSION PLAN

A series of steps are required to establish the foundation upon which a Sales Commission Plan can be built. These steps are as follows:

A. Determine Specific Sales Objectives of Positions to Be Included in Plan

For a Sales Commission Plan to succeed, it must be designed to encourage the attainment of the business objectives of the component division. Before deciding on the specific measures of performance to be used in the plan, the component should review and define its major objectives. Typical objectives might be:

- Increase sales volume
- Do an effective balanced selling job in a variety of product lines
- Improve market share
- Reduce selling expense to sales ratios
- Develop new accounts or territories
- Introduce new products

Although it is probably neither desirable nor necessary to include all such objectives as specific measures of performance in the plan, they should be kept in mind, at least to the extent that the performance measures chosen for the plan are compatible with and do not work against the overall accomplishment of the component's business objectives.

Also, the *relative* current importance or ranking of these objectives will provide guidance in selecting the number and type of performance measures to be included in the plan.

B. Determine Quantitative Performance Measures to Be Used

Although it may be possible to include a number of measures in a particular plan, there is a drawback to using so many as to overly complicate it, and fragment the impact of any one measure on the participants. A plan that is difficult to understand will lose a great deal of its motivating force, as well as being costly to administer properly.

For components who currently have a variable sales compensation plan(s) for their salespeople, a good starting point would be to consider the measures used in those plans. Although the measurements used for sales managers need not be identical, they should at least be *compatible* with those used to determine their salespeople's commissions.

However, keep in mind that a performance measure that may not be appropriate for individual salespeople may be a good one to apply to their manager. Measurements involving attainment of a share of a defined market, balanced selling for a variety of products, and control of district or region expenses might well fall into this category.

Listed below are a variety of measurements that might be used to emphasize specific sales objectives.

TAILORING COMMISSION PLAN MEASUREMENTS TO FIT COMPONENT OBJECTIVES

Objectives	Possible Plan Measurements
1 Increase sales/orders volume	Net sales billed or orders received against quota
2 Increase sales of particular lines	Sales against product lines quotas with weighted sales credits on individual lines
3 Increase market share	Percent realization (%R) of share
4 Do balanced selling job	%R of product line quotas with commissions increasing in proportion to number of lines up to quota
5 Increase profitability	Margin realized from sales Vary sales credits to emphasize profitable product lines Vary sales credit in relation to amount of price discount
6 Increase dealer sales	Pay distributor salespeople or sales manager in relation to realization of sales quotas of assigned dealers
7 Increase sales calls	%R of targeted calls per district or region
8 Introduce new product	Additional sales credits on new line for limited period
9 Control expense	%R of expense to sales or margin ratio Adjust sales credit in proportion to variance from expense budget
10 Sales teamwork	Share of incentive based upon group results.

For most components, all or most of these objectives will be desirable to some extent. The point is to select those of *greatest* importance where it will be possible to establish measures of standard or normal performance for individuals, or at least small groups of individuals working as a team.

If more than one performance measurement is to be used, the relative weighting of each measurement must be determined. If a measure is to be effective, it must carry enough weight to have at least some noticeable effect on the commission earnings of an individual.

As a general guide, it would be unusual for a plan to include more than two or three quantitative measures with a *minimum* weighting of 15 to 20% of planned commissions for any one measurement.

C. Establish Commission Payment Schedule for Each Performance Measure

1. Determine Appropriate Range of Performance for Each Measurement

The performance range for a measurement defines the percent of standard performance (%R) at which commission earnings start to the point where they reach maximum.

The minimum point of the performance range for a given measurement should be set so that a majority of the participants can earn at least some incentive pay and the maximum set at a point that is possible for attainment by some participants. These points will vary with the type of measure used, and the degree of predictability of individual budgets or other forms of measurement. In a period where overall performance is close to standard, 90 to 95% of the participants should fall within the performance range.

For the commission plan to be effective most of the participants should be operating within the performance range most of the time. If a participant is either far below the minimum of this range, or has reached the maximum, further improvement will not affect his commission earnings, and the plan will be largely inoperative as far as he is concerned.

Actual past experience of %R's attained by participants is obviously the best indicator of what this range should be for each measure used. Lacking this, it is better to err on the side of having a wider range than one which proves to be too narrow. If some form of group measure is used, the variation from standard performance is likely to be less for the group in total than for individuals within it. For example, the performance range for total district performance would probably be narrower than the range established for individual salesmen within a district.

2. Determine Appropriate Reward: Risk Ratio for Commission Earnings

This refers to the relationship of commission earned at standard performance, to maximum commission earnings available under the plan. A plan that pays 10% of base salary for normal or standard performance, and pays 30% as a maximum commission would have a 2:1 ratio. In other words, the participant can earn twice as much (20%) for above standard performance as he stands to lose for below standard performance (10%).

Reward under a sales commission plan should be related to the effort involved to produce a given result. To adequately encourage above standard results the reward:-risk ratio should generally be at least 2:1. *The proper control of incentive plan payments lies in the proper setting of performance standards,* not in the setting of a low maximum payment for outstanding results that provides a minimum variation in individual earnings. Generally, a higher percentage of base salary should be paid for each 1%R above 100% than has been paid for each 1%R up to 100%R to reflect the relative difficulty involved in producing above standard results.

Once the performance range and reward-risk ratios have been determined the schedule of payments for each performance measure can then be calculated. This will show the percentage of the participant's base salary earned for various performance results (%R) from the point at which commissions start to maximum performance.

Example: For measurement paying 20% of salary for standard performance.

% Base Salary Earned		% of Sales Quota
1% of base salary for each + 1%R	0%	80% or below
	20%	100% (standard performance)
1.33% of base salary for each + 1%R	60%	130% or above

D. Prepare Draft of Sales Commission Plan

After completion of the above steps, a draft of a sales commission plan should be prepared using the outline below as a guide.

Keys to Effective Commission Plans

1. *Get the understanding and acceptance of the commission plan by the managers who will be involved in carrying it out.* They must be convinced of its effectiveness in order to properly explain and "sell" the plan to the salespeople.
2. In turn, be sure the plan is presented clearly to the salespeople so that they have a good understanding of how the plan will work. We find that good acceptance of a sales commission plan on the part of salespeople correlates closely with how well they understood the plan and its effect on their compensation. The salesperson must be convinced that the measurements used are factors which he can control by his selling efforts.
3. Be sure the measurements used in the commission plan encourage the salespeople to achieve the marketing goals of your operation. For example, if sales volume is the only performance measure, the salespeople will concentrate on producing as much dollar volume as possible by spending most of their time on products with high volume potential. It will be difficult to get them to

spend much time on introducing new products with relatively low volume, handling customer complaints, etc. Even though a good portion of their compensation may still be in salary, you can be sure they will wind up doing the things they feel will maximize their commission earnings.

4. One good solution to maintaining good sales direction is to put at least a portion of the commission earnings in an "incentive pool" to be distributed by the sales manager according to his or her judgement. This "pool" can vary in size according to some qualitative measure of the sales group's performance, but the manager can set individual measurements for each of his or her salespeople and reward each one according to how well he or she fulfills his or her goals.

5. If at all possible, you should test the plan for a period of time, perhaps in one or two sales areas or districts. To make it a real test you should actually pay commission earnings to the participants, but the potential risk and rewards can be limited. No matter how well a plan has been conceived, not all the potential pitfalls will be apparent until you've actually operated the plan for a period of time. The test period is a relatively painless way to get some experience.

6. Finally, after the plan is in operation, take time to analyze the results. Is the plan accomplishing what you want it to do, both in terms of business results produced and in realistically compensating salespeople for their efforts?

Section 7

DISTRIBUTION CHANNELS AND DELIVERY SYSTEMS

Producers of goods and services often fail to think a lot about distribution channels, tending to take them as a given rather than as a marketing variable that needs to be planned and managed with the same care as product policy, pricing strategy, and communication efforts. No marketer should take the current distribution channel for its products as fixed, since better alternatives may be available. Distribution decisions should be taken with great care, since they may involve long-term commitments with intermediaries, raise important issues of control over marketplace activities, carry major financial implications, and affect the other elements of the marketing mix.

Distribution decisions are important to producers of both goods and services, but tend to be more complex for the former. Because goods are physical objects, their manufacturers need to find ways of transporting products from the factory to the customer. Should they choose to handle this task themselves or should they delegate it to one or more intermediaries, such as wholesalers and retailers? Service firms, by contrast, usually create and deliver their services at local outlets—"factories in the field," as they have sometimes been called. Restaurants, hotels, hospitals, and universities, for example, all share this characteristic. Services which are heavily information based—such as financial services and the reservations component of airlines, hotels, and rental cars—may centralize some of their information processing activities and then use electronic channels to transmit the desired information either to the customer or to an intermediary. (Exhibit 1 shows the commonly used distribution channel alternatives.)

Producers are not the only organizations that make distribution decisions. Intermediaries such as wholesalers and retailers are also marketing organizations with customers to consider. As service businesses operating in an often highly competitive environment, they too must worry about getting the right product to the customer at the right time and place.

A good starting point for distribution strategies is to consider the market segments the firm wishes to target. Other than looking for a good product, what specific benefits do customers in each segment seek from the buying process? Are they concerned about low prices, easily accessible locations, convenient hours of service, an extensive choice of products under one roof, expert sales assistance? Insights into the needs of each target segment can serve as criteria for selecting the most appropriate channel, since channel intermediaries may vary widely in their ability to perform well on specific attributes.

When managers make distribution decisions, they need to think carefully about the different activities involved in getting the product to the customer. What are these different tasks for a particular type of product destined for a specific market segment? What are

Exhibit 1
SOME DISTRIBUTION CHANNEL ALTERNATIVES

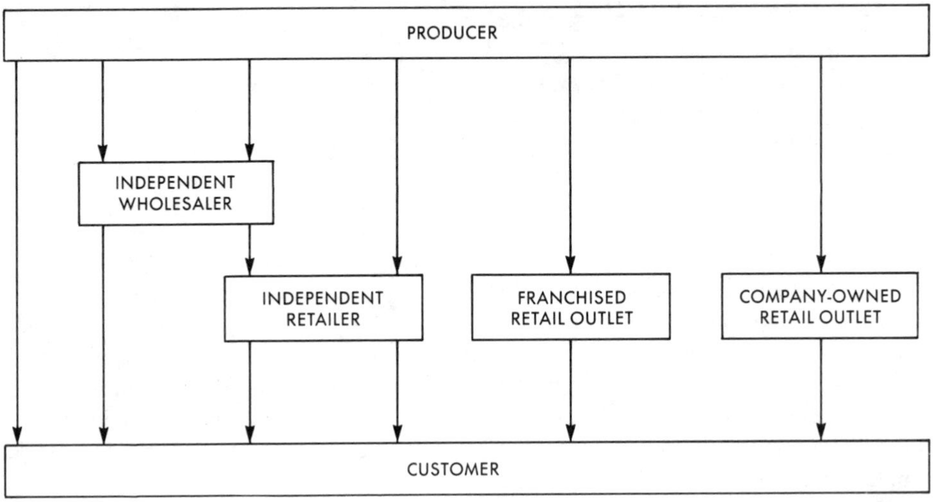

the relative costs of using an intermediary versus doing the work oneself (assuming that the latter is even feasible)? How much control does the marketer lose when certain tasks are delegated to any given intermediary? And what are the competitive implications of using one distribution and delivery strategy over another?

LOGISTICS MANAGEMENT

Logistics (also known as physical distribution management) is concerned with moving and storing goods on their way from the original point of manufacture to the customer.

Physical distribution tasks include transportation, order processing, warehousing, and inventory management. These tasks need to be managed collectively as a *system*, as opposed to focusing on each element separately. Computerization has made it easier for managers to analyze all the variables involved in taking such a systematic approach.

The criteria for selecting the most appropriate physical distribution system include

1. costs,
2. speed,
3. availability, and
4. physical protection.

In determining costs, management must examine the shipping costs associated with alternative transportation modes, the cost of using alternative storage and warehousing facilities, and additional expenses such as packaging, security, and insurance.

Speed often entails a trade-off against cost: for example, airfreight is faster but more expensive than the use of land or water-based transportation modes. On the other hand, some companies have found that by using airfreight they can do away with regional or local warehouses. New approaches to manufacturing, often characterized as Just-in-Time (JIT), may allow a firm to eliminate warehousing altogether.

Availability of the product when and where the customer needs it requires either fast, direct shipment from the factory or the use of intermediaries capable of supplying the product at times and in locations that meet the customer's needs.

Finally, there's the issue of protection. Nobody wants a damaged product or a perishable one that has "gone bad." The choice of packaging must be appropriate to the type of handling that the item will receive during transportation and storage. One reason that some marketers like airfreight is that damage due to careless handling and deterioration due to prolonged storage are often less than when other forms of transportation are used. Protection against pilferage is also an issue; one solution may be a combination of tamper-proof packaging and proper security during shipping and storage.

Distribution goals need to be concerned not only with directly measurable financial costs but also with the cost of lost sales resulting from being out-of-stock, delivering late, or generating customer ill will by delivering damaged goods that have to be replaced. As we will see below, marketers who choose not to distribute their products directly to end-users can contract out most or all physical distribution decisions to intermediaries.

SELECTING CHANNELS FOR MANUFACTURED GOODS

Managers use the term "channels" to describe the ways in which products reach the end-user. Some manufactured goods are sold directly to their ultimate buyers. Others pass through one or more intermediary organizations on their way to the final buyers.

The most common distribution channel for consumer package goods and small consumer durables is

manufacturer
↓
wholesaler
↓
retailer
↓
consumer

In the case of large consumer durables, such as automobiles, there is often no wholesaler in the channel, with cars being shipped directly from the domestic manufacturing plant to the retail showroom. With imported goods, however, an overseas factory may well ship to domestic distributors through an importer who performs certain wholesale roles.

Manufacturers of goods destined for industrial or institutional purchasers are more likely to minimize or eliminate the role of intermediaries. This strategy is most common when the product is custom designed and built for the user, when manufacturer and purchaser are geographically close, or when the product requires special expertise for installation and operator training which the manufacturer is best qualified to deliver. Large computers and specialized medical equipment are examples of goods for which direct distribution tends to be the norm. In most other instances, industrial goods pass through only one intermediary organization on their way to the end user.

Some products, of course, are sold to both industrial and household buyers. In these instances, wholesalers may sell in bulk either to end users who buy in large quantities (and require little in the way of customer service) or to retail stores who also buy in bulk but resell in small quantities.

Channels of distribution can accomplish several important functions for the marketer:

1. transfer ownership of the goods;
2. physically move the goods from the manufacturer's facility to a retail location or even to the purchaser's home or place of business;
3. store the product;
4. grade or sort products (particularly important in the case of agricultural and other natural produce);
5. combine goods from several sources, such as the components of a stereo system, to fill a buyer's needs;
6. provide sales and promotional support for the product;
7. accept orders from customers;
8. grant credit to buyers;
9. offer a variety of customer services, including information and advice, installation, and replacement or repair of items that malfunction while under warranty; and
10. relay market information to the manufacturer.

The manufacturer needs to clarify not only which of these tasks is necessary for success in the marketplace, but also which responsibilities are best assigned to which parties in a given situation.

DISTRIBUTION CHANNELS FOR SERVICES

Unlike manufactured goods, services don't need to be stored or physically transported. For this reason, service businesses are much more likely than manufacturers to create their own delivery systems. However, opportunities may exist for delegating certain tasks to intermediaries. Perhaps the most extensive form of delegation is in franchising, where the originator of the franchise concept—the franchisor—contracts with franchisees to create a tightly prescribed service and deliver it to customers.

In other instances, the service business still holds primary responsibility for creating the service but has the option of employing distributors for a fee or commission to deliver certain components of that service. For instance, banks can choose to deliver simple financial services through their own branches, through free-standing automatic teller machines, or through point-of-sale machines or booths located in retail stores. Airlines and hotels manage their own core businesses—a fleet of aircraft or a chain of hotels—but they rely heavily on travel agents to provide information and promotional support, make reservations, and collect payment in advance from the customers.

Sometimes service intermediaries will specialize in particular types of customers. For instance, some travel agents work only with business clients who make extensive use of airlines, hotels, and rental cars for their clients but have no need for the packaged vacation tours that are the bread and butter of the typical "retail" travel agent.

FINANCIAL IMPLICATIONS OF CHANNEL CHOICE

As was mentioned earlier, channel intermediaries can perform a wide variety of tasks for the producer of a good or service. However, performance of these tasks costs money.

In most instances, the intermediary is rewarded with a commission or margin that is proportional to the price of the product. Margins are usually expressed as a percentage of the final selling price. The size of the margin percentage is often pre-established within the industry, reflecting the costs and risks associated with handling particular categories of products. In situations where both wholesalers and retailers are involved in the channel, retailers usually receive a substantially higher margin, reflecting in part the higher costs associated with a retail location and of making numerous sales in small quantities.

A central issue for the marketing manager is whether he or she is getting good value for money from paying these wholesale and retail margins, which may collectively amount to more than half the recommended selling price for many consumer durables. Would it be cheaper to distribute directly to consumers and have the firm incur the distribution costs? Alternatively, should the firm assume responsibility for certain distribution tasks and seek out distributors who will accept a smaller margin in return for doing less?

A thorough analysis of alternative channel strategies should begin with identification of all distribution tasks and their associated costs, if performed by the producer.

At a minimum, these tasks might include

- Transportation
- Warehousing and other storage
- Maintenance of retail outlets
- Local promotions
- Provision of customer credit
- Handling customer service calls

Although some costs, such as transportation, may be variable costs incurred on a unit by unit basis, others—such as maintaining a warehouse or retail outlet—represent fixed costs which, within certain limits, are independent of the volume of sales. Distributors' margins, by contrast, are variable costs. So the financial desirability of performing one's own distribution functions versus using intermediaries will vary with the volume of sales.

In the case of consumer goods sold to mass markets, it is generally more cost effective for producers to use the services of distributors than to perform all the distribution tasks themselves. However, cost is not the only criterion. Marketers must also consider how much control they give up when they use one or more intermediaries in the distribution channel.

EFFICIENCY VERSUS CONTROL IN CHANNEL SYSTEMS

Marketers use intermediaries because they increase the efficiency of the distribution system. As well, distributors offer specialized skills and knowledge, particularly of local market conditions that most marketers lack and cannot afford the time and expense of acquiring themselves.

However, the use of intermediaries reduces the company's control over a number of important functions. First is price. Although the marketer remains free to suggest the retail price and terms of sale, the retailer calls the shots. Second is retail display. Retailers will tend to emphasize those products that promise the greatest financial return, either directly or as a loss leader to draw customers into the store. Local advertising and promotion are other areas of potential conflict, as are the nature of the sales presentations given by the distributor's own sales force.

The marketing manager needs to consider how much power will be yielded to the distributors. At times, channels may be marked by conflict over which members will exercise the most power: the producer who develops, produces, and markets the product; the wholesaler who controls the interaction with retail outlets (including which outlets get to sell the product); or the retailer who controls direct interactions with the ultimate buyer.

No matter who holds the most power in the channel, success in the marketplace requires that all parties be motivated to work jointly toward achieving sales of the product(s) in question. Distributors run their businesses to make a profit for their owners. Hence they will co-operate with their suppliers only to the extent that this arrangement advances their own enterprise. They are also customers of the producing organization and the marketing concept must be applied to them as well as to end users. In evaluating alternative distributors, the marketing manager needs to ask how well a particular product, backed by specific financial terms and marketing program, will fit the financial and operational goals of each potential intermediary.

LINKING DISTRIBUTION WITH MARKETING MIX STRATEGY

Distribution strategy must be consistent with product policy, pricing strategy, and marketing communication activities. Let's look briefly at each in turn.

PRODUCT POLICY

When targeting specific products at specific markets, competitive advantage is often a key consideration. This may take the form of a distinctive core product but more likely, especially in mature product categories, product differentiation centres on augmentation through a variety of service-related features. The marketing manager needs to think carefully about who will be responsible for providing these augmenting features: the producer, the distributor, or the two acting jointly.

Among the product-related responsibilities to be assigned are

1. Information and consultation
2. Installation (if any)
3. Assembly (if needed)
4. Receipt and replacement of defective merchandise
5. Repairs and maintenance of spare parts inventory
6. Other warranty-related activities

PRICING

Decisions in this area concern both dollar figures and terms of sale.

1. Does the retailer take title to the product or sell only on a consignment basis? The latter approach is sometimes demanded by distributors dealing with a new product which is being marketed by a small firm with no proven track record. Consignment increases the risk to the producer and reduces it for the intermediary.
2. Will the producer agree to accept returns of unsold or damaged merchandise? Can this responsibility be delegated? A powerful manufacturer dealing with weak distributors may be able to enforce such a policy, thereby shifting risk to the intermediaries in the channel.
3. Can the producer set and enforce a recommended retail price, without resorting to illegal behaviour? Alternatively, does the retailer have the sales volume and cost efficiencies to discount deeply without being given a more substantial margin?
4. Can the producer get the distributor to participate in promotional pricing programs, such as cents-off coupons for consumer packaged goods or special discounts? Can the retailer demand special terms from manufacturers competing for shelf space?

ADVERTISING, PROMOTION, AND PERSONAL SELLING

Distributors often play a crucial role in the marketing communication program. Some questions for the marketing manager to consider are

1. Does the distributor rely on a push strategy (generated by the skill and persistence of its own sales force) or does it emphasize a pull strategy (relying on advertising and external promotions to pull prospective customers into the store)?
2. Will the distributor participate financially in co-operative advertising and promotional activities initiated by the producer?
3. Will retail distributors be willing to use point-of-purchase display materials developed by the producer at specific times as part of a national or regional marketing campaign?

EXCLUSIVITY

Producers sometimes seek to limit the sale of a product to selected distributors. Possible reasons for such a choice include: desire to avoid head-to-head competition with competing products; avoidance of price competition between stores (especially between full-service department stores and self-service warehouse outlets); desire to position the product in a way that is consistent with the image and service provided by a certain type of store or distributor; requirement for a high level of familiarity with both the product and the producing firm; demonstrated ability to provide after sales service.

Although exclusive distribution offers important advantages, it takes time to select and nurture the most appropriate intermediaries. The latter may insist upon special terms and support. The downside of exclusivity is first that it limits geographic coverage (making it unsuitable for convenience products) and second that it may be difficult to enforce.

CONCLUSION

Providing "the right product at the right place at the right time" is the primary goal of distribution management. Whether offering physical goods or services, marketers must manage a complex set of distribution tasks and relationships if this goal is to be achieved. Because of cost constraints, distribution strategies often represent a realistic compromise between keeping costs down and maintaining control over all elements of the marketing program.

A poor distribution strategy quickly leads to lost sales and ill will among both distributors and end-users. But a well-designed and properly implemented strategy for distribution and service delivery can yield important competitive advantages.

33 AGROCHEM

Thomas Funk

Mark Vandenbosch

Mr. Stephen Applegate, marketing manager for Agrochem, a small manufacturer of agricultural chemicals in western Canada, was contemplating a major change in distribution strategy for his firm. For many years the company had sold its entire line of farm chemicals through a distribution system consisting of chemical distributors selling to a network of farm dealers who, in turn, sold to farmers. Stephen was now rethinking this policy and analyzing the option of bypassing the distributors and selling direct to farm supply dealers.

BACKGROUND

Agrochem was a relatively small firm in the agricultural chemicals business. Founded in the early 1950s, the company specialized in chemicals for flax in western Canada. It also sold some chemicals for fruits and vegetables, particularly potatoes.

The major product of Agrochem was No-Weed, a post-emergent grass herbicide for flax and potatoes. No-Weed, which has been on the market for over ten years, was the leading grass herbicide used on flax in western Canada. Annual retail sales of No-Weed for flax were estimated by Agrochem to be in excess of $5 million, which represented a market share of 30%. An additional $1 million of No-Weed was sold for potatoes. In addition to No-Weed, Agrochem sold 28 other herbicides, insecticides, and fungicides. Retail sales of the largest of these other products were less than $2 million. The suggested retail price of No-Weed was $44.60 per kilogram, and direct production costs were $20.85 per kilogram. The recommended application rate of the product on flax was one kilogram per hectare.*

In the market area served by Agrochem there were 405,000 hectares of flax. The number of hectares had remained stable over the past ten years, but was expected to decline slightly in the future.

The grass herbicide market in flax was highly competitive. Five brands accounted for the majority of total sales. Of the five, one brand, Dynomite, had the same chemical formulation as No-Weed. There were very minor differences between the two products, but in almost all major respects, they were identical. Many farmers suspected that this was the case, but still had fairly strong preferences for one brand over the other. Dealers, on the other hand, were less likely to have strong brand preferences. No-Weed sold for slightly more per kilogram than Dynomite.

* 1 acre = 0.41 hectares
2.47 acres = 1 hectare

Note: Names and data are disguised.

The other major brands of grass herbicides were different from No-Weed and Dynomite. In general they were less expensive and less effective in controlling a broad spectrum of problem grasses. Both No-Weed and Dynomite were strong chemicals that could cause some damage to the crop if not properly applied. This was not a problem with the other grass herbicides on the market.

CURRENT DISTRIBUTION SYSTEM OF AGRICULTURAL CHEMICALS

The distribution system for agricultural chemicals in western Canada consisted of a four member channel. Typically manufacturers sold to distributors, who sold to local dealers, who in turn sold to farmers. This type of system had been in place a number of years and was used by most agricultural chemical manufacturers.

A typical distributor handled a complete line of agricultural chemicals. For most products they received a 15% margin. They ordered chemicals from manufacturers in the fall and winter and took possession of these chemicals in their warehouses. All distributors had a large sales force of highly trained people who called on dealers to make sales presentations and to negotiate terms. During the busy spring season when nearly 70% of all agricultural chemicals were sold, distributor salespeople spent a great deal of their time monitoring local inventory and arranging shipments between dealers. This allowed dealers who were experiencing short supplies to obtain products from those who may have ordered more than they needed. After the product had been sold, distributor salespeople turned their attention to collecting accounts.

In order to build demand for their products, many distributors had developed elaborate dealer incentive programs. For the most part, these programs consisted of cash, merchandise, or trips the dealer and his or her spouse could earn by meeting certain sales levels. Most distributors also organized dealer meetings in the winter where they got 10 to 15 dealers together for a dinner followed by presentations covering products and programs. Manufacturers were often invited to make presentations during these meetings. Distributors did very little media advertising.

Although distributors liked to receive exclusive rights to carry a manufacturer's product, this was seldom done. Most manufacturers liked to have their product carried by two or three distributors to ensure very broad distribution among dealers. There were four major agricultural chemical distributors in the flax area of western Canada.

Agricultural chemical dealers were local farm supply organizations. Most carried a broad line of farm supplies including chemicals, fertilizer, feed, seed, and petroleum. Chemicals normally accounted for roughly 20% of a dealer's volume. The margins earned by dealers on chemicals averaged about 7%, but varied a great deal because of local competition.

Agricultural chemical dealers received shipment of chemicals in the winter and early spring and held these in local warehouses until they were needed by farmers in April and May. Most dealers simply waited for customers to come to their place of business, although some were beginning to hire salespeople to call on farmers to solicit orders. Some dealers did local advertising. Much of this was co-operative advertising in which manufacturers paid a certain percentage of the cost to have their products featured in an ad. Dealers were an important source of information for farmers and frequently were asked to give advice concerning which chemical product to use.

In the flax area of western Canada there were approximately 200 local farm supply dealers. Ten years ago, most of these were locally owned and operated businesses. However, this was changing. During the last ten years many local dealers had either gone out of business and had been replaced by branches of larger organizations, or were sold to larger organizations and became branch operations themselves. The development of retail chains at the dealer level had grown dramatically in the past ten years. It was estimated that over one-half of the retail outlets in the flax area of western Canada were controlled by five large organizations. The remaining retail outlets were still independent businesses; however, there appeared to be a continuing pressure on many of these businesses to either sell or merge.

From a manufacturer's and distributor's point of view, the growth of chain organizations had major consequences. The most important consequence was in terms of the number of customers they have to deal with. Prior to the emergence of chain organizations, each local dealer was a separate customer; with the chain organizations, many companies were set up to do central buying. As a result, instead of selling to each local outlet, one call on a corporate purchasing agent might be all that was required.

Most agricultural chemicals were highly concentrated and packaged in steel or plastic containers. As a result, transportation and storage did not present special problems. Most agricultural chemicals were produced in the late fall and early winter and shipped to distributor warehouses or, in some cases, directly to larger dealers during January. Products shipped to distributor warehouses remained in the warehouse only until dealer orders were received. Upon receipt of dealer orders, products were either shipped by the distributor to the dealer, or assembled for dealer pickup. Distributor warehouses were seldom more than 32 km away from a dealer. Shipments to dealers occurred during February, March, April, and May. Agrochem estimated shipping and warehousing costs under the current system of distribution (to either distributors or large dealers) was six cents per kilogram. Agrochem had a policy of maintaining safety stocks for all products equal to approximately 25% of expected sales.

Even though distributors take delivery of products in January, they do not pay manufacturers until mid-May. Distributors do not receive payment from dealers until mid-June. The practice of rebilling had become common in the agricultural chemical industry. Under this practice, manufacturers reimbursed distributors for unsold products as of November 1 of each year. For example, if a distributor was holding 500 kg of No-Weed on November 1, Agrochem would reimburse the distributor for that amount. The product itself remained in distributor's or dealer's warehouses, and the distributor or dealer paid for it in the following year. In the past, 15% of sales were rebilled each year. Although manufacturers seldom experienced bad debts when working with distributors, the distributors themselves normally allowed 0.75% of net sales for bad debts.

AGROCHEM DISTRIBUTION

Agrochem's current distribution system is shown in Exhibit 1. At the present time, Agrochem used three distributors—Phillips, Bailey's, and Agro Industries—to reach a total of approximately 200 retail outlets.

The major distributor used by Agrochem was Phillips, one of the larger agricultural chemical distributors in the region with annual sales in excess of $50 million. Agrochem and Phillips had been working together for many years and enjoyed an excellent relationship. Phillips handled a complete line of Agrochem products and had an exclusive distribution arrangement for No-Weed. Agrochem established this exclusive arrangement when No-Weed first came on the market because they felt it would give Phillips additional incentive to push the product. Agrochem had been very satisfied with this arrangement. Although Phillips carried other flax herbicides, they did not carry Dynomite, the major competitor to No-Weed. No-Weed was one of the top three products carried by Phillips. Phillips had 17 salespeople in the market area under consideration.

Bailey's was a small agricultural chemical distributor specializing in the fruit and vegetable markets. They carried a complete line of fruit and vegetable chemicals and only dealt with farm supply outlets in the major fruit and vegetable growing areas of the region.

Exhibit 1
AGROCHEM DISTRIBUTION SYSTEMS

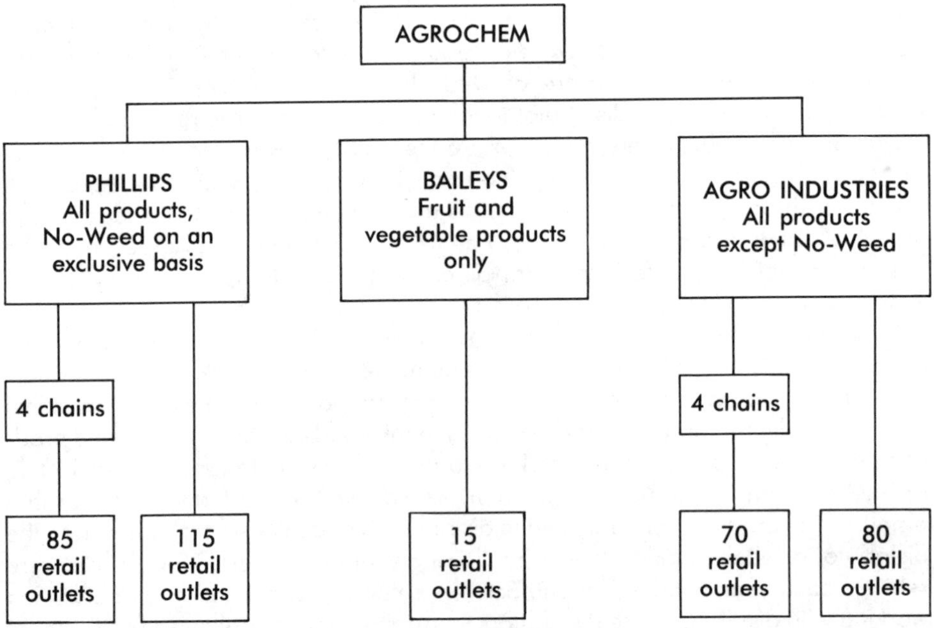

Agrochem also worked with Agro Industries, another large agricultural chemical distributor in the area. Agro Industries carried all of Agrochem's products except No-Weed, which was exclusive to Phillips. Agrochem had worked with Agro Industries for the past four years and had developed a good working relationship with the company. Agro Industries called on many of the same retail outlets as Phillips, but did not deal with as many. Agro Industries handled Dynomite, but not on an exclusive basis.

AGROCHEM SALES PROGRAM

Agrochem had a sales organization consisting of two sales managers, with each supervising five sales representatives. Most of the sales reps had been with the company for a number of years and were quite knowledgeable and experienced in the technical aspects of agricultural chemicals. The responsibilities of sales reps were: to develop a sales plan for the territory, to organize and participate in farmer meetings, to call on key farmers, to get promotional material to dealers, to line up demonstration plots, and to handle complaints. The timing of these activities throughout the year is shown in Exhibit 2.

Exhibit 2
SALES REPRESENTATIVE ACTIVITIES

Time of Year	Activities
September–October	Territory planning, training, vacation
November–January	Get promotional material to dealers Call on key farmers
February–March	Organize and conduct farmer meetings
April–May	Make key farmer calls Line up demonstration plots Check on product availability
June–August	Handle complaints Supervise demonstration plots

Sales representatives call reports indicated that the typical Agrochem sales representative called on each dealer in his or her territory four times a year and made nearly 150 farm calls. A frequency of four calls per day on either dealers or farmers was considered the norm. Agrochem calculated that it took the equivalent of two sales representatives to handle No-Weed sales in flax. On average it cost Agrochem $60,000 per year in salary and expenses to maintain one salesperson.

In addition to sales representatives, Agrochem also sponsored a substantial advertising and promotion program. Last year the company spent $180,000 to support No-Weed. The type and size of Agrochem's advertising and promotion program was very similar to that of other companies in the market.

PROPOSED AGROCHEM DISTRIBUTION CHANGES

Despite the fact that the current distribution system was working well, Mr. Applegate was thinking about making a major change. Although his long-term goal was to eliminate distributors altogether and sell directly to dealers, his short-term plan was less ambitious. As a first step in rationalizing his distribution system, he was contemplating eliminating Phillips as a distributor for No-Weed in the flax market. Phillips would continue to carry No-Weed for potatoes as well as all other Agrochem products. The rest of the distribution system would not be changed in any way. As a result, the only difference would be that Agrochem would assume the distributor's role for No-Weed in flax.

Mr. Applegate's decision to rethink the distribution strategy of his firm was prompted by several considerations. Foremost among his concerns was the fact that several competitors recently had made similar distribution changes. As a matter of fact, at the present time three major chemical companies in the area were selling all or some of their products direct to dealers. The fact that so many other companies were following this approach made Mr. Applegate wonder if he shouldn't be doing the same thing. Another consideration was the lack of market information Agrochem was able to obtain from Phillips. Phillips was very reluctant to provide any market data to Agrochem making it difficult for Agrochem to monitor sales and respond to market changes in a timely manner.

Because of the importance of this decision to the long-run success of his firm, Mr. Applegate decided to investigate his options as thoroughly as possible. Two major types of analysis were proposed: a market research study of farm supply dealers and an analysis of how the proposed change would affect the operations of Agrochem.

MARKET RESEARCH

The market research consisted of interviewing 20 randomly selected farm supply dealers in Agrochem's market area. All interviews were conducted by an independent market research firm. The key findings of the study were

- The average farm supply dealer purchases crop chemicals from three distributors. In general, dealers like to be able to purchase specific products from more than one distributor because they feel this makes price and service more competitive.
- In deciding which products to carry, dealers try to stock those they feel the farmer will want to purchase.
- Most orders are placed with distributors or manufacturers through sales representatives. Very few orders are placed by phone directly to an order desk. Dealers like placing orders through sales representatives because they feel the order will receive personal attention and will be handled promptly and correctly.
- Most dealers receive approximately 75% of their product needs in one large shipment prior to the peak selling season, and then add to this with two or three smaller shipments during the season.
- During the peak selling season, dealers expect delivery within 24 hours of

placing an order. If the warehouse is within 30 km of their outlet, they are quite prepared to pick up orders.

- In many instances, dealers order products from distributors before a final price has been negotiated. Most orders are placed in February and March on items that will not be priced until April.
- Dealers almost always extend credit to their farmer customers. The amount of credit extended and the percentage of customers having trouble meeting their obligations has been increasing.
- Dealers know very little about chemical manufacturers because most of their dealings are with distributors. In general, what they do know about Agrochem and other major chemical companies is favourable.
- Dealers think manufacturers should make a consistently good product, stand behind their product, handle farmer complaints,keep dealers up-to-date on new technology, and make sure dealers and farmers know how to handle chemicals in a safe manner.
- Phillips is the most widely used distributor in the area. In general, it has the best reputation among dealers especially for good prices and excellent sales representative service.
- Dealers have mixed feelings on direct distribution. Some very large dealers strongly favour this approach because they think it is more efficient and will result in better prices for products they buy. Other dealers are a bit skeptical about direct distribution because they think it will reduce competition and increase the number of sales representatives they have to see. Most dealers are of the opinion that direct distribution won't make a big difference one way or another.
- Almost all definitely said they do not feel direct distribution will have any effect on the amount of any manufacturer's product they sell.

OPERATION ANALYSIS

From an operational point of view, the proposed change in distribution was thought to possibly affect several areas of Agrochem's operations.

The first and, in many ways, the most obvious area that might be affected by the change in distribution strategy was physical distribution. Without the distributor, Agrochem must be concerned with obtaining more local warehouses in the market area, as well as making a larger number of small deliveries. In addition, a person to co-ordinate physical distribution would be required. A comprehensive traffic analysis revealed that the new system would result in transportation and warehouse costs of $0.20 per kilogram and the hiring of a distribution and inventory control manager at $40,000 per year.

The credit operation of the company also would be affected. Agrochem would now be responsible for assessing the credit worthiness of customers and collecting accounts. This would require hiring a credit manager at an additional cost of $40,000 per year.

An analysis of the inventory policy of the company suggested that the present 25% safety stock be increased to 35% if direct distribution were adopted. It was thought that the additional inventory would be necessary to ensure that each dealer had sufficient product quantity to meet local demands. Phillips was particularly good at doing this and, therefore, could get by with a lower level of safety stock. It was thought that the current practice of rebilling would be continued with dealers. The cost of funds to Agrochem was estimated to be 11%.

In the past, Agrochem allocated two sales representatives to No-Weed. They knew that this number would have to increase substantially in the future if direct selling were undertaken, but were unsure by exactly how much. They thought that their sales representatives would have to carry out all their existing duties plus call on each dealer an average of once a month. Another agricultural chemical company which sold all its products direct to dealers had eight sales representatives in the area.

DECISION

Mr. Applegate had convened a meeting of the Executive Committee of the company for later in the week to make a final decision on Agrochem's distribution strategy. Based on his assessment of the situation to date, he was leaning toward making the change to direct selling of No-Weed in the flax market. He knew, however, that his colleagues in the company had different points of view. Kenneth Winthrop, the president, was firmly in favour of retaining the current system of distribution; Larry Minor, the executive vice-president, seemed to favour an option in which Agrochem would sell to chains directly and let Phillips service independent accounts. Mr. Applegate wondered if there were other alternatives that might surface at the Executive Committee meeting.

Although on balance Mr. Applegate was in favour of the change, he had a couple of reservations. First of all, he was concerned about Agrochem's ability to negotiate prices with dealers. Phillips was very good at doing this sort of thing and, as a result, they were able to protect their profits. If Agrochem salespeople could not do this as effectively, margins could be eroded.

Another unanswered question concerned how he should deal with the chain organizations if the change to direct selling were implemented. He knew that some of the chains preferred central buying whereas others left the buying decision for chemicals up to local managers. Even where central buying was the preferred method, he wondered if and how often his salespeople would have to call on local dealers. With these thoughts in mind he began preparing his position for the meeting.

34 BOUTIQUE VISON

Marvin Ryder

"It happened again Sunday—Mother's Day," muttered Philip Nephelier, owner of the Boutique Vison, a furrier located in the trendy Queen Street section of Toronto. A member of the Animal Liberation Front surprised Claire Richmond, a recent customer at Boutique Vison, and sprayed her $25,000 mink coat with paint. In the first four months of 1989, three of Mr. Nephelier's customers had been attacked like this, and in each case the fur coat was ruined. "It makes me sick to think about this," he said. "I have a right to sell fur coats, and my customers have a right to wear them without harassment from fringe elements. Maybe I should sell my store. I'm getting too old to fight back."

Over the next few days, Mr. Nephelier thought more about the incident and about selling the store. His nephew, Pierre Gaston, had worked for him for three years before moving to a leading department store chain in 1985 as a retail buyer for women's clothing. While Mr. Nephelier had employed a number of his relatives in Boutique Vison, Mr. Gaston was one of the few who had both a fashion sense and business "smarts." While Mr. Nephelier had been sorry to see his nephew leave, he agreed with Pierre that it would give him broader experience in the fashion business. Two years ago, Pierre had expressed an interest in buying his business. "I'll make him an offer he can't refuse," thought Mr. Nephelier. With that, he sat down and began collecting information to prepare some financial statements.

THE FUR INDUSTRY IN CANADA

In 1985 (the most recent year for which figures were available), more than $105 million of fur pelts were produced in Canada. There were two sources of fur pelts: those taken from animals trapped in the wild (worth $49 million) and those taken from animals raised on fur farms (worth $56 million). In total, the fur trade in Canada accounted for less than one-tenth of one percent of the gross domestic product.

Originally, the settlers of Canada relied on wildlife for food and clothing, and in some remote parts of the country, Canadians still do. European voyages from England and France brought development of the fur trade which, to a large extent, guided the course of exploration, settlement, and economic development of Canada. For two centuries, fur coats were a status symbol and Canadian fur was especially prized. However, the demand for fur pelts had been declining over the last ten years due, in part, to strong anti-fur sentiments aroused by conservationists and preservationists.

Fur farms—or ranches—were a relatively new industry in Canada. In 1937, the value of farm-bred pelts accounted for approximately 40% of production. Since then, the value increased slowly, and in 1985 fur farms accounted for 53% of production.

The number of fur farms fluctuated from 1,083 (during depressed times in the mid-1970s) to 1,584 (in the booming economic period of the early 1980s). Fur farms accounted for 96% of the mink pelt harvest and 63% of the fox pelt harvest, and were located throughout the provinces, though none were located in the territories. Ontario accounted for 37% of the fur farm pelt harvest, while Nova Scotia (19%), Quebec (16%), and British Columbia (14%) accounted for most of the remainder.

To determine the value of the wild harvest, the number of animals trapped and the value per pelt must be considered. In terms of price per pelt, the most valuable furs were polar bear ($623), lynx ($599), grizzly bear ($444), wolverine ($225), and cougar ($179). These prices reflected the relative scarcity of these pelts as in 1985 only 8 grizzly bears, 294 polar bears, 831 wolverines, and 15 cougars were trapped. The pelts that made up 90% of the value of the $49 million harvest were beaver (22%), marten (17%), muskrat (11%), coyote (10%), lynx (9%), fox (8%), raccoon (6%), mink (5%), and rabbit (2%).

Wild furs were harvested throughout the country. Ontario accounted for 27% of the wild fur pelt harvest while Quebec (16%), Alberta (13%), Saskatchewan (10%), Manitoba (10%), British Columbia (10%), and the territories (9%) accounted for most of the remainder. Approximately 250,000 native Canadians were supported through the wild fur harvest. The federal government estimated that if all trapping were to stop it would cost taxpayers $36 million to replace lost food sources. Further, the Ministry of the Environment felt that there would be serious harm done to the wilderness by expanded populations of some animals if minimum trapping quotas were not enforced.

Approximately 275 companies employing 3,000 workers produced fur coats. Two-thirds of these firms were located in Quebec with another 30% located in Ontario. Employee compensation for wages and benefits averaged $20,200 per person, while the total value of fur coats manufactured was $363 million. About two-thirds of these coats were exported. In producing a rabbit coat, 15 pelts were required. Sewing, choosing, and handling pelts so that they produced a coat of uniform colour and quality was an art that could not be easily mechanized. For the most part fur coat manufacturers were small and inconspicuous, drawing little attention from fur protest groups.

There were more than 700 fur retailers operating in Canada with combined retail sales of $300 million and employing approximately 3,500 people. Most establishments operated independently and sold a combination of domestic and imported fur coats. In the United States, a new chain of Jindo fur stores had opened selling Asian pelts, but this company had not shown any interest in the Canadian market. Fur retailers and their customers were the favourite target of animal rights groups.

THE ANIMAL RIGHTS LOBBY

In 1980, only a handful of zealous people talked about animal liberation—the inherent "right" of animals to share the planet with humans, as distinct from merely being protected from wanton cruelty. But by 1989, the movement had grown. In the

United States, one source estimated that there were ten million people (7,000 groups) involved. Estimates of annual budgets of these groups ranged from $200 million to $1 billion. However, when the triple and quadruple counting of names on mailing lists was eliminated and the traditional groups like the Society for Prevention of Cruelty to Animals, voluntary animal shelters, and the city dog pounds were discounted, the movement was seen to be much smaller than headlines suggested. A retired United States Justice Department official estimated that the angry, attention-getting fringe amounted to fewer than 10,000 people.

Most of these belonged to radical-sounding groups like ''Band of Mercy,'' ''Urban Gorillas,'' and the ''Animal Liberation Front.'' These were the people who stealthily approached women and spray-painted their fur coats or liberated lobsters from holding tanks in seafood restaurants. Small though their numbers were, their voices were loud, intimidating, and unceasing. In recent years they could be heard clearly through extensive media coverage.

American game show host Bob Barker announced he would no longer host the Miss Universe pageant because fur coats were among the prizes awarded. First lady Barbara Bush chose not to wear a fur coat to the 1989 presidential inauguration. World famous designers Bill Blass, Caroline Herrera, Oleg Cassini, and Giorgio Armani decided to stop designing fur clothing. Sears, Roebuck and Company, one of North America's largest retailers, announced it would no longer sell fur coats. The core argument of the animal rights movement was well-stated by an anonymous member of the Toronto Humane Society. ''I think if people were shown how animals were raised on farms and were trapped in the wild, they would be outraged.'' Animal rights groups argued that modern fur-farming techniques meant a cruel existence for animals. They were subjected to cramped conditions and their movements were severely restrained.

''One of the things we are concerned about is fur farming and trapping in the wild,'' said Bill Bradley of the Canadian Vegans for Animal Rights group in Toronto. ''Vegans'' were a radical type of vegetarian who disdained the use of all animal products, be it leather, milk, or wool. They were against using animals for entertainment or even as pets (which was seen as confinement). ''Our fight and debate is to stop cruelty.'' Without legislation, he said, there was no incentive for farmers or trappers to do anything other than what was economically expedient. Making money and humanitarianism were not always the same thing. ''I don't think the issue will be dealt with until it is legislated,'' said Bradley.

Fighting by the ''official'' animal rights groups took many forms—protests, marches, demonstrations, advertising, brochures, and speeches. All of it had a very strong message, as illustrated by the copy from an ad sponsored by Friends of Animals:

> More than 100 million innocent are killed each year by gassing, electrocution, strangulation, neck breaking, clubbing and leg-hold trapping. All for people to indulge in the beauty of their fur. It's time to stop following the whims of fashion. Instead to set our own standards. To become less callous and more compassionate. Because it's not just our world. It's their world, too.

With this kind of campaign, the anti-fur lobby had many successes. There was no pretty way to show death, and the lobby was able to exploit this on an emotional basis. The European Parliament banned the importing of seal pelts, and left-wing members annually proposed banning all fur imports. The Princess of Wales announced she would not wear fur. In the United States more than 300 separate pieces of legislation were introduced at the federal and state levels to restrict trapping. In many cases enactment of regulations took place without the participation of the fur industry.

REACTIONS FROM THE FUR INDUSTRY

"The basic problem is that a great many animal welfare groups transpose human feelings to animals. That's not a valid thing to do. Animals aren't human. Just because something would make a human uncomfortable doesn't mean it will be uncomfortable for an animal." So said Sue Johnson spokesperson for the Ontario Federation of Agriculture. She believed attempts to promote animal welfare were "thinly disguised efforts to promote vegetarianism." She claimed it wouldn't matter if the farmer or trapper brought his animals into the house, gave them a bed and a bathroom. "The problem from their perspective is that the animals are used for meat, fur, and leather in the end."

But the fur industry was beginning to fight back against the forces of "bleeding-heart activism" using the same weapon that had ensnared them in the past—publicity. "Unless the fur industry mounts a significant and effective public awareness program," said Henry Lawson, executive director of the Fur Institute of Canada, "today's young people will be unalterably affected by anti-fur propaganda." One supporter of the fur industry is Pierre Berton, noted Canadian television personality and author. He has noted that: "The farther you are away from the wilderness, the more chance you have of becoming an animal rights advocate."

To guard against this fate, Canada's furriers formed the Fur Industry Public Awareness Committee (FIPAC) in 1985. It enlisted influential organizations representing Canadian native people in the pro-trapping cause. A delegation led by Georges Erasmus, national chief of the Assembly of First Nations, spent two weeks in Europe presenting the pro-trapping case to politicians, animal activists, and the media. As a result of such representations, both Greenpeace and the World Wildlife Fund agreed to tone down their opposition to trapping.

Through news releases, brochures, and speeches, the fur industry portrayed itself as more sensitive to the natural environment than many of its city-dwelling critics. One Fur Institute brochure invoked ancient Cree mythology and Albert Schweitzer to make the point that killing animals was part of the natural order of things. "We know that Nature is far crueler than man. It doesn't allow Bambi to sit next to the otter and mink and tell stories at night."

The Fur Institute also stressed that trappers used humane trapping methods, used the entire animal, and did not harvest endangered species. They also pointed out that the infamous leg-hold trap was now illegal in most Canadian jurisdictions.

The fur industry believed they were gaining ground against an anti-trapping, anti-farming lobby that they regarded as increasingly hysterical and misinformed. "There are people out there who believe you shouldn't even kill *rats*,'' said FIPAC Chairman Joshua Hanson. ''You can't deal with people like that on a rational level.''

Fur farming had some benefits. The use of modern genetic principles had helped to improve fur-farming techniques. New colours of mink were developed which expanded the variety of combinations and styles of fur garments, increasing potential consumption. ''Unless an animal is treated in the most humane way, is fed in the best possible manner, and is watched for diseases, we're not going to have a healthy pelt.''

The fur industry was also consumer driven. Substitutes for furs did not constitute a threat to the industry. Anti-fur activism contributed to the introduction and promotion of imitation furs in the early 1970s, but the demand was low. Although they had some effect on sales of the cheapest fur garments at the time of their introduction, this effect had not persisted. Imitation fur coats were usually purchased by women whose household disposable income was much lower than that of women who bought real fur coats.

While the anti-fur movement was very strong and effective, a consumer survey showed that only 4% of consumers or potential consumers in the core age group of 26 to 35 were against killing animals. One-third of women said they either owned or had owned a fur coat. Only 10% of this fur-owning group had stopped wearing the coat because of the animal rights issue. Still, one-third of women said they would never want to own a fur coat. More often, reasons for not planning to purchase a fur coat were lack of interest in furs, allergies to fur, dislike of furs, and, of course, inability to afford a fur coat.

Over the last three years, sales of North American furs had declined in Europe by 40% and in North America by 20%. Fur retailers blamed the recent mild winters, layoffs (due to mergers and a stock market downturn) in the affluent financial and accounting communities, and increased competition from the Jindo chain.

BOUTIQUE VISON

Philip Nephelier emigrated from France in 1950. As he had been very successful in the fashion business in Paris, he opened a women's clothing store called ''La Parisienne'' on Queen Street near Spadina Avenue in Toronto, Ontario. In his first five years of operation, he experimented with his product mix and soon settled on selling women's coats made of various materials. It was not until the 1960s, with the increasing affluence of Canadians and Torontonians in particular, that he specialized further to the field of fur coats and renamed his store ''Boutique Vison'' (translation ''Mink Shop'').

According to Mr. Nephelier, ''The 1960s were a great time to be selling fur in Toronto. All the women wanted to act like Jacqueline Kennedy. Fashion had been discovered and the height of fashion was owning two or three fur coats for formal occasions. My clientele consisted of older ladies between the ages of 35 to 70. Younger people were more interested in blue jeans and t-shirts.''

In the 1970s, Spadina Avenue became home to many retail and wholesale establishments selling furs. Rather than lose business, volume increased as more and more people travelled to the area just to shop for furs. The businesses that lost sales were located outside the district. Mr. Nephelier continued: "Tastes changed little in the seventies. Women still wanted fox and mink coats. Seal coats declined in popularity. That is when the animal rights groups first had an impact on my business. They passed out their brochures, held a few marches, and focused the media on the seal hunt. I suppose the sight of baby seals being clubbed to death did not help the matter. But people simply switched from buying seal to something else. They did not stop buying fur.

"I should have sensed that the animal rights movement wouldn't die out. The success with seals in the seventies gave them strength. In the eighties they demanded that sales of all fur end. They became more militant. One day in 1985, I found swastikas spray-painted on my front windows. After one of my neighbour's stores had been broken into and some of the merchandise shredded with knives and covered in paint, I had iron bars installed on the windows and doors to protect myself. It was like working in a war zone.

"In 1988, it got worse. Periodically small crowds of animal rights activists would gather in front of my store and harass old friends and potential customers. I called the police several times and they did what they could, but the activists were never far away. In late 1988, I came to the store one Monday morning to find several leg-hold traps filled with stuffed animals chained to the front of my store.

"But then it got even worse. In the first four months of 1989, six different women wearing fur coats were surprised while walking down the street. In each case, a group of people, wearing animal masks, sprayed her coat with paint. Three of those women were long-term customers of mine. True, they weren't injured and their insurance companies reimbursed them for the loss. Still, at 69, I don't know what to do. I don't want to fight a war. I don't have the strength or the determination I once had.

"I'm not a callous person. The treatment of animals touches on our most basic philosophical views. George Bernard Shaw said, 'animals are my friends . . . and I don't eat my friends.' Rene Descartes took the opposite view when he said, 'Beasts abstract not. I think therefore I am.' I am troubled when animals are subjected to unnecessary harm as in a cock or dog fight. We are upset about pit bulls roaming our streets, but we don't do anything about it. There is nothing illegal about selling fur coats, and it is no more harmful than having a pit bull.

"I am getting to the age where I would like to retire. I'm doing a pretty good business though sales are down 10% from a year ago. This was the first time in the last few years that sales or profits have gone down. I would really hate to close the store down, though. I don't want those animal rights people to think they've had a victory. I'll put together a proposal and talk to Pierre about buying the store."

THE PROPOSAL

In May 1989, Philip Nephelier had his accountant prepare an income statement (Exhibit 1) and balance sheet (Exhibit 2). Then he made the following offer to Pierre. He would sell the business to Pierre for $600,000 asking for half the amount in cash and the remainder to be paid over five years at 10% interest. Mr. Nephelier would take $75,000 of investments with him (see Exhibit 2). Pierre would get the land and

Exhibit 1

INCOME STATEMENT FOR BOUTIQUE VISON

Revenues	1989*	1988
Sales	$523,467	$580,432
Other income	14,327	12,213
Total income	$537,794	$592,645
Expenses		
Cost of goods sold	$245,405	$282,090
Sales staff	60,365	57,098
Interest charges	33,085	31,465
Heat, light, & telephone	10,448	9,967
Depreciation	8,543	8,706
Occupancy expenses**	32,504	29,890
Advertising/Promotion	72,554	69,651
Association membership	5,000	5,000
Total expenses	$476,904	$493,867
Income before tax	$ 60,890	$ 98,778

* Estimates based on year-end of June 30, 1989
** Includes property and city taxes

Exhibit 2

BALANCE SHEET FOR BOUTIQUE VISON

	1989*	1988
Assets		
Cash/Investments	$112,114	$103,487
Accounts receivable	25,765	22,187
Inventory	350,987	308,765
Total current assets	$488,866	$434,439
Fixed assets (land, buildings/ store fixtures)	$155,876	$152,347
Less: accumulated depreciation	113,947	105,404
Total fixed assets	$ 41,929	$ 46,943
Total assets	$530,795	$481,382
Liabilities		
Accounts payable	$ 8,763	$ 8,654
Notes payable	185,609	137,539
Total short-term liabilities	$194,372	$146,193
Retained earnings	$336,423	$335,189
Total liabilities and retained earnings	$530,795	$481,382

* Estimates based on year-end of June 30, 1989

the store on Spadina Avenue, all the store fixtures, cash (difference), and remaining assets and liabilities. The store was relatively small (about 74 m^2* with an unused one-bedroom apartment on the second floor and no real basement). The land and store were originally purchased for $45,000 and today were worth about $400,000, based on recent sales of property in the area.

After Pierre received the proposal he thought that with some cost cutting and improved sales, he could earn a good return on his investment. He would terminate one of the two full-time sales staff, add part-time help if necessary, especially if Sunday shopping came to the area, and make some needed repairs and store improvements using his own "sweat equity." Not married, he had lived for seven years with a clothing designer who enthusiastically supported the idea of buying the store and offered to help Mr. Gaston as necessary. He estimated that he could rent the apartment for $600 a month and he could drop the full association membership for an associates membership at $1,000. Finally, he thought that in 1990, he could not only get back the 10% in sales his uncle "lost" but he could add on 5% more. While financing was somewhat of a problem, Mr. Gaston had accumulated about $200,000 in savings and was confident that he could raise whatever additional money was needed.

"I think I'll accept my uncle's offer," thought Mr. Gaston, "but I'll just have one last look at everything before I make my final decision."

* 1 m^2 = 10.76 sq. ft.

35 DESCHÊNES ET FILS

Marc Dubuc

Marc Filion

In the spring of 1980, the marketing director of Deschênes et Fils Ltd. (DFL) of Montreal was asked by one of the co-owners, Mr. Jacques Deschênes, to study the possibility of expanding the business. DFL was one of Canada's largest wholesalers of plumbing and heating supplies and held a dominant position in the Montreal market. Mr. Deschênes had become concerned because the company's most important market, new housing construction, had been declining for the past few years. DFL's major source of sales was plumbing contractors who focused on plumbing installations in new residential units. Further, a growing number of plumbing supplies were being sold by retail chains to the "do-it-yourself" market. Recently, these retail chains had started buying direct from manufacturers of plumbing equipment. Mr. Deschênes asked the marketing director to prepare a plan which examined the expansion possibilities open to DFL.

THE BUSINESS

DFL began in 1940 when François Deschênes acquired the stock of a small plumbing wholesaler. Over the years the company grew, and the three sons of François Deschênes became involved and eventually took over the business from their father, who retired. In 1970, a family decision was made that saw one son, Jacques, and two employees purchase the business from the remaining two sons.

That same year, DFL joined P & H Wholesalers Ltd., a buying group of plumbing and heating wholesalers across Canada. Each member of the group of 17 wholesalers had annual sales exceeding $1 million. The buying group had considerable purchasing power which enabled them to obtain plumbing and heating products from manufacturers at very competitive prices. Each wholesaler also continued to purchase direct from manufacturers when they could obtain low prices. For several years, Jacques Deschênes was president of P & H Wholesalers.

By 1980, DFL was one of the ten largest plumbing and heating wholesalers in Canada, even though the company operated only in the Montreal area with a main office and two branches. DFL employed 135 people, including 12 sales representatives. The reasons for DFL's success was due, in large part, to the fact that the company had always focused on the wholesaling of plumbing and heating supplies. DFL considered itself a true wholesaler because it promoted products and provided technical assistance to help its clients solve their problems. The major focus of DFL's efforts were 1,500 customers in the Montreal area, most of whom were plumbing contractors.

DFL was well known and highly regarded for its customer orientation. The company frequently organized various industry activities including information clinics and product shows and exhibits. DFL contributed to the programs put on by the Canadian Institute of Plumbing and Heating, and representatives of the firm were active in making presentations in CEGEPs (Community Colleges) on the industry. The company offered many courses on various aspects of products and new developments to industry members. In brief, DFL was a leader in the plumbing and heating business in Canada and a dominant force in the Montreal area.

Product Lines

DFL stocked more than 10,000 different items and offered prompt delivery to plumbing and heating contractors via eight company-owned trucks. The principal products distributed by DFL were (1) a complete range and selection of bathroom and kitchen appliances (medicine cabinets, toilets, sinks, bathtubs, whirlpools, showers, faucets, accessories, etc.), (2) water heaters, (3) gas and wood furnaces, (4) ducting systems for heating, (5) water and sump pumps, and (6) plumbing repair equipment (pipes, joints, elbows, various repair pieces). DFL also distributed a wide variety of other products and, in total, carried approximately 500 product lines in inventory.

THE INDUSTRY

The distribution network for plumbing and heating supplies is shown in Exhibit 1. For many years, the distribution system could be described as a "traditional" channel where manufacturers sold to wholesalers, who, in turn, sold to retailers and plumbing and heating contractors. In this situation, wholesalers had a considerable amount of power in the channel because they could influence, to a degree, which manufacturer's brands were carried and promoted.

In recent years, this "traditional" channel had been changing. While there were a fair number of manufacturers, the industry was composed of a few very large firms (for example, Crane, American Standard) and a number of smaller companies. The larger manufacturers began dealing directly with retail chains (for example, Canadian Tire, Sears) and bypassing the wholesalers. In doing this, the large manufacturers could market their brands to retail buyers. These manufacturers also manufactured private brands for some of the largest retail chains. However, the majority of manufacturers' sales were still through plumbing and heating wholesalers.

DFL and other wholesalers had been supplying retail chains, plumbing stores, and plumbing and heating contractors. Now the retail chains were buying from both the wholesalers and manufacturers. Individual retail plumbing stores continued to buy from wholesalers but were losing some of their retail sales to the chain stores who were regarded as more effective marketers. The plumbing and heating contractors continued to buy all their supplies and equipment from the wholesalers. These contractors tended to specialize in a particular type of construction (for example, residential, institutional, commercial).

Another development in recent years was that some plumbing and heating wholesalers had started selling to the consumer market. Typically, these sales were a small

Exhibit 1
DISTRIBUTION NETWORK FOR PLUMBING AND HEATING SUPPLIES

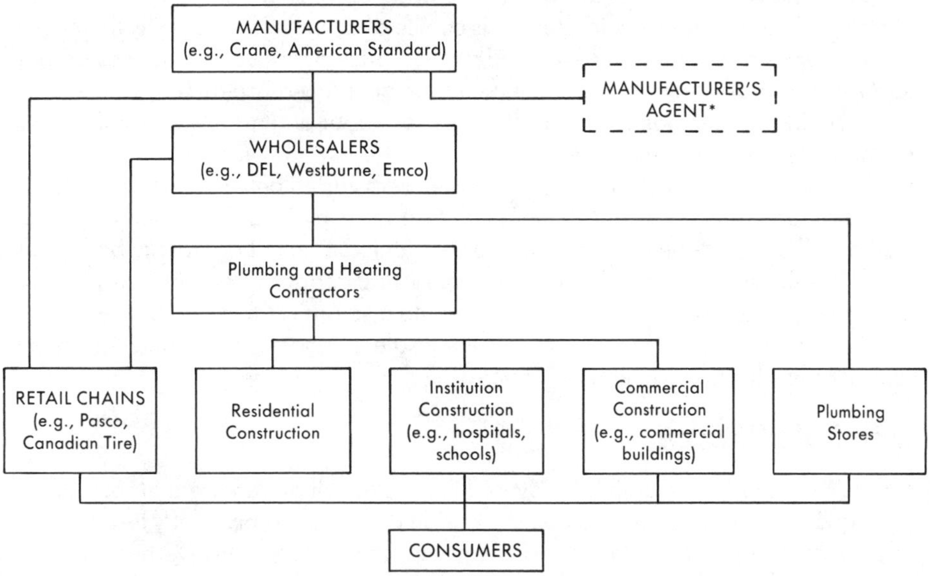

* A significant number of manufacturers used agents to promote the sale of their products to wholesalers and other channel members.

part of their business and were handled through a retail outlet that was physically part of the wholesale operation. DFL did not sell direct to customers.

Some executives in the plumbing and heating business wondered whether the "traditional" distribution system would change even more in the next few years. They pointed to the electrical products business (electrical fixtures, etc.) which had changed rather markedly. Now manufacturers sold directly to all channel members including the larger electrical contractors. In this industry the traditional influence of the wholesaler had declined dramatically, and some electrical wholesalers were fighting to survive.

Because most plumbing and heating wholesalers, including DFL, were private companies, sales and profit figures were not available. However, Dun and Bradstreet Canada provides key business ratios for various businesses. Exhibit 2 contains information for a number of wholesale businesses, including hardware, plumbing, and heating wholesalers. In addition, Statistics Canada prepares information on the sales and revenues for plumbing contractors in Canada who each had average sales of $302,800 and net profits of $15,700. Total revenues for plumbing contractors were $2.04 billion. Total sales of plumbing and heating equipment and supplies for Canada in 1979 were $1.46 billion.

Plumbing Contractor–Wholesaler Relationship

In general, a plumbing contractor used three to six wholesalers to satisfy his needs for plumbing and heating materials. Prices and purchase allowances were the most important factors for the contractor in his choice of a wholesaler. Loyalty to any given wholesaler was tenuous and depended a lot on price as the contractor was primarily interested in maximizing profits. When contractors placed orders with wholesalers it was usually on the basis of a best guess of requirements; few plumbers used sophisticated ordering methods.

On average, the gross margins for wholesalers varied between 20% and 25% for most products. However, the pricing structure used by DFL and other wholesalers was complex and depended on a number of factors. First, the quantity bought by a plumber would result in different allowances and rebates. Second, the plumber's specialty and the type of customer served would also affect the price charged. Finally, plumbers could choose between many wholesalers. In total, these factors frequently allowed the plumber to negotiate prices.

DFL Sales Force

Twelve DFL sales representatives covered the metropolitan Montreal area. All twelve were qualified technicians who could, in addition to selling products, furnish advice and practical recommendations to plumbing contractors. On average, the sales representatives had fifteen years' experience with the company.

Since most of the products that DFL sold were nondifferentiated, it was important for the sales representatives to visit customers regularly in order to fill the client's inventory needs. In addition to being an "order taker" during these visits, the representative also discussed various aspects of the business. These included inform-

Exhibit 2

WHOLESALERS—KEY BUSINESS RATIOS, 1980

Line of Business (and number of concerns reporting)	Cost of Goods Sold	Gross Margin	Current Assets to Current Debt	Profits on Sales	Profits on Tangible Net Worth
	Percent	Percent	Times	Percent	Percent
Wholesale Trade (37,355)	82.9	17.1	1.33	1.89	14.98
Hardware, Plumbing and Heating (1,457)	80.5	19.5	1.53	1.65	11.80
Lumber and Building Products (4,387)	82.0	18.0	1.46	2.19	15.12
Electrical Machinery (1,785)	76.4	23.6	1.40	1.48	10.84

Source: Dun and Bradstreet Canada

ing the clients of new products available on the market, any new developments in customer tastes, and the upcoming DFL promotions. As well, the representatives helped solve technical problems the plumber was facing.

An important task of the DFL representatives was to identify when a call for bids was forthcoming to supply plumbing materials for government or private contracts. The representatives obtained information on the project in question including the due date, the particulars of the project, and any special specifications for the project. DFL had won a large number of bidding contracts in the Montreal area.

The sales representatives also participated in activities organized by DFL. These activities, which could be classified as public relations, included information clinics and trade shows.

In an interview published in a local trade magazine, Jacques Deschênes spoke of DFL's strategy: "The technical services of DFL are our best selling tool. These are what really bring the clients to us and what makes us not just a supplier, but also a partner."

Economic Conditions

The plumbing and heating industry was closely tied to the construction industry, particularly new residential construction. As shown in Exhibit 3, a number of economic factors had had a negative impact on the construction industry in recent years, particularly with respect to the housing market.

From 1976 to 1979, real gross domestic product increased modestly, but the forecast for 1980 showed a substantial decline in the growth rate. This was attributed in part to a recession occurring in the United States. The unemployment rate was predicted to remain at approximately 7.5% for 1980. The inflation rate, as measured by the consumer price index, was forecast to increase to over 10% for the first time

Sales to Tangible Net Worth	Collection Period	Sales to Inventory	Fixed Assets to Tangible Net Worth	Current Debt to Tangible Net Worth	Total Debt to Tangible Net Worth
Times	Days	Times	Percent	Percent	Percent
7.91	43	6.4	38.4	194.5	241.7
7.71	47	5.7	25.5	164.4	200.8
6.90	44	6.3	36.5	148.3	199.0
7.33	64	5.3	28.2	222.5	269.8

Exhibit 3
SELECTED ECONOMIC INDICATORS, CANADA, 1977–1980

	1977	1978	1979	1980*
Real Gross Domestic Product (% change)	3.6	4.6	3.9	1.5
Consumer Price Index (% change)	7.9	8.8	9.2	10.2
Residential Construction ($ millions)	13,126	13,780	14,267	13,872
Housing starts ('000s)	246	228	197	159
Single detached	106.1	112.7	109.1	88.1
Semi-detached	19.0	18.4	16.3	11.2
Row	26.5	19.1	13.2	11.4
Apartment and other	94.4	77.8	58.4	48.3
(% change)	−10.1	−7.3	−13.5	−19.5
Unemployment Rate (%)	8.1	8.3	7.4	7.5
Five-year Mortgage Rate (%)	10.3	11.5	13.6	15.7

Source: Statistics Canada, various publications
* Estimates for 1980

in many years. This was accompanied by increases in mortgage rates from 10% in 1977 to over 15% in 1980. The impact of inflation, interest rates, and the general economic conditions had a serious effect on new housing starts. In 1976, 246,000 houses were built in Canada. The forecast for 1980 was 159,000, a decline of 35% in four years. In fact, if interest rates continued to climb or remained at these high levels, it was likely that housing starts would decline even further.

The net effects of these economic conditions were twofold. First, home-builders and buyers faced a great deal of uncertainty which had a negative impact on demand. Second, the market for home renovation was expanding. As the cost of new housing increased, many families decided to renovate their homes, rather than purchase new ones. It was estimated that the size of the home renovation market was worth $3.5 billion in 1976 and would increase at a rate of 30% each year. As well, it appeared that more of the renovations were being done by the home-owners on a do-it-yourself basis to combat the high cost of contractors.

Changing Distribution Systems

As a result of these economic conditions, the do-it-yourself market was growing. Most sales to this market were being captured by retail chain stores (for example, Canadian Tire, Pascal, Beaver Lumber, Sears) who aggressively pursued this market. With the heating and supply manufacturers beginning to deal directly with these retailers, wholesalers started losing sales to this segment. In response, in early 1980, two Canadian wholesalers started new programs aimed at this market.

An Ontario wholesaler, Barrie Plumbing and Electrical Supply, created a retail system called "Homestead Plumbing Warehouses." Barrie Supply set up plumber contractors in retail stores and provided a complete marketing program, including professional advertising, store layout and fixtures, materials to be sold at retail, price lists, and promotion. These retail establishments were designed to serve the handyman.

The cost to the individual plumber for obtaining a Homestead Plumbing Warehouse was $75,000. This included the cost of store design, layout and installations, participation fee, initial inventory, materials, advertising, store fixtures, etc. The plumber essentially "walked into" the store and began operations. The participation contract was for two years and was renewable on the condition that the store owner did not sell products other than those supplied by Barrie Supply or another vendor approved by Barrie Supply. Normally, Barrie Supply furnished all stock for participants.

The second program began in the Quebec City region, where a wholesaler, Roger Falordeau, originated the "Falro" plan, a variation on the Ontario operation. Here, a number of plumbing contractors joined together under the Falro umbrella and opened retail stores. The contractors all used the Falro name, paid a fee for general advertising of the name, and usually bought their supplies from Roger Falordeau. The advertising emphasized professional competence and sales and service supported by expert advice with particular reference to the renovation market.

RETAIL OPTIONS

Based on his assessment of economic conditions, the new distribution structures emerging, and the resources and objectives of the firm, the marketing director had to decide if and how DFL should enter the retail market for plumbing and heating supplies. In particular, he was concerned because the plumbing and heating market in Quebec was still primarily a traditional manufacturer-wholesaler-retailer system. If plumbing contractors felt that any new proposal was cutting into their business, they might react negatively. Thus, a major issue was whether the retail store should be operated by qualified plumbers or sales staff who had some knowledge of plumbing. The target market, the handyman, could clearly benefit from technical assistance regarding renovations and installations. On the other hand, plumbing contractors were independent businesspeople who might be unwilling to accept the role of employee or of being told how to operate the business. As well, many plumbing contractors were unfamiliar with retail marketing practices, and it was questionable whether they could effectively compete against the retail chain stores.

After carefully reviewing all the existing types of plumbing stores, the marketing director felt that if DFL opened retail stores they should have certain common characteristics and operating features.

The stores would have a retail selling area of about 185 m^2.* An initial fee of $25,000 would cover the initial inventory, renovations, and display stands (costing $3,000 to $5,000). The store would carry eight to ten bath models, ten toilet models, six sink models, and four show models of showers. Attractive displays would be used to promote the sale of these and other plumbing products.

The marketing director had thought of a name for the stores, Plomberium, which

* 1 m^2 = 10.76 sq. ft.

comes from two words, ''plumbing'' and ''atrium,'' a Latin word meaning ''meeting place.'' As well, he thought of a slogan which could be used if the stores were run by plumbing contractors. ''The real plumbing specialists.'' An advertising budget would be established and divided between newspaper ads and catalogues. The marketing director planned to have a designated trading territory for each store, and no other store would compete in that area. The marketing director calculated that a store would break even with annual sales of $250,000 based on an average gross margin of 25%. He felt that with a good marketing program, within two or three years an individual store could generate sales of $450,000.

Having completed his initial concept of the stores, the marketing director then identified the following four types of contractual arrangements that might be used: company stores, joint ventures, voluntary groups, and franchises.

Company Stores

Urban centres represented the major part of the handyman market. Large company stores with a selling area of 465 m^2 to 930 m^2 could be established to serve these markets effectively. In the urban areas, unlike the suburbs and rural areas, it would be preferable to open large stores in order to serve a more diverse range of customers. Because the cost of starting up these larger stores would exceed $25,000, DFL would own the stores. While ideally it would be useful to have plumbers own the stores, this was not feasible because few plumbers had the necessary capital to purchase the stores. It also was unlikely that many plumbers would be willing to manage these stores on a salary or commission basis. However, larger stores would probably be an effective means of competing with the retail chains in the urban areas.

It was not clear how plumbing contractors would react to DFL if the company pursued this strategy. One possibility was that the contractors would view this move as an attempt by DFL to promote the handyman business at the expense of the plumbing contracting business.

Joint Ventures

A second possibility would be for DFL and individual plumbing contractors to form partnerships in the retail stores. DFL would finance the opening of the store, and during the first year of operation, DFL would cover about 90% of the operating costs and the plumbers would pay 10% of the costs. The profits would be distributed on a 90/10 split, and in the second year the plumber would reinvest his profits in the store. The split would then be about 80/20. As the plumber continually reinvested his profits, he would take over a larger part of the operations. After some years, the split will be 50/50. In this way, DFL would be sure of maintaining a reasonable degree of control over the retail stores as well as ensuring that the plumbers would be motivated partner/owners.

Voluntary Groups

This option was based on a system similar to that developed by Barrie Supply in Ontario. Retail stores of about 185 m^2 would be established. Plumbers would join the voluntary group and own the store. The plumber would pay an initial fee of $25,000 and receive DFL's set-up services and technical advice. The fee covered an "entry cost" of about $4,000 and included initial stock, store signs, and equipment. The entry fee represented permanent access to DFL's services for store layout/setup, sales and promotion techniques, management advice, etc. As for advertising, each store would be charged about $150 per month for the first year of operation, $180 per month for the second year, and $200 per month in subsequent years. The plumber would be the legal owner of the store but would operate within certain guidelines and purchase products through DFL.

Franchises

This option closely resembled the previous alternative. The plumber would pay an entry fee of $4,000 and receive the same services from DFL. The plumber would be required to pay for the store equipment and the initial stock and would also pay a monthly fee for advertising. As in the previous options, the plumber would be required to purchase stock from DFL but, with this option, would pay a certain percentage of gross sales to DFL each month. The franchise option would require plumbers to follow policies determined by DFL with respect to store fixtures, sales methods, marketing methods, accounting methods, etc.

If franchises were adopted, DFL would prepare extensive and complete operational plans for them. All activities would be programmed in advance, and the plumber would have to do little more than follow the plan to ensure a well-managed operation. Thus, the operational plan would detail all procedures dealing with sales, promotion, advertising, accounting, personnel management, and ordering stock.

The major difference between the franchising option and the volunteer group option was that, while in both cases the plumber received advice on store management and had some latitude in day-to-day operations, the franchise option was far more constraining in that it required the plumber to follow precise methods of operation. In simple terms, the plumber was under DFL's control to a greater degree with the franchise option. This also had the advantage in DFL's view of "building" more marketing expertise into the operation.

Having reviewed the situation and laid out the options, the marketing director began to prepare a report for Mr. Deschênes. He knew that Mr. Deschênes would be very interested in whether DFL should proceed into the retail market, and if the recommendation was positive, what type of store would be opened.

36 GRANVILLE ISLAND BREWING COMPANY

Shirley F. Taylor
John D. Claxton

In early 1986, Mitch Taylor, founder and president of Granville Island Brewing Company (GIBCO), sat contemplating the future of his company. GIBCO was the first cottage brewery in British Columbia. The brewery and an attached retail outlet were located on Vancouver's Granville Island and had been in operation for nearly two years. The brewery's primary product, Island Lager, appeared to be well accepted, with demand often exceeding supply. However, the cyclical nature of the beer market and changing competitive conditions were a continuing cause of concern.

Mr. Taylor's objective for GIBCO was to build a small capacity brewery producing an ultra premium quality beer and by focusing on Vancouver eventually capture 1% of the provincial beer market. Recent expansion of production capacity and distribution coverage were steps towards these objectives. GIBCO's growth opportunities looked promising; however, Mr. Taylor's concerns included the following:

1. "cold beer stores," a new type of retail outlet, seemed both a threat to GIBCO's brewery store and an opportunity for broader distribution;
2. GIBCO's distribution in restaurants and bars was not expanding as quickly as planned;
3. Sunday beer sales were no longer exclusive to GIBCO's brewery store;
4. other cottage breweries were being licensed in the province;
5. product selection and space utilization in the brewery store needed review;
6. whether the product line should be expanded to include draft and light beers had to be examined, and
7. the idea of a "beer garden" added to the GIBCO brewery facility also required further study.

Mr. Taylor's major uncertainty was how to deal with these interrelated concerns and, in particular, how to set priorities for the GIBCO management team. His long-term goal was to open more cottage breweries in other parts of the country. However, it was clear that he first had to concentrate on making this one work.

BACKGROUND

In 1981, Mitch Taylor, a successful entrepreneur, began looking for a business opportunity that was recession proof. A local business that caught his attention was a "Brew-Pub" operating in Horseshoe Bay, a Vancouver suburb. The "Brew-Pub" had a licence to brew its own natural beer and sell it on site. It appeared to be highly successful and led Mr. Taylor to investigate the possibility of a similar venture in the Vancouver area.

After considerable interest from and discussion with the B.C. Liquor Control and Licensing Board, he developed the idea of starting a small brewery that would produce a premium quality beer and sell it through its own retail store for in-home consumption. After nearly two years of negotiations with the provincial government, permission to develop and operate the brewery was obtained. The appendix at the end of this case provides a chronological history of GIBCO.

THE BREWERY LOCATION

Mr. Taylor had wanted a building with sufficient space to house both the brewery and the retail store, as well as being convenient to a large number of potential customers. The site selected was an old warehouse on Granville Island, an urban redevelopment area in the heart of Vancouver.

In 1973, the federal government initiated a project to convert the 15 hectare Granville Island peninsula from industrial use to a retail-tourist area. By 1984, Granville Island was home to an indoor public market, as well as a number of tourist shops, restaurants and theatres (Exhibit 1). Surrounded by the newly developed and moderately affluent False Creek residential area and across the water from the downtown core, Granville Island attracted over 6 million visitors a year. Both tourists and local residents frequented the island. Approximately 65% of visitors were from the residential areas close to Granville Island. Tourists from outside the Vancouver area made up approximately 25% of its summertime traffic. A survey conducted on the island in the summer of 1985 revealed that 60% of the local visitors came to the island at least once a week in the summer and 46% at least once a week in the winter. There were no government liquor outlets on the island, and the nearest was approximately 1.5 km away. The location chosen for the brewery was just inside the entrance to the island, so that all vehicle and foot traffic had to pass the brewery upon entering Granville Island. Although technically an island, a short causeway linked the island to the mainland. Mr. Taylor considered it a perfect location for the new brewery.

THE PRODUCT AND PRODUCTION PROCESS

The product decisions centred on finding an approach to brewing a premium beer that would be of interest to the Vancouver market. Mr. Taylor hired a West German, Rainer Kallahne, who held a brew master's diploma from the University of Berlin. Mr. Kallahne directed all aspects of production following the Bavarian Purity Law, which specified that beer must be made of hops, yeast, and water and have no chemicals or preservatives. The distinctiveness of the beer was to be enhanced by a distinctive bottle. Instead of the traditional stubby brown bottle that characterized most of the domestic beers being sold in 1981, the Granville Island beer "Island Lager" was to be bottled in a tall-necked bottle, resembling the look of the imported, premium beers (Exhibit 2).

Exhibit 1
MAP OF GRANVILLE ISLAND

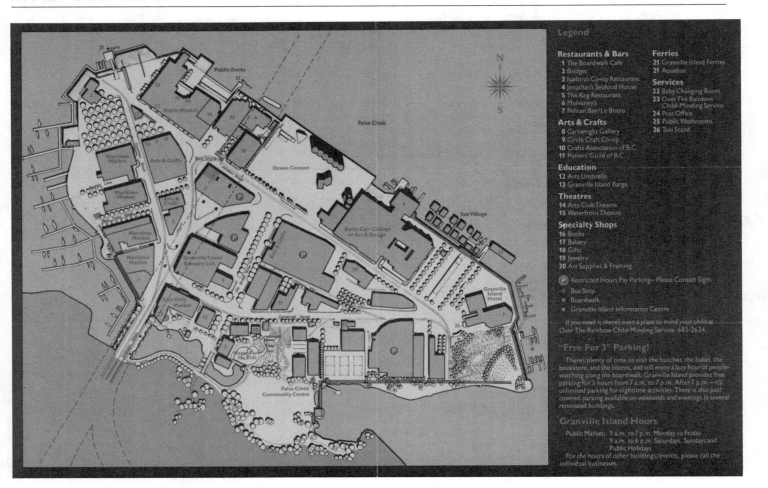

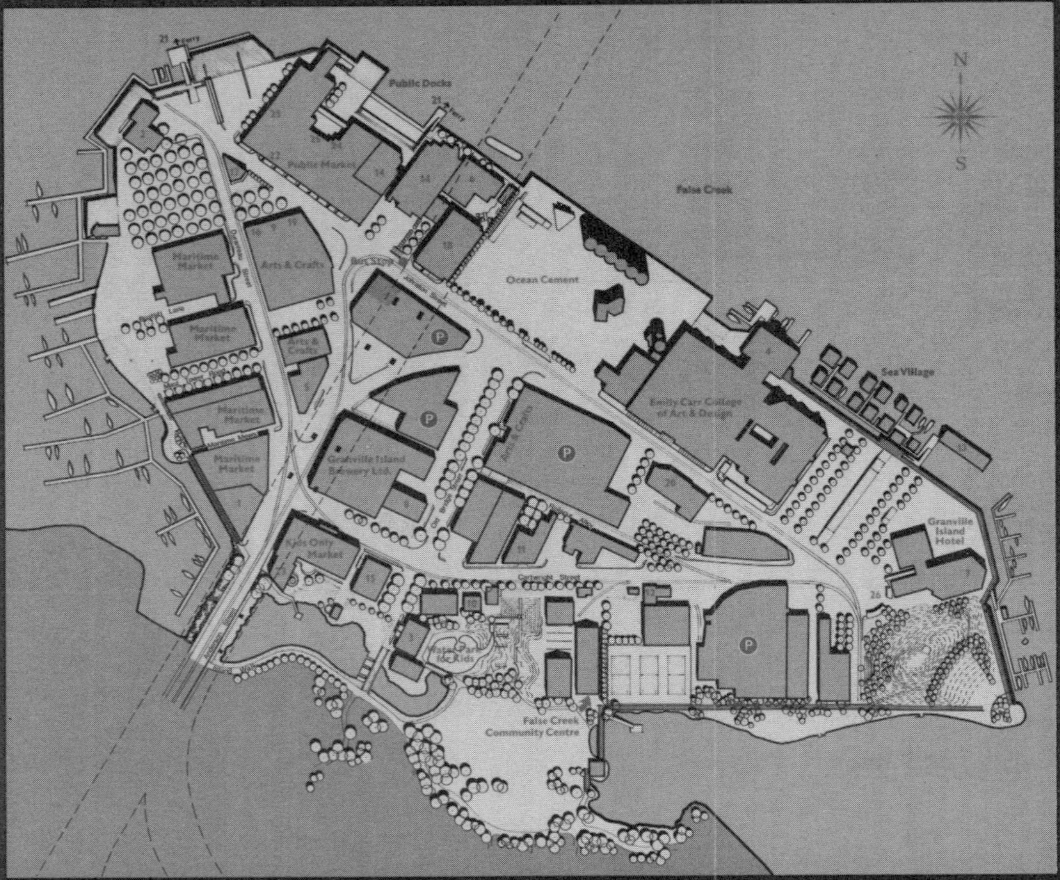

Legend

Restaurants & Bars
1 The Boardwalk Cafe
2 Bridges
3 Isadora's Co-op Restaurant
4 Jonathan's Seafood House
5 The Keg Restaurant
6 Mulvaney's
7 Pelican Bay/Le Bistro

Arts & Crafts
8 Cartwright Gallery
9 Circle Craft Co-op
10 Crafts Association of B.C.
11 Potters' Guild of B.C.

Education
12 Arts Umbrella
13 Granville Island Barge

Theatres
14 Arts Club Theatre
15 Waterfront Theatre

Specialty Shops
16 Books
17 Bakery
18 Gifts
19 Jewelry
20 Art Supplies & Framing

Ferries
21 Granville Island Ferries
21 Aquabus

Services
22 Baby Changing Room
23 Over The Rainbow Child-Minding Service
24 Post Office
25 Public Washrooms
26 Taxi Stand

(P) Restricted Hours Pay Parking—Please Consult Signs
- Bus Stop
- Boardwalk
- Granville Island Information Centre

If you need it there's even a place to mind your child at Over The Rainbow Child-Minding Service. 683-2624.

"Free For 3" Parking!

There's plenty of time to visit the butcher, the baker, the bookstore, and the bistros, *and* still enjoy a lazy hour of people-watching along the boardwalk. Granville Island provides free parking for 3 hours from 7 a.m. to 7 p.m. After 7 p.m.—it's unlimited parking for nighttime activities. There is also paid covered parking available on weekends and evenings in several renovated buildings.

Granville Island Hours

Public Market: 9 a.m. to 7 p.m. Monday to Friday
9 a.m. to 6 p.m. Saturdays, Sundays and Public Holidays

For the hours of other buildings/events, please call the individual businesses.

Exhibit 2
ISLAND LAGER PROMOTIONAL BROCHURE

With the licence, location, and product decisions set, GIBCO started to take shape. By early 1984, the building had been renovated, and the equipment installed. The first production run began in the spring. Each production run involved one day of brewing, ten days of fermentation, forty-two days of aging, and two to three days for bottling. It took nine weeks from the start of production to having bottled beer on the shelves of the brewery store. Production capacity was determined by the size and number of aging tanks. At the time of Granville Island's first production run, there were 15 sixty-hectolitre aging tanks.[1] This capacity allowed for the production of approximately 5400 hectolitres per year of lager if the brewery produced at "full-tilt" throughout the entire year. However, since beer without preservatives has a shelf life of only 60 days, it was not possible to accumulate inventory during slow periods to prepare for the highly cyclical patterns that characterized beer sales. As a result, production had to be reduced during periods of low sales.

RETAILING REGULATIONS

Island Lager sales began in June 1984 through the GIBCO retail outlet. The retail outlet operated by special arrangement with the Liquor Control and Licensing Branch (LCLB) and the Liquor Distribution Branch (LDB) of the provincial government. Since government regulations dictated that all beer sold in the province be distributed through the Liquor Distribution Branch, the Granville Island Brewery store was required to act as a government liquor outlet. This meant that government regulations affected the pricing policy for the beer.

The brewery established a price at which they would sell their beer to the Liquor Distribution Branch. This price included all production costs and desired profit, as well as federal excise duty and federal taxes. The Distribution Branch then applied their mark-up (called a "malt levy") to this price, which was based on the alcoholic content of the beer. The 5% alcohol level in Island Lager resulted in a 50% mark-up. To this figure, the 7% provincial sales tax was added, resulting in a final price to the consumer. The LDB would allow only one price change per month, and prices were uniform across all retail outlets within the province. The prices set to the consumer for Island Lager in June 1984 were: $4.60 for a four-pack, $8.90 for an eight-pack, and $12.50 for a twelve-pack. From these sales, the brewery would receive, after deducting the federal excise duty and taxes, $2.33 for four-packs, $4.60 for eight-packs, and $6.45 for twelve-packs.

Although the pricing structure allowed for the desired profit to be set by the brewery, this profit was essentially determined by competitive forces. Granville Island Brewery established a retail price and worked backwards from there to determine profit. The retail price was based on the positioning of Island Lager relative to its competitors. Since Mr. Taylor wanted Island Lager positioned as an ultra-premium product, it was priced as such—Island Lager's retail price was marginally below the price of imports and substantially above the price of domestic beers. In June 1984,

[1] 1 hectolitre = 100 litres = 22 gallons
1 dozen beer = 4.092 litres = approximately 11 gallons
1 barrel = approximately 28 dozen bottles

a six-pack of domestic beer ranged in price from $4.05 to $5, while imported beer ranged from $5.50 to $9.

VANCOUVER BEER MARKET

Three major breweries dominated the national beer market and together accounted for approximately 98% of the domestic beer sales in British Columbia. Mr. Taylor had hoped that Island Lager would compete directly with imported beer, which had risen to a 4.7% market share in the 1983–84 fiscal year (Exhibit 3). The recent upswing in import sales had not gone unnoticed as all three major breweries had taken action to produce their own versions of U.S. brands. For example, after Labatt introduced a Canadian version of Budweiser in March 1981, Carling O'Keefe (in May 1984) and Molson (in October 1985) followed with U.S. brands brewed in Canada. Lager was the most popular type of beer consumed in the province, accounting for 98% of packaged beer sold; ale, porter, and stout made up the remaining 2%. When Island Lager first entered the market in the spring of 1984, total provincial beer sales exceeded 200 million litres a year, accounting for approximately 40% of total provincial alcohol dollar sales—75% of total volume in litres (Exhibit 3). It was estimated that the Metro Vancouver area accounted for approximately 68% of provincial beer sales.

Exhibit 3

LITRE BEER SALES IN B.C.
FOR EACH FISCAL YEAR ENDING MARCH 31

Year	Domestic (000)	Imported (000)	Total (000)
1980/81*	182,853	13,382	196,235
1981/82	222,080	5,378	227,458
1982/83	225,235	6,807	232,042
1983/84	216,389	10,726	227,115
1984/85	221,458	9,806	231,264
1985/86	214,411	8,783	223,194

* A labour strike at B.C. breweries in 1980 resulted in increased sales of imported beer.

GIBCO BUSINESS MISSION

While setting up GIBCO, Mr. Taylor spent many months on the product and location decisions, adjusting these decisions to government regulations and evaluating market potential. The objectives that he used as guidelines were

1. To build a small capacity brewery and add incremental expansion as demand increased to a maximum of 25,000 barrels (approximately 700,000 dozen or 2,864,440 L).
2. To realize gross margins of approximately 50%; control expenses and achieve a net operating income after tax of 15 to 20%.

3. To produce high quality ultra-premium products in bottles and kegs.
4. To service markets in the Greater Vancouver region only, where distribution and shelf life can be controlled.
5. To staff the operation with qualified and experienced employees who would eventually participate as shareholders.

GIBCO OPERATIONS JUNE 1984 TO DECEMBER 1985

Initial sales of Island Lager were promising, resulting in total sales through the brewery store of close to $300,000 (about 40,000 dozen bottles) in the first seven months of operation (Exhibit 4). The Granville Island Brewery became one of the tourist attractions on Granville Island, and line-ups for beer at the store were common. The inability to store the beer because of its limited shelf life resulted in stockouts during periods of heavy traffic. These stockouts were infrequent and never lasted more than one or two days. Yet, the stockouts served to enhance the image of Island Lager as a "hot item."

From the beginning beer sales were supplemented by sales of Granville Island Brewery souvenirs, such as beer mugs, sweaters, wine glasses, bottle openers, and various other items. Souvenir sales grossed close to $40,000 in the first seven months, with retail margins varying between 30% and 40%. Free tours of the brewery were also offered through the retail store. These tours, held at various times throughout the day, helped to establish the brewery as a tourist attraction, differentiating it from other government liquor stores. The brewery's store manager estimated that three quarters of those customers taking the tour were out-of-towners.

When Island Lager was first introduced to the public in June 1984, it was sold through the brewery's own retail store, through some local restaurants and pubs, and later through cold beer stores.[2] Sales to these outlets, referred to by the brewery as licenses, were also channeled through the Liquor Distribution Branch, but the physical distribution of the lager to the licensees were handled by the brewery. By the end of 1984, Island Lager was sold in 60 local restaurants and pubs, resulting in total licensee sales of over $54,500 (about 9,000 dozen bottles).

During 1985 Mr. Taylor implemented two major initiatives designed to (1) smooth sales patterns and (2) expand distribution to government liquor stores.

Smoothing Sales Patterns

While successful, Island Lager sales followed the traditional patterns for beer sales. Summer volume substantially surpassed winter volume, leaving summer sales to offset the high fixed overhead costs of running the brewery and maintaining its excess capacity in the winter months. In an attempt to utilize this excess production capacity and establish a more stable flow of revenue, plans for a "bock" beer were initiated in early 1985. Bock, a darker, heavier beer, goes through the same production process as lager but requires a longer aging time (11 to 12 weeks). One batch of

[2] In May 1985, the provincial government announced that certain hotels and neighbourhood pubs would be allowed to open Licensee Retail Stores on their premises for the sale of B.C. packaged beer, cider, wines, and coolers. These are referred to as "cold beer stores."

Exhibit 4

MONTHLY SALES SUMMARY: JUNE 1984 TO DECEMBER 1985

1984	Store Beer ($000)	Souvenir ($000)	Wine ($000)	Store Total ($000)	LDB* ($000)	Licensee ($000)
June	37.4	3.0	0.0	40.4	0.0	2.6
July	66.8	5.3	0.0	72.1	0.0	7.4
Aug.	53.2	7.2	0.0	60.4	0.0	7.6
Sept.	41.5	5.0	0.0	46.5	0.0	4.8
Oct.	30.6	5.0	0.0	35.6	0.0	9.9
Nov.	28.4	4.3	0.0	32.8	0.0	12.8
Dec.	41.9	9.7	0.0	51.6	0.0	9.3
Total	299.8	39.5	0.0	339.3	0.0	54.5
1985	**Store Beer ($000)**	**Souvenir ($000)**	**Wine ($000)**	**Store Total ($000)**	**LDB* ($000)**	**Licensee ($000)**
Jan.	27.0	2.4	0.0	29.4	0.0	10.7
Feb.	29.9	2.4	0.0	32.3	0.0	9.5
Mar.	47.7	4.6	0.0	52.2	0.0	16.2
Apr.	47.1	4.4	1.3	52.9	0.0	17.2
May	61.3	6.0	8.8	76.0	0.0	20.6
June	74.4	9.1	13.1	96.6	0.0	17.9
July	75.2	11.1	12.6	98.9	0.0	21.9
Aug.	75.3	12.8	17.0	105.1	0.0	19.1
Sept.	58.1	9.3	15.2	82.5	2.4	12.5
Oct.	42.9	5.6	15.6	64.1	7.1	13.9
Nov.	37.9	6.0	13.4	57.2	5.7	11.4
Dec.	50.5	12.4	14.8	77.6	7.8	11.6
Total	627.4	85.9	111.7	825.0	23.1	182.5

* LDB refers to sales through government retail outlets.

3,000 dozen bottles was planned for every March and November, with the first batch (at half the ultimate capacity) to be available in March 1985, in twelve-packs through the brewery store. Bock not only made use of facilities in slow lager periods, it also fit nicely into the Octoberfest and Easter celebration times, and both spring and fall batches sold out quickly.

In another attempt to establish a more stable flow of revenues, GIBCO obtained a licence to sell wines through the brewery store. In April 1985, Okanagan Estate wines (a collection of wines from one winery in British Columbia's Okanagan region) were sold in a self-serve fashion from shelves at the front of the store. Approximately 25 varieties were carried on a 10% commission basis. The terms of the wine licence had two important implications. First, the licence stipulated that a cash system be maintained for wine sales that was separate from beer sales. This meant that customers had to wait in two lines when purchasing both wine and beer. Second, the wine licence allowed the store to be open on Sunday. Normally, Sunday beer sales were not allowed in the Vancouver area (government liquor stores and pubs were closed on Sundays). However, the terms of the wine licence designated Granville Island Brewery as an Estate Wine Store, and hence allowed for Sunday sales. Of the six Estate Wine Stores in the province, five were in the greater Vancouver area. These six establishments were the only stores in the province that were authorized to sell wine for off-site consumption on Sundays. Granville Island Brewing was the only one that also sold beer. Sunday openings proved to be a big asset for Granville Island Brewing, with more beer sold on Sunday than any other day of the week. For example, in July 1985, Sunday beer sales averaged 800 dozen bottles of Island Lager. This was more than three times the weekday average of 260 dozen bottles per day and more than twice the average 370 dozen bottles sold on Saturdays. Sunday sales were similarly higher for wine and souvenir sales.

Expanding to Government Liquor Stores

With the brewery store successfully underway, Mr. Taylor looked for expanded distribution of Island Lager. In the summer of 1985, the brewery's sales manager, Turk Whitehead, began negotiations with the managers of several government liquor stores. Each liquor store had to be solicited individually, since the decision of whether to carry Island Lager was to be made by each store manager. In addition, all proposals to carry Island Lager had to be approved by the Liquor Distribution Branch (LDB). Thus, upon acceptance of arrangements by a liquor store manager, an application in writing was presented to the LDB.

Solicitation of the liquor store accounts was handled primarily by Turk Whitehead, who as general manager and sales manager oversaw all sales activities. He had been with Granville Island Brewing since the fall of 1983, after ten years with Carling O'Keefe Breweries. Although he held two management titles, his primary responsibility concerned the soliciting of liquor store accounts. There were 70 local liquor stores, and Mr. Taylor hoped to have Island Lager in all of these by 1987. While some of these accounts were actively sought by Mr. Whitehead, other placements resulted from initiatives taken by liquor store managers themselves. The first liquor store agreements were completed in September 1985, and by the end of that year Island Lager was being sold through seven LDB outlets. Mr. Taylor decided to limit LDB store sales to the eight-pack. He considered the eight-pack more "marketable" in that it allowed consumers to see the distinctive Island Lager bottle, while the twelve-pack was in an enclosed case. Over $23,100 (about 5,000 eight-packs) were sold in the first four months that Island Lager was on liquor store shelves.

These sales were accompanied by minimal advertising support. Granville Island Brewing had relied primarily on word of mouth and any free publicity given by the media, such as a short spot on a news broadcast featuring "cottage breweries." Flyers advertising the brewery had been distributed throughout Granville Island and placed in racks at liquor stores. Paid advertising through the media had not been used. Mr. Taylor felt that since the brewery did not appear to be suffering from the lack of advertising, it was unnecessary to spend money on it until the brewery had built itself up.

Results as of December 1985

The combination of brewery sales, licensee sales, and sales through LDB outlets resulted in steady growth over the initial 19 months of GIBCO operations. As shown in Exhibit 4, July through December 1984 saw sales of $262,400 (about 35,000 dozen bottles) through the brewery store, $51,900 (about 8,600 dozen) through licensees, and $36,500 in souvenirs. During the same six months of 1985, the corresponding sales figures had grown to $333,900, $94,400 and $57,200 plus $23,100 through LBD outlets and $88,600 in wine sales. Based on this initial success, Taylor decided to expand the brewery's production capacity and look for further opportunities for growth.

DEVELOPMENTS IN 1986

The first five months of 1986 were a busy time for Mr. Taylor. He prepared an operating statement for GIBCO for the year based on certain assumptions that he hoped would become reality. As well, he took steps to improve distribution, added more capacity to the brewery, began producing a draft beer, added a new line of wines to his retail store, and contemplated changes in his retail operations. On top of this, Mr. Taylor was concerned about pending changes in the provincial legislation to the distribution and sale of liquor in the province. In late May he began reviewing these activities prior to making some fundamental decisions about the future of the business.

GIBCO PROFITABILITY

Mr. Taylor prepared an operating statement that projected total sales for the year from the store operations of $1,129,500, with a total net income of $486,800, and from the off-island operations a total net income of $282,000 leading to a profit of $670,400 (Exhibit 5). However, Mr. Taylor knew that the operating statement was based on the overriding assumption that everything would go well during the year. He was not sure it would happen as much depended on GIBCO sales during Expo '86, the world's fair taking place in Vancouver between April and October.

As well, the forecasted revenue from beer sales was dependent on the distribution method; different sizes were carried by the various outlets, and similar sizes had higher margins. With federal duty and taxes subtracted, GIBCO revenue per dozen averaged $7.25 through the brewery store, $7.43 through LDB outlets, and $6.99 through licensees and Expo pavillions. These figures were based on May 1986 retail prices of $5.25 per four-pack, $10.20 for an eight-pack, and $14.50 for a twelve-pack. These prices were about 30% above domestic beer prices, yet marginally below the prices of premium import beer.

In addition to revenue differences by outlet, there were variations in marketing expenses. GIBCO paid $0.75 per dozen for sales to licensees by Mark Anthony representatives (see below), $0.75 per dozen to the Expo Corporation for sales through Expo pavillions, and delivery costs for all beer sold off the brewery site. On the other hand, beer sold through the brewery store received a commission from the

Liquor Distribution Branch of 10% of the retail price. This commission was paid because of the licensing agreement designating the brewery store as a government liquor store.

Exhibit 5

GIBCO OPERATING STATEMENT ($000s) 1986

	First Quarter Actual	Second Quarter Budget	Third Quarter Budget	Fourth Quarter Budget	Total
Store Operations					
Beer Sales and Cost of Goods					
Beer Sales	90.6	201.6	270.2	138.0	700.4
Operating Fee[1]	17.2	38.8	50.1	23.5	129.6
Total Revenue	107.8	240.4	320.3	161.5	830.0
Cost of Goods	47.8	94.4	121.2	62.0	325.4
Gross Income	60.0	146.0	199.1	99.5	504.6
Wine Sales and Expenses					
Wine Sales	22.9	59.8	89.7	84.1	256.5
Wine Commissions[2]	3.4	9.0	13.5	12.6	38.5
Rental Expense	0.6	1.6	2.4	2.2	6.8
Gross Income	2.8	7.4	11.1	10.4	31.7
Souvenir Sales and Expenses					
Souvenir Sales	18.6	43.0	73.0	38.0	172.6
Rental Expense	0.0	2.2	3.7	1.9	7.8
Cost of Goods	11.3	23.7	40.2	20.9	96.1
Gross Income	7.3	17.1	29.1	15.2	68.7
Other Income	0.2	0.1	0.2	0.1	0.5
Store Administrative Expenses					
Tours & Hospitality	0.6	2.0	2.6	1.2	6.4
Sales Promotion	0.7	1.5	1.5	1.5	5.2
Salaries & Benefits	18.9	26.0	25.0	20.3	90.2
Store Supplies	3.2	3.0	3.0	3.0	12.2
Credit Card Sales Expense	0.7	1.3	1.7	0.9	4.6
Total Expenses	24.1	33.8	33.8	26.9	118.6
Total Store Sales	132.1	304.4	432.9	260.1	1129.5
Net Income[3]					
Beer	43.5	123.6	178.0	85.2	430.3
Wine	(1.3)	0.8	4.1	1.7	5.3
Souvenir	4.0	12.4	23.5	11.3	51.2
Total Store Net Income	46.2	136.8	205.6	98.2	486.8

(continued)

Exhibit 5 continued

	First Quarter Actual	Second Quarter Budget	Third Quarter Budget	Fourth Quarter Budget	Total
Off-Island Operations					
Liquor Distribution Branches (LDB) Sales and Expenses					
LDB Sales	33.0	85.3	81.9	134.0	334.2
Cost of Goods	17.0	39.0	35.8	58.8	150.6
Gross Income	16.0	46.3	46.1	75.2	183.6
Car and Salary Expense	8.0	9.6	10.3	10.3	38.2
Delivery	2.1	3.0	3.0	2.9	11.0
Promotion	3.5	6.5	11.0	3.5	24.5
Net Income	2.4	27.2	21.8	58.5	109.9
Licensee Sales and Expenses					
Licensee Sales	39.4	82.0	97.4	162.8	381.6
Cold Beer Store Sales	2.4	20.3	27.3	24.5	74.5
Total Sales	41.8	102.3	124.7	187.3	456.1
Cost of Goods	22.9	49.7	58.0	87.3	217.9
Gross Income	18.9	52.6	66.7	100.0	238.2
Commission Expense	3.4	19.7	20.0	30.2	73.3
Delivery	2.8	3.8	4.9	4.3	15.8
Promotion	3.5	6.5	11.0	3.5	24.5
Net income	9.2	22.6	30.8	62.0	124.6
Expo Sales and Expenses					
Expo Sales	0.0	43.6	65.6	14.4	123.6
Cost of Goods	0.0	21.2	30.5	6.7	58.4
Gross Income	0.0	22.4	35.1	7.7	65.2
Advertising	0.0	4.7	7.0	1.5	13.2
Delivery	0.0	1.6	2.6	0.3	4.5
Net income	0.0	16.1	25.5	5.9	47.5
GIBCO Total Net Income	57.8	202.7	283.7	224.6	768.8
Other Company Expenses					
Advertising	3.2	18.1	26.7	9.5	57.5
Car and Salary	8.0	9.6	10.3	10.3	38.2
Travel	0.3	0.8	0.8	0.8	2.7
Total	11.5	28.5	37.8	20.6	98.4
PROFIT	46.3	174.2	245.9	204.0	670.4

[1] GIBCO received an operating fee from the Liquor Distribution Branch for running the beer store.

[2] GIBCO received a 15% commission on wine sales.

[3] Net income was calculated by allocating "Store Administrative Expenses" based on proportion of total sales.

DISTRIBUTION CHANGES

In the first four months of 1986, Turk Whitehead continued his efforts to have Island Lager stocked in local liquor stores. By the end of April, the number of local liquor stores carrying Island Lager had grown to 26. Exhibit 6 lists these store accounts, the date GIBCO started supplying them, and the estimated sales of Island Lager supplied to these outlets in April 1986.

Exhibit 6
GREATER VANCOUVER GOVERNMENT LIQUOR STORE SALES

Store*	Date of First Sales of Island Lager	Total Fiscal 1986 Store Sales** ($ mil)	Estimated April 1986 Sales of All Brands of Beer (Dozens)	Sales in April 1986 (Dozens)
GIBCO	June 1984	1.4		4,528
Lansdowne	Sept. 1985	7.1	26,700	100
39th & Cambie	Sept. 1985	12.6	42,200	260
Thurlow	Sept. 1985	7.0	20,300	80
Park Royal	Sept. 1985	8.9	22,700	90
Lougheed Mall	Sept. 1985	8.8	36,100	100
Whistler	Sept. 1985	3.0	12,200	60
Middlegate	Sept. 1985	10.2	44,300	80
Westwood	Feb. 1986	7.4	30,000	60
Tsawwassen	Feb. 1986	5.1	17,200	—
Kennedy Heights	Feb. 1986	11.0	48,500	60
North Burnaby	Feb. 1986	10.5	46,000	80
Westview	Feb. 1986	10.8	42,200	100
Seafair	Feb. 1986	6.9	26,100	60
White Rock	Feb. 1986	7.8	28,500	80
Guilford	Feb. 1986	7.7	31,500	80
Marpole	Feb. 1986	9.1	46,100	100
Kerrisdale	Feb. 1986	4.4	13,600	80
Kingsgate	Feb. 1986	7.7	34,700	64
Robson	Feb. 1986	8.9	32,800	240
Senlac	Feb. 1986	9.7	44,200	50
4th & Alma	Feb. 1986	8.5	33,200	270
Broadway & Maple	Feb. 1986	11.4	45,000	270
West Vancouver	Feb. 1986	8.0	23,800	140
New Westminster	Feb. 1986	8.3	36,500	100
Gibsons	Feb. 1986	2.9	11,900	60
AVERAGE (not including GIBCO)		8.2	32,900	107

* There were an additional 45 LDB outlets in Metro Vancouver that did not stock Granville Island Lager.

** The 1986 fiscal year ended March 31, 1986.

The number of licensee accounts had not grown as rapidly as the liquor store distribution, and Mr. Taylor felt that changes were necessary. In March 1986, with only 200 of an estimated 800 potential licensee accounts in the Vancouver area stocking Island Lager, Mr. Taylor commissioned the Mark Anthony wine and spirit merchants to act as exclusive sales representatives for Island Lager. The Mark Anthony company had ten representatives serving the Vancouver area. They carried approximately 150 products, none of which were beer. These reps were contracted to represent Island Lager to the licensees. Turk Whitehead would continue his contacts with the liquor stores.

ADDING CAPACITY

The distribution improvements and the preparation for Expo '86 led, in April 1986, to the addition of 12 sixty-hectolitre aging tanks, almost doubling production capacity. As well, an additional 36 aging tanks were planned for the fall of 1986. With this increase in capacity, Mr. Taylor began production of a draft beer. British Columbia in contrast to other provinces was a strong draft beer market, averaging 20% of domestic beer sales. A new draft product would be sold through licensees, and by packaging it in a party keg, it could also be sold through the brewery store. However, Mr. Taylor had made commitments to supply both bottled and draft beer to Expo '86. Since the Expo demand for Island Lager was difficult to predict, it seemed best to delay the introduction of non-Expo draft until the fall.

As of May, production of draft beer was underway and shipments of both draft and bottled beer were being readied for Expo. If the Expo demand turned out to be less than expected, Mr. Taylor considered introducing draft kegs through the brewery store earlier than planned. Mr. Taylor thought that 10% of GIBCO's beer sales would consist of draft beer by the fourth quarter of 1986.

THE NEW LINE OF WINES

To increase sales revenue in the retail store, Mr. Taylor completed a deal with the Mark Anthony representatives to carry another line of estate wines, Mission Hill, starting in May. Mission Hill offered a selection of over 70 wines, a selection deemed by the store manager to be much broader than the currently carried Okanagan Estate wines. In addition to Mission Hill wines, five kinds of cider and two kinds of wine coolers were to be carried. All of these products were currently offered in the government liquor stores and would be priced comparably in the brewery store. Mission Hill wines carried a commission of 15%, whereas Okanagan Estate wines carried only a 10% commission. However, Okanagan wines responded to the proposed introduction of Mission Hill wines by increasing their commission to 15%.

POSSIBLE CHANGES IN THE RETAIL OPERATIONS

Decisions regarding store operations were also concerning Mr. Taylor. How many Okanagan Estate wines to keep and how many Mission Hill wines to carry in the store had not been decided. The store had the capacity to carry between 60 and 70 types. However, if both wines were carried, a third cash till would be required.

This requirement of the wine licence was essentially the same as stipulated in the Okanagan Estate wine licence—a separate cash system must be maintained for all types of wines carried. If both types of wines were carried, a customer might have to wait in three line-ups to purchase all of his selections. Exhibit 7 provides a diagram of the store's floor plan at that time.

Plans for changes in the brewery store did not stop at product line decisions. The daily tours of the brewery conducted by the store's staff were also scheduled for revision. Mr. Taylor was considering an extended tour and tasting, and eventually

Exhibit 7
GRANVILLE ISLAND BREWERY RETAIL OUTLET

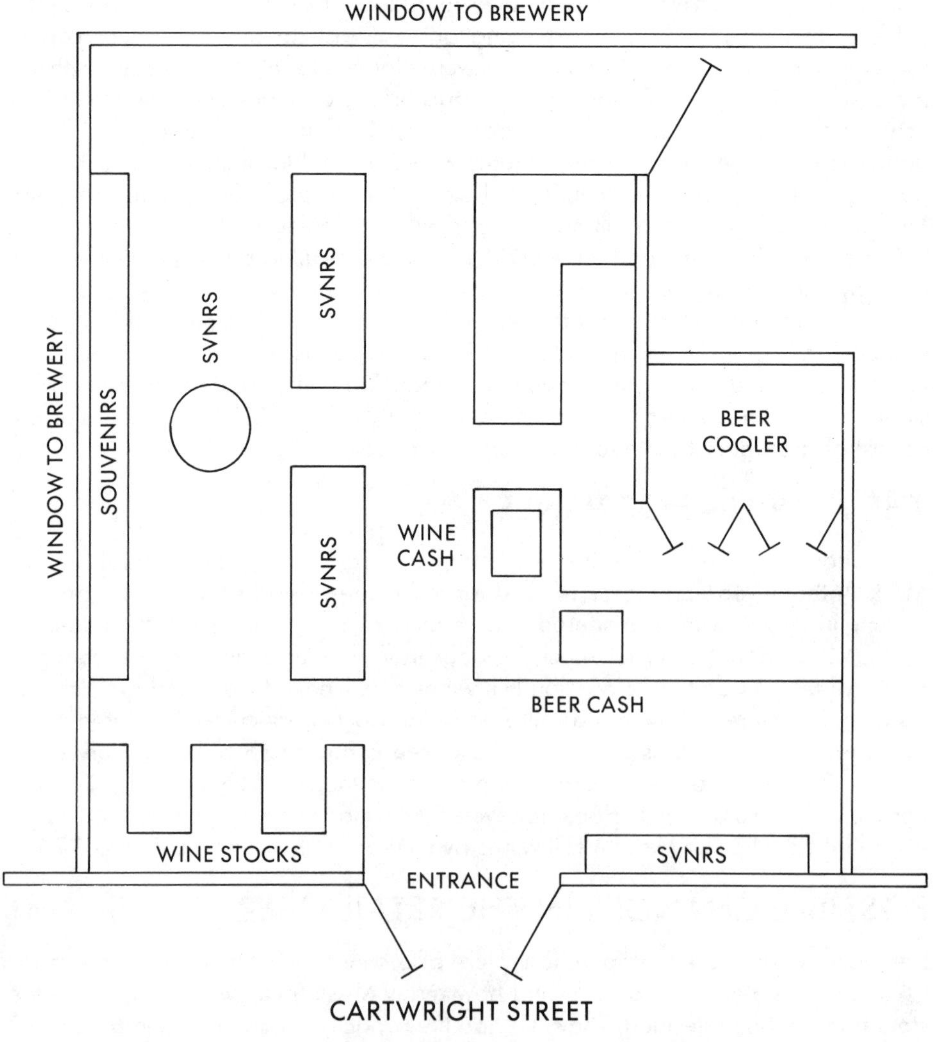

the addition of beer garden. The brewery had a mezzanine floor of approximately 435 m^2. This area could serve to enlarge the tour area allowing for bigger groups. Further development of this area would involve its conversion to a facility with a pub-like atmosphere where customers could purchase their beer for on-site consumption. It was estimated that this area could house a 200-seat beer garden. However, the beer garden concept was subject to the approval of the Liquor Control and Licensing Branch. The decision of whether to staff the beer garden with brewery store employees or lease it out would have to be examined.

THE FUTURE

As Mr. Taylor reflected on the past two years he was pleased with GIBCO's initial progress and felt that future prospects looked very promising. His main concern was to set priorities that would help him to achieve the hoped-for growth. He believed in keeping his management team limited to a small number of people. As a result, the effective allocation of management energies was a key concern. It was clear to Mr. Taylor that growth priorities must be based on the relative profitability of his various options and on continual awareness of market trends that might affect future profitability.

With respect to market developments, Mr. Taylor noted several developments that could have a negative impact on his business. First, the uniqueness of Island Lager's tall-necked bottles was eliminated. By the end of 1985, all of the major breweries switched from the brown, stubby bottles to the tall-necked bottles for many of their domestic brands.

As a side issue, Mr. Taylor noted that all three major breweries had introduced and heavily promoted light beers in the past few years. Feedback from licensees indicated that consumer preference was shifting to light beer. This raised the question of introducing a light, low-alcohol beer.

Second, although it had only been a short period of time since the Mark Anthony group had been commissioned, the number of licensee accounts was increasing very slowly. Mr. Taylor wondered if his hopes for additional licensee accounts were too optimistic or that he might be going about it the wrong way.

Third, there was several recent developments that could adversely affect brewery store sales. Mr. Taylor was concerned that the increased availability of Island Lager in liquor stores would cut sales of Island Lager at the brewery store. Also, the Granville Island Trust, the managing body for Granville Island, was considering plans to open an Estate Wine Store in the Granville Island market. This outlet would provide direct local competition to the brewery store's wine sales and, being an Estate Wine Store, would also be open for business on Sunday.

The brewery store's Sunday wine sales were not the only Sunday sales threatened. A more immediate problem existed with Sunday beer sales. The provincial government announced that during Expo pubs and bars could open on Sundays. At these locations beer could be purchased for off-site consumption. Although the government stipulated that this would only be the case during Expo, public speculation was that these openings would continue past October. As well, the number of cold beer stores in the province had increased to seventeen. These outlets were similar to the brewery store in that they carried cold beer, a variety of B.C. wines, and souvenirs.

Fourth, the uniqueness of the Granville Island Brewery was also threatened. There were now four more cottage breweries in the province—two on the outskirts of Vancouver and two in other regions of the province. However, none of these sold their products through government liquor stores.

As Taylor reviewed these market developments, he wondered what impact they would have on GIBCO profitability. He had hoped to capture 1% of the provincial beer market by 1987. Whether this goal was realistic was uncertain, but even if it were, questions as to how to proceed remained. Should he emphasize new products, such as draft or light beer? Should he put his efforts into sales through the brewery store, LDB outlets, or licensees? Further, he wondered what impact his distribution emphasis would have on other aspects of GIBCO, such as product line decisions. Mr. Taylor determined that he had five general options for growth (draft beer introduction, light beer introduction, focus on LDB sales, focus on licensee sales, or focus on store sales). He needed to set priorities that would ensure the future profitability and growth of Granville Island Brewing.

Appendix
CHRONOLOGICAL HISTORY OF GIBCO

Spring 1982	Negotiations with the Liquor Control and Licensing Branch of the provincial government begin.
Spring 1984	Licensing arrangements are complete. Granville Island Brewing Company begins production of Island Lager. Brewing capacity: 900 hectolitres (hL).
June 1984	Granville Island Brewing retail store opens its doors to the public with sales of Island Lager (four-, eight-, and twelve-packs) and GIBCO souvenirs. GIBCO begins sales of Island Lager through local licensees.
March 1985	GIBCO introduces Island Bock in twelve-packs through the Brewery store.
April 1985	GIBCO starts selling Okanagan Estate wines through the Brewery store.
September 1985	Island Lager is first sold through government liquor stores (LDB).
March 1986	Mark Anthony wine and spirit merchants are engaged to act as sales representatives for Island Lager for sales to licensees.
April 1986	Production capacity to GIBCO is expanded. The addition of 12 sixty-hectolitre tanks brings capacity to 1620 hL.
Fall 1986	Proposed capacity expansion to 3750 hL.

Section 8

INTERNATIONAL MARKETING

Over the last four decades, international marketing has received increasing attention from nations and businesses across the world. Since 1970, almost every industralized country's ratio of merchandise exports and imports to Gross National Product (GNP) has increased substantially. This means that countries are exporting more of what they produce domestically each year and are buying more from other countries. Canada is no exception to this trend with both imports and exports more than doubling in the 1980s (Exhibit 1). Nations are realizing that it is advantageous for them to purchase goods and services that represent the best value, no matter where these products or services originate. Of course, total international free trade does not exist as many countries impose quotas and tariff barriers to protect domestic industries from foreign competition.

WHY COUNTRIES TRADE

There are various theories as to why trade occurs between countries. Put simply, trade occurs because people (as individuals, as managers in firms, or as government officials) seek to generate funds by exploiting a competitive advantage they enjoy. A competitive advantage can take many forms including: raw materials, technological expertise, management skills, low wage rates, and distribution strategies. Countries, both industrialized and nonindustrialized, trade in order to strengthen their domestic economies.

International trade has become so important for many businesses that the world is now viewed as a single global marketplace. Today, many business people realize that they can no longer afford to restrict themselves to one geographic market, they must "think global." The notions of international trade, competitive advantage, and scale economies have become so important that in 1992, twelve European countries (otherwise known as the European Community) are planning to drop all tariff and nontariff barriers between them. The rationale behind this action is to create one European economic market versus many smaller markets.

IMPORTANCE OF INTERNATIONAL TRADE TO CANADA

As indicated previously, Canada is a trading nation; exports have risen every year since 1970. Canadians export everything from raw materials to finished goods, from technology to services. Canada trades with many countries around the world, but the United States is still this nation's main trading partner, accounting for 70% of Canada's exports. Nevertheless, other countries have become very important to the economic well-being of

Exhibit 1

CANADA'S MAJOR TRADING PARTNERS (1979 TO 1989)

	Exports To		Imports From	
	$ millions 1989	% change 1979–89	$ millions 1989	% change 1979–89
UNITED STATES	103,732	+130	93,322	+110
EUROPE				
Switzerland	719	+290	600	+86
Norway	635	+127	785	+780
France	1,260	+103	2,017	+159
Belgium/Luxembourg	1,231	+84	567	+135
Sweden	319	+84	939	+145
Spain	398	+83	567	+220
Italy	1,096	+50	2,012	+216
Netherlands	1,533	+42	823	+227
Britain	3,538	+41	4,604	+145
West Germany	1,777	+30	3,708	+138
AUSTRALIA	1,032	+85	618	+34
JAPAN	8,472	+117	8,262	+291
NEWLY INDUSTRIALIZED COUNTRIES (NICs)				
Taiwan	882	+750	2,352	+350
Hong Kong	1,014	+637	1,161	+172
South Korea	1,592	+336	2,441	+427
Singapore	243	+112	503	+207
EMERGING NICs				
Indonesia	295	+371	192	+356
Thailand	340	+289	420	+1,224
Malaysia	219	+235	320	+232
Philippines	219	+159	205	+162
OTHERS				
Mexico	600	+154	1,680	+706
China	1,116	+85	1,182	+606
Saudi Arabia	337	+34	253	−80
India	297	+32	224	+140
Brazil	521	+24	1,130	+261
U.S.S.R.	685	−11	118	+83
Algeria	292	−26	30	−66
Total	138,934	+112	134,255	+120

Source: *The Financial Post 500*, Summer 1990, p. 21.

Canada. Japan is now Canada's second largest trading partner (6% of exports), and Europe as a whole accounts for 9% of Canada's trade. Growth rates of trade in some of the Asian Pacific countries are quite high and business executives need to pay attention to both established trading partners and newly emerging ones.

International trade not only means more markets for Canadian goods but also more competition from foreign firms. As a result, Canadian managers must become more efficient and effective in their businesses if they want to compete not only internationally but domestically as well. This notion was the driving force behind the recent introduction of the Canada–U.S. Free Trade Agreement (FTA). The FTA gradually removes, over a ten-year period, almost all tariffs on Canadian and American goods. This allows firms in both countries greater access to larger markets and provides them with an opportunity to achieve greater scale economies. Becoming more efficient means that these North American firms will have an increased likelihood of successfully competing in the global marketplace as well.

IMPORTANT FACTORS IN INTERNATIONAL TRADE

There are many important factors for a business to consider when trading internationally. Similar to a domestic strategy, a thorough assessment of the important environmental opportunities and threats is needed. However, three factors deserve special attention when considering international opportunities: (1) trade barriers and quotas, (2) the political environment, and (3) the cultural environment. These factors need to be considered for *every* prospective market and are likely to differ from one country to another.

TRADE BARRIERS AND QUOTAS

Almost all countries have some type of trade barriers and quotas on certain products. These restrictions are placed on imported goods and are designed to limit the quantity of foreign products allowed into a country. Import restrictions are designed to protect domestic industries—often to safeguard the jobs of workers in an industry. Trade barriers and quotas are acts of law established by governments, but political officials are frequently lobbied by management and labour representatives of domestic industries who desire favourable barriers and quota structures. As such, it is important for firms entering a foreign nation to understand the political process of import restrictions affecting an industry, and to fully recognize the impact of barriers and quotas on their business.

Canada has barriers and quotas on a variety of foreign goods including apparel and textiles. Tariffs on imports can range from 1% to upwards of 15% depending on the product.

THE POLITICAL ENVIRONMENT

One of the most important factors in the political context of a country is its relationship with other nations. A country that offers stable and open political and economic policies may provide an attractive climate for potential foreign businesses. Nations in the Middle East do not provide promising opportunities for many foreign enterprises as the governments in these countries are frequently viewed as unstable and unpredictable.

The political climate of a nation also dictates, in part, the economic policies of other nations. For example, the oppressive political mandates of the South African government regarding its black population led to many national governments passing laws severely restricting trade with South Africa during the 1980s. Actions such as these are fuelled by political rather than economic motives. Consequently, domestic firms desiring to export to a politically unpopular country such as South Africa have little chance to do so.

THE CULTURAL ENVIRONMENT

The cultural environment is one of the most poorly researched areas by firms considering entry into a foreign marketplace. Many questions need to be answered regarding the specific culture of a new international market before a product or service is introduced. These questions include

- Who is the primary decision-maker for purchasing the product/service?
- Do strong values regarding work, morality, or religion play a large role in the purchase decision?
- Do members of the culture exhibit impulsive or calculated methods in their purchase behaviours?
- What role does advertising play in the country?
- Is there a cultural or social significance to the purchase or use of certain products?
- Where does the purchaser typically buy the product?

Firms must do their "homework" before entering a new market in order to avoid cross-cultural marketing mistakes. Many firms have blundered by taking a domestic brand name or package colour and directly introducing it into a foreign market. Some examples include

- A British firm's tonic sales in Italy were minimal as the firm inadvertently advertised its product as "bathroom water."
- In Malaysia, a major ad campaign by an American firm did not work as it was discovered that the Malaysian people associate the colour green with death and disease; the ads were predominately green.
- General Motors' Chevrolet Nova did not sell well in Latin America initially; the word Nova, when spoken as two words in Spanish, means "it doesn't go."

ROLE OF COMPANIES

While international trade is frequently examined on a country by country basis, trade is a result of a series of decisions made by companies. While countries can set up incentives to encourage international trade, businesses must be able to plan and implement an international strategy if an advantage is to be gained. Canadian companies that decide not to compete globally, comforting themselves with the thought that they can succeed by operating in the Canadian market only, must recognize that firms in other countries are looking for new opportunities and may pursue Canadian ones. More positively, by the beginning of the 1990s, many Canadian companies have gone global: Northern Telecom in communications, Alcan in aluminum, Moore in business forms, and Bombardier in transportation. These firms recognize that to grow and prosper they must compete in international markets. In fact, with the Free Trade Agreement and falling trade barriers, Canadian firms may no longer have a choice—they will have to think and act globally.

Canadian firms should realize that in order to successfully compete in the long-run they must look beyond the domestic situation. Today governments are protecting fewer and fewer industries with import restrictions. Firms must remember that industries that are currently protected may not enjoy the same import restrictions in the future. This was the case for the Canadian wine industry where the adoption of the Canada–U.S. Free Trade Agreement caused a major exodus and restructuring by many firms in this industry; relaxed import tariffs on U.S. wines made these products cheaper for Canadian consumers, and thus made it more difficult for Canadian companies to compete. Even long-protected service businesses, such as banks and law firms, are finding that decreased barriers are bringing both new threats and new opportunities.

INTERNATIONAL MARKETING STRATEGY CONSIDERATIONS

Upon deciding to enter a foreign market, a company must determine what mode of entry to use. The main alternatives are export, joint ventures (which can vary from simple licensing to complex joint ownership/management agreements), and direct ownership and investment. The various forms involve differing degrees of commitment and risk, as well as the ability to control both local and international strategies. For manufacturers of goods, the simplest way to enter a market is through export to a local firm which then handles all local decisions; service providers (and some manufacturers) view licensing in a similar vein. While such arrangements can be viewed as add-on business and a source of increased return with minimal effort, the lack of control often proves unsatisfactory to managers who think beyond their domestic markets.

Increased commitments to international marketing occur when a firm takes over more of the management, production, and marketing functions outside of its original market. Examples of this increased commitment include not only exporting from the home country, but running the distribution system as well; going from licensing the use of the corporate logo for the delivery of services to actively participating in the management of service facilities and ensuring that standards are met; and buying local companies to understand and gain a foothold in local markets. As firms become more sophisticated in international business, they begin to see that fewer of their decisions turn on home market versus foreign markets, but on what is the best way to compete internationally.

A firm makes many decisions when developing an international marketing strategy. In some cases, it is difficult for a company to take a domestic strategy and implement it in its entirety in a foreign market. A global competitive strategy, in which the directives and the goals of a firm are "in sync" across all divisions and countries, must be balanced against the autonomy that each domestic business requires in order to effectively compete in local markets. Each country, to a certain degree, must be treated as its own marketplace–each nation possesses varied political, legal, social, and cultural requirements. Also, each nation has its own currency and interest rate structure.

In terms of the marketing mix, important decisions must be made regarding all four mix components. Some of the more important considerations are highlighted in the following sections.

PRODUCT

The primary concern for any firm in international product policy decisions is the fit of the product with the needs, desires, or wants of a foreign market segment. Almost without exception, before considering other issues, a company must determine that their product strategically fits with a particular international market. Once a proper fit has been determined, other factors to take into account are product/service positioning and the degree of uniformity or standardization to adopt.

Effective foreign product/service positioning can be a difficult task to accomplish, unless a firm has a substantial base of experience in a particular region. Positioned properly, a foreign product can often command a premium price (as evidenced in the Canadian garment industry), but positioned poorly, a firm may waste a substantial amount of money and achieve a small market share.

Marketing a standardized product in foreign markets offers advantages such as lower manufacturing costs, easier service requirements, and greater performance monitoring capabilities. Few companies, with exceptions such as McDonald's and IBM, have been able to maintain a high degree of product uniformity. Products and services must frequently be adapted to address the needs and desires of a particular international market segment.

PRICE

Price probably is the most difficult component to control for an international firm. Standardized pricing is virtually impossible to achieve due to different tax laws, exchange rates, and interest rates.

In determining a price for a product or service in a foreign country, international firms must carefully consider many factors. Some of these factors are similar to domestic pricing decisions, but considerations that are unique to international pricing are the stability of the foreign currency, the rate of inflation (for example in the mid-1980s, Peru experienced inflation of 40% per month), and in the case of less developed countries, the method of payment. An additional factor that firms must consider is countertrade where instead of receiving money for goods, the international marketer receives payment in kind. Finally, some marketers have to consider the risk of transhipments or "grey markets," when differing pricing strategies and tax systems make it economical to buy goods in one country and sell them in another. A cosmetics firm, for example, pursuing an upscale strategy in developed markets and a mid-range policy elsewhere, may find its differentiated strategy upset by transhipments between countries.

DISTRIBUTION

There are two types of systems that a firm may utilize in distributing products internationally: direct and indirect. With the direct approach, the domestic firm deals with foreign firms. Using the indirect method, the domestic firm deals with another firm that acts as a sales agent for the producer of the product.

The type of distribution system utilized will depend, in part, on the level of involvement the manufacturer has with the overseas market; the more sales a firm is seeking from a particular market, the more involved the company will want to be in the distribution process. Also, the type of distribution method used will depend on the system(s) that are available to a company in a particular country. For example, in Saudi Arabia the most common distribution channel for manufactured goods is manufacturer to wholesaler to retailer, while many Japanese markets are characterized by the distribution of imported products via a variety of channels—one of the more popular is the multi-wholesaler system. Several agents may be needed to distribute products to the many small retailers who play a very important role in Japan as they account for a substantial portion of retail sales for some goods.

COMMUNICATION

Communication techniques, including promotion, advertising, and personal selling, are often more difficult to co-ordinate and integrate in international markets. This is primarily a result of the fact that firms may be restricted by the media vehicles available and the existing regulations within a country.

Another factor a firm must consider when designing an international communication strategy is the degree of uniformity to use with an advertising message that is being employed across two or more foreign markets. While opinions differ on this issue, it is clear that over the last decade, international communication messages have become more standardized. This has occurred because many nations have achieved a higher standard of living; manufacturers have responded with products that are more globally uniform, and with advertising and personal selling initiatives that are more internationally standardized. This strategy primarily applies to the more developed nations; in the less developed countries, promotion techniques must vary due to limited accessibility to some mass-media vehicles (for example, television and radio) and differing literacy rates. Instead, firms may have to rely on unique promotions such as sponsorships of a sporting event or free information clinics to show potential customers how to use a product.

CONCLUSION

For many firms around the world, international marketing is becoming an integral part of their business operations. Companies are no longer restricting themselves to domestic markets, instead they are utilizing competitive advantages to exploit global opportunities. Over the last decade, many governments have decreased national and international trade barriers, thus encouraging more foreign trade. As a result, a global perspective must be adopted by many companies to prosper in the 1990s and beyond.

To compete on an international level, firms frequently must redefine their businesses and become more specialized; business focus leads to greater efficiencies and increased economies of scale. Marketing on a global level also requires a company to define their "sustainable" competitive advantage on a country by country basis. Firms should define an advantage by reviewing their business operations and comparing them to the socioeconomic, political, and cultural environments of potential markets.

As companies enter the global marketplace, there are many factors to consider. Firms must first determine if a strategic fit exists between their product or service and the wants of the peoples of a particular foreign market. Companies must also understand the impact of barriers and quotas and the political, legal, cultural, and economic environments of foreign countries. Once these elements have been examined, a firm must develop a marketing plan that requires managers to examine a broad range of global and local factors. This process must be undertaken, at least in part, with every prospective country. While this is a time-consuming and somewhat intimidating task for many firms, it appears that many companies must develop their competitive advantages on a global level to succeed in the twenty-first century.

37 ROSS PACIFIC FOODS

Katherine Gallagher
Charles B. Weinberg

"Well, I'm still not convinced that we should get into the Korean honey market," said Geoff Taub, one of two executive vice-presidents of Ross Pacific Foods. "We've built a $15 million business by doing what we know best, importing Asian foods into Canada. I can see that exporting Canadian honey to Korea has potential, but is it sound enough for us to go ahead with it now?"

"Geoff, we built this business by taking risks," said Beth Wine, the firm's other executive vice-president. "The marketing plan is well researched and the time to move is now. If anything, I thought you'd think the plan was too cautious. I admit it'll take several years until it's profitable, but it's a real opportunity. Pardon the pun, but it's a 'honey' of a deal."

Michael Chan, president and founder of Ross Pacific, felt it was time to make a decision. It was early February 1988, and his staff had spent considerable time, with the help of outside consultants, putting together a marketing plan for exporting Canadian honey to South Korea. "Okay, let's review this one more time. Let's meet Monday at 8 a.m. to go through all the details again. We'll stay as long as necessary to reach a decision. Can you both clear your schedules for Monday?"

COMPANY BACKGROUND

Ross Pacific, a Vancouver firm specializing in the import, distribution, and wholesaling of foods from Asian Pacific countries, employed about 50 people in its Vancouver head office. It had branch offices in several Asian cities, including Seoul, Hong Kong, Taipei, Bangkok, and Jakarta. (Exhibit 1 provides a financial summary.)

Ross Pacific started modestly 20 years earlier when Michael Chan, then a recent immigrant from Hong Kong, began importing Chinese specialty foods to sell in his Ross Avenue grocery store in Vancouver's Chinatown area. Ross Pacific had grown steadily, although it had experienced a few setbacks. In its first few years, overly optimistic estimates of market potential for some items led to losses. It also had intermittent problems with getting suppliers to provide consistent product quality; occasionally, lapses in product quality had been very costly. However, during the 1980s, increasing numbers of Asian immigrants in Canada, as well as greater acceptance of and curiosity about Asian cultures in the Caucasian population, had led to market growth for many Asian food imports.

Ross Pacific's management had lately been investigating opportunities for exporting Canadian products. Over the years, they had built an extensive network of

Note: Some data are disguised. Unless otherwise noted, all figures are in Canadian dollars.

contacts in Asia. Many of these, in appreciation for the job that Ross Pacific had done in selling their products in Canada, had expressed a willingness to reciprocate in their home markets. This seemed like a worthwhile opportunity. Also, Michael Chan believed that it would be prudent to balance the company's risks and vulnerability by being both an exporter and an importer. Canadian honey was the first product considered for export.

CANADIAN HONEY

Honey is a sweet, sticky substance made by honeybees from the nectar of flowers. According to a recent market research survey, 82% of Canadians claim to be users of honey; it is perceived as a wholesome, natural food. Honey consists mostly of glucose and fructose, although there are also traces of proteins and vitamins.

The two forms of honey, liquid and solid, do not differ in content. Conversion between liquid and solid forms is easily accomplished by temperature changes. There are also two types of honey, pasteurized and unpasteurized. In pasteurized honey, yeasts, which might ferment the honey, have been killed by heat. The Canadian government allows pasteurized honey to contain no more than 18.6% moisture; unpasteurized honey may contain no more than 17.6% moisture.

The flavour of the honey depends on the flowers from which the honeybees collect nectar. For instance, honey from alfalfa and clover is golden coloured, with a light smell and taste; buckwheat honey is dark-chocolate coloured and has a very strong smell. In western Canada, there are several source flowers: alfalfa, clover, buckwheat, fruit-tree flowers, and wildflowers. Honey from different flowers can be mixed to get special characteristics. In addition, flavours such as strawberry or cream can be added to the honey.

There are four grades of Canadian honey, unimaginatively labelled No. 1, No. 2, No. 3, and No. 4, with No. 1 honey being the highest quality. The grade depends on the honey's colour, smell, taste, water content, total sugar content, amount of crystallization, stickiness, and so on. "Good" honey should be golden coloured, the smell and the taste should be "good," specific gravity should be 1.4 or higher, the total sugar content should be high (the less saccharase [a sugar compound] the better), and the honey should crystallize very well at room temperature. Stringent government regulations control the quality of Canadian honey.[1]

THE KOREAN HONEY MARKET

When they first considered exporting Canadian honey to Korea, Ross Pacific's management outlined what they believed the firm's strengths and weaknesses would be in this market. They saw three main strengths. First, they were in a strong financial position, with retained earnings of several million dollars. Second, their experience dealing with Asian food concerns had given them "connections" in most Asian countries, including Korea. Finally, there was an existing infra-structure in place to

[1] Canadian regulations required at least 78% sugar content and allowed no saccharase, no artificial sweeteners, and no artificial colour in honey.

Exhibit 1

FINANCIAL SUMMARY OF ROSS PACIFIC OPERATIONS (000s)

	1978	1979	1980	1981	1982	1983	1984	1985	1986	1987[1]
Net sales	$3,026.31	$3,859.80	$4,745.16	$5,829.39	$6,920.34	$8,079.12	$9,610.86	$12,671.82	$13,652.52	$14,700.63
Cost of products sold	2,467.50	3,071.88	3,701.04	4,561.41	5,363.19	6,248.55	6,996.57	8,637.72	9,269.82	9,819.81
Gross profit	558.81	787.92	1,044.12	1,267.98	1,557.15	1,830.57	2,614.29	4,034.10	4,382.70	4,880.82
Marketing, administrative, and general expenses	289.38	399.84	577.29	749.07	900.06	1,081.50	1,579.20	2,562.42	2,797.83	3,132.99
Operating income	269.43	388.08	466.83	518.91	657.09	749.07	1,035.09	1,471.68	1,584.87	1,747.83

[1] In 1987, sales of imports of food products to Canada were $11.4 million (78% of total sales), sales of imports of non-food products were $2.9 million (20%), and sales of exports of all products were $0.3 million (4%). The import of food products accounted for 85% of operating income, the import of non-food products accounted for 13% of operating income, and exports accounted for 2% of income. The percentages for both sales and income had remained virtually unchanged (within ±2%) over the past three years.

Exhibit 2

KOREAN EARNINGS AND PRICE OF HONEY (IN WON)

Year	1979	1980	1981	1982	1983	1984	1985	1986
Average monthly income per worker	142,665	176,058	212,477	245,981	273,119	296,907	324,283	350,965
Price of honey per kilogram (at farm)	5,478	7,629	9,262	9,700	10,104	10,090	10,052	9,827
Price ratios (%)	3.8	4.3	4.3	3.9	3.6	3.3	3.1	2.8

Note: In 1986, $1.00 CDN = 640 Won

ensure the efficient movement of food products. Of particular importance were the shipping, customs brokerage, and telecommunications networks.

These strengths were balanced by two serious weaknesses. First, the company had no experience exporting to Korea. Even though Ross Pacific had done some limited exporting to Japan, management recognized that Korean culture and the business environment there were different. Second, Ross Pacific was a trading house—the intermediary—not the producer. It therefore had little control over suppliers, especially with respect to such crucial factors as quality, quantity, and packaging technology. The positive relationships with its Asian suppliers that Ross Pacific had developed and cultivated over the years had meant that this had largely ceased to be a problem on the import side of the business, but the reliability of Canadian honey suppliers was unknown.

What was known, however, was quite a bit about the Korean honey market. A few months earlier, Beth Wine had been put in charge of researching the market. She had organized an extensive review of the situation. A Korean consultant had collected data on Korean attitudes toward honey, as well as the regulatory situation.

Korean Consumers

Koreans traditionally regard honey, not as a food, but as a medicinal substance. It is thought to be both a source of vigour and a "miracle medicine" that sustains good health. For instance, honey is used after medical operations to speed recovery. Diluted with hot water, it is said to cure a hangover. More commonly, sliced ginseng is pickled with honey and eaten a couple of times a day to maintain good health. Although Western medicine has not demonstrated that it has any curative or preventative properties, Koreans maintain that honey is an invaluable instrument of preventative medicine.

Canadian honey was perceived to be of higher quality and lower cost than the domestic product. Many Korean visitors to Canada bought 20 to 30 kg of honey to take back to Korea, and Canadian honey was one of the most popular gift items sent by Korean immigrants to their relatives back home.

In Korea, honey was bought at oriental herb stores or honey specialty stores, usually by women—not for themselves, but for their husbands, fathers-in-law, and mothers-in-law—in their role as guardians of family health.[2] Korean shoppers did not seem to have confidence that domestic honey was "pure." Several shoppers were overheard querying shopkeepers, "Is it pure honey? I hope I'm buying real (pure) honey this time." Wealthy Koreans sometimes went as far as seeking out farmers directly to find "real" honey, often at very high prices.

Demand and Supply

Even given the lack of consumer confidence in the product, there was strong demand for honey in Korea, and Ross Pacific's research led management to believe that

[2] Korean tradition calls for women to put the needs and desires of their in-laws and husband ahead of their own.

Exhibit 3
NUMBER OF KOREAN HONEY FARMS AND PRODUCTION

Year	1982	1983	1984	1985	1986 Est.
Farms (000s)	51.9	54.5	53.2	51.5	52.8
Hives (000s)	395	444	451	467	475
Production (mil. kg.)	14.13	15.98	16.24	16.81	18.45
Growth rate of production	N.A.	13%	2%	4%	10%

demand would increase. At the same time, it seemed likely that the domestic supply of honey would not keep up with demand.

In 1988, there were about 41 million people in Korea.[3] In 1986, the last year for which there were figures, per capita consumption of honey had increased to about 0.45 kg from 0.20 kg in 1979. In comparison, Canadian consumption was about 1.2 kg per person.

Beth Wine believed that Korean demand for honey would continue to increase. She saw three reasons for the expansion of the market. First, Koreans appeared to be becoming more health conscious. Expenditures on food and beverages as a percentage of total household expenditure had decreased from 48.1% in 1980 to 44.6% in 1985, while medical and health-related expenditures had increased from 3.9% in 1980 to 4.3% in 1985. Second, honey was becoming more affordable. The average monthly earning power of workers was increasing while the per unit price of honey was decreasing (Exhibit 2). Finally, Ms. Wine anticipated that, as they used it more frequently, Korean consumers would start to consider honey a food, rather than just a medicinal substance.

The growing demand for honey in Korea was not being met by domestic production. In 1986, total domestic honey production was only 18.5 million kilograms (Exhibit 3). There were several reasons for low honey production. First, the average Korean honey farmer kept only about nine hives. Beekeeping was rarely a farmer's primary occupation; it tended to be a sideline or hobby. Second, unit production per hive was low. This was a result of scarcity of source flowers due to widespread rice farming (rice does not produce source flowers), short blooming seasons for what source flowers there were, and the fact that the time of greatest source flower bloom coincided with heavy rains, preventing bees from collecting nectar. Finally, many Korean beekeepers were still using "non-improved" bees, which are not highly productive.

[3] Major cities are the capital, Seoul (population 10 million), Busan (3.5 million), Taegu (2 million), and Incheon (1.3 million). The population growth rate is about 1.25% and population density is 419 per square kilometre. Recently the government recommended that families have only two children, and imposed penalties on families with more children. Koreans are well-educated: almost everyone finishes high school, and most go to university.

It was Beth Wine's contention that the supply of domestic honey would only increase marginally and might even decrease or become uneconomical in the next few years. As Korea's population increased, more and more farmland was being developed for urban use. As honey production is heavily dependent on the availability of land, geographical environments, and proper weather conditions, this decrease in farmland would limit or decrease honey production.

Price

As one might expect in a situation of excess demand, honey in Korea was not cheap. The price ranged from $11 Canadian to $100 Canadian per kilogram. Honey at the lower end of the price range had recently been introduced in grocery and department stores by a food processing company, Dong Seo Foods, as one of its food lines. Honey at the higher end of the price range was supposedly collected from the honeycombs of wild bees, and was sold either at oriental medicine stores, at honey specialty stores, or directly by farmers. The bulk of Korean honey was sold through oriental medicine stores and honey specialty stores.

Distribution

Although no one firm dominated the distribution system, the wholesale herbal medicine distributors, which supplied Chinese medicine stores, were major players. Major competitors were the domestic honey producers, who often sold honey (as a medicine) directly to customers, to oriental herb stores in the cities, or to the Agricultural Co-op.

Recently, several Korean food companies, such as Dong Seo Foods, had started marketing honey through domestic food channels. Dong Seo Foods was well known in the Korean food processing industry. They bought their honey directly from domestic producers, processed, packaged, and labelled it, then sold it through large food stores. The product was not high quality, as was typical of most Korean honey. Other distributors sold honey through department stores.

Regulatory Changes

Until 1987, honey could be imported only by firms approved by the Ministry of Agriculture, or by the Head of the Agriculture Co-op with permission from the Ministry of Agriculture. There was a 25% tariff. At the end of 1987, however, a trade surplus, coupled with political pressure from the outside, notably the United States, prompted the Korean government to relax certain import restrictions. As a result, honey imports were allowed, but for hotel use only, and imported honey was required to have a sugar content of at least 78%, higher than the 76% required for the domestic product.

The consultant hired by Ross Pacific reported that Korean consumer groups were complaining that the price for honey was too high. Indications were that import restrictions on honey would be relaxed soon. The consultant also expected that eventually the government would eliminate the protection of domestic honey production, since honey was not the main source of income for honey farmers, and they were relatively inefficient. This move would be consistent with recent de-regulation

Exhibit 4

EXPORT COST ANALYSIS

Honey Price per kg	Description
$2.75	Wholesale price in Canada ($2.60 to $2.90).*
0.13	Shipping cost; 12 (1 kg) jars/case, 1000 cases in a container
0.14	Insurance, custom fees, etc.
0.68	Tariff; 25% of invoice price
$3.70	Price at the Korean port

* The Canadian wholesale price is for Canada No. 1 white honey (Alfalfa-Clover).

in the wine industry, where the government had announced its intention to open up 40% of the market within two years. If and when this happened, Korean importers might consider several countries. The major producers of honey were the U.S.S.R. (190 million kilograms), China (150 million kilograms), the U.S.A. (91 million kilograms), Mexico (47 million kilograms), Canada (38 million kilograms), and Australia (27 million kilograms).

Although the U.S.S.R. and China were the biggest producers, under the present administration, it seemed unlikely that the Korean government would encourage substantial imports from Communist countries. Mexico and Australia were major producers but did not have as much political clout as Canada, due to the Korean trade surplus with Canada. The United States was also a large producer, but was not much of a threat because domestic production was insufficient for export—the United States was a net importer of honey. Therefore, Ross Pacific's expectation was that the Korean government would look favourably at Canadian imports of honey.

CANADIAN HONEY IN THE KOREAN MARKET

Ross Pacific's management believed that Canadian honey was superior to Korean honey in several ways. The Canadian government imposed higher quality specifications than the Korean government.[4] Canadian honey contained less moisture, more total sugar, and finer particles. Many Canadian brands of honey exceeded the minimum specifications. In contrast, Korean honey production practices were not regulated. Beekeepers often added sugar to the honey to increase volume.

Second, the flavour of Canadian honey was preferred to that of Korean honey. In Canada, alfalfa, clover, buckwheat, and fruit-tree blossoms are the main source flowers. These produce better-testing honey than do the source flowers commonly found in Korea. In addition, lower levels of air pollution in Canada and a longer collection season (due to the absence of a rainy season) contribute to better taste.

Canadian honey also had a price advantage. The lowest-priced honey in Korea retailed for $11 (Canadian) per kilogram, far above the average retail price of $6 in Canada. As shown in Exhibit 4, Ross Pacific could be very price competitive because the basic cost was only $3.70 for high-quality honey landed in Korea.

[4] Korean government specifications required the sugar content to be at least 76%, allowed up to 21% moisture, and saccharase up to 7%. No artificial sweeteners nor artificial colours were allowed.

Supplier Decision

Of the three major Western Canadian suppliers—Bee Cee Ltd. and KB Ltd. in B.C., and Bee Maid Co-op in the Prairies—Ross Pacific had decided on Bee Maid. Bee Maid, a beekeepers' co-operative in Alberta, Saskatchewan, and Manitoba, was the largest honey supplier in Canada. It collected honey from farmers, then processed and packaged it for wholesalers. Bee Maid also did some promotion in Canada and the United States.

Bee Maid was already exporting honey to more than 20 countries, so the brand was well recognized internationally, including Japan. Bee Maid had shown an interest in expanding its market in association with Ross Pacific, and it seemed clear that they could consistently supply honey for export. Moreover, Bee Maid would agree to give Ross Pacific an exclusive license for Korea provided minimum quantities (to be specified in contract negotiations) were ordered each year.

In order to take advantage of the positive reputation of Canadian honey, packaging and labelling would emphasize the origin of the "Canadian" product and the "purity" of the honey. Consequently, the product would be packaged and sealed in Canada, and labelled "Sealed in Canada."

MARKETING PLAN

Michael, Geoff, and Beth had all agreed that the Korean honey market was worthy of further investigation. Consequently, Beth had been put in charge of a three-person team to develop a marketing plan. The basic planning assumptions were that Ross Pacific was to enter the Korean honey market, supply of Canadian honey was viewed as assured, and no more than $500,000 would be invested. The following consists of the main points from the four-phase plan that the team developed.

A Four-Phase Marketing Plan

The first phase (hotels) deals with the current situation, where we can only import honey for use in hotels under current import regulations. In this stage, efforts will be focused on hotels to develop goodwill with the government and gain a foothold in the Korean market.

The second phase (hotels and medicine) will go into action when the Korean government opens the honey market and relaxes import restrictions. (Some restrictions may still apply.) At this stage, consumers still consider honey as a medicine rather than food. The main strategy is to build sales in the medicine market and eventually obtain dominance in this market segment. At the same time, a minor thrust into the food market will be attempted.

The third stage (medicine and food) will come into effect when consumers' attitudes toward honey change. In this phase most consumers will have undergone a cultural change and consider honey as food, rather than medicine. Although honey-as-medicine sales will remain strong, the food market will grow considerably. The main strategy is to hold and maintain the medicine market segment and to build the food market segment.

The fourth stage (food) will be reached when the abundance of honey turns it into a commodity. Similar to the current situation in Canada, Koreans will have sufficient income to purchase honey as a regular item. The strategy in this phase is to hold and maintain profits, in the face of anticipated competitive pressures. At the present time, this phase of the marketing plan has not been developed in detail.

Phase One

Environment. There are several significant aspects of the market to consider. This will be the first time Canadian honey will have been introduced to Korea for commercial purposes. Many Koreans have tasted Canadian honey, but it was as a souvenir of travel or a gift from relatives who had emigrated to Canada. In addition, Canadian honey will not be available directly to Koreans, because all imported honey will be used only in hotels. We need to consider the special business environment of this phase.

On the legal side, there is an import restriction at this time: honey can be imported for hotel use only. We expect this to change, but it will likely be done step-by-step because of pressure from Korean honey producers.

In terms of market size, there are roughly 300 hotels in Korea, with about 160 concentrated in the four largest cities: Seoul, Busan, Taegu, and Incheon.

Major foreign competitors will be the United States and Australia. The strongest selling point for Canadian honey is the image of Canada as a big, unspoiled, natural country. In addition to foreign competitors, there are several local honey companies like Dong Seo Food and Han Yang Food. Since the local honey price is very high, if Ross Pacific introduces Canadian honey at a low price, we expect the competition will give up the small hotel market.

Product. The main consumers of honey in Korean hotels will be foreigners; we will offer only high-quality liquid honey (Canada No. 1 White), because most foreigners prefer it. This will not only please foreigners, it will also give us a small foothold with Korean consumers, as Koreans with high incomes are also an important segment of the hotel market. This is very important, because we plan to import Canadian honey for consumer use in the next phase.

We have decided against introducing other forms of high-quality honey during this phase, since the goal is simply to gain a strategic foothold in Korea in anticipation of the next phase. Profitability is not a major goal in Phase One.

Price. We will charge the lowest price possible in order to get into more hotels, thereby allowing more Koreans to be exposed to Canadian honey. The low price of Canadian honey, which Koreans might take as a signal of low quality, will not be known to potential consumers, since the hotels will mark it up, so it should not have a negative impact on the image of Canadian honey.

The lowest price for breakeven is $6 per kilogram (Exhibit 5). We do not know the likely price of other imported honeys, but transportation and other related costs will be similar to ours. As for production costs in the United States and Australia, we believe that costs are slightly higher in the United States than in Canada, and that Australian costs are about the same as ours. We could price as much as $4 per kilogram more and still be substantially below current Korean prices.

Distribution. At present, honey used in hotels bears the brand name of the distributors, such as Dong Seo or Han Yang. The main focus of Dong Seo and Han Yang is coffee and various drinks, respectively; honey is not their chief interest. They gather honey directly from producers, process it minimally, and then distribute it through their own channels. The larger hotels purchase honey directly from the company-owned distribution agency, but the smaller hotels usually buy at nearby supermarkets. The quality of this honey is lower than Canadian honey, and the price is considerably higher.

Our strategy for distribution is to set up our own office with two salespeople in Seoul. This location has been chosen because it is the political, economic, cultural, and social centre of Korea. It also has one-third of the total hotels in the nation. Once the Seoul office has been established, we will use it as a base to open direct channels to hotels in other main cities.

Promotion. We will pursue three different promotion strategies. The first is person-to-person and door-to-door. This is possible because the hotel market is limited in terms of location and number. Main targets will be restaurant managers and/or cooks. A close relationship between a salesperson and a manager (and/or a cook) is a very important factor for sales in Korea, and we need to establish and maintain good relationships. Our second strategy is to distribute free samples to hotels. Because we are certain that Canadian honey is of much better quality than the local product, as well as lower in price, we feel this will be a good way to establish relationships with the hotels. The sample will be the same in size and shape as the honey we will be selling. The salespeople will carry these samples with them when they visit the hotels.

Third, we will print and distribute recipe booklets which also tell the Canadian honey story. The booklets will give hotel cooks new ideas for using honey, and can also be used in the consumer phases.

Exhibit 5

DERIVATION OF BREAKEVEN PRICE (THREE-YEAR AVERAGE, BEFORE LOBBYING COSTS)

Cost/kg (at Korean port)	$3.70
Annual sales (kg) (80 hotels at 500 kg/hotel) =	40,000 kg
Cost of goods sold (40,000 * $3.70) =	$148,000
Administration and promotional costs	$92,000
Total cost	$233,000
Approximate minimum price $240,000/40,000 =	$6/kg

Assumptions:
1. Average hotel purchase = 500 kg/yr
2. Market size and share (at end of phase I): 160 hotels in 4 cities * 50% = 80 hotels
3. Incremental personnel costs = $40,000

Incremental personnel costs	= $40,000
Office rental	= $20,000
Set-up costs (written off over three years)	= $17,000
Sampling program (average over three years)	= $ 5,000
Recipe book	= $10,000
Total:	$92,000

Marketing Budget. We can allocate up to $500,000 for this phase, which we believe will last about three years. We estimate that this will be sufficient to set up and operate the Seoul office. One manager, currently based in Korea, will be responsible for the initial business and two salespeople will be employed locally. At this time, we have no plans to send additional people to Korea. Space adjacent to our current offices in Seoul is available. Incremental personnel costs will be $40,000 annually and office rental (and related expenses) will be $20,000 annually.

Set-up costs are estimated to be roughly $50,000: $30,000 for two cars and $15,000 for furniture and fixtures. Another $5,000 is allocated for other expenses, such as handling charges.

The cost of the sampling program is expected to be $10,000 (at most) in the first year, and minimal thereafter. The recipe booklet will cost $10,000 in each of the three years. We feel it is important to update the recipe books on a regular basis.

The major portion of the budget for this phase will be allocated to government lobbying. We estimate it at up to $225,000 ($75,000 for each of three years).

Timing. Ross Pacific will start exporting Canadian honey to Korea in January 1989. We expect to concentrate on Seoul in the first year and gradually expand to Busan, Taegu, and Incheon. The Phase One strategies will be continued until the Korean government opens up the honey market. Although we cannot pinpoint when this will be, we do not anticipate that it will be more than three years, given Korea's current trend toward a more open market.

Marketing Action Plan. The three goals are (1) take 50% of the hotel restaurant market in the four major cities by the end of three years, (2) open the market as soon as possible, and (3) accumulate experience. Two potential problems exist. The first is Korean honey producers may resist the government's opening of the market. The strength of their resistance will be an important determinant of the timing of the lifting of import restrictions. Thus, the Korean government must be cultivated in a careful (and silent) way. The second potential problem is that other exporters will see, and go after, the same opportunity.

Phase Two

Environment. With import restrictions removed, the potential for the honey market is huge. The food market will be larger than the medicine market. At this time, the medicine market is over $200 million annually. Consequently, in this phase, we will begin to target consumers. We expect to achieve substantial market share and commensurate profits. At this stage, special business environments become crucial.

First, we anticipate that the Korean government will not open the market completely, chiefly because of political pressure from honey producers and the possibility of a swing in public opinion against opening agricultural markets to international competition. On the other hand, the precedents in Korea point to a more open economy. Furthermore, agricultural trade restrictions are a major issue in the 1992 GATT negotiations. Our main concern is the size of the honey quota and the way it will be allocated among various countries. We are guessing that the size of the initial quota will be 5% of local production and that the allocation will be based on previous trade volumes in other goods. This puts us in a good position.

We expect that local honey production will reach 22 million kilograms per year by 1992, up from about 18 million kilograms in 1986, and honey imports will reach 1.1 million kilograms per year. The value of the Korean honey market (local and imported) is estimated to be roughly $231 million (Canadian) a year, at retail; the imported honey market will be about $11 million a year (based on $10 per kilogram).

Consumer behaviour must also be considered. The traditional Korean view of honey is as a medicine or health tonic. Although we believe this attitude can be changed so that consumers view honey as food, such a change will take time to accomplish. That is the overriding goal of Phase Two. Closely related to this is the need to ensure consistently high quality. Because honey has been so expensive and quality has been so low, the reputation of the honey trade is poor: hence the Korean proverb that "the father does not believe the son in the honey trade."

Another important aspect of consumer behaviour is that housewives purchase the honey. This must be taken into account in all strategies. We have made contacts with a leading Korean market research firm. They are prepared to, and capable of, doing a major market research survey of consumers, but advise against doing so until a year before we are ready to enter the consumer market directly.

There will be powerful local competition from companies such as Dong Seo and Han Yang Food.

Product. Until recently, Koreans have been unfamiliar with liquid honey. Whenever they think of honey, Koreans imagine creamy honey. One food company started distributing liquid honey at a low price a few years ago, but the introduction was unsuccessful, because creamy honey is so well established as a medicine.

Thus, in this phase, we will export two different kinds of Canadian honey. For hotels, liquid honey will still be provided, but creamy honey will also be available. For the consumer market, creamy honey will be offered, except for department stores, where liquid honey will also be available. No matter what the form, market, or channel, the Canadian honey we export will be the premium product.

Packaging will differ in the hotel and consumer markets, in order to allow us to charge different prices. It is crucial that honey will be labelled and sealed in Canada for authenticity.

Price. For the hotel market, we will continue the previous pricing policy, for two reasons. First, profit from the hotel market is negligible no matter what the price, and, second, our high-quality image will be reinforced if our product is widely available in hotels.

For the consumer market, we plan to charge a premium price, equivalent to at least $11 (Canadian) per kilogram (in today's dollars). The important thing in the Korean honey trade in Korea is, as mentioned before, authenticity. The higher price will reassure customers that quality is high. Furthermore, under quota restrictions, products with higher prices are more profitable.

Distribution. Channels for the hotel market will continue as set up.

During this phase of the marketing plan, we will begin distributing Canadian honey to consumers through herbal medicine dealers. We will focus on the largest four cities, because under a 5% import quota, distribution to the smaller cities will be less profitable, given the higher costs of reaching these markets.

The department store channel will be a second focus. It is not unusual for department stores in Korea to sell imported or gourmet foods in a special section of the store. Since it is recognized in Seoul that the department stores deal with the high quality and expensive commodities, it is consistent with our product strategy to place Canadian honey here. In addition, through this channel, we will be able to monitor changes in the perceptions of honey (as a medicine or as a food). This will become important factor in Phase Three.

We will avoid supermarkets at this stage, because the honey in supermarkets is inexpensive and therefore incompatible with our high-quality image.

Promotion. We will, at this stage, establish one more office with two salespeople in Busan, the largest port and second-largest city in Korea. The Seoul office will be in charge of the northern part of the country and the Busan office will take care of the south.

We are also considering three advertising strategies. The first is advertising through herbal medicine periodicals. There are over 3,000 herbal medicine clinics in Korea, and the influence of the herbal medicine doctor is strong. Advertisements in these periodicals will be based on a chemical analysis of honey, and we expect that herbal medicine doctors will begin recommending Canadian honey to their patients.

We will also advertise in women's magazines, because women make most honey purchases. The high quality and the authenticity of Canadian honey will be emphasized.

Finally, recipe booklets will be distributed to department store customers. These booklets will be similar to those used for hotels in Phase One. Here we intend to introduce the idea that honey is a food, and show housewives how to use it.

Marketing Budget. During Phase Two, we expect to become profitable. For setting up the Busan office, we will allocate the same amount of money as for the Seoul office and have similar staffing policies. Additional sales assistants will be hired in both cities as necessary to provide sufficient market coverage. We anticipate that all personnel costs (including salary and expenses) will be 10% of sales.

Lobbying of the government will also be necessary, to encourage either the complete opening of the market or a larger quota. But the government lobbying at this stage will be at a lower rate, but protracted. Thus we allocate $50,000 annually for ten years.

The cost of the advertising program can only be roughly estimated. Personal selling will be strongly supported by the advertising strategies described above. We budget advertising at 5% of sales, though market research will be undertaken to better understand the response to differing advertising strategies.

Timing. In the first half of Phase Two, we will concentrate on medicinal use of honey, but in the second half, the focus will shift to honey as food.

Marketing Action Plan. The goals of Phase Two are (1) 50% market share of the 5% import quota, (2) maintain and enhance a high-quality image, (3) convince Korean consumers that honey is also a food, (4) continue to open the market, and (5) make a profit, with full recovery of costs, by 1995.

Phase Three

Phase Three will begin when the market is open. While we can set the general direction of Phase Three, all numbers are highly speculative. In brief, being successful at Phases One and Two will put us in the position of being able to pursue a highly profitable competitive strategy that late entrants will have difficulty in matching.

Environment. Phase Three of the marketing plan will be reached when consumers perceive honey as a food rather than as a medicine. We think that this change is inevitable, based on the theory of "cultural convergence", that is, as Koreans interact more with the West, they will adopt more Western attitudes, including the attitude that honey is a food. This effect will be hastened by increasing supplies of honey.

Despite the expected demand increase in the food market and the decrease in the medicine market, the medicine market will still remain relatively large compared with the food market during this phase of the marketing plan. In the long run, the traditional medicine market is not of much interest to us, but as a service, high-quality honey will continue to be sold through medicine stores in a market maintenance mode.

The general market condition will be "growth." As honey changes from being a medicine to being a food, sales volume is expected to increase rapidly. Early converts to the food market will influence other consumers to use honey as a food, accelerating demand. This market condition is expected to persist for between two and five years before growth in demand flattens.

We anticipate an intense competitive situation. Although foreign competition will be minimal (probably only temporarily) due to the exclusive marketing agreements secured in Phase Two of the marketing plan, domestic producers of honey are expected to put up an intense fight for market share. The government, more specifically the Korea Trade Commission, will likely take measures to protect the approximately 50,000 honey farmers. Import quotas or tariffs may be imposed, but probably only to help farmers adjust to the new market realities. The Korean government will recognize that Korea does not have a comparative advantage in the production of honey, and that it would be more efficient and economical to import in the long run. As long as the government restricts imports, the price level will be maintained at a relatively high level, and the target market will continue to be high- and middle-income families.

Product. In the food market segment, only medium quality (Canada No. 2 and No. 3) honey will be sold; Canada No. 1 will be reserved for the medicine market.

Price. In the medicine market, the target retail price will be considerably higher than that of domestically produced honey. The profit margin is difficult to estimate because the tariff rate during this phase is unknown. However, a minimum 20% profit margin is required to cover the potential risks in a declining market.

In the food market, the retail price will likely be set at parity with domestic honey. Since the quality of Canadian honey is superior, at parity pricing, it will be a better value. Parity pricing also prevents accusations of dumping, which might provoke the Korean government to invoke protectionist measures. We see here why it is important to have secured exclusive rights or agreements for honey distribution, so that we can maintain an orderly growth, minimizing disruptive competition from other foreign competitors in this sensitive phase of growth.

Distribution. In this phase, because of the large volume (about 6 million kilograms) of honey to be distributed, we will require a warehouse—either our own or a joint venture with a large distributor—near a seaport. The number of sales representatives will be increased in order to deal with the larger number of customers. The exact number of sales reps will depend on the number of customers we have. As a rule of thumb, each customer should be called on at least once every two months.

In the medicine market, the traditional herbal distribution system will continue to be followed.

In the food market, the traditional food distribution system is far too complex to be used. Currently, food passes through at least five distribution steps before it reaches a retailer. The large number of small wholesalers in the Korean food distribution system makes the servicing of all wholesalers unwieldy. Therefore, in this phase only department stores, supermarkets, and the larger distributors will be used. Our honey will not be retailed through grocery stores, as it is in Canada; this channel will be left to local producers, should they want to pursue this opportunity (an unlikely eventuality). This distribution plan is congruent with the goal of targeting only the upper-middle income segment of population which tends to frequent department stores and the supermarkets.

Promotion. In the medicine market, the promotion strategy will remain the same as in the previous phase.

In the food market, magazine advertising, introductory discount coupons, and posters in department stores will be used in an awareness campaign. In this phase, promotions will be aimed at middle- and high-income earners, as the price of honey will still be relatively high.

Budget. The total size of the honey market is (crudely and very conservatively) projected to be at least equal to the current market size:

$$\begin{aligned} \text{Market} &= \text{Current Domestic Production} * \text{Wholesale Price} \\ &= (18.5 \text{ million kg}) (\$6/\text{kg}) \\ &= \$111 \text{ million} \end{aligned}$$

The targeted market share is between 30% and 60%. With a wholesale margin of 15%, the projected annual profit will be $5 million as summarized in the following table.

	Minimum	Maximum
Market size:	$111 million	$111 million
Market share:	30%	60%
Annual sales:	$33 million	$67 million
Margin:	15%	20%
Contribution:	$5 million	$13 million

It should be noted that the operating profit calculated above does not include the expected growth in demand prior to and during Phase Three. Therefore, the projected profit will be more accurate near the beginning of the phase; towards the end of the phase, market size is expected to increase but operating margins are expected to shrink.

THE MONDAY MORNING MEETING

At precisely 8:00 a.m. on Monday, Michael Chan called the meeting to order. ''We've all had a chance to review Beth's marketing plan. I think we agree that she and her team have done a very thorough job, and should be congratulated.

''Obviously, the honey market in Korea has great potential, despite the fact that it is closed to foreign imports at this time. It seems pretty clear that the Koreans will relax the import restrictions in the near future. It is also pretty obvious that if we want to benefit from this situation, we have to act immediately to gain first mover advantage before other competitors step in. But I have to be honest. I'm not in favour of this plan.''

There was silence in the room. The management team at Ross Pacific waited for the boss to elaborate. They all thought the plan, while it had its weaknesses, was viable, and it certainly was consistent with the strategic direction they wanted to take.

Michael Chan paused, and then continued, ''This company has always operated with the highest ethical standards. Sometimes it has cost us money. But I believe that in the long run, doing the right thing makes good business sense. Can we and should we go into another country and convince the people to change centuries of tradition? Can we and should we try to change cultural values so that we can make a profit?''

Beth Wine almost choked on her herbal tea. ''Don't you think you are being a little melodramatic, Michael?'' she asked.

Geoff Taub, who had never been in favour of the idea of exporting honey to Korea, had nevertheless been impressed with Beth's plan. He knew she would put up a good fight for it. Geoff thought it was going to be an interesting meeting.

38 CURTIS AUTOMOTIVE HOIST

Gordon H. G. McDougall

In September 1990, Mark Curtis, president of Curtis Automotive Hoist (CAH), had just finished reading a feasibility report on entering the European market in 1991. CAH manufactured surface automotive hoists, a product used by garages, service stations, and other repair shops to lift cars for servicing (Exhibit 1). The report, prepared by CAH's marketing manager, Pierre Gagnon, outlined the opportunities in the European Economic Community and the entry options available.

Mr. Curtis was not sure if CAH was ready for this move. While the company had been successful in expanding sales into the United States market, Mr. Curtis wondered if this success could be repeated in Europe. He thought, with more effort, that sales could be increased in the United States. On the other hand, there were some positive aspects to the European idea. He began reviewing the information in preparation for the meeting the following day with Mr. Gagnon.

CURTIS AUTOMOTIVE HOIST

Mr. Curtis, a design engineer, had worked for eight years for the Canadian subsidiary of a U.S. automotive hoist manufacturer. During those years, he had spent considerable time designing an above-ground (or surface) automotive hoist. Although Mr. Curtis was very enthusiastic about the unique aspects of the hoist, including a scissor lift and wheel alignment pads, senior management expressed no interest in the idea. In 1980, Mr. Curtis left the company to start his own business with the express purpose of designing and manufacturing the hoist. He left with the good wishes of his previous employer who had no objections to his plans to start a new business.

Over the next three years, Mr. Curtis obtained financing from a venture capital firm, opened a plant in Lachine, Quebec, and began manufacturing and marketing the hoist, called the Curtis Lift (Exhibit 1).

From the beginning, Mr. Curtis had taken considerable pride in the development and marketing of the Curtis Lift. The original design included a scissor lift and a safety locking mechanism that allowed the hoist to be raised to any level and locked in place. As well, the scissor lift offered easy access for the mechanic to work on the raised vehicle. Because the hoist was fully hydraulic and had no chains or pulleys, it required little maintenance. Another key feature was the alignment turn plates that were an integral part of the lift. The turn plates meant that mechanics could accurately and easily perform wheel alignment jobs. Because it was a surface lift, it could be installed in a garage in less than a day.

Mr. Curtis continually made improvements to the product, including adding more safety features. In fact, the Curtis Lift was considered a leader in automotive lift

Exhibit 1
EXAMPLES OF AUTOMOTIVE HOISTS

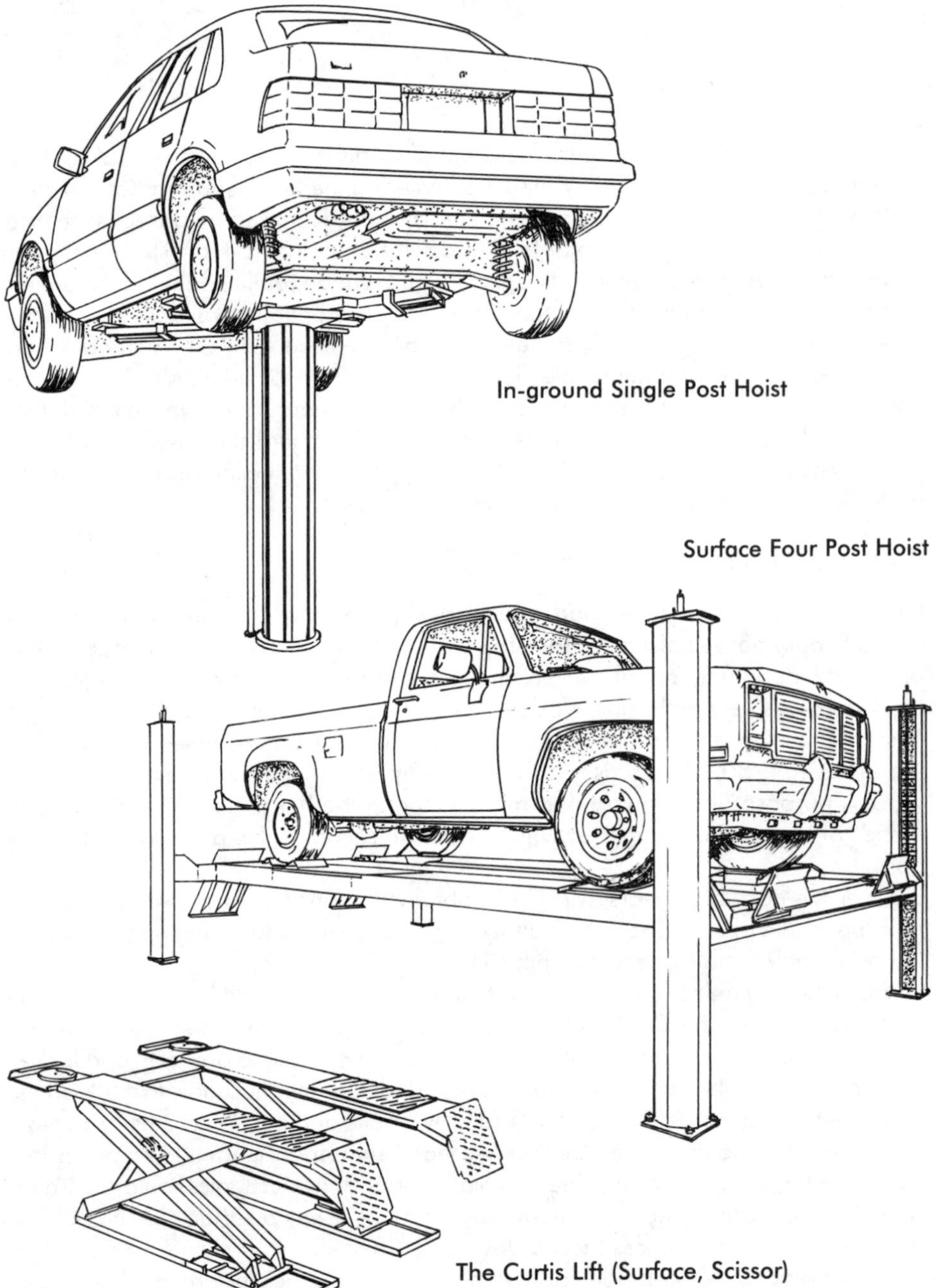

Exhibit 2

CURTIS AUTOMOTIVE HOIST—SELECTED FINANCIAL STATISTICS (1987 TO 1989)

	1989	1988	1987
Sales	$9,708,000	$7,454,000	$6,218,000
Cost of sales	6,990,000	5,541,000	4,540,000
Contribution	2,718,000	1,913,000	1,678,000
Marketing expenses*	530,000	510,000	507,000
Administrative expenses	840,000	820,000	810,000
Earnings before tax	1,348,000	583,000	361,000
Units sold	1,054	847	723

Source: Company records

* Marketing expenses in 1989 included advertising ($70,000), four salespeople ($240,000), marketing manager and three sales support staff ($220,000).

safety. Safety was an important factor in the automotive hoist market. Although hoists seldom malfunctioned, when they did, it often resulted in a serious accident.

The Curtis Lift developed a reputation in the industry as the "Cadillac" of hoists; the unit was judged by many as superior to competitive offerings because of its design, the quality of the workmanship, the safety features, the ease of installation, and the five-year warranty. Mr. Curtis held four patents on the Curtis Lift including the lifting mechanism on the scissor design and a safety locking mechanism. A number of versions of the product were designed that made the Curtis Lift suitable (depending on the model) for a variety of tasks, including rustproofing, muffler repairs, and general mechanical repairs.

In 1981, CAH sold 23 hoists and had sales of $172,500. During the early years, the majority of sales were to independent service stations and garages specializing in wheel alignment in the Quebec and Ontario market. Most of the units were sold by Mr. Gagnon, who was hired in 1982 to handle the marketing side of the operation. In 1984, Mr. Gagnon began using distributors to sell the hoist to a wider geographic market in Canada. In 1986, he signed an agreement with a large automotive wholesaler to represent CAH in the U.S. market. By 1989, the company sold 1,054 hoists and had sales of $9,708,000 (Exhibit 2). In 1989, about 60% of sales were to the United States with the remaining 40% to the Canadian market.

INDUSTRY

Approximately 49,000 hoists were sold each year in North America. Typically hoists were purchased by an automotive outlet that serviced or repaired cars including new car dealers, used car dealers, specialty shops (for example, muffler shops, transmission, wheel alignment), chains (for example, Firestone, Goodyear, Canadian Tire), and independent garages. It was estimated that new car dealers purchased 30% of all units sold in a given year. In general, the specialty shops focused on one type of repair, such as mufflers or rustproofing, while "non-specialty" outlets handled a variety of repairs. While there was some crossover, in general, CAH competed in the specialty shop segment and, in particular, those shops that dealt with wheel alignment. This included chains such as Firestone and Canadian Tire as well as new car dealers (for example, Ford) who devote a certain percentage of their lifts to the wheel alignment business and independent garages who specialized in wheel alignment.

The purpose of a hoist was to lift an automobile into a position where a mechanic or service person could easily work on the car. Because different repairs required different positions, a wide variety of hoists had been developed to meet specific needs. For example, a muffler repair shop required a hoist that allowed the mechanic to gain easy access to the underside of the car. Similarly, a wheel alignment job required a hoist that offered a level platform where the wheels could be adjusted as well as providing easy access for the mechanic. Mr. Gagnon estimated that 85% of CAH's sales were to the wheel alignment market to service centres such as Firestone, Goodyear, and Canadian Tire and to independent garages that specialized in wheel alignment. About 15% of sales were made to customers who used the hoist for general mechanical repairs.

Firms purchasing hoists were part of an industry called the automobile aftermarket. This industry was involved in supplying parts and service for new and used cars and was worth over $54 billion at retail in 1989, while servicing the approximately 11 million cars on the road in Canada. The industry was large and diverse; there were over 4,000 new car dealers in Canada, over 400 Canadian Tire stores, over 100 stores in each of the Firestone and Goodyear chains, and over 200 stores in the Rust Check chain.

The purchase of an automotive hoist was often an important decision for the service station owner or dealer. Because the price of hoists ranged from $3,000 to $15,000, it was a capital expense for most businesses.

For the owner/operator of a new service centre or car dealership the decision involved determining what type of hoist was required, then what brand would best suit the company. Most new service centres or car dealerships had multiple bays for servicing cars. In these cases, the decision would involve what types of hoists were required (for example, in-ground, surface). Often more than one type of hoist was purchased, depending on the service centre/dealership needs.

Experienced garage owners seeking a replacement hoist (the typical hoist had a useful life of 10 to 13 years) would usually determine what products were available and then make a decision. If the garage owners were also mechanics, they would probably be aware of two or three types of hoists but would not be very knowledgeable about the brands or products currently available. Garage owners or dealers who were not mechanics probably knew very little about hoists. The owners of car or service dealerships often bought the product that was recommended and/or approved by the parent company.

COMPETITION

Sixteen companies competed in the automotive lift market in North America: four Canadian and twelve United States firms. Hoists were subject to import duties. Duties on hoists entering the U.S. market from Canada were 2.4% of the selling price; from the U.S. entering Canada the import duty was 7.9%. With the advent of the Free Trade Agreement in 1989, the duties between the two countries would be phased out over a ten-year period. For Mr. Curtis, the import duties had never played a part in any decisions: the fluctuating exchange rates between the two countries had a far greater impact on selling prices.

A wide variety of hoists were manufactured in the industry. The two basic types of hoists were in-ground and surface. As the names imply, in-ground hoists required that a pit be dug "in-ground" where the piston that raised the hoist was installed. In-ground hoists were either single post or multiple post, were permanent, and obviously could not be moved. In-ground lifts constituted approximately 21% of total lift sales in 1989 (Exhibit 3). Surface lifts were installed on a flat surface, usually concrete. Surface lifts came in two basic types, post lift hoists and scissor hoists. Surface lifts, compared to inground lifts, were easier to install and could be moved, if necessary. Surface lifts constituted 79% of total lift sales in 1989. Within each type of hoist (for example, post lift surface hoists), there were numerous variations in terms of size, shape, and lifting capacity.

The industry was dominated by two large U.S. firms, AHV Lifts and Berne Manufacturing, who together held approximately 60% of the market. AHV Lifts, the largest firm with approximately 40% of the market and annual sales of about $60 million, offered a complete line of hoists (that is, in-ground and surface) but focused primarily on the in-ground market and the two post surface market. AHV Lifts was the only company that had its own direct sales force; all other companies used (1) only wholesalers or (2) a combination of wholesalers and company sales force. AHV Lifts offered standard hoists with few extra features and competed primarily on price. Berne Manufacturing, with a market share of approximately 20%, also competed in the in-ground and two post surface markets. It used a combination of wholesalers and company salespeople and, like AHV Lifts, competed primarily on price.

Exhibit 3

NORTH AMERICAN AUTOMOTIVE LIFT UNIT SALES, BY TYPE (1987 TO 1989)

	1987	1988	1989
In-ground			
Single post	5,885	5,772	5,518
Multiple post	4,812	6,625	5,075
Surface			
Two post	27,019	28,757	28,923
Four post	3,862	3,162	3,745
Scissor	2,170	2,258	2,316
Other	4,486	3,613	3,695
Total	48,234	50,187	49,272

Source: Company records

Most of the remaining firms in the industry were companies that operated in a regional market (for example, California or British Columbia) and/or offered a limited product line (for example, four post surface hoist).

Curtis had two competitors that manufactured scissor lifts. AHV Lift marketed a scissor hoist that had a different lifting mechanism and did not include the safety locking features of the Curtis Lift. On average, the AHV scissor lift sold for about 20% less than the Curtis Lift. The second competitor, Mete Lift, was a small regional company with sales in California and Oregon. It had a design that was very similar to the Curtis Lift but lacked some of its safety features. The Mete Lift, regarded as a well-manufactured product, sold for about 5% less than the Curtis Lift.

MARKETING STRATEGY

As of early 1990, CAH had developed a reputation for a quality product backed by good service in the hoist lift market, primarily in the wheel alignment segment.

The distribution system employed by CAH reflected the need to engage in extensive personal selling. Three types of distributors were used: a company sales force, Canadian distributors, and a U.S. automotive wholesaler. The company sales force consisted of four salespeople and Mr. Gagnon. Their main task was to service large "direct" accounts. The initial step was to get the Curtis Lift approved by large chains and manufacturers and then, having received the approval, to sell to individual dealers or operators. For example, if General Motors approved the hoist, then CAH could sell it to individual General Motors dealers. CAH sold directly to the individual dealers of a number of large accounts including General Motors, Ford, Chrysler, Petro-Canada, Firestone, and Goodyear. CAH had been successful in obtaining manufacturer approval from the big three automobile manufacturers in both Canada and the United States. As well, CAH had also received approval from service companies such as Canadian Tire and Goodyear. To date, CAH had not been rejected by any major account but, in some cases, the approval process had taken over four years.

In total, the company sales force generated about 25% of the unit sales each year. Sales to the large "direct" accounts in the United States went through CAH's U.S. wholesaler.

The Canadian distributors sold, installed, and serviced units across Canada. These distributors handled the Curtis Lift and carried a line of noncompetitive automotive equipment products (for example, engine diagnostic equipment, wheel balancing equipment) and noncompetitive lifts. These distributors focused on the smaller chains and the independent service stations and garages.

The U.S. wholesaler sold a complete product line to service stations as well as manufacturing some equipment. The Curtis Lift was one of five different types of lifts that the wholesaler sold. Although the wholesaler provided CAH with extensive distribution in the United States, the Curtis Lift was a minor product within the wholesaler's total line. While Mr. Gagnon did not have any actual figures, he thought that the Curtis Lift probably accounted for less than 20% of the total lift sales of the U.S. wholesaler.

Both Mr. Curtis and Mr. Gagnon felt that the U.S. market had unrealized potential. With a population of 248 million people and over 140 million registered vehicles, the U.S. market was over ten times the size of the Canadian market (population of 26 million, approximately 11 million vehicles). Mr. Gagnon noted that the six New England states (population over 13 million), the three largest mid-Atlantic states (population over 38 million), and the three largest mid-eastern states (population over 32 million) were all within a day's drive of the factory in Lachine. Mr. Curtis and Mr. Gagnon had considered setting up a sales office in New York to service these states, but they were concerned that the U.S. wholesaler would not be willing to relinquish any of its territory. They had also considered working more closely with the wholesaler to encourage it to "push" the Curtis Lift. It appeared that the wholesaler's major objective was to sell a hoist, not necessarily the Curtis Lift.

CAH distributed a catalogue type package with products, uses, prices, and other required information for both distributors and users. In addition, CAH advertised in trade publications (for example, *Service Station & Garage Management*), and Mr. Gagnon travelled to trade shows in Canada and U.S. to promote the Curtis Lift.

In 1989, Curtis Lifts sold for an average retail price of $10,990 and CAH received, on average, $9,210 for each unit sold. This average reflected the mix of sales through the three distribution channels: (1) direct (where CAH received 100% of the selling price), (2) Canadian distributors (where CAH received 80% of the selling price), and (3) the U.S. wholesaler (where CAH received 78% of the selling price).

Both Mr. Curtis and Mr. Gagnon felt that the company's success to date was based on a strategy of offering a superior product that was primarily targeted to the needs of specific customers. The strategy stressed continual product improvements, quality workmanship, and service. Personal selling was a key aspect of the strategy; salespeople could show customers the benefits of the Curtis Lift over competing products.

THE EUROPEAN MARKET

Against this background, Mr. Curtis had been thinking of ways to continue the rapid growth of the company. One possibility that kept coming up was the promise and potential of the European market. The fact that Europe would become a single market in 1992 suggested that it was an opportunity that should at least be explored. With this in mind, Mr. Curtis asked Mr. Gagnon to prepare a report on the possibility of CAH entering the European market. The highlights of Mr. Gagnon's report follow.

HISTORY OF THE EUROPEAN COMMUNITY

The European Community (EC) stemmed from the 1953 "Treaty of Rome" in which five countries decided it would be in their best interest to form an internal market. These countries were France, Spain, Italy, West Germany, and Luxembourg. By 1990, the EC consisted of 12 countries (the additional seven were Belgium, Denmark, Greece, Ireland, and the Netherlands, Portugal, and the United Kingdom) with a population of over 325 million people.[1] In 1992, virtually all barriers (physical, technical, and fiscal) in the EC were scheduled to be removed for companies located

[1] As of September 1990, West Germany and East Germany were in the process of unification. East Germany had a population of approximately 17 million people.

within the EC. This would allow the free movement of goods, persons, services, and capital.

In the last five years many North American and Japanese firms had established themselves in the EC. The reasoning for this was twofold. First, these companies regarded the community as an opportunity to increase global market share and profits. The market was attractive because of its sheer size and lack of internal barriers. Second, in 1992, companies that were established within the community were subject to protection from external competition via EC protectionism tariffs, local contender, and reciprocity requirements. EC protectionism tariffs were only temporary, and would be removed at a later date. It would be possible for companies to export to or establish in the community after 1992, but there was some risk attached.

MARKET POTENTIAL

The key indicator of the potential market for the Curtis Lift hoist was the number of passenger cars and commercial vehicles in use in a particular country. Four countries in Europe had more than 20 million vehicles in use, with West Germany having the largest domestic fleet of 30 million vehicles followed in order by France, Italy, and the United Kingdom (Exhibit 4). The number of vehicles was an important indicator because the more vehicles in use meant a greater number of service and repair facilities that needed vehicle hoists and potentially the Curtis Lift.

An indicator of the future vehicle repair and service market was the number of new vehicle registrations. The registration of new vehicles was important as this maintained the number of vehicles in use by replacing cars that had been retired. Again, West Germany had the most new cars registered in 1988 and was followed in order by France, the United Kingdom, and Italy.

Based primarily on the fact that a large domestic market was important for initial growth, the selection of a European country should be limited to the "Big Four" industralized nations: West Germany, France, the United Kingdom, or Italy. In an international survey companies from North America and Europe ranked European countries on a scale of 1 to 100 on market potential and investment site potential.

Exhibit 4
NUMBER OF VEHICLES (1988) AND POPULATION (1989)

Country	Vehicles in Use (000s) Passenger	Commercial	New Vehicle Registrations (000s)	Population (000s)
West Germany	28,304	1,814	2,960	60,900
France	29,970	4,223	2,635	56,000
Italy	22,500	1,897	2,308	57,400
United Kingdom	20,605	2,915	2,531	57,500
Spain	9,750	1,750	1,172	39,400

The results showed that West Germany was favoured for both market potential and investment site opportunities while France, the United Kingdom, and Spain placed second, third, and fourth respectively. Italy did not place in the top four in either market or investment site potential. However, Italy had a large number of vehicles in use, had the second largest population in Europe, and was an acknowledged leader in car technology and production.

Little information was available on the competition within Europe. There was, as yet, no dominant manufacturer as was the case in North America. At this time, there was one firm in Germany that manufactured a scissor-type lift. The firm sold most of its units within the German market. The only other available information was that 22 firms in Italy manufactured vehicle lifts.

INVESTMENT OPTIONS

Mr. Gagnon felt that CAH had three options for expansion into the European market: licensing, joint venture, or direct investment. The licensing option was a real possibility as a French firm had expressed an interest in manufacturing the Curtis Lift.

In June 1990, Mr. Gagnon had attended a trade show in Detroit to promote the Curtis Lift. At the show, he met Phillipe Beaupre, the marketing manager for Bar Maisse, a French manufacturer of wheel alignment equipment. The firm, located in Chelles, France, sold a range of wheel alignment equipment throughout Europe. The best-selling product was an electronic modular aligner that enabled a mechanic to utilize a sophisticated computer system to align the wheels of a car. Mr. Beaupre was seeking a North American distributor for the modular aligner and other products manufactured by Bar Maisse.

At the show, Mr. Gagnon and Mr. Beaupre had a casual conversation in which each explained what their respective companies manufactured, they exchanged company brochures and business cards, and both went on to other exhibits. The next day, Mr. Beaupre sought out Mr. Gagnon and asked if he might be interested in having Bar Maisse manufacture and market the Curtis Lift in Europe. Mr. Beaupre felt the lift would complement Bar Maisse's product line and the licensing would be of mutual benefit to both parties. They agreed to pursue the idea. Upon his return to Lachine, Mr. Gagnon told Mr. Curtis about these discussions, and they agreed to explore this possibility.

Mr. Gagnon called a number of colleagues in the industry and asked them what they knew about Bar Maisse. About half had not heard of the company, but those who had, commented favourably on the quality of its products. One colleague, with European experience, knew the company well and said that Bar Maisse's management had integrity and would make a good partner. In July, Mr. Gagnon sent a letter to Mr. Beaupre stating that CAH was interested in further discussions and enclosed various company brochures including price lists and technical information on the Curtis Lift. In late August, Mr. Beaupre responded stating that Bar Maisse would like to enter a three-year licensing agreement with CAH to manufacture the Curtis Lift in Europe. In exchange for the manufacturing rights, Bar Maisse was prepared to pay a royalty rate of 5% of gross sales. Mr. Gagnon had not yet responded to this proposal.

A second possibility was a joint venture. Mr. Gagnon had wondered if it might not be better for CAH to offer a counter proposal to Bar Maisse for a joint venture. He had not worked out any details, but Mr. Gagnon felt that CAH would learn more about the European market and probably make more money if they were an active partner in Europe. Mr. Gagnon's idea was a 50–50 proposal where the two parties shared the investment and the profits. He envisaged a situation where Bar Maisse would manufacture the Curtis Lift in their plant with technical assistance from CAH. Mr. Gagnon also thought that CAH could get involved in the marketing of the lift through the Bar Maisse distribution system. Further, he thought that the Curtis Lift, with proper marketing, could gain a reasonable share of the European market. If that happened Mr. Gagnon felt that CAH was likely to make greater returns with a joint venture.

The third option was direct investment where CAH would establish a manufacturing facility and set up a management group to market the lift. Mr. Gagnon had contacted a business acquaintance who had recently been involved in manufacturing fabricated steel sheds in Germany. On the basis of discussions with his acquaintance, Mr. Gagnon estimated the costs involved in setting up a plant in Europe at: (1) $250,000 for capital equipment (welding machines, cranes, other equipment), (2) $200,000 in incremental costs to set the plant up, and (3) carrying costs to cover $1,000,000 in inventory and accounts receivable. While the actual costs of renting a building for the factory would depend on the site location, he estimated that annual building rent including heat, light, and insurance would be about $80,000. Mr. Gagnon recognized these estimates were guidelines but he felt that the estimates were probably within 20% of actual costs.

THE DECISION

As Mr. Curtis considered the contents of the report, a number of thoughts crossed his mind. He began making notes concerning the European possibility and the future of the company.

- If CAH decided to enter Europe, Mr. Gagnon would be the obvious choice to head up the "direct investment" option or the "joint venture" option. Mr. Curtis felt that Mr. Gagnon had been instrumental in the success of the company to date.
- While CAH had the financial resources to go ahead with the direct investment option, the joint venture would spread the risk (and the returns) over the two companies.
- CAH had built its reputation on designing and manufacturing a quality product. Regardless of the option chosen, Mr. Curtis wanted the firm's reputation to be maintained.
- Either the licensing agreement or the joint venture appeared to build on the two companies' strengths; Bar Maisse had knowledge of the market and CAH had the product. What troubled Mr. Curtis was whether this apparent synergy would work or would Bar Maisse seek to control the operation.

- It was difficult to estimate sales under any of the options. With the first two (licensing and joint venture), it would depend on the effort and expertise of Bar Maisse; with the third option, it would depend on Mr. Gagnon.
- CAH's sales in the U.S. market could be increased if the U.S. wholesaler would "push" the Curtis Lift. Alternatively, the establishment of a sales office in New York to cover the eastern states could also increase sales.

As Mr. Curtis reflected on the situation he knew he should probably get additional information—but it wasn't obvious exactly what information would help him make a "yes" or "no" decision. He knew one thing for sure—he was going to keep his company on a "fast growth" track—and at tomorrow's meeting he and Mr. Gagnon would decide how to do it.

39 JANTZEN CANADA

Craig R. Pollack
Charles B. Weinberg

It was January 1990 as Mr. George F. Daley sat at his desk and read the latest newspaper headline aloud to one of his fellow managers, Mr. Morris VanAndel: "Canada's Clothing Industry Unravels." As vice-president of sales for Jantzen Canada, and the manager responsible for the men's sweater division, Mr. Daley wondered how a small manufacturer like Jantzen Canada could compete in an increasingly difficult Canadian men's sweater industry. He began to think about all the problems his firm faced, and he commented to Mr. VanAndel, "You know, Morris, the competition is getting more aggressive, and the business is drastically changing. Men's sweaters in Canada are subject to more and more environmental influences, including rapidly changing fashion trends and the Canada–U.S. Free Trade Agreement to name only two. If we don't think of something, we may end up being a distributor—with all the manufacturing done in the States or off-shore." After Mr. VanAndel left his office, Mr. Daley began to think of some alternatives that would enable Jantzen to meet its strategic goal of increasing unit sales while improving profitability.

THE COMPANY

Jantzen Canada is a wholly owned subsidiary of Jantzen USA. In turn, the entire Jantzen company is owned by Vanity Fair—a conglomerate with annual sales of $2.5 billion (U.S.) that controls a number of well-known clothing manufacturers including Blue Bell ("Wrangler" jeans) and Lee Sportswear. The Jantzen name is best recognized for swimsuit apparel; the firm is one of North America's leading manufacturers of this product line. Jantzen also operates a successful sportswear business in North America. Additionally, Jantzen Canada manufactures a line of men's sweaters for the Canadian market which account for about 20% of Jantzen Canada sales across all divisions.

While Jantzen Canada operates primarily as an autonomous company from its American parent (for example, Jantzen Canada manufactures swimsuits, sportswear, and sweaters in its Vancouver, B.C. plant) the firm takes its general directives from its American parent company. For example, Jantzen USA informs Jantzen Canada which sweater styles and stitch and pattern designs are available for manufacturing in Canada. Jantzen Canada then chooses which sweaters to manufacture and decides how to market them in Canada.

Note: Some data have been disguised.

Jantzen Canada also utilizes the resources of Jantzen USA for marketing research. Jantzen Canada conducts very little of its own research on Canadian consumers, relying instead on information generated by its American parent. This method is cost-efficient as the two companies share the same information, but some individuals in the garment industry question the reliability of using American data to understand Canadian consumer buying habits. Using American research, Jantzen Canada has defined its primary target market of men's sweater buyers as well-educated, middle-income, 25- to 45-year-old males who enjoy a casual lifestyle. Jantzen Canada recognizes that sweater style and consumption patterns are influenced by women, but no specific research on this issue is available to the firm. The only information that Jantzen Canada has on the role of women in men's garment purchases is a recent article in *Report on Business Magazine* that quotes some figures compiled by International Surveys Ltd. (ISL). According to ISL, Canadian women spent about $8 billion on clothes in 1988, while men spent only half that. Also, a 1989 ISL survey found that women buy 58 units of male underwear out of every 100 and that number increases to 76 for men's robes and pyjamas.

As Mr. Daley sat at his desk, he reviewed the strengths and weaknesses of Jantzen Canada's sweater division, at least as far as he saw them (Exhibit 1). Mr. Daley felt this was a useful exercise to conduct as he recognized that Jantzen would have to become more "lean and mean" as the Canadian clothing manufacturing sector had gone through some tough times in recent years. According to a Statistics Canada

Exhibit 1
JANTZEN CANADA'S STRENGTHS AND WEAKNESSES

Strengths

Product	• manufacture a good quality (Canadian) sweater (it is uncertain whether producing a *Canadian* garment is an advantage or a disadvantage)
Distribution	• established among independent stores (two-thirds of Jantzen's business is generated via independent retailers) • good reputation with retailers for delivering products on-time and for helpful customer service • can offer retailers shorter lead times due to Canadian location of manufacturing operations

Weaknesses

Pricing policy	• higher than Pacific Rim competitors due to higher labour and overhead costs (retailers may receive lower margins from carrying Jantzen sweaters)
Promotion policy	• limited promotion (presently includes personal selling, point-of-purchase displays, and some co-op advertising) • rely on USA parent company's research

Exhibit 2
JANTZEN CANADA SWEATER DIVISION FINANCIAL DATA (000s)

	1988	1989
Net sales	4,050	4,286
Cost of sales		
Materials	647	672
Labour	1,318	1,388
Overhead (allocated)	541	563
	2,506	2,623
Gross profit	1,544	1,663
Sales force	524	556
Marketing	293	326
General & administration	596	638
	1,413	1,520
Net profit	131	143

labour force survey, 18,000 jobs (about 18% of the clothing manufacturing work force) were lost during the period of March 1988 to March 1989. Additionally, some Canadian clothing industry sources predicted that, with the passage of the Canada–U.S. Free Trade Agreement, some Canadian garment manufacturing operations might relocate south of the border to take advantage of potentially lower wage rates.

After hearing all these doom and gloom statistics, Mr. Daley was concerned about Jantzen Canada's sweater operations. Compounding his concern was the fact that the firm's sweater division had experienced limited profitability over the last few years. On the other hand, Mr. Daley was somewhat pleased with the fact that Jantzen Canada had not laid off an employee in the last three years, and that the sweater division had been able to maintain annual sales of approximately 125,000 units, or $4.1 million in sales, during the last two years (Exhibit 2). Total Jantzen Canada sales had also remained relatively stable in recent years.

THE CANADIAN SWEATER INDUSTRY

Manufacturing

The Canadian sweater industry can be divided into four primary groups of manufacturers:

1. Pacific Rim manufacturers—some produce lower-quality/lower-price sweaters and others manufacture high-quality/high-price garments.
2. Italian manufacturers—produce high-quality/high-price goods.
3. Canadian domestic manufacturers—produce a range of quality/price sweaters.
4. Other manufacturers from the United States and elsewhere—produce a full range of quality/price sweaters.

Pacific Rim Manufacturers

Pacific Rim manufacturers account for approximately 70% of Canadian sweater imports. The major producers are located in Korea, Hong Kong, and Taiwan. Some of these producers have high "mass" technology plants and equipment, and consequently, these Pacific Rim manufacturers require large minimum orders as small production runs do not generate economic margins. Mass production Pacific Rim manufacturers are able to offer a reasonable quality sweater for an inexpensive price due not only to the economies of scale generated via large production runs but also due to low labour costs. The majority of mass-produced types of sweaters are private label garments. Private labels account for the majority of all Pacific Rim sweater exports and include labels such as Bay Club (Hudson's Bay Company), Club International (Tip Top, a major chain of men's wear stores), and Birkdale (Eaton's). All of these sweaters are priced in the low- to mid-price range (up to $40).

The Pacific Rim manufacturers that produce fine quality sweaters have gained considerable market share in recent years and are now responsible for a large portion of all high-quality/high-price sweaters that are imported to Canada on an annual basis. Some of the more popular Orient produced brand-name sweaters include the Ralph Lauren line, Gant, and Nautica. Import brand-name sweaters are typically priced at a minimum of $100, and some are as expensive as $500.

Italian Manufacturers

Even with the increased demand for fine-quality sweaters produced in the Orient, Italian manufactured sweaters still enjoy reasonable popularity with Canadian garment consumers. The Italian producers are known for their fashionable styles and rich colours. Because of the fine quality of their sweaters, and because their labour rates are comparable to Canadian wages, Italians sweaters are frequently priced at the high end of the Canadian sweater market. Private labels account for most of Italian sweater import sales. Additionally, the popular Giorgio Armani brand-name sweater, priced from $200 to $500, is manufactured in Italy.

Canadian Manufacturers

There are six major Canadian manufacturers of men's sweaters. Two produce recognized national brand names, while the others concentrate on private labels. Included among the Canadian manufacturers are: Standard Knitting based in Winnipeg, marketer of "Tundra" sweaters, priced between $40 and $100, and distributed through Eaton's and various independent stores; Dorthea Knitting Mills Ltd. based in Ontario and primarily a private label manufacturer for Eaton's and others; and Jantzen Canada which produces brand-name sweaters, priced from $55 to $85, and distributed via Woodward's (a western Canadian chain), The Bay, Eaton's, and various independent stores.

Other Manufacturers

Manufacturers from the United States, Europe, and China also produce sweaters for the Canadian market. These manufacturers market a range of sweaters that vary in price, quality, and design. While many of these sweaters are sold via large department stores and discount stores, some of the sweaters are retailed through independent shops that specialize in various cultural garments. For example, some Scottish wool sweaters are sold in stores that specialize primarily in Scottish garments. It is estimated that all other manufacturers account for approximately 22% of Canadian sweater imports.

Market

The Canadian sweater market is a mature industry. Over the years, increases in sales have traditionally paralleled increases in the Canadian population. Although the types of sweaters sold have changed over time, these garments have remained fairly popular as many Canadians view sweaters as a "stable" clothing item. One major fashion trend that occurred during the 1980s was that the "plain" sweater went out of style. Although plain sweaters are still being produced by Pacific Rim manufacturers, these sweaters are now only found in the lower price category. For some foreign and domestic manufacturers, including Jantzen Canada, a considerable portion of their sales had been generated from the sale of medium price range plain sweaters, but now these firms have been forced to either exit the industry or change the focus of their manufacturing operations. For example, the majority of Jantzen's revenue is now based on intricate patterned sweaters that are produced on expensive machines with highly skilled labour.

During the mid-1980s, based on unit volume, Canadian sweater manufacturers maintained a market share in the range of 30 to 32% of national sales. Imports, during that time, held a market share of between 68 and 70%. In 1988, sales of men's sweaters in Canada amounted to 12.5 million sweaters, for a total retail value of $400 million.

During the 1980s, the sales distribution across various price segments for men's sweaters remained static. A slight change occurred only in the low and high segments with the high end gaining approximately 3% of total units sold due to a strong national economy during the latter half of the 1980s. See Exhibit 3 for the distribution of sweater sales by price range in 1988.

Canadian retailers purchase the majority of their sweaters from overseas manufacturers a year in advance and "fill" the rest of their orders from Canadian manu-

Exhibit 3
MEN'S SWEATER SALES BY PRICE

Price Segment	Total Units Sold[1]
Less than $20.00	55.4%
$20.00 to $39.99	30.9%
$40.00 to $79.99	10.5%
$80.00 and up	3.2%

[1] Total units sold in 1988 in Canada were 12.5 million.

facturers six months before delivery is required or when there is a shortfall in the retailer's inventory. As a result of this process, some retailers, including the large department, discount, and chain stores spend a significant portion of their budget overseas before considering domestically produced sweaters.

Retailers

The Canadian sweater market is composed primarily of three types of retailers:

1. Department stores.
2. Discount stores.
3. Men's Wear Speciality stores.
   a. Chain stores.
   b. Independently Owned Stores.

During the mid-1980s, the unit sweater sales of each type of retailer remained relatively constant (Exhibit 4). The exception was the specialty stores which increased sales by approximately 4% primarily at the expense of the department stores. Within the specialty store category, the chain stores accounted for the vast majority of the growth due to their strategic locations within the increasingly popular malls. The growth of the independent stores remained relatively static as these types of outlets did not increase in popularity or number.

Department store sales are concentrated among Sears, Eaton's, The Bay, and Woodward's, with Sears holding the largest market share at 13.7% of total department store sweater sales. Within department stores, there has been a trend towards private labels which now account for over 50% of sweaters sold in these types of outlets.

The major discount store sweater buyers are Zellers, K mart, and Woolco. These retailers tend to carry sweaters that are purchased from Pacific Rim manufacturers as their target customers prefer garments that are at the lower end of the price range.

The major specialty chain stores are Tip Top, Jack Fraser, and Big Steel. Tip Top and Big Steel are owned by Dylex, a large multinational firm that also owns other clothiers such as Fairweather and Suzy Shier. Due to the increasing popularity of

Exhibit 4

MEN'S SWEATER SALES BY STORE TYPE (100% = TOTAL UNITS)

	1985	1986	1987	1988
Department stores	34.7%	35.8%	30.9%	28.6%
Discount stores	25.8	22.3	25.6	26.9
Independent and specialty stores	34.9	37.1	39.2	38.5
All other stores	4.6	4.8	4.3	6.0
Total	100.0%	100.0%	100.0%	100.0%

specialty chain stores with Canadian consumers, these retailers are becoming stronger within the garment industry. Some specialty chain stores are requiring higher margins from their suppliers and some stores are switching to (or promoting more) their own private labels; private labels generate higher margins than brand-name garments. Chain specialty store retailers usually price their sweaters in the mid-price range. Most of these stores are located in malls and in shopping centres.

The independent stores consist of many small, independently run "Mom and Pop" retail stores. This segment holds a 9% sweater market share based on units sold and a 16.1% share based on dollar sales volume. Because independents do not possess the large order purchasing power of the department or chain stores, they frequently target consumers who desire high-quality/high-price garments. The main advantage these types of outlets have over their competition is their high level of service. Many independents have loyal customers as a result of the personal and friendly service customers frequently receive.

For the 1990s, it is expected that the traditional "lines of competition" between the various retailers will decrease as the department stores adopt a more aggressive strategy regarding garment sales. For example, some department stores are beginning to offer high-quality/high-price designer sweaters in order to expand their customer base. As well, some department stores are setting aside boutique-like areas devoted to the products of one manufacturer, often sharing the costs and profits with the manufacturer, who has a role in managing the space. Such arrangements are common with perfumes and cosmetics marketers. Additionally, department stores are attempting to target the low-price segment by opening subsidiary stores/departments—The Hudson Bay Company with Zellers, Eaton's with Eaton's Annex, and Woodward's with Woodwyn.

LAWS AND REGULATIONS

As Mr. Daley leaned back on his chair, he began to think about the many laws that have an impact on the Canadian men's sweater industry. While Mr. Daley understood the laws well, many of the more significant regulations were expected to change in the 1990s. Additionally, a new tax law—the Goods and Services Tax—and tariff reductions as a result of the Canada–U.S. Free Trade Agreement would have a significant impact on all Canadian garment firms. Mr. Daley did not know whether the effect of these new regulations would be positive or negative for Jantzen.

The Multi-Fibre Agreement (MFA)

The MFA provides a framework for regulating global textile and apparel trade of wool, cotton, and synthetic fibres. The agreement came into effect on January 1, 1974 and has been renewed approximately every four years. Endorsed by 45 countries, the MFA's stated objectives are (1) to expand orderly trade of such products, while avoiding market disruptions in the importing and exporting countries, and (2) to further the export economies of developing countries.

Over the years, the MFA has come under considerable criticism due to its inability to meet its objectives. For example, in 1981 the developed nations, and especially the European Community (EC), highlighted the fact that problems of declining employment and rising imports occurred in their countries despite the existence of the MFA. On the other hand, developing countries complained that their economies suffered because industrialized nations were using the MFA to protect their uncompetitive industries. Some critics argue that these problems, or forms of these problems, still exist today.

The current version of the MFA expires in 1992. The future of the agreement is uncertain as many low-cost countries want liberalization of trade barriers. However, only a few countries appear to be ready to grant such trade concessions. If Canada and the USA were to reduce import barriers, many North American manufacturers would not be able to compete in the garment industry.

Canada–U.S. Free Trade Agreement (FTA)

Textiles and apparel fall under Category C of the FTA where the tariff rate prior to the FTA was 25%. Effective January 1, 1989, these goods were subject to yearly tariff reductions of 2.5%. By January 1, 1998, all remaining tariffs will be eliminated.

It is expected that during the early part of the 1990s, tariff reductions will not have a significant impact on the Canadian garment industry. However, as the reductions continue, considerable changes will occur as Canadian sweater prices may decline due to increased competition from U.S. manufacturers. As well, Canadian export opportunities to the United States are likely to increase. Although it is unclear whether Canadian garment manufacturers will be able to effectively take advantage of U.S. sweater export opportunities, the United States does offer a large market for Canadian producers; U.S. expenditures in 1990 on outerwear (sweaters, coats, hats, etc.) were predicted to be approximately $16.5 billion and sweaters (both men's and ladies') were expected to reach $2.7 billion in retail sales.

Goods and Services Tax (GST)

The GST is scheduled to be implemented as of January 1, 1991. Many experts in the garment industry are unsure as to how the GST will affect the sales of men's sweaters in Canada. Some individuals believe that the GST may hurt the sales of mid-priced sweaters as the cost of all goods may increase by as much as 7%; lower priced sweaters will not increase in price as much due to their lower retail price and it is likely that individuals purchasing higher priced sweaters will be better able to afford the additional tax. Others pointed out that countervailing effects from decreased or eliminated federal sales taxes on manufactured goods would also need to be considered.

ALTERNATIVES AVAILABLE TO JANTZEN

After reviewing the situation, Mr. Daley concluded that Jantzen had at least six alternatives that could assist in meeting the firm's goal of increasing unit sales while improving profitability. Mr. Daley recognized that some of the alternatives were more direct in addressing this goal, but he believed that some of the more indirect options could also aid Jantzen.

Alternative 1—Status Quo

While some Canadian firms had recently dropped out of the men's sweater market (White Ram and Dimitri), Jantzen Canada had remained profitable. Additionally, regular reports from the sales force, and Mr. Daley's own contacts with buyers, indicated that all major customers intend to maintain current buying relationships with Jantzen. Mr. Daley recognized that with other firms exiting the industry, maintenance of the status quo would probably allow Jantzen to slowly improve its market position. To do this Jantzen would have to continue pursuing its past strategy (which was similar to almost all domestic manufacturers) of relying on shorter lead times for orders and deliveries, better customer service, and a "Canadian Made" sweater. Maintaining the status quo would not only require the continued success of past strategies but would also require tight cost controls and high service standards. Although this appeared to be a lot for the company to tackle, Mr. Daley felt that all these requirements were within Jantzen's ability.

Alternative 2—Conduct Consumer Research

Conducting consumer research may be useful for Jantzen Canada in understanding the needs, wants, and purchasing habits of present and potential Canadian consumers of their products. Marketing research might be helpful in resolving an important brand question. Do Canadian consumers associate the Jantzen name with men's sweaters or just with swimsuits? Other important research issues include the role of sweaters as gift purchases, the price sensitivity of consumers buying these garments, and whether sweaters are bought more as a current fashion need or as a long-term stable clothing item.

While Mr. Daley thought that marketing research was usually beneficial, he knew it was a costly and time-consuming procedure. Based on discussions with a major market research firm, Mr. Daley knew that a telephone market research study, conducted with approximately 400 (actual and potential) consumers from across Canada, would cost between $25,000 and $35,000.

Alternative 3—Increase Promotional Efforts

Jantzen may be able to increase sales by concentrating more on promotional activities such as advertising, personal selling, publicity, and/or point-of-purchase displays. Mr. Daley felt quite strongly that, if Jantzen were to utilize promotions to increase sales, the firm should concentrate on advertising and personal selling as they have been the most effective vehicles in the past.

Few manufacturers in the sweater industry did any advertising. Consequently, Jantzen has an opportunity to effectively use this vehicle to gain market share. Mr. Daley felt that any print advertising would have to be focused on colour ads in magazines, since black and white ads (in newspapers or magazines) would not show off the vibrant colours in some of the sweaters and television was too expensive. Given the success of Jantzen's swimwear line, Mr. Daley had access to high-quality talent in producing fashion ads. However, magazine ads were costly: a full page, four-colour ad in *Maclean's*, a national news magazine with a readership of over one million adults weekly (55% male), would cost nearly $20,000. Much cheaper rates would prevail in men's fashion magazines with smaller circulations. The major drawback to this option is that most sweater companies, including Jantzen, operate on limited budgets. As a recurring cost, Mr. Daley was uncertain as to whether Jantzen could afford to use print media.

Personal selling is an essential element in securing orders from retailers. At present, Mr. Daley has primary responsibility for the ten key national accounts (for example, Woodward's, The Bay, Sears). The remaining larger outlets plus the 1,200 independent retailers were covered by an 11 person sales force. The territories were geographically aligned and a salesperson represented all Jantzen lines when calling on a customer. Mr. Daley thought that Jantzen could increase sales by concentrating more on personal selling, by either increasing productivity from their existing sales force or by hiring additional salespeople. As the firm's present sales force is paid on a commission basis, Jantzen had to make sure that if additional people were hired that they would not take sales away from their present employees. To hire an additional salesperson, Mr. Daley knew that support costs of at least $20,000 (travel expenses primarily) plus a partially guaranteed salary during the first year would be necessary. Mr. Daley noted that a good salesperson with Jantzen earned approximately $75,000 per annum.

Alternative 4—Lower Costs by Introducing "Veriloft" Fabric

In order to become more profitable, Jantzen could lower the cost of manufacturing its sweaters. To do this the firm could introduce a sweater made of a less expensive fabric. One such fabric is an acrylic that is currently being used in some garments in the United States, a product called "Veriloft." Veriloft is different from traditional acrylic—it looks more expensive and has the texture of good sweaters. Although the new acrylic has received most favourable reviews from American consumers who have purchased garments made from the material, Mr. Daley questioned how well it would be received by Canadian consumers; it was well known in the North American garment industry that acrylic has traditionally been associated with "cheap" goods. Despite the potential problems with Veriloft, Mr. Daley was encouraged by the product as it could save Jantzen Canada as much as 50% on materials costs. Fortunately for Jantzen, manufacturing the Veriloft would not require the purchase of new machinery.

Another concern for Jantzen was that a sweater made from a new, unknown product would likely require considerable ad support to make customers aware of the product and its attributes. Jantzen USA had run four-colour, full-page ads in four issues of *USA Today* in October–November 1989 as part of its introductory program for its Veriloft line. The sales impact of these ads was not known as the firm could not separate the results of the ads from the other parts of the introductory promotional campaign. Jantzen USA was satisfied with the initial sales of the Veriloft sweaters.

To maximize any monies Jantzen might spend on promoting the Veriloft product, Mr. Daley contemplated conducting a test market in one region in order to receive some feedback on the new fabric. A test market would entail gaining the cooperation of retailers in the chosen region and could cost anywhere from $10,000 to $50,000 depending on the media support employed during the test period. Despite the considerable hurdles Jantzen faced in possibly introducing the new fabric, Mr. Daley felt that the product could help increase the firm's overall sales. A good-quality Veriloft fabric sweater could be sold at a lower price than any of the sweaters that the firm currently sells and could generate increased unit and dollar sales. A sweater made from Veriloft would likely be sold at retail from $50 to $60. A comparable wool or cotton sweater that Jantzen currently manufactures sells at retail for about $10 more. One other important factor Mr. Daley noted was that a Veriloft sweater would generate similar margins as the firm's wool or cotton sweaters for the trade.[1]

Alternative 5—Open "Jantzen" Retail Stores

In order to increase sales, Jantzen could open its own retail outlets. These outlets could be regular retail stores and/or factory outlets. Mr. Daley was excited by the possibility of this option as there appears to be numerous advantages for Jantzen in opening up their own retail outlets. These include gaining maximum exposure for their products, choosing which products should be sold at the retail level (store executives choose the garments they wish to sell from the range Jantzen offers), and immediate feedback from customers. This last advantage was very important to Mr. Daley as Jantzen presently relies on retailers for any information regarding customer's preferences and dislikes about sweaters in general and about Jantzen's garments.

The primary disadvantage to this alternative is cost. Mr. Daley recognized that it is expensive to open any sort of retail outlet. Rental costs for one retail store in a small location can cost anywhere from $6.00 per square foot per year at Hull Quebec's Place Cartier to $30.00 per square foot per year at Burnaby B.C.'s Station Square (rents can even be higher at some Canadian malls). Also, prices within a city can fluctuate substantially—for example, Exhibit 5 provides prices and other information on some Edmonton-based malls. The space required for a typical garment outlet varies considerably but, on average, a clothing store requires 1000 to 1500 square feet of space. Additionally, a staff of at least two full-time and four part-time people are needed to properly operate a retail garment operation.

While it is expensive to open and maintain one outlet, opening many stores, in order to gain national coverage, would be a major undertaking for Jantzen. There was no doubt in Mr. Daley's mind that, although retailing could potentially provide good returns, it was an expensive and risky business. Further support of the uncertain nature of retailing was the fact that many small stores had been forced to close in recent years and even such large department store chains as Woodward's had reported losses.

In addition to the "traditional" garment retail outlets that are found in many malls and in popular shopping districts, Jantzen could open up a factory outlet. Factory outlets could be a viable alternative for Jantzen as they would facilitate the selling

[1] It is standard practice for retailers to mark up goods 100%, from the wholesale cost, in determining an appropriate retail price.

Exhibit 5
INFORMATION ON EDMONTON MALLS

Centre Name	Store Count	Gross Leasable Area (sq. ft.)	Market Population	Distance to Competition	Average Rent (sq.ft./year)
Terra Losa Centre	55	240,000	175,000	1 mile	$20
Thorncliffe Centre	10	53,197	N/A	3 blocks	$12
West Edmonton Mall	828	3,800,000	700,000	1 mile	$35
Westgate Centre	18	105,000	75,000	1 mile	$16
Westmount Mall	115	620,000	100,000	1.8 miles	$30

of seconds, returns, and/or in-season surpluses. A considerable disadvantage of these outlets is that this type of operation may be viewed negatively by other retailers. The outlets would likely be considered a direct threat by retailers as the prices in factory outlets are usually lower than those found in regular retail stores. As a result of opening up factory outlets, Jantzen could experience a backlash in the form of reduced orders from regular retailers. Nevertheless, Jantzen already successfully operated a small factory outlet (of 1200 square feet) adjacent to its Vancouver factory. This outlet was essentially a breakeven proposition. A number of garment manufacturers had opened outlets in several locations, often in cities far from their factories.

Alternative 6—Seek New Markets

The two primary new markets in which Jantzen could possibly expand its current sales are: high-end private label and specialty orders.

Although, at the present time, there are a number of manufacturers that produce garments for the high end of the Canadian sweater market, Jantzen has an opportunity to manufacture a high-end private label sweater for a retailer like Harry Rosen. Jantzen possesses the technology required for producing high quality, intricately designed sweaters, and the firm can provide much quicker service than overseas manufacturers. Faster service could be a substantial advantage, particularly when certain styles become "hot" and foreign manufacturers cannot resupply Canadian retailers. Adopting this strategy would require negotiating agreements with the U.S. parent to give Jantzen Canada more flexibility in style requirements. Also, to develop a team of professionals capable of designing and marketing fashionable sweaters would require several years of effort and an investment of between $150,000 and $200,000.

A more immediate opportunity was the specialty order business. In recent years, it had become fashionable for groups of all sorts to have logos and trademarks placed on tee-shirts and sweatshirts. This fashion had now spread to jackets and, according to trade magazines, it was about to become very popular with sweaters. Groups that Jantzen could initially target in developing a specialty order business include: government agencies (the army and the navy); corporations (airlines, banks, and restaurants); special events groups (the Muscular Dystrophy Association, the

Heart Foundation); and schools (high schools, colleges, and universities). Specialty orders may be viable for Jantzen as it is feasible for the firm to deliver small quantity orders in a short period of time. Mr. Daley was somewhat unsure about the competition in the specialty business but he concluded that overseas producers could not likely compete in this market due to the relatively short delivery requirements. Mr. Daley knew that there were domestic firms that concentrated solely on the specialty order business, but he did not think that there were any large national firms—only small regional companies. Mr. Daley knew that one advantage that some of the competition had over Jantzen was their ability to provide a wide range of products. For example, Jantzen did not have the manufacturing capabilities to produce constructed jackets (jackets with shoulder pads), although Jantzen did have the machines to fill almost every other kind of speciality order.

Mr. Daley thought that the specialty order business could be a high-profit, low-risk opportunity for Jantzen. He recognized that it would entail opening up relationships with a new line of retailers—sporting goods stores, trophy sellers, and others—but he foresaw no unusual difficulties in doing so. Mr. Daley did recognize that opening up new accounts would also mean servicing these stores which could require considerable sales support. Mr. Daley was uncertain about the size of the speciality market, but he felt quite confident it would not be as price sensitive as others that Jantzen currently competed in. Since the U.S. parent company had not entered this business, he had little reliable data to use. On the other hand, if the venture was successful, then perhaps the U.S. company would follow the Canadians for a change.

As the end of the business day approached, Mr. Daley realized that he had been so busy that he had not opened some of his mail. One letter was from head office at Vanity Fair and it indicated that all divisions of the company were going to undergo a complete operations analysis over the next few months. This worried Mr. Daley somewhat as he recognized that, being a small unit of a large multinational firm, Jantzen Canada's sweater division could be subject to closure. Despite that discomforting thought, Mr. Daley believed that, with the successful implementation of the alternative(s) he had generated, the division could provide a healthy return.

40 BAROSSA WINERY

Gordon H. G. McDougall

Mr. George Steen, marketing manager for the Barossa Winery, had just been given an interesting assignment: to evaluate the feasibility of launching a major export drive. The Barossa Winery, an Australian producer of quality table wines, had experienced rapid growth in the early 1980s, but in 1986 and 1987 sales and profits had slowed considerably. At a strategy meeting held in early July 1988, the senior management group, which included Mr. Steen, decided that a growth opportunity existed in export markets and Mr. Steen agreed to prepare a feasibility study for the next strategy meeting.

As Mr. Steen sat in his office, Mr. Tony Clark, the general manager came in and they began discussing the assignment. Mr. Steen said, "There will never be a better opportunity for us to get into foreign markets in a big way. The world has now heard of Australia because of Crocodile Dundee and the Bicentennial Celebration, we've got a very favourable exchange rate, and we produce great wines." Mr. Clark replied, "I agree, it's a good opportunity for growth and we've got the capacity of doing it and making a profit. I know our wines are as good and, in some instances better than comparable European wines, but the consumer doesn't know that." Mr. Steen replied, "That's true, but we only need a small share of any one of a number of markets to sell a large volume of wine. I think it's a matter of selecting one of two markets and going after them." Mr. Clark responded, "You are probably right, but I'm more cautious. I'll be very interested in hearing what you recommend. Our future growth may depend on your report."

THE COMPANY

The Barossa Winery, located in the Barossa Valley of South Australia, was started in the early 1960s by a winemaker, Mr. Rolf Mann, who had obtained a degree in viticulture from a well-regarded French school and emigrated to Australia. Since 1970, the firm had captured numerous awards every year at national and regional wine shows for both its red and white wines. By 1980, the company had established a solid reputation in Australia as a consistent producer of high-quality premium table wines.

The company was also known for its marketing skills. Mr. Steen, who joined the company in 1976, instituted various marketing initiatives including a series of labels that were regarded by many industry analysts as exceptional in terms of communicating the quality of the wines and "standing out" among the many competitive brands. As well, Mr. Steen established a distribution system that resulted in the prominent display of the company's products in many retail outlets. Finally, many of the advertising campaigns prepared for the Barossa Winery were judged as innovative and had contributed to the recognition and acceptance of the company's brands.

These efforts had resulted in rapid growth for the company. Between 1980 and 1985 sales increased from $17,500,000 to $33,900,000 and profits before tax from $1,600,000 to $3,100,000 (Exhibit 1).[1] However, in 1986 and 1987 sales grew more slowly and profits were unchanged. Company officials felt that recent results were due, in part, to a slowdown in the growth of both the overall market and the table wine market (Exhibit 2). As well, increased competition in the quality premium bottle table wine market had led to price discounting by some wineries. As a policy, the Barossa Winery did not engage in price discounting.

With respect to export activity up to now the company could best be described as a passive exporter. While George Steen had made one overseas trip in the past two years (the trip covered stops in the United States, Canada, and the United Kingdom) to "drum up" some business with wine importers, no explicit export strategy had been established. In fact, the company's export sales had been generated by wine importers who had approached the Barossa Winery.

The interest of those wine importers (primarily from the United Kingdom) in Barossa Winery products was due to the increasing recognition by many knowledgeable buyers of the quality of Australian and the company's wines. In the early 1980s, wine experts from the United Kingdom visited Australia and sampled numerous wines. Upon their return home, many wrote glowing reports on the quality of these wines, including Barossa Winery's products.

In 1987, the company exported 37,400 cases of wine valued at $2,094,400, an increase of 42% in volume and 70% in dollar value compared to 1986 (Exhibit 1). In fact, 1987 was the first year the company received the same average price for its wine in both the domestic and export markets. In prior years it was estimated (no records had been kept) that export sales generated a price per case of approximately 15% less than the average price received in the domestic market.

THE AUSTRALIAN WINE INDUSTRY

In many ways, the Australian wine industry is similar to other world wine markets. The first requirement for producing good wines was to have the appropriate climate and soil conditions. Many regions of Australia had these conditions and produced wine grapes including such classics as Cabernet Sauvignon, Grenache, and Pinot Noir for red wines, and Clare, Rhine Riesling, and Traminer for white wines. Most medium- and large-sized wineries in Australia made a complete range of wines, each with their own individuality. The Barossa Winery made six different white wines with two brands, Barossa Chardonnay and Barossa Rhine Riesling, making up over 80% of the company's white wine sales. The company produced five different red wines and again, two brands Barossa Cabernet Sauvignon and Barossa Hermitage accounted for the majority of sales. Dry white wines accounted for 85% of total company sales.

[1] All figures in this case are quoted in Australian dollars, unless otherwise noted. At the time of the case, $1.00 Australian = $0.99 Canadian.

Exhibit 1

BAROSSA WINERY—SELECTED COMPANY STATISTICS (1980 TO 1987)

	1980	1981	1982	1983	1984	1985	1986	1987
Profit and Loss Statement (in $000,000)								
Sales	17.5	20.6	23.6	26.8	30.5	33.9	35.3	36.8
Cost of goods sold	11.7	13.8	15.6	17.9	20.8	23.2	24.4	25.7
Gross margin	5.8	6.8	8.0	8.9	9.7	10.7	10.9	11.1
Marketing expenses	3.0	3.5	3.9	4.5	4.8	5.5	5.7	5.8
Net margin	2.8	3.3	4.1	4.4	4.9	5.2	5.2	5.3
Administration and overheads	1.2	1.5	1.7	1.8	2.0	2.1	2.2	2.2
Profit before tax	1.6	1.8	2.4	2.6	2.9	3.1	3.0	3.1
Sales by Volume								
(000 litres)	4,120	4,520	4,830	4,950	5,210	5,680	5,800	5,900
(000 cases)[a]	468	502	537	550	579	631	644	656
Average selling price per case ($)	37.40	41.00	44.00	48.70	52.70	53.70	54.80	56.10
Export statistics								
Export sales (000 litres)	84.2	122.0	115.9	158.4	187.6	215.8	237.8	336.3
Export sales (000 cases)	9.4	13.6	12.9	17.6	20.8	24.0	26.4	37.4
Average selling price/case ($)[b]	31.80	34.90	37.40	41.40	44.80	45.60	46.60	56.00
Export sales ($000)[c]	298.9	474.6	482.5	728.6	931.8	1094.4	1230.2	2094.4
Consumer Price Index	100.0	109.8	120.8	135.5	148.7	160.9	176.7	186.0

Source: Company records

[a] One case equals 9 L (12 bottles containing 750 mL each).

[b] Up to 1987 detailed sales records on prices were not kept. Company officials estimated that between 1980 and 1986 the average selling price per case was approximately 15% less than the domestic price per case.

[c] It was estimated that marketing expenses and administration and overheads amounted to 3% of sales for export sales versus around 8% for domestic sales.

Exhibit 2

AUSTRALIAN WINE MARKET—SELECTED STATISTICS (1980 TO 1987) (000 LITRES)

	1980	1981	1982	1983	1984	1985	1986	1987
Total Wine Sales	245,040	262,872	278,595	293,582	305,802	320,478	325,183	329,952
Table	160,867	179,278	197,904	216,948	227,805	245,400	253,045	258,231
Fortified[a]	45,587	45,868	45,189	43,027	42,587	38,617	36,819	36,246
Sparkling[b]	29,915	29,577	27,749	27,022	29,021	31,277	30,413	30,098
All other[c]	8,671	8,158	7,753	6,585	6,389	5,182	4,907	5,378
Table Wine Sales by Variety								
Dry white	121,093	138,016	155,310	172,334	175,341	179,286	171,780	176,227
Sweet white	3,497	3,912	4,529	4,929	10,060	20,840	36,936	34,657
Red	27,667	29,258	30,362	31,856	34,480	37,805	37,188	40,192
Rose	8,610	8,091	7,706	7,830	7,924	7,466	7,140	7,155
Table Wine Sales by Package								
Soft pack—white	51,148	69,525	84,680	103,585	111,486	137,675	140,788	138,787
Bottled—white	34,300	36,709	39,368	38,644	36,278	39,559	38,851	41,743
Soft pack—red	7,451	8,871	11,263	12,787	14,425	16,191	16,927	17,659
Bottled—red	11,507	12,455	12,252	12,657	14,058	16,779	16,838	19,004
All other[d]	56,461	51,718	50,341	49,275	51,558	35,196	39,641	41,038

Source: Australian Wine and Brandy Corporation

[a] Includes sherry and dessert wines.

[b] Includes champagne and carbonated wines.

[c] Includes flavoured and vermouth.

[d] Includes white, red, and rose sold in bulk and in bottles over one litre in size.

A second requirement for producing good wines was to have a skilled winemaker. Mr. Mann had quickly established a reputation throughout Australia for producing high-quality wines on a consistent basis. He was renowned for his ability to purchase the finest grapes (the company did not own any vineyards, but instead purchased its grapes from among the over 4,000 grape growers in Australia), and he used the latest technology in producing many award-winning wines.

The third requirement was the ability to market the company's wines. Few, if any, product categories offered the consumer as wide a choice of varieties and brands as the wine category. For example, one of the large wholesalers of beer, wine, and spirits in Australia listed 577 brands of bottled table wines, including 256 red wines and 273 white wines. Most of these listed wines would be supplied by the 50 medium to large wineries in Australia.

Retail liquor outlets would not carry the complete range of wines offered by a wholesaler, but a typical outlet would handle at least 100 different brands of red and white bottled table wines. This large selection meant that marketing was critical in getting a brand known and recognized by consumers. While wine connoisseurs understood the differences between the varieties and brands of wines, these consumers constituted a very small percentage of the wine buying public. A second group, who knew a reasonable amount about wines, and could identify the major and some minor brands, tended to purchase the majority of the bottled table wines.

In terms of quantity, most table wine in Australia was sold in two or four litre casks to consumers who were relatively price sensitive. Retail liquor outlets in Australia could advertise and offer beer, wine, and spirits at any price. A consumer could purchase a four litre cask of average quality Riesling for about $7.00 on sale (regular price $10.00) or a 750 mL bottle of slightly higher quality Riesling for $3.50 on sale (regular price of $6.50). As shown in Exhibit 2, soft pack or cask sales of table wine constituted about 61% of total table wine sales, while bottled table wines constituted about 24% of total table wine sales by volume.

A further indication of the price sensitivity of the market was the impact of government taxation policies on the level of wine consumption. In late 1984, a 10% tax was placed on wines, and in 1985 the tax was increased to 20%. As shown in Exhibit 2, the total market growth rate, which averaged 5% between 1980 and 1984, declined to 1.5% in 1985.

On a broader scale, the consumption of wine in Australia appeared to have peaked in 1985 at 21 L per capita. This compared to per capita consumption of 9 L in 1970, 12 L in 1975, and 17 L in 1980.

Against this backdrop, the Barossa Winery competed in the bottled table wine markets. Its target market was the relatively sophisticated wine drinker who was somewhat knowledgeable about wines and was likely to drink wine with his or her evening meal two or more times a week. Within this target market, the Barossa Winery competed with virtually all the wineries in Australia as this was the most profitable segment. However, only a few companies, such as Wolf Blass and Leasingham had been as successful as the Barossa Winery within this segment. While no market data was available, some industry observers felt that Wolf Blass and Leasingham were increasing their share of the market at a faster rate than the Barossa Winery.

THE WORLD WINE INDUSTRY

On a world-wide basis, the wine market was dominated by the European Community (EC) and within the community, by three countries, France, Italy, and Spain. The EC vineyards accounted for approximately 27% of the total area of the world under vines, 38% of the world's grapes, and 60% of the world's production of wines. Because of price supports within the EC for the wine industry in the past, the EC countries typically produced more wine than could be consumed within the EC. Consequently, there was considerable pressure to export wine. Due to declining consumption within the EC countries and revised price support policies, in recent years the production of wine by EC nations had declined (Exhibit 3). However, a surplus of wine was still produced within the EC, and the countries collectively exported over four billion litres of wine annually. Exporting of wine was encouraged by governments as the EC provided export refunds and subsidies for table wine exported outside the EC.

Exhibit 3
WORLD WINE INDUSTRY—SELECTED DATA (000,000 LITRES)

	Production			Exports	Imports	Per Capita Consumption (Litres)	
	1983–84	1984–85	1985–86	1985	1985	1983	1985
France	6,855	6,436	7,015	1,189	701	85	80
Italy	8,228	7,090	6,258	1,803	n/a	91	85
Spain	3,247	3,625	3,277	731	n/a	57	48
Portugal	845	850	855	152	n/a	89	87
West Germany	1,340	889	540	292	962	27	26
Greece	525	503	478	140	n/a	44	43
United Kingdom	—	—	—	—	580	9	10
Total EC	21,058	19,409	18,431	4,307			
Europe—All Others (incl. U.S.S.R.)	7,031	6,692	5,804	—	—	—	—
United States	1,476	1,670	1,810	—	519	8	9
Australia	396	451	480	11	8	20	21
Canada	47	50	50	—	140	9	10
Africa, Latin America, and South Africa	3,312	2,931	3,124	—	—	—	—
All Others	1,002	918	981	—	—	—	—
Total	34,323	32,120	30,680	5,303	5,364		

Source: Australian Wine and Brandy Corporation

AUSTRALIAN WINE IMPORTS AND EXPORTS

Between 1980 and 1985 only a small portion (about 3%) of Australia's total wine production was exported. In the 1985–86 period exports increased to 11 million litres, and in 1986–87 exports rose to 21 million litres (Exhibit 4). This was due primarily to a more favourable exchange rate as the Australian dollar had fallen sharply against most foreign currencies (Exhibit 5). Two other factors also contributed to this increase. First, the Chernobyl nuclear incident (a nuclear reactor exploded in Poland in 1986 and nuclear waste was spread across Europe) had raised concern in a number of countries (particularly in Scandinavia) about contamination of European grapes. Second, there was a growing awareness in many countries of the quality of Australian wines.

The vast majority of Australian wine exports were table wines and most of these exports went to seven countries with the United States, the United Kingdom, and Canada being three of the largest markets. The value per litre of export sales varied considerably by country. At the lower end, Sweden purchased wine in bulk (it was

Exhibit 4
AUSTRALIAN WINE IMPORTS AND EXPORTS, 1986–1987

	IMPORTS*			EXPORTS		
	Litres (000)	Value ($000)	Value/ Litre ($)	Litres (000)	Value ($000)	Value/ Litre ($)
Champagne	1,134	19,628	17.31	370	1,484	4.00
Table wine	4,852	17,084	3.52	18,627	37,967	2.04
All others	1,573	4,899	3.11	2,326	5,170	2.22
Total	7,559	41,611	5.50	21,323	44,621	2.09

EXPORTS FROM AUSTRALIA BY DESTINATION (000 LITRES OR $000)

	Champagne		Table Wine		All Others		Total		Value/ Litre
	L	Value	L	Value	L	Value	L	Value	
United States	36	$ 171	2,455	$ 9,029	422	$1,255	2,913	$10,455	$3.59
United Kingdom	34	122	2,190	6,775	96	352	2,320	7,249	3.12
Sweden	—	—	5,223	5,257	—	—	5,223	5,257	1.01
New Zealand	183	611	1,054	3,397	177	540	1,414	4,548	3.22
Canada	—	—	1,228	3,017	791	1,283	2,019	4,300	2.13
Hong Kong	28	149	527	1,009	108	246	663	1,404	2.12
Fiji	14	67	230	426	72	136	316	629	1.19
All Other	75	364	5,720	9,057	660	1,358	6,455	10,779	1.67
Total	370	$1,484	18,627	$37,967	2,326	$5,170	21,323	$44,621	$2.09

* Largest imports (in 1000 L) come from Italy (2,714), France (1,981), and Portugal (777).

Exhibit 5
EXCHANGE RATES (UNITS OF FOREIGN CURRENCY PER $ AUSTRALIAN)

June	United States Dollar	Canadian Dollar	U.K. Pound Sterling	West German Mark	French Franc	Italian Lira	Trade Weighted Index*
1984	0.86	1.14	0.64	2.40	7.36	1,477.13	79.2
1985	0.67	0.91	0.51	2.03	6.19	1,294.40	65.0
1986	0.68	0.94	0.44	1.48	4.73	1,019.90	56.3
1987	0.72	0.96	0.45	1.31	4.40	955.48	56.6
1988	0.81	0.99	0.44	0.99	3.97	1,099.32	56.8

Source: Reserve Bank of Australia, *Bulletin*, Publication No. NBP4521

* Trade-weighted index of average value of the Australian dollars vis-a-vis currencies of Australia's trading partners. May 1970 index = 100.

shipped from Australia in large containers) at a value per litre of $1.01. The wine was bottled and sold by the Swedish liquor control board. At the upper end, all of the wine exported to the United States was in bottle form at an average price to the exporter of $3.59 per litre.

THE EXPORT DECISION

In preparing the report, Mr. Steen first considered the possible countries where the Barossa Winery could achieve significant sales. Based on a preliminary screening, he decided to limit his investigation to the three countries that he felt offered a good potential for the company's products: Canada, the United States, and the United Kingdom.

Canada

Canada was an attractive market because the domestic wine industry was not well developed and was not recognized as producing quality wines (Exhibit 6). The marketing of wine and spirits in Canada was strictly controlled by the ten provincial governments, and most sales were made through government liquor stores. In March 1988, the Australian Wine and Brandy Corporation sponsored a tour of the listing agents for the ten liquor control boards of Canada. The agents visited the major wine-growing areas and sampled many of the wines available for export. The main objective of the tour was to acquaint the agents with the quality, variety, and availability of Australian wines.

The two major drawbacks to the Canadian market were the difficulties in getting a general listing and the restrictions placed on marketing activities. Australian wines would compete against all other wine producing countries for listings. It was estimated that up to 1,000 listing requests were received by each of the ten boards every year and a selection committee might list 75 new wines. Chances of acceptance were improved by a personal visit to present the listing application. Primarily, it was felt that price (within a given quality range) was the dominant criteria in getting accepted on the list. Government restrictions placed on marketing activities (for example, no price discounting, restrictions as to the amount and type of advertising, no point-of-purchase displays) made it difficult to develop brand awareness and trial by consumers.

Exhibit 6
FACT SHEET ON CANADA

- Canadian consumption of wine, particularly imported wine, is increasing despite severe marketing restrictions. The import and retailing of all alcoholic beverages is controlled by individual provincial monopolies, as are all aspects of product marketing (for example, advertising, sampling).
- Import licensing as such is not required. However, distribution is controlled by the provincial government liquor monopolies who will only list a brand if convinced it will achieve the required sales volume.
- Import duties are $12 Canadian per imperial gallon (one imperial gallon equals 4.546 L). Excise taxes are $0.35 Canadian per litre. Federal sales taxes are 12% on the landed duty and excise paid value. As of June 1988, import duties in Australian dollars would be $2.64 per litre, excise duties would be $0.35 per litre, and federal sales tax would be $10.29 per litre.
- No major difficulties in terms of certification, packaging, etc. However, with respect to labels, the label information must be in English and French.
- Canada produces less than one-half of its wine requirements and Canada's climate is not conducive to grape growing.
- Prices to the provincial monopolies should be quoted in Canadian dollars CIF (cost, insurance, freight). Each province arbitrarily sets the retail price of a product by applying a fixed mark up to the landed cost (C$CIF). For example, Alberta has a mark up of 55%; British Columbia has a mark up of 50% on B.C. produced table wines, 110% on other Canadian produced table wines, and 110% on imported wines; Ontario has a mark up of 58% on Ontario produced table wines, 98% on other Canadian produced table wines, and 123% on imported wines; Quebec has a mark up of 80% on Quebec produced table wines, 114% on other Canadian produced table wines, and 120% on imported table wines.
- Distribution of all wine and spirits sold in Canada is controlled by government monopolies and/or liquor boards. Each of the ten provinces has its own liquor board. Since each province will only stock a limited range of wines out of the hundreds of different types and brands available, it establishes a price list giving the names of those wines available for sale. However, even when a wine is listed, it will probably not be available in every store.
- The majority of Canada's 26 million people reside in Ontario, Quebec, British Columbia, and Alberta.

Primary source: Australian Wine and Brandy Corporation, *Export Market Grid.*

In preparing his report Mr. Steen obtained information on the largest Australian wine exporter's operations in Canada (Hardy's Wines). It was rumoured that Hardy's held somewhat over 40% share of the Canadian table wine market for Australian wines. As well, Hardy's was thought to have about a 50% share of the "All Other" wines category. It had achieved this position by spending approximately $200,000 each year in Canada. Hardy's had two full-time employees, one in Ontario and one in Quebec (total costs for both employees including salaries, office space, cars, and expenses were $100,000), and the company spent about $100,000 on all types of promotions, including visits by the Australian export manager. The two employees spent the majority of their time making regular calls on the liquor board head office, checking stocks, and calling on individual liquor stores to ensure that the product was available. As well, the employees would have the product on hand at any wine tastings within the provinces. A further important duty was to encourage Canadian wine writers for newspapers and magazines to write about Hardy's Wines. Hardy's also employed agents in Alberta and British Columbia who received a 10% commission plus up to 5% more for expenses.

Most Australian wine producers who exported to Canada used agents to perform the marketing function. The agents worked on a commission basis (usually 10% of the landed cost in Canada) and their prime role was to obtain product exposure. This could be done by convincing restaurants and hotels to include the product on wine lists, by conducting tastings, and by obtaining good press for the product. Agents could be valuable because the need for personal selling was considerable in Canada. Wine consumption in Canada had been increasing and per capita consumption had risen from 6.3 L per year in 1976 to 10 L in 1985. Over 50% of the wine sold in Canada was imported and over 80% of that came from the wine-producing countries of the EC. Some well-known European brands such as Blue Nun, Black Tower, and Mateus had substantial sales in Canada. Of the 140,000,000 L of wine imported to Canada in 1985, 90% were table wines.

United States

By Australian standards, the magnitude of the U.S. market was staggering (Exhibit 7). Imports of table wine alone were about 313 million litres in 1986, most of it coming from Italy (48%), France (30%), and West Germany (11%). The Italian wine imports tended to be lower priced ($1.52/L on average), while the French imports were relatively high priced ($4.43/L). The German imports ($2.89/L) were close to the average of all imports ($3.09/L).[2] In 1986, the Australian share of the U.S. table wine market was estimated at 0.06%.

The top-selling import brands in the U.S. market included Riunite from Italy (8,500,000 cases), Blue Nun from Germany (1,000,000 cases), and Mateus from Portugal (800,000 cases). It was estimated that the wholesale price per case for these brands were: Riunite $19.35 ($2.15/L), Blue Nun $33.12 ($3.68/L), and Mateus $21.30 ($2.37/L). Promotion expenditures for many of the imported wines were extensive, and while total expenditures were not available it was estimated

[2] Value at foreign export port exclusive of shipping costs and taxes.

that Riunite spent over $12,000,000 in television advertising and Blue Nun spent approximately $2,400,000 in radio advertising.

With respect to markets, the top ten markets for table wine in the United States accounted for 65% of all sales. The New York metropolitan area had sales of 5.9 million cases of imported table wine, and Detroit (ninth ranked) had sales of 550,000 cases in 1986.

Selection of an agent or importer was obviously an important consideration. Numerous spirit agents were available ranging from small companies that specialized in a few product lines in one area of the country to national distributors that had a vast product line and covered the entire country.

Marketing activities for wine companies, particularly in the non-monopoly states could be extensive and include advertising, in-store promotions, and price specials. Many United States wine producers, particularly from California, had established well-known brand names and were recognized as producing quality wines.

Exhibit 7
FACT SHEET ON THE UNITED STATES

- The United States consumption of wine, both domestic and imported, has been increasing and the absolute size of the market is one of the most attractive in the world. Estimated sales for 1988 are 2 billion litres.
- Import licenses may only be held by U.S. citizens.
- Import duties on table wines are $0.375 U.S. per U.S. gallon (one U.S. gallon = 3.785 L). Excise taxes are $0.17 U.S. per U.S. gallon. As of June 1988, import duties in Australian dollars would be $0.12 per litre and excise taxes would be $0.06 per litre.
- No major difficulties in terms of certification, packaging, labelling, etc.
- Seventy-two percent of the table wine sold in the U.S. was produced in California, 24% was imported, and 4% was produced by other states in 1986.
- The U.S. market, because of its size and complexity, should be treated on a state-by-state basis. The sale of alcoholic beverages is controlled by state organizations, the degree of authority ranging from minimal licensing requirements to complete control of retail outlets. There are 18 "monopoly" states that operate in a similar manner to Canada. Most of the larger states, including California and New York, are non-monopoly states. The "non-monopoly" states operate in a similar manner to the Australian system. In these states, the product can only enter the U.S. through a licensed importer, who, in turn, can only then sell to a wholesaler. A direct sale to the retailer or consumer level is not permitted. Importers' or agents' margins range from 10% to 25% of landed cost, wholesalers' around 15% to 30%, and retailers' 30% to 40%.
- In 1968, the majority of table wines sold in the U.S. retailed in Australian dollars between $3.40 and $5.25 (69%), $5.26 and $7.10 (15%), and $7.11 and $9.26 (9%).

Primary source: Australian Wine and Brandy Corporation, *Export Market Grid.*

United Kingdom

The third market under consideration was the United Kingdom (Exhibit 8). In the past few years, per capita wine consumption in the United Kingdom had increased and stood at ten litres in 1985. A review of the U.K. wine market in 1986 noted that Australia had less than 2% of the table wine market.

The U.K. market was very competitive and extensive advertising, point-of-purchase displays, and price specials were used at the retail level to promote individual brands.

The major drawback for any exporter in developing the U.K. market was the potential threat that import regulations for wines might be changed. In the past France had engaged in certain activities that "changed the rules" resulting in a new set of regulations that disrupted the marketing activities of exporters to the EC.

Most of the larger and some of the medium-sized Australian wine producers had entered the export market by focusing first on the United Kingdom. For example, one of the largest Australian producers, Orlando Wines, had been very active in the United Kingdom. Orlando regarded the U.K. as an important market. As one executive of Orlando stated: "If you can be successful in the U.K., it will stand you in good stead in other export markets." Orlando had established their own company in the U.K. and the subsidiary performed the role of the importer. The export marketing manager visited the U.K. four times a year, spending two weeks on each visit. His main activities were to motivate the distributor of the company's brands and to discuss the brands with wine writers, if possible. The distributor was a medium-

Exhibit 8
FACT SHEET ON THE UNITED KINGDOM

- The U.K. consumption of wine has been increasing and all wine consumed in the U.K. is imported. The U.K. is a member of the EC.
- Import licenses can be easily obtained although there are major difficulties in complying with various EC requirements for import.
- Import duties on table wines entering the EC are £8.58 per hundred litres. It should be noted that wines entering the EC must exceed a minimum threshold price. Excise taxes in the U.K. are £0.980/L on table wine. As well, a Value Added Tax of 15% is placed on all products. As of June 1988, import duties in Australian dollars would be $0.20 per litre, excise taxes would be $2.23 per litre, and the Value Added Tax would be $1.34 per litre.
- Considerable efforts are required to comply with EC standards with respect to certification, packaging, and labelling. In particular, an EC analysis certificate that describes the wine's characteristics including actual alcohol strength, total dry extract, total acidity, and residual sugar must be completed (the analysis can be done in Australia) and meet EC requirements.
- In 1985, the United Kingdom imported 580 million litres of wine, most of it from member countries of the EC.

Primary source: Australian Wine and Brandy Corporation, *Export Market Grid.*

sized wholesaler who sold to retail liquor chains, primarily in the London area. While no figures were available on Orlando's export sales it was estimated that in 1988, their sales into the U.K. market would be approximately 40,000 cases.

Orlando did some advertising in both consumer and trade magazines in the United Kingdom. In a recent issue of *Decanter* (a consumer magazine targeted at wine buffs) Orlando had a full-page ad emphasizing the quality of their brands and stated, "They [the two brands] compare beautifully with similar wines from France, yet only cost around half as much."

Another company that was actively involved in export marketing was Wolf Blass, a well-known medium-size producer of quality wines. In 1985, they set up distributorships with agents in both the United States and the United Kingdom. Wolf Blass was one of the few companies that received the same price of wine in both the domestic and export markets (in 1987, the average price received was approximately $65 per case). In selecting the distributors in both the U.S. and the U.K., Wolf Blass had decided on large agents to give them access to the markets they wanted. In 1987, Wolf Blass had sold a total of 50,000 cases in the export market, but it was not clear whether they had made any profits. Some experts felt that the money Wolf Blass invested to develop the exports markets (estimated annual marketing expenditures for both major markets were $600,000) had been substantial and that no profits would be obtained for at least four years.

PRELIMINARY COST DATA

Mr. Steen prepared some rough calculations on the costs of getting a case of wine to each of the three markets and what it might sell for at retail (Exhibit 9). With respect to costs of production, Mr. Steen had read a recent newspaper article on the costs of wine and was surprised at how closely those costs were to those of the Barossa Winery. As shown in Exhibit 10, the production cost for a 750 mL bottle of good quality Chardonnay was $3.02. By the time the consumer purchased it, the price was $11.08. While the cost of grapes for some of the other varieties of wines could be considerably less (for example, $600 per tonne for Semillon), most of the price of a bottle of wine ($8.06 per the example) was made up of margins and taxes.

Mr. Steen also worked out some preliminary estimates of what it would cost to actively enter all three export markets. In terms of personnel, the cost of an export sales manager was about $60,000 and if the manager made six overseas trips a year, this expense would be about $100,000. One or two sales clerks might be required at a cost of $30,000 each. Preparation of custom requirements including documentation, obtaining label approvals, and sending samples could cost up to $30,000. Promotion costs were difficult to estimate, but they could exceed $100,000 for expenditures on wine tastings and shows for both the public and the trade, advertising expenditures for consumers and the trade, and public relations.

A portion of these expenditures could be recovered from the federal government through the Export Market Development Grant. Firms engaged in export marketing were eligible (for the first five years) to receive up to 70% of certain export costs including printing of special labels, preparation and printing of point-of-sale material, a portion of the cost of any personnel who were located in the export market,

Exhibit 9

ESTIMATED RETAIL PRICE OF A CASE OF BAROSSA WINE IN THE THREE MARKETS

	United Kingdom	United States	Canada
Barossa Winery price	$ 56.00	$ 56.00	$ 56.00
Transport to destination[1]	2.55	2.85	2.85
Landed cost	58.55	58.85	58.85
Import duties and excise tax[2]	21.90	1.60	26.90
Other taxes[2]	12.05	—	10.30
Landed cost with duties/taxes	92.50	60.45	96.05
Importer/agent margin[3]	27.75	9.70	9.60
Importer price	120.25	69.55	105.65
Wholesale margin[4]	—	13.90	—
Wholesale price	120.25	83.45	105.65
Retail margin[5]	60.15	29.20	64.75
Retail price	180.40	112.65	170.40
Bottle price (750 mL)	$ 15.00	$ 9.40	$ 14.20

Assumptions:

[1] It costs $347 to ship a container from the Barossa Valley to Port Adelaide. On average, a container holds 1,000 cases. One case contains 9 L or 12 bottles (750 mL). Port Adelaide to U.K. is $2,200 per container; to U.S. or Canada, approximately $2,500.

[2] Based on information in fact sheets.

[3] Importer margin in U.K. ranges from 25% to 40% of landed cost (assume 30% for estimation purposes); in U.S. range is 10% to 25% (assume 15%); in Canada agents average 10%.

[4] Wholesale margins in U.S. range from 15% to 30% (assume 20%).

[5] Retail margins in U.K. are about 50%; in U.S. from 30% to 40% (assume 35%); in Canada, range from 55% to 123% of landed cost (assume 110%).

air travel, and a portion of accommodation expenses for managers visiting the export markets, samples, and expenses related to wine trade shows. While it was difficult to estimate the precise proportion of costs that would be recovered, depending on the type of expenditure, Barossa Winery could receive up to $100,000 each year.

Although the Barossa Winery had not aggressively pursued the export market, Mr. Steen was quick to capitalize on any export opportunity that was presented. For example, if a British importer expressed interest in any of the company's products, Mr. Steen, or a member of the marketing group, would provide free samples, information on the wines, and product availability. If an importer placed an order, Mr. Steen ensured that the order was shipped as quickly as possible with proper documentation. As Mr. Steen once joked to a colleague, "We may not go after the export business, but if anybody comes to us, we'll offer better service and support than any other winery in Australia."

Exhibit 10
TYPICAL COST STRUCTURE OF A BOTTLE/CASE OF WINE

	Per Bottle	Per Case
Product*	$ 1.61	
Packaging	1.07	
Bottling	.22	
Transportation	.12	
Total production cost	3.02	$ 36.24
Manufacturer margin (50% of costs)	1.50	
Price to wholesaler	4.52	54.24
Wholesaler margin (25%)	1.13	
Wholesaler price before taxes	5.65	
Federal tax (20%)	1.13	
Wholesaler price after federal tax	6.78	
State tax (9%)	.61	
Wholesaler price after taxes	7.39	88.68
Retailer margin (50%)	3.69	
Retail price	11.08	132.96

* Based on premium Chardonnay fruit at a price per tonne of $1,200. One tonne will produce 744 bottles of 750 mL wine. A case contains 12 bottles (9 L).

Mr. Steen was pleased with the growth of exports in the past few years, but he was concerned about the tenuous nature of the business. While the export business had experienced steady growth, the source of sales often changed substantially on a yearly basis. For example, sales to the United Kingdom had been made through two different U.K. importers in the past three years. Between 1981 and 1984, Star Importers, a U.K. importer who specialized in Australian wines, had purchased up to 10,000 cases of Barossa Wines in a given year. In late 1984, Star Importers switched their major buying from Barossa to a competitive winery in New South Wales. In 1985, the Reid Company, another U.K. importer, began buying Barossa Wines and in 1987 purchased 18,000 cases for the U.K. market.

Similarly, the company had been approached in the past five years by six different United States importers. The Barossa Winery had conducted business with all six (sales in a given year to any one of the importers ranged from 400 to 4,500 cases) over the years and in 1987 sold a total 9,000 cases through four importers to the U.S. market. Two sales agents in Canada (who have been importing the product for about four years) had generated sales of about 800 cases in Ontario and Alberta. As well, the company had sold about 10,000 cases to the "rest of the world" through two Australian exporters. These two firms approached Australian wine producers and obtained products that they would sell to distributors at the wholesale or retail level in other countries. As far as Mr. Steen could tell the two exporters who sold Barossa Wines had most of their sales in New Zealand, Micronesia, and the Far East (for example, Japan, Taiwan, Thailand, Hong Kong).

Mr. Steen realized that the Barossa Winery did not have strong links with these importers or exporters in that no formal contracts were signed with any of them in terms of an exclusive agreement. In all cases, both parties were free to buy from or sell to anyone. Further, the company had little expertise in exporting as most of the work and all of the marketing was done by the importer or exporter. In the final analysis, Mr. Steen felt that the company's success to date had been a combination of good service, good prices, and good quality wine.

THE DECISION

Having gathered the preliminary data, Mr. Steen began thinking about the report. He was not certain what he should recommend. On the one hand, export sales were growing with little effort and expense on the company's part. Possibly with a little more effort, sales could be increased without going "full speed ahead" into exporting. On the other hand, the tenuous nature of the company's relationship with its exporters and importers suggested that some action should be taken.

Mr. Steen knew that the senior management group was expecting a report that contained specific recommendations including whether the Barossa Winery should aggressively enter the export market and, if so, how many markets to enter. As well, the group would expect to receive details of the proposed strategy Mr. Steen would pursue for the next three years in the export area. With these thoughts in mind, Mr. Steen began writing the report.

41 CANADIAN FOREMOST LTD.

Talaat Abdel-Malek

After reviewing Canadian Foremost Ltd.'s activities over the past four years to develop its sales potential in China, Jack Nodwell summed up the situation: "What can be seen here is a continually moving target. We have been trying to identify the Chinese requirements and approach to business and at the same time work to our company philosophy. The essential question now is whether we are doing the right things." As president of Canadian Foremost Ltd., Mr. Nodwell had successfully negotiated several sales contracts with the U.S.S.R. since 1968 and was now directly involved in efforts to promote Foremost's business prospects in China. In early 1985, he was anticipating an invitation for another visit to China, probably in late May or June. His immediate task was to decide whether a change in strategy was necessary and to determine what further actions were required to enter that market. China was believed to hold considerable long-term potential for the company.

BACKGROUND

Canadian Foremost specialized in the design, manufacture, and marketing of high-mobility vehicles and hydraulic oilfield pumping systems. Through three operating divisions, the company served a broad range of primarily energy-related industries throughout the world. In fiscal 1983, more than 80% of total revenues were derived from sales to customers outside Canada. With its expertise in moving heavy loads over soft ground, the company had placed its large vehicles in 23 countries throughout the world. A five-year financial summary of the company's operations is given in Exhibit 1.

Product Line

For three decades, Canadian Foremost had been providing industry with heavy-duty, off-highway transportation vehicles (Exhibit 2). Payload capacities varied from 4 to 70 tons. Because of their mobility in marginal terrain and high-load capacities, Foremost's vehicles were used by many industries for resource development projects in remote areas, for example in pipeline and powerline construction, geophysical exploration, mining, construction, and oilfield handling. About 200 custom-built vehicles were produced each year.

Canadian Foremost's policy was to provide a comprehensive warranty program, on-site operator start-up, training and maintenance instruction, as well as complete after-sales maintenance with every vehicle purchased. In addition, Foremost insisted on providing to foreign customers spare parts for two years of operation with each vehicle sold as part of the sale contract at a cost to the client of approximately 18% of the vehicle(s) sold.

Exhibit 1
CANADIAN FOREMOST LTD.—FIVE YEAR FINANCIAL SUMMARY*

	1983	1982	1981	1980	1979
Financial Results					
Revenue	$17,124	$13,817	$28,563	$20,390	$8,689
Research and development	542	1,027	1,340	1,525	803
Income (loss) before taxes and extraordinary loss	1,559	(887)	2,089	768	(631)
Income taxes	474	(393)	718	146	(325)
Net income (loss)	1,085	(494)	1,371	622	(306)
Earnings (loss) per share	.29	(.13)	.37	.17	(.09)
Funds from operations	1,743	(543)	2,289	878	(664)
Financial Position					
Assets	19,085	10,836	14,489	13,957	9,924
Liabilities	10,333	2,722	5,434	5,826	1,970
Shareholders' equity	8,752	8,114	9,055	8,131	7,954
Working capital	7,068	6,064	7,634	6,101	6,272
Property, plant and equipment, at cost	2,438	2,248	2,179	1,766	1,441
Long-term debt	—	—	—	—	—

* Dollar amounts are in thousands, except in case of per share figures.

Prices of vehicles depended on size, type, and special features built in the vehicles to meet specific needs. However, prices ranged from $190,000 for a Delta-3 model to $300,000 for a Pioneer to as much as $500,000 or more for a Husky-8.

The Competition

Foremost had very few competitors and was considered by many to be the Cadillac of its industry. The other Canadian producer of off-road vehicles was the Quebec-based Bombardier, which received significant support from the Quebec government. Bombardier produced a wide product line, of which off-road vehicles represented a small portion beside such products as sailboats, subway cars, and skidoos.

Oshkosh was another competitor. This was a very large U.S. company which built large trucks primarily for use by the military. Oshkosh modified conventional trucks for heavy-duty use and had secured several military contracts. Foremost's management believed that it would be difficult for Oshkosh to do custom work, and that its trucks lacked the manoeuvreability and mobility of Foremost's all-terrain vehicles. However, Oshkosh had appointed an agent in Beijing and was actively pursuing market opportunities in China.

Markets

Canadian Foremost's management realized that its highly specialized custom-built products required a world-wide market for viable operations. The North American market, regarded by the company as its domestic market, was subject to cyclical fluctuations in demand caused by changes in economic conditions and in government policies aimed at key sectors, like oil and gas.

The depressed state of the North American market since the late 1970s induced Foremost to pursue a more aggressive export policy. As a result, the share of offshore markets rose from 40% of sales in the early 1970s to 60% in the early 1980s.

Offshore markets included mainly the U.S.S.R., Peru, Venezuela, Iran, and Antarctica. Mr. Nodwell felt that his company had gained a good position in these markets, many of which continued to show good potential for Foremost's vehicles. Recalling his experience in the Russian market, he said, "It took us two years at the beginning to get to the negotiating stage with the Soviets. But since then we have sold them over 350 machines valued at more than $100 million over a 15-year period. Future prospects look good. We feel we now have a good understanding of how a centrally planned economy works."

EARLIER EFFORTS IN CHINA

Canadian Foremost had made considerable efforts, especially during the past four years, to ascertain China's needs for Foremost-type vehicles. To gain first-hand familiarity with the market, executives had made a number of trips to Beijing and oilfield sites. They also appointed China Traders Inc. (CTI), an American agency with offices in the U.S. and Beijing, as its agent in China. This firm was recommended by another heavy equipment manufacturer and represented several foreign suppliers of industrial and oilfield equipment in China. Foremost agreed to pay the agent a retainer of $12,000 plus a commission of 5% of net selling price or 2.5% on third party sales.

Mr. Nodwell led a company team on a visit to China in 1983. During that visit the team was satisfied that its vehicles could effectively meet transportation needs arising from China's expanding oilfield exploration and development activities. This assessment was confirmed by the Chinese technical and managerial personnel with whom the team met during company-organized technical seminars and other functions. The next step was to identify specific types and models of vehicles which would be required by the Chinese. Requests had been made earlier to Foremost for detailed sales and technical proposals with respect to four models, namely, the Delta-3, Commander-C, Chieftain, and Husky. The proposals were delivered to the Chinese side shortly thereafter.

Meanwhile, the Chinese intimated on several occasions that Foremost's vehicles were overpriced by something like 30%, although no explanation was given as to how this percentage was arrived at. The team's visit also revealed the complexity of pursuing equipment sales contracts in China. While end-users had to be convinced of the technical merits of the vehicles, the decision to purchase rested with other

Exhibit 2
CANADIAN FOREMOST PRODUCT LINE

TRACKED VEHICLES

NODWELL 60

Payload	8,000 lbs., 3,630 kg
Ground Bearing Pressure (Max. Load)	2.13 P.S.I., 0.15 kg/cm²
Maximum Speed	12.2 mph, 19.6 km/h
BHP (SAE)	92 HP (68.6 kW) @ 2800 RPM
Suspension	Walking beam
Length	16 ft. 11 in., 5.16 m
Width	8 ft. 2 in., 2.50 m
Height	8 ft. 0 in., 2.44 m

NODWELL 110

Payload	20,000 lbs., 9,080 kg
Ground Bearing Pressure (Max. Load)	3.6 P.S.I., 0.25 kg/cm²
Maximum Speed	10.8 mph, 17.4 km/h
BHP (SAE)	197 HP (147 kW) @ 2800 RPM
Suspension	Torsional coil spring
Length	20 ft. 0 in., 6.10 m
Width	9 ft. 11 in., 3.02 m
Height	8 ft. 10 in., 2.69 m

NODWELL 110 C

Payload	20,000 lbs., 9,080 kg
Ground Bearing Pressure (Max. Load)	3.11 P.S.I., 0.22 kg/cm²
Maximum Speed	10.8 mph, 17.4 km/h
BHP (SAE)	197 HP (147 kW) @ 2800 RPM
Suspension	Torsional coil spring
Length	23 ft. 8.5 in., 7.23 m
Width	9 ft. 8 in., 2.95 m
Height	8 ft. 11 in., 2.72 m

CHIEFTAIN

Payload	30,000 lbs., 13,600 kg
Ground Bearing Pressure (Max. Load)	3.5 P.S.I., 0.25 kg/cm²
Maximum Speed	14.7 mph, 23.6 km/h
BHP (SAE)	197 HP (147 kW) @ 2800 RPM
Suspension	Torsional coil spring
Length	32 ft. 10 in., 10.01 m
Width	9 ft. 7.5 in., 2.93 m
Height	8 ft. 10 in., 2.69 m

PIONEER

Payload	50,000 lbs., 22,700 kg
Ground Bearing Pressure (Max. Load)	4.8 P.S.I., 0.34 kg/cm²
Maximum Speed	8.4 mph, 13.6 km/h
BHP (SAE)	267 HP (195 kW) @ 2100 RPM
Suspension	Torsional coil spring
Length	35 ft. 10 in., 10.92 m
Width	10 ft. 10 in., 3.30 m
Height	9 ft. 7 in., 2.92 m

HUSKY 8G

Payload	80,000 lbs., 36,300 kg
Ground Bearing Pressure (Max. Load)	4.7 P.S.I., 0.33 kg/cm²
Maximum Speed	9.0 mph, 14.5 km/h
BHP (SAE)	362 HP (270 kW) @ 2100 RPM
Suspension	Torsional coil spring
Length	46 ft. 7 in., 14.20 m
Width	12 ft., 3.60 m
Height	13 ft. 6 in., 4.10 m

NODWELL 240 VIBROCARRIER

Payload	24,000 lbs., 10,900 kg
Ground Bearing Pressure (Max. Load)	3.98 P.S.I., 0.28 kg/cm²
Maximum Speed	13.1 mph, 21.1 km/h
BHP (SAE)	197 HP (147 kW) @ 2800 RPM
Suspension	Walking beam
Length	25 ft. 10 in., 7.87 m
Width	11 ft. 8 in., 3.82 m
Height	10 ft. 1 in., 3.30 m

WHEELED VEHICLES

DELTA 2B

Payload	20,000 lbs., 9,080 kg
All wheel drive	
Ground Bearing Pressure (Max. Load)	18 P.S.I., 1.27 kg/cm²
Maximum Speed	27.9 mph, 44.9 km/h
BHP (SAE)	197 HP (147 kW) @ 2800 RPM
Suspension	Multi-leaf spring, front; rigid, rear
Length	27 ft. 2 in., 8.28 m
Width	10 ft. 10 in., 3.30 m
Height	9 ft. 6 in., 2.90 m

DELTA 2C

Payload	20,000 lbs., 9,080 kg
All wheel drive	
Ground Bearing Pressure (Max. Load)	
Off-road tires	17.0 P.S.I., 1.2 kg/cm²
On-road tires	75.0 P.S.I., 5.2 kg/cm²
Maximum Speed	
Off-road tires	20.9 mph, 33.6 km/h
On-road tires	36.1 mph, 58.1 km/h
BHP (SAE)	175 HP (130 kW) @ 2500 RPM
Suspension	Multi-leaf spring, front; rigid, rear
Length	30 ft., 9.14 m
Width	10 ft. 9 in., 3.28 m
Height	9 ft. 11 in., 3.02 m

DELTA 3B

Payload	30,000 lbs., 13,600 kg
All wheel drive	
Ground Bearing Pressure (Max. Load)	16.0 P.S.I., 2.3 kg/cm²
Maximum Speed	23.7 mph, 38.1 km/h
BHP (SAE)	197 HP (147 kW) @ 2800 RPM
Suspension	Multi-leaf spring, front; walking beam, rear
Length	30 ft. 1 in., 9.17 m
Width	10 ft. 10 in., 3.30 m
Height	9 ft. 11 in., 3.02 m

MARAUDER

Payload	30,000 lbs., 13,600 kg
All wheel drive	
Ground Bearing Pressure (Max. Load)	16 P.S.I., 1.12 kg/cm²
Maximum Speed	29 mph, 47.3 km/h
BHP (SAE)	304 HP (227 kW) @ 2100 RPM
Suspension	Multi-leaf spring, front; walking beam, rear
Length	33 ft. 6 in., 10.2 m
Width	9 ft. 0 in., 2.74 m
Height	9 ft. 11 in., 3.02 m

Product Line

COMMANDER C

Payload	60,000 lbs., 27,200 kg
All wheel drive	
Ground Bearing Pressure (Max. Load)	35 P.S.I., 2.44 kg/cm²
Maximum Speed	27.9 mph, 44.9 km/h
BHP (SAE)	362 HP (270 kW) @ 2100 RPM
Suspension	Multi-leaf spring, front; Walking beam, rear
Length	47 ft. 7 in., 14.53 m
Width	11 ft. 6 in., 3.50 m
Height	11 ft. 9 in., 3.58 m

SUPER COMMANDER C

Payload	80,000 lbs., 36,300 kg
All wheel drive	
Ground Bearing Pressure (Max. Load)	34.0 P.S.I., 2.4 kg/cm²
Maximum Speed	25.3 mph, 40.7 km/h
BHP (SAE)	525 HP (392 kW) @ 2100 RPM
Suspension	Walking beam, front and rear
Length	49 ft. 8 in., 15.14 m
Width	11 ft. 6 in., 3.50 m
Height	12 ft. 2 in., 3.71 m

MAGNUM 4

Payload	140,000 lbs., 63,300 kg
All wheel drive	
Ground Bearing Pressure (Max. Load)	48 P.S.I., 3.4 kg/cm²
Maximum Speed	22.9 mph, 36.9 km/h
BHP (SAE)	465 HP (347 kW) @ 2100 RPM
Suspension	Walking beam, front and rear
Length	53 ft. 4 in., 16.30 m
Width	13 ft. 1 in., 4.00 m
Height	9 ft. 5 in., 2.90 m

TERRA BUS

56 passenger (Max.)	
All wheel drive	
Ground Bearing Pressure (Max. Load)	15 P.S.I., 1.05 kg/cm²
Maximum Speed	26.5 mph, 42.7 km/h
BHP (SAE)	210 HP (157 kW) @ 2100 RPM
Suspension	Multi-leaf spring, front; walking beam, rear
Length	42 ft. 8 in., 13.00 m
Width	11 ft. 10 in., 3.61 m
Height	12 ft. 8 in., 3.86 m

POWERED CHASSIS

Gross Axle Ratings	70,000 lbs. to 100,000 lbs., 31,800 kg to 45,400 kg
Horsepower Range BHP (SAE)	228 HP to 600 HP, 170 kW to 448 kW
Axle Configurations	4 x 2 drive, 5 x 2 drive
Speed	45 mph, 72 km/h
Suspension	Multi-leaf spring, front; Walking beam, rear

agencies such as national or provincial foreign trade corporations and the Ministry of Petroleum. Moreover, many equipment purchases were subject to international tender arrangements especially when external financing was provided by such agencies as the World Bank. Foremost had not yet sold vehicles under these terms.

In December 1983, shortly after their return from China, executives at Canadian Foremost received a proposal to consider a co-production arrangement that would enable China to assemble vehicles locally. These vehicles would then be used in all Chinese oilfields.

Co-production Proposal

The co-production proposal was made by Mr. Zhang Chief Mechanical Engineer, Petroleum Administration, Bureau of Zhongyuan Oilfield. Foremost had earlier identified that major oilfield area as its initial prime target market.

Mr. Zhang suggested that "Foremost's vehicles would be assembled in China from components supplied by the company." He indicated that preliminary approval for the project had been received from the Ministry of Petroleum. Co-production was not a favoured option for Canadian Foremost since it represented a major undertaking for a company its size. Among other things, such an arrangement would require a minimum of four key technical people spending at least one year in China. It also meant dealing with a different ministry and a different foreign trade organization in Beijing, with which the company did not presently have contacts. In any case, Foremost's preference (next to a straight equipment sale) would be for a licensing agreement under which the company would supply components and technical know-how in return for an acceptable royalty.

Shortly after the co-production proposal was transmitted through CTI, Mr. Nodwell called a meeting of the senior management committee to consider it. At that meeting, it was agreed that the company should be prepared to discuss the proposal but that additional information was required. Estimates of production volume, models to be assembled, time period for the proposed agreement, adequacy of local production and assembly facilities, and arrangements for selling the assembled vehicles to other oilfields were all matters to be clarified. Although co-production was not likely to be technically and managerially viable, Foremost decided to respond in a positive way in order to maintain contact with Chinese officials.

FURTHER ASSESSMENT OF PROSPECTS

In the meantime, it was decided that a further assessment of prospects be undertaken by consulting with knowledgeable Canadian government officials and other sources. These consultations led to several findings. Historically, Zhongyuan was *the* oilfield which other oilfields in China emulated. It commanded both political and financial power due to its size. However, the Minister of Petroleum, who originally came from that region, resigned in 1979. The new minister did not have an oil-related background but had visited Foremost during a mission to Canada in 1972. Some of his senior staff appeared to be anti-Zhongyuan. However, Zhongyuan still produced 50% of China's oil.

Recently officials at Zhongyuan recommended a purchase of drilling rigs from both Alberta and the United States, but the Minister authorized purchase from one source only—and the United States got the order, for reasons that were not clear. Central government agencies had the final say in equipment purchases.

It was noted that twinning arrangements between Canadian provinces and cities and Chinese counterparts were on the rise. These would make it feasible for a company such as Canadian Foremost to be introduced and endorsed at the political level to the appropriate authorities in China.

In addition, the Export Development Corporation (EDC) had extended to China $2 billion in credit facilities, which had so far been virtually unused. It was worth discussing the use of some of these facilities to make equipment purchases by the Chinese more cost attractive to them.

It was also suggested that Foremost stick to "bare essentials" in technical specifications. This would bring prices down and be in line with China's relatively less sophisticated needs. Foremost's management had some difficulty accepting this advice as they pointed out that "the price difference between us and our competitors is in the guts of the unit we sell. We are unwilling to supply substandard equipment. We have also noted that the specs for required vehicles in China are written in such a way that the Chinese can get anything from a farm tractor to a Foremost unit." This was illustrated when a wide range of vehicles competed for the World Bank tender for two-tracked vehicles, announced in December 1983. Foremost proposed a Nodwell-110 vehicle but lost to the lowest bidder, a French company, which proposed a much lighter-duty vehicle that was unlikely to meet the requirements of the terrain the Chinese had in mind.

Foremost waited patiently for an invitation to visit China while these consultations continued. CTI was advised by the Chinese that the situation was still under review. In the meantime, CTI learned that the Minister of Petroleum suggested to Mr. Zhang that he view in person the Dawson-5 unit which had been purchased from Foremost in 1972.[1] Anxious that this not cause Zhang to receive the wrong impression, the company instructed its agent to explain once again the circumstances in which that unit was purchased by the Chinese and how different Foremost's marketing policies were now.

June 1984 Visit

An invitation was subsequently received, and Mr. Yost visited China in June 1984 to discuss the co-production proposal. A lot of technical preparations had been made for that trip including a detailed submission which dealt with Foremost's technical

[1] In 1972, Canadian Foremost displayed one of its earlier vehicles, the Dawson-5, at a Canadian Oilfield Equipment Show in Beijing. Despite instructions not to sell the vehicle, company representatives did just that when approached by a Chinese buyer who expressed greater interest in Foremost's product than in competing products. The vehicle was sold for $40,000. Foremost subsequently tried to contact the Chinese customer in order to provide manuals and training and to sell him the necessary spare parts. But its efforts failed. It was learned later on that the vehicle had been sent to Liaohe—a tidal swamp area. No spare parts went with it and the operators received no training. Very quickly the machine ran out of spare parts and was left idle after logging a mere 890 hours of operation. It was put in storage in 1975.

capabilities, key components, materials management procedures, manufacturing time, inspection procedures, and so on. Discussions with the Chinese side illustrated the complexity of production requirements and the necessity of meeting the exacting standards. It became evident to the Chinese that co-production was not feasible at that time. This led to the idea of testing Foremost's vehicles in China prior to entering into any negotiations. It was agreed that Foremost would prepare a test program proposal for discussion at the next visit a few months later.

October 1984 Visit

Certain objectives were set for the October visit. These included the selection of a suitable test site and agreement on specific models to be tested and the terms under which the vehicles would be sent to China. Foremost also saw an opportunity to convince the Chinese of the company's ability to determine the most suitable models and load sizes. Achieving these objectives could lead to setting a tentative date for commercial negotiations.

Arriving in Zhongyuan on October 17, the team consisted of Fred Holmes (Vice-President and General Manager, Tracked Vehicle Division), Richard Yost, and a representative from CTI in Beijing. The following day began with a meeting attended by 15 people on the Chinese side, led by Mr. Zhang who represented the Zhongyuan Petroleum Administration Bureau. Others represented various drilling companies in the oilfield, the auto repair shop, and the newly created Zhongyuan Petroleum Technical Import Office.

Although four test vehicles were on the agenda, discussion soon centred on the Husky-8 and the Commander-C. Mr. Zhang disclosed that the 30 amphibious vehicles they purchased in 1981 from Rolligon Corporation in the United States (for $40,000 each) for work in the Liaohe Oilfield did not work well as the tires kept balling up with mud. These vehicles were too small (5-ton capacity) for oilfield operations and were assigned to a tidal flat area in which they had not been tested beforehand. The result was that while the vehicles stayed on top of the silty mud, they ceased to be mobile.

Other discussions revealed that the biggest operating problem facing the Chinese was mobility during March and April, when the thawing ground was muddy on top and frozen underneath. Maximum travel distance was 300 km through scattered swamps. There was no continuous road to the outer edge of the oilfield. The maximum load requirement was 40 tons, but this was likely to be needed only once a year. The trade-off between the number of trips and alternate payloads was discussed at length. Foremost advised that only the Husky-8 would operate in the most difficult circumstances, and that a different vehicle-mix from that proposed initially might be advisable. For example, if a Husky unit were to get stuck, only another Husky could retrieve it. This made it important that all test units be put to work in the same area. Meanwhile, the team explained that the Commander model was not really necessary since it was required only once a year (to haul a 40-ton load).

Mr. Zhang wanted the vehicles on site by April 1985, if at all possible. Allowing for production and delivery schedules, Mr. Yost said that negotiations would have to be finalized by mid-December 1984 to meet that target date. Mr. Zhang responded by saying that they would try their best and later added that "price may be the key problem." In any case, Foremost's proposal would have to be submitted to the authorities in Beijing.

In the afternoon, a visit was made to the first test site which was classified as "normal but slightly on the worse side." It was still the dry season. The swamp area turned out to be silt quicksand with a hard bottom one to two metres down. A Husky unit could operate in the swamp area only marginally. As certain parts of this region were even worse, Foremost did not feel this site to be acceptable. A second site was inspected the following day. Here, the water table was about three feet down with the top three feet consisting of a combination of sand and clay. Below it was a wet silty material. Chinese rigs, each weighing 60 tons, were being used. Distance between drilling locations ranged from half a kilometre to two kilometres. A Husky unit could be used year round and a Commander unit would be non-operational only during the worst time in the spring. This area, however, had many swamps, which the Chinese said were too far to visit in the time available. Both sides agreed not to use this as a test site.

Subsequent discussions led to the selection of the first site for testing purposes but vehicles would be tested only on existing rig roads and rig pads where equipment presently on site could not function during the spring breakup and rainy seasons. These discussions were interrupted with a message that the Ministry of Petroleum was unlikely to approve any deal unless the price was lowered. Foremost was requested to do so before negotiations could commence. No clear agreement was reached about the cost of testing. Canadian Foremost was to ship the units and test them under its supervision. If the vehicles did not perform, the company was to take them back.

The visit was concluded with both sides confirming that test vehicle models should be selected quickly, that testing be conducted as agreed, and that the Chinese would try to begin commercial negotiations by the end of November. As Mr. Zhang was due to be away until the end of December, Mr. Yost and his colleagues felt that not much was likely to happen before January 1985. The test program was tentatively scheduled for the spring of 1985, although it could be delayed to late summer during the rainy season.

In early November, through CTI, Mr. Zhang advised that the Ministry of Petroleum was not enthusiastic about the test arrangement and preferred a 25-ton unit instead of the Husky-8 which was "too big." The Ministry reiterated that the price was too high. Mr. Zhang had yet to select the test vehicles and, when asked by CTI, did not know when negotiations could begin. CTI felt that the Ministry of Petroleum might suspect that Foremost was trying to push something down their throat by promoting the Husky vehicle only.

CHANGING OF THE GUARD

A week later Mr. Yost learned from CTI that Mr. Zhang was being phased out of the project and a new man was being put in charge. This was Mr. Lu, Head of the Planning Department at the newly formed Zhongyuan Petroleum Technical Import Office. Mr. Lu had been summoned by the Minister of Petroleum to discuss the project and offered the opinion that Zhongyuan did not have adequate facilities to assemble Foremost's vehicles. He recommended that the co-production proposal be dropped. At the same time, the Minister did not like the test proposal, as it was going to create "an obligation" to purchase Foremost's equipment. He proposed instead that a company be selected and units be purchased outright for the test. Mr. Lu was instructed to find similar (that is, competing) vehicles to allow price comparisons to be made. The lower priced unit would then be selected, as per normal policy. With this in mind, Mr. Lu was to visit the United States to inspect a military vehicle which sold at a lower price. Mr. Lu was also entering into negotiations with American suppliers to purchase well drilling and servicing equipment. On learning of these developments, Mr. Yost asked the CTI office in Houston to arrange a meeting for Mr. Nodwell and himself with Mr. Lu during the latter's U.S. tour.

The Houston Meeting

The meeting took place at the end of November in Houston. Mr. Nodwell outlined his company's experience, types of vehicles and conditions under which they were used, stressing custom design to meet specific needs. A brief review was then made of earlier visits to China and key points discussed with various officials. Reference was also made to the test program and to test areas inspected. Mr. Lu said he appreciated Foremost's efforts to identify China's needs over many months but pleaded for patience as he was not yet familiar with Foremost's vehicles. His priorities now were to ask his engineers to determine load requirements for the Zhongyuan oilfield operations, then consider the much bigger needs beyond Zhongyuan and how to cope with the swamp areas. He was not clear on why some people suggested a payload of 15 tons, while others suggested 25 tons, and Foremost was recommending 40 tons. He was anxious not to repeat the mistake of purchasing vehicles which could not be utilized properly. He was also concerned that the Husky-8 would damage their roads and did not want to stock too many spare parts. He appealed again for patience until these matters had been discussed with his officials and hoped to have the answers by January 1985.

In the meantime, Mr. Lu asked for information about the Commander vehicle, which he thought might be appropriate due to the large pot holes on the roads in the spring. He also stated that "experience with the Dawson-5 left doubt in some minds about Foremost's equipment." Finally, he had to ensure cost effectiveness in future purchases and was planning to compare Canadian Foremost with Oshkosh. Mr. Nodwell responded by stressing the importance of differences in specifications and the fact that his company did not initially inflate its prices in anticipation of requests for discounts. He also restated Foremost's willingness to go ahead with the test program if the Chinese so desired. Mr. Lu promised to have his staff draw up an overall plan and then invite Foremost for a visit. Mr. Nodwell learned that Mr. Lu's new department was now responsible for all allocations of foreign funds acquired by Zhongyuan oilfields. This department was not associated with Techimport (one of the foreign trade corporations) in Beijing. The Ministry of Petroleum was not likely to be involved in the decision but had to be kept aware of what was happening. Negotiations for equipment sale would be conducted with Machimpex (National Machinery Import/Export Corporation) in Beijing with Mr. Lu representing the end-user in this instance.

OTHER DEVELOPMENTS

In assessing Foremost's prospects in China, Mr. Nodwell and his team had taken note of other important developments. The first was the conclusion of a loan agreement under which Japan extended $2.4 billion of credit to China to develop the latter's oilfields, including Zhongyuan. Mitsui, a major Japanese company, had recently contacted Canadian Foremost to discuss the possibility of building the Husky unit in Japan under licence for mounting drill rigs. Foremost had yet to respond to that inquiry.

Secondly, Bombardier had just signed an agreement in principle to build snowmobiles in China and was promoting an older style TF-900 for the oilfield market. This vehicle was higher priced than the Husky-8 and had a 50-ton capacity. However, Bombardier also had a 21-ton vehicle which was lower priced than Foremost's Pioneer and might appeal to the Chinese "buy cheap" philosophy despite the fact that it did not match Pioneer's specs.

Thirdly, following Mr. Lu's visit to Oshkosh in Houston, that supplier was now proposing a military-type truck capable of negotiating marsh and water up to one metre deep. This vehicle was limited to a five- to ten-ton load and had poor traction. Although Oshkosh planned to modify it for oilfield use, Foremost engineers believed the vehicle would still be deficient in tests of load capacity, mobility, and loading area requirements. However, Oshkosh was pursuing Chinese prospects aggressively and Foremost suspected that Mr. Lu was being actively romanced by that supplier. The Chinese were apparently impressed with the vehicle. Oshkosh had already sold 24 units of another type of vehicle which were being used for crash and fire rescues at Chinese airports, at an estimated price of $300,000 per unit.

In the meantime, many Chinese perceived Canada as being industrially underdeveloped relative to the United States. They believed they could buy more cheaply from American companies than from their Canadian subsidiaries or other Canadian suppliers. Added to this was the fact that many American and European manufacturers offered large discounts in attempting to sell to China in recent years due to a sluggish world market.

In January 1985, Mr. Lu requested the Beijing office of CTI to obtain a more detailed proposal on Foremost's 25, 30, and 40 ton vehicles and alluded to prices being "not clear." CTI suggested that Foremost resubmit a photocopy of the detailed proposals presented earlier in case the Chinese had misplaced them.

Jack Nodwell estimated that Foremost had spent at least $500,000 (including the equivalent of two person-years of its technical and marketing managers' time) to develop sales prospects in China. Most of this sum was spent in the past two years. He wondered what results might have been obtained had these resources been directed to other market areas. Meanwhile, he was optimistic that the knowledge acquired and contacts made in China would lead to an agreement soon. The task facing him and his executives now was to put together a plan of action in anticipation of making another visit to China during which negotiations could be resumed. If all went well, the initial order was likely to be for three vehicles, (two Husky-8's and either a Pioneer or a Commander) with a sales value of $1.5 million. It was also estimated that the Zhongyuan oilfield alone would ultimately require 180 vehicles of the types produced by Foremost.

Section 9

NEW VENTURE MARKETING

Success of a new venture depends on meeting the same requirements as a business of any size—finding a market need and filling it on a basis that allows a company to earn profits and differentiate itself from competitors. However, the small size and resources of most new businesses give a different flavour to new venture marketing. Sometimes this is an advantage—small businesses tend to have greater flexibility than large ones, give more attention to detail, and generate enormous commitment from the entrepreneur and his or her closest co-workers. On the other hand, small businesses often have very limited resources, so that short-term problems, particularly financial ones, can cause a good long-term strategy to fail. In addition, new ventures often start with a product idea or an innovation, and not with a market need. These small businesses can become too technical or product-oriented. They frequently fail because they focus on product and technological innovation, not on what consumers want.

To avoid the pitfalls of a misdirected focus or orientation, the new venture should develop a business plan. The plan is the foundation for the future of the firm and requires the entrepreneur to consider all facets of the business.

The first part of this section discusses the preparation of a business plan, placing particular emphasis on meeting market needs. New ventures are typically very dependent on the one or two individuals who start the business. We next suggest desirable characteristics for an entrepreneur. In analyzing the cases in this section, the student needs to judge whether the person proposing the business idea has the characteristics required for success. Finally, we conclude by outlining some of the competitive advantages available to small businesses.

BUSINESS PLAN[1]

A comprehensive, carefully thought-out business plan is essential to the success of entrepreneurs. A business plan is valuable not only as a guide for management, but is also the principal means used by the entrepreneur to attract capital from outside investors—venture capitalists, and bank managers—needed to support a new business in its first years of existence. Given the high failure rate of new businesses in Canada, no entrepreneur should expect outside investors to be easily persuaded to invest in his or her new venture. Yet, on the other hand, many thousands of new businesses succeed every year.

A business plan should describe the new venture accurately and attractively. The plan should detail the venture's current status, immediate needs, and expected future. In

[1] Adapted in part from Stanley P. Rich and David E. Gumpert, "How to Write a Winning Business Plan," *Harvard Business Review* (May–June 1985), pp. 156–166.

addition, it should both state and justify ongoing and changing resource requirements, marketing decisions, financial projections, production demands, and personnel needs.

A successful plan should reflect three viewpoints:

1. The market, including an analysis of existing and prospective customers of the planned product. The user benefits and competitive edge must be convincingly demonstrated.
2. The investors or providers of financial and other resources that will be committed to the venture.
3. The producer or entrepreneur.

Many business plans reflect just the producer's viewpoint, As such, they describe the underlying technology or creativity of the proposed product in glowing terms, but neglect the components that give the venture its financial viability—the market and the investor. This is particularly true of those entrepreneurs with a scientific or engineering background, or "backyard" inventors.

Take the case of a group of engineers seeking financing to establish their own engineering consulting firm. In their business plan, they listed a dozen types of specialized engineering services based on their own skills and preferences. Without an analysis of the market, they estimated first year sales based on what their revenue needs were and suggested that their sales would grow at the same 20% rate that characterized recent industry trends. The forecast downturn in the economy was not considered. More significantly, the engineers did not determine which of the proposed dozen services their potential clients really needed and which would be most profitable. By not examining these issues closely, they ignored the possibility that the marketplace might want some services not among the dozen listed. Their plan represented an attractive set of numbers and a wish list of services, but not market reality.

In fact, the engineers had only considered their own perspective, including the new company's services, organization, and projected results. Because they hadn't convincingly demonstrated why potential customers would buy the services or how investors would make an adequate return (or when and how they could cash out), their new venture would be unlikely to succeed. However, they never got the chance because their business plan lacked the credibility necessary for raising the investment funds needed.

Investors usually want to put their money into market-driven rather than technology-driven or service-driven companies. The potential of the product for sales and profit is far more important than its technical features. A convincing case for the existence of a good market can be made by demonstrating user benefits, identifying marketplace interest, and showing competitive superiority.

SHOW THE USER BENEFITS

The premise for a new venture must be based on user benefits, not on what appeals to the entrepreneur. This point, seemingly known to all, seems to need constant re-emphasis. To illustrate, consider the case of the developer of an instrument designed to control certain aspects of the production process in the textile industry. In this entrepreneur's presentation to a group of potential investors, he emphasized the technical aspects of the product and how the cutting of fabrics could be improved. This project was rejected immediately after the presentation by one investor because, in his opinion, the product was aimed towards a depressed industry. However, when further questioning revealed that the product paid for itself within six months, the investor reversed his original opinion. He said he would back a company in almost any industry if it could prove such an important user's benefit—and emphasize it in its sales approach.

The entrepreneur rewrote his business plan so that it emphasized the short payback period and only briefly discussed the product innovation. This company succeeded and made the transition from a technology-driven to a market-driven company.

Many entrepreneurs develop a product for the consumer market based on their dissatisfaction with existing products. Paint cans that don't drip, garbage cans that don't tip over, and floor mats that don't slip are all products that individuals have designed for the consumer market. Unfortunately, in many instances, the "problem" the inventor solved was not viewed as serious by most of the marketplace. In fact the new products did not offer distinct advantages for the potential user over existing products. On the other hand, many new consumer products have been developed and successfully marketed by individuals who analyzed and understood the benefits of their offering against competitive products. These products provided real and distinct advantages that satisfied consumer needs.

DETERMINE THE MARKET'S INTEREST

Establishing the user benefits is only the first step. An entrepreneur must also show that customers are interested in obtaining this benefit and that they like the proposed good or service. The business plan must reflect clear positive responses from customer prospects to the question, "Having heard the pitch, will you buy?" Methods of showing such success vary according to whether the product is sold to consumer or industrial markets, the amount of money required for production of samples of goods or demonstrations of the service, and the size of the expenditures on the customer's part.

For a new industrial product, letters of support and appreciation from significant potential customers or early users, successful "reference installations," and commitments from sales representatives or distributors all help to support the soundness of a new venture. For a consumer good or service, demonstrated success in a small market helps considerably in building confidence in a business plan.

Having established a market interest, carefully analyzed data are needed to support assertions about the market and the growth rate of sales and profits. Too often executives think, "If we're smart, we'll be able to get about 10% of the market," and "Even if we only get 1% of such a huge market, we'll be in good shape." But there's no guarantee a new company will get any business, regardless of market size. One company developed a chemical ingredient that could be used in the making of tiles. This company, which would be the sole supplier of the product, was able to show the cost benefits of the project and persuade a number of small, growing companies to adopt it. Only 1% of the market was needed for profitability of the product, but in fact only 1/10 of 1% was achieved. Customers balked because use of the chemical required the replacement of old dies with new ones, reformulation of the ingredient mix, and time to learn how to use the product. Coupled with this single source dependence, these factors limited sales to only a few companies for whom these factors were less important.

A realistic business plan needs to specify the number of potential customers in the best market segments, their likely purchase patterns, the rate of acceptance for the new good or service, etc. From such marketing research data, a credible sales plan and plant and staff needs can be projected.

Start-up ventures often cannot afford large-scale market research projects. However, secondary data, government reports, interviews with knowledgeable executives, and other information are often inexpensively available to the resourceful entrepreneur.

In Canada, there is considerable secondary data available for the entrepreneur to estimate the total market size, trading areas, and per capita expenditures on various product and service categories. Statistics Canada offers a wealth of information in this area as do companies such as Maclean-Hunter whose publications include *Canadian Markets*, a synopsis of Canadian consumers by geographic area. These and other information sources are found in many public, college, and university libraries.

The entrepreneur can also conduct small, inexpensive research studies that provide valuable insights for his or her venture. The use of precoded advertising flyers can help in determining the size of a retail trading area. Universities and colleges often look for small businesses to serve as "real world" projects for marketing research classes. Finally, informal surveys can be conducted with small convenience samples to learn the consumer's response to a new product idea.

An entrepreneur needs to be particularly careful in extremely fast-growing and fast-changing operations such as franchised weight-loss clinics and computer software companies. Here the problem is the reverse of the typical ones of a small business. While some companies have achieved multi-million dollar sales in just a few years, they are vulnerable to declines of similar proportions due to changing consumer tastes and competitive forces. Market pioneers must innovate constantly so that potential competitors will be discouraged from entering the marketplace.

A successful new venture requires the company not only to satisfy a market need, but also to do it better than present competitors are willing or able to do it. As we discuss later in this section, small companies have some advantages over larger established firms because they are willing to be satisfied with the profit results from smaller markets or because they have the flexibility to meet the needs of certain customers who have highly specialized demands.

A new venture's competitive advantage must be sustainable. It is not enough to find a market need that is presently not served; the entrepreneur must also consider whether a competitor will react to the new development in a way that will close off its profitability. When Polaroid first introduced instant photography, patent protection assured it of a long-run position in the market. On the other hand, the small, natural foods companies that introduced granola cereal to the market had success for only a short period of time. When Quaker introduced its own granola to the Canadian market with heavy advertising and widespread distribution, many previously successful entrepreneurs ceased operations.

ADDRESS INVESTORS' NEEDS

Entrepreneurs, by deciding to start and manage a business, are committed to years of hard work and personal sacrifice. Early on, they must try to evaluate objectively their own businesses to decide whether the opportunity for future rewards truly justifies the work and the risk. When an entrepreneur looks at an idea objectively rather than through rose-coloured glasses, the investment decision may change.

Even if the entrepreneur doesn't take a hard look at the new venture, the investors will. The marketing issues just discussed are critical to satisfying the investors. Once entrepreneurs make a convincing case for their sales penetration over a one- to five-year horizon, they can make the financial projections that help determine whether investors will be interested in evaluating the venture, how much they'll commit, and at what price.

Investors' primary considerations beyond the investment required and the returns expected are as follows.

CASHING OUT Entrepreneurs frequently do not understand why investors have a short attention span. Many who see their ventures in terms of a lifetime commitment expect that anyone else who gets involved will feel the same. When investors evaluate a business plan, they consider not only whether to get in, but also how and when to get out.

SOUND PROJECTIONS One- to five-year forecasts of profitability help lay the groundwork for negotiating the amount investors will receive in return for their money. Investors see such financial forecasts as yardsticks against which to judge future performance.

Entrepreneurs often go to extremes with their numbers. Some entrepreneurs think that the financial statements *are* the business plan. They may cover the plan with a smog of numbers. Such "spreadsheet merchants," with their pages of computer printouts covering every business variation possible and analyzing product sensitivity, completely turn off many investors. In contrast, other entrepreneurs present sales and other data that are so skimpy or overly optimistic that an outside analyst will dismiss them quickly.

DEVELOPMENT STAGE OF THE PROJECT All investors wish to reduce their risk. In evaluating the risk of a new and growing venture, potential investors frequently assess two primary aspects of a business:

1. the status of the project, and
2. the management team.

The farther along an enterprise is, the lower the risk for investors. The more "homework" entrepreneurs undertake regarding their ventures (for example, examining the industry in which the product is likely to compete, conducting marketing research, etc.) the greater the chance of attracting capital from investors.

Similarly, the more competent and well-trained a management team, the lower the risk for investors. In many cases, entrepreneurs develop creative products or services, but frequently these individuals do not have the expertise to successfully run a business based on their new idea. Unless the inventor is well-versed in many business disciplines (for example, marketing, finance, manufacturing, etc.), venture capitalists are unlikely to invest in a new, unproven business. A well-staffed management team can aid in overcoming this problem by providing expertise in areas where an entrepreneur may lack knowledge.

WELL-WRITTEN, RELEVANT BUSINESS PLAN While important aspects of a business plan can be specified, the actual writing of effective business plans is as much an art as a science. The idea of a master document with blanks that executives can merely fill in—much in the way lawyers use sample wills or real estate agreements—is appealing but unrealistic.

New ventures differ in key marketing, production, and financial issues. Each venture's plan should emphasize appropriate areas and de-emphasize minor issues. Potential investors view a plan as a distillation of the objectives and character of the business and its executives. A business plan should reflect the vision of the entrepreneur, but it must also look externally towards both customers for the product to be successful and investors to obtain the necessary resources for achieving market success.

CHARACTERISTICS OF ENTREPRENEURS

Successful new ventures are critically dependent on the people who lead the enterprise. Because these businesses are so small, the abilities and efforts of the individuals involved are critical. The willingness of such individuals to devote long hours and their full intellectual capacities is often a key strength of a start-up business.

While new ventures are occasionally begun with a large team of people, one or two individuals are usually the key or lead entrepreneurs in the project. As with all aspects of a new business, the leader must evaluate himself or herself on an objective, realistic basis. The entrepreneur should know his or her own entrepreneurial strengths *and* weaknesses; what skills and experiences he or she already has and which ones need to be acquired to make the particular venture succeed. Except in the smallest of ventures, the entrepreneur should also have a highly committed and motivated team of co-workers. These people should be chosen for reasons other than friendship. Their skills and experience should complement the founder's, according to the needs of the business.

Just as there is no single personality type or skill base that ensures success in any field—from being the prime minister to managing a restaurant—successful entrepreneurs do not fit a common mould. On the other hand, we can identify some characteristics that seem important for entrepreneurs to have. These include

- a high level of drive and energy. New ventures are only for those who are willing to work extremely hard.
- the self-confidence to take carefully calculated, moderate risks. The successful entrepreneur is not reckless, but is willing to take risks.
- a conception that money is a way of keeping score and a tool for growth. Money is necessary both to satisfy the needs of investors and to fund growth, but a short-term payout is seldom available.
- unusual skill in motivating and obtaining productive collaboration from other people. New enterprises are resource-constrained so that extra efforts from people are always needed.
- high but realistic and achievable goals. Impossible goals only lead to frustration, but realistic, demanding goals stimulate new venture management.
- the ability to learn from their own failures. Few new entrepreneurs do everything right. But many mistakes, if recognized, are correctable and can lead to improvements in business functioning.
- a long-term vision of the enterprise.[2]

[2] Adapted in part from Jeffrey A. Timmons, "Careful Self-Analysis and Team Assessment Can Aid Entrepreneurs," *Harvard Business Review* (November–December 1978), pp. 198–206.

Few entrepreneurs have strength in all of these areas, but they will in many of them. They will also recognize their own shortcomings and seek ways to limit their impact.

COMPETITIVE ADVANTAGES OF SMALL BUSINESSES

New businesses are typically small, so they often lack the resources necessary to sustain themselves when projects get delayed or market demand doesn't develop as planned. Their lack of money often limits their ability to do proper research—both technical and market oriented—so entrepreneurs tend to live with a higher degree of risk than managers in large companies. Even when new ventures are successful in market terms, they can fail because they run out of cash to fund their growth—suppliers and employees need to be paid well before customers receive their goods and, more importantly, pay their bills. But being small in size also has its advantages. The new venture team can be very carefully selected and the members often work together directly without many layers of bureaucracy. Decision making can be fast and related directly to the problem or opportunity at hand.

Additionally, small businesses can be very low cost operations. The combination of concentrating on a specialized market segment and offering a limited product line can lead to reduced costs for attentive managers. While such a viewpoint seems contrary to the notion of economies of scale, economies of scale assume all other factors are equal. In a tightly managed, low overhead small business they often are not.

While small businesses always have to be wary that their success will provoke retaliation from competitors, their smallness can often assist them in finding ways to outmanoeuvre their competitors.[3] One area is the development of market concepts that would not be attractive for larger businesses. For example, Emergency Parts Service Ltd.'s (disguised name) competitive edge was to specialize in locating and shipping urgently needed spare parts in 24 hours. Very few large manufacturers or distributors of spare parts could consistently fill orders on such short notice. One premise underlying Emergency Parts Service's (EPS) business plan was to avoid head-on competition with large parts manufacturers and industrial supply houses. Since competitors either could not or would not attempt to fill emergency needs (except for "standard" items) within 24 hours, this position was protected. In general, a successful new venture strategist should be able to come up with creative designs in the first place and then be able to continue to keep them aligned with changes in the firm's environment. EPS, for example, exploited the fact that large parts manufacturers and distributors were slow in filling single item orders on a very short notice since such orders were unprofitable for them to process. Moreover, competitors' cost structures were unlikely to change in ways that would allow them to take this market away from EPS. In this case, EPS's existence may be of benefit to the larger companies since it provided a means to satisfy customers in emergency situations.

A second area in which a small business can outmanoeuvre larger businesses is in the choice of a specific niche or market segment to serve. Emergency Parts Service chose, as its niche, manufacturing concerns that need parts in a hurry at virtually any cost. This is

[3] Adapted in part from Megeed A. Ragab, "A Concept of Strategy for a Small Business," *Journal of Small Business—Canada*, Vol. 1, No. 1, 1983.

a small segment, but it can generate considerable profits if well served. On the other hand small niches can grow into large markets as the success of Federal Express attests.

Small businesses can also devlop unique capabilities that are difficult for its larger competitors to duplicate. These can be technical know-how, customer knowledge, supplier contacts, etc., EPS, for instance, established contacts with parts suppliers around the world and constructed air freight arrangements that allowed it to deliver needed items in 24 hours to virtually any place around the world.

CONCLUSION

Launching a new venture is extremely challenging. The needs of the market, investors, and the entrepreneur must all be considered; yet the entrepreneur typically focuses on the inherent appeal of the good or service proposed and not on the viability of the new venture to external constituencies. Management of a small business can put extraordinary demands on the individual, but successful ones can bring considerable personal satisfaction to the entrepreneur.

42 THE STRESS CENTRE

Robert Cohen

For the past six months Donna Cohen had been preparing for the launch of a new business idea; a nonprofit charitable organization catering to the physical needs of female office workers. The idea fit in very well with Donna's background and interests. Donna, a physical fitness instructor, recognized that physical activity was an extremely viable method of reducing stress. The problem was that many office workers suffered from low activity and simultaneously had a high level of job-related stress. To complicate matters, most office workers did not really understand stress and had been conditioned by society into believing that their jobs were relatively low stress. Donna was interested in starting a new organization for two prime reasons: to teach people about stress and how to deal with it, and to create a job for herself that would be rewarding as well as meaningful, challenging, and enjoyable.

STRESS AND ITS MANAGEMENT

Stress management research was traditionally concerned with how stress affected people in management positions. Most writers on stress started with the basic conservative presumption that the more responsibility people have at their place of work the more they were candidates to suffer from distress.

Stress cannot be avoided; it is a natural part of life. Complete freedom from stress only comes as a by-product of death. Job stress refers to conditions arising from interaction of people and their jobs. Stress is not necessarily detrimental, since it is activated by any environmental, emotional, or physiological arousal.

Positive stress (eustress) can and does spur efficiency and improve performance by giving people the initiative and the desire to compete. Unfortunately, excessive amounts of stress that are not properly channelled eventually wear down the body's defenses. Once the saturation point is surpassed, the arousal can no longer be effectively channelled into positive activity. Normally, one is unaware of stress and stress build-up until negative stress (distress) has already begun to take its toll.

There had been numerous and widely differing methods of dealing with stress. Common methods included transcendental meditation, encounter groups, transactional analysis, biofeedback, yoga, and many other behavioural modification techniques. All the methods were attempts to handle stress by changing the situation causing the emotional distress, by altering the victim's perception of the distress-causing events' significance, or by altering the negative feelings without making any attempt to change the distress-causing situation.

Recent research showed that high-stress jobs fell into two broad categories: jobs that demanded either too much (burn-out) or too little (rust-out) from employees. This research implied that previous work done in the area of stress management neglected a major group of people employed in high-stress jobs. Jobs that were repetitive, requiring low levels of skill and lacking in challenge, were often viewed as boring, meaningless, or insignificant. Individuals in such jobs became alienated from their place of work and suffered from stress-related problems if they valued challenge and personal growth.

THE OPPORTUNITY

Donna became interested in the results of this new research. The findings indicated that there existed an enormous number of workers who fit into the high-stress group of having jobs that did not offer enough challenge or demand to be satisfying. Some of the jobs in this group included secretaries, video-display terminal operators, clerical office staff, bookkeepers, receptionists and lower level managers. The majority of these workers had the following demographics: female, 18 to 29 years of age, single, living in a metropolitan area in their own apartments, and interested in thinking about physical fitness but lacking the time to make any serious effort to become and stay fit. In Canada, female clerical workers numbered about two million—roughly 14% of the total workforce.

In January, Donna wrote her first article, which presented a short exercise program for video-display terminal operators. The program was a five-minute set of nine exercises to be undertaken every two hours or when tension was felt. The exercises were designed to be done while in the operator's chair and would help to alleviate neuro-muscular disorders of the neck, back, arms, and legs. The article ran in the February issue of *Toronto Business Magazine* in a special supplement section entitled "Secretary's Efficiency Guide." Immediately upon the article's release Donna got some interesting calls: women's magazines wanting pemission to reprint the article, other magazines wanting follow-up articles or similar articles, and government offices inquiring about permission to reprint and circulate the article. As well, several secretaries wrote or called to express thanks for the interesting article. Unsure of where to go next, Donna started typing again. The second article, "How to Reduce Secretarial Stress Without Having to Leave Your Desk," appeared in *Canadian Office Magazine* in May of the same year. The interest again was very high. Donna submitted articles to other magazines, with each article catering to a specific group of these "under-demand" jobs. The articles called workers in these jobs "pink-collar workers," as opposed to blue- or white-collar workers.

The need appeared to be very real. Somehow this large group of workers had to be reached and educated. Donna knew that stress led to all sorts of problems, including gastrointestinal, respiratory, musculoskeletal, skin, metabolic, and cardiovascular disorders, menstrual irregularities, cancer, accident proneness, and even death. Most of the common methods of relieving stress did not fit in with the schedules and lifestyles of the target market. To make the situation even more alarming, most of the target market had been conditioned to believe that they were in low-stress jobs.

THE CHALLENGE

The challenge facing Donna was that she wanted to create a means of educating pink-collar workers about the stress involved in their jobs and what stress could do to them, then help get them started in an exercise program designed to help them channel stress before it became dangerous.

The obvious place to offer this education, Donna felt, would be at the workers' place of employment. She could put together a slide show that would last about fifteen minutes and a follow-up demonstration of about ten minutes that would supply sufficient information. This meant she could be in and out of a particular office in half an hour and accomplish her objectives. The questions she now had were: (1) how much to charge, (2) who should pay, and (3) how could she get employers to let her in.

FINANCIAL DATA

After consultation with her lawyers and accountants, Donna decided that the only viable manner to set up an organization that could address her objectives would be a charitable nonprofit organization. (See Exhibits 1 and 2 for financial data.) Such an organization would be able to solicit funds from government bodies, private donations, and corporate donors. To the extent that stress management services were sold for a fee, fewer donations than estimated would be required.

In looking over the expenses Donna said that she should be willing to reduce her salary initially to $24,000 from her current $34,000 as her donation to the organization. However, she still did not know how to go about soliciting the necessary funds. She also realized that she would need market research done on an on-going basis to ascertain whether she was reaching the right target group and how they perceived her program. The estimated annual cost of this research was around $5,000. The calculations assumed that Donna would open the organization in Toronto and would only serve the Toronto area. In late August, Donna Cohen opened a nonprofit, charitable organization called Pink Performance Inc. (PINC). The organization was to operate out of rented space in Thornhill, a suburb of Toronto, and initially was to serve only the working population of Toronto and the surrounding southern Ontario area.

Exhibit 1

PRO FORMA STATEMENT OF SOURCES AND USES OF FUNDS FOR YEARS ONE TO THREE

	Year 1	Year 2	Year 3
Sources			
Government agencies	$ 40,000	$ 30,000	$ 25,000
Corporate donations	50,000	55,000	55,000
Private donations	10,000	15,000	24,000
Sale of shirts, buttons, and bumper stickers	2,000	3,125	4,375
Total Sources	$102,000	$103,125	$108,375

(continued)

Exhibit 1 continued

	Year 1	Year 2	Year 3
Uses			
Salaries	$ 24,000	$ 25,500	$ 27,000
Wages	15,000	15,900	16,900
Promotion	15,000	15,000	15,000
Marketing and research	7,500	7,500	7,500
Consulting	7,500	6,500	5,500
Rent, heat, hydro	3,500	3,850	4,300
Transportation	5,000	5,500	6,050
Course material	1,000	1,000	2,000
Printing			
stationery	3,000	1,800	3,000
reprints	1,500	2,000	3,000
shirts	1,050	1,500	2,000
buttons	350	500	750
bumper stickers	350	500	750
Postage	400	450	500
Telephone	500	500	500
Legal and audit	2,000	1,500	1,500
Computer analysis	5,000	3,500	3,500
Assets (see Exhibit 2)	8,075	3,000	5,000
Miscellaneous (3%)	3,025	2,900	3,150
Total uses	$103,750	$ 98,900	$107,950
Total sources less uses	$ (1,750)	$ 4,225	$ 425

Exhibit 2

STATEMENT OF ASSETS NEEDED IN FIRST YEAR

Microcomputer with software	$ 5,000
Desks	1,000
Chairs	600
Filing cabinets	500
Book cases	500
Tape player	150
Slide projector	225
Screen	100
	$ 8,075

43 GRENADIER CHOCOLATE COMPANY LIMITED

Robert E. M. Nourse

"I've gotten into this for several reasons," explained Mr. Ronald Begg, president and founder of Grenadier Chocolate Company. "The potential of financial reward is one of them, although it will likely be some time before we begin to show a profit. I also wanted, however, to be in a position where I would make my own decisions. Procter & Gamble, where I spent seven years, provides great sales training. But as you develop you begin to want to flex your muscles. There are layers of managers up there above you, and they don't end in Canada. They go on and on. Finally, I have five children and, when they grow up, they're going to ask me where I was in the 1960s and 1970s when Canada was being sold out to the U.S. I don't want to have to say to them that I was there, helping the Americans take over."

Ronald Begg, 34, quietly explained his reasons for leaving a promising career with a large multinational food company. His background in sales, mass merchandising, and promotion was extensive. For seven years, Mr. Begg had been a Procter & Gamble brand manager for products such as Duncan Hines cake mix, Secret deodorant, and Crisco shortening. Subsequently, he had become national sales manager of Frito-Lay, a division of Pepsico Inc. In late 1973, Mr. Begg had left Pepsico with the objective of forming his own company.

The first task had been to find a suitable product. Dozens of product categories were systematically examined and a "hundred-odd" product concepts were reviewed. Each was assessed against a set of criteria that attempted to recognize market opportunities while, at the same time, taking into account the limited financial resources at Mr. Begg's disposal. The criteria, for example, included market size, growth rate, competitors active in the category, their costs, degree of consumer satisfaction with existing products, feasibility of new product development, ease of product formulation and suitability for custom packaging by an outside source. Of the original product concepts three were selected for intensive study. Formulations were prepared, and small-scale consumer testing was undertaken. The eventual choice was a new, milk modifying, instant chocolate syrup for household use. Subsequently, the product was given the name Milk Mate.

By November 1974, the formulation of Milk Mate had been improved to a point where extensive consumer testing yielded highly satisfactory results. Arrangements with ingredient suppliers had been finalized. An outside blender had been contracted to manufacture the Milk Mate concentrate, and a similar contract with a custom packer approved the final addition of bulk ingredients and packaging. Several crucial marketing decisions, nonetheless, remained to be made. Selling prices and trade margins had to be decided upon. A program of advertising and promotion, if undertaken, would have to be preceded by establishing product availability through retail grocery outlets. Selling effort would be needed, and it would be necessary to decide whether to employ company salespeople or commissioned sales agents. A plan indicating rate of market penetration to national distribution would need to be formulated.

THE CANADIAN MILK MODIFIER MARKET

Milk modifiers were used by consumers to create a flavoured milk drink. The product was sold as a powder, with typical label instructions calling for two teaspoons of powder to be added to an 8-ounce glass of milk. Well-known brands included Nestle's Quik, Hershey, and Cadbury's Choc-O. Chocolate was the dominant flavour, estimated to account for about 80% of total sales.

In 1974, total Canadian sales of milk modifiers were estimated at 23 million pounds. Market size had been relatively stable in recent years, growing roughly in proportion with population increase. Total sales were estimated to divide as follows:

British Columbia	—	10%
Prairies	—	14%
Ontario	—	38%
Quebec	—	30%
Atlantic Provinces	—	8%

Nestle was thought to hold a 50% market share, Hershey 20%, Cadbury 10%, with the remaining 20% being accounted for by a number of small, regional brands. All major producers offered a one-pound package size, which accounted for one-third of total sales, and a two-pound package size, which comprised virtually all of the remainder.

In November 1974, the major brands sold to retailers at a price of $10.00 per case of 12 one-pound packages. Typical retail price was $0.99 for a one-pound package. Throughout 1974, however, rapid escalations in sugar prices, which made up 85% of a manufacturer's ingredient cost, had drastically reduced or eliminated manufacturer profitability on milk modifiers.[1] Estimates prepared by Mr. Begg, shown in Exhibit 1, indicated that the market leaders were currently losing $1.00 to $1.25 per case relative to their full costs. On this basis, Mr. Begg was momentarily expecting a trade price increase to $11.50 per case.

MILK MATE

Milk Mate possessed several important qualities. Unlike existing products, it was a liquid that dissolved instantly and completely. By comparison, powdered milk modifiers had low solubility, were difficult to mix, and often left a residue in the glass

[1] Sugar was priced at $60 per hundredweight in November 1974, compared to $20 per hundredweight at the start of 1974.

Exhibit 1

ESTIMATED MANUFACTURERS' COSTS FOR NESTLE'S QUIK, NOVEMBER 1974[1]

Ingredients	$ 7.25
Packaging	0.75
Manufacturing	0.50
Distribution (warehouse, cartage, cash discount, etc.)	0.50
Selling expense	0.50
Total, exclusive of advertising and promotion	$ 9.50
Advertising and promotion expenses[2]	1.50
Total	$11.00

Source: Estimates prepared by Mr. Begg.

[1] Based on a case of 12 one-pound packages.

[2] Hershey costs were thought to be similar except for advertising and promotion expenses of $1.75 per case. No estimates were prepared for Cadbury.

after drinking. Standard 20-ounce and 36-ounce plastic containers could be used in packaging, thereby minimizing costs.[2] The Milk Mate formulation required proportionately less sugar than competitors, resulting in lower ingredient costs. No specialized formulating or blending processes were needed. Refrigeration was unnecessary because the product contained a preservative.

Twelve generations of the Milk Mate formulation had been tested until an optimum blend was found. In the fall of 1974, the final blend was subjected to extensive consumer testing. Each of 100 families selected as heavy users of milk modifiers was given an unidentified sample of Milk Mate and a one-pound package of the market leader, then asked to use both products in their home for two weeks. In a follow-up survey, just under 50% of the sample indicated an overall preference for Milk Mate. Mr. Begg viewed these results as encouraging, particularly since a new product form (a liquid) was being tested against an established one (a powder). Further, as shown in the reported results in Exhibit 2, Milk Mate was preferred on many specific dimensions such as taste, colour, ease of mixing, sweetness, and convenience.

Throughout the past year, Mr. Begg had worked out of his home and had kept business and personal expenses to a minimum. Product formulation and consumer testing, however, had been carried out by well-established professionals. To date, slightly under $25,000 had been invested in the project.

Mr. Begg hoped for a market launch by May 1975. In anticipation, he had recently hired a secretary and rented a second storey, walk-up office in an older North Toronto building. He estimated that office expenses (secretary, rent, telephone, bookkeeping, legal, supplies, and other general expenses) and his own salary would together total approximately $40–50,000. At current sugar prices, and *exclusive* of advertising and promotion costs, Grenadier's costs for ingredients, packaging,

[2] The 20-ounce size of Milk Mate yielded roughly the same quantity of beverage as a one-pound container of powder.

Exhibit 2

RESULTS OF CONSUMER BLIND PAIRED COMPARISON TEST CONDUCTED IN FALL 1974

Methodology

Milk Mate was tested against the leading chocolate powder brand by an independent research company. The test sample was carefully selected to comprise approximately 100 heavy users of instant chocolate powders. Each family was given one pound of the market leader and a sample of Milk Mate and asked to use both products in their home for two weeks.

Results

	Percent of Consumers Liking Milk Mate Better than Market Leader	Percent of Consumers Liking Milk Mate as Well as or Better than Market Leader
Taste, flavour	39%	54%
Colour	49%	75%
Ease of mixing	91%	93%
Sweetness	41%	64%
Convenience	90%	94%

Consumer Intention to Buy

After the consumers had tried both Milk Mate and the leading powder in their homes for two weeks, they were asked about their intention to buy Milk Mate.

—52% of families said they would definitely or probably buy Milk Mate if it was the same price as the leading powder brand.

—43% of families said they would definitely or probably buy Milk Mate if it was 5¢ per pound higher than the leading powder brand.

manufacturing, and distribution were expected to be about 10% to 20% lower than the comparable amounts shown for the market leader in Exhibit 1. These costs were almost fully variable since manufacturing and packaging were to be contracted to outside sources.

While Grenadier was small, Mr. Begg felt that big company advertising and promotion techniques would be needed to introduce and sustain Milk Mate. Television, magazine, and newspaper advertising were all strong possibilities, but the objectives and budget for such a campaign would require close scrutiny. Mr. Begg also wondered if couponing would not be appropriate at the outset to induce trial. Selected advertising space cost statistics are shown in Exhibit 3. Advertising production costs, Mr. Begg estimated, would average 10 to 15% of space costs.

A related question was the primary theme to be used in advertising. Milk Mate's principal consumer benefit was its ease of mixing. Mr. Begg felt, however, that taste was the ultimate choice criterion of consumers, and he wondered which feature to stress in his advertising.

Exhibit 3
SELECTED MEDIA ADVERTISING COSTS, NOVEMBER 1974[1]

Television	Cost per Minute (Bracketed figures are 30-second rates) Class AA Time (Prime)		Class B Time (noon to 6:00 p.m. weekdays)	
CBC National Network (43 English Stations)	$4,775		$2,621	
CBC Mid-Eastern Region (16 Ontario and Quebec English Stations)	2,303		1,222	
CBLT, Toronto (spot)	700	(420)	270	(165)
CFTO, Toronto (spot)	850	(525)	325	(225)

Radio	Rates for Prime (Class AA) Time One Minute	30 seconds	15 seconds
CFCO, Chatham	$ 23	$ 20	$18
CFPL, London	70	49	35
CFRB, Toronto	185	145	—
CHUM, Toronto	120	80	—

Newspaper Supplements and Magazines	Circulation (in thousands)	B & W Rates (4-colour rates in brackets) ½ page	Full page
The Canadian Magazine			
National Edition	1,903	$7,960(11,300)	$14,490(18,075)
Ontario Edition	1,243	7,895(9,885)	11,790(13,925)
Chatelaine (English)[2]			
National Edition	984	4,860(6,930)	8,450(10,828)
Ontario Edition	444	2,820(4,020)	4,900(6,280)
Toronto Calendar Magazine[3]	172	2,005(2,600)	3,195(3,960)

Newspapers	Circulation (in thousands)	Rate per Agate Line
Barrie Examiner	11	$0.18
Kingston Whig-Standard	33	0.30
Toronto Star	507	2.70
Windsor Star	86	0.58

(There are approximately 2,500 agate lines on a newspaper page.)

[1] All rates for one-time airing or insertion.

[2] Inserted cents-off coupon, printed in 4 colours on heavy offset paper, available in national edition for $8,950. Also available regionally.

[3] Cents-off coupon may not be run in regular advertising space, but may be inserted at cost of $4,500 (committal to firm date basis) or $3,000 (first available date basis).

Exhibit 4

MAJOR CANADIAN GROCERY CHAINS, VOLUNTARY AND CO-OPERATIVE GROUPS, 1974

Name		Estimated Number of Stores by Region				
Chains	Total Canada	B.C.	Prairies	Ontario	Quebec	Maritimes
A & P	174	—	—	142	32	—
Canada Safeway	269	89	169	11	—	—
Dominion Stores	394	—	14	228	109	43
Loblaws	188	—	32	156	—	—
Steinberg's	194	—	—	55	138	1
Becker Milk	411	—	—	411	—	—
Mac's Milk	432	41	71	320	—	—
Perrette Dairy	180	—	—	—	180	—
(29 other chains in Canada with a total of approximately 900 stores)						
Voluntary and Co-operative Groups						
Associated	255	255	—	—	—	—
Atlantic Wholesalers	189	—	—	—	—	189
IGA	730	50	172	271	201	36
Lucky Dollar	519	28	166	161	—	82
Maple Leaf	752	—	—	752	—	—
Much More	589	70	519	—	—	—
Provigo	2,049	—	—	—	2,049	—
Red & White	831	145	119	254	—	66
(70 other voluntary and co-operative groups with a total of approximately 4400 stores)						

Source: *Blue Book of Food Store Operators and Wholesalers*, 1974, pp. 119–122.

If an introductory advertising campaign was scheduled, it would be necessary in advance to gain as widespread retail distribution as possible. To obtain distribution in a supermarket chain, the first step would be to make a presentation to the chain's buyer. The actual decision, however, would be made by the chain's buying committee. Typically, sales representatives were never invited to buying committee meetings. Mr. Begg was concerned about Grenadier's credibility to the buying committees, since the company was new and unknown. For this reason, he felt that highly professional sales presentation material would be necessary.

Some major chains might be willing to give a general order in which the product was sent to every store. More likely, however, the chain would give a "listing" by which individual store managers would make their own choice about stocking the product. Some chains might refuse even to give a listing.

Selected data on retail grocery outlets in Canada are shown in Exhibit 4.

If company salespeople were employed, Mr. Begg estimated that salary and expenses for each person would amount to about $25,000 per year. Alternatively, trade sources indicated that the costs of commissioned sales agents could range from three to ten percent. A sales agent would be responsible for his or her own expenses.

A final question was the rate of market penetration. Mr. Begg hoped to achieve national distribution for Milk Mate within two years, but was unsure about how quickly he could move toward his goal. Rapid penetration seemed desirable, but financing and cash flow requirement could prove to be a limiting factor.

''There are two kinds of companies in the food industry,'' Mr. Begg concluded, ''small Canadian firms and dominant U.S. multinationals. Both have their drawbacks. The multinationals, with their huge overheads, are locked into economies of scale. They are their best with a $20 million brand, but not the $2 million one. Canadian companies can handle the $2 million product, but are reluctant to invest in marketing and promotion support programs. Somewhere in the middle, there's room for a company that combines a small-scale product with multinational marketing techniques.

MARKETING PROGRAM

In considering a marketing program for Milk Mate, Mr. Begg was aware that the financial requirements of his plan would require almost total bank financing. In turn, the bank's willingness to extend funds would depend on the amount required and the perceived viability of his program.

One important decision to be made was pricing. Milk Mate seemed superior, but could it support a premium price in the marketplace? Since the liquid product concept was new, it was important to get consumers to try Milk Mate, and this might prove easier at price parity with competition. On the other hand, a lower price might speed up market penetration, thereby establishing a consumer franchise before possible introduction of other imitative products.

A related question was that of trade margins. Retailers, Mr. Begg felt, were unhappy with existing margins and would be far more receptive to a figure closer to 20%.

44 SPACEMAX

Marvin Ryder

As part of the Entrepreneurialism course in the M.B.A. program at McMaster University, Ashton So, Tony Valaitis, and Kirk Sabo had developed a business plan for a new company. Their plan was judged to be the best submitted in the course, and in early April 1984 they were awarded a $500 prize. The next day, over coffee in the cafeteria, the three Hamilton-area students were trying to decide whether they should pocket the prize money or use it to start a new company.

THEIR COMPANY

The three students named their company "SPACEMAX" as the mission of this business was "to provide inexpensive space saving devices for non-commercial applications." Initially, SPACEMAX was to produce and market only one product—a portable, inexpensive, and easy-to-install locker shelf (called the "Lockermate Shelf"). The primary market for the product was students in high schools, community colleges, and universities. Secondary markets included senior elementary schools and non-educational institutions such as fitness/leisure centres, factories, hospitals, and police stations.

For the remainder of 1984, their plan was to penetrate the school market in the Hamilton–Toronto area. This area included a substantial portion of the total school market in Canada. They estimated that sales of $70,000 could be obtained in this area in 1984. They wanted to earn a before tax profit of 35% of sales and maintain a gross margin (after cost of goods sold) of 52%. All these estimates were best guesses. Actual performance could be quite different.

In future years, they felt they could geographically expand the school market while penetrating the non-school market. They thought the business could expand by launching one new product each year in the space-saving device field. Further they projected growth in sales dollars of 90% in 1985 and 32% in 1986.

The students felt they had a competitive advantage because of

1. their knowledge of and closeness to the school environment;
2. their emphasis on personal service; and
3. low overhead costs (SPACEMAX would subcontract out the manufacture of shelf components).

They recognized that the school market was highly seasonal, with over 80% of sales expected to occur in September and October, and thus penetration into the non-school market was essential to smooth out sales during the year.

THEIR PRODUCT

The Lockermate Shelf could be broken down into two components: (1) a single shelf board (12" × 12") and (2) a pair of wire legs. The shelf board was made of particle board (½" thick), finished with a wood veneer on one side while the legs were made of zinc plated wire 0.144" thick (Exhibit 1). When inserted in a locker, the Lockermate Shelf would stand approximately 12" high. The shelf could be collapsed into a flat unit for ease of packaging and shipping. As well, the shelf would not become a permanent part of the locker so that the purchaser could reuse the shelf in many different situations.

Before arriving at the final design, the team of students tried ten different prototypes. Wire legs were used with various shelf materials in seven of the designs. Thick corrugated cardboard, Coroplast, sheet metal, moulded plastic, hardwood, and some combinations were all tested and rejected. Sheet metal and moulded plastic were rejected because they were too expensive. Coroplast and the cardboard were

Exhibit 1
THE LOCKERMATE SHELF

LOCKERMATE SHELF Installation Instructions

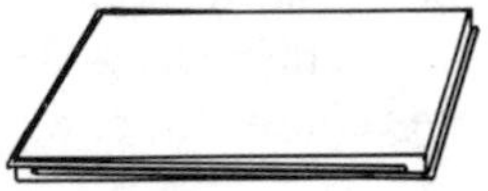

1. The LOCKERMATE shelf folded flat for convenient carrying.

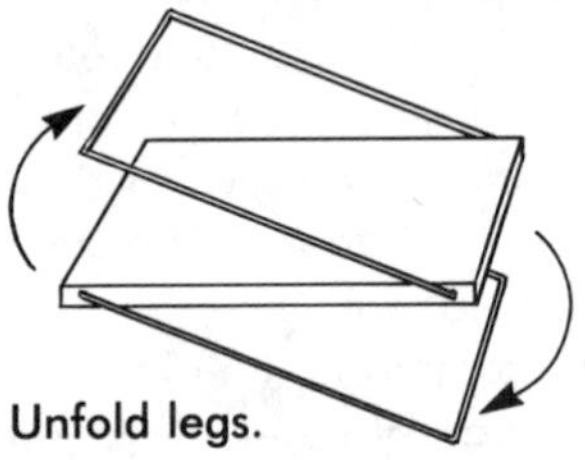

2. Unfold legs.

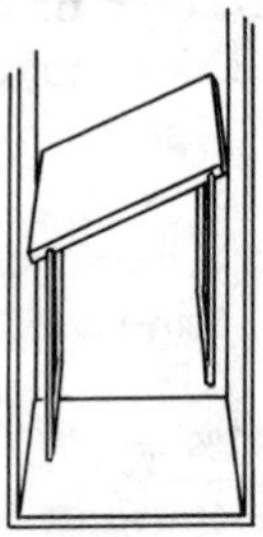

3. Tilt shelf sideways and insert into locker.

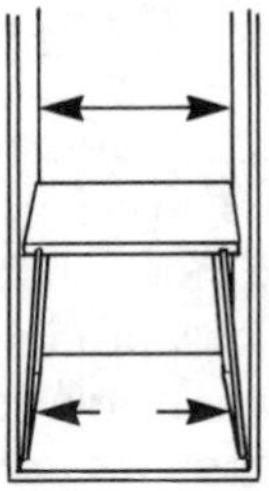

4. Set shelf into bottom of locker and press legs up against side walls.

NO SCREWS, BRACKETS or TOOLS are REQUIRED

CAUTION: Do Not Step On The Lockermate Shelf Once Installed.

not strong enough. Hardwood had a tendancy to warp. The veneer-covered particleboard was sturdy enough to take a stack of textbooks, yet cheap enough for production purposes.

Suppliers quoted a cost of $0.80 for the particleboard with the holes drilled and $0.50 for the wire legs. Assembly, shrink wrapping, and labelling would cost an additional $0.20. Cardboard boxes for shipping orders of 25 would cost $1.25. Suppliers required cash-on-delivery for all businesses with no previous credit history.

For the first year, the product would be distributed through university and community college bookstores. There were 17 universities and 22 community colleges in Ontario. Distribution to the high schools would be arranged through student councils who would sell the product as part of a fund-raising drive. There were approximately 700 high schools in Ontario. As well, student-run stores and clubs in high schools could be used as alternative sales outlets. All of these outlets would not require any intermediaries. Retail stores (like Coles, Grand & Toy, K mart, etc.) would not be approached until 1985 as purchase deadlines for the "Back-to-School" merchandise could not be met in 1984.

Market research had indicated that $5 appeared to be the upper price limit. To allow mark-ups of 50–55%, the planned selling price to the campus bookstores and students councils was to be $3.25. A recommended selling price of $4.95 would allow student councils and campus bookstores to make $1.70 profit per unit.

The promotion plan for community colleges and universities was somewhat different from the approach used for high schools. For the first market, campus bookstores would be contacted to identify the appropriate buyer. That person would be mailed a promotional package, at an estimated cost of $10, which would introduce the product and the company. The mailing would be followed up with a personal sales call by one of the three partners. If the bookstore agreed to carry the shelf, SPACEMAX would provide a point of purchase display/dump bin unit to stack the shelves at an estimated cost of $40. The shelves would be sold on consignment to the bookstore to minimize its financial risk. As well, shelves would be delivered to the bookstore in time for the September "rush" when lockers would be issued and bookstore traffic would be highest.

For high schools, the process began with identifying newly elected student council presidents. A package introducing the product, the company and the fund-raising potential of the shelf would be mailed to that person at an estimated cost of $10. If possible, personal contact would be made and a presentation given. If the product was accepted SPACEMAX would again provide a point-of-purchase display for the shelves. The shelves would again be sold on consignment with free delivery and pickup (if necessary). As well, special recordkeeping forms would be given to the student councils to ease the bookkeeping problems.

MARKET AND ENVIRONMENTAL ANALYSIS

There were approximately 1.4 million lockers in the Canadian school market (high schools, community colleges, and universities). The largest regional markets were Ontario (40%) and Quebec (24%), and the largest market by school type was

Exhibit 2
LOCKERS BY LOCATION AND SCHOOL TYPE

	Ontario	Quebec	Rest of Canada	Total
High Schools	485,000 (41%)	250,000 (21%)	440,000 (38%)	1,175,000 (100%)
Community Colleges	40,000 (30%)	70,000 (51%)	26,000 (19%)	136,000 (100%)
Universities	25,000 (42%)	14,000 (23%)	21,000 (35%)	60,000 (100%)
Total	550,000 (40%)	334,000 (24%)	487,000 (36%)	1,371,000 (100%)

Market size was calculated by multiplying the number of students by a locker-to-student ratio. The ratios were determined to be 15% for universities, 50% for community colleges, and 75% for high schools.

represented by the high schools (85%). A breakdown of the locker market by region and type of school is shown in Exhibit 2.

The students determined that a standard locker (72″ × 18″ × 12″) was widely used in Canadian schools. The dimensions were obtained by measuring lockers in and around the McMaster University campus. The most prominent weakness of the standard locker was that it offered very limited space and usually had only one shelf, located at the top. The lack of shelving space was an even greater problem when two individuals shared the same locker. As far as SPACEMAX could determine, no company manufactured and sold a portable shelf for use in lockers.

To understand the student purchaser of a Lockermate Shelf, surveys were taken of university, college, and high-school students. The first two groups were surveyed using a face-to-face interview, while the high-school students completed a self-administered survey. The surveys were administered during the winter in the first week of February. For this work "student" refers to a student using a locker. A total of 580 usable responses were obtained from the following sources: McMaster University, 83; Mohawk College, 101; St Mary's, Lorne Park, Central Clarkson, and Oakville Secondary Schools, 396. Some of the survey results are presented in Exhibit 3.

Finally, the SPACEMAX team measured the intent to purchase the Lockermate Shelf at two price points. Students were made aware of the product (through diagrams and verbal explanation) before being asked about their purchase intentions. Results of this part of the survey are presented in Exhibit 4.

THE SPACEMAX TEAM

The three students who developed the SPACEMAX Business Plan came from different backgrounds. Tony Valaitis was enrolled in the Co-op M.B.A. program at McMaster. His first two work terms were spent with Gulf Canada in the Human Resources Department. His third work term would begin on May 1, and as yet no co-op work placement could be found. Tony had graduated with a B.A. in Geography from

Exhibit 3
SELECTED SURVEY RESULTS

	Yes	No
Do you share a locker?	Yes	No
University Students	50%	50%
Community College Students	67%	33%
High School Students	54%	46%
60% of people sharing a locker were women		
Do you need 1 extra locker shelf?	Yes	No
University Students	76%	24%
Community College Students	73%	27%
High School Students	46%	54%
33% of High School Students wanted two extra locker shelves		
Do you use the bottom of your locker to stack books?	Yes	No
University Students	77%	23%
Community College Students	77%	23%
High School Students	50%	50%
Do you feel your locker is well-organized and well-kept?	Yes	No
University Students	67%	33%
Community College Students	67%	33%
High School Students	50%	50%
Is having a well-organized locker important to you?	Yes	No
University Students	61%	39%
Community College Students	65%	35%
High School Students	53%	47%
Are you dissatisfied with your current locker facility?	Yes	No
University Students	14%	86%
Community College Students	48%	52%
High School Students	55%	45%

McMaster in 1978 and had spent three years as the Office Manager for a Hamilton firm. While pursuing his B.A., Tony had been a member of the Varsity Basketball team, and he hoped to use his last year of eligibility in the fall while completing his M.B.A.

Kirk Sabo was enrolled as a full-time M.B.A. student. He came to McMaster after completing a B.B.A. at Wilfrid Laurier University in 1982. His work experience had been limited to summer jobs on the assembly line at the Ford Motor Company plant in Oakville and with pool cleaning companies as Crew Chief. Kirk was a member of the W.L.U. Varsity hockey team but upon being accepted to McMaster he pursued the objective of a career in marketing.

Ashton So was the only married man of the three. His undergraduate degree was a B.A.Sc. in Chemical Engineering which he obtained from the University of Waterloo

Exhibit 4
PURCHASE INTENTIONS AT TWO PRICE POINTS

If the Lockermate Shelf sold for $3

	Definitely Buy	Probably Buy	Neutral	Probably Not Buy	Definitely Not Buy
University Students	48%	19%	11%	7%	15%
College Students	48%	31%	11%	5%	5%
High School Students	38%	29%	12%	7%	14%

If the Lockermate Shelf sold for $5

	Definitely Buy	Probably Buy	Neutral	Probably Not Buy	Definitely Not Buy
University Students	28%	19%	16%	15%	22%
College Students	25%	26%	26%	13%	10%
High School Students	11%	25%	29%	11%	24%

in 1979. He immediately went to work for Gulf Canada, working in process engineering to improve the efficiency and energy conservation of the Edmonton and Clarkson refineries. He was also a full-time M.B.A. student.

THEIR PROBLEM

The $500 that the team won for their business plan was intended to be an incentive for them to start a new business. They could pocket the money or use it to go ahead with the plan to sell the Lockermate Shelf.

On the other hand, the preliminary investment would be much more than $500. Being students, banks would probably be wary of giving them a loan. Further, even with all their work on the business plan, they were not sure that they wanted to take a risk and begin a new venture with an untried product. There could be problems with the survey, and they had yet to do any breakeven analysis. They had not worked out what their fixed costs would be, so in any breakeven analysis some assumptions would have to be made.

They would need to make a decision soon. The lead time for one production cycle was six weeks. After exams finished at the end of May, they would not have any shelves in stock until the middle of June. Time was already slipping by if they were to have the Lockermate Shelf in bookstores for the September rush.

45 THE PERFECT PACE

Ian Spencer

Shauna White

Early in March 1986, Patricia Cameron, 25, sat at her parents' kitchen table reviewing the hectic schedule of the previous two months and began to map out what was likely to be an even busier schedule for the two months ahead. At the start of the year she had returned to her hometown, Antigonish (pronounced Auntie-gun-ish), Nova Scotia, to open a fitness club for women. Since her return Ms. Cameron had created a name for the club; found a suitable location; contacted several equipment suppliers, local contractors, and office furnishings dealers to obtain estimates or quotations; studied the Antigonish market; met with insurance agents, media reps, bankers, and government officials; and had tentatively lined up two experienced instructors. In the weeks ahead Ms. Cameron knew that she would have to supervise and finalize all of these arrangements as well as develop in some detail a tentative program of activities for members, price and sell memberships, and effectively promote the opening. The target date for the opening of the club was May 1.

Ms. Cameron had chosen Antigonish not only because it was her home town but also because it had no fitness club to serve the needs of women. From her experience as the assistant manager of a fitness club in Truro, Nova Scotia, and having taught fitness and aerobics classes at the Halifax YWCA and Mount Saint Vincent University during the previous four years, she believed that The Perfect Pace could achieve a membership base of 400 by the end of the first year. As she sat at the table Ms. Cameron realized that the longstanding dream of owning her own business soon would come true. She was excited, enthusiastic, and determined to succeed.

THE FITNESS CRAZE

In the mid-1970s Participaction generated widespread awareness of a massive Canadian fitness problem. The average 60-year-old Swede, Participaction had discovered, was fitter than the average 30-year-old Canadian. Widespread awareness soon led to widespread guilt which, in turn, led to widespread action. In the early to mid-1980s hundreds of thousands of Canadians made a commitment to better physical health. Some did it on their own and some through company or recreation department programs. Others did it through television "The 20 Minute Workout" or books (Jane Fonda's or Christie Brinkley's) or joined private fitness centres.

By 1985, all Canadian cities and most larger Canadian towns had one or more fitness centres that offered members workout gymnasiums, exercise mats and equipment, weight equipment for body building and muscle toning programs, a variety of fitness and aerobics classes, fitness assessments, diet planning, saunas, showers, and locker facilities. Some centres even had squash and racquetball courts, colour and beauty consultations, tanning beds, and child-minding services.

THE ANTIGONISH MARKET

Although the population of the Town of Antigonish was only 5,500, its trading area contained an estimated 35,000 people. Most families from Antigonish County (population 18,000) and Guysborough County (population 13,000) shopped in the Town of Antigonish with some regularity. As well, a minority of families from Richmond, Victoria, and Inverness Counties to the east and Pictou County to the west shopped in Antigonish. Antigonish County occupied the northeast corner of mainland Nova Scotia and was about 250 km west of Sydney and 250 km northeast of Halifax. The town of Antigonish was the home of Saint Francis Xavier University which generated an annual influx of 2,300 students each September to April. The Antigonish Town Office had provided Ms. Cameron with age, sex, and labour force profiles for Antigonish County (Exhibit 1).

Ms. Cameron had not conducted any formal marketing research, but, informally, from listening to her peers and some of her mother's friends, she had sensed a strong interest in the idea of a women's fitness club. She felt that they were tired of doing nothing, that many had been bored for too long, and that her club would be an ideal outlet for them.

A further indication of interest, Ms. Cameron discovered was the fact that Linda Steeghs, one of the two qualified instructors she had approached about working for her, had offered fitness classes for women with great success during 1983 and 1984

Exhibit 1

POPULATION AND LABOUR FORCE STATISTICS FOR ANTIGONISH COUNTY

Age Group	Male	Female	Total
0–14	2,744	2,570	5,314
15–24	1,760	1,725	3,485
25–34	1,399	1,398	2,797
35–44	957	944	1,901
45–64	1,354	1,444	2,798
65+	812	999	1,811
Totals	9,026	9,080	18,106

Labour Force			
Population 15+	6,282	6,510	12,792
Labour force	4,485	2,940	7,425
Participation rate	71%	45%	58%
Employed	4,405	2,570	6,975

Source: Statistics Canada, 1981 Census

through a franchise called Dance Fit. Ms. Steeghs had been unable to continue these classes after 1984 because the large and very inexpensive space that she had rented became unavailable when the building was sold and later torn down.

Ms. Cameron also discovered that the university posed limited competition on two fronts. First, some physical education students had offered aerobics classes for a nominal fee to their fellow students. Second, the university offered public memberships in a Fitness and Recreation Association. Ms. Cameron was not too concerned about this competition. The aerobics classes were taught by students just trying their hand at it, and not qualified personnel. The Fitness and Recreation Association offered no fitness classes and tended to be a do-it-yourself facility. Its main attraction for families was access to the only indoor swimming pool in the area. It also offered a weight room, squash, racquetball, handball and tennis courts and access to the university gymnasium. The only overlapping facilities with The Perfect Pace Ms. Cameron could see were the weight room, the sauna and showers. A family membership in the Association cost $195 and a single adult membership $160. To Ms. Cameron's knowledge there were no other organized fitness organizations in Antigonish, but the ever-present risk that someone else might be planning to start one heightened the urgency to open The Perfect Pace as soon as possible.

THE HECTIC JANUARY AND FEBRUARY PACE

Ms. Cameron's first two actions in January were to see the family's bank manager and decide on a name. The bank manager indicated that with favourable revenue and profit projections he could probably lend her up to 100% of the value of her equipment, repayable over five years, if the equipment were pledged as security. She would have to raise the balance of the initial investment privately, but believed that with favourable projections this would be possible.

The club needed an appropriate name—one that was somewhat feminine, connoted fitness, and suggested a club without also suggesting exclusiveness or snobbishness. After much deliberation and some consultation with family members she chose the name, The Perfect Pace.

A few days later Ms. Cameron heard about some space available above a dry cleaning business just off Main Street at the east end of town. Substantial renovations and improvements would be required and parking on the short side street would not always be available for members. However, the room was large enough, had windows on three sides, a fairly high ceiling, a solid floor, and its rent was only $650 per month plus utilities. Near the end of January, Ms. Cameron signed a one-year lease with an option to renew for two years with rent to be determined. Her sketch for organizing the space is reproduced in Exhibit 2.

Ms. Cameron solicited cost estimates from several equipment suppliers, two general contractors, several tradesmen and two office furnishings dealers. By early March the file folder of estimates was both thick and virtually complete. It appeared that renovations and improvements—all wiring, plumbing, heating, insulation, carpentry, tiling, drywalling, and painting—would cost about $16,000. The fitness equipment including mats, bikes, benches, rowing machines, a central weight machine, a quality tape deck, and assorted hoops and balls, would come to about $15,000. The office furniture and furnishings, including carpeting, chairs, a table, a stool, locker room benches, a reception counter, planters, and pictures, would come to $6,000.

With a little assistance from a friend Ms. Cameron estimated that monthly operating expenses, aside from rent and interest on the loan, would be about $3,500. This figure included salaries and benefits, utilities, telephone, office supplies, maintenance and instructional supplies, insurance, property taxes, and advertising. In developing the expense estimates she had assumed that The Perfect Pace would be open approximately 70 hours each week from Monday to Saturday. As the membership wished or needed, this assumption could change. The instructors would be paid on an hourly basis at a higher rate for teaching a class and at a lower one for working at the reception desk. Ms. Cameron planned to act as both manager and instructor and expected to work 60 to 70 hours per week for the first year if necessary.

Ms. Cameron also had a file folder on the program of activities to be offered which contained a summary of the Truro club's facilities and services and some of

Exhibit 2
SKETCH OF THE LAYOUT

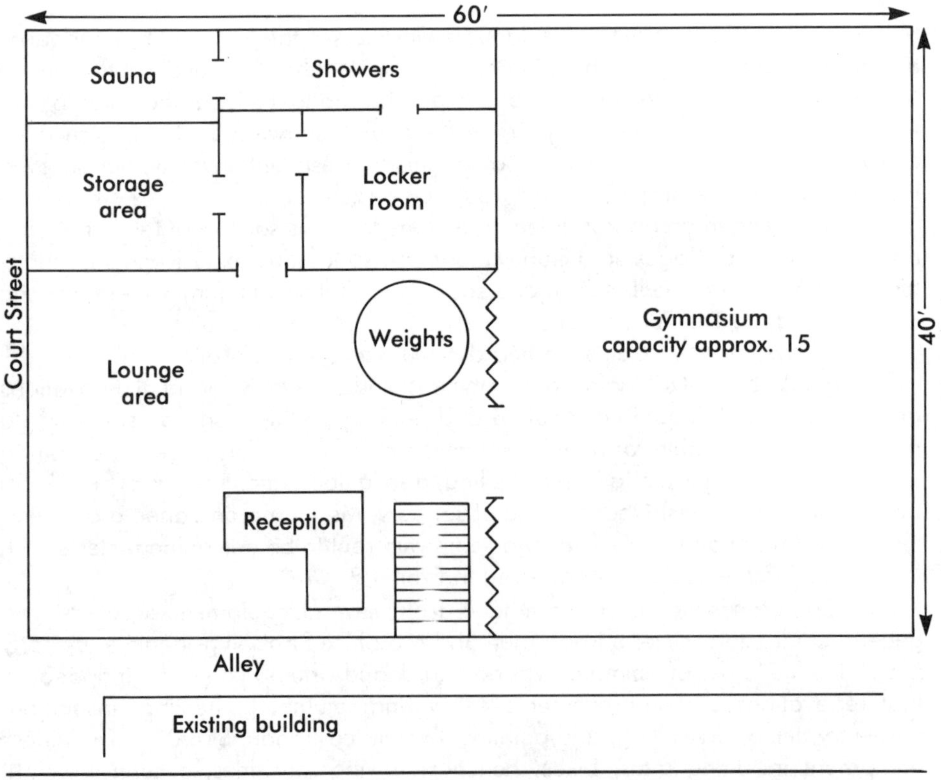

her own programming notions. The Truro club charged a membership fee of $325 per year. The membership bought unlimited access to all facilities and classes. The facilities available to members were a series of exercise machines, called the Nautilus System, on which an individual program of body building or muscle toning could be developed, six stationary bikes, free weights, a sauna, two tanning beds, showers, a change area with hair dryers, and a lounge area with a television and a video cassette recorder. The two classes offered were introductory and advanced aerobics. Each class, including change, warm-up, cool-down, and class time, ran about an hour. Some days there were only a few classes, while on others the exercise gym was booked solidly. Ms. Cameron recalled that the average was about five classes per day. The Truro fitness club was open Monday to Thursday from 7 a.m. to 10 p.m., Friday from 7 a.m. to 9 p.m., Saturday from 9 a.m. to 5 p.m., and Sunday from 11 a.m. to 6 p.m.

Ms. Cameron planned to offer aerobics classes at the beginner, intermediate, and advanced levels, weight toning and body building programs, and fitness assessments. In time, if demand seemed to warrant it, The Perfect Pace would add a child-minding service for mothers. She wanted The Perfect Pace to be known for quality instruction and service. Each member would be assured careful attention and guidance as she advanced in the program. She also wanted to ensure that members who were inexperienced did not injure themselves, become discouraged, or lose interest. She was highly committed to the proper education of every member.

THE HECTIC PACE AHEAD

Ms. Cameron believed that 90% of the members of The Perfect Pace would be women from Antigonish County, including some students from the university. She felt that few women from the adjacent counties would travel the 50 to 100 km to take advantage of her fitness classes and facilities. Hence, to create awareness and sign up members, she planned initially to focus on the town, the county within a radius of about 30 km of the town, and the university campus.

How to price a Perfect Pace membership would be a critical decision. Ms. Cameron felt that the Truro club's fee might be a little too high, while the University Fitness and Recreation Association's fee might be a little too low. She had thought about offering introductory memberships for three or six months in addition to the regular full-year memberships, but she was unsure whether they would lead to a larger membership base. She had also thought about a user pay plan, whereby someone could pay by the hour or the activity, but she wondered what the regular members might think of sharing the facility with casual users. Finally, she believed that she should offer an eight-month student membership but had not determined what this might be.

Decisions on advertising and promotion also would be critical to the success of The Perfect Pace. From her discussions with media reps Ms. Cameron had learned that the local newspaper had a weekly circulation of 8,500, with most copies sold in Antigonish County. A very small ad—one column wide and one inch high—would cost $4, a one-eighth page ad would cost $60, and a one-quarter page ad $120. The local radio station had a total six-county reach of over 70,000 different people each week. On average, the number of listeners during a quarter hour period between 6 a.m. and midnight was about 8,000. The radio station would charge $15 for each 30-second commercial. Advertising in the campus newspaper would cost about half as much as the local newspaper, while advertising on the campus radio station would cost about a quarter as much as the local radio station. Flyers could be printed and distributed for as little as $0.10 each for a one-colour, one-side only, 8½" × 11" page. Larger, four-colour flyers printed on both sides could cost $2–3 or more. To date Ms. Cameron had not done any detailed planning for advertising, special promotions, or publicity. In the operating expense budget, she had tentatively estimated advertising at a total of $1,000 for the first year.

As she began to mull over issues like pricing memberships, and advertising for the opening, Ms. Cameron became a bit concerned. She certainly had not lost her enthusiasm or her determination to succeed. However, the importance of these factors in motivating women to join The Perfect Pace, coupled with the uncertainty of making the right decisions, really made her wish she had someone else she could turn to for help.

46 BOOT-DRYER (PIED-O-SEC)

Jacques M. Boisvert
Carole Duhaime

In January 1983 Réginald Lecor was examining the possibility of marketing a new product developed by his sister Nicole. Boot-Dryer is an electrical appliance designed to dry out winter boots and mittens. The Lecors did not have any business experience but they had both taken an introductory course in marketing, as part of the Certificate in Administration course given by the University of Québec in Rouyn-Noranda. They thus knew that the stage following the development of an idea for a new product is to examine the market opportunities for the product and if necessary, to develop a prototype. The two Lecors were interested in the product and they were already discussing the possibility of creating a company, Réginord, to manufacture and sell the Boot-Dryer. Before thinking about the financing for the project, M. Lecor wondered if it was worth the effort (in terms of the opportunity cost of their time vs. the potential benefits), and if so, how they should proceed to market the new product.

PRODUCT CHARACTERISTICS

The idea for the new product came to Nicole Lecor when she heard one of her friends complaining about the high cost of winter boots for children. Her friend, who had three children under the age of twelve, was telling her that every year she had to make sure that each child had one pair of boots for going out in the rain and two pairs of winter boots; even then, these were not sufficient. Indeed, quite often her children, who liked playing outside, would come back home with their feet completely soaked. Their boots took hours to dry even when they were turned upside down on the radiator or were placed on the hot-air register. Sometimes the children were prevented from playing outside if the boots were not dry. The problem was the same for wet mittens and gloves. The friend, knowing that Mlle Lecor was very imaginative, asked her to think about a way to dry out boots and mittens more rapidly. The Boot-Dryer was Mlle Lecor's solution.

The Boot-Dryer has pegs for warming both boots and mittens by means of electricity (Exhibit 1). Five pairs of boots of all sizes can be fitted on the pegs. The boots are placed upside down on these pegs. In addition, another set of pegs located at the back can hold five pair of mittens, gloves, or even hats. To retain the drained-off water until it evaporates, the rim of the appliance is somewhat raised in relation to the platter.

The corners of the appliance are rounded in order to prevent children from injuring themselves. A ventilation grille is located in the front of the appliance. The electrical system, a fan with a heating element, and a thermostat that keeps the inside termperature at 39°C are located inside the appliance. The thermostat automatically switches off the appliance after the expiration of the time chosen by the user (minimum time is 45 minutes).

The operation of the Boot-Dryer is simple. Air enters through the grille located at the front, flows through the fan, which forces it onto the heating element, and then up and through the pegs on which the boots and mittens hang to dry. A small container inside the applicance holds some concentrated deodorant. This deodorant can slowly be added to the hot air, one drop at a time, when the appliance is turned on.

The top of the pegs are bevelled to prevent the boots or mittens from resting against the pegs and blocking the exit of the hot air. In addition, several slots on the sides of the pegs allow a more uniform distribution of air on the items to be dried. The pegs and the base of the appliance are made with a plastic alloy (ABS) that conforms to government sanitary norms

Deodorant is the only accessory and its use is optional. Any concentrated liquid deodorant sold on the market may be used, for example Boréal, Biloder, or Des Bois. These deodorants work by a simple evaporation process. A single drop saturates approximately 43 cubic metres. If the reservoir has deodorant, a drop is automati-

Exhibit 1
DIAGRAM OF THE BOOT-DRYER

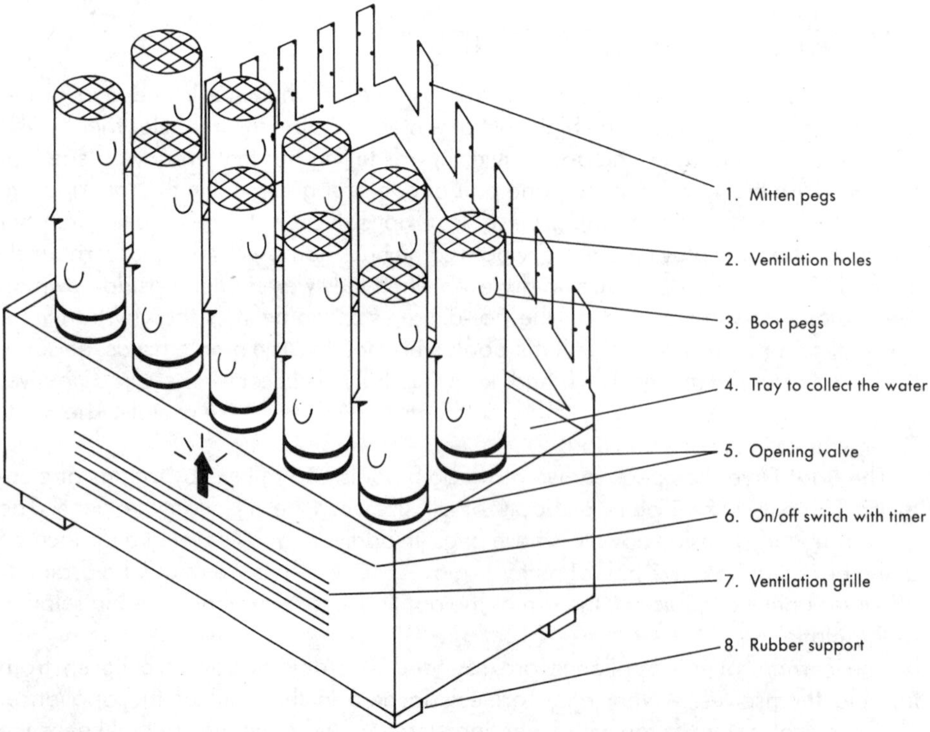

cally released to the air when the appliance is turned on. Use of deodorant can remove the unpleasant odour associated with feet and wet boots.

Like most electrical appliances, the product is extremely easy to use. The user simply has to connect the pegs to their support and plug the Boot-Dryer into a standard electrical outlet of 100 volts with a minimum of 850 watts. In order for the appliance to function well, the user should ensure that the entrance of air through the grille is not blocked.

Other Product Characteristics

Each unit of the Boot-Dryer was to be presented to consumers in a cardboard box measuring 30 × 45 × 92 cm. A label glued on each box would show a picture of the appliance with the brand name of the product and a brief explanation for use of the product. For transportation to the distributors, the boxes were to be packed in larger containers measuring 92 × 92 × 122 cm, each containing eight appliances.

Regarding the brand name, the Lecors chose to call the product Boot-Dryer because this name is short, easy to remember, easy to pronounce, and identifies the product (even though it only mentions the feet and not the hands or head). Boot-Dryer is also compatible with the promise made to the consumer to have dry feet. For the French market the product name was to be Pied-O-Sec.

The average life of the Boot-Dryer was estimated at five years. The Lecors agreed that they should offer a one-year warranty. M. Lecor wondered if the after-sale service mentioned in the warranty should be the responsibility of the manufacturer or the distributor. He believed that the service would be better if the manufacturer was responsible for it. On the other hand, he was not sure if the company would have sufficient resources to do the servicing itself.

Product Introduction

M. Lecor thought that it would be a good idea if the product introduction included a promotion. He proposed that with each purchase consumers should receive a bottle of concentrated deodorant valued at five dollars. He believed that this incentive would prevent customer disappointment if a perspiration odour occurred when the product was tried for the first time.

For distribution, he wondered if he should ask the help of his friend Charles Bérubé, who was the owner of the Rouyn Canadian Tire outlet. The two friends often went cross-country skiing together. M. Lecor thought that maybe M. Bérubé could recommend the product to head office. If a chain as large as Canadian Tire agreed to distribute the Boot-Dryer and even to promote it, M. Lecor felt that he would not have to worry about those two marketing variables. For these reasons, he believed that a retail margin of 50%, in addition to an exclusive contract, would be necessary to ensure the services and co-operation of each outlet. A sales representative could also be equipped with a demonstrator Boot-Dryer and a folder of technical cards emphasizing the product characteristics, for visits to each Canadian Tire outlet.

M. Lecor knew that his alternative was not ideal. Among other things, it had the drawback of restraining the market for the new product and it also made M. Lecor a captive of the retail chain. Another alternative would be to try to sell the product to several shoe store chains such as Lewis, Trans-Canada, and Yellow. This alternative required that the Lecors set up a co-operative advertising program in which they would pay half the advertising costs of the retailers. In this case the retail margin would be 40% and the minimum advertising cost would be around $50,000.

A third alternative involved distributing through wholesalers who would promote the product to retailers. If this last solution was adopted, the Lecors would be able to sell through a larger number of outlets. Of course, as for the preceding alternative, a co-operative advertising budget would be necessary. In addition, a margin of 10% would have to be given to obtain the co-operation of the wholesalers. Mlle Lecor prepared a cost analysis of the project (Exhibit 2). The suggested retail price turned out to be about $35. To find out whether this price was reasonable, the Lecors conducted a mini-survey. They asked a sample of their friends the following question: "If the Boot-Dryer was sold at $35, would you be a lot, a little, or not at all interested in buying it?" The answer was positive in the majority of the cases.

Finally, M. Lecor went to the university library to consult Statistics Canada publications in order to get some information on the size of the potential market (Exhibit 3).

At this point they felt that they had enough information to develop a marketing plan. If an in-depth analysis of the information in their possession revealed that the project would be successful, they were prepared to make an appointment with their bank manager to discuss financing for the project.

Exhibit 2
COST ANALYSIS FOR THE BOOT-DRYER

Fixed Costs for a Year		
Prototype manufacturing		$ 200
Equipment, furniture, tools for the warehouse: $5,000 amortized over 5 years		1,000
Telephone: $40.00/week × 50 weeks		2,000
Labour cost: (one specialized worker to assemble and pack the product)		18,000
Salesperson salary: (without taking into account commission)		15,000
Salesperson's expenses gasoline: $0.18/km × 56,000 = $10,000 room and board: $51/day × 4 days/week × 48 weeks = $10,000		20,000
Rent: (renovated barn, heated, or a large warehouse) $400/month		4,800
Taxes and permits		
Business tax	$ 200	
Patent	4,000	
Incorporating fees	750	
Insurance	300	5,250
Accounting costs		1,000
Administration costs, stationery, etc.		1,000
		$68,250

Variable Costs		
Product cost per unit		
plastic moulding	$5.00	
ventilator with thermostat and heating element	5.00	
electric control with timer	3.00	
electric connections and material for the deodorant	0.50	$13.50
Wrapping and labelling cost per unit		
small individual box	0.50	
large box: $0.80 (contains 8 small boxes)	0.10	
paper, label, printing	0.05	0.65
Salesperson commission per unit sold		0.12
		$14.27

Exhibit 3

CENSUS FAMILIES BY AGE OF CHILDREN AT HOME
Canada and the Provinces, June 1, 1980*

Province	Total Families with Children at Home	All Children 5 Years and over	All Children 14 Years and over	All Children 17 Years and over	All Children 24 Years and over	All Children under 6 Years	All Children under 15 Years	All Children under 18 Years	All Children under 25 Years
					(In Thousands)				
Total Families									
Nfld.	104.3	59.2	21.6	13.1	5.7	22.9	59.6	72.2	95.6
P.E.I.	22.6	13.5	6.1	3.4	1.4	5.0	11.8	14.8	20.4
N.S.	146.4	91.5	36.1	21.7	8.0	29.3	83.1	102.3	134.7
N.B.	127.8	75.5	30.0	18.5	6.4	30.0	73.9	90.7	113.4
Que.	1,144.7	727.7	338.4	219.5	61.2	258.3	601.8	749.5	1,043.9
Ont.	1,509.6	948.9	415.0	243.2	64.1	334.5	832.3	1,049.1	1,411.1
Man.	171.5	103.7	45.4	26.1	7.9	39.4	96.5	123.8	160.3
Sask.	152.2	89.9	37.0	19.8	6.6	37.2	86.0	112.4	143.4
Alta.	363.5	221.2	81.3	41.5	11.7	87.9	220.5	274.7	346.0
B.C.	420.7	273.9	112.5	63.3	14.8	90.5	237.4	299.3	400.2
Canada	4,163.4	2,604.9	1,123.4	670.3	187.8	935.1	2,302.9	2,888.7	3,881.0

Source: Statistics Canada, *Estimates of Families for Canada and the Province*,1980, Cat. 91-204, Table 3

Note: Numbers are rounded to the nearest hundred

* Not including the Yukon and the Northwest Territories

Section 10

STRATEGIC MARKET PLANNING

Managers often don't devote enough attention to strategic market planning because they are too busy reacting to immediate market situations. This can lead to a long-term decline of the company's established market position and inadequate development of profitable new opportunities.

At the highest level of the organization, strategic planning involves defining the corporate mission or purpose, setting objectives, and formulating strategy. However, a number of layers of strategy are necessary in a large company, each layer being progressively more detailed, to provide operational guidance for the next level of subordinate managers. At each level (business unit, product line, market, brand) the strategy must be co-ordinated with those above and below. Critical to the success of a strategy is the marketing plan, which summarizes the strategy and its development as well as laying the framework for its implementation.

Strategic market planning integrates all elements of marketing. Consequently, this section serves not only to introduce new material, but also as a review of many of the concepts discussed throughout this book.

Marketing's concern ranges from the overall design of strategy to the implementation of a myriad of programs. Even superb execution cannot save a misdirected stategy; only good execution can transform a sound strategy from plans on paper to reality. Marketing success depends on all elements of a plan working together to accomplish the organization's goals.

THE STRATEGIC PLANNING PROCESS

MISSION

Fundamental to a firm's overall strategy is a definition of its mission or purpose, a basic statement of what the organization seeks to do in the long term, and the rationale for its existence. A company's mission is determined by answering such simple questions as, What business are we in? Who are our customers? and What value do we provide to our customers? Profit making, often said to be every firm's goal, is not so much the purpose of a company, but the outcome that results from the successful fulfillment of its mission.

Probably the most important test for a good mission statement is that it is both externally and internally oriented. Many organizations define themselves solely in product or technological terms, not in market terms. They suffer from "marketing myopia."

For instance, many metal can manufacturers ran into difficulties because they defined themselves in just that way—not as being in the packaging business. They therefore did not take advantage of innovations in materials to meet changes in customer needs. Of course, in using a market definition, an organization must be careful not to move too far away from its resources and abilities. Defining a metal can manufacturer as being in the packaging business does not necessarily mean that it should be supplying paper bags to supermarkets.

OBJECTIVES AND GOALS

Once defined, the purpose should be translated into a set of goals or objectives that indicate the specific accomplishments to be attained in fulfilling it. Objectives, which should be based on a realistic assessment of what can be done, can have varying time horizons, degrees of interrelatedness, and levels of priority. However, too many goals for a manager result in an effort that is not well focused. The manager becomes the proverbial "Jack of all trades, master of none." Without a few key, specific, measurable objectives, strategy becomes merely a statement of good intentions. Efficient achievement of these objectives within the available resources is key.

STRATEGY

If the objectives specify *what* is to be accomplished, the strategy specifies *how*. Strategic decisions include both where to commit resources and how to use the resources, once committed.

There are a number of analytic tools available that can help management formulate strategy. A *product-market growth matrix* (Exhibit 1) categorizes opportunities for growth in terms of the business's current products (or technologies) and markets. A growth oriented company can then look for expansion through *market penetration* (increased usage of current products by current market segments), *product development* (adding new products that appeal to current markets), *market development* (offering existing products to new markets), or *diversification* (growth strategies encompassing both new markets and new products). In addition, some growth opportunities arise from forward integration (for example, by buying out wholesalers or retailers) or from backward integration (for example, by taking over suppliers, as some department stores have done with clothing manufacturers). When considering any growth strategy, even one based on diversification, management should look for attractive opportunities that use at least some of the firm's strengths and have some link to current activities. The product-market growth matrix helps a firm to identify which opportunities rely primarily on its strengths in marketing and which on its strengths in technology or other areas. Further analysis can then be done to determine the specific abilities required to compete successfully in the attractive growth opportunities that were identified.

Portfolio management can also be a useful aid to making strategic resource allocation decisions. In *portfolio analysis*, divisons or strategic business units are usually evaluated along two dimensions: the overall attractiveness of the market and the unit's competitive strength in the market. Portfolio analysis helps in highlighting critical strategic issues and in deciding whether to invest, maintain, or withdraw resources from a unit.

Exhibit 1
PRODUCT-MARKET GROWTH MATRIX

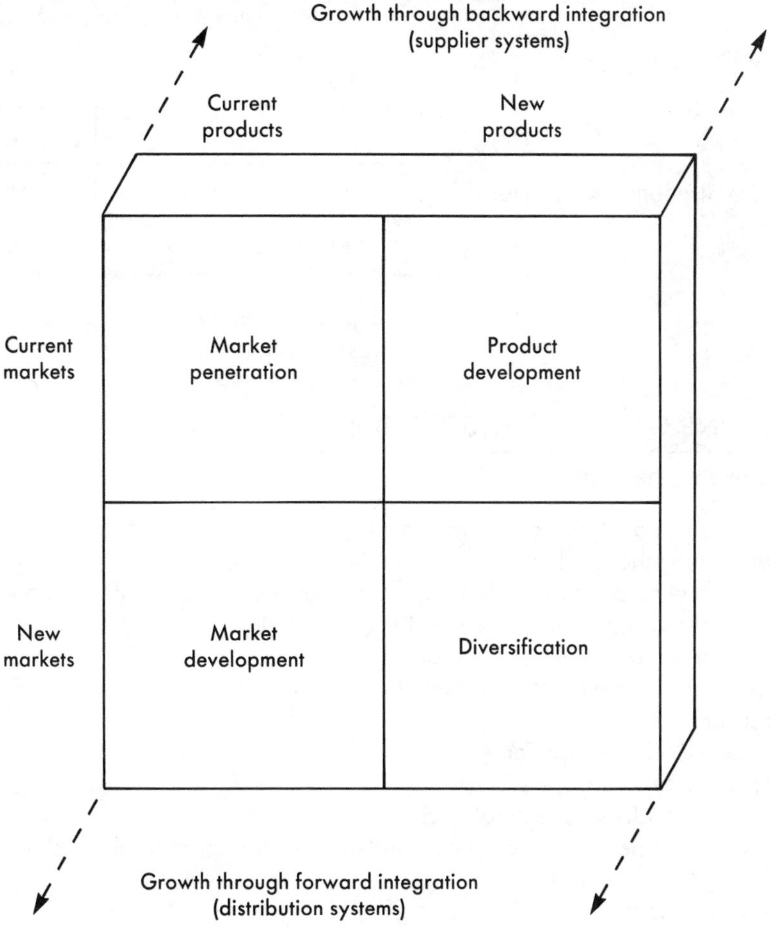

One popular approach to portfolio management, the *growth/share matrix*, uses growth to represent market attractiveness and share to represent competitive strength. While these two dimensions have the advantage of concreteness and are readily quantifiable, provided that relevant markets can be properly defined and future growth rates can be well estimated, the dimensions of growth and share may not be sufficiently comprehensive for decision making. For example, current market share may not be a good indicator of a company's ability to increase its future market share, and growth leaves untouched such factors as present and potential competitive threats and technological, regulatory, and social trends. Consequently, companies are increasingly turning to the use of *multifactor portfolio matrices*. While the dimensions underlying such firm's portfolio matrix vary, typical

Exhibit 2
MULTIFACTOR PORTFOLIO MATRIX WITH TYPICAL DIMENSIONS

Attractiveness of Market

Competitive Strength		High	Medium	Low
	High	I	I	M
	Medium	I	M	W
	Low	M	W	W

I = Invest or Build Commitment
M = Maintain or Hold Position
W = Withdraw Resources

DIMENSIONS OF A MULTIFACTOR PORTFOLIO MATRIX

Attractiveness of the Market

1. What is the industry sales growth rate?
2. How large is the market?
3. Are industry sales susceptible to cyclical, seasonal, or other fluctuations?
4. What is the competitive structure of the industry?
5. What is the profitability of the industry?
6. Does extensive government regulation constrain actions or pose uncertainties?
7. How powerful are suppliers?
8. How powerful are buyers?
9. What is the industry's technological status?
10. What environmental, social, etc., trends have an impact on the industry?

Competitive Strength

1. How strong is our market share? What is our competitive position?
2. What trends are there in market share?
3. How are we perceived by customers?
4. Are our distributors well established and supportive?
5. Do we have reliable suppliers?
6. Does our cost structure enable us to compete profitably?
7. Are our production facilities modern and efficient?
8. Do we have the technology required for innovation and product development?
9. Do we have the managerial skills needed to compete?
10. What environmental, social, etc., factors have an impact on our firm and its market position?

dimensions for (1) attractiveness of the market and (2) competitive strength are given in Exhibit 2.

Portfolio models are not without their weaknesses. They do not allow a full consideration of the interrelationships among businesses and concentrate on current products. Nevertheless, they provide an overview of a company's various businesses and can highlight areas for resource investment and help to set goals (for example, generate money in the short term, build market share) for each division or unit. Combined with a manager's knowledge of his products and markets, portfolio models can provide useful insight into resource allocation decisions.

COMPETITIVE MARKETING STRATEGY

Competitive marketing strategy focuses on determining the critical factors necessary for success in the chosen markets and determining the means by which to compete. Once the critical success factors are identified, management must objectively evaluate its strengths and weaknesses in meeting those requirements as compared to those of present and potential competitors. True strength is usually based on accumulated experience and consistent success; occasional flashes of brilliance are rarely dependable in the long run.

Strategies can be broadly summarized as being the overall *low cost producer* and/or establishing a *differential competitive position* (through [1] product or other forms of differentiation and/or [2] market segment specialization). However, the next questions to ask are, How is cost leadership to be attained? and What are the bases for a differentiation or segmentation strategy? These in turn lead to a long list of alternatives. Ultimately, strategy formulation is a creative process; no analyst can really claim to offer a complete list of strategy types.

The proposed strategies must be evaluated on such criteria as:

1. direct financial analysis,
2. ability to meet the objectives set,
3. external and internal consistency, and
4. degree of risk undertaken and robustness of the strategy in the light of market and environmental uncertainty.

One reason strategic choice is difficult is that seldom does one alternative uniformly exceed the others on all criteria.

DEVELOPING A MARKETING PLAN

The marketing plan is a systematic way of structuring an analysis of a market, an organization's position in that market, and a program for future marketing activities. The elements of a plan are interrelated, so that its development may involve cycling through its components several times before satisfactory results are achieved. The following discussion briefly highlights selected portions of the marketing plan format suggested in Exhibit 3. In addition to providing an integrated format for marketing decision making, the discussion of the marketing plan provides a means to review topics discussed earlier in the book.

Exhibit 3
MARKETING PLAN FORMAT

Executive Summary
Situation Analysis (Where Are We Now?)
- External
  - Environment (Political, regulatory, economic, social, technical, and other relevant areas)
  - Consumers and markets
  - Employees
  - Suppliers and distributors
  - Competition
- Internal
  - Objectives
  - Strengths and weaknesses
- Problems and opportunities
  - Momentum forecast
  - Gap identification

Marketing Program Goals (Where Do We Want to Go?)
Marketing Strategies (How Are We Going to Get There?)
- Positioning
  - Target segments
  - Competitive stance
  - Usage incentive
- Marketing mix
  - Product
  - Price
  - Distribution
  - Marketing communication: Advertising, personal selling, promotion, etc.
- Contingency strategies

Marketing Budget (How much do we need and where should we allocate it?)
- Resources (Money, people, time)
- Amount and allocation

Marketing Action Plan (What do we need to do?)
- Detailed breakdown of activities required
- Responsibility by name
- Activity schedule in milestone format
- Tangible and intangible results expected from each activity

Monitoring System (Are we performing?)

SITUATION ANALYSIS

The situation analysis examines the relevant external and internal environment. It includes a historical summary, an evaluation of previous marketing efforts, an analysis of the present situation, and an assessment of future trends.

Identifying and assessing threats and opportunities is the purpose of a situation analysis. A forecast of year-end position, which assumes that present conditions continue, can be constructed based on the situation analysis. This momentum forecast is then compared with the desired year-end position and also with the gaps between the forecast and the desired position identified.

MARKETING STRATEGY

As discussed earlier, strategy specifies the means by which the marketing goals are to be achieved. It is the core of the marketing plan.

Positioning is a fundamental statement of what the organization and its products represent to chosen market segments. In brief, the first step in positioning is defining the target segments. Next is setting the organization's competitive stance, which is the degree to which its products will be similar or different in each of the target segments. Depending on the segment and the competition, the most profitable competitive stance can vary considerably. The final step in positioning is to establish the usage incentive, that is, the primary benefits to be offered to current and potential users in each segment. The positioning strategy is vital not only for reaching consumers, but also because it provides a focus for management efforts and ultimately channels the efforts of the entire marketing organization.

The *marketing mix* is a convenient way of summarizing a set of activities that support the marketing goals of the organization. Given the target market and competitive stance, the manager must ensure that the products offered will serve customer needs; the price is appropriate; the products are distributed so that consumers in the target segments can easily purchase them; and communication with the target segment is efficient and effective.

Because the marketing mix activities are the most visible, many people think that that's all there is to marketing. In fact, some people think advertising is synonymous with marketing. On the contrary, advertising is only one of several communication activities, which are themselves only one element in the marketing mix, and the marketing mix is only one part of marketing.

A marketing plan should include *contingency strategies*. Since it is difficult to predict the future precisely, the manager should anticipate and be prepared for major surprises. Having well-thought-out, timely contingency strategies can provide a competitive advantage, especially in a crisis situation.

MARKETING BUDGET

For each element in the plan, the resources required to operate at different levels and the results at these different levels should be determined and evaluated. Trade-offs must often be made and interrelationships among marketing elements need to be considered.

MARKETING ACTION PLAN

The marketing action plan is a detailed breakdown of the activities necessary to achieve each of the goals. Planning without implementation is worth little; much effort in planning is wasted because of inadequate execution, as is discussed more fully in the next section.

MONITORING SYSTEMS

The marketing plan and its action implications serve as the basis for a firm's monitoring system. Significant deviations from the marketing plan and unanticipated events may require management to make adjustments to the original plan, or substitute a contingency strategy.

IMPLEMENTING MARKET PLANS

Meaningful implementation requires a marketing orientation throughout the company, starting with the chief executive officer. Managers at all levels in each function must understand what marketing is and how it can contribute to the organization. Employees must be service-oriented and be prepared to act as if they were users instead of providers of the product. Often organizations seem not to be marketing oriented at all. This, however, can be an illusion—the marketers and the production people may simply not be speaking the same language. In such a case, the marketing manager has to communicate in terms that are meaningful—and not threatening—to other areas in the firm. Sometimes, however, the organization just isn't marketing oriented. The marketer's task in this case is to market marketing to his or her colleagues.

Once market sensitivity has been achieved, maintaining such an orientation is a continuous process. Long-run vitality of a company requires responsiveness to change and maintenance of the external perspective that market-focused management brings.

Marketing is a demanding discipline; even successful organizations face the danger of slipping back into a product or inward-looking orientation. Executives must constantly be on the lookout for indications of product-oriented management. Not tailoring marketing strategies to meet segment needs and seeing the product as inherently desirable for the target market may cause the organization to blame lack of consumer interest in the offering on ignorance or lack of motivation. Consequently, management places too much emphasis on communication strategies, and uses research, not to understand consumer needs, but to confirm management beliefs. Similarly, generic competition is largely ignored in a product-oriented firm. Successful implementation requires that a business maintain a market orientation at all levels and throughout all functional and management areas that interact directly or indirectly with consumers.

GOOD PRACTICE IN MARKETING

There are no magic formulas for good practice in marketing or sure-fire routes to success. But there are some areas that need to be emphasized, including, as just discussed, consumer orientation throughout the firm and a supportive relationship based on mutual trust and respect among the functional areas.

Particularly important in the successful execution of marketing strategies is establishing a clear, powerful, shared theme, a vision of what the company does. For example, a company may emphasize customer service so that no consumer problem is too small to be disregarded. Products are to be highly reliable, and virtually instantaneous service is provided nation-wide, 24 hours a day, every day of the week. All personnel then know that customer satisfaction comes first in decision making.

Success also requires a high degree of competence in carrying out the marketing mix functions—advertising, pricing, and distributing the product. Often a company will have one or a few selected functions in which it excels. One consumer-goods firm, for example, dominates its markets through its skills in obtaining display space in stores for its heavily advertised branded products.

In addition to skills in the marketing-mix functions themselves, there needs to be a program to co-ordinate the functions. In other words, management must make sure the elements operate as an integrated marketing mix, not as individual components. For example, one organization's mail order campaign to sell Christmas gifts was enormously successful in generating orders, but produced huge embarrassment when stocks were exhausted early in the campaign, because of someone's failure to ensure access to adequate supplies.

Good implementation requires the development of a monitoring system to measure and control the results of marketing activities. The marketing plan can be the basis of a management-control system. An action plan can detail the specific activities that need to be carried out and list responsibilities and targets, by name or functional area. By monitoring against the targets on a continuing basis, usually monthly or quarterly, management has time to make changes before the situation deteriorates to a crisis. It is usually easy for managers to get information to keep track of how well they are doing. Nevertheless, many marketing departments do not have reliable, understandable monitoring mechanisms. The marketing strategy may set the direction and excellent execution may carry the organization along, but a reliable, timely monitoring and control system is needed to make sure the program is on the right path.

SUMMARY

Strategy at all levels of the organization is the means of guiding management action and resource allocation. It is rooted in a clearly articulated mission and a well-defined set of objectives. For long-run profitability, planning is needed to help the organization overcome the vagaries of the immediate environment and do more than just react to competitive initiatives. A well-conceived, creative marketing plan that recognizes the capabilities and limitations of the organization and environmental threats and opportunities is a critical tool for successful marketing management. Excellence in marketing requires a marketing orientation throughout the firm and commitment to success in implementing programs.

47 ARCTIC POWER

Gordon H. G. McDougall
Douglas Snetsinger

"We've got some important decisions to make on Arctic Power for 1988," said Linda Barton, Senior Product Manager for the brand. "As I see it, we can continue to develop our strong markets in Quebec, the Maritimes, and British Columbia or we can try to build market share in the rest of Canada." Ms. Barton was discussing the future of Arctic Power, one of Colgate-Palmolive Canada's leading laundry detergents, with Gary Parsons, the Assistant Product Manager on the brand.

"Not only do we have to consider our strategic direction," replied Mr. Parsons, "but we also have to think about our positioning strategy for Arctic Power. I'm for running the Quebec approach in all our markets." Mr. Parsons was referring to the Quebec advertising campaign which positioned Arctic Power as the superior detergent for cold water cleaning.

"I'm not sure," said Ms. Barton. "We're making great progress with our current advertising in British Columbia. It might be more effective outside of Quebec. Remember, cold water washing is a newer concept for the western provinces. We have to overcome that obstacle before we can get people to buy Arctic Power. Let's go over the data again, then make our decisions."

THE COMPANY

Colgate-Palmolive Canada is a wholly-owned subsidiary of Colgate-Palmolive, a large multinational with divisions in 58 countries. World-wide company sales in 1986 were $4.9 billion with profits of $178 million. The Canadian subsidiary sales exceeded $250 million each year. Colgate-Palmolive Canada (CPC) manufactures a range of household, health, and personal care products. Among CPC's major brands are ABC, Arctic Power and Fab (laundry detergents), Palmolive (dishwashing liquid), Ajax (cleanser), Irish Spring (bar soap), Ultra Brite and Colgate (toothpastes), Halo (shampoo), and Baggies (food wrap).

Under the product management system at CPC, product managers are assigned responsibility for specific brands, like Arctic Power. Their overall goals are to increase the sales and profitability of their brand. To meet these goals, the product manager supervises all marketing functions including planning, advertising, selling, promotion, and market research. In planning and executing programs for a brand the product manager usually is assigned an assistant product manager, and they work closely together to accomplish the brand goals.

Prior to the late 1970s CPC essentially followed the strategy of nationally supporting most of its brands. The result was the CPC was spread too thin with too many brands. There were insufficient resources to properly promote and develop all of the CPC line, and profits and market share were less than satisfactory. Beginning in the late 1970s and continuing to the early 1980s the Canadian division altered its strategy. An extensive review of the entire product line was conducted, and CPC moved to what was referred to as a regional brand strategy. Where a brand had regional strength, resources were focused on that area with the objective of building a strong and profitable brand in that region. For example Arctic Power had a relatively strong market share in Quebec and the Maritimes where the proportion of consumers using cold wqter to wash clothes was considerably higher than the national average. Promotional support was withdrawn from the rest of Canada and those resources were focused on Quebec and the Maritimes. Arctic Power was still distributed nationally but by the end of 1981, national market share was 4% consisting of an 11% share in Quebec, a 5% share in the Maritimes, and a 2% share in the rest of Canada. Over the next four years, marketing efforts were concentrated primarily on Quebec, and to a lesser extent the Maritimes. This approach worked well for Arctic Power. By the end of 1985, Arctic Power's national share had increased to 6.4%, share in Quebec had risen to 18%, share in the Maritimes was 6%, and less than 2% in the rest of Canada. With the increase in sales and profitability, the decision was made to target Alberta and British Columbia for 1986. The results of these efforts exceeded expectations in British Columbia but were less than satisfactory in Alberta.

THE LAUNDRY DETERGENT MARKET

The laundry detergent market was mature with unit sales increasing by approximately 1% annually and dollar sales increasing by about 5% each year. (Exhibit 1). Three large consumer packaged goods companies, Procter and Gamble, Lever Detergents, and CPC dominated the market. All three were subsidiaries of multinational firms and sold a wide range of household and personal care products in Canada. Procter and Gamble Canada had annual sales exceeding $1 billion, and its major brands included Crest (toothpaste), Ivory and Zest (bar soaps), Secret (deodorant), Pampers and Luvs (disposable diapers), and Head & Shoulders (shampoo). P&G held a 44% share of the laundry detergent market in 1986, due primarily to the large share (34%) held by Tide, the leading brand in Canada.

Lever Detergents with annual Canadian sales in excess of $400 million operated primarily in the detergent, soap and toiletries categories. Major brands included Sunlight (dishwasher detergent), Close-up (toothpaste), and Dove and Lux (bar soaps). Lever held a 24% share of the laundry detergent market, and its leading brand was Sunlight with a 13% share.

CPC was the only one of the three companies to gain market share in the laundry detergent market between 1983 and 1986. In 1986, CPC's total share was 23%, up from 16% in 1983. ABC, a value brand from CPC positioned to attract consumers interested in "value for less money," more than doubled its share between 1983 and 1986 and was the second leading brand with a 14% share.

Exhibit 1

LAUNDRY DETERGENT MARKET—MARKET SHARES (PERCENTAGES)

	1983	1984	1985	1986
Colgate				
ABC	6.0	9.8	11.8	13.9
Arctic Power	4.7	5.6	6.4	6.5
Fab	2.1	1.3	1.6	1.4
Punch	2.0	.7	.4	.3
Dynamo	1.0	.8	.6	.5
Total Colgate	15.8	18.2	20.8	22.6
Procter and Gamble				
Tide	34.1	35.1	32.6	34.1
Oxydol	4.9	4.2	4.0	3.3
Bold	4.8	4.2	3.2	2.3
Other P&G brands	4.7	4.8	4.4	4.3
Total P&G	48.5	48.3	44.2	44.0
Lever				
Sunlight	13.9	12.2	14.2	13.4
All	4.1	3.7	3.8	3.2
Surf	2.6	2.6	2.7	2.2
Wisk	3.8	4.1	4.1	4.4
Other Lever brands	.9	.8	.6	.4
Total Lever	25.3	23.4	25.4	23.6
All other brands	10.4	10.1	9.6	9.8
Grand total	100.0	100.0	100.0	100.0
Total Market				
Tonnes (000s)	171.9	171.9	173.6	175.3
(% change)	2.0	0.0	1.0	1.0
Factory sales (000,000s)	$265.8	$279.1	$288.5	$304.7
(% change)	6.2	5.0	3.0	6.0

Source: Company records

COMPETITIVE RIVALRY

Intense competitive activity was a way of life in the laundry detergent business. Not only did the three major firms have talented and experienced marketers, but they competed in a low-growth market where increased sales could be achieved only by taking share from competitive brands. A difficult task facing any product manager in this business was to identify the marketing mix that would maximize share while maintaining or increasing brand profitability—a task that had both long-term and short-term implications. In the long term, competitors strove for permanent share gains by building a solid franchise of loyal users based on a quality product and a strong brand image or position. These positioning strategies were primarily executed through product formulation and advertising campaigns. However, companies also competed through consumer and trade promotions (for example, coupons, feature specials in newspaper ads), tactics that were more short term in nature. Trade and consumer promotions were critical to maintain prominent shelf display and to attract competititors' customers. In virtually every week of the year, at least one brand of detergent would be "on special" in any given supermarket. The product manager's task was to find the best balance between these elements in making brand decisions.

Reformulating brands, the changing of the brand ingredients, was a frequent activity in the laundry detergent business. Reformulating a brand involved altering the amount and kinds of active chemical ingredients in the detergents. These active ingredients cleaned the clothes. Each of these cleaning ingredients was efficacious for particular cleaning tasks. Some of these ingredients were good for cleaning clay and mud from cotton and other natural fibres, while others would clean oily soils from polyesters, and yet others were good for other cleaning problems. Most detergents were formulated with a variety of active ingredients to clean in a wide range of conditions. As well, bleaches, fabric softeners, and fragrances could be included.

Thus laundry detergents contained different *levels* and *mixes* of active ingredients. The major decision was the *amounts* of active ingredients that would be used in a particular brand. In simple terms, the greater the proportion of active ingredients, the better the detergent was at cleaning clothes. However, all detergents would get clothes clean. For example, in a recent test of 42 laundry detergents, a consumer magazine concluded, "Yes, some detergents get clothes whiter and brighter than others—but the scale is clean to cleanest, not dirty to clean."

The Canadian brands of laundry detergent contained various amounts of active ingredients. As shown in the following table, Tide and Arctic Power had more active ingredients than any other brand.

Level of Active Ingredients of Laundry Detergents*

1	2	3	4	5
Some private labels	Bold 3 Oxydol Surf All	ABC Fab Cheer 2 Sunlight	—	Arctic Power Tide

* The scale of active ingredients increases from 1 to 5.

In fact, Tide and Arctic Power were equivalent brands in terms of the level of active ingredients. These two, referred to as the "Cadillacs" of detergents, had considerably higher levels of active ingredients than all other detergents. While the actual *mix* of active ingredients differed between the two brands (with Arctic Power having a greater mix of ingredients that were more suited to cold water washing), the cleaning power of Tide and Arctic Power was equal.

As the amount of active ingredients in a brand increased, so did the cost. Manufacturers were constantly facing the trade-off between cost and level of active ingredients. At times they had the opportunity to reduce unit costs by switching one type of active ingredient (a basic chemical) for another, depending on the relative costs of the ingredients. In this way, the level of ingredients remained the same, only the mixture changed. Manufacturers changed the physical ingredients of a brand in order to achieve an efficient per unit cost, to provide a basis for repositioning or restaging the brand, and to continue to deliver better consumer value.

Maintaining or increasing share through repositioning or other means was critical because of the profits involved. One share point was worth approximately $3 million in factory sales, and the cost and profit structures of the leading brands were similar. While some economies of scale accrued to the largest brands, the average cost of goods sold was estimated at 54% of sales, leaving a gross profit of 46%. Marketing expenditures included trade promotions (16%), consumer promotions (5%), and advertising expenditures (5%), leaving a contribution margin of 18%. Not included in these estimates were management overheads and expenses (for example, product management salaries, market research expenses, sales salaries, and factory overheads), which were primarily fixed. In some instances, lower share brands were likely to spend higher amounts on trade promotions to achieve their marketing objectives.

One indication of competitive activity was reflected in advertising expenditures between 1982 and 1986. Total category advertising increased by 12% to $14.4 million (Exhibit 2). As well, substantial increases in trade promotions had occurred during that period. While actual expenditure data was not available, some managers felt that twice as much was being spent on trade promotions as on advertising. For example, in Montreal over a nine-month period in 1986, Tide was featured in weekly supermarket advertisements 80 times and Arctic Power 60 times. Typically, the advertisement cost for the feature was shared by the manufacturer and the retailer. At times during 1986, consumers could have purchased Arctic Power or Tide for $3.49 (regular price $5.79). There was also a strong indication that the frequency and size of price specials on detergents was increasing. The average retail price of laundry detergents (based on the volume sold of all detergents at regular and special

Exhibit 2

SHARE OF NATIONAL MEDIA EXPENDITURES (1982 TO 1986)

			Percentages		
	1982	1983	1984	1985	1986
ABC	6.4	8.9	12.3	14.0	13.6
Arctic Power	6.1	6.1	6.7	7.2	9.3
Tide	21.0	17.8	19.1	16.4	29.7
Oxydol	5.1	4.5	5.9	6.6	6.4
Sunlight	14.1	10.8	10.5	9.1	11.3
All	10.3	5.5	6.9	7.7	4.0
Wisk	9.9	12.8	10.3	10.4	14.6
All other brands	27.1	33.6	28.3	28.6	12.1
Total	100.0	100.0	100.0	100.0	100.0
Total spending (000s)	$12,909	$13,338	$14,420	$13,718	$14,429
Percentage change	29.2	3.3	8.1	−4.9	5.2

Source: Company records

prices) had increased by only 4% in the last three years, whereas cost of goods sold had increased by 15% during the same period.

One final observation was warranted. Between 1983 and 1986, the four leading brands—Tide, ABC, Sunlight and Arctic Power—had increased their share from 58.7% to 67.9% of the total market. The three manufacturers appeared to be focusing their efforts primarily on their leading brands and letting the lesser brands decline in share.

Positioning Strategies

While positioning strategies were executed through all aspects of the marketing mix, they were most clearly seen in the advertising execution.

Tide was the dominant brand in share of market and share of media expenditures. Tide's strategy was to sustain this dominance through positioning the brand as superior to any other brand on generic cleaning benefits. In 1986, four national and four regional commercials were aired to support this strategy. These commercials conveyed that Tide provided the benefits of being the most effective detergent for "tough" situations, such as for ground-in dirt, stains, and bad odours. Tide also aired copy in Quebec claiming effectiveness in all temperatures. Tide's copy was usually developed around a "slice of life" or testimonial format.

Other brands in the market faced the situation of going head-to-head with Tide's position or competing on a benefit Tide did not claim. Most had chosen the latter route. CPC's ABC brand had made strong gains in the past four years, moving from sixth to second place in market share based on its value position. ABC was positioned as the low-priced, good quality, cleaning detergent. Recent copy for ABC utilized a demonstration format where the shirts for twins were as clean when washed in ABC versus a leading higher priced detergent with the statement: "Why pay more, I can't see the difference." Sunlight, a Lever brand, had for several years attempted to compete directly with Tide and build its consumer franchise based on efficacy and lemon-scented freshness. Advertising execution had been of the upbeat, upscale lifestyle approach and less of the straightforward problem solution or straight-talking approaches seen in other detergent advertising. More recently, Sunlight had been moving towards ABC's value position while retaining the lemon freshness heritage. Sunlight was positioned in 1986 as the detergent which gave a very clean fresh wash at a sensible price. The final brand which attempted to compete for the value position was All. The advertising for All also claimed that the brand particularly whitens white clothes and gives them a pleasant fragrance.

Arctic Power had been positioned as the superior cleaning laundry detergent, especially formulated for cold water washing. For the eastern market, Arctic Power advertising had utilized a humorous background to communicate brand superiority and its efficacy in cold water. For the western market a nontraditional, upbeat execution was used to develop the cold water market.

Wisk, which had received much attention for its "ring around the collar" advertising, competed directly with Tide on generic cleaning qualities and provided the additional benefit of a liquid formulation. Tide Liquid was introduced in 1985, but received little advertising support in 1986.

Fab and Bold 3 competed for the "softergents" market. Both products, which had fabric softeners in the formulation, were positioned to clean effectively while softening clothes and reducing static cling. Another detergent with laundry product additives was Oxydol, which was formulated with a mild bleach. Oxydol was positioned as the detergent that kept colours bright while whitening whites.

The other two nationally advertised brands were Cheer 2 and Ivory Snow. Cheer 2 was positioned as the detergent that got clothes clean and fresh. Ivory Snow, which was a soap and not a detergent, was positioned as the laundry cleaning product for infants' clothes which provided superior softness and comfort.

The Cold Water Market

Every February, CPC commissioned an extensive market research study to identify trends in the laundry detergent market. Referred to as the tracking study, its findings were based on approximately 1800 personal interviews with female heads-of-households across Canada each year. Among the wealth of data provided by the tracking study was information on cold water usage in Canada. Regular cold water usage was growing in Canada and, by 1986, 29% of households were classified as regular cold water users (Exhibit 3). Due to cultural and marketing differences, Quebec (55%) and the Maritimes (33%) had more cold water users than the national average. A further 25% of all Canadian households occasionally (one to four times out of ten) used cold water for washing.

For households that washed occasionally or regularly with cold water, the most important benefits of using cold water fell into two broad categories (Exhibit 4). First, it was easier on or better for clothes in that cold water stopped shrinkage, prevented colours from running, let colours stay bright, and was easier on clothes. Second, it was more economical in that it saved energy, was cheaper, saved hot water, and saved electricity. Households in Quebec and the Maritimes mentioned the "economy" benefits more frequently, whereas households in the rest of Canada mentioned the "easier/better" benefit more often.

Exhibit 3
PROPORTION OF HOUSEHOLDS WASHING WITH COLD WATER (1981 TO 1986)

	Percentages					
	1981	1982	1983	1984	1985	1986
National	20*	22	26	26	26	29
Maritimes	23	25	32	40	32	33
Quebec	35	41	49	48	53	55
Ontario	14	13	18	16	11	17
Prairies	12	12	13	11	10	17
British Columbia	13	19	20	17	22	21

Source: Tracking study

* 20% of respondents did 5 or more out of 10 washloads in cool or cold water.

N ≃ 1800

Exhibit 4
MOST IMPORTANT BENEFIT OF COLD WATER WASHING, 1986

Reason	National	Maritimes	Quebec	Ontario	Man./Sask.	Alta.	B.C.
• Stops shrinkage	22.7*	19.4	5.2	32.7	35.4	35.4	30.2
• Saves energy	16.5	12.5	32.1	8.2	2.1	9.9	12.9
• Prevents colours from running	11.6	17.4	0.0	21.8	21.3	9.9	2.9
• Cheaper	11.1	19.4	10.4	10.2	2.8	9.3	16.5
• Saves hot water	9.7	9.7	15.5	6.8	11.3	3.1	3.6
• Colours stay bright	8.8	4.2	7.8	11.6	9.2	6.8	7.9
• Saves on electricity	8.7	19.4	0.5	8.2	5.7	16.1	25.9
• Easier on clothes	8.5	11.1	6.7	8.8	10.6	13.7	5.0

Source: Tracking study

* When asked what they felt was the most important benefit of cold water washing, 22.7% of all respondents said, "it stops shrinking." Sample included all households that washed one or more times out of last ten washes in cold water.

N = 956

Only the eight most frequent responses are reported.

Arctic Power

Having achieved reasonable success in eastern Canada and having returned the brand to profitability, Linda Barton, product manager for Arctic Power, decided, for 1986, to increase the brand's share in Alberta and British Columbia. The brand plan is reported below.

THE 1986 BRAND PLAN FOR ARCTIC POWER

Objectives

Arctic Power's overall objective is to continue profit development by maintaining modest unit-volume growth in Quebec and the Maritimes while developing the Alberta and British Columbia regions.

Long Term (by 1996) The long-term objective is to become the number three brand in the category with market share of 12%. Arctic Power will continue to deliver a minimum 18% contribution margin. This will require

1. maintenance of effective creative/media support,
2. superior display prominence particularly in the key Quebec market,
3. continued investigation of development opportunities, and
4. cost of goods savings programs where possible.

Short Term The short-term objective is to sustain unit growth while building cold water washing dominance. This will require current user reinforcement and continued conversion of warm water users. Specifically, in fiscal 1986, Arctic

Power will achieve a market share of 6.5% on factory sales of $22 million and a contribution margin of 18%. Regional share objectives are Maritimes—6.3%, Quebec—17.2%, Alberta—5%, and British Columbia—5%.

Marketing Strategy

Arctic Power will be positioned as the most effective laundry detergent which is especially formulated for cold water washing. The primary target for Arctic Power is women 18 to 49 and skewed towards the 25 to 34 segment. The secondary market is all adults.

Arctic Power will defend its franchise by allocating regional effort commensurate with brand development in order to maintain current users. In line with the western expansion strategy, support will be directed to Alberta and British Columbia in promoting the acceptance of cold water washing in those areas and thereby broadening the appeal among occasional and non-users of Arctic Power.

Media Strategy

The media strategy objective is to achieve high levels of message registration against the target group, through high message continuity and frequency/reach. Media spending allocation for regional television will be 75% on brand maintenance and 25% on investment for brand and cold water market development. Arctic Power will retain its number five share of media expenditure position nationally while being the number three detergent advertiser in Quebec.

		TV Spending	GRPs* per Week
1985	Plan	$1,010,000	92
	Actual	$ 990,000	88
1986	Plan	$1,350,000	95

* GRP (Gross Rating Points) is a measurement of advertising impact derived by multiplying the number of persons exposed to an advertisement by the average number of exposures per person.

Arctic Power's 1986 media spending of $1.35 million is a 36% increase over 1985. This returns Arctic Power to its reach objective of 90% in Quebec, five points ahead of a year ago. In addition, two new television markets have been added with enhanced support in British Columbia and Alberta. Reach objectives will be achieved by skewing more of Arctic Power's spending into efficient daytime spots which cost less than night network and are more flexible in light of regional reach objectives.

Scheduling will maintain flighting[1] established in 1985 with concentrations at peak dealing time representing 40 weeks on-air in the east and 32 weeks in the west.

[1] Periodic waves of advertising, separated by periods of low activity (as opposed to continuous advertising).

Copy Strategy: Quebec/Maritimes

The creative objective is to convince consumers that Arctic Power is the superior detergent for cold water washing. The consumer benefit is that when washing in cold water, Arctic Power will clean clothes and remove stains more effectively than other detergents. The support for this claim is based on the special formulation of Arctic Power. The executional tone will be humorous but with a clear, rational explanation (Exhibit 5).

Copy Strategy: British Columbia/Alberta

The creative objective is to convince consumers that cold water washing is better than hot and to use Arctic Power when washing in cold water. The consumer benefit is that cold water washing reduces shrinkage, colour run and energy costs. The executional tone needs to be distinct from other detergent advertising in order to break through traditional washing attitudes and to do so will be young adult-oriented, light, "cool," and up-beat (Exhibit 6).

Consumer Promotions

The objective of consumer promotions in Quebec and the Maritimes is to increase the rate of use by building frequency of purchase among existing users. The objective in B.C. and Alberta is to increase the rate of trial of Arctic Power. In total $856,000 will be spent on consumer promotions.

Jan. $0.50 In-pack Coupon—to support trade inventory increases and retain current customers in the face of strong competitive activity 400,000 coupons will be placed in all sizes in the Quebec and Maritimes distribution region. The coupon is for 6 L or 12 L sizes and expected redemption is 18% at a cost of $50,000.

April To generate a 17% recent trial of regular-sized boxes of Arctic Power in B.C. and in Alberta a 500 mL saleable sample prepriced at $0.49 will be distributed through food and drug stores. In addition, a $0.50 coupon for the 6 L or 12 L size will be placed on the pack of all samples. The offer will penetrate 44% of households in the region at a total cost of $382,000.

June $0.40 Coupon through Free Standing Insert: to sustain interest and foster trial a $0.40 coupon will be delivered to 30% of homes in Alberta and B.C. The coupon is redeemable on the 3 L size and expected redemption is 4.5% at a cost of $28,000.

April/July Game: Cool-by-the-Pool—Five in-ground pools with patio accessories will be given away through spelling POWER by letters dropped in boxes of Arctic Power. Two letters will be placed in each box through national distribution and will coincide with high trade activity and the period in which the desirability of the prizes is highest at a cost of $184,000.

Exhibit 5
QUEBEC CAMPAIGN

Arctic Power . . . is made to work in cold water . . . some detergents are not . . .

Look . . . Arctic Power

. . . is formulated to release more power and energy in cold water

. . . some detergents are formulated to

. . . work well in hot water

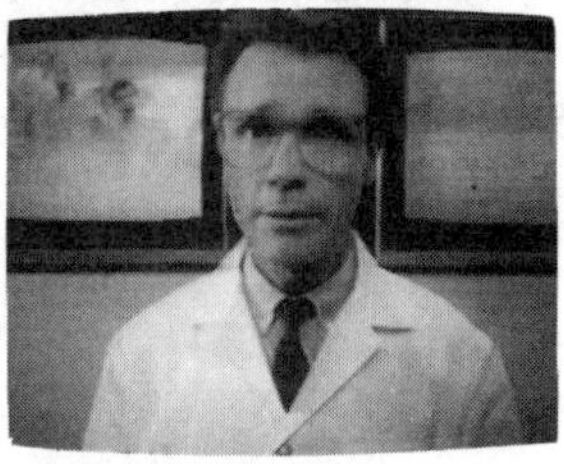

. . . but

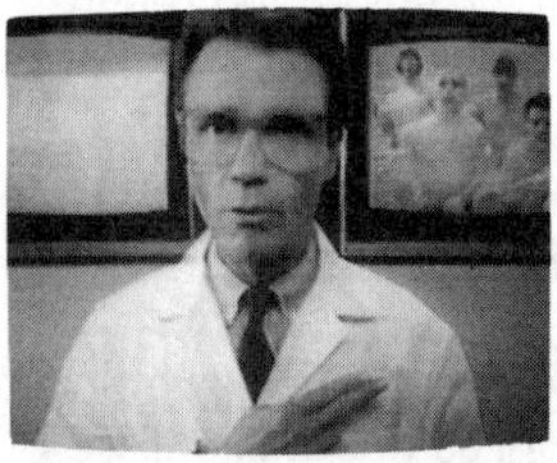

. . . put them in

. . . cold and they start to freeze up

In cold water . . . it makes a difference which detergent you use . . . you want clean like this

. . . and bright like this

Look for a pack like this

. . . and you'll get more power in cold water.

Exhibit 6
WESTERN CAMPAIGN

CLIENT: COLGATE PALMOLIVE
PRODUCT: Arctic Power
TITLE: "Cool It"
LENGTH: 30 Sec. TV

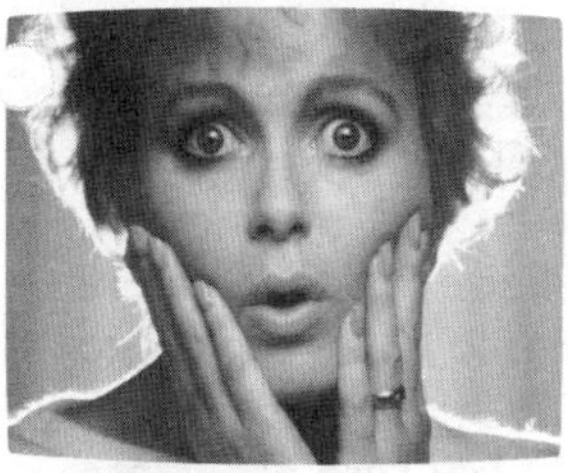

SINGERS: No!

Cool it.
Cool it.

Get some Arctic Power and cool it.

Cold water washing that's the way.

Up to date people save money today . . .

they cool it.
Cool it.

Get some Arctic Power and cool it.

You get less shrink.

You get less run.

And the laundry looks great when you get it all done.

So cool it.
Cool it.

Get some Arctic Power and cool it.

Sept. $0.75 Direct Mail National Coupon Pack (excluding Ontario)—To maximize swing buyer volume (from competition) in Quebec and encourage trial in the West a $0.75 coupon for the 6 L or 12 L size will be mailed to 70% of households in the primary market areas generating a 3% redemption rate at a cost of $212,000.

Trade Promotions

The objectives of the trade promotions are to maintain regular and feature pricing equal to Tide and encourage prominent shelf facing. An advertising feature is expected from each key account during every promotion event run in Quebec and the Maritimes. Distribution for any size is expected to increase to 95%. In the west, maximum effort will be directed at establishing display for the 6 L size and four feature events will be expected from each key account. Distribution should be developed to 71% in B.C. and 56% in Alberta. Average deal size will be 14% off regular price or $5 per 6 L case. In addition, most trade events will include a $1 per case allowance for co-op advertising and merchandising support. The total trade budget is $3.46 million which includes $1 million investment spending in the West. The promotion schedule is shown below.

Arctic Power 1986 Promotional Schedule

Trade Promotions	Jan	Feb	Mar	Apr	May	Jun	Jul	Aug	Sep	Oct	Nov	Dec
Maritimes	X			X		X			X		X	
Quebec	X	X		X		X	X		X		X	X
Alberta/B.C.	X			X		X		X	X			
East $0.50 coupon	X	X										
West sample/ coupon				X								
West $0.40 coupon						X						
National game				X	X	X	X					
National $0.75 coupon									X			

Results of the Western Campaign

In August of 1986, during the middle of the western campaign, a "mini-tracking" study was conducted in the two provinces to monitor the program. The results of the August study were compared with the February study. (Both studies are reported in Exhibit 7.) Market share for Arctic Power was also measured on a bi-monthly basis and the figures are shown below.

The campaign clearly had an impact—brand and advertising awareness had increased, particularly in Alberta (Exhibit 7). Brand trial within the six months had more than doubled in Alberta and was up over 25% in B.C. However, market share had peaked at 2.8% in Alberta and by the end of the year had declined to 1.9%. Market share in B.C. had reached a high of 7.3% and averaged 5.5% for the year.

Arctic Power Market Share

				1986						
	1983	1984	1985	D/J	F/M	A/M	J/J	A/S	O/N	Total 1986
Alberta	0.7	2.3	1.7	1.4	1.1	2.8	2.8	2.4	1.9	2.1
B.C.	3.2	4.0	3.9	4.0	4.0	6.1	6.1	7.3	5.4	5.5

In attempting to explain the different results in the two provinces, Linda Barton and Gary Parsons isolated two factors. First, B.C. had always been a "good" market for Arctic Power with share figures around 4%, whereas Alberta was less than half that amount. Second, there had been a considerable amount of competitive activity in Alberta during the year. Each of the three major firms had increased trade and consumer promotions to maintain existing brand shares.

ARCTIC POWER—1987

The 1987 brand plan for Arctic Power was similar in thrust and expenditure levels to the 1986 plan. Expenditure levels in Alberta were reduced until the full implications of the 1986 campaign could be examined. Market share in 1987 was expected to be 6.7% up marginally from the 6.5% share achieved in 1986 (Exhibit 8).

Each year, every product manager at CPC conducted an extensive brand review. The review for Arctic Power included a detailed competitive analysis of the four leading brands on a regional basis and was based primarily on the tracking study. In July 1987, Linda Barton and Gary Parsons were examining the tracking information which summarized regional information on four critical aspects of the market—brand image (Exhibit 9), brand and advertising awareness (Exhibit 10), brand trial and usage in last six months (Exhibit 11), and market share and share of media expenditures (Exhibit 12). Future decisions for Arctic Power would be based, in large part, on this information.

THE DECISION

Prior to deciding on the strategic direction for Arctic Power, Ms. Barton and Mr. Parsons met to discuss the situation. It was a hot Toronto day in early July 1987. Ms. Barton began the discussion. "I've got some estimates on what our shares are likely to be for 1987. It looks like we'll have a national share of 6.7%, broken down as follows: Maritimes (6.3%), Quebec (18%), Ontario (1%), Manitoba/Saskatchewan (0.1%), Alberta (2%), B.C. (6%).

Exhibit 7
RESULTS OF WESTERN CAMPAIGN

	Prelaunch (February, 1986)		Postlaunch (August, 1986)	
	Alberta	B.C.	Alberta	B.C.
Unaided Brand Awareness[a]				
Brand mentioned total (%)	13.3	20.3	18.1	24.2
Advertising Awareness				
Advertising mentioned (unaided)[b] (%)	1.9	7.9	20.3	11.5
Advertising mentioned (aided)[c] (%)	18.5	27.9	31.4	34.6
Brand Trial				
Ever tried[d] (%)	25.0	43.0	36.3	48.0
Used (last six months)[e] (%)	6.8	15.1	17.1	19.4
Image Measure[f]				
Cleaning and removing dirt	1.0	1.2	1.2	1.5
Removing tough stains	.7	.9	.9	1.4
Being good value for the price	.5	.9	1.0	1.4
Cleaning well in cold water	1.2	1.3	1.7	1.8
Conversion to cold water				
Average number of loads out of 10 washed in cold water	1.8	2.2	2.0	2.3

Source: Tracking study

[a] *Question:* When you think of laundry detergents, what three brands first come to mind? Can you name three more for me? *Brand Mentioned Total* is if the brand was mentioned at all. On average, respondents mentioned 4.5 brands.

[b] *Question:* What brand or brands of laundry detergent have you seen or heard advertised? *Advertising Mentioned (Unaided)* is any mention of brand advertising mentioned.

[c] *Question:* Have you recently seen or heard any advertising for *Brand? Advertising Mentioned (Aided)* is if respondent said yes when asked.

[d] *Question:* Have you ever tried *BRAND?*

[e] *Question:* Have you used *BRAND* in the past six months?

[f] Respondents rated the brand on the four image measures. The rating scale ranged from −5 (doesn't perform well) to +5 (performs well).

Exhibit 8

ARCTIC POWER MARKET SHARE AND TOTAL VOLUME BY REGION (1983–1987E)

Region	1983	1984	Market Share 1985	1986	1987E	1986 Total Volume* (000s litres)
National	4.7	5.6	6.4	6.5	6.7	406,512
Maritimes	5.3	5.7	6.3	6.3	6.3	32,616
Quebec	12.3	13.8	17.7	17.5	18.0	113,796
Ontario	.9	1.1	1.1	.8	1.0	158,508
Manitoba/Saskatchewan	.2	.2	.1	.1	.1	28,440
Alberta	.7	2.3	1.7	2.1	2.0	40,644
British Columbia	3.2	4.0	3.9	5.5	6.0	32,508

Source: Company records
1987E = Estimated
* All laundry detergents

Mr. Parsons responded, "I think our problem in Alberta was all the competitive activity. Under normal conditions we'd have achieved 5% of that market. But the Alberta objective is small when you think about what we could do in our other undeveloped markets. I've been giving it a lot of thought, and we should go national with Arctic Power. We've got a brand that is equal to Tide and we've got to stop keeping it a secret from the rest of Canada. If we can duplicate our success in B.C., we'll turn this market on its ear.

"Wait a minute, Gary," said Ms. Barton. "In 1986 we spent almost $2 million on advertising, consumer and trade promotions in the west. Even though spending returned to normal levels this year, that was a big investment to get the business going, and it will be at least four years before we get that money back. If we go after the national market, you can well expect Tide to fight back with trade spending which will make our share or margin objectives even harder to achieve. On a per capita basis we'd have to spend at least as much in our underdeveloped markets as we spent in the west. We've got a real problem here. Our brand may be as good as Tide, but I don't think we can change a lot of consumers' minds, particularly the loyal Tide users. I hate to say it but for many Canadians, when they think about washing clothes, Tide is the brand they think will clean their clothes better than any other brand. I agree that the size of the undeveloped market warrants another look. But remember, any decision will have to be backed up with a solid analysis and a plan that senior management will buy."

"I know that even if I am right it will be a tough sell," Mr. Parsons replied. "I haven't got it completed yet, but I'm working out the share level we will need to break even if we expanded nationally."

Ms. Barton responded, "Well, when you get that done, we will talk about national expansion again. For the moment we have to resolve this positioning dilemma. I don't like a two-country approach, but it does seem to make sense in this case. I

Exhibit 9

BRAND IMAGES, BY REGION, 1986

Image Measure	National	Maritimes	Quebec	Ontario	Man./Sask.	Alberta	B.C.
Arctic Power							
• Cleaning and removing dirt	1.4	2.0	2.5	0.8	0.4	1.0	1.2
• Removing tough stains	1.1	1.6	1.9	0.7	0.3	0.7	0.9
• Being good value for the price	1.1	1.4	2.6	0.3	0.2	0.5	0.9
• Cleaning well in cold water	1.6	2.1	2.8	1.0	0.4	1.2	1.3
ABC							
• Cleaning . . . dirt	1.0	1.9	0.5	0.9	1.1	1.2	1.6
• Removing . . . stains	0.5	1.1	0.0	0.6	0.8	0.7	0.9
• Being . . . price	1.5	2.4	0.8	1.5	1.3	1.7	2.1
• Cleaning . . . cold water	0.6	1.0	0.1	0.7	0.7	0.7	0.7
Sunlight							
• Cleaning . . . dirt	2.0	1.9	1.8	2.4	1.9	1.6	1.6
• Removing . . . stains	1.6	1.6	1.5	1.9	1.4	1.2	1.2
• Being . . . price	2.0	1.7	1.9	2.4	1.8	1.7	1.5
• Cleaning . . . cold water	1.4	1.1	1.5	1.7	1.2	1.1	0.7
Tide							
• Cleaning . . . dirt	3.4	3.7	3.2	3.6	3.5	3.3	3.2
• Removing . . . stains	3.0	3.1	2.8	3.3	3.0	2.7	2.7
• Being . . . price	3.1	3.1	3.3	3.1	2.8	3.0	2.4
• Cleaning . . . cold water	2.4	2.3	2.6	2.5	2.4	2.3	1.9

Source: Tracking study

Respondents rated each brand on the four image measures. The rating scale ranged from −5 (doesn't perform well) to +5 (performs well).

N = 1816

A difference of 0.2 is likely to be significant in statistical terms.

Exhibit 10
BRAND AND ADVERTISING AWARENESS BY REGION, 1986

	Percentages						
	National	Maritimes	Quebec	Ontario	Man./Sask.	Alberta	B.C.
Unaided Brand Awareness[a]							
1. Brand Mentioned First							
Arctic Power	4.4	7.0	12.5	.0	.0	1.0	2.6
ABC	8.1	18.4	4.6	7.3	4.7	8.4	12.8
Sunlight	9.3	8.4	9.6	9.3	12.0	9.1	7.9
Tide	57.9	55.5	41.9	69.7	63.1	59.7	54.4
2. Brand Mentioned Total							
Arctic Power	23.0	43.5	49.8	5.0	3.0	13.3	20.3
ABC	61.3	82.6	47.9	64.0	56.1	67.5	64.9
Sunlight	58.1	60.2	50.8	65.0	58.5	62.0	46.6
Tide	94.8	95.7	88.8	98.0	97.3	97.4	94.4
Advertising Awareness							
1. Advertising Mentioned (Unaided)[b]							
Arctic Power	7.0	10.7	17.5	.7	.0	1.9	7.9
ABC	25.2	32.8	20.8	27.0	17.3	30.5	24.9
Sunlight	8.6	4.7	5.9	13.0	5.0	6.8	8.2
Tide	44.0	40.1	32.7	55.0	46.2	48.4	35.4
2. Advertising Mentioned (Aided)[c]							
Arctic Power	29.2	38.8	55.1	15.3	5.6	18.5	27.9
ABC	56.1	61.5	55.1	56.0	51.5	60.4	53.4
Sunlight	29.9	20.1	26.4	40.3	21.3	21.1	24.9
Tide	65.3	60.9	54.8	78.0	68.1	65.3	48.4

Source: Tracking study

[a] *Question:* When you think of laundry detergents, what three brands first come to mind? Can you name three for me? *Brand Mentioned First* is the first brand mentioned. *Brand Mentioned Total* is if the brand was mentioned at all. On average, respondents mentioned 4.5 brands.

[b] *Question:* What brand or brands of laundry detergent have you seen or heard advertised? *Advertising Mentioned (Unaided)* is any mention of brand advertising mentioned.

[c] *Question:* Have you recently seen or heard any advertising for *BRAND*? *Advertising Mentioned (Aided)* means respondent said yes when asked.

N = 1816

Exhibit 11

BRAND TRIAL AND USED IN LAST SIX MONTHS, BY REGION, 1986

Brand Trial	National	Maritimes	Quebec	Ontario	Man./Sask.	Alberta	B.C.
1. Ever tried[a]							
Arctic Power	42.4	67.9	75.6	19.7	20.3	25.0	43.0
ABC	60.4	83.9	50.8	60.0	53.5	62.7	67.9
Sunlight	66.3	65.6	59.4	75.0	67.1	58.1	58.7
Tide	93.6	91.0	90.1	97.3	95.0	91.9	92.1
2. Used (last six months)[b]							
Arctic Power	19.4	29.8	46.5	4.3	2.3	6.8	15.1
ABC	37.2	56.2	34.7	32.3	29.2	39.3	47.5
Sunlight	38.3	29.8	38.0	44.3	36.2	36.7	28.5
Tide	68.1	66.6	66.0	73.3	67.8	69.5	54.8

Source: Tracking study

[a] *Question:* Have you ever tried *BRAND?*

[b] *Question:* Have you used *BRAND* in the past six months?

Note: On average, respondents had 1.3 brands of laundry detergents in the home.

N = 1816

Exhibit 12
MARKET SHARE AND SHARE OF MEDIA EXPENDITURES, BY REGION, 1986

	Percentages						
	National	Maritimes	Quebec	Ontario	Man./Sask.	Alberta	B.C.
Market Share							
Arctic Power	6.5	6.3	17.5	.8	.1	2.1	5.5
ABC	13.9	27.8	8.6	13.8	11.6	16.1	21.5
Sunlight	13.4	7.7	12.1	16.4	14.2	10.4	11.3
Tide	34.1	24.5	28.3	39.3	40.0	36.9	28.5
All other brands	32.1	33.7	33.5	29.7	34.1	34.5	33.2
Total	100.0	100.0	100.0	100.0	100.0	100.0	100.0
Share of Media Expenditures[a]							
Arctic Power	9.3	13.1	16.1	.5	1.4	16.0	13.1
ABC	13.6	14.7	9.1	18.4	17.3	12.1	12.1
Sunlight	11.3	11.1	11.1	12.6	10.2	10.1	9.8
Tide	29.7	27.8	25.1	33.1	38.1	30.2	28.7
All other brands	36.1	33.3	38.6	35.4	33.0	31.6	36.3
Total	100.0	100.0	100.0	100.0	100.0	100.0	100.0
Total $ ('000)	14,429	695	4,915	4,758	928	1,646	1,487

Source: Company records

[a] The total amount of advertising spent by all brands was determined. The amount spent by each brand as a percentage of total spending was calculated.

think we might still want to focus on the brand in the east and continue to develop the cold water washing market in the west.''

Mr. Parsons would have preferred to continue the discussion of national expansion but realized he would have to do some work and at least produce the share estimate before he raised the subject again and so replied, ''I agree that Canada is not one homogeneous market, but that perspective can be taken to extremes. I worry that all of this data we get on the regional markets is getting in the way of good marketing judgement. I prefer a unified strategy and the Quebec campaign has a proven track record.''

''Let's go over the data again, then start making our decisions,'' Ms. Barton concluded. ''Remember, our goal is to develop a solid brand plan for 1988 for Arctic Power.''

48 TURNER LUBRICANTS AND SUPPLIES

Peter Gilmour

In July 1989, Brian Harper, president of Turner Lubricants and Supplies, asked the newly appointed marketing manager, Jim McCloughin, to examine Turner's marketing effort to industrial customers and to propose strategies for improving sales and sales force productivity. Turner had numerous small (less than $1,000 per annum) accounts including a large number of inactive accounts. Currently these accounts were, to varying limited degrees, serviced by visits from sales representatives, telephone calls, and, intermittently, by direct mail.

Jim's immediate thoughts were that probably all that was needed was a certain amount of pruning of small unprofitable accounts to reduce selling costs, and to help the sales force develop a more focused selling emphasis. Jim had heard that this approach had been tried with some success by one of Turner's competitors—Canwest Oil.

However, after pondering the problem for several days, Jim began to have doubts. Firstly, although Turner had many small-account customers, Jim believed that some contained unrealized potential business for Turner. Secondly, some of these small accounts could well become big accounts in several years. Thirdly, perhaps there were some new ways these small accounts could be adequately serviced more efficiently.

Jim decided that he needed more information about Turner's marketing practices, customer purchasing patterns, and new selling techniques before he could propose a new strategy to Mr. Harper.

THE COMPANY

Turner, a lubricant blending, packing, and wholesaling company, supplied lubricants and related products to most industries across Canada. Turner had a high quality image and a reputation as a leader in lubricant technology. This reputation was complemented by its premium pricing strategy.

Turner divided its market into three major segments, each serviced by one of three marketing divisions: reseller, where products were sold through resale outlets including distributors; industrial, where products were sold directly to industrial consumers; and new ventures, where the products were non-oil agency lines marketed to Turner's non-traditional markets, for example, the hospitality industry.

THE LUBRICANT INDUSTRY

The industry was highly concentrated with sales dominated by six companies (83% of sales in 1988). Except for Turner, which was a specialist lubricants company, the principal competitors were the major oil companies. Additionally, a large number of smaller companies serviced specific product and user areas.

The Canadian lubricants market was at a mature stage with projected volume growth of only 0.9% for 1989 from a level of between 440 to 450 million litres in 1988. Total lubricant sales in 1988 were approximately $850 million. Although there were large price increases in early 1989 as a result of additional federal and provincial taxes, demand for lubricants was consistent; consumption had declined only marginally at the start of the year.

For the user, lubricants were a small percentage of their costs as they represented only a minor portion of total maintenance and operating costs. As products were difficult to differentiate, with no observable differences in appearance and performance, users could easily switch from one brand to another.

Companies tried to differentiate products on the basis of quality and brand image. As a result, the industry was characterized by considerable cost competition with decreasing margins, although higher margins were obtained for specialty and premium products.

COMPETITOR SELLING PRACTICES—INDUSTRIAL MARKETS

Turner's principal competitors (Canwest, Collins, Bowen, Lomtil, and Martin), in contrast with Turner, did not use a direct sales force to market to industrial user groups. Except for the very large accounts, they relied almost entirely on their distributors. Smaller specialist lubricant companies such as Varsone had their own dedicated direct sales force like Turner. The low market share held by Turner in the industrial segment was mainly attributed to the ability of the major oil companies to offer combined fuel/lubricant packages and aggressive pricing. The major competitors were able to secure many of the larger contracts through more specific attention. Competitors generally paid little attention to small customers who were either serviced by distributors or who purchased from retail outlets.

TURNER'S MARKETING STRATEGIES

Turner's broad mission was to remain a producer and marketer of high-quality, differentiated lubricants and to use that base to pursue growth through new investments by exploiting their existing skills and resources. The overall company strategy was to differentiate its products through product superiority in quality and performance, which was achieved by emphasizing research and development. This was supported by an extensive marketing effort.

The company's product range was characterized by breadth and depth; there were 450 separate lubricant products, each available in up to six containers to suit the full requirements of most users in all segments of the lubricants market. However, Turner was very dependent on just three automotive lubricant products that made up 43% of its sales. In 1988, lubricant products constituted some 92% of Turner's sales. The company was also an agent for several nonlubricant lines including disposable wipers, dispensing equipment, and oil absorbants. Although most of the firm's marketing effort was on the premium products, Turner had product lines for all price and quality segments in the market.

In 1988, the company spent 5% of sales on advertising and promotions. Television advertising was the major media used for the retail market. Newspapers and trade magazines were used mainly for targeting the industrial and reseller markets. Sponsorships of car racing and community safety campaigns were also used, mainly for promoting retailer products. Promotions, including gifts and prizes, were used on specific industry groups such as the transport industry.

Turner products were sold to end users through a combination of distributors and retailers and via direct sales. The company divided its marketing efforts into two broad categories: resellers (distributors and retailers) and industrial (direct sales). Conflict between the company and its resellers was generally avoided because of differing buying practices as direct sales were aimed at industrial markets. However, the company and its distributors did compete in a few segments for some of the smaller-volume purchasers of lubricants. The company had a total of 195 people in sales and marketing throughout Canada, of whom 130 were sales representatives. Most sales representatives focused on broad industry segments (for example, chemicals, textile manufacturing) except for most rural representatives who handled geographic areas (for example, northern Manitoba). Of the 130 sales representatives, 46 were allocated in the industrial segment, 78 to the reseller segment, and 6 to new ventures.

While the sales force was largely allocated according to industry segmentation, many of the products were common to all segments. Turner's accounts were serviced by the sales representatives at a calling frequency generally proportional to account size.

Turner's Existing Industrial Customers

Turner's industrial segments, the subject of Jim's investigations, had approximately 23,000 accounts with projected 1989 sales of approximately $33 million (Exhibit 1). Included in the industrial segments were 4,900 accounts classified as Miscellaneous Territory (Unserviced) accounts. Although this group received mailings (brochures, promotional material, and so on) it was not serviced by a representative. Sales to this group were initiated by the customer. The policy was that customers were placed into the Miscellaneous Territory group if their annual purchases were under $300, and if there did not appear to be potential for an increase in the foreseeable future. Exhibit 2 provides an analysis of annual sales by size of Miscellaneous Territory accounts. Jim confirmed from this analysis that the majority of these accounts had grown dramatically above $300 per year in purchases. Indeed, in the "over $750" accounts, he found 294 accounts that were forecasted to purchase over $370,000 in total in 1989.

Jim drew two conclusions from the data in Exhibit 2:

1. growth potential existed in Miscellaneous Territory and other poorly serviced small-customer groups, and
2. this potential was very difficult to identify.

Exhibit 1

TURNER INDUSTRIAL SEGMENTS—ANALYSIS OF SALES AND CONTRIBUTION BY ANNUAL SALES

	$ Annual Sales								
	Inactive	0–300	300–500	500–750	750–1,000	1,000–2,000	2,000–4,000	4,000+	Total
Calls per account[1]	0	1	1	2	3	5	8	12	
Estimated cost per call[2]	$5	$50	$50	$60	$70	$80	$90	$100	
No. of accounts	11,029	3,830	1,952	875	1,172	1,704	1,262	1,768	23,592
Sales ($000)	—	396	641	501	824	2,071	3,108	25,948	33,489
Contribution ($000)	—	158	256	200	329	828	1,243	10,379	13,393
Less selling and distribution ($000)	55	192	98	105	246	681	908	2,121	4,406
Contribution ($000)	(55)	(34)	158	95	83	147	335	8,258	8,987

[1] Estimated average representative calls to each customer per year.

[2] Estimated cost per call to cover selling and distribution costs. Inactive accounts did not have representative calls; however, they were allocated $5 per year for mailings. The cost of each call has been determined on a sliding scale, that is, increase in sales volume requires higher service.

Exhibit 2

TURNER MISCELLANEOUS TERRITORY (UNSERVICED) ACCOUNTS

Annual Sales ($) per Account	Accounts	Total Sales ($)
Inactive	1,960	—
0–300	1,764	11,500
301–500	686	296,400
501–750	196	127,400
751–1,000	147	138,500
1,001–1,500	147	231,800
	4,900	805,600

Jim thought there was a danger in arbitrarily setting up groupings of Miscellaneous Territory accounts unless the servicing of these groupings was co-ordinated in a total service policy. Currently there was no mechanism to periodically identify and move the larger accounts (for example, annual sales over $750) from Miscellaneous Territory back into represented territories. Similarly, dormant or small sales revenue accounts in represented territories were not periodically transferred into the Miscellaneous Territory group.

In analyzing the approximately 23,000 accounts with $33 million in forecast sales for 1989 (Exhibit 1), Jim noted that the "80–20" principle (where a small portion of customers account for a large portion of sales) certainly applied. He found that 7.4% of customers accounted for $26 million or 77% of annual sales (that is, 1,768 customers over $4,000 per year). Also, 63% of customers accounted for only 1.2% of sales (Exhibit 3). The contribution data in Exhibit 3 raised Jim's concern about the cost of servicing existing accounts. Turner lost $89,000, before administration and advertising expenses, to provide services to the "less than $300" group. Administration and advertising expenses were not allocated due to the arbitrary nature of any allocation system and because Jim believed that those costs were essentially fixed.

Exhibit 3

INDUSTRIAL SEGMENT—SUMMARY OF ACCOUNTS, SALES, AND CONTRIBUTION

Annual Sales ($) per Account	Number of Accounts	Total Sales ($000s)	Total Net Contribution[1] ($000s)
<300	14,859	396	(89)
300–1,000	3,999	1,966	336
1,000+	4,734	31,127	8,740
	23,592	33,489	8,987

[1] Based on an analysis of the number of calls and call notes gathered from a cross-section of sales representatives.

Based on this analysis, Jim felt that a new comprehensive marketing program should be developed to service (or not service) each customer group, particularly small-account customers, defined as "those existing Turner accounts which purchase goods and services of less than $1,000 per year."

SMALL ACCOUNT ANALYSIS

To establish a "picture" of the small-account customers, Jim used a variety of market research approaches that allowed him to prepare an assessment of Turner and its major competitors (Exhibit 4).

Based on information provided by the sales representatives and other available data, a comparison of Turner's customers with total Canadian firms was compiled (Exhibit 5). Jim realized that Turner's current market segmentation of industrial accounts was somewhat imprecise. This was caused by the difficulty in categorizing certain companies and the marked perceptual differences between small customers and the larger customers. As noted in Exhibit 5, some problems existed in categorizing companies.

As well, Jim estimated that 90% of Miscellaneous Territory sales were obtained from just three segments: 43% from Manufacturing—General, 34% from Transport, and 13% from Manufacturing—Production.

Several significant observations emerged from the market research studies. Specifically, within the transport segment the key determinants of choice for non-Turner users were (1) price, (2) availability, and (3) quality. However, Turner users were clearly sold on (1) quality, (2) availability, and (3) value for money.

The determinants of choice for the manufacturing segments were (1) quality, (2) service, and (3) price. For the construction, building, and mining segments, the key factors were (1) having a contract, and (2) price. Interestingly, for this last group, quality was near the bottom of the list.

EVALUATION OF OPTIONS FOR SMALL-ACCOUNT CUSTOMERS

Jim found it was essential in evaluating strategy options to segment existing accounts into three groups by annual sales:

1. accounts currently purchasing under $300.
2. accounts currently purchasing between $300 and $1,000, and
3. accounts currently purchasing over $1,000.

Jim then focused on the small-account customers, namely the first two groups.

Group 1: Accounts Currently Purchasing under $300

Turner had approximately 15,000 accounts in this category. As noted, Turner lost approximately $89,000 (before overheads) in servicing these accounts by mailings and some sales representation.

A study conducted by mail in December 1988 of 6,900 Miscellaneous Territory accounts revealed that many accounts were not "small" but, in fact, were purchasing

Exhibit 4

PERCEPTIONS OF MAJOR OIL COMPANIES BY SMALL ACCOUNTS

Positive	Company	Negative
High quality product Good brand awareness Very progressive company Oil experts Technological expertise first class Standard of sales reps highly regarded High brand loyalty	Turner	Expensive Hard to find stocklists Delivery/stock-out a problem Cost prohibitive Non-users' limited knowledge of full product range
Well regarded Wide product range Canwest credit card	Canwest	Canwest reps • unreliable • ill-informed • few in number Strike prone Unreliable deliveries Customers not very aware of Westside's technical services
Customers very loyal Reliable service Efficient order handling Technical back-up well regarded	Collins	Customers not easily able to negotiate price deals Limited product range
Value-for-money perception Adequate service Comprehensive range Products well regarded by users	Bowen	Limited product range Poor and unreliable service
Number of loyal users Flexible approach to total product usage Unobtrusive sales reps	Martin	Representatives call only when requested More expensive than Bowen or Canwest
No strong positive or negative perceptions	Lomtil	Higher prices Adequate product range Reluctant to do oil/fuel tests

Source: Company records

over 200 L of lubricants, with total purchases of over $500 annually. Further, as a result of increased sales attributed to the "mailer," over 1,000 accounts were placed back into represented territories. Telephone research with a very small sample conducted by Turner sales representatives in June 1989 indicated that many "small" accounts were high lubricant users but were purchasing only a fraction of their total lubricant purchases from Turner; that is, of 34 "small" accounts contacted, five revealed that their total lubricant purchases exceeded 1,000 L of lubricants per year with total purchases, including related products, of over $3,000.

Jim estimated that of the existing 15,000 customers in the "small account" category, 200 could be transferred to represented territories, 2,000 could be serviced by alternative direct marketing programs, and approximately 13,000 could be offered to distributors, or they could be completely eliminated.

Exhibit 5
TURNER INDUSTRIAL CUSTOMERS COMPARED WITH TOTAL CANADIAN FIRMS

Key Segments[2]	Number of Firms by employees[1] A 1–19	B Over 19	C Total Firms	D Turner Customers	Turner Coverage (%) D/C
Manufacturing—Production	8,652	6,473	15,125	2,345	15.5
Manufacturing—General	29,422	29,789	59,211	8,905	15.0
Transport (including wholesale and retail)	89,986	146,501	236,487	8,052	3.5
Transport (excluding wholesale and retail)	13,956	17,122	31,078	8,052	25.9
Mining/quarry	1,647	1,269	2,916	769	26.4
Building/earthmoving/ construction	47,682	74,751	122,433	2,455	2.0
Earthmoving/construction[3]	40,293	599	40,892	2,455	6.0
Total[4]	177,389	258,783	436,172	29,196	6.7

[1] Although it would have been informative to group Turner customers by number of employees to give some indication where the bulk of Turner's trading really lies, such data was not readily available. The number of employees by company is not a good gauge of potential volume; for example, a transport firm with four employees (which may be the operator, spouse, and two children) can potentially purchase more lubricants and supplies than a Manufacturing—General firm with nineteen employees.

[2] Turner customer classification did not exactly match Statistics Canada classifications; for example, Turner representatives sometimes miscoded essentially Transport firms as Manufacturing—General. For example, assemblers or manufacturing equipment wholesalers whose prime function was storage and distribution were classified by Turner reps as Manufacturing—General.

[3] Excluding concreting, bricklaying, tiling, and special construction trades, the earthmoving and construction market reduces to 40,892 firms.

[4] Total is calculated by summing Manufacturing—Production, Manufacturing—General, Transportation (including wholesale and retail), Mining/quarry, and Building/earthmoving/ construction.

Group 2: Accounts Currently Purchasing Between $300 and $1,000

Turner had 4,000 accounts in industrial segments in this category. Jim believed this group had a strong potential for development. Evidence for this belief was gained from a survey of Turner sales representatives and a telephone survey of small accounts in Quebec. However, despite the potential, Jim found that present servicing of this group was poor.

The group represented the "middle ground" of customers providing a respectable contribution of $336,000 annually (before overheads), although they did not justify regular service by the current sales force.

Jim considered that feasible options for servicing this group could be via distributors, direct mail, or telephone solicitation. Assigning these customers to distributors would allow the existing sales force to focus their attention on the larger accounts with the aim of obtaining increases in sales from the larger accounts. Jim estimated that the transfer of these accounts to distributors would result in an increase of $16,000 in contribution to Turner (Exhibit 6). He wondered if the use of distributors would ultimately generate conflicts between Turner and the distributors over accounts that became large.

Exhibit 6
GROUP 2 SMALL-ACCOUNT CUSTOMERS—CONTRIBUTION OF DIRECT SALES VERSUS DISTRIBUTORS

	Sales to Small Accounts by	
	Turner ($ million)	Distributor ($ million)
Revenue to Turner	1.966[1]	1.573[2]
Cost of goods sold	1.180	1.180
Gross profit	0.786	0.393
Selling cost	0.449[1]	0.040[3]
Contribution to Turner	0.337	0.353

[1] From Exhibit 4
[2] 20% distributor margins
[3] Ten distributors, $4,000 selling costs (each)

DIRECT MARKETING ALTERNATIVES

Direct mail had been used by Turner with considerable success. When combined with inserts in magazines and trade journals, Turner achieved a high degree of reach to and response from targeted segments. In a campaign run between February and April 1989, Turner sent a mailing to 20,000 account customers and placed 80,000 inserts in trade magazines. Total costs of $94,000 for this campaign consisted of (1) $16,000 for "mailers" (estimated at $0.80 per mailing to cover postage, brochures, and insertion costs), (2) $52,000 for inserts (covering costs of brochures and publication insertion costs), and (3) $26,000 for promotional coupons.

As a direct result of this campaign, sales for the two major products promoted increased by more than 210,000 L, with a net marketing contribution increase of $163,000. In addition, it was believed that about 330 new account customers were gained. Moreover, sales remained at the new higher level in the following two months.

In addition, opportunities existed for the selective use of mailing lists. There were currently over 436,000 industrial firms with lubricant usage potential in Canada, Turner estimated they had coverage of only 6.7% of these firms (Exhibit 5).

Jim examined various mailing-list services and considered that two were promising: Jackson Listings and Bartholomew's. Both services provided a vast range of highly segmented lists, and although costs vary by type of list, the average cost was approximately $100 for each list of 1,000 names. Careful vetting of lists to eliminate duplications of current customers would need to be undertaken. However, benefits of closely segmenting customers would provide specific targeting of the company's products, for example, hygiene applications targeted to architects for inclusion in building design.

The use of the telephone as a marketing tool in Canada had increased considerably during the 1980s and many sophisticated campaigns had been developed. Some companies achieved higher sales volumes and reduced selling costs by conducting specific and highly structured telephone solicitation campaigns. Telephone

Exhibit 7
ANALYSIS OF TELEPHONE SELLING

- Companies who used telephone selling estimated a call rate of 50 effective calls per day.
- Turner has 1,145 Quebec metropolitan customers who purchase between $300 and $1,000 annually, with total purchases of $620,000 annually.
- The cost of establishing a telephone salesperson was estimated at $34,500 based on a salary of $27,000 and benefits of $7,500. In addition, a cost allocation for office space would need to be made.
- Based on a call rate of twenty-five effective calls per day and 250 work days per annum, it was estimated that a single salesperson could cover the 1,145 Quebec customers with an average contact of 5.5 times per year. The current average calls per customer in this group annually was estimated at 1.5.
- To "break even" on contribution, the telephone salesperson would need to increase current sales by 14% per year:

Increase sales	$85,000 ($620,000 × 14%)
Increase contribution	$34,000
Costs	$34,500

- Currently a salesperson covers an average of 200 active accounts per year.

selling was one of the few marketing techniques where the actual direct benefits could easily be identified. When compared with the specific costs, the net results of each call could be calculated accurately.

For Turner there appeared to be an excellent opportunity for promoting not only lubricants but also high-margin agency-line products (that is, nonlubricant lines). Although it was difficult to quantify benefits, Jim prepared a brief analysis to help determine the viability of telephone solicitation (Exhibit 7). This analysis suggested to Jim that telephone selling could cost-effectively service and develop over 1,000 customers in Quebec using one salesperson. Jim thought that if this alternative was chosen, it should be tested in one province first.

Jim believed he faced a number of major questions in reviewing the industrial marketing program for Turner products. In particular, he wondered what the possible advantages and long-term consequences were for each of the three proposed options for improving sales force performance. This required an assessment of each option's implications for existing channels and sales force activities. Specifically, he thought he needed to recommend a plant to the president for increasing sales force productivity at Turner.

49 THE LIVELY ARTS AT HANSON (I)

Kenneth Shachmut

Charles B. Weinberg

"I'm very frustrated about our attendance figures," noted Barbara Lynn, associate director of the Office of Public Events at Hanson University in Ontario. "Our programming is high quality—and for the whole season we have only about 27,000 seats to sell, but we have a significant seasonal attendance problem. Our spring term attendance has been running at only 50% of capacity over the last few years, down from about 85% in the fall. Winter term figures are just marginally better than those for spring, averaging about 60%."

It was May 1982, and both she and Tom Bacon, who was finishing his fourth year as director of the Office of Public Events, saw this seasonal attendance pattern as their most pressing management problem.

PROGRAM CHANGES

Over the past three seasons, Mr. Bacon had implemented a number of changes in the "Lively Arts at Hanson" program. Attendance as a percentage of capacity had increased from 54% in the three academic years 1976–79 to 68% in the most recent three years. These changes are summarized below.

Programming

The number of performances was reduced from 41 in 1978–79 to 31 for the 1979–80 season. This figure rose again to 36 in 1980–81 and was reduced once more to 25 in 1981–82. Additionally, Mr. Bacon had attempted to make the program commercially more viable during the last three seasons than it had been previously. He accomplished this by scheduling relatively more performances by string quartets and guitarists, which usually did very well at Hanson. Attendance data by type of programming for the past three years were: guitar—104% of capacity; chamber music—79%; jazz—75%; dance—62%; and young concert artists—51%. Detailed attendance statistics by term for 1981–82 are shown in Exhibit 1.

Personnel

The size of Mr. Bacon's staff was increased, permitting more and more effective promotional activities. Even with this increase, however, the total time devoted to the program was not greatly in excess of one person-year, owing to the fact that the

Office of Public Events was responsible for managing four other university programs in addition to the Arts program during the school year.

The first of these was general administration (mainly scheduling) of all public events on the Hanson campus. This function required considerable time and represented a steady workload throughout the academic year. Secondly, the office was responsible for co-ordinating all university public ceremonies. Most significant of these was the annual Commencement exercise, held in May. Although some aspects of Commencement required advance planning and co-ordination, by far the biggest push came during the two months preceding the event. The third major responsibility of the office was co-ordination of various university lecture programs. As with general administration, the lecture series imposed a relatively steady workload throughout the year.

In addition, Mr. Bacon was responsible for a travel film and lecture series which ran throughout the academic year. Also, during the summer, he scheduled a number of "commercial" attractions (for example, the Preservation Hall Jazz Band) for community enjoyment.

The university administration considered all of these activities to be important in helping fulfill the multiple goals of a major university in the community.

PROMOTIONAL CHANGES

Name

The name of the program was changed to "The Lively Arts at Hanson" for the 1979–80 season in order to attract more attention to the program and to identify it more positively as a performing arts program. This new name was incorporated in a redesigned logo and used in all media advertising.

Brochures

The season brochure (now called "The Lively Arts at Hanson") was made much more elaborate and eye-catching, starting with the 1979–80 brochure. Its physical size was doubled (to 8½ by 11 inches), and it was printed in three colours on glossy paper stock. These changes increased the costs substantially. By 1981–82 the total cost of the brochure (45,000 copies printed, of which 30,000 were mailed and 15,000 bulk distributed) had risen to $16,800 (including mailing costs) from approximately $6,500 in 1978–79.

The brochure included listings not only for the Lively Arts program but also performances by various university departments (for example, drama and music departments). These nonprofessional performances were clearly separated from the Lively Arts offerings within the brochure. In addition, the sponsoring departments were required to fully absorb their pro-rata share—$2,000—of total brochure costs. Mr. Bacon planned to maintain this policy in the foreseeable future.

Brochures were sent in accordance with a mailing list at the beginning of each season in early September. The mailing list was composed of three separate lists. The first contained approximately 15,000 names of people who had previously purchased Lively Arts season tickets, who had purchased individual tickets by cheque

Exhibit 1
1981–82 ATTENDANCE STATISTICS FOR LIVELY ARTS

	Percentage of capacity*				
	Student	Nonstudent	Total	Capacity	Day
			Fall		
Performance					
Canadian Brass (CM)	49%	55%	104%	720	Tuesday
Mann Jazz Quartet (Jazz)	39	59	98	1,694	Friday
Royal Winnipeg Ballet 1 (Dance)	38	28	66	1,694	Thursday
Royal Winnipeg Ballet 2	27	27	54	1,694	Friday
Contemporary Chamber Ensemble	19	19	38	720	Friday
Guarneri Quartet 1 (CM)	49	63	112	720	Tuesday
Guarneri Quartet 2	53	62	115	720	Friday
Guarneri Quartet 3	50	71	121	720	Sunday
Ron Thomas (YCA)	22	37	59	350	Friday
Liona Boyd (Guitar)	39	69	108	1,085	Friday
Breakdown (average figures)					
Chamber Music (5)	44%	54%	98%	720	
Guitar (1)	39	69	108	1,085	
Jazz (1)	39	59	98	1,694	
Dance (2)	33	28	60	1,694	
Young Concert Artist (1)	22	37	59	350	
Totals (10)	38	48	86	10,117	
			Winter		
Performance					
AMAN! (Dance)	31%	69%	100%	1,694	Friday
Music by Three (YCA)	14	37	51	350	Friday
Nicanor Zabaleta (Harp)	38	66	104	720	Friday
Pilobolus Dance Theater 1	6	37	43	1,694	Thursday
Pilobolus Dance Theater 2	26	25	51	1,694	Friday
Tel Aviv Quartet (CM)	19	64	83	720	Friday
Fernando Valente (Harpsichord)	26	68	94	720	Friday
Hiroko Yajima (YCA)	7	41	48	350	Friday
Murray Dance Company 1	7	12	19	1,694	Thursday
Murray Dance Company 2	22	21	43	1,694	Friday
Music from Marlboro (CM)	14	52	66	720	Friday
Breakdown (average figures)					
Chamber Music (2)	17%	58%	75%	720	
Dance (5)	18	33	51	1,694	

(continued)

Exhibit 1 continued

	Percentage of capacity*				
	Student	Nonstudent	Total	Capacity	Day
Young Concert Artist (2)	11	39	50	350	
Other (2)	32	67	99	720	
Totals (11)	19	41	60	12,050	
			Spring		
Performance					
Mummenschanz (Mime)	17%	26%	43%	1,694	Tuesday
Early Music Consort of London (CM)	35	69	104	720	Friday
Paul Winter Consort (Jazz)	21	24	45	1,694	Friday
Arthur Renner (YCA)	11	51	62	350	Friday
Breakdown (not applicable)					
Totals (4)	21%	34%	55%	4,458	

* Chamber music events were held in the 720-seat hall, dance and jazz in the 1,694-seat hall, and the Young Concert Artist series in the 350-seat hall. For the guitar concert, the balcony and back rows of the 1,694-seat hall were not made available for sale, leaving a capacity of 1,085 seats. Other events were scheduled for either the 720- or 1,694-seat hall depending upon the nature of the event. The average production cost per performance was $3,000 in 1981–1982.

Note: Some names are disguised.

(from which a name and address was obtained), or who had specifically requested to be put on the list (by filling out cards available at all performances).

A second list of about 6,000 (the so-called "Sunset Hills Cultural List") was obtained from the Council for the Arts in Sunset Hills, a large suburban community adjacent to Hanson. The remainder of the brochures (approximately 9,000 for 1981–82) was sent to local Hanson alumni, with priority determined by the proximity of residence to the university campus.

These three lists were not cross checked against each other for duplication. A spokesperson from University Computing Services, which maintained the lists, said that because of their different coding systems, reprogramming and integrating the lists would be costly and time consuming. Mr. Bacon was uncertain about the extent of duplication within the lists. However, he noted that he himself received three mailed copies of the brochure each year.

In addition to program information, the annual brochure included a calendar of all performances (professional and nonprofessional), season ticket information, and ticket order forms for all performances.

Supplemental one-page brochures in a postcard format were mailed at the beginning of winter and spring terms to the Lively Arts mailing list, briefly outlining the coming term's program offerings.

Posters and Flyers

When available from the performers' agents, posters and flyers were displayed around the Hanson campus on centrally located information kiosks, in student residences, and other places about two weeks prior to each performance. Depending on availability, additional posters were distributed to willing local merchants. These posters were of varied quality, and public events staff had no control over their format. Typically the posters included a blank area at the bottom in which was printed program time and location information. The posters did not include the Lively Arts logo or any other mention of the program itself.

Advertising and Other Promotional Activities

Each performance was advertised for about two weeks prior to the performance date in the local press and, for some performances, on classical music radio stations. Typical newspapers used were the *Hanson Daily*, the *Sunset Hills Free Press*, and the *Globe and Mail*. Additionally, miscellaneous promotional pieces, such as Lively Arts bookmarks, were printed in large quantities and made widely available on campus at the beginning of each season (Exhibit 2).

Pricing

Greater flexibility was introduced into the pricing scheme, with price levels varying across different performances according to program cost, expected drawing power of individual performers, and other factors. For example, during the winter term, 1982, the best nonstudent tickets for the Murray Dance Company sold for $9, while the Tel Aviv Quartet seats went for $7, and Young Concert Artist series performances sold at $5 for nonstudents. Additionally, the overall price level was increased to an average ticket price paid (including student and season discounts) of $4.97 for 1981–82, compared to $4.01 for 1979–80.

STUDENT PROMOTIONS

Student Introductory Program (SIP)

Under the program, initiated in 1979–80, each new Hanson undergraduate or graduate student was given a free pass to any one performance during the fall term and also a coupon allowing that student to buy a ticket at 75 cents for any other performance during the year.

Response to the initial free ticket was good, but only a very limited number of students exercised the follow-up 75-cent option. Consequently, the 75-cent coupon was discontinued after only one season. However, the initial free SIP ticket had been maintained up to the present time.

Student Discount Tickets

The price of a ticket to any performance for students was set substantially below the average nonstudent ticket price. During the 1981–82 season the student price was

Exhibit 2

APPROXIMATE PROMOTIONAL EXPENDITURES—1981–82 SEASON

Annual Costs			
Season brochure*	$16,800		
Program covers	1,200		
Promotional material (bookmarks, surveys, etc.)	1,650		
			$19,650
Fall Term Costs			
Advertising			
Newspaper	$ 7,500		
Radio	900		
Other	300	$ 8,700	
Posters and flyers		600	
Other		300	
			$ 9,600
Winter Term Costs			
Advertising			
Newspaper	$ 7,650		
Radio	1,050		
Other	450	$ 9,150	
Posters and flyers		600	
Winter brochure*		3,150	
Other		450	
			$13,350
Spring Term Costs (estimate)			
Advertising			
Newspaper	$ 3,750		
Radio	750		
Other	150	$ 4,650	
Posters and flyers		300	
Spring brochure*		1,350	
Other		150	
			$ 6,450
Total promotional costs			$49,050

* Includes mailing cost.

$4.50 per ticket. Mr. Bacon felt that this price level was appropriate and equitable, and he desired to maintain it as long as possible.

PROGRAM ATTENDANCE

In May 1982, Mr. Bacon was undertaking a reappraisal of the entire Lively Arts marketing program employed over the past three seasons to determine what changes, if any, might be warranted. Although he felt strongly that many of his program changes had been successful, he still faced significant problems. Most worrisome of these was a marked pattern of seasonal attendance. While fall term audiences had been very good, averaging nearly 85% of capacity, the comparable figures for winter and spring were 60% and 50% respectively (Exhibit 3). To compound this difficulty Mr. Bacon noted that student attendance had slipped from a high of over 45% of the audience during the 1979–80 season to an all-time low of 32% for the winter term 1981–82.

Mr. Bacon was concerned about both of these trends and made the following comments to Ms. Lynn.

> "The Lively Arts at Hanson" presents first-rate artists in a varied program that should appeal to a broad base of individuals. Look at this season's offerings, for example: The Guarneri and Tel Aviv string quartets; Canadian Brass; AMAN! (a folk dance group); Pilobolus and the Murray Company in dance; the Early Music Consort of London. These artists are representative of the best in their fields.
>
> Our Young Concert Artist series brings some of the most promising young talent in the world to the Hanson audience. Already they have received laudatory reviews by major music critics. Moreover, our prices are quite low compared to what one would have to pay to see comparable performers in Toronto. The average nonstudent ticket price this year was only about $6 to $9. Most city performances cost twice as much.
>
> Student attendance also bothers me. As a group, Hanson students should be very interested in the Lively Arts program. However, from a number of sources, I have the strong impression that they're really not as aware of our program as I would like. For example, take the Student Introductory program (SIP). By and large, new students were very willing to take a complimentary ticket, but very few of them exercised the option to purchase a second ticket for 75 cents plus the SIP coupon. Somehow we have to get through to the students that "The Lively Arts at Hanson" is something very special and very professional, to be distinguished from the whole host of other performance activities with which we must compete for their attention on campus.

"The Lively Arts at Hanson" was not alone in facing a seasonal attendance problem. The performing arts programs at the other Ontario universities experienced similar difficulties. Mr. Bacon's counterpart at University of Toronto commented that she had had some success in combatting this problem by scheduling relatively

Exhibit 3
ATTENDANCE BY TERMS, 1976–82

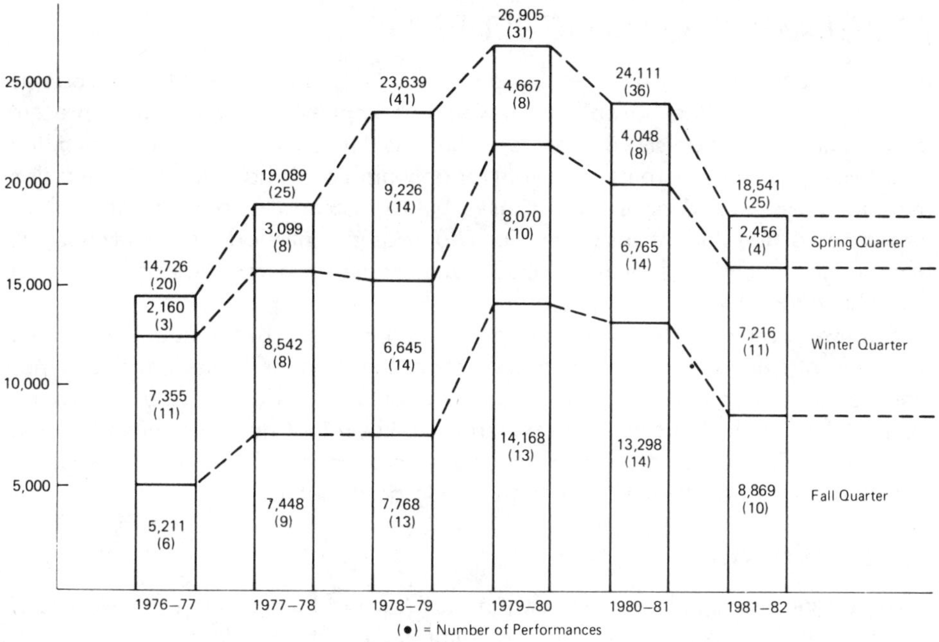

more "light" and fewer "heavy" performances during spring term, her toughest attendance period. The "light" category encompassed performances which typically sold well at the university, including string quartets, early music, and anything by Bach. "Heavy," on the other hand, included contemporary music and vocalists, which were always difficult to sell. The university manager also tended to favour more well-known performers in the spring.

PROGRAM GOALS

Mr. Bacon felt strongly that the program had, and must of necessity have, multiple goals reflecting the multiple dimensions of managing an arts program. For purposes of control and evaluation of the program's progress, Mr. Bacon decided after much thought that the following four goals were paramount:

- Establish "The Lively Arts at Hanson" as a major source of first-rate performing arts talent for the extended community as well as for the immediate Hanson University community.
- Run the series on a close-to-breakeven basis, incurring only a minimal deficit as approved by the university administration.
- Keep prices as low as possible in order to make performances widely accessible.

- Target the total season for overall attendance at 75 to 80% of capacity. Further, maintain the following overall audience proportions: students, 35%; nonstudents, 65%.

PROGRAMMING DIFFICULTIES

In order to achieve the first of these goals, which he and his staff felt was probably the most important, Mr. Bacon knew it would be imperative to continue to present a varied program of artists each season. This was difficult for two reasons. First, the scheduling problems were impressive. Not only did Bacon have to book the artists more than a year in advance in most cases, but he also had to compete with various departmental and student arts productions (for example, music department concerts, drama department, and theatrical club productions) for a very limited number of available auditoriums on campus and suitable dates.

However, even more troublesome was the second factor. By maintaining a varied program, Mr. Bacon was including each season a number of performance types which did not seem to do very well in drawing large audiences, such as the Young Concert Artist series and dance in general. He knew that he would have to try to lessen the variations in attendance by performance type for the 1982–83 season if possible, but he wasn't sure of the best way to go about it.

Segmentation

Barbara Lynn, who had been working in the Office of Public Events for two years, had some strong feelings about the potential audience:

> I think we have, basically, three groups of people who come out to our performances. First there are the students. Our sources on campus seem to indicate that Hanson students are not very aware of our program. The students have heard of performers like the Canadian Brass and the Guarneri Quartet—and they know they will be performing—but they don't seem to know that the "Lively Arts" is bringing them to campus. I don't know, but maybe our posters and *Hanson Daily* advertising aren't doing the job. They sure cost enough, though!
>
> Second is the group I like to call "Hanson affiliated"—university faculty and staff members and their spouses. We haven't made any special attempt to get them interested, but feel they should respond to the advertising both on campus and in the local press.
>
> Finally we've got the community at large—mostly in and around Hanson and Sunset Hills. Many of these people receive our annual brochure and the subsequent postcard mailings. In addition, they probably read the *Globe and Mail* or the *Free Press*, in which we advertise regularly. They're all great fans in the fall, but when we have to compete with spring weather their loyalty runs thin. Their allegiance during the winter is also poor.
>
> There are other groups, too. For example, local music teachers and their pupils—maybe even some of the companies in the nearby industrial

parks. We could probably do a lot here in the way of group discounts. This also might apply to faculty and staff—especially those living nearby. I've got a million ideas I'd like to try out, but not nearly enough time. Especially now, with Commencement to worry about . . .

Image Advertising

Both executives were concerned that the perceived image of "The Lively Arts at Hanson" was not as good as it could be. Precise information was not available on this issue, but a number of informal sources supported this belief:

- The manager of the Campus Ticket Office reported that very few buyers ever mentioned the program when purchasing individual performance tickets. Additionally, she said that over the past few years only one of the many students who had worked part-time in the ticket office had heard of the program before beginning work.
- Informal polling of students in the campus cafeterias indicated that only 5 to 10% of them had heard of the program.

These and other indicators led Mr. Bacon and Ms. Lynn to consider the possibility of an image advertising campaign during the summer in the local press as well as on campus at the beginning of the academic year in September 1982. Ms. Lynn also thought that students in Hanson's several graduate professional schools (Business, Law, Medicine, and Education) might be a good target segment. She reasoned that these students were much more dedicated to a particular field than were undergraduates, and therefore probably were less involved in the many competing general university activities.

Audience Questionnaire

To get a handle on some of the characteristics of the audience and formulate an appropriate marketing plan for next year, Lively Arts staff prepared an audience survey. This questionnaire was distributed to most of the audience at ten of the winter term performances in early 1982. A random sample of about 100 (when fewer than 100 questionnaires were turned in, the whole group was used) was selected from each performance (in all, over 850 responses were sampled) and the results were analyzed using the computer program available through the university computer centre.

By mid-May Mr. Bacon had the results of the analysis (Exhibit 4). By and large the questionnaire reconfirmed many intuitive feelings he and his staff had had prior to the survey. But they gained several new insights as well. As a result of the questionnaire, Bacon was seriously rethinking some of his marketing strategies for next season.

The 1982–83 Season

Due to the long-range planning needed to arrange bookings for performing artists, the 1982–83 season was already scheduled (Exhibit 5). Of the 26 performances,

Exhibit 4
AUDIENCE PROFILE

	Students*	Nonstudents
Median:		
Age group	18–24	35–44
Number of children	0	1
Educational level	University	Graduate work
Annual family income	—	$25–49K
Hanson affiliation:		
Students	73%	3%
Faculty	—	10
Staff	1	9
Alumni	3	15
Place of residence:		
Hanson	44%	10%
Sunset Hills	26	35
Other	30	55
Performing arts performances attended in Hanson within the past year:		
1–3	64%	49%
4–7	27	27
8–10	4	10
Over 10	5	13
Time of ticket purchase:**		
At the door	19%	12%
Day of performance	11	9
1–3 days before	23	12
4–7 days before	16	11
2–3 weeks before	11	12
1 or more months before	20	45
Lively Arts at Hanson:		
Current subscribers	8%	34%
Received brochure in mail	21	56
Information sources for this performance:		
Brochure by mail	15%	48%
Newspaper advertising	34	27
Newspaper story	9	14
Poster or flyer	42	14
Word of mouth	46	29

(continued)

Exhibit 4 continued

	Students*	Nonstudents
Sources usually consulted for upcoming arts events:		
Hanson Daily	72%	27%
Campus Report	12	17
Chronicle	9	14
Globe and Mail	32	46
Free Press	21	54
CBC	18	17
CKSL	13	18
Listen to classical music radio regularly:	57%	73%
Station most often listened to (if yes):		
CBC	20%	37%
CKSL	39	40
Performance preferences:		
Theatre	81%	77%
Contemporary Music	41	33
Symphony	63	68
Modern Dance	58	51
Instrumental Recitals	47	51
Opera	25	32
Chamber Music	47	55
Ballet	58	62
Vocal Recitals	11	17
Factors important in deciding to attend a performance:		
Name of performers	68%	75%
Repertoire	79	87
Ticket price	68	49
Find hall easily	28	29

Source: Audience survey questionnaire

* Student/Nonstudent categories were developed according to the response to an occupation question. About 80% of respondents were nonstudents.

** Among nonstudents attending 1 to 3 performances, 30% bought their tickets at the door or on the day of the performance; among nonstudents attending 4 or more performances, the comparable percentage was 11%. For students, the percentage was about 30%, regardless of attendance level.

Exhibit 5

1982–83 SEASON SCHEDULE

	Fall term
October 22	Orford String Quartet
October 28	"Billy Bishop Goes to War" (drama)
October 29	Oba Koso (Nigerian opera)
November 5	Roman de Fauvel (medieval secular music drama)
November 9	Music from Marlboro (chamber music)
November 12	Young Concert Artist
November 14, 16, 19	Guarneri String Quarter—Beethoven Quartet Series (chamber music)
	Winter term
January 18	"An Evening of George Orwell" with José Ferrer (celebrity)
January 21	Young Concert Artist
February 1, 2, 3	Eliot Feld Ballet Company (dance)
February 11	Young Concert Artist
February 18	Bach Aria Group (chamber music)
February 22, 25, 27	Guarneri String Quartet—Beethoven Quartet Series (chamber music)
	Spring term
April 1	Narcisco Yepes (guitar)
April 7, 8	Repertory Dance Company
April 15	Young Concert Artist
April 17	Canadian Brass (chamber music)
April 24, 26	Fine Arts Quartet (with viola)—Mozart Quintet Series (chamber music)

nine were scheduled for the fall term, ten for winter, and seven for spring. Within this programming context, Mr. Bacon sought to use all the market information he had gathered during the season to formulate a well-integrated, specific marketing plan.

To put his strategic planning into operation, he thought it would be a good idea to set a specific attendance objective. After much thought he decided on a season attendance goal of 75%, with a 35 to 65% student/nonstudent mix. This was clearly a stretch target, but by setting his overall season goals high, Mr. Bacon hoped to really come to grips with what had historically been his most pressing problem—seasonal attendance. He further thought that, at a minimum, his plans should address the following issues:

Brochures Was the "lavish" annual brochure with postcard follow-ups sent at the start of each term sufficient, or should each mailing be more like the current elaborate annual brochure?

Exhibit 6
ESTIMATED MARKETING EXPENSES—FORTHCOMING SEASON

Newspaper Ad Rates[a]			
Free Press	$11.00		
	8.50[b]		
Hanson Daily	5.00		
Globe and Mail	54.00		
Radio Ad Rates[c]			
CKSL	$43.00		
CKMS	24.00		
Lively Arts Brochure (annual)			
Typesetting	$165 per page		
Printing—Plates	150 per page		
Variable cost per page:			
First 10,000 copies	$0.022		
Next 20,000 copies	0.077		
Next 30,000 copies	0.005		
Labels and bulk mailing	0.11 per brochure		
Typesetting	$165 × 20 pages		$ 3,300
Printing:			
Fixed (plates)		$3,000	
Variable			
$.022 × 10,000 × 20		4,400	
$.007 × 20,000 × 20		2,800	
$.005 × 15,000 × 20		1,500	11,700
Labels and bulk mailing $.11 × 30,000			3,300
Total			15,000
Winter and Spring Brochures			
Printing			
Fixed cost (plate)	$15.00		
Variable cost per item			
First 25,000	0.03		
Next 50,000	0.022		
Labels and bulk mailing	0.09 each		
Bookmarks			
Printing	$ 0.019 each		

[a] costs quoted are "per column inch" for each time the ad is run
[b] if there are no changes and the ad is run a minimum of four times
[c] costs for a 30-second announcement

Notes:

1. A typical Lively Arts ad in 1981–82 was 2 columns wide and 3 inches long, or 6 column-inches. In the *Free Press* these ads typically ran for about two weeks prior to the performance.
2. *Globe and Mail* advertising for 1981–82 was restricted to the Saturday edition.
3. For the 1981–82 season the brochure had 20 pages; 45,000 copies were printed and 30,000 bulk-mailed at a total cost (including mailing) of $16,800.

Advertising How should he allocate his advertising budget? What media should he expand? Contract? Why? What were the possibilities of image advertising over the summer to develop demand?

Pricing How might he alter his pricing policy further? What level of prices would be tolerable and consistent with his goals?

Season Tickets Was the "choose-your-own" program[1] viable? Why or why not? What might be employed as an alternative? For example, should the six Guarneri Quartet performances be packaged as a series to be sold at a discount?

Segmentation What would be an effective way to target his marketing pitch at each of the segments that Lynn had identified? Were there other viable segmentation possibilities?

As Mr. Bacon mulled over these issues he recognized that his total promotional budget could not exceed about $50,000 for the 1982–83 season. To assist in formulating the marketing plan, Ms. Lynn had put together an estimate of the major advertising, brochure, and other promotional expense items for the 1982–83 season (Exhibit 6). Mr. Bacon also thought it would not be too early to begin formulating some strategy regarding the more long-term issue of programming (that is, how many of what type of performances to schedule when?). Although he wanted to maintain program diversity, he knew that university financial pressures would force his program's funding implications into prominence in future interdepartmental budget battles.

[1] The "choose-your-own" program allowed season ticket purchasers to structure their own discount season, choosing only those performances they wished to attend, as long as a minimum number of performances was selected.

50 O & E FARM SUPPLY

Thomas F. Funk

E. Gimpel

O. Guindo

On a cool, rainy day in November 1986, Len Dow, manager of O & E Farm Supply, was sitting in his office looking over the past season's records. He felt he had brought the fertilizer outlet a long way since he purchased it in February of 1985. Volume, which had declined to 7,000 tons in 1984 due to poor management, increased to 8,400 tons in 1985, and to 10,000 tons in 1986 (Exhibit 1). Total sales for 1986 reached $2,400,000. Profit margins, which were also lower in 1984, had returned to their normal 6% level in 1986 due to Mr. Dow's good managerial abilities. In spite of all this, he was not completely satisfied; he wanted to increase the volume and profitability of the outlet, but was not sure what direction he should take.

Exhibit 1

O & E FERTILIZER SALES

Year	Tons Liquid and Dry Fertilizers	Tons Micronutrients
1982	11,000	—
1983	11,000	—
1984	7,000	—
1985	8,400	10
1986	10,000	100

THE COMPANY

O & E Farm Supply was located in Goodland, a town centrally located in a major corn- and potato-producing area of Ontario. O & E does most of its business within a five-mile radius of Goodland (60%); however, it did have some sales and distribution extending 20 miles from its plant (35%), and a very small wholesale market over 100 miles away in northern Ontario (5%). At the time, O & E was involved only in the sale of fertilizers and related services. Dry bulk blends and bagged blends made up the majority of O & E's fertilizer volume (9,000 tons) with 28% liquid nitrogen making up a much smaller portion (1,000 tons). Potato and vegetable farmers purchased almost 60% of O & E's production, corn and cereal farmers accounted for 33%, and sod farmers purchased the remaining 7% (Exhibit 2).

Exhibit 2
O & E FERTILIZER SALES BY FARM TYPE, 1986

Farm Type	Percentages of Dry Fertilizer Sales	Percentages of Acres Served
Potato and vegetable	60	35
Corn and cereals	33	60
Sod	7	5

O & E sold a custom application service for bulk fertilizers and rented application equipment to farmers who wished to apply their own fertilizer. Current equipment consisted of two dry fertilizer spreader trucks, two feeder delivery trucks to refill spreader trucks on the farms, and three four-ton tractor-pulled spreaders which were rented out to customers who spread fertilizer themselves. Since Mr. Dow purchased the organization he had cut the full-time staff from seven to five including himself. One of his newest employees was a young agricultural university graduate who spent most of his time in a sales capacity calling on present and potential customers in the area. He also spent some of his time making farm calls.

Of O & E's 85 local customers in 1986, five were merchant dealers who resold to farmers. These five dealers accounted for 2,000 tons of O & E's business and ranged in volume from 100 to 1,000 tons each. For the most part these dealers were located on the fringes of O & E's 20-mile trading area. Of the remaining 80 local customers, Mr. Dow's records showed that 70 were within five miles of the Goodland plant and ten were at a greater distance. Almost all of these customers purchased more than 50 tons of fertilizer a year from O & E.

O & E sold 10 tons of micronutrients in 1985 and over 100 tons in 1986. Micronutrients were basic elements that a plant requires in relatively small amounts, compared to the larger amounts of nitrogen phosphorus, and potassium found in most regular, blended fertilizers. Micronutrients had been proven by university and industry research in the United States to improve the quality and yield of crops. Commercial trials carried out in Ontario had indicated similar positive results.

THE MARKET AND COMPETITION

The total market for fertilizers in O & E's trading area had been remarkably stable at approximately 50,000 tons for the past several years. This was not expected to change significantly in the future although some shifts in types used were possible. Within five miles of Goodland there were four major fertilizer outlets competing with O & E for approximately 25,000 tons of fertilizer business, and within 20 miles there were an additional three fertilizer outlets competing for the remaining 25,000 tons. Mr. Dow estimated that there were approximately 550 farmers within a five-mile radius of Goodland.

Although the market for fertilizer was very competitive, Mr. Dow felt that he had been able to better his competition by offering excellent service, remaining open extended hours, offering advice and timely delivery to his customers, and knowing how to deal with the large farmer. He had quickly come to realize that farmers placed service ahead of price when deciding where to buy fertilizer as long as the price was close to that of competitive outlets. He felt that by offering a superior service, he had nurtured a high level of dealer loyalty in his customers which resulted in a lower turnover relative to his competition.

GROWTH OPPORTUNITIES

Although the business had been doing well, Mr. Dow realized that growth was essential to future success. He had therefore been giving this matter considerable thought the past couple of months. So far, he was able to identify several avenues of growth, and now his aim was to evaluate each and arrive at some plan for 1987 and beyond.

Liquid Nitrogen

Mr. Dow had been toying with the idea of getting into 28% liquid nitrogen in a bigger way. He estimated that the total current market in his 20-mile trading area was 4,000 tons, of which he sold 1,000 to three corn farmers. This type of fertilizer was of interest mainly to the larger corn farmer because it could be mixed with herbicides for combined application and because of its ease of handling. Although its price per ton was less than the price per ton for dry fertilizers, it was comparable in terms of price per unit of actual nitrogen. This was because it was usually less concentrated than other forms of nitrogen such as dry urea, which contained 45% nitrogen compared to the 28% concentration in the liquid form. The product was very corrosive, which meant that the farmer must also purchase a stainless steel sprayer costing about $2,000 if he were to use 28% liquid nitrogen. This relatively high initial capital outlay restricted use to fairly larger farmers. Of the 400 corn farmers in his trading area, approximately 200 had sufficient acreage to be possible 28% liquid nitrogen users, and Mr. Dow estimated that about 20 farmers were using 28% liquid nitrogen in 1986. Price was the major purchase criterion since the product was a commodity and little service was involved. Most of the volume of 28% liquid nitrogen was sold in December for delivery in the spring. Prices and margins for O & E's fertilizers are provided in Exhibit 3. O & E's current holding capacity was 10,000 gallons or 50 tons. If output was increased, additional storage and nurse tanks would have to be purchased, as well as another pumping system. A pumping system was priced at $4,000, storage tanks were $0.15 per gallon, and a 1,400 gallon nurse tank was $1,000. Mr. Dow felt one additional pumping system, one more 10,000 gallon storage tank and two more nurse tanks should allow a large increase in sales. No matter what Mr. Dow decided to do, he wanted to stay ahead of his competition by at least two years. Because he felt 28% liquid nitrogen could be a big thing in the future, he was excited about this possibility. He had seen a new type of potato planter which required only liquid fertilizer. If this type of planter became popular, the potential for liquid fertilizer would increase dramatically. Despite these positive feelings about this market, he was concerned about a number of things, including the relatively low liquid nitrogen margins and the slow growth of this market in the past. He also wondered whether he should offer a weed and feed service in which

Exhibit 3
FERTILIZER PRICES AND MARGINS

	Dry Fertilizers		28% Liquid Nitrogen				Micronutrients	
			Winter		Spring			
	$/ton	%	$/ton	%	$/ton	%	$/ton	%
Average selling price	248	100	138	100	170	100	700	100
Cost of sales	203	82	131	95	136	80	595	85
Gross margin	45	18	7	5	34	20	105	15
Estimated fixed costs	$260,000			$20,000			$5,000	

O & E would apply liquid fertilizer and herbicides for the farmer all in one operation. He was not really sure of the demand for this service or what was involved in operating a weed service. There was no one currently offering such a service in his area.

Micronutrients

Another opportunity facing Mr. Dow was to try to expand micronutrient sales in a major way. At the present time, O & E was a dealer for the Taylor Chemical Company which produced and sold a complete line of micronutrients. Included in their line were manganese, zinc, iron, copper, molybdenum, boron, calcium, and sulfur. These materials were sold separately or in various combinations designed to treat specific crops. An example of the latter was the company's vegetable mix which contained magnesium, sulfur, copper, iron, manganese, and zinc in fixed proportions. The individual materials and mixes were sold in two ways: in a dry form for mixing by the dealer with other fertilizer products, and in liquid form for spray application by the farmer on the foliage of the growing crop. Although foliar (that is, leaf) application was more bother for the farmer and may have resulted in some leaf burning, some farmers preferred it because they could postpone micronutrient application until visible signs of deficiencies occurred. Also, there was some research which indicated that micronutrients could be most effective if absorbed through the leaves at the peak growth period of the plant. Despite the apparent advantages of foliar application, Mr. Dow had not sold any micronutrients in this form during the first two years in this business. If properly applied, he felt liquid micronutrients offered the most value to his customers, yet he noticed a great deal of reluctance and skepticism on the part of even the most progressive farmers in his area to try this product form.

Sales of the dry, mixed micronutrients had grown considerably over the past year and it appeared that the products offered real value to customers. One of Mr. Dow's customers applied micronutrients to half of a large potato field and treated the other half as he normally did. The treated field yielded 327 hundredweight, whereas the untreated portion only yielded 304 hundredweight. This 23 hundredweight gain resulted in a $111.55 higher revenue per acre when computed at the $4.84 per hundredweight price to the farmer. Unfortunately, the University of Guelph, which farmers looked to for technical information, was not promoting or even recommending the use of micronutrients. Their soil testing service, which analyzed soil samples for most Ontario farmers and made fertilizer use recommendations, didn't even include an analysis for micronutrients. The competition did not want to get involved in this business unless there was a very high demand and they started to lose their other fertilizer business. Of the 100 tons sold in 1986, 75 went to six large potato farmers representing 3,500 acres, 10 tons went to vegetable farmers, and 15 tons went to corn farmers (Exhibit 4).

Mr. Dow had been receiving excellent service and advice from the company distributing the micronutrients. He felt that the use of micronutrients was becoming accepted by the farmers using them, and that sales should rise in the future. He chuckled to himself as he recalled the day two very large potato farmers who were brothers were sitting in his office and the subject of micronutrients came up. One of the brothers, Jack, asked the Taylor sales rep if he thought they should be using micronutrients. The sales rep related all of the advantages of using micronutrients to them, whereupon Jack turned to his brother and asked, "Well, what do you think?" Peter replied "Yes, I think we should be using them." With that, Mr. Dow landed a micronutrients order worth several thousand dollars.

Mr. Dow was convinced that micronutrients had potential in his area. His major concern was how he could convince farmers to spend an additional $10 to $15 per acre on a product for which there was no objective basis for determining need.

Exhibit 4
MICRONUTRIENT SALES BY CROP, 1986

Crop	Tons Sold	Acres	Application Rate	Cost/Acre
Potatoes	75	3,500	50 pounds per acre	$15.90
Corn	15	1,300	25 pounds per acre	$ 8.00
Vegetables	10	400	50 pounds per acre	$15.90

Northern Ontario

Mr. Dow was also considering expanding sales in northern Ontario. He had three dealers selling bagged fertilizer for him in Sault Ste. Marie, New Liskeard, and Kenora. O & E's volume was approximately 500 tons of bagged fertilizer only—several co-op outlets had most of the market in this area. Prices were very competitive and there appeared to be strong dealer loyalty to the co-ops. There were many small farms in the region with 75 to 100 acres of workable land per farm. The crop types in the area were mixed grain, barley, hay, and a few hundred acres of potatoes near Sudbury. On the average, farmers in northern Ontario who used fertilizer purchased 2 to 3 tons of bagged fertilizer per year and did their purchasing in the winter months. Because the retail price of fertilizer in northern Ontario was similar to that around Goodland, the margin to O & E was reduced by about $17 a ton, the sum of the $12 dealer commission and the $5 freight cost. The lower margin was offset to some extent by lower personal selling costs, since dealers were used. Although the growing season was only two to three weeks behind that of Goodland, because most sales in the area occurred in the winter months, O & E's ability to service the Goodland area in the spring was not affected. One reservation about dealing with the distant northern Ontario market was that credit could be a problem, particularly because the cost of collection could run very high due to the distance involved. On the more positive side Mr. Dow was quite optimistic about the long-run potential growth of this market. He felt that there was an ultimate total industry potential in this market of 50,000 to 60,000 tons of dry fertilizer, of which perhaps 10 to 20% had been developed at the present time.

Agricultural Chemicals

So far, O & E's product line consisted only of fertilizers. However, Mr. Dow observed that all of his competitors carried insecticides, herbicides, and fungicides as well, and he wondered if he should be getting into this business too. He had always believed that concentrating on one line was the way to go. Agricultural chemicals were very competitively priced, leaving small margins in the neighbourhood of 5 to 10% for the dealer. He felt that farmers in his trading area bought fertilizer and chemicals each on their own merits. For example, if a dealer had a great price on fertilizer, this would not mean that farmers also would buy their chemicals from the same dealer unless, of course, they were also the lowest price. At any rate, he sized up his customers as not wanting to buy everything from one dealer, so he was satisfied to receive all of their fertilizer business and to leave the other lines to the other dealers. The set-up costs for carrying chemicals would be approximately $20,000 for an additional warehouse. No other direct costs would be attributable to the chemical line, but he knew that servicing the line would take valuable time away from servicing and selling the fertilizer line, which could possibly result in lower sales and profits. He estimated that the average farmer in his trading area spent $3,000 to $5,000 per year on agricultural chemicals.

Dry Fertilizers

An alternative Mr. Dow thought particularly attractive was to expand dry fertilizer sales in his local trading area. Although he had a substantial share of this market already, he felt he could pick up more through aggressive pricing and continued good service. He was especially interested in this alternative because, no matter what he did, he knew his present plant, which was over 20 years old, would have to be upgraded. As part of his plant improvement program, he planned to set up a new mixing system that would be adaptable to adding micronutrients without any downtime. This mixer could be purchased in two sizes: the smaller size was similar to his present system with a maximum capacity of 15,000 tons and cost $100,000, while the larger size had an annual capacity of 20,000 tons and cost $160,000. Because of this opportunity to increase his capacity, he wondered if he shouldn't just try to sell more dry fertilizer to both his current customers and possibly some new ones in his local trading area. To do this, he was thinking of adding another person to his staff who would act as a second salesperson to develop and offer a comprehensive crop management service to interested farmers. He was also considering the possibility of developing a local advertising program aimed at developing more awareness and interest among farmers outside his immediate five-mile concentrated area. The total cost of the new sales specialist would be about $35,000 per year, and the local advertising would cost about $10,000 per year.

THE DECISION

Mr. Dow knew he would have to make a decision soon if he were to make some changes for 1987. Although he had identified what he thought were several good opportunities for future growth, he knew he could not pursue all of them right away, and, therefore, he would have to establish some priorities. To help in this assessment, he recently wrote away to the University of Guelph and received a publication entitled "Farmer Purchasing and Use of Fertilizers in Ontario." (The Appendix provides a summary of the study.) With this new information, plus his own analysis of the situation, he began planning for 1987 and beyond. He knew that economic conditions in 1987 were not expected to be good. This made the necessity of coming up with a successful plan all the more important to him.

Appendix

RESULTS OF FERTILIZER MARKETING RESEARCH STUDY

1. Only 7% of total crop acreage in southern Ontario is not fertilized at the present time. This acreage is almost entirely in soybeans, pasture, and forages.
2. The average fertilizer application rate for southern Ontario farmers is 384 pounds per acre. Most farmers use soil test recommendations from the University of Guelph to determine the application rate. There is some tendency for farmers to apply more fertilizer than recommended by their soil tests.
3. The major types of fertilizer used by southern Ontario farmers are dry bulk blends and liquid nitrogen. Of less importance are dry bagged fertilizers, anhydrous ammonia, and liquid mixes (N-P-K). Liquid nitrogen fertilizers are almost exclusively used by very large farmers.
4. Most farmers find the quality and availability of fertilizers very good.
5. In southern Ontario as a whole, a relatively small percentage of farmers purchase a large percentage of the fertilizer products sold. The breakdown is as follows:

	% of Farmers	% of Purchases
Under 25 tons	30	10
26–50 tons	35	25
51–100 tons	20	20
Over 100 tons	15	45

6. Over 70% of all dry fertilizers are sold to farmers in April and May. This figure is somewhat lower (50%) for liquid nitrogen.
7. Thirty percent of Ontario farmers use dealer custom application services, while

75% apply the fertilizer themselves using rented dealer application equipment. There is some preference by larger farmers for custom application services.

8. In the course of a year, farmers discuss their fertilizer program with a number of parties to get information and advice on various aspects of fertilizer use and dealer selection. The influence groups most widely consulted are the local fertilizer dealer, other farmers, and family members. In addition to these influence groups, fertilizer company representatives, agricultural extension officials, and university scientists are consulted by some farmers. Proportionately more larger farmers visit company representatives and university scientists than smaller farmers.
9. Farmers also obtain fertilizer information from soil test results, various government publications, company-sponsored farmer meetings, dealer demonstration plots, and company and dealer displays at farm shows and fairs.
10. Over 60% of all farmers contact more than one fertilizer dealer before making a purchase. Larger farmers have a tendency to contact more dealers than smaller farmers.
11. Over 50% of all farmers reported receiving an on-farm call by a fertilizer dealer in the last year. Larger farmers reported receiving more dealer calls than smaller farmers.
12. In addition to fertilizers, southern Ontario farmers purchase, on the average, more than three other products from their fertilizer supplier. Of these, the most common are herbicides, insecticides, general farm supplies, and seeds. Large farmers are more likely to purchase herbicides and insecticides from their fertilizer supplier than are small farmers.
13. Six dealer services were identified as essential to all but a very small proportion of farmers: application equipment which is available when needed and in good repair; custom application services; custom fertilizer blending; fertilizer information through a well-informed staff, brochures, newsletters, and farmer meetings; soil testing; and demonstrations.
14. Other dealer services which were reported as being important to smaller groups of farmers were: crop management assistance, help in securing expert assistance with problems, and custom herbicide application.
15. Dealer location, price, and availability of product when needed are the major factors farmers consider when selecting a fertilizer dealer. In general, dealer location and availability of product when needed are more important to smaller farmers, while price is more important to larger farmers.
16. Over 45% of all farmers purchase fertilizer from their nearest dealer. On the average, farmers purchase from dealers located less than five miles from their farms.
17. Thirty percent of all farmers purchase from more than one dealer. Larger farmers have a greater tendency to spread their purchases over more dealers than do small farmers.
18. Analysis of dealer switching showed that one-third of the farmers made no dealer changes in the past five years, one-third made only one change, and the remaining one-third made two or more changes. Those farmers making several dealer changes are the larger, younger farmers.

51 WILD WEST ORGANIC HARVEST CO-OPERATIVE

Katherine Gallagher

In the autumn of 1990, the members of the Wild West Organic Harvest Co-operative were contemplating the ramifications of their success. For more than a decade, they had been the only company in western Canada specializing in the distribution of organic produce. By 1989, annual sales were over $3.25 million, profits were steady, dividends to members were significant and growing, and the Wild West name was well known and respected in the food business from Winnipeg to Victoria. Building the business from scratch to its present strong position had not always been easy. For most of the 1980s, consumers seemed more interested in their clothes and their cars than in what they put into their mouths. Yet there had always been a solid core of consumers who cared about their food. Wild West's strategy had been to focus on serving this segment well. But now the environment was a popular concern, and people were starting to wonder whether the way their food was grown might be poisoning both them and the planet. Fastidiousness where food was concerned was no longer confined to a relatively small group of consumers; it was suddenly popular, even trendy. It was motivated by both health and environmental concerns.

The market, in short, was expanding. While this brought new opportunities for growth, the members of Wild West recognized that it might also bring new threats. As Darcy Hamilton, the buyer and 13-year member of the co-op put it, "It's a mixed blessing. We're pleased because we think organic food is good for people, so this growth means that more people are eating healthy food, but we're also worried. The organic market is now attracting the attention of the big produce distributors. Customers want *real* organic food, and we're not sure that the big wholesalers will be as careful as we are about providing certified organic produce. Even then, certification standards vary, and the big wholesalers may have an economic incentive to use the most lenient standards they can get away with. That wouldn't be good for the organics industry, and it certainly wouldn't be good for consumers."

Now the members of Wild West were taking a critical look at the organization's marketing strategy. They wanted to take advantage of opportunities for long-term growth, as well as protect themselves as much as possible from competitive threats. The strategy they were considering was unusual for a produce wholesaler: branding their products and promoting them directly to consumers, as well as increasing the level of promotion to the trade.

NOT JUST ANOTHER PRODUCE WHOLESALER

Incorporated in 1977, Wild West Organic Harvest Co-operative had grown out of a Vancouver food co-op. The idea of a food co-op was to make buying food simple and cost effective for consumers: a group of people would get together and buy certain items in bulk directly from a wholesaler, then divide them up. A food co-op could, for instance, save its members a lot of money by purchasing a whole round of cheese, then cut it up into amounts suitable for each member. Each member would then pay for the proportion he or she had taken. The problem was that many wholesalers, for fear of offending their retail clients, would not sell to individuals, and they considered small food co-ops to be individuals.

Consequently, several small food co-ops got together to form FEDUP, a much larger food co-operative. This organization was successful in getting around the "individuals" problem with the wholesalers. It was also large enough to have some influence on wholesalers' product selection. Some of FEDUP's members were interested in organic food, and in 1977 half a dozen of them got together to form the Wild West Organic Harvest Co-operative.

The founders of Wild West hoped eventually both to grow the food and distribute it. Their plan was to use profits from the distribution arm to fund the purchase of land, equipment, and other requirements for organic agriculture. However, there was so little money to be made in distribution that assembling the required capital seemed less and less likely. By the time of the recession of the early 1980s, the co-op had virtually abandoned the idea of growing the organic food it distributed. Wild West was focused solely on wholesaling.

By 1990, however, the co-op was thriving. Sales and profit figures for the years from 1985 to 1990 appear in Exhibit 1. Wild West's members were proud of their co-op's success for all the obvious reasons, but also because Wild West showed that nontraditional businesses could work, and work well. For the organization was not only a co-op, it was a worker-owned co-op.

The organizational structure was completely flat: there were no superiors or subordinates. Each of the 17 members of the co-op had an area of responsibility, such as sales, buying, or truck-driving, and they made all the routine decisions in their own areas. Major decisions affecting the co-op as a whole, such as whether to purchase a new warehouse, truck, or capital equipment, were made by the whole group. The truck drivers had just as much influence on the decision as the marketing person or the buyer. Surprisingly for such a large group, this was not a cumbersome process. Darcy Hamilton laughed about "Myth No. 42: It takes ages to make a decision in a co-op." Various people had different areas of expertise (often wider

Exhibit 1

SELECTED FINANCIAL RESULTS

Year	Net Income	Sales
1985	$25,678	$ 954,000
1986	$13,390	$ 978,000
1987	$34,082	$1,866,000
1988	$22,995	$1,704,000
1989	$43,938	$3,252,000

than their area of responsibility would suggest) and the others respected their colleagues' knowledge and experience. Everyone's voice was heard. Obviously, it worked.

Many co-ops had tried to implement a completely flat organizational structure and a consensual decision-making process, but once the group exceeded about eight individuals, it tended to break down. Usually, a traditional hierarchical organizational structure was then adopted. The 17 members of Wild West attributed their unusual success with a flat organizational structure in such a large group to the fact that, until 1989, the workers in the co-op were all women.[1] The explanation offered by two of the workers at Wild West was that women were socialized to be more co-operative than competitive, so group decision making was viable in relatively larger groups of women than men. The consensual style of decision making translated into effective implementation of decisions, since each co-op member had contributed to the decision.

Another reason for the success of the flat organizational structure was the care that went into choosing members. Individuals interested in joining Wild West had to work first as "prospective," rather than full-fledged members, for a period of six months. During this time, both the prospective member and the people already involved in Wild West could evaluate their mutual fit. After the waiting period, there was a formal performance evaluation and, assuming the latter was favourable and the worker still wanted to become a member of the co-op, she (or he) was accepted as a member, with all the accompanying rights and responsibilities: a share in the decision making and profits, and the payment of share capital. Each member, regardless of number of years as a member, experience, or area of responsibility, was paid the same hourly rate, which was competitive with rates for skilled labour in the industry.[2]

ORGANIC AGRICULTURE IN CANADA

Wild West's success in co-operative decision making was matched by its financial success. In the last ten years, annual sales had risen from just under $750,000 to over $3.25 million. This was not a trivial achievement, since margins in produce wholesaling were squeezed by costs of spoilage, and fluctuating demand and supply. These costs tended to be higher for organic produce, since organic agriculture tended to be small scale. Briefly, organic farming methods were based on maintaining the health of the soil by following the regenerative cycles found in nature. Rather than using chemical fertilizers, which could deplete the soil's fertility, organic farmers used well-composted plant and animal materials and green manure crops to provide a healthy growing environment for their crops. Fortunately for Canadian farmers, the

[1] In 1989, two men became involved with the co-op. One had since become a member; the other had been hired on a limited term contract.

[2] Having a uniform rate of pay meant that some of the workers, such as the accountant, were receiving less than they might in a traditional business. However, on average, the workers at Wild West earned more for their work than they would elsewhere, because women in traditional warehouses usually worked at low-paying unskilled jobs, while the better-paying skilled jobs, such as operating a forklift, were usually done by men.

cold Canadian winters simplified pest control naturally, but when pests did become a problem, organic farmers used purely biological methods such as target-specific bacterial insecticides and predacious insects. In contrast, conventional farmers used chemical means to control pests. By the late 1980s, Canadian farmers were using 88,000 tons of 5,000 different pesticides, herbicides, and chemical fertilizers each year. Many pesticides and herbicides were systemic toxins that penetrated the skins of fruits and vegetables (such as lettuce) and could not be washed off.

Production costs were inherently no higher for organic food than for conventionally raised food. However, much of the non-organic agriculture in Canada was done on large corporate farms that could take advantage of economies of scale. Organic farms required more intensive management and therefore tended to be small. Nevertheless, by the end of the 1980s, organic produce was a significant factor in the market for fruits and vegetables. Many organic farmers sold everything they could grow directly to consumers who came to their farms to pick up produce.

In the United States, it was estimated that organically grown produce constituted a $5 billion portion of that country's $36 billion annual fruit and vegetable market. However, organic certification standards in Canada were much more stringent than in the U.S., so the organic share of the produce market in Canada was about one-third the size of the U.S. market. In Canada, the market for fresh produce had been growing at about 12% per year for the past decade, compared with annual growth in frozen fruits and vegetables of 10%, and an annual decrease in sales of canned fruits and vegetables of 20%.

Wild West had been the first organization in British Columbia to set specific standards for organic produce. Their certification program required that growers' fields be free of chemicals for at least four years (versus the one-year requirement for certified organic produce in California). Farmers who wanted to become certified as organic growers had to make an application. Their knowledge of organic farming methods and their farm records would then be reviewed and their farms would be classified as either "certified" or "transitional." Transitional farmers became certified after they had met the growing standards for four years. Each year, all of Wild West's Canadian suppliers had to submit to a stringent review of their farming practices. Anyone not conforming to the standards would be dropped. By 1990, more and more conventional farmers were expressing an interest in converting to organic methods.

CONSUMER EXPECTATIONS

Organically grown produce did not always have the "eye-appeal" that conventionally grown produce did. For instance, organically grown apples were not waxed, so they were not as shiny as the apples usually found in big supermarkets. These visual differences were only cosmetic. Yet in focus group research commissioned by Wild West in the last months of 1989, consumers indicated very strongly that the appearance of fruits and vegetables was very important to them; they said that they would prefer "less" rather than "no" chemicals in order to maintain the appearance they had come to expect in supermarket produce. Exhibit 2 provides excerpts from a 1989 consumer survey of 482 respondents, designed to assess attitudes and beliefs about food, as well as food purchasing patterns.[3] The same survey also indicated that most consumers expected to pay more for organically grown food, but the maximum they would be willing to pay was 25% more than the price of the conventionally grown equivalent. In addition, about 25% of respondents indicated that they would be very likely or somewhat likely to buy organic vegetables; and 18% of respondents said they would be very likely or somewhat likely to buy organic fruit.

The members of Wild West found the survey results interesting and helpful, but their own experience told them that the situation was a little more complicated. They viewed the consumer market for produce as having three segments: committed organic customers, borderline customers, and conventional customers. They were most interested in the first two groups.

Committed organic customers were convinced that organic produce was healthier. Consequently, they were willing to pay a premium for chemical-free food, and they were used to having to go to some trouble to find it. People in this group were careful consumers, aware that certification standards for organic produce varied, and not hesitant to make the effort to find out exactly where their food came from. Committed organic customers were estimated to make up about 65% to 70% of Wild West's consumer base, but probably only 8% of the total consumer market for produce.

Borderline customers were more fickle. Whenever media stories about the health risks associated with agricultural chemicals appeared, there would be a huge increase in sales of organically grown fruits and vegetables. For instance, during the alar on apples scare of 1989, demand for organically grown apples doubled, and Wild West was temporarily unable to meet it. (This partially accounts for the substantial sales increase in 1989). However, once media attention faded, so did sales, although more slowly. The health consequences for the majority of pesticides in use in Canada were unknown, but research was ongoing. The news was generally not good. The members of Wild West expected that fear-induced runs on organically grown produce would occur more frequently as research results were released over the next few years.

The difference in loyalty between the committed and borderline customers might have been due to differences in motivation: one was positive; the other, negative. Committed customers seemed to buy organic food because they believed it to be healthier; borderline customers seemed to buy organic food because they were worried that the food they usually bought might be unhealthy. Thus, when they were no longer being reminded of these fears, the borderline customers reverted to their old habits. It seemed that the extra cost and inconvenience associated with the purchase of organically grown fruits and vegetables were hurdles too great to overcome if fear was not top of mind. Nevertheless, every time there was disturbing news about chemicals in food, some borderline customers became committed customers, and some people who had previously ignored the organic option started to think about it. By 1990, borderline customers probably made up at least 15% of the

[3] The survey was carried out among supermarket shoppers in the Greater Vancouver area as part of a government-sponsored survey about food expenditures.

Exhibit 2
SELECTED RESULTS FROM THE CONSUMER SURVEY

A. Current Food Consumption Patterns: Amount of Food Eaten Today as Compared to 5 Years Ago

Food	More Today	Same	Less Today
Vegetables	46%	48%	6%
Red Meats	8%	42%	50%
Poultry	50%	40%	10%
Fish	40%	42%	18%
Cheese	43%	45%	12%

B. Current Consumption and Purchase of Organic Foods

Category	Purchased or Consumed	Not Purchased or Consumed	Don't Know
Vegetables	35%	55%	10%
Fruits	20%	65%	15%
Meats	10%	75%	15%
Dairy products	10%	72%	18%
Other foods	12%	70%	18%

C. Where Consumers of Organic Produce Buy

Source	Fruits	Vegetables
Farmers' market	33%	22%
Grocery store	21%	14%
Health food store	15%	12%
Farm gate	11%	11%
Grow own	10%	31%
Combination of places	10%	11%

D. Perceptions of Organically and Conventionally Grown Vegetables by Purchase Status

Product Attributes	Superiority	Organic Buyer*	Organic Non-Buyer
Better quality	• Organic	66%	52%
	• Conventional	11%	18%
	• Same	23%	30%
Better tasting	• Organic	72%	49%
	• Conventional	7%	18%
	• Same	21%	33%

(continued)

Exhibit 2 continued

Product Attributes	Superiority	Organic Buyer*	Organic Non-Buyer
More appealing	• Organic	26%	24%
	• Conventional	50%	42%
	• Same	24%	34%
Healthier	• Organic	87%	75%
	• Conventional	5%	8%
	• Same	8%	17%
More nutritious	• Organic	78%	62%
	• Conventional	4%	9%
	• Same	18%	29%

* Defined as those who said they had ever purchased or consumed organic produce.

E. Opinions About Pesticides and Herbicides

Respondents were asked which of the following statements about pesticides and herbicides most closely matched their own opinion.

Statement 1: I'm totally opposed to the use of any pesticides and herbicides on crops that are to be used for food.

This statement was chosen by 14% of respondents.

Statement 2: I'm not opposed to the use of pesticides and herbicides, but I am concerned about their use and would like to see more controls on their use.

This statement was chosen by 67% of respondents.

Statement 3: Pesticides and herbicides are a reality and a necessity today if we are going to produce the foods that are needed.

This statement was chosen by 10% of respondents.

consumer produce market; they represented about 30% of Wild West's ultimate customers.

The remainder of the produce market was made up of people who did not buy organics. It seemed unlikely that they did not care about healthy food; numerous consumer surveys have shown both an increasing awareness of the importance of eating a nutritious diet and the dangers of pesticides. Results from some surveys seemed to indicate that many people who did not buy organic fruits and vegetables were interested in doing so, but didn't know how to go about it. Other than that, little was known about this group.

THE PATH FROM GROWER TO CONSUMER

The typical distribution channels for fruits and vegetables were fairly simple. The grower raised produce and sold it either to a wholesaler or grower co-op. The price paid to the grower was determined almost completely by supply and demand. Organic produce commanded a higher price than conventionally raised produce, partly because demand generally exceeded supply. But Wild West also recognized the importance of keeping their suppliers in business, so they generally offered their growers a premium price. Growers and suppliers often developed loyal relationships, and this was especially the case with Wild West and its growers. The members of Wild West viewed this as a particular area of strength.

The wholesaler or grower co-op could then do any of three things with the produce. They could sell it to a large chain of grocery stores such as Safeway or Overwaitea. The wholesaler's usual margin would be about 20% of the price the wholesaler had paid for it. In this case, the produce would move from the wholesaler's warehouse to the chain's warehouse, and then on to the chain stores, along with a 45% to 50% mark-up above the wholesale price. Often large chains had a policy that the same produce would appear in all stores in the organization, so if the Vancouver stores had organically grown produce, so did every store in British Columbia. This meant that the wholesaler had to be able to provide sufficient quantities to stock stores across the province,[4] but it also meant that the wholesaler would get a large sale, so margins were often shaved. Wild West had recently begun to supply Safeway stores in British Columbia. So far, they had not had too much difficulty supplying adequate quantities, although it was sometimes complicated dealing with Safeway. There were several produce buyers who bought for the whole chain, then each store had a produce manager who decided on specific quantities of each type of produce for his or her store. Wild West had access to the corporate produce buyers, but they had little opportunity to influence produce managers in individual stores.

Another alternative for the wholesaler would be to sell its produce to an independent distributor. The wholesaler's margin would still be, as with sales to the chain stores, about 20%. The independent distributor would then resell the produce to independent grocers, convenience stores, restaurants, and sometimes even chains. For this, they would get a margin of anywhere between 20% and 50% of their selling price. The retail prices charged to consumers could vary widely. Wild West did not see any particular advantage to this alternative, so they had never pursued any opportunities to deal with the independent distributors.

Wild West's traditional strength was in the third area: selling directly to retailers. Their customers included over 400 health food stores, health food restaurants, gourmet restaurants, independent grocery stores, buying clubs, and food co-ops from Winnipeg to Vancouver. The typical order was small compared to a Safeway

[4] In the autumn of 1990, there were 86 Safeway outlets in British Columbia, 59 Overwaitea (including Save-on-Foods) stores, and more than 40 IGA branches. Competition among the big retail chains could be intense. For example, the small community of 100 Mile House in the Interior of the province had both a Safeway and an Overwaitea, but the total population of area was only about 15,000.

order. Wild West's mark-up for small customers was larger than it was for Safeway, but the smaller orders were more costly to ship, since they usually required that a pallet be broken up, so in the final analysis, Wild West was no better off financially with its smaller customers. For most of Wild West's history, however, these retailers had been the only ones interested in carrying organic produce.

COMPETITION

Wild West faced competition for both their suppliers and their customers. The co-op had built strong relationships with its grower-suppliers, of which there were about 40 local farmers and more than 100 American farmers, whose crops Wild West bought when local supplies were depleted. Most of the local farmers had been selling to Wild West for several years. The fact that the co-op had had a policy of paying the growers "a fair price," which was frequently higher than the law of supply and demand might dictate, had engendered considerable loyalty, or so Wild West believed. Now that consumer demand for organic produce was growing, the large produce wholesalers, who had until recently virtually ignored the organic market, were starting to become active in this area—but not all of them: one of the large produce wholesalers believed that interest in organics was already waning, and that there was hefty consumer resistance based on price, so they intended to continue treating organics as special order items only. Nevertheless, since the number of certified organic growers was limited, it was becoming increasingly likely that other produce wholesalers would compete directly with Wild West for supply. In this case, Wild West might be at a disadvantage, since the large produce wholesalers could, if necessary, pay the grower a higher price and take a smaller margin, since organics made up a relatively small proportion of their business.

On the other hand, competitors might decide instead to import organic produce from the United States, where supplies were more plentiful, and organic requirements less stringent. Even this might have an adverse impact on Wild West, since the co-op also imported organic produce that was not grown in Canada, or not grown in sufficient quantities in Canada, from the United States, Mexico, and Central America.[5]

If the large produce wholesalers decided to get into the organic market in a big way, Wild West would have to watch its client list carefully. The competition's ability to shave margins might mean that they could charge lower prices to their retail customers. However, the members of Wild West were confident that price was not the only consideration their customers had. Stores and restaurants also wanted to be sure that what they were getting was truly organic, and they wanted reliability in terms of delivery and quality. In fact, one of the reservations that the large grocery chains had about organic produce was the varying certification standards. If they called something "organic," they wanted to be sure that their customers used the same definition they did; the last thing they needed was to have to fend off accusations of deception. Fortunately, it seemed that national standards (requiring four years of chemical-free farming for certification) were close to introduction.

[5] Wild West dealt with differences in certification standards by indicating on its price list which items satisfied which standards.

There was also a good possibility that completely new competitors would enter the market, taking advantage of increased consumer interest in organics.

The possible effects of competition on consumers was also a concern. Wild West had, for over a decade, been the dominant force in organic produce wholesaling in western Canada. During that time, they had placed considerable emphasis on nonfinancial goals: consumer education about the benefits of organically raised food, support and education of growers, and the provision of truly organic food. Wild West worried that some of the larger wholesalers, who did not operate from the same ideological base, might act in ways that might erode some of the progress that had been made in these areas.

Notwithstanding all the potential threats, Wild West was in a favourable competitive position. They had excellent relations with their suppliers, a good client list, and considerably credibility. In addition, the market seemed poised to grow rapidly: in a recently released national survey, 90% of Canadians said they were unhappy about current pesticide practices.

A CHANGE IN APPROACH?

Given the new opportunities and threats that rapid market growth could yield, the members of the Wild West Organic Harvest Co-op decided to take a close look at their marketing strategy. Before 1990, they had done very modest promotion, with fair success. Wild West's main communication vehicle was their quarterly catalogue, supplied to all regular clients. This was supplemented by informational brochures on differences between organic and conventional farming, distributed to retailers to help them better understand the product. Wild West had also participated in the annual Canadian Health Food Association trade convention, and had placed print ads in trade magazines such as *The Packer*. Exhibit 3 shows an advertisement that had recently appeared. These activities, added to Wild West's established reputation as a dependable supplier of organic produce, had put the company in a good position with retailers. A 1989 telephone survey of 20 randomly chosen food retailers in the Vancouver area revealed strong recognition and recall of the Wild West name, even among retailers who did not do business with the co-op.

Wild West had also done some consumer promotions. These had mainly been in-store demonstrations, and they had not been very successful, attracting few customers and requiring a great deal of time to execute. Total advertising expenses for 1989 had been $10,000. Based on industry standards, this level of consumer advertising was not low, because there was very little branding in the produce industry and many wholesalers did no consumer advertising or promotion at all.

The new market growth had recently led co-op members to re-examine their goals. They decided that their marketing objective should be to build the Wild West brand name to encourage consumer loyalty in the future. In order to achieve this objective, they would have to convince the large grocery chains to broaden their current organic produce sections, and demonstrate to consumers the quality and safety of their product, as well as its nonhazardous effect on the environment. Wild West's members believed that the concern they had demonstrated over the years for the best interests of consumers and the environment would contribute to their success

Exhibit 3
SAMPLE ADVERTISEMENT

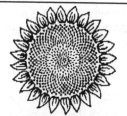

Wild West Organic Harvest Co-op

FRESH ORGANIC FRUIT

FRESH ORGANIC VEGETABLES

FRESH ORGANIC B.C.
Cherries
Apricots
Peaches
Apples

One box or two hundred...!

The more you learn about the way your food is grown, the more you want to buy organic!

Organically grown produce from Wild West, a co-op 13 years committed to sustainable agriculture.

Organics is THE positive alternative to the major environmental impact of conventional agriculture. We are working with organic farmers and retailers to be this alternative—the consumers best food choice!

Carrots to Kumquats, Watercress to Watermelon, Wild West draws from near and far to provide year round availability. Phone, fax, or write for a complete list of our products. Taste the organic difference.

2471 Simpson Rd., Richmond B.C.
V6X 2R2 (604) 276-2411

in this area. Consumers could be loyal to Wild West because Wild West had been and would be loyal to them.

The first step in a new, more aggressive approach would have to be labelling. The large grocery chains had made it clear that they required that organic produce be either bagged or stickered, to distinguish it from conventional produce. (The irony of having to package food that had been raised in an environmentally sensitive manner was not lost on Wild West.) Some items, such as apples, would best be stickered individually, to allow consumers to buy varying amounts, while other items, such as carrots or potatoes, would have to be bagged. This would add slightly to the cost, but it fit with Wild West's desire to encourage brand loyalty. Designs for bags and stickers with the Wild West logo (a sunflower and the brand name), along with the word "organic," had been submitted by a small advertising consulting group.

A STRATEGY UNDER CONSIDERATION

In the fall of 1990, the members of Wild West sat down to consider a new promotional strategy suggested by the advertising consultants. Basically, it was a campaign directed at getting Wild West's products listed and supported with reasonable shelf space by large grocery chains such as IGA, Overwaitea, and Safeway.

Consumer Advertising

The advertising portion of the proposed campaign involved informing consumers about the dangers of pesticides and suggesting that they ask their grocers to stock more organically grown food.

Specifically, the objective was to inform consumers of the nutritional and environmental benefits of organic produce, while linking it to the Wild West brand name. The target audience was to be the primary food shopper. The best potential was expected to be among younger females with above average income and education, the group most likely to be nutritionally and environmentally conscious.

The primary message would be that organic produce offers a chemical-free alternative to conventional produce, thereby offering a nutritious and healthy product in a form that is better for the individual and the environment. The back-up claim would be that the purchase of organic produce allowed the consumer to participate in saving the environment from chemical pollutants: the use of natural methods ensured that organic farming did not contaminate soil or ground water, harm wildlife, or present a health threat to farming communities. The style of the ads was to be "serious, impactful, and interesting." The brand's character was to be "honest, appealing, and awakening." The portrayal would be such that "if the brand were a person, it would be someone like David Suzuki or Meryl Streep," both of whom had campaigned against pesticides.

Several headlines, all simple and eye-catching, had been developed. Three of the headlines considered were

- *An organic apple a day keeps the doctor away.* This elaboration on the old saying would be attention-getting and easy to remember, but it dealt only with the health aspect of organics, omitting the larger environmental concern. In addition, there was concern that the headline could be construed as implying that conventionally grown apples *would* bring the doctor (that is, be unhealthy), which had not been empirically demonstrated. Wild West did not want to make any deceptive claims.
- *Don't play with your food.* This was intended to show that eating chemical-laden produce was gambling with danger, while playing on the well-known maternal exhortation. However, many people who saw the ad would not read the supporting copy, and this headline might conjure up the wrong images,such as juggling apples.
- *Do you have questions about pesticides? So do we.* This headline was less "clever" or "cute" than others, but it was still attention-getting. The headline was appropriate to deal with a serious issue in a serious way. The implication was that Wild West and the consumer were on the same side. In addition, the

headline seemed to be person-specific: consumers who had mostly health concerns could interpret it as a statement about the health risks associated with pesticides, while consumers whose primary concern was the environment could interpret it as referring to the environmental consequences of pesticide use (groundwater contamination, etc.).

General findings from advertising research suggested that a closing line such as "Make the switch to organic," should be used. It would let the consumer know what action to take to solve the problem.

Promotion

The advertising campaign would be complemented by an integrated promotional campaign designed to broaden the current organic produce sections of grocery chains in the Greater Vancouver area. The product chosen to lead this action was locally grown organic apples.

To accomplish the objective of getting the product listed and well-placed in the major grocery chains, Wild West would promote organically grown apples directly to consumers, while simultaneously marketing the product to the trade. Once the desired listings had been arranged, incentives for trial would be the focus of the campaign. The advertising consultants suggested a multi-event, three-stage campaign, including direct mail, publicity releases, sales calls, professional specification sheets, backer cards, health club trials, and in-store demonstrations.

A direct mail piece would be sent to 5000 environmentally active consumers in the Lower Mainland. The mailing list could either be obtained from local environmental groups or from a market research firm. The mailing would remind consumers of the environmental threats posed by conventional farming methods, and suggest that one appropriate action would be to request environmentally safe produce at their local grocer. A draft of the suggested copy appears in Exhibit 4.

Publicity releases would also be used. The members of Wild West had a great deal of knowledge about organic farming methods and their benefits, as well as the dangers of chemical farming. Publicity releases would focus on facts about pesticides in a newsworthy way. The releases would always include an indication of what consumers could do in this area (including buying organic produce).

In order to compete effectively with large produce distributors, Wild West would have to upgrade its trade-oriented marketing tools. The simple price list would have to be replaced with a specification sheet (including a full-color product shot) highlighting the incremental benefits of organic produce. Since the price of organics was higher, emphasis would be placed on other benefits. As well, the spec sheets would emphasize volume discounts for large orders.

To reinforce its advertising, Wild West would provide the food stores with large backer cards (posters mounted on cardboard that stand behind a display) showing the headline, highlighting one or two key problems with pesticides, and closing with the "Make the switch to organic" line and the company logo. This visual aid would provide information to consumers while benefiting the trade by attracting attention and increasing sales.

Once listings with the large grocery chains had been obtained, the plan was to

Exhibit 4
SUGGESTED COPY FOR TARGET MAIL

**DO YOU HAVE QUESTIONS ABOUT PESTICIDES?
SO DO WE!**

Actually, here at the Wild West Organic Harvest Co-op, we have questions about all synthetic chemicals used in growing produce. One thing we do know is that these chemicals have a *negative* effect on our environment and we want it to stop. These chemicals decrease the soil's fertility and stability, they pollute the air, and when oversprayed, these chemicals seep into our water tables. In addition to the environmental concern, did you know that in the U.S., of the 25 pesticides detected most frequently in food, nine have been identified as causing cancer in laboratory animals?

Although research has shown that over 85% of consumers are concerned about the current use and testing of pesticides, some of the big name stores are hesitating to carry a full line of organic produce.

Wild West Organic Harvest Co-op was founded 13 years ago by a group of environmentally concerned people, in an attempt to demonstrate that people could grow produce naturally, without the use of environmentally harmful chemicals. Currently Wild West carries a wide variety of organic fruits and vegetables. Unfortunately, it has been an uphill battle for us to get this certified organic produce to you.

It is here that we are asking for your help. All of us environmentally concerned consumers need to ask our store managers for more organics. We need to voice our opinions about the use of chemicals in food. We need to ask for *organic fruits and vegetables.*

Please . . . the next time you are in one of the big chain food stores, tell the store manager that you care about your health and the environment, and you would like to make the switch to organic. Thanks for caring.

The people at Wild West Co-op.

---

increase volume by offering free apple samples at health clubs in Greater Vancouver. A display, including a basket of organic apples, the backer card, and informational brochures would be placed near the main entrance so that health club members could pick up an apple and a brochure after a healthy workout. The majority of health club members were 18 to 34 years old and female, a group that overlapped with primary food shoppers. Several local health clubs had been contacted to determine whether they would be receptive to participating in such a promotion. Most were enthusiastic, since they quickly identified with Wild West's health and environmental goals. Club managers suggested that 80% of their members could be reached in a three-day span.

As an added benefit to the trade, Wild West would offer to do introductory in-store demonstrations during the first month of a new listing. The in-store demonstra-

Exhibit 5
CRITICAL PATH

Stage	Timing	Activities
Preliminary	a.s.a.p.	• develop new sticker • develop all ad/publicity material
Stage 1	Weeks 1 to 3	• target mail • news releases and publicity generation • preliminary sales calls to grocers • trade print ads
Stage 2	Weeks 4 to 8	• sales calls on all produce buyers in major food chains
Stage 3	Weeks 9 to 12	• begin in-store demos • health club trials • backer cards • in-store flyers
Stage 4	Weeks 13 to 16	• in-store demos in new stores

tor would give slices of Wild West apples to consumers, encouraging trial. Since the consumer research commissioned by Wild West had shown that consumers perceive organic apples to be better tasting, the combination of tasting an apple and having a demonstrator talking about the benefits of organically grown produce would likely have a strong positive effect on sales. The increase would likely decay slowly, since once consumers tried the apples and became aware of the dangers of the alternative, many would decide not to switch back to conventional apples, provided that the price differential did not exceed 25%.

Radio and magazine ads were also options, but they were very costly, and everyone at Wild West agreed that these opportunities would not be seriously entertained until the rest of the campaign had been successful.

Exhibit 5 shows the planned critical path, and Exhibit 6 shows a preliminary budget for the campaign. The budget required Wild West to spend $12,000 more than the $10,000 they were currently spending, and this substantial increase made some members of the co-op nervous.

THE AUGUST MEETING

In mid-August, the members of the Wild West Organic Harvest Co-op met to discuss a variety of issues facing them. Among these was the question of how best to deal with the growth of the market and the dynamic competitive situation. They had built their business on serving one segment of the produce market better than anyone

Exhibit 6
BUDGET

Target Mail	
(5,000 pieces/$600 production/$1,000 postage)	$ 1,600
Spec Sheet	
(8.5 × 11"/one side colour/2,000 sheets)	700
Backer Cards	
(per design/50 @ $20 ea.)	1,000
Brochures	
(per design/20,000 @ $0.10 ea.)	2,000
In-Store Demo	
(20 stores/2 days/$75 per day)	3,000
Health Club Promos	
(80 events @ $50 ea.)	4,000
Total	$12,300
Other Options	
Radio	
(10 spots weekly/afternoon drive/ CKNW,CKWX,CHQM)	$ 2,500/wk
Magazines	
(3 issues/one third page)	
Western Living	$ 3,000
Vancouver Magazine	$ 4,000

else did. Now they had an opportunity to sell to a much wider segment of the population. They were going to have to decide to what extent they should pursue that opportunity. They also had to address the problem of increased competition.

On a more tactical level, the members of Wild West also wanted to consider the advertising and promotion proposal submitted by the consultants. They wanted to make sure it was consistent with their overall marketing strategy. The apple season was fast approaching, and they had to decide whether the campaign should go ahead and, if so, whether it should include all the suggested elements.

Everyone at the meeting was convinced that organic food was superior to conventionally raised food, and they knew that the increased interest in the environment was an opportunity they could take advantage of. But some members were concerned about getting too involved in advertising, which they saw as manipulative. They also worried that they might face new pressures to compromise their standards if they were successful in getting listings with the large grocery chains. Some members thought that Wild West had built a solid, loyal group of customers by serving their specialized needs well, and that they risked losing this advantage if they became too big.

Consensus under these conditions might be difficult, but the co-op had faced complicated issues before, so they were confident that a decision that was satisfactory to everyone would be found.

52 VASELINE INTENSIVE CARE LOTION[1]

Tara Tomlinson was concerned—it was June 19, 1989, and she had just heard that a new brand, Eversoft, from a formidable competitor, Jergens, was entering the Canadian market. As the senior brand manager for hand and body lotions for Chesebrough-Pond's, Tara was responsible for the growth and profitability of the product category, including Vaseline Intensive Care Lotion (VICL). The news had been brought by Katy Morton, the assistant brand manager for VICL. Katy added: "The sales representative I talked to said that Eversoft will be in the stores in late July or early August. That gives us about a month to prepare and launch a counterattack."

"It's going to be tough," said Tara. "Eversoft made a big impact in the United States. Let's review the information we have and come up with a game plan. I want to keep VICL in the number one position."

VICL was the market leader in the hand and body lotion category with a 28% share, based on volume, in 1988. Chesebrough-Pond's had recently reversed the brand's falling market position by investing heavily and making significant changes to the brand, creative, media, and trade strategies. This translated into a substantial growth in volume and profits. Both Tara and Katy knew it was imperative that VICL maintain its leadership, and the action plan developed should halt Eversoft from making major inroads in Canada.

THE U.S. EXPERIENCE

Eversoft was launched in the United States in September 1988, and started to advertise in November 1988. Estimated spending for Eversoft in the first year was $27 million of which $10 million was in advertising and $17 million was in couponing and sampling. These large promotion expenditures gave this new brand a 15% to 20% share of total advertising expenditures for the product category.

By March/April of 1989, Eversoft attained a market share of 4% in dollars and 3% in volume (Exhibit 1). This share was achieved with a retail price that was 60% higher than VICL. Tara and Katy had watched these events and felt that it was just a matter of time before Eversoft was introduced in Canada. Now, the time had come.

THE COMPANY

Chesebrough-Pond's is a division of Unilever, the second largest consumer packaged goods company in the world. Unilever, an Anglo-Dutch conglomerate, with world-wide sales of $40 billion, has grown mainly through acquisition in three major

[1] Written by executives at Chesebrough-Pond's (Canada) Inc.

Exhibit 1

U.S. NIELSEN RESULTS—PERCENT SHARE OF MARKET (SELECTED BRANDS)

	March/April 1988	January/February 1989	March/April 1989
Value (Retail $)			
VICL	16	17	17
Vaseline Hand & Nail	N/A	5	4
Jergens	10	9	8
Eversoft	N/A	3	4
Keri	10	8	9
Volume (Units)			
VICL	20	21	21
Vaseline Hand & Nail	N/A	4	3
Jergens	12	10	9
Eversoft	N/A	2	3
Keri	5	4	5

categories: detergents, food, and most recently personal care products. Unilever Canada operates a number of divisions (and brands) including Lever Brothers (Sunlight detergent, Dove soap), Thomas J. Lipton (Red Rose Tea), Unox Meats (Shopsy's), Monarch Fine Foods (Blue Bonnet margarine), and A & W (A & W Restaurants, A & W Soft Drinks). Total sales for Unilever in Canada in 1988 were $926 million and net profits were $17 million. Estimates were that 1989 sales could exceed $1 billion and net profits could exceed $24 million. The Chesebrough-Pond's division operated in a number of core markets including hand and body lotions (VICL, Vaseline Petroleum Jelly), dentifrice (Close-up, Aim), shampoos (Pears), conditioners (Pears), colour cosmetics (Cutex lipsticks), and fragrances (Cachet, Brut). VICL is Chesebrough-Pond's number one brand in sales and number two brand in contribution (Exhibit 2). Building on that success, Chesebrough-Pond's launched Vaseline Intensive Care Hand & Nail Formula in August 1988.

THE PRODUCT

Functionally, hand and body lotions are all formulated to (1) soften and moisturize hands, (2) leave no tacky feeling or greasiness, (3) apply easily and absorb quickly, (4) have a pleasing scent, and (5) stay on and have an appealing application.

Formulations vary in their raw material composition. This affects the lotion's ability to deliver moisturizing efficacy and changes the product. Eversoft, which is similar to VICL in efficacy, is composed of different ingredients that are considered to be appealing on application.

Exhibit 2

VASELINE INTENSIVE CARE LOTION—1989 PROFIT AND LOSS STATEMENT (ESTIMATED)

		% of Sales
Net sales	$7,700,000	100
Cost of goods	2,700,000	35
Gross margin	5,000,000	65
Advertising	1,270,000	16
Trade promotions	1,150,000	15
Consumer promotions	200,000	3
Total promotion	2,620,000	34
Gross profit	3,380,000	31
Administration expenses	1,540,000	20
Profit before tax	840,000	11

Source: Company records

CONSUMER ATTITUDES

A national survey conducted in the spring of 1989 provided information on consumer attitudes and usage of lotions. Incidence of use is very high at 70% to 75% of females using hand and body lotions, with 45% of them using lotions at least once a day (Exhibit 3). As a result, consumers repurchase their lotions on average every six to eight weeks. Per capita consumption was approximately 2.5 L per annum and growing. Lotions are used most commonly on hands, but approximately half use these lotions on other parts of the body. On average, consumers have two brands at home suggesting multiple users and/or uses. VICL has the highest awareness scores[2] as well as ever used scores.[3]

In the same survey, respondents rated "dry skin relief" as being an important purchase decision, followed by "smoothes rough skin." The percentage of respondents rating the product attributes as "extremely desirable" were

Attribute	Percent
Relieves skin dryness	70
Smoothes rough skin	53
Helps heal red, sore, chapped hands	30
Moisturizes the skin	25
Protects hands from dry/chapping	20

[2] Percentage of consumers who mention VICL, when asked to name a brand of hand lotion.

[3] Percentage of consumers who state they have used VICL at some time since its launch.

Exhibit 3
FREQUENCY OF USAGE, BODY CARE, AND BRANDS USED (PERCENTAGES)

Hand Care Product Users

			Age*				Household Income*				Region*				
	Total Canada	Total English Canada	18–24	25–34	35–49	50+	Under $20K	$20K to $35K	$35K to $50K	$50K or More	Atl.	Que.	Ont.	Man./ Sask.	Alta. B.C.
Frequency of Using Hand-Care Products															
Hand Lotion/Liquid															
Daily or more often	43	47	31	46	45	56	44	47	46	50	36	46	47	53	48
2–6 times a week	17	17	19	19	18	15	13	10	17	20	25	15	16	15	19
Once a week	4	4	7	6	3	3	6	5	4	3	3	3	4	4	6
Less than once a week	8	9	12	10	10	6	9	8	11	7	13	11	9	6	8
Not stated	28	23	32	19	24	20	29	22	23	20	23	25	24	22	19
Total	100	100	100	100	100	100	100	100	100	100	100	100	100	100	100
Hand Cream															
Daily or more often	16	16	17	11	15	18	20	15	15	14	12	16	17	21	13
2–6 times a week	9	8	8	7	10	6	6	9	8	7	8	8	8	5	8
Once a week	3	2	5	3	2	1	3	2	2	2	4	3	3	–	2
Less than once a week	5	3	3	3	5	3	2	3	3	5	3	4	4	5	2
Not stated	67	71	66	77	68	72	69	72	73	71	73	70	69	70	76
Total	100	100	100	100	100	100	100	100	100	100	100	100	100	100	100
Use Hand Care Product For Body Care															
Yes	69	72	75	78	69	68	71	74	70	71	71	70	73	69	71
All over/Entire body	31	33	34	45	31	26	34	30	33	35	36	29	33	31	36
Arms	22	23	20	19	20	28	24	23	22	22	25	19	23	26	21
Elbows	32	32	32	26	30	37	32	36	32	28	39	36	31	33	21
Legs	25	26	31	23	24	28	25	27	25	26	24	33	28	25	23
Feet	25	25	22	19	25	31	25	26	25	24	28	24	26	27	22
Face	1	1	–	1	1	1	1	1	1	–	2	–	–	1	1

(continued)

Exhibit 3 continued

	Total Canada	Total English Canada	Age*: 18–24	25–34	35–49	50+	Household Income*: Under $20K	$20K to $35K	$35K to $50K	$50K or More	Region*: Atl.	Que.	Ont.	Man./ Sask.	Alta. B.C.
No (use only on hands)	25	25	22	19	26	28	20	23	28	26	26	23	23	28	26
Not stated	6	4	3	3	5	4	8	4	3	3	3	6	4	3	3
Total	100	100	100	100	100	100	100	100	100	100	100	100	100	100	100
Total Respondents	2,784	2,257	329	506	581	840	367	645	520	660	195	108	1,080	265	606
Brands of Hand Lotion/ Liquid Used															
Vaseline Intensive Care	24	26	33	25	24	26	24	29	24	26	36	25	25	18	27
Jergens	12	13	10	14	14	13	12	11	10	12	12	9	13	14	14
Vaseline	10	9	13	6	11	9	9	8	8	11	9	13	9	6	10
Keri Lotion	7	7	5	8	5	8	3	8	8	6	5	10	6	7	8
Avon (any Avon)	7	7	3	6	9	7	7	8	6	6	5	10	6	7	8
Soft Sense	5	5	8	7	6	3	7	4	5	4	3	3	6	8	4
Nivea	2	2	–	2	3	2	2	–	2	3	3	2	2	–	2
Store brand/ private label	2	2	–	1	3	2	4	2	2	1	3	1	2	–	2
(Note: All other brands 2% or less)															
Total Brands Mentioned	1,944	1,701	223	399	422	657	251	494	392	513	146	79	792	202	481

Source: Chatelaine, Chatelaine Spotlight on Beauty, 1989 Consumer Council Study.

* Breakdowns for age, household income, and region based on "Total English Canada" respondents.

There is a seasonal skew towards the fall, winter, and spring months when people's skin tends to be drier. However, usage during the summer months is still frequent, often for moisturizing after sitting in the sun.

Not only do environmental factors such as weather and central heating affect skin dryness, in addition, as people age their skin naturally loses its ability to retain moisture. Some consumers perceive their skin to be particularly dry and problematic and are willing to pay more for a ''therapeutic'' brand.

THE HAND AND BODY LOTION MARKET

The hand and body lotion market in Canada was profitable and growing. In the past year, the hand and body lotion market volume increased by more than 5% and dollar sales by more than 8%. The total size of the market at retail prices was approximately $50 million and at factory prices approximately $35 million. Competition is strong with frequent new product introduction, consumer advertising, and promotional pack activity. Lotions are found in most retail outlets; however, drug stores account for 80% of all sales with food stores at 15% and all others accounting for 5%. The brands in the market tend to be categorized on a price basis; however, price is not necessarily an indication of lotion effectiveness at moisturizing skin (Exhibit 4).

The market is characterized by having heavy trade promotion (8% allowances off list prices) and frequent bonus pack activity (30% of volume sold via bonus packs).[4] There is a seasonal sales skew towards the winter months due to the drying effects of cold weather on people's skin. This seasonally has also been influenced by heavier trade and bonus pack activity during the fall and winter.

Advertising expenditures have increased substantially in the past two years as the category underwent rapid growth and as new competitors entered the market (Exhibit 5).

BRAND COMPETITION

VICL History

Prior to VICL's launch in 1970, the only significant hand lotion was Jergen's. VICL, with its unique blend of moisturizers, was a product that consumers wanted and quickly achieved a 30% share. In 1980, Chesebrough-Pond's launched Vaseline Dermatological Formula (VDF), a highly therapeutic product, and in 1988 launched Hand & Nail Formula, a product that strengthens nails while it softens hands.

Corporately, Chesebrough-Pond's Inc. was by far the leader in 1988 (Exhibit 6). Competitors had taken a run at VICL but never succeeded in establishing a major brand.

Throughout VICL's history there had been many changes in its strategy and in particular its advertising strategy. Possibly the most successful advertising strategy

[4] A bonus pack could be offering a larger size (for example, 33% more) at a special price or two packs for a special price.

Exhibit 4

HAND & BODY LOTION MARKET—PRICE AND EFFICACY OF BRANDS

Price	Share of Market (%)[a]	Brand	Moisturizing Efficacy[b]
Low-price brands	25	Store brands	Lower
		Suave	Lower
Mid-price brands	55	VICL	Middle–High
		Jergens	Lower–Middle
		Soft Sense	Middle
		Nivea	Lower–Middle
Premium-price brands	20	Keri	Lower
		Vaseline Dermatological	High
		Curel	Middle–High
		Eversoft	Middle
		VIC Hand & Nail	Middle–High

[a] Based on volume.

[b] Moisturizing efficacy is a measure of the ability of the product to produce the desired effect, in this case, moisturizing the skin.

Exhibit 5

HAND & BODY LOTIONS—SHARE OF MEDIA EXPENDITURES (1987 TO 1989)

	Percentages		
	1987	1988	1989 Est
VICL	50	40	42
Hand & Nail	—	10	15
VDF	5	10	8
Total Cheseborough-Pond's	55	60	65
Soft Sense (S.C. Johnson)	10	5	5
Curel (S.C. Johnson)	—	3	2
Jergens	9	5	11
Keri Lotion	7	13	10
Nivea	—	5	5
Other	19	9	2
Total Competition	45	40	35
Total Spending ($000s)	2,200	2,540	3,025
Change versus year previous (%)	+13	+15	+19

Source: Media Measurement Bureau

Exhibit 6

HISTORICAL HAND & BODY MARKET SHARES (PERCENTAGES)

	Litres											Dollars		
	1978	1979	1980	1981	1982	1983	1984	1985	1986	1987	1988	1986	1987	1988
Chesebrough-Ponds														
Vaseline Intensive Care Lotion	25	26	29	32	31	30	29	28	30	26	28	23	20	22
Vaseline Dermatological Formula	—	—	—	—	2	2	2	3	3	4	5	5	6	6
Hand & Nail Formula	—	—	—	—	—	—	—	—	—	—	1	—	—	2
Total (includes a minor brand)	25	27	29	34	37	36	34	33	34	31	35	30	27	30
Others														
Keri (Westwood)	—	—	—	2	3	5	8	8	9	10	12	12	12	16
Jergens (KAO)	20	17	15	16	14	13	13	12	10	10	12	8	8	9
Soft Sense (S.C. Johnson)	—	—	—	—	—	—	—	6	9	12	9	7	8	7
Wondra (Procter & Gamble)	2	12	8	6	3	1	—	—	—	—	—	—	—	—
All others*	53	44	48	42	43	45	45	41	38	37	32	43	45	38
Total	100	100	100	100	100	100	100	100	100	100	100	100	100	100

* All others account for approximately 20 brands.

began in 1971 with the "Leaf" campaign. The slogan used was "The Lotion That Works" and the copy used the analogy of a leaf:

> Your hard working hands, just like leaves, are exposed to the elements. They can dry out or be soft and healthy looking. What makes the difference is moisture. Vaseline Intensive Care Lotion's greaseless formula goes to work instantly sealing in protective moisture while preventing its loss. So your hands become soft and supple. Vaseline Intensive Care. The lotion that works.

In the 1980s competitive activity increased, putting pressure on VICL. By the end of 1987, the brand had exhibited a series of declines, resulting in its lowest share (26%) in eight years. The Brand Group and Advertising Agency did an extensive brand review involving market analysis and qualitative and quantitative market research.

An action plan involving significant changes to the brand strategy, advertising, and trade marketing plans was implemented in the late 1980s. Brand share had responded despite continued competitive pressure.

Competition

Andrew Jergens & Company is a division of a huge Japanese conglomerate, KAO Corporation. In Japan, KAO is the dominant company in the personal care market especially in the large hair care and face care categories. Andrew Jergens Inc. was acquired in 1987 to provide KAO with an entry into the North American personal care market. Eversoft is the first product launch since the takeover.

KAO, like Unilever, is willing to invest heavily over the long term to obtain a large market share. Success in the hand and body lotion market would provide experience and serve as an introduction for KAO into the larger face care and hair care categories.

Keri Lotion is a premium-priced hand and body lotion produced by Westwood Pharmaceutical, a division of Bristol-Myers. Westwood, being a pharmaceutical company with many specialty medical and dermatological products, has achieved an excellent reputation with medical professionals through a large sales force which target doctors. Keri Lotion has benefited through doctor sampling programs where the product is handed out by doctors to their patients. This "halo" effect has allowed Keri to give the impression of being highly therapeutic and recommended by doctors.

S.C. Johnson markets two brands, Soft Sense and Curel. Both products have historically been heavily supported by promotions directed to the trade (for example, retailers). Their other personal care products are primarily in haircare and include Agree and Halsa Shampoo & Conditioner.

In the past three years, there has been a flurry of competitive activity including: in 1987 the introduction of Nivea Professional Care and Jergens Vitamin E; in 1988 the introduction of Nivea Moisturizing Lotion, Moisturel (Westwood), Curel (S.C. Johnson), and the repositioning of Soft Sense (S.C. Johnson); and now, in 1989, the Eversoft launch.

Exhibit 7

EVERSOFT INTRODUCTORY PROGRAM

	1989		1990			
	3rd Quarter	4th Quarter	1st Quarter	2nd Quarter	3rd Quarter	4th Quarter
Advertising						
TV 30/15 second	5 weeks—275 GRP/wk		5 weeks—275 GRP/wk		5 weeks—275 GRP/wk	
Magazines full page, four-colour			6 Insertions		6 Insertions	
Consumer Promotion						
Free-standing inserts	50¢ coupon 3.5 million printed		$1.00 coupon 3.5 million printed		50¢ coupon 3.5 million printed	
On-pack couponing 50¢ & 75¢	Coupon—Neck Tags					
Pre-pack trial size displays (number of stores)	←→ 1,000		←→ 1,000			
Direct mail sampling with 75¢ coupon	215,000 Households Start Sept. 11		835,000 Households Start Jan.1/90			
Professional Program						
Dermatologist samples		← 1,100 →				
Patient samples		← 100,000	→	→		

Exhibit 8

EVERSOFT MARKETING PROGRAM—INFORMATION PROVIDED TO RETAILERS

Television

- Begins September 1989, and will deliver over 80 million gross impressions in first year (275 GRPs per week in 15 weeks of year).

Magazine Campaign

- Full-page, full-colour ads in 12 issues of *Chatelaine* and *Canadian Living* to generate over 15 million gross impressions.

Couponing

- Thousands of 75¢ and 50¢ instant-redeemable coupons on pack.
- Fall, 1989 National Free-Standing Insert (F.S.I.)—3.5 million 89¢ coupons
- Winter, 1990 National F.S.I.—3.5 million $1.00 coupons

Consumer Sampling

- Over 1,250,000 15 mL sample tubes will be delivered beginning fall 1989.
- Sample pack includes information piece and 75¢ coupon for first purchase.

In-store Merchandising

- Pre-pack floor displays will be available fall 1989 to boost consumer trial.

Professional Program

- Nearly 200,000 28 mL unscented patient samples will be distributed through 550 dermatologists beginning fall 1989.
- Extensive direct marketing campaign will be targeted to professionals.

Note:

1. GRPs (gross rating points) are an aggregate of the total ratings of a given advertising schedule. GRPs equal reach times frequency where reach is a measure of the total unduplicated target audience potentially exposed one or more times and frequency is the average number of exposures among those reached. For example, 275 GRPs could be 50% of the target audience exposed 5.5 times.

Eversoft Launch in Canada

Fortunately, Tara and Katy had managed to get a copy of Eversoft's plans via Chesebrough-Pond's sales force. The introductory program for Eversoft (Exhibit 7) was massive and it was estimated that total launch expenditures would be $1.7 million over 18 months. The introductory program was also highlighted for the Eversoft sales force as they persuaded retailers to carry the product (Exhibit 8). The published marketing mix for Eversoft was as follows:

Product Eversoft is an effective formula for moisturizing skin. It is a non-greasy lotion that has a very appealing silky feel. In addition, although most lotions including

VICL will last through handwashing, due to a different emulsion, Eversoft will stay on a laboratory plastic film through a rigorous detergent bath better than either Keri Lotion or VICL. Soft Sense or Curel would perform as well on this laboratory test.

Positioning Eversoft has a unique new formula that leaves hands soft, even after a handwashing.

Packaging The packaging is modern with contemporary colours emphasizing the name Eversoft, with very little "Jergen's" identification. The copy emphasizes "softness that lasts" and "lasts through handwashing" with a line mentioning dermatologist recommendations and concentrated skin care. The product is labelled "satisfaction guaranteed."

Pricing Eversoft is premium priced at approximately 42% more than the market average and 20% more than Keri lotion. In addition, during the first three months, retailers can purchase quantities for inventory and not pay for three months.

Advertising The advertising features a pediatrician who washes her hands regularly, but must have soft hands when dealing with her young patients. The advertising clearly communicates the brand's positioning and indirectly supports it with a doctor's endorsement. The copy of the television commercial is

> Introducing new Eversoft lotion . . . for softness that lasts for hours . . . even after a handwashing. That's important to Dr. Paula Couture because she washes her hands throughout the day. So she uses Eversoft from Jergens. Eversoft is the remarkable lotion that . . . won't wash off the next time she washes up yet Eversoft is not greasy. Keep your hands soft for hours. Eversoft lotion for softness . . . that lasts for hours even after a handwashing.

Consumer Promotions Consumer promotions consist of on-pack coupons, prepack trial size displays, and direct mail sampling. For the introduction, all bottles will have instantly redeemable 50 cent and 75 cent coupons as neck tags to encourage trial.

Competitive Positioning The Eversoft plan then went on to describe the competitive positioning of the major brands:

Brand	Positioning
Vaseline Intensive Care Lotion	• The all over body lotion that restores lost moisture to your skin
Jergens Extra Dry	• Contains extra ingredients to smooth and moisturize even rough dry skin
Soft Sense	• A specially formulated lotion for each skin type

(continued)

Brand	Positioning
Keri	• Therapeutic lotion for best care of dry skin
Vaseline Intensive Care Hand & Nail Formula	• The lotion which is guaranteed to strengthen nails while it softens hands
Vaseline Dermatological Formula	• The therapeutic lotion that is clinically proven to be superior to Keri Lotion
Curel	• The all-body moisturizing lotion that is preferred three to one versus Keri

As well, a competitive price analysis had been conducted and was contained in the report (Exhibit 9).

Exhibit 9
COMPETITIVE PRICE ANALYSIS

	Size (mL)	Price to Retailer (Case of 12)	Price/Unit	Price/Litre
VICL	200	$24.24	$2.02	$10.10
	400	$40.92	$3.41	$ 8.53
	600	$53.16	$4.43	$ 7.38
Vaseline Dermatology Formula	190	$38.16	$3.18	$16.74
	380	$69.60	$5.80	$15.26
	580	$87.48	$7.29	$12.57
Hand & Nail Formula	100	$29.28	$2.44	$24.40
	190	$38.16	$3.18	$16.74
	380	$69.60	$5.80	$15.26
Curel	300	$58.97	$4.91	$16.38
Soft Sense	360	$36.03	$3.00	$ 8.34
Keri	190	$41.40	$3.45	$18.16
	380	$74.28	$6.19	$16.29
	580	$93.24	$7.77	$13.40
Jergens	200	$25.20	$2.10	$10.50
	400	$34.20	$2.85	$ 7.13
Jergens (Vitamin E)	240	$32.76	$2.73	$11.38
	360	$44.10	$3.68	$10.21
Eversoft	170	$35.40	$2.95	$17.35
	300	$58.28	$4.86	$16.19

Confirming the Threat

Consumer research was conducted in the United States by Chesebrough-Pond's after Eversoft's launch. Anticipating the Canadian launch, research had been conducted in Canada as well. Clinical tests had proven that Eversoft was more effective as a moisturizer than Keri, but less effective than the Chesebrough-Pond's brands. In consumer tests, the concept test showed high purchase intent for Eversoft with the majority of consumers believing the formula was unique.

The advertising creative used by Eversoft tested particularly well in Canada. Not only was the advertising intrusive, but the doctor and baby both scored as credible and memorable. The Eversoft name was very well liked. Purchase interest went up substantially after advertising exposure. After trial, surprisingly, purchase intent scores were slightly lower than pretrial.

THE ACTION PLAN

The VICL brand group had gathered the facts including the rough costs of some tactical alternatives (Exhibit 10). Now it was time to develop the action plan. Tara recognized that management would not approve any additional funding unless the plan was comprehensive and well justified with sound strategic rationale.

It was clear the objective was to minimize the impact of Eversoft's launch on Chesebrough-Pond's Hand & Body lotion business and VICL in particular. Tara and Katy began to determine the strategy and the corresponding tactics to achieve this objective.

Exhibit 10
APPROXIMATE COST OF VARIOUS TACTICAL ALTERNATIVES

• Shelf-Wobbler	$ 20,000
• Neck Tags—Rest of year (50¢)	60,000
• Increase TV ad's frequency (5 weeks @ 275 GRPs/week) (Gives VICL +7% Share of Voice)	280,000
• Consumer Research	30,000
• Add Print Advertising—13 insertions (current TV only)	200,000
• National Coupon (Free-standing insert) 75¢ off (4% redemption) or Buy 1 get 40¢ off Buy 2 get $1 off (3% redemption)	160,000
• National Sample Drop	250,000
• In-store Display Program—2 months	50,000
• Buy One Get One Free	150,000
• Bonus Pack	80,000
• Increase Trade Rate (+5%)	100,000
• Sticker Flashes	30,000
• In-store Demonstration and Sampling (National)	150,000

53 IBM CANADA LTD.

Douglas Snetsinger

If it were as easy as a smile and good manners, we would be the world leaders in service quality,'' Graham Bradley, manager for Service Quality, quipped to his team in the Information & Marketing Services Group of IBM Canada Ltd. He had called the meeting in August 1990 to describe a critical task: to create a service quality revolution at IBM. Sounding more like an evangelist than a seasoned IBM executive, Graham continued: ''Everyone here, I believe, is absolutely committed to giving our customers the very best we have to offer. However, there is hard work ahead of us before we are recognized as 'Best-of-Breed' for service quality in every aspect of our dealings with our customers.'' The team had been commissioned by the president of IBM Canada to propose broad-based changes to the service delivery system for the high-volume personal computer business.

In 1986, the president determined to make customer service at IBM the standard against which all firms would judge their performance, regardless of industry. As well, the president was committed to reducing costs and increasing operating efficiencies. Since 1986, substantial progress had been made in several areas of customer service, particularly in IBM's relationship with its network of dealers and resellers. Now the focus was on improving IBM's relationship with corporate accounts purchasing high-volume products (for example, personal computers).

For many years the majority of IBM's business was the marketing of large computers, custom packaged for individual firms. More recently, a growing component of their business was in low-margin, high-volume personal computers and related products. Internal IBM systems for delivery management, billing, and other support services that had been designed, and continued to work effectively for large computer sales, were not as effective for the new product lines.

Under review were the systems for managing the high-volume business. However, Graham Bradley knew that the internal systems were only one aspect of the solution. He envisioned a cultural revolution at IBM in which service quality would radiate from every part of the business. Based on his experience, the new plan would have to include changes to the infra-structure and systems within the department; the relationships between departments; changes to the human resource policies on how employees were trained, given authority, encouraged, and compensated; changes to quality measurements that were gathered internally as well as on customers and competitors; and finally changes to the positioning and communication strategies.

As he reached for his first overhead, Graham made his final introductory remarks: ''At IBM we sell and deliver 'Total Solutions' to our customers. It is the task of this group to find and propose a total solution for service quality in the high-volume business at IBM. To do this, we need to propose: (1) a service quality measurement system, (2) a human resource management plan, and (3) an internal and external communication plan.''

THE COMPUTER INDUSTRY

The computer industry has been described as a "dynamic, revolutionary industry." Annual growth rates in sales of over 20%, frequent introduction of new, dramatically improved products, a proliferation of software products, and intense competition characterized the industry.

In 1989, over 300 hardware, software, and service corporations competed for revenues of $12.4 billion in Canada. The dominant industry competitors were: IBM, with revenues of $4.18 billion; Digital Equipment Corporation with revenues of $826 million; Unisys Corporation with revenues of $744 million; and Hewlett Packard with revenues of $409 million.

Traditionally, the industry was made up of either hardware vendors, software vendors, or service-related firms. Over the past decade, these distinctions were blurred as many hardware companies like IBM expanded their product lines and competed in all three markets.

Hardware Market

There are three general classifications of hardware: mainframes, minicomputers, and single-user systems. The mainframe, a category dominated by IBM, is a multi-user system, typically costing more than $1 million, and frequently used to run multiple business applications. Minicomputers are multi-user systems typically serving from 5 to 500 users and costing more than $100,000. The major competitors within this market are IBM, DEC, Unisys, and Hewlett Packard. The single-user system consists of personal computers and high-resolution graphic workstations, priced from $1,000 to $100,000. In the personal computer (PC) market, the dominant competitors are IBM, Apple, and Compaq while Sun Microsystems, Hewlett Packard/Apollo, and DEC dominate the workstation sector. In July 1990, IBM launched its version of workstation technology. With respect to growth, the mainframe market was experiencing moderate growth, the minicomputer market somewhat stronger growth (6% in 1989), and the single-user system market more rapid growth (15% in 1989).

Software Market

The software market is composed of two basic products, system software and application programs. System software provides the "brains" of the computer. Each hardware vendor such as IBM has traditionally developed their own proprietary operating system resulting in high switching costs for users and, in turn, high customer loyalty. More recently, a large independent software industry has developed that was founded on application software for personal computers (for example, word processing and accounting applications). Often, these independent companies are now working with companies such as IBM to write software applications for their (for example, IBM's) operating system. These partnerships can be very advantageous to both parties, as hardware manufacturers can improve sales through the availability of the newer applications of these software companies. The major competitors in the software market are IBM, Lotus, DEC, Microsoft, and Computer Associates. Some industry experts have forecast that software could increase to as much as 30% of total industry sales (currently it is 5% of industry sales) within the next few years.

Services Market

The services market, consisting of vendor service, third-party maintenance, and consulting, makes up the remaining revenues in the computer industry. Previously, hardware vendors simply honoured standard warranty contracts on their products. Today, vendors have recognized extended after-sale service can lead to added value for the customer, as well as provide additional revenues. The large computer vendors now include maintenance of their own warranty and post-warranty products as well as for their competitors' products. Many customers would prefer to source their service for all of their computer equipment from a single company, resulting in a flood of mergers, acquisitions, and strategic allliances within the industry.

These shifts in growth, structure, and alliances have led, in part, to an increasing importance of factors such as software capabilities and the quality of service. While leading-edge technology is the primary basis for competing, factors such as service are also becoming important buyer criteria.

IBM CANADA LTD.

IBM Canada is a wholly owned subsidiary of IBM World Trade Corporation, which operates in 132 countries. IBM Canada, like many subsidiaries, dominates the Canadian computer business. It manufactures some of the parent company's product line, conducts research and development for new products and services, and has an extensive marketing and service network. IBM Canada employed approximately 13,000 people in 1989 and has 23 branch offices in 13 cities across Canada.

In 1964, IBM launched the first family of compatible multi-user systems, the IBM mainframe, and for 25 years this product was IBM's main source of revenue and profits. Despite the large marketing costs associated with the mainframe, margins were lucrative (a $2.5 million mainframe might only cost $100,000 to produce). During the mid-1980s the mainframe market began to mature with annual growth rates of less than 10%. This situation had an adverse effect on IBM's sales and profit performance, particularly from 1985 to 1988 (Exhibit 1).

Five years after the introduction of personal computer (PC) technology, IBM entered the market in 1981, and by 1990 held a substantial share of the PC market. As the computing needs of their customers changed, IBM found itself largely dependent for growth in this highly competitive market with these PC products which cost less than $10,000 and yielded profit margins as low as 30%. The low profit margins meant that IBM could not employ its own sales force. As a result, IBM contracted with 350 dealer outlets and 55 independent agents to sell their PC and other high-volume product lines.

IBM's success has been established by its popularity within the commercial environment. For some prospective customers, it has been a risk to buy non-IBM products. IBM is able to offer customers quality products, stability, a large software product line, excellent service, and a knowledgeable sales force.

Exhibit 1
IBM CANADA LTD.—FIVE-YEAR FINANCIAL SUMMARY ($ MILLIONS)

	1985	1986	1987	1988	1989
Statement of Earnings					
Gross revenue	3,148	2,924	3,104	3,693	4,188
Domestic revenue	2,226	2,096	2,111	2,341	2,602
Export revenue	922	828	993	1,352	1,586
Costs	2,568	2,469	2,630	3,214	3,568
Income before tax	580	455	474	479	620
Income taxes	283	232	243	219	271
Net income	297	223	231	260	349
Assets					
Current assets	932	796	1,178	1,658	1,376
Non-current assets	1,132	1,143	1,202	1,318	1,543
Total assets	2,064	1,939	2,380	2,976	2,919
Liabilities					
Current liabilities	554	344	383	512	510
Non-current liabilities	216	197	369	576	795
Shareholder equity (SE)	1,294	1,398	1,628	1,888	1,614
Total liabilities and SE	2,064	1,939	2,380	2,976	2,919

Several basic beliefs and principles are key to IBM's operating practices. These principles stress the importance of effective management and excellence in all tasks that are undertaken, and most importantly, place high regard on and respect for its stakeholders, whether they be employees, customers, shareholders, or individuals in the community at large.

INFORMATION & MARKETING SERVICES (I&MS)

I&MS was one of six operating areas within IBM Canada (Exhibit 2). In the past, I&MS was primarily involved in order fulfillment and billing maintenance; but today, along with Marketing & Service, it was responsible for customer contact and service delivery.

Marketing representatives from Marketing & Service retained the lead role in developing new business, marketing new products, and building strong customer relationships. However, for many of IBM's customers, representatives from I&MS were as critical in maintaining and fostering good customer relations.

The origin of the I&MS group was in the support function that maintained customer records and oversaw the internal ordering and delivery of equipment to customers. The growth in the personal computer business made these support functions more complex and resulted in more frequent contact with the customer. With multiple manufacturing plants and outside vendors, complex terms and conditions, many dealers and resellers as well as direct corporate accounts, many product variations, and substantial sales volumes, the volume of customer contacts at IBM had increased dramatically (Exhibit 3).

I&MS consisted of three operational units: Branch Offices, Business Centres, and a Distribution Centre. Branch officers were in close contact with the marketing representatives to ensure that the customer requirements were met (for example,

Exhibit 2

IBM CANADA LTD.—SENIOR EXECUTIVE ORGANIZATIONAL STRUCTURE

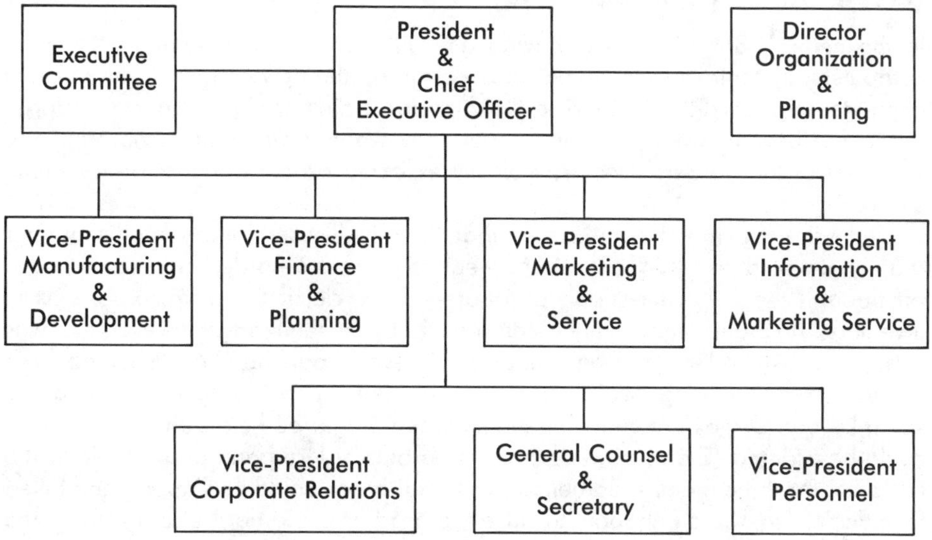

Exhibit 3

IBM DAILY CUSTOMER CONTACTS

	Early 1980s		Late 1980s	
	Calls	%	Calls	%
I&MS	10,000	18	50,000	59
Marketing	40,000	74	31,000	36
All Other	5,000	8	4,000	5
	55,000	100	85,000	100

Source: Company records

Note: A customer contact is any contact between a customer and an IBM employee, whether originated by the customer or IBM. Examples would include a telephone call from a customer enquiring about the status of an order or a formal IBM presentation to a major corporation on mainframe computers.

determining what, when, etc., the customer requested and how to meet the request). The three Business Centres in Canada were designed to provide centralized support for various activities including marketing of high-volume products through telemarketing efforts, recordkeeping, and managing the internal systems that ensured superior customer service. The Distribution Centre was responsible for ordering, inventory, and shipping the product to the customer. In general, I&MS, was involved with selling, ordering (from suppliers), supply (managing inventory), distributing, and settling the account. A detailed description of the activities of I&MS is provided in Exhibit 4.

SERVICING THE SMALL COMPUTER MARKET (DEALERS AND RESELLERS)

In the early 1980s, I&MS was having difficulty servicing the demand for small computers. In contrast to the mainframe customer, the new customers in the small computer segment did not require technical support, did not want to work with a large number of IBM employees, and most importantly, wanted immediate turnaround and shipment of their orders. Dealers typically expected orders to be delivered within seven days.

Under the old "mainframe" system that IBM initially used for the small computer market, it would take IBM at least one week to process an order as it was handed-off through the sell-order-supply-distribute-settle cycle. If the entire order was in inventory, the order might hit the loading docks by the tenth day. However, that was a big "IF." An order could be made up of several part numbers, sourced from separate manufacturing locations, and inventoried separately. If one of the parts, say a keyboard, was not available the shipment might be held up until new stock could be ordered. The missing part might be backordered and unavailable to the customer for three months. Sometimes a partial order would be shipped and billed to a dealer, who was unhappy because the product could not be sold without the missing part. With more than 1,600 part numbers which could be combined into numerous unique product configurations, forecasting the monthly or weekly demands of dealer market was a frustrating experience that was straining I&MS to its limits.

The first solution to the problem was a parallel system, which was not integrated with the old system, and was designed specifically for the high-volume business. I&MS kept "larger than necessary" inventories of product parts to facilitate the short-term needs of its customers, and additional I&MS staff were assigned to the high-volume business. These staff helped to improve the flow of orders through the system and to work more closely and frequently with the customer. These steps improved customer relations, but increased overhead expenses that could not be justified for this low margin business. Even with the changes, IBM's competitors in the small computer market were achieving much higher customer satisfaction ratings on key requirements.

In 1986, a task force of cross-functional IBM executives was commissioned by the president to examine and propose a total quality system for the dealer market. The task force held several meetings with dealers and resellers seeking information on their expectations on vital operational issues. A break-through occurred when IBM executives showed one dealer group a "blueprint" of the IBM service system. "Blueprints" were flowcharts that showed the major activities in order fulfillment from both the customer and company perspective. This new concept, of blueprinting, had recently been used at IBM to identify problems with service encounters and to facilitate design change. This simple tool illustrated the sell-through-settle process at IBM identifying the several points of contact with the customer and the systems supporting the IBM personnel at the contact points. A simplified version of that blueprint is shown in Exhibit 5. Although simply drawn, this prototype blueprint provided an effective communication device to the dealer on IBM's process problems. Working together, blueprints were drawn up for the dealer market and solutions began to emerge. Out of all of these discussions, a broad-based program was implemented. Highlights of that program were

1. A revised forecasting system with monthly inputs from the dealers on expected requirements for the upcoming quarter.
2. Centralization of the ordering system into the Business Centres. Telemarketing systems were installed to improve communications with the dealers and to accept orders which would be expedited to shipping within two days. Contact personnel provided systems support to answer almost all questions or initiate any actions that came in from the dealers without having to pass the enquirer on to another IBM contact person. An automated ordering system installed at the dealer's location was created to provide an electronic link to IBM product information and permit immediate ordering and confirmation of delivery date.
3. A new customer quality perception tracking system of dealers was created, the results of which were reported to the president at his newly created, monthly Quality Assurance Council meetings.
4. A complete change in human resource management was undertaken which promoted the office skills self-sufficiency of all IBM employees and virtually eliminated the need for secretarial and clerical staff. All I&MS employees were provided with sophisticated workstation capabilities and training to enable them to be self-sufficient in communications, word processing, financial analysis, and other internal systems utilization. Existing secretarial and clerical staff were provided with training and new skills which improved productivity.
5. Path managers were created to help the managers with functional responsibilities (for example, functional responsibility for billing or distribution) to ensure the quick flow of an order through the system.
6. New sophisticated distribution systems were developed that (1) provided an effective storage and retrieval system, (2) maximized storage retrieval speed, (3) minimized labour and energy costs, (4) maximized space utilization, and (5) improved information tracking. A state-of-the-art distribution centre was created which applied robotic, automated crane and other new distribution technologies to ensure efficient inventory storage and retrieval.

Exhibit 4
I&MS ACTIVITY BY LOCATION

Activity	Location		
	Branch Office	Business Centre	Distribution Centre
Sell	Complete worksheets to configure contacts Interact with marketing and customer providing the details on the what, when, why, who, and how of the sell-through-settle process Co-ordinate new product announcements	Prepare contracts from branch worksheets Configure contracts for high-volume products Maintain the customer record files Co-ordinate new product announcements Conduct customer demonstrations Conduct marketing programs for selected products Outbound telemarketing activity	
Order	Generate worksheets	Activate worksheet data into order system Conduct credit risk assessment Inbound telemarketing information and order requests Administer contracts—terms and conditions of contracts Administer special bids—qualify contract terms Lease administration	

(continued)

Exhibit 4 continued

Activity	Location		
	Branch Office	Business Centre	Distribution Centre
Supply	Negotiate with distribution centre Interact with marketing and customer on supply issues	Negotiate with distribution centre for high-volume supply Conduct forecasting and backlog reviews Interact with marketing and customer on supply issues	Build interlock between sales forecast and manufacturing Conduct supply analysis Negotiate manufacturing delivery schedule Track delivery
Distribute	Verify customer shipment details Ensure installation	Verify customer shipment details Update ship and install status in tracking system Initiate shipping process	Manage delivery of new stock Manage inventory Customize orders as per customer requirements Expedite shipment to customer
Settle	Ensure all documentation is complete Follow-up on overdue accounts	Create and mail invoice Accounts receivable collection Credit note processing	

Exhibit 5
CUSTOMER ORIENTED VIEW OF PROCESS PATH

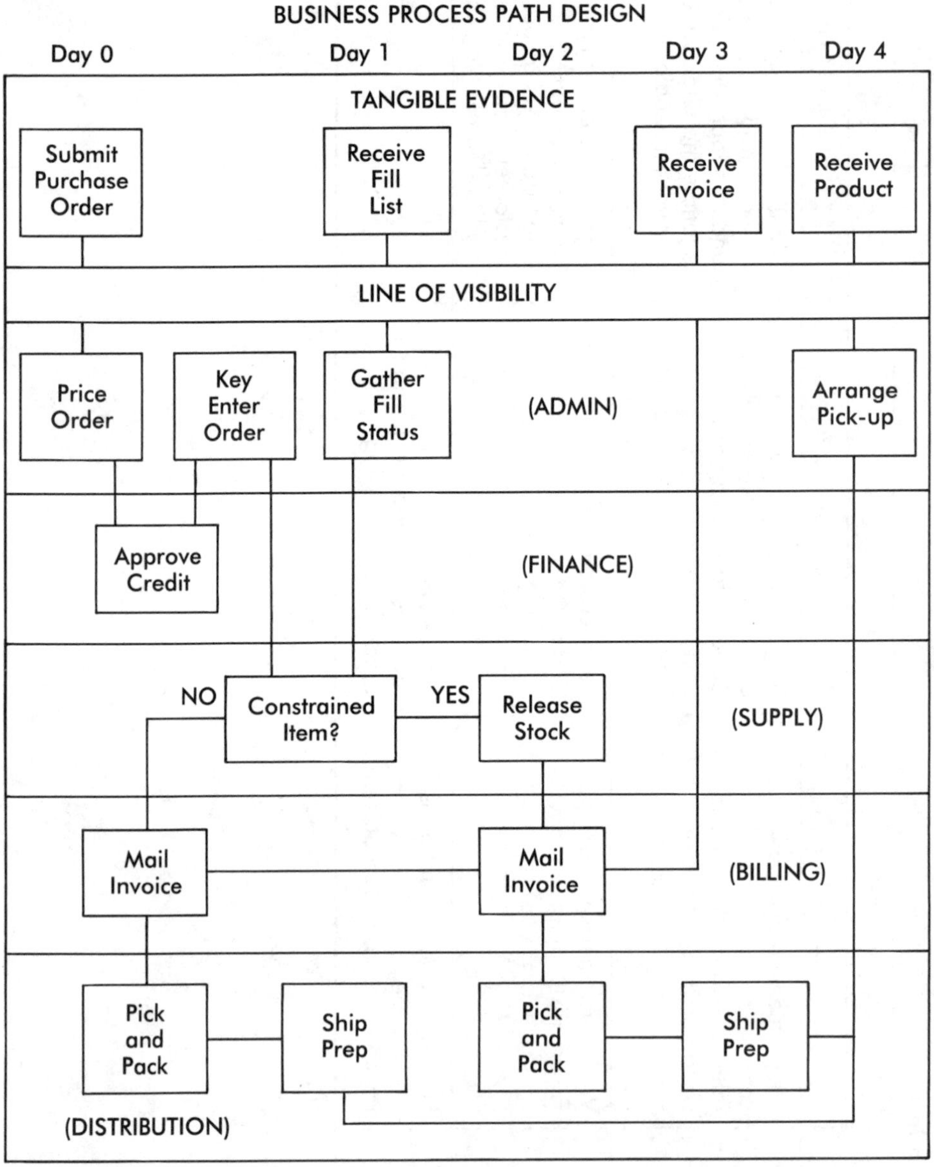

Exhibit 6
DEALER SERVICE QUALITY MEASUREMENTS

Order Fulfillment Rates (in %)

	1986 IBM	1986 Competition	1989 IBM	1989 Competition
Orders Shipped				
Within 5 days	25	65	70	71
Within 6 days	45	70	78	75
Within 7 days	62	77	86	81
Backorder Resolution				
Within 10 days	55	75	80	81
Within 20 days	65	85	85	87

Dealer Attitudinal Response (1 is strong disagreement and 10 is strong agreement)

	1986 IBM	1986 Competition	1989 IBM	1989 Competition
Reliable	5.5	6.8	7.8	8.1
Understands customer needs	5.7	7.3	7.9	7.9
Overall satisfaction	6.2	7.8	8.5	8.6

Source: Company records

The implementation program had been an enormous undertaking but the efforts were proving to be effective. The dealers, who now were regarded as partners with IBM, saw the improvements in terms of order fulfillment rates. As well, their view of IBM improved substantially between 1986 and 1989 (Exhibit 6). Another significant accomplishment of the new program was an increase in cost savings and efficiency. One method of viewing efficiency is shown in Exhibits 7 and 8, in which revenues and orders per I&MS employment are charted for the 1984 to 1990 period. These changes in organizational structure and distribution management had improved the dealer high-volume business. With this success in the dealer network, the next stage on improving the service quality of the entire high-volume business would be through a focused effort on the corporate account business.

HIGH VOLUME CORPORATE ACCOUNT BUSINESS

The broad-based use of microcomputers and workstation technology has had a significant impact on managerial work. The increased power and flexibility of small computers led to changes that include how office tasks are performed, such as in IBM's own drive for managerial self-sufficiency, and in how specific information inquiry and analysis tasks are conducted. Microtechnology now provides the manager with analytical and database applications that, even ten years earlier, would

Exhibit 7
REVENUE PER HEAD COUNT—I&MS

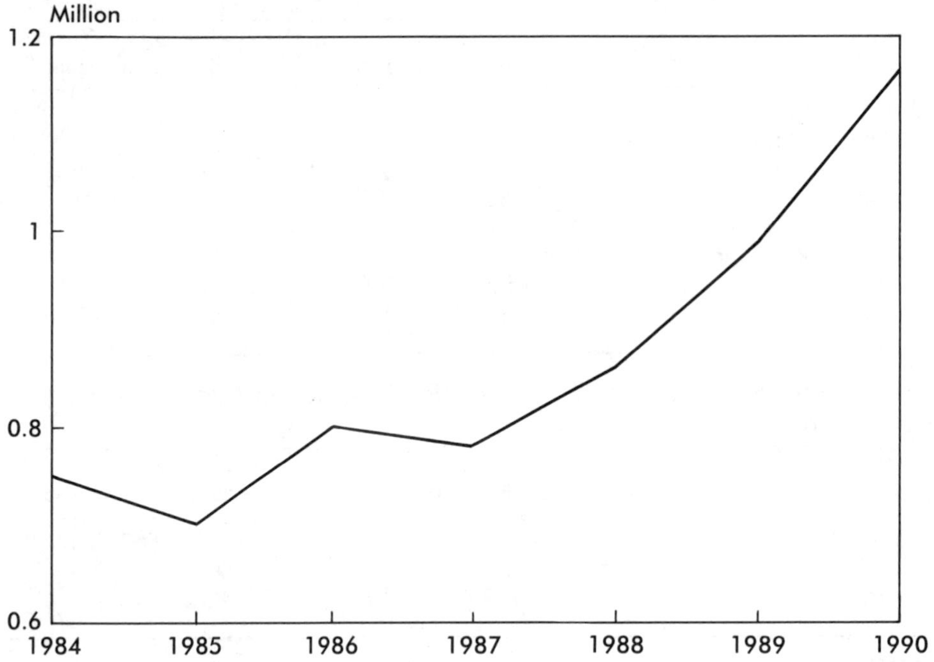

Source: Company records

have been available only to the most highly trained computer specialist using mainframe tools. Across Canadian corporations there has been a widespread adoption of micro-based technology and/or workstation capability.

As some of the largest Canadian companies invested in the use of microcomputers and workstations, they preferred to deal directly with IBM and avoid potential intermediary issues or costs. A single corporate account could result in the sale of several thousand units of a variety of small computers and peripherals. The delivery of the units were often to several hundred locations over a period of a year or longer. At the time of signing the contract, the size of the order was established in terms of the quantity of each general machine type. However, what usually was not detailed at the signing were the specific requirements of a branch or regional office and the time at which they would require delivery. The challenge for I&MS was being able to ship the required and customized machine as soon as that branch requested delivery.

In many respects, the corporate account business was similar to the dealer business. Many of the systems improvements which had been instituted for the dealer business would benefit the corporate account business. However, some develop-

Exhibit 8
CUSTOMER ORDERS PER HEAD COUNT—I&MS

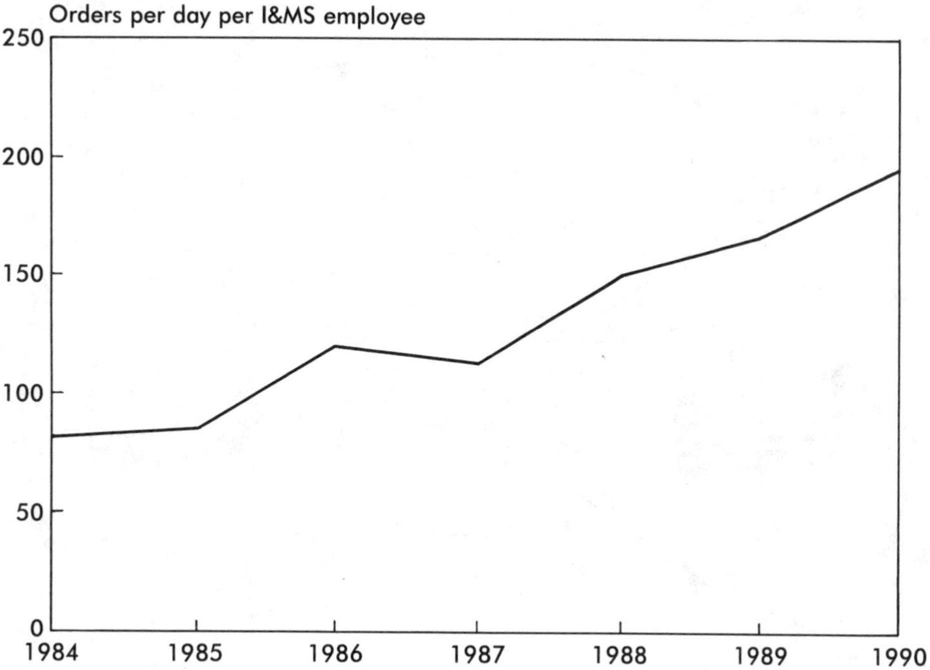

Source: Company records

ments had not been instituted for the corporate accounts, such as a service quality measurement program specific to the corporate account business, automated ordering systems, and process path management. In addition, a particular problem with the corporate account business was created because multiple ordering systems continued to be used for different aspects of the contract. The old mainframe ordering systems, which provided the flexibility of customizing a specific computer configuration, was still being used for some of the unique requirements of a corporate contract. The new high-volume ordering system (prepared for the dealers) was being used for standard product configurations. The two systems continued to work in parallel but were not integrated, making it difficult to determine the status, in total, of a single order and to control its dispatch. On a more general level, new developments in services marketing practices were being widely discussed at I&MS.

THE NEW TASK FORCE ON SERVICE QUALITY

Graham Bradley pulled out his "Gap Chart" (Exhibit 9) to lay out the specific issues which he felt should be the focus of the task force's efforts. The use of gap analysis

Exhibit 9
GAP PERSPECTIVES ON SERVICE DELIVERY AT IBM

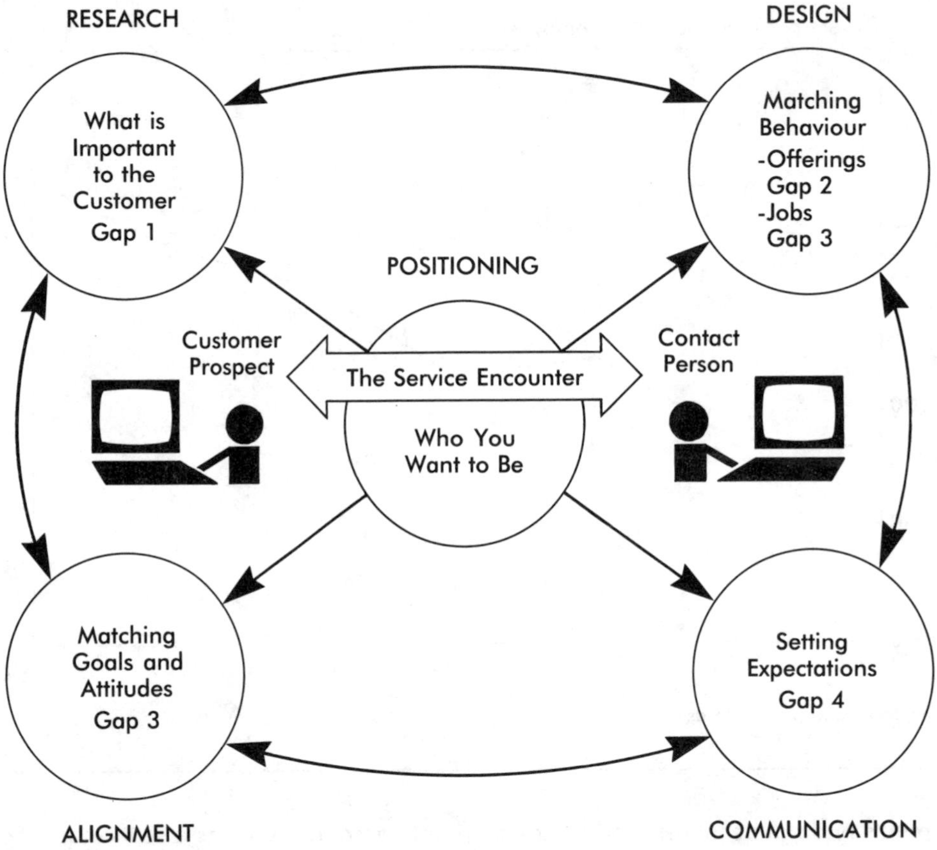

had been proposed in the marketing literature as a method of identifying potential problem areas in the service delivery system. Graham had been exposed to gap analysis in a Service Quality Seminar and regarded it a comprehensive tool for thinking about improving the business: "If we are to meet the challenge, it will be by narrowing the gaps in four strategic areas of our high volume business."

Gap 1—Research: Customer's Expectations versus Management Perceptions

"The experience with our success in dealer relations was in a reciprocal and deep understanding of each other's business. To date, our corporate account business suffers from the following limitations:

1. insufficient and inadequate use of marketing research;
2. lack of interaction between service delivery management and the customer; and
3. insufficient communication between contact employees (marketing and service) and I&MS employees."

Gap 2—Design: Management Perceptions versus Service Quality Specifications

"The design and implementation of the service system will not reach full potential until we are able to address the following issues:

1. a total commitment by every IBM employee that the customer's expectations will, can, and must be met;
2. the development of a formal process for setting service quality goals for corporate accounts which will be endorsed and monitored by senior management; and
3. an overhaul of our internal and multiple ordering systems to achieve one simple order entry system which is integrated with the forecasting and distribution systems and results in continuous tracking and management of the contract."

Gap 3—Alignment: Service Quality Expectations versus Service Delivered

"The size of IBM and the variety of contact personnel and supporting personnel is obstructing the next quantum leap in service delivery. To narrow this gap a revamped human resources perspective needs to be examined which will address the following issues:

1. role ambiguity and conflict with the various contact employees;
2. a revised evaluation, recognition, and compensation scheme which rewards or possibly penalizes employees for attainment or failure to attain service excellence standards;
3. the enhancement of perceived control and empowerment of all employees; and
4. a culture predicated on total commitment to service excellence through individual dedication to personal and team objectives."

Gap 4—Communication: Service Delivered versus Communicated

"To ensure that IBM Canada is personified by our customers as embodying the characteristics of reliability, credibility, empathy, and having superior integrity, we will need to tackle the issues of:

1. inadequate internal communications between sales, advertising, and service employees, to avoid

2. inappropriate claims in either mass or personal communications which would create unrealistic customer expectations."

Graham pulled out his next overhead which provided a blueprint of the service system for the corporate account business (Exhibit 10). Blueprinting or Line of Visibility (LOV) Charts were now extensively employed within I&MS and had become known as "Love Charts." "The service encounter begins with Marketing taking a lead role supported by the Branch and Business Centre in the Promise Creation. Once the order has been established, I&MS manages the Promise Fulfillment process from ordering through billing. There are several points of customer contact and consequently several opportunities to enhance or harm service perception. As the order moves both horizontally and vertically through the system, there are several "hand-off" points which, potentially, could cause a failure in the service delivery through inadequate communication from one function to the next. Because there are multiple hand-off points, whether it be from Marketing to I&MS or crossing functional responsibilities within I&MS, responsibility and accountability for the total service delivery is spread thinly and potentially diluted across several IBM employees."

Having summarized the problems and the issues that needed to be addressed, Graham subdivided the group into task forces asking them to prepare solutions in three specific areas. The issues were not independent, but Graham felt that solutions generated on intersecting problems from multiple perspectives would achieve the best results. Prior to the meeting, a fourth group had been formed within the computer system group, to address the issue of a unified ordering and account management system. This system would replace the existing parallel ordering systems now being used. Graham asked each group to assume that the new system would be in place and operational within six months.

The mandates for the groups were to propose

1. a new quality intelligence system,
2. enhancement of human resource management to achieve total service quality dedication,
3. a method of improving internal communication and an external communication posture for the long-run positioning of IBM Canada in the minds of its current customers and prospects.

Task Force I—Service Quality Measurement

Task Force I was required to propose a service quality measurement system that would be used within a regular reporting and control system. The new system would be developed through extensive interaction with existing customers. A substantial understanding of the customer needs already existed, and a prototype system needed to be roughed out for feedback in these customer meetings. The system could be based on internal measures, external measures, or some combination of both. Internal measures on service quality were easily accessible at any point in the process as illustrated on the blueprint (Exhibit 10). For example, the timing of the order cycle was maintained from order to supply to inventory to shipping. All process errors

Exhibit 10
BLUEPRINT FOR TOTAL SOLUTION FULFILLMENT

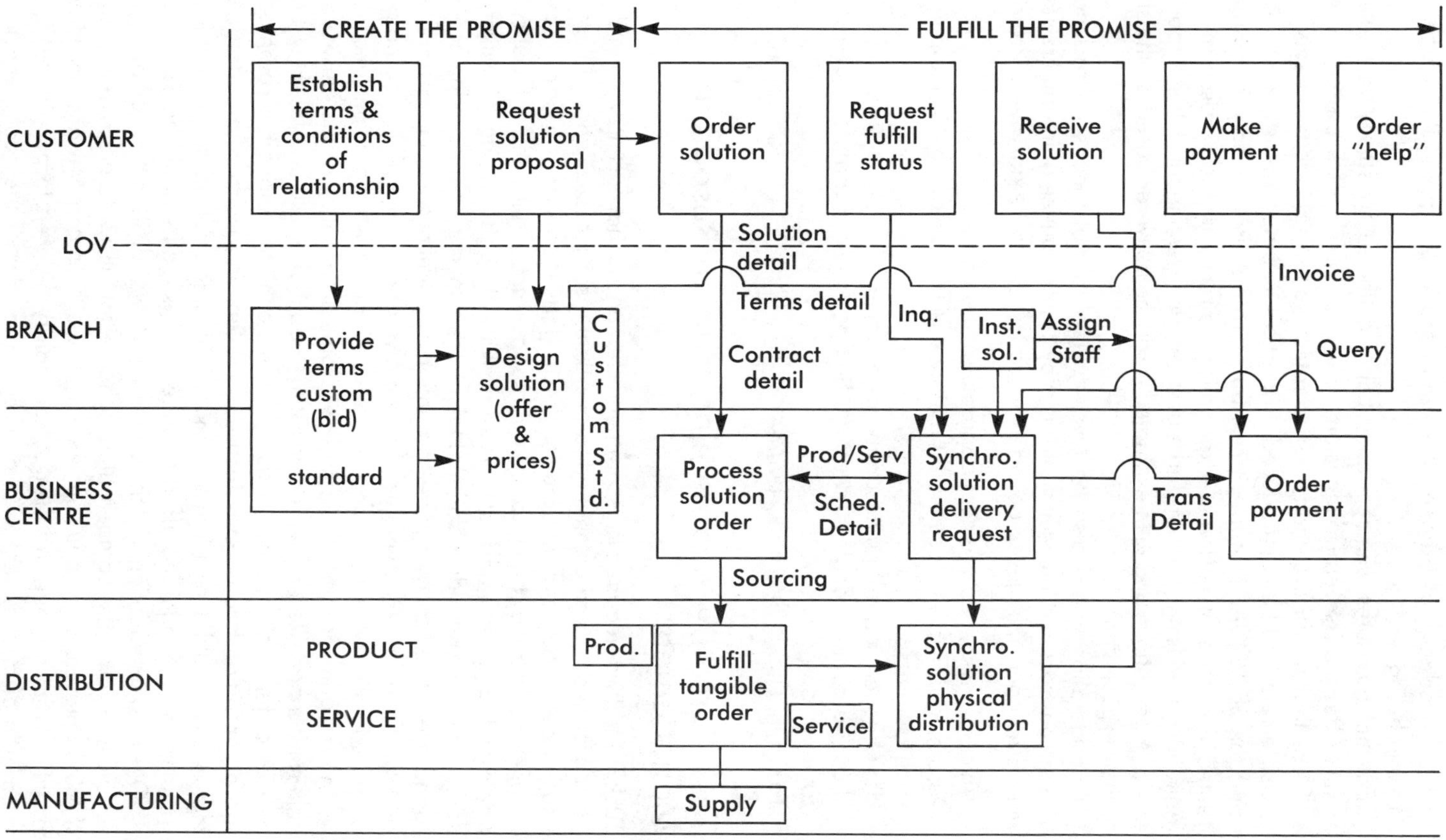

were collected such as ordering the wrong product, shipping the wrong order, or errors in billing.

External measures were currently being collected by surveying dealers on a monthly basis on several dimensions, some of which were presented in Exhibit 6. Since those measures had been created, some new ideas on service quality measurement had been introduced. In particular, a new measurement approach, using the SERVQUAL instrument was built around a gap analysis approach and treated the issue of customer expectations directly in the measurement system (Appendix 1). Using a three-part questionnaire, respondents first reported their service expectations and then evaluated a service deliverer based on the standards of their expectations.

Consideration would also be given to less formal means of tracking quality through unstructured interviews, site visits by key personnel, or internal review. There were a number of issues to consider and questions to be answered including:

- Which of these measurement approaches should be used?
- Assuming multiple measurement methods will be used, what is the purpose of each method?
- How frequently should measurements be taken?
- Should a panel of dealers be established or should a sample of dealers be surveyed over time?
- To whom should the results be reported?

Task Force II—Augmenting Human Resource Management

Task Force II was required to recommend changes so that each I&MS member would be challenged by and committed to live by the service excellence philosophy. The issues were largely summarized in the previous discussion of Gap 3 (Exhibit 9). Progress had already been achieved through improving the self-sufficiency of managers and improving work and decision skills through training. However, like the sports team with abundant skill and talent, the final and winning edge needed to be found in team dedication and determination. In a similar spirit, the focus of employee activity needed to be continually directed away from "doing" to "accomplishing," and accomplishing meant a focused drive to meet customer expectations.

The assignment for Task Force II was difficult because of the illusive nature of cultural change. Recommendations they would propose would likely be subtle. Service culture enhancement was by nature a highly intangible commodity, and the organization had already focused its attention towards the customers needs. However, it would likely be in the small steps of job design, training, encouraging initiative, and recognizing effort that the greatest gains would be achieved.

One recommendation, which was not subtle, was an idea that had been proposed to totally revamp the compensation scheme for all I&MS employees. Virtually all I&MS employees were paid on a salary basis. This compensation scheme would result in employees having their current salary reduced to possibly 90%, 75%, or even 50% of their current level and the remainder of their compensation tied to service goals and/or team contributions. For example, if the 75% level were proposed, employees would be at risk for the remaining 25% of their current salary if their work team did not meet their goal. If the employee's team surpassed their goal, they could earn as much as 125% of current salary. At issue with this proposal, was whether it should be instituted at all, should it be voluntary or mandatory, how broadly it would be instituted and on what criteria would the service goal portion of the compensation be based? Some employees had little direct contact with customers, for example, those managing the billing system. Should these employees be compensated based on global service quality indicators, or based on more local measures generated by their operating unit, such as minimizing accounts receivable? Was IBM ready for a compensation system that was driven by team productivity rather than individual productivity?

Clearly, this was going to be a challenging assignment. Task Force II would have to engage in creative problem solution generation because whatever recommendations proposed would have a substantial impact on organizational dynamics and services marketing practice.

Task Force III—Communications

Task Force III was mandated to enhance communication efforts internally and externally. Part of that task intersected with Task Force II. However, specific recommendations needed to be directed at improving the interaction between Marketing and I&MS and the communications within I&MS. As well, Task Force III was required to prepare an external communication plan which would effectively position IBM as a leader in service quality.

In the past, the roles of Marketing and I&MS were more clearly defined; Marketing's purpose was to market, and I&MS's purpose was to administer. However, over the years there had been more customer contact on the part of I&MS personnel as they supported Marketing. Long-standing problems simmered between Marketing and I&MS and occasionally boiled over regarding issues of (1) who should be interfacing with the customer and (2) promises that were not fulfilled.

After a contract has been signed, I&MS staff were the most intimate with the details of ordering, sourcing, delivery, and billing. Often by necessity and obligation, and also through telemarketing and 800 number support, I&MS staff made frequent contact with the customer. However, the customer preferred to deal with a small number of IBM staff, in particular the Marketing employee who had established a relationship with the customer. Recommendations by Task Force III need to be found that achieved strong customer relations but could also take advantage of both the Marketing representatives customer linkages and the I&MS employees resources and knowledge.

The second issue arose because of over-promise or under-delivery depending on whose view was taken: Marketing or I&MS. The solution that was required was to devise a plan to break down the functional barriers between the two IBM operational units.

The final recommendation would assume that the goal of "Best-of-Breed" for service quality would be and was achieved. Given that assumption, what external communications would be recommended that would effectively position IBM Canada as a leader in service quality? How public should the message, along with the solutions, be made? Should efforts be taken to engage in promoting service quality awareness by sharing the message with groups such as community,business, trade, school, and government organizations? Should employee leadership and involvement be encouraged in quality activities of professional, trade, business, and education groups and in national and international standards activities?

WRAP-UP

With the requirements of the three task forces clarified, Graham Bradley reminded them that the report would be personally delivered to the president. The group could be assured that every part of the proposal, no matter how far-reaching the implications, would receive measured and serious consideration. Graham Bradley invited each of his colleagues to rise to the challenge of the revolutionary mandate they had been given, and closed the meeting with this final remark: "Every revolution began in the minds of a few individuals. Our job will have been in vain if we do not lead the service quality uprising at IBM Canada."

Appendix 1
SERVQUAL INSTRUMENT

SERVQUAL, a service quality measurement instrument, was designed to understand fundamental dimensions of service quality in various settings.[1] The team that developed the measurement instrument has identified five dimensions of service quality which determine customer impression and evaluation of a service. These five dimensions are tangibles, reliability, responsiveness, assurance, and empathy. Multiple items have been developed which assess what the customer expects and how well the service provider delivers on each of these five dimensions. The questionnaire consists of three parts. The first part solicits the respondent's expectations on twenty-two statements about service quality at an excellent company. The second part has five statements used to determine the relative importance of each of the five service quality dimensions. The third part is identical to the first part, except that the service provider's name is substituted for 'the excellent company' and ratings are gathered for that service provider. The designers of the questionnaire recommend that a SERVQUAL score should be calculated by subtracting the expectations score from the service provider's score on each of the twenty-two dimensions. Examples of the questions used in the first part of the instrument are provided below. Respondents indicate the extent of agreement or disagreement on a five-point scale.

[1] A more complete discussion of SERVQUAL can be found in A. Parasuraman, Valerie A. Zeithaml, and Leonard L. Berry, "SERVQUAL: A Multiple-Item Scale for Measuring Consumer Perceptions of Service Quality," *Journal of Retailing,* Spring 1988, pp. 12–40.

Tangibles

1. Excellent companies will have modern-looking equipment.
2. Materials associated with the service (such as pamphlets or statements) will be visually appealing in an excellent company.

Reliability

1. When excellent companies promise to do something by a certain time, they will do so.
2. When a customer has a problem, excellent companies will show a sincere interest in solving it.

Responsiveness

1. Employees in excellent companies will tell customers exactly when services will be performed.
2. Employees in excellent companies will never be too busy to respond to customers' requests.

Assurance

1. Employees in excellent companies will have the knowledge to answer customers' questions.
2. The behaviour of employees in excellent companies will instill confidence in customers.

Empathy

1. The employees of excellent companies will understand the specific needs of their customers.
2. Excellent companies will have the customer's best interests at heart.

Appendix 1

GLOSSARY OF SELECTED MARKETING AND MANAGEMENT TERMS

advertising Any paid form of nonpersonal presentation and promotion of a product or organization by an identified sponsor.

agent A business unit that negotiates purchases or sales (or both) of goods and services. Agents are commonly remunerated by payment of a commission or fee.

attitudes Enduring systems of positive or negative evaluations of, or emotional feelings toward, an object.

augmented product The core product plus any additional services and benefits that may be supplied.

backward integration Obtaining ownership or increased control of an organization's supply systems (see also *forward integration* and *vertical integration*).

benefit segmentation Dividing the population into different groups on the basis of the benefits they want or require and the costs they wish to avoid.

billings The total charges for advertising space or time, production, and other services provided by an advertising agency to its clients.

bottom-up planning Designing, developing and implementing of programs by middle- and lower-level managers and other personnel who work out the details and follow through on them (see also *top-down planning*).

brand A name, term, sign, symbol, design, or combination of these that seeks to identify the product of an organization and differentiate it from those of competitors.

branding The process of creating, assigning, and publicizing a brand name, term, sign, symbol, etc., to one or more products.

breakeven The volume of sales necessary, at a specific price, for a seller to recover all relevant costs of a product.

broker See *agent*.

cannibalization The erosion of sales of an existing product by a new product marketed by the same firm.

cash cow A product in the mature or declining stage of the product life cycle that can be "milked" for as much profit as possible.

catchment area The geographic region or area from which the bulk of an organization's customers are drawn.

centralized management The decision-making power concentrated among a relatively small number of managers at the head office (see also *decentralized management*).

chain store One of a group of centrally owned retail stores of similar type with some degree of centralized control over operations.

channels of distribution See *distribution or delivery system.*

clutter See *noise.*

cognitive dissonance Perceived inconsistency within an individual's own beliefs or attitudes or between these and one's behaviour. A person will attempt to reduce the dissonance through changes in either behaviour or cognition.

commodity A generic product category or product that cannot be distinguished by potential customers from similar products offered by competitors.

communication The transmission of a message from a sender (or source) to a receiver (or recipient).

communication medium The personal or impersonal channel through which a message is transmitted to an audience or individual (see also *mass media*).

communication mix The combination of elements (personal selling, media advertising, signage, public relations, publicity, and onsite display) used by an organization to communicate its message(s) to its target market(s).

comparative advertising Advertising messages that make specific brand comparisons using actual product names.

competition See *direct competitor* and *generic competitor.*

concentrated marketing strategy The efforts, in a segmented market, of an organization that is focusing on one target group and designing its marketing strategy specifically to reach that group, rather than trying to be all things to all people.

consignment sales Sales not completed until products placed by a supplier with a retailer are resold to customers, at which point payment becomes due from the retailer to the supplier.

consumers Individuals or households or organizations that are current or prospective purchasers or users of goods and services.

contingency budget Funds set aside in advance to finance contingency plans and respond to unanticipated events.

contingency plans Plans, prepared in advance, outlining a course of action to deal with situations that might potentially arise.

contribution (or gross contribution) The monetary difference between total sales revenues (gross income) and variable expenses (see also *margin*).

convenience products Products the consumer usually purchases frequently, immediately, and with a minimum effort in comparison and shopping (see also *shopping products* and *specialty products*).

convenience store A small store, with a limited stock of groceries and household products, that remains open for long hours.

co-operative advertising Local or regional advertising whose costs are shared jointly by a national advertiser and a retail or wholesale institution.

copy testing A preliminary test of alternative advertising copy appeals or selling messages to assess their relative effectiveness for specific audiences.

core product The central elements of a product that serve a basic consumer or societal need (see also *augmented product*).

cost-per-thousand The cost of advertising for each 1,000 homes reached in TV or radio, or for each 1,000 circulated copies of a publication (often abbreviated CPM).

coupons Certificates that are mailed, handed out, or incorporated in print advertising and that entitle the bearer to a specified monetary savings on a purchase of a specific product.

cost centre An organizational unit whose costs are clearly identifiable.

crisis management The result of the occurrence of an unexpected event for which management has not prepared and that requires immediate action (see also *contingency plans*).

cross-sectional data or study Research information gathered from a whole population (or a representative sample of that population) at single point in time (see also *longitudinal data*).

cumulative audience ("Cume") The net unduplicated radio or TV audience delivered by a specific program in a particular time slot over a measured period of time usually one to four weeks.

customer service A collective term that describes all the supplementary services provided by an organization to satisfy customers and combat competitors, such as technical aid, information, order taking, complaint handling, refunds, or substitutions.

decentralized management The result of the dispersion of decision-making power to relevant personnel at lower levels within an organization (see also *centralized management*).

decision-making unit (DMU) An individual or group of individuals involved in making decisions on the purchase of a specific product.

demographic segmentation Categorizing or differentiating people based on demographic variables such as age, sex, religion, income, etc.

differentiated marketing strategy Developing different products and/or marketing programs for each market segment that the organization plans to serve.

direct competitor An organization suffering a product that meets similar consumer needs and is broadly similar in substance or process to one's own product.

direct selling Selling to the end user by the producer without use of retail or wholesale intermediaries.

discretionary income Funds remaining to an individual or household after paying for necessities out of disposable income (see *disposable income* below).

disposable income Personal (or household) income remaining after deduction of income taxes and compulsory payments such as social security.

dissonance See *cognitive dissonance.*

distribution or delivery system The combination of internal organizational resources and external intermediaries employed to move a product from production or creation to the final consumer. Goods necessarily move through physical distribution channels, involving transportation, storage, and display. Services may be delivered to the customer directly at the production site or, in certain instances, transmitted electronically.

diversification The process of entering new markets with one or more products that are new to the organization.

drive time The weekday commute hours when many motorists are listening to their car radios.

durable goods Goods such as appliances, furniture, and automobiles that are expected to last several years or more.

elasticity of demand (to price) The responsiveness of sales volume to a change in price. Demand is said to be *price inelastic* when raising (or lowering) price by a certain percentage has a proportionately smaller impact on sales volume, and *price elastic* when the impact on volume is proportionately greater than the price change.

evoked set The array of specific brands for a product category consciously considered by a consumer in making a purchase decision.

experiment An attempt to measure cause-and-effect relationships under controlled or natural conditions.

fixed costs Costs that remain unchanged in total for a given time period despite wide fluctuations in activity, such as property taxes, executive salaries, rent, insurance, and depreciation (see also *variable costs*).

flight of advertising A part of an advertising campaign that is divided into groups of ads, with periods of time between each group.

focus-group interviews A small group discussion method of obtaining qualitative information from individuals who are broadly representative of the target market.

forward integration Obtaining ownership or increased control of the means by which an organization distributes its products to end users (see also *backward integration* and *vertical integration*).

four Ps See *marketing mix.*

franchise The licencing of a production and distribution business, dealership, or complete business format where one organization authorizes a number of independent outlets to market a product or service and engage in a business using the franchisor's trade names and methods of operation.

frequency The number of times an accumulated audience has the opportunity to be exposed to the same advertising message within a measured period of time.

generic competitor An organization offering a product that, while possibly different in substance or process, is capable of satisfying the same general consumer needs as one's own product (see also *direct competitor*).

geographic segmentation Segmentation of a market on the basis of region, city/metropolitan area size, population density, climate, or terrain.

gross rating points (GRPs) A measurement of advertising impact derived by multiplying the number of persons exposed to an advertisement by the average number of exposures per person (see also *reach* and *frequency*).

horizontal integration The process of obtaining ownership or increased control of one's competitors (see also *vertical integration*).

impulse purchase A purchase decision made on the spur of the moment without prior planning.

industrial/institutional marketing Selling goods and services to corporate, institutional, or government purchasers as opposed to individuals and households.

intermediary An organization or individual that serves as a go-between, or facilitator, between producer, marketer, and customer.

list price The price shown on the marketer's sales list and used as the basis for computing discounts.

longitudinal data or study Research information gathered over time (usually at periodic intervals) from the same population or sample; this allows the researcher to monitor individual changes among participants in the study.

loss leaders A product of known or accepted quality priced at a loss or no profit for the purpose of attracting consumers who may then purchase other regularly priced products.

manufacturer's agent/representative An intermediary who handles noncompeting but related lines of goods usually on an extended contractual basis within an exclusive territory.

margin The difference between the selling price of a product and its production cost (for a manufacturer or service provider) or purchase cost (for a wholesaler or retailer). The margin may be expressed in monetary units or as a percentage of the selling price.

markdown A reduction in the originally established price of a product.

market The set of all current and potential consumers of a particular product.

market aggregation See *undifferentiated marketing strategy*.

market definition An attempt by the organization to determine which segment of the market its operations are or should be serving.

market development An organization's marketing of its current line of products to new markets or segments.

market niche A segment of a market where there is demand for a product with specific attributes distinguishing it from competing offerings.

market penetration An organization's attempt to increase consumption of its current products in its current markets.

market potential A calculation of maximum possible sales (in units of currency values) or usage opportunities in a defined territorial area for all marketers of a product during a stated period of time.

market segment A homogeneous subset of the total market that may require a marketing plan tailored to the segment's distinctive characteristics.

market segmentation The process of identifying distinctive submarkets or segments within the total market.

market share The ratio of an organization's sales volume for a particular product category to total market volume on either an actual or potential basis.

marketing audit A systematic, critical, unbiased, and comprehensive review and appraisal of an organization's or subunit's marketing objectives, strategies, policies, and activities.

marketing mix The four basic ingredients (or elements) in a marketing program that influence consumers' decisions on whether or not to patronize the organization. These four elements are product, price, distribution or delivery systems, and communication. (Note: Some people use the phrase the *four Ps*—product, price, place, and promotion—to describe the elements of the marketing mix, but we regard the terms "place" and "promotion" as too narrow and potentially misleading.)

marketing planning The tasks of setting up objectives for marketing activity and of determining and scheduling the steps necessary to achieve such objectives.

marketing research The systematic gathering, recording, and analyzing of data to provide information for marketing decision making.

markup The amount by which a seller increases the selling price of a product over its original purchase price; markup is generally computed as a percentage of the final selling price rather than of the original price.

mass media Informational networks, reaching large numbers of people, that carry news, features, editorial opinion, and advertising—specifically newspapers, magazines, radio, and television; the term can also be applied to other communication vehicles, such as billboards, poster sites, and mail service, that can be used to convey marketing messages to large numbers of people.

members Individuals who join nonprofit organizations and pay dues or support the organization on a periodic basis with funds, services, or their time and efforts.

merchandising Selecting, displaying, and promoting products in a retail store or other distribution outlet.

national account A customer operating over extended geographic areas whose service and sales needs are typically co-ordinated out of a head office.

noise (or clutter) Conflicting, counter, or unrelated communications that distract from an advertiser's ability to communicate a specific message to members of a target audience.

nondurable goods Consumer goods such as food, health and beauty aids, and items that are consumed or otherwise used up relatively quickly (see also *durable goods*).

opinion leader An individual who influences other people's purchase and consumption behaviour.

opportunity cost The maximum benefit foregone by using scarce resources (e.g., money, management time, physical facilities) for one purpose instead of the next best alternative.

penetration strategy An aggressive marketing strategy, based upon low price and heavy advertising and promotional expenditures, that is designed to gain quickly a large share of the market for a specific product.

point-of-sale advertising Promotional displays used by retailers at in-store locations, such as shelf, window, counter, aisle, or checkout, to promote specific products (also known as point-of-purchase, or P-O-P, advertising).

price Defined narrowly as the monetary cost to the purchaser of obtaining a product; more broadly it includes other monetary outlays associated with purchasing and using the product, as well as all nonmonetary costs associated with purchase and use of a good or service (or adoption of a social behaviour), such as time and physical and psychological effort.

price elasticity See *elasticity of demand.*

price leader A firm whose pricing policies are followed by other companies in the same industry.

pricing strategy The mix of monetary price level charged to the final purchaser, terms and methods of payment (e.g., cheques, credit cards, exact change), and discounts offered to both intermediaries and final purchasers.

primary data Information the researcher collects through observation, experimentation, or survey research (see also *secondary data*).

primary demand The current level of demand for all sources for the entire product class in question.

prime time The evening hours of broadcasting (typically 8:00 p.m. to 11:00 p.m.) when audience size is usually the largest and advertising rates are highest.

private label brands Brands owned by retailers or other channel intermediaries, as distinct from manufacturers' brands.

proactive selling Actively seeking out prospective customers (see also *reactive selling*).

product What the organization offers to prospective customers for their acquisition, use, consumption, or adoption; the term includes physical goods, services, and social behaviours or causes (such as driving safely, giving blood, etc.).

product class A group of products that serves the same general function or fulfills the same basic need.

product development The process of developing or acquiring new or improved products for an organization's current market (see also *diversification*).

product differentiation Creating and communicating product attributes that cause consumers to perceive the product as being different from the other offerings on the market.

product life cycle The movement of a product from introduction ("birth") through growth, maturity, and decline to eventual termination; each of these phases requires a distinctive marketing strategy.

product line All the products marketed by a given organization, sometimes subdivided into sets of product lines.

product portfolio Mix of products offered by an organization, grouped with reference to market share, cash flow, and growth characteristics.

product recall Retrieval by the manufacturer of products (usually defective) that are already in the hands of customers and/or channel intermediaries.

profit centre An organizational unit whose revenues and costs are clearly identifiable and whose management is held responsible for controlling both sides of the income statement.

promotional activities Various nonrecurrent selling efforts, usually of a short-term nature, such as contests, discount coupons, special displays, and introductory offers.

psychographic segmentation Dividing the market into segments using variables such as people's life styles, values, attitudes, personalities, and interests.

public relations The managing of public perceptions of an organization and its products by making available news about the organization to the media, or by interacting directly with opinion leaders.

publicity The end result of the staging and publicizing of special events and activities to attract community attention, often via the news media.

pull strategy A marketing strategy based upon heavy advertising by the manufacturer to potential end users, with the objective of "pulling" the product through the channels of distribution (see also *push strategy*).

push strategy A marketing strategy in which the channels of distribution take major responsibility for promotional and personal selling efforts to end users, designed to "push" the product out of the store (see also *pull strategy*).

reach The number (or percentage) of target audience members who are exposed to an advertising campaign at least once.

reactive selling Letting customers take the initiative in seeking out the vendor, who then tries to complete the transaction (see also *proactive selling*).

roll out The process of extending distribution and advertising/promotion for a new product from a limited geographic area to a wider (or national) area.

secondary data Existing information in an accessible form that can be used to provide insights for management decision making or serve as inputs to newprimary data collection efforts (see also *primary data*).

shopping products Products that the consumer, in the process of selection and purchase, characteristically compares on such bases as suitability, quality, price, and style (see also *convenience products* and *specialty products*).

specialty products products with unique characteristics and/or brand identification for which a significant group of buyers are habitually willing to make a special purchasing effort (see also *convenience products* and *shopping products*).

spot advertising The purchase of TV or radio time on a station-by-station or market-by-market basis rather than nation-wide.

stockkeeping-unit (SKU) The lowest level of disaggregation at which a product can be ordered; it reflects size, style, colour, and other distinctive variations.

store audit Retail and wholesale audits track the movement of goods through the distribution channel to provide manufacturers with sales and market share data (see also *marketing audit*).

strategic business (management) unit (SBU/SMU) A unit within a larger organization that is essentially treated as a separate entity and established as an independent profit centre, usually with a distinct mission, objective, competitive environment, and managerial requirements (see also *profit centre*).

target market That portion of the total market the organization has selected to serve.

target marketing Focusing the marketing efforts on specific segments within the total market.

test marketing Evaluating customer response to a new product by putting it on the market in a limited geographic area.

time-series data See *longitudinal data*.

top-down planning Designing programs to be implemented by top-level management; participation filters down to the lower levels (see also *bottom-up planning*).

trademark A brand or part of a brand that is given legal protection and whose use is restricted to its owner.

trading up Encouraging current or prospective customers to purchase a more expensive version of a given product.

undifferentiated marketing strategy A plan whereby the organization treats the market as an aggregate and designs its products and marketing program to appeal to the greatest number of consumers possible.

usage segmentation Subdividing the total consumer market on the basis of where, when, why, and in what quantities the product is used.

value pricing Establishing price levels on the basis of how the buyer perceives the value of the product rather than on the basis of the costs to be recovered by the seller.

variable costs Costs that change in direct proportion to changes in activity, such as materials and parts, sales commissions, and certain labour and supplies (see also *fixed costs*).

vertical integration The process of purchasing or acquiring control over one's suppliers (see *backward integration*), or one's distributors (see *forward integration* and *horizontal integration*), or both.

wholesaler A business unit in the channel of distribution which buys goods or services from producers and resells them to other merchants or to institutional purchasers but not to household consumers.

Appendix 2

USE OF COMPUTERS FOR MARKETING DECISION MAKING

A student recently commented to one of us that he couldn't imagine how we studied for our degrees (in the 1960s) without pocket calculators. The immediate reply was, "Soon, students won't be able to imagine completing their degrees without a personal computer."

In the early days of computer development, some observers predicted that at most the world market for all computers would be a hundred or less. Others suggested that computers would replace managers and lead to sharp reductions in their numbers. Fortunately for everyone, neither forecast proved accurate. Instead, computers and computer-based systems have become important aids in managerial analysis and decision making. Computers, when properly used, can lead to better decisions or decisions being made more rapidly or more efficiently. Successful computer applications provide help to managers trying to deal with an uncertain, competitive, dynamic environment.

A computer is not necessary for the study of the cases in this book. However, availability of a personal computer will reduce the time in which cases can be analyzed, increase the depth of analysis of alternative courses of action, and allow for an examination of a broader set of options. The course instructor will suggest the appropriate level of computer involvement, depending on the objectives of the course, the availability of computers, and your own computer skills.

COMPUTER AIDS AND MANAGERS

A computer can help in analyzing some, but not all, cases. The optional computer disk that accompanies this book lists the cases for which computer aids are available.

ECONOMIC AND PROFITABILITY ANALYSIS

For most students, the first type of computer aid to be used in a marketing course will be a relatively straightforward program to do breakeven and profitability analyses. This kind of program allows the user to evaluate quickly the financial and economic implications of alternative courses of action from a set of assumptions about future demand, price, cost, and other factors. The program asks the user to input such data in a conversational format and then does the calculations necessary to generate income and other statements. The real challenge lies not in running the analysis but in establishing the appropriate assumptions, as will be seen in cases such as "Windsor Miniature Golf" and the "Fraser Company." Set within the context of a "spreadsheet" system, these programs are specially designed to be used easily by the beginner. They greatly reduce the computational burden in testing assumptions, thereby allowing a more thorough evaluation of the cases.

For other cases, the computer programs assume some familiarity on the student's part with the use of spreadsheet programs. In these cases, data from a case and its exhibits have been transferred to the computer disk in a framework that makes it easy to analyze case information. For example, in the "Cascade Foods" case, data from a test market that examined the sales impact of different price and advertising levels at various stores and times are stored on the computer disk. By combining the data from the different stores and time periods, the effect of different marketing mix strategies can be assessed. Spreadsheet programs such as this one primarily involve application of the four basic arithmetic operations of addition, subtraction, multiplication, and division to tables of case data to derive meaningful information. Only limited knowledge of the use of spreadsheet programs is required; most students can learn to use the programs needed for this book's cases in less than a day. The payoff from this knowledge is the ability to carry out quickly both a thorough analysis of case data and a test of the impact of alternative plans.

MARKETING MODELS

Several cases in this book allow the use of specially developed marketing models. These models typically develop a structure that estimates the effect of marketing variables such as price, advertising, and product design on sales. For example, an important question in "Castle Coffee" is how much money to spend on advertising. A successful analysis requires the manager to estimate the relationship between advertising and sales. While a computer is not necessary for such an analysis, using an appropriately designed computer model will help the manager to specify the nature of that relationship and predict the sales and profit consequences of changes in advertising levels. Computer models also help a manager estimate possible market repsonses to different actions. For instance, in the "Lively Arts at Hanson" case, a student can use the product planning computer system employed at Hanson University to forecast attendance at performing arts events and help identify which events should be presented and promoted during the year. This model, in a slightly different form, was used by the managers of the Lively Arts Program to help them make such decisions.

Detailed descriptions of these models and the management problems that stimulated their development are given later in this appendix.

CONCLUSION

The cases in this book do not require access to a computer. However, the increasing use of personal computers by managers and the potential of computers to help managers suggest the benefit of analyzing cases with the aid of computers and spreadsheet programs. Some of the cases in this book can be studied at various levels of sophistication with the aid of specially developed computer programs. Remember, however, that the objective of any computer model—simple or sophisticated—is to help analyze and understand a marketing situation. Responsibility for discovering problems and developing, testing, and implementing sound, creative decisions rests with the manager.

54 CASTLE COFFEE LIMITED (II)

William F. Massy

David B. Montgomery

Charles B. Weinberg

Since returning from a one-week management development course, Adrian Van Tassle had been working with Jack Stillman on the adaptation of a small "marketing planning model" to help him plan Castle Coffee's advertising budget for the coming fiscal year. Stillman, director of research for Castle, was quite experienced in computer models applied to a broad range of management problems. While Stillman had little or no experience in the marketing area, he had welcomed the opportunity to work with Van Tassle.

The model being developed was designed to aid a brand manager or advertising manager in determining a reasonable advertising budget for a product.[1] Van Tassle felt that the model might help him to clarify his own thinking, make sounder decisions, and communicate better with management.

THE MARKETING PLANNING MODEL

After reviewing the marketing planning model with Jack Stillman, Van Tassle asked Stillman to provide a list of the basic inputs required for the model. After much thought and several conferences with Stillman, Van Tassle arrived at a preliminary set of estimates for the basic inputs. The input list and the preliminary estimates are presented in Exhibit 1. Some of these factors were obvious; only the ones relating to market share and the advertising plan itself required a lot of thought.

Although Adrian Van Tassle had to develop a quarterly plan, he decided that the best first step would be to determine the size of the annual advertising budget. He felt that developing an annual plan would be relatively easier in that seasonal effects could be ignored and questions of how fast sales and market share respond to advertising could be postponed. In addition, he felt that the experience of developing an annual plan would sharpen his understanding of the model and his ability to use it.

After some reflection, Van Tassle concluded that if his advertising were reduced to zero for that year, he would lose perhaps half his market share in the first year, cutting it to a mere 2.7%. This would result partly from a slackening in consumer demand and partly from an accelerating erosion of Castle's distribution. If a zero rate of advertising were to be continued, he was relatively certain Castle would lose

[1] A general description of the model is provided at the end of this case, under the heading, "A Note on the Structure of an Advertising Planning Model."

Exhibit 1
PRELIMINARY VALUES FOR INPUTS TO THE ADVERTISING PLANNING MODEL (ANNUAL PLAN)

Variable	Preliminary Value
Number of periods	1
Reference market share	.054
Maintenance advertising per year (millions of dollars)	.8
Market share at end of year if during the year:	
(a) No advertising	.027
(b) Saturation advertising	.10
(c) 20% increase in advertising	.060
Market share in long run with no advertising	0
Media efficiency	1
Copy effectiveness	1
Contribution ($/unit)	0.45
Brand price ($/unit)	2.72
Initial market share (the March-April result)	.054
Annual product sales (industry sales, in millions of units)	88
Product price ($/unit)	2.72

all its distribution and hence market share. On the other hand, pushing advertising to saturation might nearly double the company's share, to about 10%. "Of course," he commented to Stillman, "that figure could well be 9% or even 11% or 12%. We've never come close to blitzing the ad budget. He also believed that the most likely result of a 20% increase in advertising would be a 6% market share (up from 5.4%) though here again there was considerable uncertainty. Van Tassle still wasn't sure when to expect this increase to a 6% market share, but felt that it would surely occur by the fourth quarter after the change.

Van Tassle had run the model using data that represented his plans as they were at the beginning of the 1982 fiscal year. At that time, the late spring of 1981, he had estimated the previous period's market share at 5.5%; however, the market share report he later received estimated market share at 5.4%. According to the results of the theatre tests, the copy effectiveness for the autumn-winter-spring campaign, he had recently learned, was rated at 0.90. (Curiously, the "old" advertising copy used in the summer of 1981 had been rated at 1.0). In addition, as compared to last year, Van Tassle now had judgements concerning maximum and minimum shares, a subject he had not thought about last year. In using the advertising planning model, Van Tassle first set the levels of brand advertising at the amounts he had planned for the year, not the amounts actually expended. Given the confusion with the media schedule caused by the abrupt cancellation of 20% of Castle's advertising spending during the winter quarter, Van Tassle wondered whether a run of the model with actual expenditures would be meaningful. The inputs and outputs for this run are shown in Exhibit 2.

Exhibit 2
RUN OF ADVERTISING PLANNING MODEL (ANNUAL)

This spreadsheet contains two advertising planning models to help plan Castle's advertising budget. The first is an ANNUAL plan which may be used to determine the size of the annual budget and sharpen the understanding of the models. The second is a more detailed QUARTERLY plan for developing the actual budget.

HIT <Home> TO BEGIN
HIT <ALT-C> TO CHANGE SCREENS

Screen 1A: Planned Spending — Annual Model

Annual Industry Sales (millions of units)	{88}	Market Share at YEAR END if...	
Maintenance Advertising $mm	{$.800}	No Advertising	{2.70%}
Market Share and Maintenance	{5.40%}	20% incr. in adv'g	{6.00%}
Most recent Market Share	{5.40%}	Saturation adv'g	{10.00%}
Long Run Shr Without Adv'g	{.00%}	Brand Advertising $mm	{$.928}

YEAR END OUTCOMES * (in thousands)

Market Share	5.89%
Industry Unit Sales	88,000
Brand Unit Sales	5,180
Brand Dollar Sales	$14,089
Gross Contribution (Bef Adv)	$2,331
Net Contribution (After Adv)	$1,403
Slope : Net $ Contrib/$ Adv	.41

* Outcomes are based on a price of $2.72 and unit contribution of $0.45

Enter Decisions and Estimates Between { }'s. Hit <F9> to Recalculate. Hit <Tab> for Quarterly Model, <PgDn> for Advertising Response Function.

SCREEN 1A: Actual Spending — Annual Model

Annual Industry Sales (millions of units)	{88}	Market Share at YEAR END IF ...	
Maintenance Advert'g $mm	{$.800}	No Advertising	{2.70%}
Market Share @ Maintenance	{5.40%}	20% Incr in Adv'g	{6.00%}
Most Recent Market Share	{5.40%}	Saturation Adv'g	{10.00%}
Long Run Shr Without Adv'g	{.00%}	Brand Advertising $mm	**{$.864}**

YEAR END OUTCOMES (in thousands)

Market Share	5.65%
Industry Unit Sales	88,000
Brand Unit Sales	4,971
Brand Dollar Sales	$13,521
Gross Contribution (Bef Adv)	$2,237
Net Contribution (After Adv)	$1,373
Slope : Net $ Contrib/$ Adv	.48

Note: Format of the print out will vary slightly according to the version of the program used.

Exhibit 3

CHANGES IN PRELIMINARY VALUES OF REFERENCE CASE CONDITIONS FOR INPUTS TO THE ADVERTISING PLANNING MODEL

Variable	Preliminary
Number of periods	4
Maintenance advertising per quarter (million of dollars)	0.2
Market share at end of quarter if during the quarter:	
(a) No advertising	.0454
(b) Saturation advertising	.0686
(c) 20% increase in advertising	.0559
Quarterly product sales (industry sales in millions of units)	22

Quarterly Plan

Van Tassle next decided to test a quarterly plan. Stillman indicated that some changes in the values of the variables would have to be made. Some were obvious: average sales rate per quarter is the annual rate divided by four. Other changes were more difficult. For example, if there were no advertising for a year, market share would drop by 50% (that is, to 0.027) at the end of the year. Stillman suggested that market share falls off by quarter in approximately the same way that a bank compounds interest—in this case at the rate of 16% per quarter. Thus, if there were no advertising for four quarters, market share would drop to approximately 84%, 71%, 60%, and 50% of the initial value. This seemed to be a reasonable approach, so Van Tassle let Stillman make the calculations which led to the data in Exhibit 3. Van Tassle made some trial runs of a quarterly plan, as shown in Exhibit 4.

Next Year's Budget

Van Tassle gave a final pull to his moustache and turned to the evaluation of the results of running his model on quarterly data. He expected he would want to make a series of additional runs, including tests of alternative plans for fiscal year 1983 before making his advertising budget presentation and recommendation to management.

A NOTE ON THE STRUCTURE OF AN ADVERTISING PLANNING MODEL

The advertising planning model available to Van Tassle was designed to help him evaluate the impact of different advertising budget levels primarily on market share. While advertising and other effects on industry sales could be represented in the model, this was not its main focus.

The model was intended to help a manager translate both subjective estimates and data from past events and market research studies into a systematic framework. The model encompasses enough critical variables to provide acceptable outputs—given reasonable judgement in estimating the variables. Yet at the same time it does

Exhibit 4
RUN OF ADVERTISING PLANNING MODEL (QUARTERLY)

Quarterly Industry Sales (millions of units)	{22}
Maintenance Advertising/Quarter ($ millions)	{.2}
Market Share at Maintenance Advertising	{5.40%}
Most Recent Market Share	{5.40%}
Long Run Market Share With No Advertising	{.00%}
Market Share at END OF QUARTER if ...	
No Advertising	{4.54%}
20% Increase in Advertising	{5.59%}
Saturation Advertising	{6.86%}

Enter Model Inputs Between {}'s. Hit <F9> to Recalculate
Hit <PgDn> for Decisions, Estimates, and Outcomes.

ADVERTISING DECISIONS	Qtr 1	Qtr 2	Qtr 3	Qtr 4
Brand Advert'g (millions)	{ $.160	$.240	$.288	$.240 }
SEASONALITY AND OTHER ESTIMATES				
Product Seasonality Index	{ .85	1.00	1.15	1.00 }
Advert'g Maintenance Index	{ .80	1.00	1.20	1.00 }
Media Efficiency Index	{ 1.00	1.00	1.00	1.00 }
Copy Effectiveness Index	{ 1.00	1.00	1.00	1.00 }
OUTCOMES (000's Unless Noted)				
Market Share	5.40%	5.59%	5.75%	5.88%
Industry Unit Sales	18,700	22,000	25,300	22,000
Brand Unit Sales	1,010	1,230	1,455	1,294
Brand Dollar Sales	$2,747	$3,345	$3,957	$3,521
Gross Contribution (Bef Adv)	$454	$553	$655	$583
Net Contribution (After Adv)	$294	$313	$367	$343
Cumulative Net Contribution	$294	$608	$974	$1,317
Slope: Net $ Contrib/$ Adv	.90	.38	.15	.35

ACTUAL SPENDING

Enter Model Inputs Between { }'s. Hit <F9> to Recalculate.

ADVERTISING DECISIONS	Qtr 1	Qtr 2	Qtr 3	Qtr 4
Brand Advert'g (millions)	{ $.160	$.240	$.264	$.200 }
SEASONALITY AND OTHER ESTIMATES				
Product Seasonality Index	{ .85	1.00	1.15	1.00 }
Advert'g Maintenance Index	{ .80	1.00	1.20	1.00 }
Media Efficiency Index	{ 1.00	1.00	1.00	1.00 }
Copy Effectiveness Index	{ 1.00	1.00	1.00	1.00 }
OUTCOMES (000's Unless Noted)				
Market Share	5.40%	5.59%	5.66%	5.62%
Industry Unit Sales	18,700	22,000	25,300	22,000
Brand Unit Sales	1,010	1,230	1,431	1,236
Brand Dollar Sales	$2,747	$3,345	$3,893	$3,361
Gross Contribution (Bef Adv)	$454	$553	$644	$556
Net Contribution (After Adv)	$294	$313	$380	$356
Cumulative Net Contribution	$294	$608	$988	$1,344
Slope: Net $ Contrib/$ Adv	.90	.38	.23	.53

Hit <Alt-C> to Change Screens

Exhibit 5
INPUTS FOR ESTIMATING SHARE RESPONSE TO ADVERTISING IN ONE PERIOD

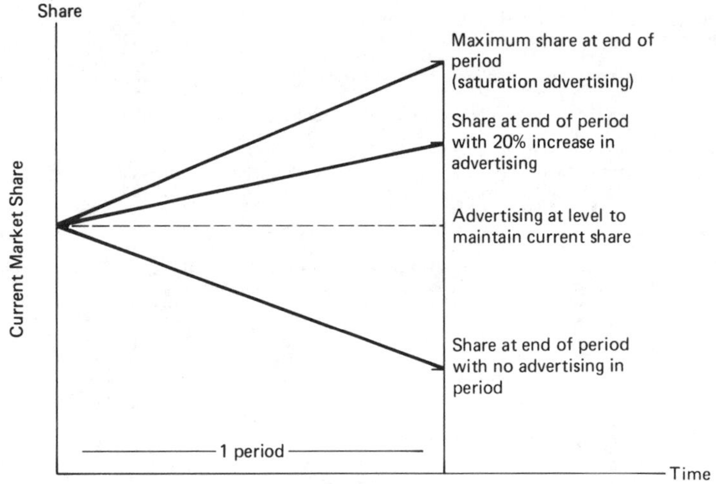

not become so complex and cluttered that it is difficult for the manager to understand and apply it.

To use the model the manager first needs to estimate four quantities (Exhibit 5).

1. If a brand's advertising is reduced to zero, there is a minimum point (min) to which brand share will fall from its current or initial value by the end of one time period.
2. If a brand's advertising is increased a great deal, to a saturation level, there is a maximum point (max) beyond which sales will not rise by the end of one time period.
3. There is some advertising rate that will maintain current market share, called the maintenance level of advertising.
4. If there is a 20% increase in a brand's advertising over the maintenance rate, share would increase to a new level by the end of one time period.

The estimates of these four quantities are used to estimate an advertising response function for one period, as shown in Exhibit 6. Algebraically, the relationship can be written as follows:

$$\text{share} = \text{min} + (\text{max} - \text{min})(\text{adv})^b/[a + (\text{adv})^b].$$

The min, max, a and b are implicitly determined by the input data. The diagram in Exhibit 6 shows an S-shaped curve, that is, at low levels of spending there is very little effect of advertising on share and there is first increasing and then decreasing

Exhibit 6
ADVERTISING RESPONSE FUNCTION

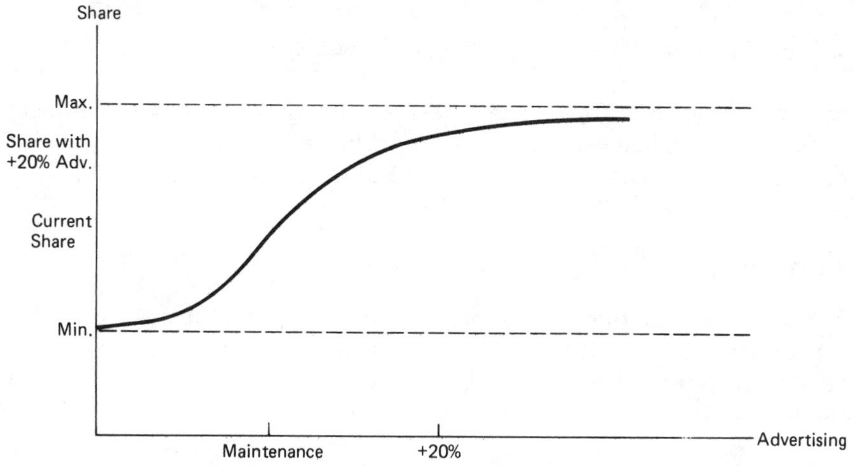

returns to scale. (This is not required by the equation. If $b > 1$, the curve will be S-shaped, for $0 < b \leqslant 1$, a concave function. The particular value of b will depend on the estimate provided in response to item 4 above.)

Carryover Effects and Time Delays

To take into account carryover effects and time delays, the model assumes:

1. In the absence of advertising, share would eventually decay to some long run minimum value (long run min). Its value can possibly be zero.
2. The decay in one time period will be a constant fraction of the gap between current share and the long run minimum, that is, decay is exponential.

The term "persistence" denotes the fraction of the difference between share and long run minimum that is retained each period after decay. For Castle Coffee, where the long run min is estimated as zero, these relationships can be written algebraically as:

$$\text{persistence} = \text{min/current share}$$

$$\text{share}(t) = (\text{persistence})[\text{share}(t-1)] + (\text{max} - \text{min})[\text{adv}(t)]^b/\{a + [\text{adv}(t)]^b\}.$$

In this model, share is based on a carryover from last period's share plus the effect of current advertising.

To adjust advertising for media and copy, the following two time-varying indices are constructed: (1) a media efficiency index and (2) a copy effectiveness index. Both will be assumed to have reference values of 1.0. The model then hypothesizes that the delivered advertising, that is, the adv(t) that goes into the response function, is given by:

adv(t) = [media efficiency(t)][copy effectiveness(t)][adv dollars (t)].

The media efficiency and copy effectiveness indices can be determined subjectively, but better alternatives exist. Copy testing is helpful; data on media cost of exposures by market segment and relative value of market segments can be used to develop a media index.

Other Factors

In addition to the response of market share to advertising, product class sales also need to be considered. Two important phenomena here are seasonality and trend. These and any similar effects can be combined into a product class sales index that varies with time. Thus,

product class sales(t) = [reference product class sales] [product class sales index (t)].

In addition there may be a product class response to brand advertising and corresponding time lags. The treatment of this is analogous to that for share, but is not a factor for Castle to consider.

A variety of other factors affect share. Some of these factors are promotions, competition, distribution, price, product changes, and package changes. These factors are treated, in a simple way, through a composite index of nonadvertising effects. Brand share is modeled as the product of the nonadvertising effect index and the share developed from the advertising response relation. For clarity the latter will be called the unadjusted share, and its effect is represented as:

brand share(t) = [non adv effects index(t)] [unadj share(t)].

Contribution and Slope

On looking at the output in Exhibits 2 and 4, Van Tassle was somewhat puzzled by the rows, "NET CONTRIBUTION (AFTER ADV)" and "SLOPE: NET $ CONTRIB/ $ ADV." Stillman explained that slope (marginal profit) and contribution measure two different elements. Contribution measures the aggregate results in only one period; slope estimates the marginal return (marginal revenue − marginal cost) from advertising. In addition, when used for the quarterly model, slope includes an estimate of the revenue impact of the carryover effect of advertising. That is, a fraction of the customers attracted to Castle Coffee in one quarter by advertising may repeat their purchase of Castle's products in future quarters, so that advertising in one period may have an impact on future profits. This is a particular concern in planning the quarterly budget. Slope attempts to measure this carryover effect by estimating repeat sales in future periods. In the quarterly model, repeat sales for a full year are included in the estimate of slope.

55 THE LIVELY ARTS AT HANSON (II)

Charles B. Weinberg

In the fall of 1983, Tom Bacon and Barbara Lynn of Hanson University's Office of Public Events began planning the 1984–85 season for the Lively Arts at Hanson (LAH) program. In December, they would go to the performing arts industry's annual booking meeting at which time almost all the commitments for 1984–85 would be made.

In preparation, the two managers had prepared a list of events they might wish to schedule for LAH. Exhibits 1 to 5 list the performers who were being actively considered, a brief description from promotional brochures about the performer, the month the performer was available, and the seating capacity of the hall they would perform in if they were booked as part of the LAH program.[1] Each performer listed went on tour at various times in the year and would be available for Hanson during these tour periods. Sometimes, however, performers would adjust their schedule to be available for such programs or events as LAH.

The LAH season generally ran from October to early May. Most of December and early January were excluded because of winter holidays at the university, and much of March, because of spring holidays.

As in the current year, LAH planned to offer approximately 25 performances. In general, performers made only one appearance on campus during a year. However, because of the expense of setup, any dance group that was booked appeared a minimum of two, and usually three, times. In addition, the Guarneri String Quartet, which had become virtually a Hanson tradition (and a sellout), performed three times, and it was possible to book one other chamber music group for more than one night. Booking too many groups for more than one night would detract from LAH's objective of presenting a mix of events.

It was decided that the "Young Concert Artist" designation be abandoned for 1984–85. The name seemed to doom concerts so categorized to low attendance. Consequently, younger artists would not be separately identified but would be described by type of performance.[2]

Bacon and Lynn were trying to develop a 25-event schedule. They had already scheduled the following ten performances:

[1] The seating capacity of the large hall was approximately 1,700 (usually 1,694) seats. When the balcony and back rows were closed off, then approximately 1,100 (usually 1,085) seats were available for sale.

[2] Among the artists who were being considered by LAH, the following could be classified as Young Concert Artists: Elly Ameling, Sour Cream, Il Divertimento, and Robert Cohen.

Edward Albee, Playwright	October (to open the season)	1 night
Guarneri String Quartet	November	3 nights
Misha and Cipa Dichter, Pianists	January	1 night
Nicanor Zabaleta, Harpist	February	1 night
Terminal City Dance	February	3 nights
Michael Lorimer, Guitarist	May	1 night

While the financial aspects could not be ignored, at this stage LAH management was more concerned with scheduling a season that would help LAH to meet its non-financial objectives. Indeed, the artistic fees of the performers listed in Exhibits 1 to 5 were such that LAH would have a deficit of between $1,000 and $2,000 if ticket sales were at the historically average level for the type of event. Ticket prices were expected to be in the $9–10 range, but a pricing decision would not be required for some time.

In planning for next year, LAH management had available an interactive computer model, called ARTS PLAN, to help forecast attendance and choose events to schedule. A brief report describing this system follows in the latter part of this case. The system had provided accurate forecasts when previously used by LAH management.

Tom Bacon and Barbara Lynn expected to use ARTS PLAN as an aid in developing next year's schedule. However, from past experience, they knew it was best to develop a limited list of alternative schedules before using the computer system. They also found it more efficient to prepare the fall (October, November, December), winter (January, February, March), and spring (April, May) schedules separately at first, and then, after some test computer runs, to consider a full schedule. One year, when the computer was unavailable, Mr. Bacon and Ms. Lynn simply used the ARTS PLAN forecasting rule (see below) with a pocket calculator to test scheduling alternatives. They were thinking of having a student write a program so that ARTS PLAN could be run on their newly acquired personal computer.

Meeting attendance goals was just one of the tasks that they faced. They had to deal with the practical problem of matching performers' availability with a schedule that would present a relatively balanced number of events in the major months of October, November, January, February, and April. Beyond this, the programming schedule also had to help achieve the goal of establishing LAH as a major source of first-rate performing arts talent in a variety of fields.

EXCERPTS FROM A REPORT DESCRIBING THE DEVELOPMENT AND USE OF ARTS PLAN

To gain a better understanding of the factors influencing attendance at Lively Arts at Hanson (LAH) events, LAH management asked a marketing faculty member at Hanson University for help. By employing a statistical technique known as regression analysis, a fairly accurate attendance forecasting system was developed. Moreover, the professor and a student assistant were able to transform the technical, statistical

Exhibit 1
CHAMBER MUSIC

Name	Description	Month Available	Seating Capacity
Tokyo String Quartet	Four young musicians who burst on the musical scene eight years ago and are now ranked with the world's top quartets. ''If you care at all about chamber music, you won't want to miss them.''	October	720
Guarneri String Quartet	The talents of the Guarneri can barely be described, so supreme is the Quartet's playing. Has played here every year since 1970.	November	720
Juilliard String Quartet	Veterans of more than 3,000 sold-out concerts and participants in every major music festival around the world, the Juilliard is hailed for its superb chamber music performances.	November	720
Pittsburgh Symphony Chamber Players with Barry Tuckwell, French Horn	Tuckwell has subjected this most difficult instrument to a degree of obedience that approaches perfection. His performance with the principal players of the Pittsburgh Symphony Orchestra provides a delightful evening of music.	January	720
Bartok Quartet	Acclaimed world-wide as one of the most distinguished chamber groups on the concert scene. ''The sense of ensemble could hardly be more intimate and the tonal blend of the instruments more homogeneous.''	January	720
Music from Marlboro	Join us for what has become a tradition at Hanson: the annual visit of Music from Marlboro. Performing with the ensemble on this year's tour will be Isidore Cohen, famous violinist with the Beaux Arts Trio.	March	720
Chilingirian String Quartet	Four polished musicians who produce an elegant, exquisite sound. ''Once you've heard them, you'll never forget them.''	April	720

Exhibit 2
DANCE

Name	Description	Month Available	Seating Capacity
Bella Lewitzky Dance Company	Lewitzky is a revelation . . . a major choreographer . . . a great dancer . . . a superb teacher. With herself and her company, there is a body awareness that transcends mere muscular discipline.	October	1,700
Kathryn Posin Dance Company	One of the bright new stars on the dance horizon. "Posin's choreography is simply brilliant, employing both space and body in fresh, formful ways."	October	1,700
AMAN*	Colourful, authentic costumes, exotic instruments, and an exciting repertory of more than 70 folk dances from the Balkans, Middle East, North Africa, and the U.S.	January	1,700
Joffrey II	The best small classical ballet on the continent. Their remarkable control and technique will dazzle you.	January	1,700
Terminal City Dance Company	Vancouver's exciting dance company includes in its repertory some intriguing works in modern dance.	February	1,700
Alvin Ailey American Dance*	Modern, jazz, and classical dance technique which reflects America's heritage, black and white.	March	1,700
Pilobolus	An ever-changing flow of linked body shapes that mold and remold in space with skill and sophistication. Pilobolus is gymnastics, acrobatics, applied physics, theories of leverage, and contemporary dance!	April	1,700

*Can be considered a well-known dance group.

Exhibit 3
GUITAR

Name	Description	Month Available	Seating* Capacity
Eugenia Zukerman, Flutist/ Carlos Bonell, Guitarist	Zukerman, one of the finest flutists to be found anywhere, teams up with Bonell, one of Europe's leading guitarists, for a program of works primarily from the Baroque period.	February	1,085
Ronald Radford, Flamenco Guitar	One of the few American masters of the Flamenco guitar shares Spanish gypsy music with you through performance and dialogue.	April	1,085
Michael Lorimer, Guitarist	A protégé of Andres Segovia, Lorimer has carved an enviable reputation as a classical guitarist.	May	1,085

*Guitarists usually perform in the 1,700 seat hall, but some 600 of these seats are not made available for sale.

Exhibit 4
JAZZ

Name	Description	Month Available	Seating Capacity
New England Conservatory Ragtime Ensemble with Gunther Schuller	The toe-tapping sounds of Joplin, Morton, Marshall, Hampton, and others are played by this very famous ensemble. Gunther Schuller will conduct and discuss this marvelous Ragtime music.	October	1,700
Richard Stoltzman, Clarinet	Consistently acclaimed as "an artist of indescribable genius." Often compared to the legendary Reginald Kell.	October	720
Billy Taylor Trio	Jazz pianist, composer, arranger, teacher, and actor, Billy Taylor performs in company with a drummer and bassist. Taylor is among those musicians who have elevated jazz to new heights of recognition and appreciation.	December	1,700
Toshiko Akiyoshi/Lew Tabackin, Big Band	An outstanding jazz orchestra in the tradition of the great Duke Ellington. Akiyoshi is composer, conductor, pianist. Tabackin plays tenor sax and flute and is the principal soloist.	February	1,700
Sonny Rollins, Tenor Saxophone	"A giant. A man who has altered the course of music to which he still contributes mightily." Hear the musician who has converted a new generation to the meaning and joys of jazz!	February	720
Dizzy Gillespie, Trumpeter	Revered throughout the world. An artist with absolute mastery of his instrument and seemingly unlimited musical ideas.	March	1,700

Exhibit 5
OTHER ARTISTS

Name	Description	Month Available	Seating Capacity
	Theatre		
Edward Albee, Playwright	Edward Albee is one of the world's most important contemporary playwrights. A cast chosen and directed by Albee will present his prize winning plays *The Zoo Story* and *The American Dream*.	October	1,700
The World of Gilbert & Sullivan	Artists from the Canadian Opera Company present in concert some of Gilbert & Sullivan's finest tunes and patter. Produced in co-operation with the university chorus and orchestra.	October	1,700
The Acting Company	Presenting the *White Devil*, a work by John Webster, author of the Elizabethan classic, *The Duchess of Malfi*.	January	1,700
Ruby Dee & Ossie Davis, Theatre	Two of America's foremost black performers share their love of stories, poems, legends, and experiences in *Inside/Outside*, a project of personal love and dedication that has become internationally famous.	April	720

(continued)

Exhibit 5 continued

Name	Description	Month Available	Seating Capacity
	Soloists and Duets		
Elly Ameling	Truly one of the foremost masters of the art of song in the world.	October	720
Igor Kipnis, Harpsichordist	The foremost harpsichordist of today. "He need bow to no one in the intelligence and scrupulousness with which he approaches the various stylistic requirements of Renaissance, Baroque, and Classical music."	November	720
Misha and Cipa Dichter, Pianists	Husband and wife, Misha and Cipa Dichter win accolades wherever they perform for their assurance, virtuosity, and unique sense of musical spirit.	January	720
Nicanor Zabaleta, Harp	The harp virtuoso of our era. A veteran of more than 4,000 concerts around the world and a sellout at every previous Lively Arts concert.	February	720
Robert Silverman, Piano	"His playing is all one could wish for. It has taste, intelligence, and artistic insight." From Vancouver.	April	720
Robert Cohen, Cello	Winner of the 1978 Gregor Piatigorsky Award, Cohen is known for his combination of high virtuosity and genuine eloquence.	May	720

(continued)

Exhibit 5 continued

Name	Description	Month Available	Seating Capacity
	Groups		
Sour Cream	Frans Brueggens' avant garde recorder trio. Join him, Kess Boeke and Walter van Hauwe for an informal session of music making, featuring works from the Renaissance to the present.	October	720
Il Divertimento	Eight master woodwind players performing on 18th-century instruments. Hear Haydn, Beethoven, and Mozart played the way the composers themselves heard it.	November	720
Greenwood Consort	Music of the late Middle Ages and Renaissance, delivered with verve, enthusiasm, humour, and top-notch musicianship. Brings early music to life by combining voices with flute, recorder, lute, pipe and tabor, krummhorns, and viols.	April	720
Waverly Consort	Hear gentle pastorales and madrigals, ribald drinking songs, lusty cries of chimney sweeps, delicate airs for the recorder and viheula, gay gigues and galliards, sedate minuets—all played on instruments of the Medieval, Renaissance, and Baroque periods.	May	720

analysis into a "user-friendly" computer system called "ARTS PLAN," that LAH management used to help plan a season. What follows is a brief description of the development and usage of the system.

Development of a Forecasting Model

A number of factors beyond the distinctive appeal of an individual performer could influence the attendance at any given performance. The first step was to determine these factors and to measure their importance via the use of regression analysis. The resulting model forms a preliminary base case forecast for a planning model. The manager can override the forecast, if necessary, because of factors not captured in the model.

Data were available on attendance by performance for 93 LAH performances over three years. Preliminary analyses of these data revealed that there were seasonal influences on attendance. An average performance drew 85% of capacity in the fall, 60% in the winter, and 50% in the spring. Similarly, attendance was affected by type of performance. Chamber music performances drew 80% of capacity, dance 60%, guitar 105% (seats on the stage or tickets for standing room were sometimes sold), and jazz 75%. Performers classified as Young Concert Artists (YCA) drew 50% of capacity. These five performance types accounted for 81 of the 93 performances. The remaining 12 events averaged 60% of capacity. It was also believed, although not specifically tabulated, that performances on Friday nights drew better than performances during the week. There were too few Saturday night or Sunday performances to examine other weekend nights.

Approximately 15% of the performers who were booked appeared for more than one performance. There were a number of reasons for multi-performance bookings. Some groups had a varied repertoire and fairly broad appeal. Dance groups were generally booked for multiple performances because of the fixed costs involved in bringing such a group to campus. The number of performances for some groups was determined by their availability or the availability of auditoriums on campus. Because of the various reasons for having multiple performances, the effect on attendance was problematic. Multiple performances could spread out a limited audience over several days, provide opportunities for word-of-mouth to build second or third day audiences, and allow devotees to attend several times.

Examination of the data revealed that there was only one group (the Guarneri String Quartet) that appeared more than five times over the three years. A specific variable was set up to represent this group. Although no dance group appeared more than five times, there appeared to be a subset of dance groups that were particularly well known. A specific variable was established for dance groups belonging to this subset.

The performances were held (with three exceptions out of 93) in three halls on campus whose capacities were approximately 350, 720, and 1,700 seats. Thus, the capacity of the hall could be a factor in the attendance. However, the hall chosen was dictated by the musical and technical requirements of the performance type and not by an estimate of attendance. For example, chamber music concerts are usually held in the 720-seat hall, and dance groups always perform in the 1,700-seat hall. Because of the direct association between type of performance and capacity of hall, it was not possible to separate the effect of capacity from performance type. Consequently, the performance type, "dance," denotes a performance held in a 1,700-seat auditorium. (If a dance performance were to be held in a 2,000-seat auditorium, some extrapolation would be required.)

Data on several other potentially important factors (such as competing events held on the same night and weather conditions) were not readily available in LAH records. For example, concert attendance might suffer if a basketball game were being played on the same night. Also, the effect of any special promotion was not included. However, to account for any temporal shift, variables representing the year were included.

Statistical Model

The mathematical model tested was the following:

$$Y = a_0 + a_w W + a_s S + a_{T1} T_1 + a_{T2} T_2 + a_{T3} T_3 + a_{T4} T_4 + a_{T5} T_5 + a_{F1} F_1 + a_{M1} M_1 + a_{G1} G_1 + a_{G2} G_2 + a_{Y1} Y_1 + a_{Y2} Y_2$$

Where,

Y = attendance
W = 1, if held in winter, 0 otherwise,
S = 1, if held in spring, 0 otherwise,
T_1 = 1, if chamber music, 0 otherwise,
T_2 = 1, if dance, 0 otherwise,
T_3 = 1, if guitar, 0 otherwise,
T_4 = 1, if jazz, 0 otherwise,
T_5 = 1, if young concert artist, 0 otherwise,
F = 1, if held on Friday, 0 otherwise,
M = 1, if part of a series of multiple performances, 0 otherwise,
G_1 = 1, if by group performing more than five times, 0 otherwise,
G_2 = 1, if by well-known dance group, 0 otherwise,
Y_1 = 1, if held during year 1, 0 otherwise,
Y_2 = 1, if held during year 2, 0 otherwise.

The independent variables are all 0, 1 dummy variables which represent different effects and, as is usual, are defined to omit one class in order to preserve the non-singularity of the independent variables.

Statistical Results

When regression analysis was run, five variables, Y_1 for year one, M for multiple performances, F for Friday, W for winter, and T_1 for chamber music were not statistically significant at the 0.05 level. When these variables were deleted, all the remaining variables were significant at the 0.05 level. The regression results are shown in Exhibit 6. The adjusted R^2 was 0.79. When a split-half double crossover

Exhibit 6

REGRESSION RESULTS FOR PREDICTING ATTENDANCE

Variable	Coefficient	Beta Weight	Value of F*
S (Spring)	−127	−0.12	5.5
T_2 (Dance)	231	0.22	12.3
T_3 (Guitar)	481	0.26	27.0
T_4 (Jazz)	732	0.46	79.6
T_5 (YCA)	−400	−0.30	33.0
G_1	178	0.10	4.1
G_2	804	0.50	74.1
Y_2 (Year 2)	−113	−0.12	6.0
Constant	647		

*As discussed in the text, all coefficients are significant at the 0.05 level or above.

validation was run, the R^2 turned out to be 0.70. These results were considered very good and superior to what was expected by both management and the analyst. All the significant effects were in the expected direction.

There was a clear effect for performance type: four of the five dummy variables for performance type were significant and, in addition, were significantly different from each other. Although the dummy variable for chamber music did not achieve significance, this only implies that its attendance is not significantly different from that of the 12 nonclassified performances. The attendance estimate for chamber music is significantly different than that of the other four performance types.

Year 3 was the base case for the annual effects. No particular explanation for the comparative drop-off in year two attendance (unlike year one) has been developed. In the absence of an apparent trend, it was decided to assume $Y_2 = 0$ in the forecasting model.

Forecasting Rule

In brief, the forecasting model was

Attendance = 647
−127 (if Spring)
+231 (if Dance)
+481 (if Guitar)
+732 (if Jazz)
−400 (if YCA)
+178 (if well known chamber group)
+804 (if popular dance group)

For example, the base case forecast for a dance event to be held in the spring is 647 − 127 (Spring) + 231 (Dance) = 751; the forecast for jazz in the fall would be 647 + 732 (Jazz) = 1379.

Planning Model

The planning model is designed to help the manager determine whether a tentative or planned schedule will meet attendance objectives for the year and what the impact of promoting certain events would be on the attendance predictions.

The model has three main stages. The first stage establishes a base case forecast for the season being planned, using the forecasting model discussed in the previous section. The second stage allows the manager to *override* the regression forecast because of unique factors of which the manager is aware. For example, although the expected attendance for jazz groups booked in the fall is 1,379 people, one group may be expected to do particularly well at the university because of its local reputation or a previous successful appearance. The manager may wish to test alternative estimates for groups falling in the "other" category. When this stage is completed, a forecast of attendance by performance, season, or year is available.

In the third stage, the manager can test the impact of alternative strategies. The strategic options are to make scheduling changes (add, omit, or substitute a performance) and to promote particular performances. For example, if the manager wants to schedule a dance company instead of a guitarist as the second performance of the season, the impact of this scheduling change on attendance can be assessed.

Implementation Experience

The ARTS PLAN system has been used at LAH as an aid in the management of an on-going season and in the planning of a future season. Before the start of the last season, attendance forecasts were made for the 26-performance schedule. Adjustments were made to the regression analysis forecast to account for the several chamber music concerts that were to be given in a 1,300-seat hall and to reflect other factors that the manager thought important. Selected performances in the winter and spring were scheduled for intensive promotion. In December, results to data were checked. At the end of the season, the actual and predicted attendances were compared. An R^2 of 0.80 between actual and predicted was obtained. Furthermore, the total attendance prediction was within 5% of the actual attendance.

Sample Application of Usage

Exhibit 7 is an illustration of the usage of the ARTS PLAN system. The number of options considered is relatively small because of space limitations, but, in an actual application, can be considerably increased. The exhibit is largely self-explanatory. The following comments briefly describe the use of the model in this example.

After identifying the time period to be examined and setting the number of performances, the program prints out the historical record. The program then requests the user to identify each performance by name and type, give the capacity of the hall it is in, and indicate any special effects. When all the required information has been submitted, the program provides a forecast of attendance.

An option is then provided to override the base case projections to accommodate any additional information the manager has. For example, the jazz group, Sari, may

Exhibit 7
SAMPLE RUN

```
ARTS PLANNING MODEL
DO YOU WISH TO INVESTIGATE AN ENTIRE SEASON, OR A
SINGLE QUARTER?  (S = SEASON; Q = QUARTER)?Q
WHICH QUARTER DO YOU WISH TO INVESTIGATE
   (FALL = 1, WINTER = 2, SPRING = 3)       ?3
NO. OF PERFORMANCES PLANNED FOR QUARTER (MAX = 17)?4
THE FOLLOWING TABLE PRESENTS THE BASE-CASE ATTENDANCE
PERCENTAGES WHICH WILL BE USED IN GENERATING THE
FIRST-ROUND ATTENDANCE PROJECTION

                  ESTIMATED ATTENDANCE PERCENTAGES (HISTORICAL)*
                     FALL           WINTER          SPRING
(1)  CHAMB MUSIC      90              90              72
(2)  DANCE            52              52              44
(3)  GUITAR          104             104              92
(4)  JAZZ             81              81              74
(5)  YCA              71              71              34
(6)  OTHER-(720)      90              90              72
(7)  OTHER-(1700)     38              38              31
*IN ADDITION THE FOLLOWING SUPPLEMENTARY EFFECTS HAVE BEEN OBSERVED
     (G)  GALA QUARTET          +22 PERCENT
     (P)  POPULAR DANCE GROUP   +47 PERCENT
AT THIS STEP YOU ARE ASKED TO PROVIDE SPECIFIC INFORMATION ON
THE PROGRAM YOU ARE PLANNING.
*****************************************************************
PERFORMANCE NUMBER 1
ENTER PERFORMANCE NAME (MAXIMUM 12 CHARACTERS)?BETH
ENTER PERFORMANCE TYPE (USE CODE NUMBER:)
     1=CHAMBER MUSIC   3=GUITAR  5=YOUNG CONCERT ARTISTS(YCA)
     2=DANCE           4=JAZZ    6=OTHER-(720)  7=OTHER-(1700)
?2
ENTER CAPACITY OF HALL?1700
   POPULAR DANCE GROUP  (Y=YES, N=NO)?Y
*****************************************************************
 † (Remainder of initial input deleted)

ATTENDANCE PREDICTIONS FOR SPRING QUARTER
PERFORMANCE     PERFORMANCE     PERCENTAGE      CAPACITY
NUMBER          NAME            ATTENDANCE      OF HALL        ATTENDANCE
  1             BETH                91            1700            1547
  2             SARI                74            1700            1258
  3             AMY                 34             350             119
  4             MICHELLE            72             720             518
--------------------------------------------------------------------------
TOTALS          *                   77            4470            3442
**************************************************************************
DO YOU WISH TO MAKE ANY CHANGES?  (Y=YES, N=NO)?Y
ENTER NUMBER OF PERFORMANCE YOU WISH TO CHANGE?2
CURRENT STATUS OF PERFORMANCE NUMBER 2
     NAME        SARI
     TYPE        (4) JAZZ
   PCT ATTEND    74
   CAPACITY      1700
   ATTENDANCE    1258
INDICATE BY CODE NUMBER THE PARAMETER YOU WISH TO CHANGE
ENTER ONE ONLY  1=PERFORMANCE NAME  3=PERCENTAGE ATTENDANCE EXPECTED
                2=PERFORMANCE TYPE  4=CAPACITY OF HALL
?3
OLD PERCENTAGE ATTENDANCE IS:         74
NEW PERCENTAGE ATTENDANCE EXPECTED: 85
ANY OTHER CHANGES TO THIS PERFORMANCE  (Y=YES, N=NO)?N
```

(continued)

Exhibit 7 continued

```
ATTENDANCE PREDICTIONS FOR SPRING QUARTER
PERFORMANCE     PERFORMANCE        PERCENTAGE      CAPACITY
NUMBER          NAME               ATTENDANCE      OF HALL         ATTENDANCE
  1             BETH                   91            1700              1547
  2             SARI          RV       85            1700              1445
  3             AMY                    34             350               119
  4             MICHELLE               72             720               518
----------------------------------------------------------------------------
TOTALS              *                  81            4470              3629
****************************************************************************
DO YOU WISH TO MAKE MODIFICATIONS TO THE PLANNED
SEASON?       (Y=YES, N=NO)?Y

INPUT TYPE OF CHANGE DESIRED.  (ONE ONLY)

     1 - ADD A NEW PERFORMANCE
     2 - DELETE AN EXISTING PERFORMANCE
     3 - REPLACE AN EXISTING PERFORMANCE WITH ANOTHER
     4 - MAKE CHANGES TO AN EXISTING PERFORMANCE
?2

WHICH PERFORMANCE DO YOU WISH TO DELETE (ENTER PERFORMANCE NUMBER)?2


DO YOU WISH TO EXAMINE PROMOTIONAL IMPACT  (Y=YES, N=NO)?Y

AT THIS STAGE YOU ARE ASKED TO ESTIMATE THE IMPACT OF DEVOTING
CONSIDERABLE PROMOTIONAL EFFORT TO A PARTICULAR PERFORMANCE.

PERFORMANCE                PROJECTED              ESTMATED % ATTENDANCE
NAME                       % ATTENDANCE           WITH PROMOTION
BETH                          91                  ?95
AMY                           34                  ?34
MICHELLE                      72                  ?95

THE FOLLOWING TABLE LISTS PERFORMANCE BY ORDER OF INCREASE
IN ATTENDANCE DUE TO PROMOTION

PERFORMANCE    PERFORMANCE        PROJECTED        INCREASE       ATTENDANCE WITH
NUMBER         NAME               ATTENDANCE       FROM PROMO     PROMOTION
  3            MICHELLE               518             166            684
  1            BETH                  1547              68           1615
  2            AMY                    119               0            119

WHICH PERFORMANCE, IF ANY, DO YOU WANT TO PROMOTE?  INDICATE BY
  PERFORMANCE NUMBER OR ZERO IF NO MORE . . . .?3
PERFORMANCE NUMBER OR ZERO IF NO MORE . . . .?0
ATTENDANCE WITH PROMOTIONS CHOSEN IS NOW ESTIMATED
****************************************************************************
ATTENDANCE PREDICTIONS FOR SPRING QUARTER
PERFORMANCE     PERFORMANCE        PERCENTAGE      CAPACITY
NUMBER          NAME               ATTENDANCE      OF HALL         ATTENDANCE
  1             BETH                   91            1700              1547
  2             AMY                    34             350               119
  3             MICHELLE               95             720               684
----------------------------------------------------------------------------
TOTALS              *                  85            2770              2350
****************************************************************************
```

be particularly well known and, consequently, may be expected to do better than the average jazz group, even without special promotion. The adjustment may either be upwards or downwards. The manager can also examine the impact of adding, deleting, or replacing a performance with another. When all the adjustments are completed, a planning base forecast for the quarter is established.

The user then selects the performances to be promoted in light of the above results and any other information available. An attendance projection by performance and by quarter, including the effect of promotion and a variety of summary statistics, are then displayed. The user has the option to revise estimates or make programming changes before terminating the program.

CUT HERE

STUDENT REPLY CARD

In order to improve future editions, we are seeking your comments on *Canadian Marketing: Cases & Exercises*, 2/e by Weinberg & McDougall.

After you have read this text, please answer the following questions and return this form via Business Reply Mail. *Thanks in advance for your feedback!*

1. Name of your college or university: ______________________________

2. Major program of study: ______________________________

3. Your instructor for this course: ______________________________

4. Are there any sections of this text which were not assigned as course reading? __________
   If so, please specify those chapters or portions:

5. How would you rate the overall accessibility of the content? Please feel free to comment on reading level, writing style, terminology, layout and design features, and such learning aids as chapter objectives, summaries, and appendices.

CUT HERE

FOLD HERE

6. What did you like *best* about this book?

7. What did you like *least?*

If you would like to say more, we'd love to hear from you. Please write to us at the address shown on the reverse of this card.

CUT HERE

CUT HERE

FOLD HERE

BUSINESS REPLY MAIL

No Postage Stamp Necessary If Mailed in Canada

Postage will be paid by

Canada Post Postes Canada

7115

Attn: Sponsoring Editor, Business and Economics
The College Division
McGraw-Hill Ryerson Limited
300 Water Street
Whitby, Ontario
L1N 9Z9

TAPE SHUT